Great Lives from History

Latinos

Latinos

Volume III
Eduardo Padrón – Patricia Zavella
Appendixes
Indexes

Editors

Carmen Tafolla
University of Texas - San Antonio

and

Martha P. Cotera
University of Texas - San Antonio

SALEM PRESS
Ipswich, Massachusetts   Hackensack, New Jersey

Library of Congress Cataloging-in-Publication Data

Great lives from history. Latinos / Carmen Tafolla, Martha P. Cotera, editors.
   p. cm.
  ISBN 978-1-58765-810-5 (set) — ISBN 978-1-58765-811-2 (vol. 1) — ISBN 978-1-58765-812-9 (vol. 2) — ISBN 978-1-58765-813-6 (vol. 3)
  1. Hispanic Americans—Biography—Encyclopedias.   I. Tafolla, Carmen, 1951-   II. Cotera, Martha.
III. Title: Latinos.
  E184.S75G75 2012
  920.009268—dc23
  [B]

   2011043168

Contents

KEY TO PRONUNCIATION

Many of the names of personages covered in *Great Lives from History: Latinos* may be unfamiliar to students and general readers. For difficult-to-pronounce names, guidelines to pronounciation have been provided upon first mention of the name in each essay. These guidelines do not purport to achieve the subleties of all languages but will offer readers a rough equivalent of how English speakers may approximate the proper pronunciation.

Vowel Sounds

Symbol	Spelled (Pronounced)
a	answer (AN-suhr), laugh (laf), sample (SAM-puhl), that (that)
ah	father (FAH-thur), hospital (HAHS-pih-tuhl)
aw	awful (AW-fuhl), caught (kawt)
ay	blaze (blayz), fade (fayd), waiter (WAYT-ur), weigh (way)
eh	bed (behd), head (hehd), said (sehd)
ee	believe (bee-LEEV), cedar (SEE-dur), leader (LEED-ur), liter (LEE-tur)
ew	boot (bewt), lose (lewz)
i	buy (bi), height (hit), lie (li), surprise (sur-PRIZ)
ih	bitter (BIH-tur), pill (pihl)
o	cotton (KO-tuhn), hot (hot)
oh	below (bee-LOH), coat (koht), note (noht), wholesome (HOHL-suhm)
oo	good (good), look (look)
ow	couch (kowch), how (how)
oy	boy (boy), coin (koyn)
uh	about (uh-BOWT), butter (BUH-tuhr), enough (ee-NUHF), other (UH-thur).

Consonant Sounds

Symbol	Spelled (Pronounced)
ch	beach (beech), chimp (chihmp)
g	beg (behg), disguise (dihs-GIZ), get (geht)
j	digit (DIH-juht), edge (ehj), jet (jeht)
k	cat (kat), kitten (KIH-tuhn), hex (hehks)
s	cellar (SEHL-ur), save (sayv), scent (sehnt)
sh	champagne (sham-PAYN), issue (IH-shew), shop (shop)
ur	birth (burth), disturb (dihs-TURB), earth (urth), letter (LEH-tur)
y	useful (YEWS-fuhl), young (yuhng)
z	business (BIHZ-nehs), zest (zehst)
zh	vision (VIH-zhuhn)

COMPLETE LIST OF CONTENTS

VOLUME 1

Volume 2

Contents

Volume 3

P

EDUARDO PADRÓN

Cuban-born college administrator

Padrón is a well-known college administrator who has significantly advanced opportunities for Latinos at Miami Dade College and, through high-profile service on national boards and commissions, improved the prospects and opportunities for minorities in higher education nationwide.

Latino heritage: Cuban
Born: June 26, 1944; Santiago, Cuba
Also known as: Eduardo José Padrón
Area of achievement: Education

EARLY LIFE

Eduardo José Padrón (pah-DROHN) was born in Santiago, Cuba, on June 26, 1944. At the height of the Cuban Revolution, he fled Cuba with his family, arriving in Miami in 1959 at age fifteen. After graduating from high school, he entered Miami Dade Junior College and received his A.A. in finance and then went on immediately to earn his B.A. in economics from Florida Atlantic University and an M.A.(1967) and Ph.D. (1970) in economics from the University of Florida with a doctoral thesis on post-World War II economic development in Colombia.

Padrón began his college teaching career at his first alma mater, Miami Dade Junior College, as an assistant professor in 1970. Rising quickly to the attention of senior administrators, he was made president of the downtown Wolfson campus, where he served from 1980 to

1995, building strong relationships with the corporate community that would pay enormous dividends in the future. When the presidency of the entire college—then

Eduardo Padrón. (AP Photo)

689

known as Miami Dade Community College—became available, Padrón won the enthusiastic support of the board of trustees and became president in 1995.

LIFE'S WORK

As an American citizen and a refugee from Cuba within a large Cuban American community, Padrón well understood the challenges facing many Latino and minority youths in urban America. As president of Miami Dade Community College, he led a series of changes and skillfully navigated many challenges as he relentlessly focused on improving student learning, opportunity, and facilities and strengthening the city that had become his refuge from the political turmoil of his youth.

Over his more than forty years at the college, Padrón oversaw the creation of more than sixty new programs, expansion of campuses, the launch of a four-year degree in 2003, and an accompanying name change to Miami Dade College. The college experienced explosive growth from around 15,000 students when he first became a professor to more than 170,000 students by 2011, the largest institution of higher education in the nation.

The college has been a well-recognized innovator in higher education with a minorities-majority campus almost from its inception. It was one of the first community colleges to provide an expansive welcome to part-time students and provide the flexibility they needed to succeed. Miami Dade also was one of the first community colleges to introduce multimedia classrooms, a virtual college, an honors college, and the Emerging Technologies Center of the Americas. It launched the Books by the Bay exposition in 1984 to bring literature to the attention of Miami burgeoning and ethnically diverse populations. This well-attended event grew into the well-known Miami Book Fair International. The college took over the Miami Film Festival when it was in danger of disappearing and has built it into a regional powerhouse. Above all, Padrón has overseen outstanding achievements by large numbers of Latinos and African Americans.

A widely sought-after leader, speaker, and adviser, Padrón has served five presidents of the United States in various advisory capacities. In 2010, he was named by President Barack Obama to chair the White House Initiative on Educational Excellence for Hispanic Americans. *Time* magazine hailed him in 2009 as one of the ten best college presidents in the nation and *People* magazine declared him one of the world's most influential Hispanics. He has received awards from France, Argentina, and King Juan Carlos II of Spain, who bestowed upon him the Order of Queen Isabella.

The list of awards Padrón has garnered from civic, cultural, educational, and government entities is long and august. He has been the board chair of the Association of American Colleges and Universities and served on or chaired numerous other prestigious boards, including the Carnegie Foundation for the Advancement of Teaching, American Council on Education, League for Innovation in the Community College, Hispanic Association of Colleges and Universities, the Woodrow Wilson Foundation's Commission on the High School Senior Year, National Institute for Literacy Advisory Board, National Association for the Advancement of Colored People, Hispanic American League against Discrimination, International Association of University Presidents, Council on Foreign Relations, the College Board, and the (U.S.) Congressional Hispanic Caucus Institute.

Padrón also has written countless columns for *Hispanic* magazine and *The Miami Herald* and editorials for *The Chronicle of Higher Education*, *Community College Week*, *Diverse Issues in Higher Education*, *Education Week*, and numerous other publications. He has been a champion for the underprivileged, always explaining the need for sustained and strategic investment in the nation's youth and its workforce through equitable access to educational opportunities. During his tenure, Miami Dade College has won numerous awards for its programs, services, and achievements and has shared its methods and approaches with other institutions in the United States and around the world.

SIGNIFICANCE

One of the most well-known Latino college administrators in the nation and the world, Padrón has given a professional lifetime of service to Miami-Dade College and the citizens of Miami. He has influenced major national educational debates and issues regarding both higher education and primary-secondary education while using his large, diverse, and innovative multicampus institution to demonstrate that what he advocates can, with appropriate planning and execution, become reality.

Dennis W. Cheek

FURTHER READING

Bowens, Raymond C., and Gilbert H. Muller. *Gateways to Democracy: Six Urban Community College Systems*. San Francisco, Calif.: Jossey-Bass, 1999. Miami Dade College and the influence of its president are central features of this academic study.

Padrón, Eduardo J. "In the Center of It All: An Exclusive Interview with Miami Dade College

President Eduardo Padrón." Interview by David Pluviose. *Diverse Issues in Higher Education* 27, no. 9 (June 10, 2010): 24-25. In this interview, Padrón displays his acumen and grounded insights into higher education.

_____. "What Community Colleges Can Do." *Community College Week* 15, no. 3 (September 16, 2002): 5. A brief exposition that demonstrates the clarity of Padrón's vision and the graceful way he encourages others to experiment with educational change that benefit students.

See also: José A. Cárdenas; Lauro Cavazos; Joseph A. Fernández.

RAFAEL PALMEIRO

Cuban-born baseball player

Palmeiro had an impressive two-decade career in professional baseball, winning praise for both his hitting and fielding. In 2005, however, Palmeiro's reputation was tarnished by charges that he used performance-enhancing drugs during his playing career.

Latino heritage: Cuban
Born: September 24, 1964; Havana, Cuba
Also known as: Rafael Palmeiro Corrales
Area of achievement: Baseball

EARLY LIFE

Rafael Palmeiro Corrales (pahl-MEH-roh) was born in Havana, Cuba, on September 24, 1964, to Maria Corrales and Jose Palmeiro. In 1971, Palmeiro and his family legally left Fidel Castro's communist-controlled Cuba for Miami, Florida. In 1982, he graduated from Miami's Jackson High School. Palmeiro played baseball for Mississippi State University, where he set single-season records for runs scored (87), total bases (209), and slugging percentage (.886). He also became the school's career home run leader (67).

LIFE'S WORK

In 1985, before graduating from Mississippi State, Palmeiro signed a contract with the Chicago Cubs. He was their first draft choice that year and the twenty-second player selected overall. He saw limited action in 1986 and 1987, but in 1988 he made the All-Star team and batted .307.

Despite this success, in 1989 Palmeiro was traded to the Texas Rangers, where he spent the next five years. In 1990 and 1991, he finished fourteenth and nineteenth, respectively, in the voting for the American League most valuable player (MVP) award. In 1991, he made the All-Star team for the second time. In 1992, Palmeiro's batting average dipped to .268 (he had hit .322 and .319 the previous two seasons). The next season, though, his average returned to .295 and he had a career high in home runs with 37 (his previous high had been 26 in 1991).

Having finished eighth in the voting for American League MVP that year, Palmeiro became a hot commodity on the free agent market. In 1994, the Baltimore Orioles signed him to a five-year contract worth $30 million, making him at the time the highest-paid player in that franchise's history. Palmeiro's next five years were his most productive; he averaged 36 home

Rafael Palmeiro. (AP Photo)

runs and 110 runs batted in. He won two Gold Glove awards for his defensive work as a first baseman, and in 1998, he garnered the Silver Slugger award (given to the best offensive player at each position as voted by each league's managers and coaches).

When Palmeiro's contract with Baltimore ended, he returned to the Rangers, where he spent the next five years (1999-2003). The 1999 season was Palmeiro's best—he hit 47 home runs and recorded a .324 batting average. For the second straight year, he made the All-Star team and won Gold Glove and Silver Slugger awards. During his next four seasons, Palmeiro's home run totals remained high (ranging from 38 to 47 per year), but his batting average dropped steadily, going from .288 in 2000 to .260 in 2003. Still, in 2002, Palmeiro reached a milestone by hitting his 500th career home run.

In 2004, Palmeiro returned to Baltimore, where he spent the last two years of his career. Although his performance during this time was mediocre, on July 15, 2005, Palmeiro became just the twenty-sixth player in Major League Baseball history to record 3,000 hits. Palmeiro's baseball career ended soon after, on August 1, 2005, when he was suspended after testing positive for the steroid stanzolol. Just a few months earlier, in March, Palmeiro had flatly denied using steroids before a session of the U.S. House of Representatives' Committee on Government Reform, which was investigating allegations of widespread performance-enhancing drug use in baseball.

This investigation had been sparked by a tell-all book written by former major leaguer Jose Canseco, who claimed that he and Palmeiro had used steroids as early as 1992 when they were teammates on the Rangers. Palmeiro denied knowingly using steroids and said he injected himself with what he thought was vitamin B12 from a vial given to him by Orioles teammate Miguel Tejada. He continued to maintain his innocence after retiring from baseball following the 2005 season.

SIGNIFICANCE

By July, 2005, Palmeiro was considered a likely (if not guaranteed) inductee into the Baseball Hall of Fame. He was only the fourth player in major league history to record more than 500 home runs and 3,000 hits. In light of his positive test for steroids, though—and especially after his public testimony to the contrary before Congress—his election to the Hall of Fame became highly unlikely.

John E. Thorburn, Jr.

FURTHER READING

Arangure, Jorge, Jr. "Palmeiro Suspended for Steroids Violation." *The Washington Post*, August 2, 2005. Describes Palmeiro's reaction to his positive drug test and his previous testimony before Congress on the issue of steroids.

Brandt, Ed. *Rafael Palmeiro: At Home with the Baltimore Orioles*. Childs, Md.: Mitchell Lane, 1998. A biography of Palmeiro that pays special attention to the history of Latino baseball players and the Baltimore Orioles franchise.

Canseco, Jose. *Juiced: Wild Times, Rampant 'Roids, Smash Hits, and How Baseball Got Big*. New York: Regan Books, 2005. Controversial work by a former professional baseball player who describes his own use of steroids and accuses other players of using them as well.

_____. *Vindicated: Big Names, Big Liars, and the Battle to Save Baseball*. New York: Simon Spotlight Entertainment, 2008. When Canseco's *Juiced* came out, many declared him a liar, including Palmeiro. In *Vindicated*, Canseco continues his accusations and defends his claims.

Connolly, Dan. "Palmeiro Speaks." *The Baltimore Sun*, June 30, 2006. Profile written after Palmeiro's retirement in which he repeats his assertion that he never knowingly took steroids.

See also: Roberto Alomar; Sandy Alomar, Jr.; José Canseco; David Ortiz; Manny Ramirez; Alex Rodriguez; Miguel Tejada.

CHARLIE PALMIERI

American musician

Palmieri was an authoritative voice in Latin American piano styles, an accomplished classical player, an outstanding arranger, and an virtuoso soloist. His melodic and harmonic ideas distinguished Palmieri as one of the *great creative Latino voices. His technical facility was astounding, and he had an unrivaled command of the entire range of his instrument, with a variety of styles represented, including tango, bolero, cha-cha, and mambo.*

Latino heritage: Puerto Rican

Born: November 21, 1927; South Bronx, New York

Died: September 12, 1988; Bronx, New York

Also known as: Carlos Manuel Palmieri; The Giant of the Keyboard

Area of achievement: Music

EARLY LIFE

Charlie Palmieri was born Carlos Manuel Palmieri on November 21, 1927, in the South Bronx section of New York City. Palmieri's parents had migrated to New York City from Ponce, Puerto Rico, in 1926 and settled in the South Bronx. As a child, Palmieri displayed a penchant for playing the piano, and by the age of seven he was enrolled at the Juilliard School. By 1940, he had participated in many local talent contests, at which he had earned multiple prizes with his five-year old brother, Eddie. In 1943, Palmieri made his professional debut as a piano player for the Osario Selasie Band. He graduated from high school in 1946 and immediately went to play for various bands. He made his recording debut with the song "Se Va La Rumba" as a member of the Rafael Muñoz Band. In 1948, Palmieri made several recordings for the Alba label with his first band, Conjunto Pin Pin, featuring Sabú Martinez on congas. During the remainder of the1940's and 1950's, Palmieri worked as a sideman, accompanying such bandleaders as Xavier Cugat, Tito Puente, Tito Rodriquez, Vicentico Valdés, and Pete Terrace.

LIFE'S WORK

Palmieri made his debut as a leader in 1960 for the United Artists label. The recording *Let's Dance the Charanga!* focused on a Cuban style of music that fused African rhythms with Spanish-tinged melodic lines. Subsequent to the success of the album, he became the music director of a series of groundbreaking studio albums by the Alegre All-Stars.

The public's interest in the charanga waned by the mid-1960's and Palmieri's career suffered. This lull would be temporary because his friend, Latin percussionist Tito Puente, hired Palmieri as the musical conductor for Puente's television show *El Mundo de Tito Puente* in the latter part of the decade.

During the 1970's, the Latin style of the salsa had exploded on the New York scene. Palmieri joined his brother's band, La Perfecta, and together they initiated a progressive aggregate that would prove to be the harbinger of the New York Latin jazz scene, incorporating daring melodic improvisations and complex musical arrangements. Palmieri played a virtuoso organ solo on the classic Eddie Palmieri tune, "Vamonos pal Monte," on the *Harlem River Drive—Live at Sing Sing, Volume 1* album (1971). Charlie Palmieri played with his brother's band on the *Concert at the University of Puerto Rico* (1971) and *Live at Sing Sing, Volume 2* (1972) recordings. Palmieri helped to elevate salsa to a new level, bringing in blazing improvisations and daring arrangements of the repertory. This proved to be integral to Palmieri's career. He consequently was offered to make a trio of albums between 1972 and 1975, and by the end of the decade, for the Alegre label, he had formed a new ensemble, El Combo Gigante, which featured vocalist Jimmy Sabater. However, the 1970's were not without their tragedies: Palmieri suffered a heart attack, which caused him to lose the use of his hands. He ultimately demonstrated great tenacity and resilience by recovering from his paralysis and returned to performing, although not with the full capacity of his hands, at New York's Avery Fisher Hall on March 7, 1977.

Following the three Alegre recordings, Palmieri went on to release five more albums as a leader on the Coco, Alegre, and Tropical Budda labels between 1974 and 1984. His most ambitious album was *A Giant Step* (1984) on Tropical Budda, reviving the piano and rhythm section of bass, timbales, conga, and bongo format. His seemingly voracious appetite and unhealthy lifestyle caused his health to deteriorate, and he suffered another heart attack. He died on September 12, 1988, at Jacobi Hospital in the Bronx, New York.

SIGNIFICANCE

Palmieri served as an ambassador of Latin jazz, propagating the style through his virtuoso facility on his instrument and passion for the music. He helped to fuse Latin elements such as the rhythmic patterns of the mambo, salsa, charanga, and tango with the established jazz canon along with creating an interest in Latin culture. His work was illustrative of the evolutionary process of jazz: he highlighted African and Latin American influences in his arrangements while staying true to the improvisatory nature of the music.

Palmieri's mission to spread the jubilance of Latin jazz was not relegated to the bandstand—as a true ambassador, he lectured frequently in his later years, taught aspiring musicians at institutions such as Schuylerville Music Center, and traveled the globe to unlikely audiences in cities such as London, England.

Michael Conklin

FURTHER READING

Baron, Robert. "Syncretism and Ideology: Latin New York Salsa Musicians." In *Western Folklore* 36, no. 3 (July, 1977): 209-225. An examination of how New York salsa musicians create their music, including drawing upon and reworking their tradition while experimenting with the music of several different Latin ethnic groups in the complex, cultural setting of New York City.

Pinckney, Warren. "Puerto Rican Jazz and the Incorporation of Folk Music: An Analysis of New Music Directions." In *Latin American Music Review* 10, no. 2 (Autumn/Winter, 1989): 236-266. An in-depth analysis of Latin jazz, beyond its bebop influences, which includes Afro-Caribbean, Latin American, and North American forms and structures, both instrumental and vocal.

Schroeder, Pollyanna. "The Growth of Latin American Pop Music in the United States." In *College Music Symposium* 18. No. 2 (Fall, 1978): 124-129. An exquisite article on the rise of Latin culture in the United States, focusing on the indelible mark of Latin musicians throughout the United States.

See also: Celia Cruz; Paul Gonsalves; Noro Morales; Poncho Sánchez; Tito Puente.

AMÉRICO PAREDES

American writer, scholar, and educator

An accomplished writer and educator who was particularly concerned with the history and culture of Mexican Americans in Texas, Paredes was an important early contributor to scholarship on Latino art and literature, particularly music and folktales.

Latino heritage: Mexican

Born: September 3, 1915; Brownsville, Texas

Died: May 5, 1999; Austin, Texas

Also known as: Américo Paredes Manzano; Guálinto Gómez

Areas of achievement: Literature; scholarship; education

EARLY LIFE

Américo Paredes Manzano (ah-MEH-rih-koh pah-REH-dehs mahn-ZAH-noh) was born on September 3, 1915, in Brownsville, Texas. Paredes's father, Justo Paredes Cisneros, was a Mexican citizen, and his mother, Clotilde Manzano Vidal, had family on both sides of the U.S.-Mexico border. As a youngster, Paredes attended public school in Brownsville but spent his summers with family in Matamoros, Mexico, where he learned not only the Spanish language, but also the folklore of Mexico, including *corridos* (folk ballads) and *dichos* (proverbs and other sayings). Paredes's early poems (collected in 1937's *Cantos de adolescencia*) reveal his commitment to speaking to and about Mexican Americans ("Pochos"), a responsibility that would inform his creative and scholarly work throughout his life.

Growing up as a Mexican American in the early twentieth century, Paredes often experienced discrimination. As he notes in "The Mexico-Texan," a poem written when he was in high school, "For the Mexico-Texan he no gotta lan',/ He stomped on the neck on both side of the Gran'." At school, Paredes and other "Mexicanos" were grouped in special classes with diminished academic expectations. Outside of school, Mexican American children and Anglo children were not allowed to play together.

Guálinto, the protagonist in Paredes's novel *George Washington Gómez: A Mexicotexan Novel* (1990), has obvious similarities to the young Paredes—in fact, Paredes used the pen name "Guálinto Gómez" for a time. Like Guálinto, the main character in his novel, Paredes corrected teachers who taught U.S. history exclusively from the perspective of the Anglos; Paredes and Guálinto also both felt pressure to conform to Anglo society even though Anglos looked down upon "Mexicanos."

LIFE'S WORK

After Paredes graduated from Brownsville Junior College in 1936, he volunteered to serve in World War II. While stationed in Japan, he worked as editor of the Pacific edition of the military publication *Stars and Stripes*. In 1950, Paredes enrolled at the University of Texas at Austin. He completed his bachelor's degree in English and philosophy in 1951, his master's degree in 1953, and his Ph.D. in 1956. His graduate degrees were in English (folklore) and Spanish. In 1958, Paredes became a professor of English and anthropology at the University of Texas at Austin,

Also in 1958, Paredes published his dissertation, *With His Pistol in His Hand: A Border Ballad and Its Hero*, an analysis of a *corrido* about Gregorio Cortez, a Mexican American outlaw and folk hero. The *corrido* questions Cortez's guilt and the motivation of the Texas Rangers who pursued him, implying that they were seeking the reward money rather than justice. Through books such as *Folktales of Mexico* (1970), *A Texas Mexican Cancionero: Folksongs of the Lower Border* (1976), and *Uncle Remus con Chile* (1993), Paredes continued in his scholarship to showcase folklore originating from both sides of the Rio Grande.

In 1989, Paredes was one of the first recipients of the Charles Frankel Prize from the National Endowment for the Humanities for his lifelong contributions to the humanities, and in 1990, he became one of the first Mexican American inductees into the Order of the Aztec Eagle, given by Mexico to non-citizens for the advancement of Mexican culture.

Also in 1990, Paredes published *George Washington Gómez*, which he had originally written thirty years earlier. In the novel, Paredes explores the ramifications of the 1848 Treaty of Guadalupe Hidalgo, which ceded much Mexican territory to the United States, including the region that became south Texas. Although initially this reconfiguration of national borders led to resistance by Mexican Americans, exemplified by the activities and stories of the older generation in the novel, the main character, Guálinto/George Washington Gómez represents the generation who opted to assimilate into the dominant U.S. culture. The main character Anglicizes his name, marries an Anglo woman, and becomes a U.S. Army officer tasked with border security. Although many readers criticized Paredes for seemingly advocating assimilation, Paredes purposefully kept the text as he wrote it in 1960 in order to reflect a period before the Chicano movement and widespread Mexican American cultural pride. On May 5, 1999, Paredes died after a lengthy illness.

SIGNIFICANCE

Paredes's writings demanded respect for the Mexican American people and their culture. His work moved Mexican Americans from the margins to the center of attention and challenged readers to question the status quo, especially with regard to voices that have been historically silenced. As an anthropologist and folklore scholar, Paredes preserved folktales and folk songs of the border and established their scholarly significance. In so doing, he helped to create the field of Chicano studies. In 1970, Paredes also helped to create the Center for Mexican American Studies at the University of Texas, a national leader in the field.

Nancy Effinger Wilson

FURTHER READING

Medrano, Manuel F. *Américo Paredes: In His Own Words, an Authorized Biography*. Denton: University of North Texas Press, 2010. Compiled from interviews with Paredes and his family. Also contains photographs and transcripts from the interviews that Medrano conducted with Paredes over a five-year period before Paredes's death in 1999.

Morín, José R. López. *The Legacy of Américo Paredes*. College Station: Texas A&M University Press, 2006. A general and accessible introduction to the life and scholarship of Américo Paredes, including historical background on the Lower Rio Grande region.

Paredes, Américo. *George Washington Gómez: A Mexicotexan Novel*. Houston: Arte Público Press, 1990. A bildungsroman about a young Mexican American man living in the early twentieth century in Texas near the Mexico border.

Saldívar, Ramón. *The Borderlands of Culture: Américo Paredes and the Transnational Imaginary*. Durham, N.C.: Duke University Press, 2006. Saldívar theorizes that Paredes's life on the border and his time spent in Asia enabled him to become transnational long before that term was coined.

See also: Rudolfo Anaya; Rolando Hinojosa; Luis Leal; Felipe de Ortego y Gasca.

CESAR PELLI

Argentine-born architect

Pelli is one of the world's leading architects. His designs are innovative and influential, earning him several awards. In 2010, his Petronas Towers were the largest twin buildings in the world. Pelli also pioneered a method of collaboration on projects that changed the nature of architectural business.

Latino heritage: Argentinean
Born: October 12 1926; Tucumán, Argentina
Area of achievement: Architecture

EARLY LIFE

Cesar Pelli (SEH-sahr PEH-lee) was born October 12, 1926, in Tucumán, Argentina. His mother worked as a teacher, lecturer, and writer. Pelli was exposed to European and American cultural influences as well as Argentine culture while growing up. As a boy, he read that architects needed to be good at drawing and appreciate history; Pelli liked both, so he decided to pursue architecture as a career.

Pelli attended the National University of Tucumán, graduating with a bachelor's degree in architecture in 1949. It was during this time that the modernist movement in architecture began. Modernism is defined by simple, cubic forms and relies on glass, steel, and concrete as building materials. Pelli married Diana Balmori, a landscape designer, in 1950. They later had two children, Denis and Rafael.

For the next two years, Pelli worked as the director of design for a government agency that built subsidized housing in Tucumán. He won a scholarship from the Institute of International Education in 1952 to study architecture in the United States. Pelli and his wife moved to Illinois, where he studied at the University of Illinois School of Design. He graduated with a master's degree in architecture in 1954. After graduation, Pelli began his apprenticeship with the firm of Eero Saarinen. Saarinen, considered a master in architecture, had a great impact on Pelli. While working for Saarinen, Pelli was a project designer on the Trans World Airlines terminal building at John F. Kennedy International Airport in New York. In 1960, Pelli briefly taught architectural design at the National University of Tucumán in Argentina.

LIFE'S WORK

Pelli returned to the United States and continued working for Saarinen until 1964. That year, he became a naturalized American citizen. He moved with his family to Los Angeles, where he became vice president and director of design at the firm of Daniel, Mann, Johnson, and Mendenhall. Pelli worked there until 1968, when he became a partner in the Gruen Associates firm. For two years he also was a visiting professor at the University of California at Berkeley. Pelli worked for Gruen until 1976, after which he accepted the position as dean of Yale University's School of Architecture.

When Pelli moved to New Haven, Connecticut, he also started his own design firm with two associates from Los Angeles. The small firm soon was hired to handle the expansion and remodeling of New York's Museum of Modern Art. Because Pelli's firm was not equipped to handle a job of that size, he began what became a new mode of practice in architecture: collaboration. He hired a large New York firm to help with the production drawings, while Pelli's firm handled the creative design aspects. His idea showed that a small firm could maintain creative control and still execute large national and international projects. Pelli retired from

Cesar Pelli. (Getty Images)

Yale in 1984 but continued to lecture occasionally while working with his design firm, Pelli Clarke Pelli.

Pelli received the American Institute of Architects' Gold Medal in 1995. Among his most famous buildings are the Petronas Twin Towers in Kuala Lumpur, Malaysia, which were completed in 1997. The two eighty-eight-story skyscrapers include a pyramidal pinnacle and spire. Their total height is 1,483 feet, which made them the world's tallest buildings until 2004. A walkway connects the forty-first and forty-second floors of the two towers. In 2004, Pelli received the Aga Khan Award for Architecture for the design. Pelli has designed a number of skyscrapers and finds them fascinating. In 2008, he received an honorary doctorate from Yale University. He also has received several other honorary degrees.

SIGNIFICANCE

Pelli's buildings have changed the skylines of numerous cities throughout the world. In 1991, the American Institute of Architects named Pelli one of the ten most influential living American architects. He approaches new designs without any preconceived ideas; each has its own context. He embraces new building and construction technology because it allows him to design taller, more elegant buildings using thinner metal and glass. By 2011, the firm of Pelli Clarke Pelli had more than 150 employees and offices in New Haven and New York City. The firm also is a leader in environmentally friendly design.

Jennifer L. Campbell

FURTHER READING

Crosbie, Michael. *Cesar Pelli: Buildings and Projects 1988-1998.* New York: Birkhauser Basel, 1998. The author explains Pelli's method, motivation, and design behind his major architectural projects. Includes data on his designs from 1969 to 1997, including pictures, facts, and figures for each.

Pelli, Cesar. *Observations for Young Architects.* New York: Monacelli Press, 1999. Pelli explains the factors an architect should consider when formulating a design. Includes an in-depth discussion of his own work as examples.

Pelli, Cesar, and Michael Crosbie. *Petronas Twin Towers: The Architecture of High Construction.* New York: Wiley-Academy, 2005. Describes the creation of the Petronas Twin Towers in Kuala Lumpur.

See also: Eduardo Catalano; Juan Estanislao Cotera.

ELIZABETH PEÑA

American actor and director

Known for her compelling work in such films as Jacob's Ladder (1990), Lone Star (1996), and How the Garcia Girls Spent Their Summer (2005), Peña is a Cuban American performer who insists on artistic and personal integrity and supports artistic ambition in people of diverse backgrounds.

Latino heritage: Cuban
Born: September 23, 1959; Elizabeth, New Jersey
Also known as: Elizabeth Anne Dickinson
Areas of achievement: Acting; filmmaking; radio and television

EARLY LIFE

Elizabeth Peña (PAYN-yuh) was born in Elizabeth, New Jersey, to actor, writer, and director Mario Peña and producer and arts administrator Estella Marguerita Toirac Peña. When Peña was nine months old, the family moved back to her parents' native Cuba. Her parents believed that, since Fidel Castro had unseated corrupt dictator Fulgencio Bautista, they could have a better life on the island. However, Mario soon was imprisoned for what were considered subversive philosophical views and writings; after his prison term, he was exiled from Cuba, while Estella, Peña, and Peña's younger sister were forced to remain in the country for eight more years.

When the family finally reunited in 1968, the Peñas moved to New York. There on Manhattan's Upper West Side, Peña grew up following in her artistic, theatrical parents' footsteps. In 1970, Peña's father founded the New York City Latin American Theatre Ensemble (LATE). While her mother hoped for a more stable career for her daughter, Peña was eager to pursue acting and enrolled at New York's High School for the Performing Arts.

Peña's passion for acting soon landed her a place as professional actor in repertory theatre as well as in a number of television commercials. By the time she had

Elizabeth Peña. (AP Photo)

graduated from the well-known school, she was studying with private teachers and training as an actor in a variety of genres and styles.

LIFE'S WORK

Peña worked tirelessly at her craft, and by 1979, she was acting on stage and in films. That year, she was cast as Juliet in *Romeo and Juliet* (1595-1596), as Beba in *La noche de los asasinos* (1965; *The Criminals*, 1971), and as Aurelita in the film *El Super* (1979). She went on to more roles in independent films, such as *Times Square* (1980), *They All Laughed* (1981), and *Crossover Dreams* (1985), and episodes of the television shows *Cagney and Lacey* and *T. J. Hooker*, both in 1985.

Having convinced her mother that acting was the right career for her, Peña set her sights on mainstream film work. She moved to Los Angeles, designed a plan, and bombarded the office of the casting director for *Down and Out in Beverly Hills* (1986) with demonstration tapes, photographs, and messages, often sent through a friend who worked for security on the studio lot. She was rewarded with the role of Carmen, for which she won critical praise. Peña used similar strategies to earn roles in numerous hit films, television projects, and animated works. She has received numerous honors for her acting and her work as mentor and advocate for aspiring filmmakers. Her career grew to include dozens of acting credits; she also directed episodes of the series *The Brothers Garcia* and *Resurrection Blvd.* in the early 2000's.

SIGNIFICANCE

Peña's career is built on a rigorous work ethic and a robust passion for acting. As a female, Cuban American performer, she is a staunch advocate of diversity in front of and behind the camera. She resists stereotypical Latino roles and promotes the work of Latino artists. She took part in the founding of the National Association of Latino Independent Producers in her role as a board member for Film Independent and established the Elizabeth Peña Fellowship in Project: Involve. She also has been featured in such initiatives as Target's Dream in Color diversity program.

Roxanne McDonald

FURTHER READING

Garcia-Johnson, Ronie-Richele. "Elizabeth Peña." In *Latinas!: Women of Achievement*, edited by Diane Telgen and Jim Kamp. Detroit, Mich.: Visible Ink Press, 1996.

Otfinoski, Steven. "Elizabeth Peña." In *Latinos in the Arts*. New York: Facts On File, 2007. A comprehensive entry that addresses Peña's experiences as a Latina performer.

Peña, Elizabeth. "My Interview with Elizabeth Peña." Interview by Greg Hernandez. *The Los Angeles Daily News*, May 19, 2008. Peña discusses Hollywood typecasting and her role in the film *How the Garcia Girls Spent Their Summer* (2005).

See also: María Conchita Alonso; Catherine Bach; Benjamin Bratt; Andy Garcia; Rosie Pérez; Jimmy Smits.

FEDERICO PEÑA

American politician

As a two-term mayor of Denver, and later as President Bill Clinton's secretaries of transportation and energy, Peña established a national reputation for progressive, activist leadership with a broad interest in cutting-edge strategies that relied on the use of ecologically friendly technologies to enhance the urban landscape.

Latino heritage: Mexican
Born: March 15, 1947; Laredo, Texas
Also known as: Federico Fabian Peña
Area of achievement: Government and politics

EARLY LIFE

Born in Laredo, Texas, and raised in Brownsville, an industrial hub in south Texas along the Rio Grande, Federico Fabian Pena (fehd-eh-REE-koh FAY-bee-ahn PAYN-yah) enjoyed a comfortable middle-class upbringing as the son of a successful commodities broker in the Texas cotton industry. His parents encouraged their children to succeed through diligence and commitment. Early on, Peña excelled in school, and in 1965,

Federico Peña. (AP Photo)

he matriculated at the University of Texas at Austin. Attending college at the height of nationwide campus resistance to the Vietnam War, Peña was drawn to politics and joined campus protest demonstrations and campaigned for local liberal politicians. By the time he graduated in 1969, he was committed to law as a career and was accepted at the University of Texas School of Law, completing his law degree in 1972.

Peña moved to Denver, Colorado, to join the law firm in which his older brother was practicing. Living in Denver was something of a cultural shock for Peña, who grew up within the Tex-Mex culture of border towns in southern Texas and now lived in a Rocky Mountain metropolis in which Hispanics accounted for less than 18 percent of the population. In his brother's firm, Peña specialized in civil rights litigation involving Hispanics, particularly cases involving police brutality and voting irregularities. A charismatic presence, articulate and handsome, Peña made a forceful impression and quickly became one of the Denver's leading Hispanic advocates, championing bilingual education and better funding for schools in predominantly Latino neighborhoods.

LIFE'S WORK

Concerned by the lack of progress in these areas, Peña in 1978 ran successfully for a seat in the Colorado general assembly. Quickly establishing himself as a rising star, he was named outstanding freshman Democrat by Colorado's Social Action Committee. Despite being reelected two years later and then selected as the party's minority leader, Peña, frustrated by the cumbersome machinery of state politics and convinced that local politics was more effective, announced his intention in early 1983 to run for mayor of Denver. His candidacy appeared at best a long shot as Peña, a neophyte to city politics, was running against William "Mayor Bill" McNichols, an institution in Denver Democratic politics. McNichols was in his fifteenth year in office, the second-longest mayoral term in the city's history, and a man credited with a building boom that had transformed Denver. More problematically, the Hispanic voting bloc in the city, which would presumably be Peña's strength, had yet to be organized; only 7 percent of the city's Hispanics were actually registered to vote.

Peña, a charismatic campaigner, took advantage of voter discontent over McNichols's perceived mismanagement of the city's catastrophic 1977 Christmas Eve blizzard, a monstrous snowstorm that had paralyzed Denver for almost ten days. The city's forty-five plows proved ineffective against three-inch-per-hour snowfalls accumulating in ten-foot drifts. Moreover, McNichols had refused to pursue federal disaster relief, making the city entirely responsible for the cost of recovery operations. Peña seized on voters' discontent and crafted a narrow victory through a coalition of minority advocacy groups, liberal think-tank visionaries, and business-savvy entrepreneurs ready to reshape Denver into an international center. In becoming the city's first Hispanic mayor, Peña was catapulted onto the national political stage.

Peña's first term was uneven. New to city management, he proposed far more programs than entrenched interests wanted to undertake, focusing primarily on construction of a massive new downtown convention center. Peña was stung by the rancorous criticism aimed at him over his lack of management finesse. In the months before the 1987 mayoral race, it appeared he would be soundly defeated for reelection because he was down by more than 20 percent in the polls. Drawing on his base of support in the minority communities, Peña narrowly won reelection by less than 2 percent of the vote in a June runoff after an acrimonious and often ugly campaign against Dan Bain, a corporate lawyer with no political experience.

After surviving a recall—ironically, after charges of mismanaging a snowstorm—Peña enjoyed a far more successful second term. Many of his visionary ideas for Denver's development were approved. Although he was considered a shoo-in for a third term, Peña retired to spend time with his family. He founded an investment firm that focused on recruiting the best Hispanic talent in the country.

In late 1992, Peña's achievements in improving Denver's transportation system led to his being approached by President-elect Bill Clinton's transition team to serve as a cluster adviser, shaping the incoming administration's policies on alternative energies, public transportation, environmental research, and infrastructure rebuilding. Clinton later named Peña to serve as the secretary of transportation, the first Hispanic to head this department. Peña became one of the administration's most recognized cabinet members, spearheading activist efforts to develop overseas routes for American-based airlines, to rebuild Los Angeles's devastated infrastructure after the 1993 earthquake, to develop urban programs that supported mass transit and biking as

---

Peña's Accomplishments as Mayor of Denver

"Imagine a Great City"–the uplifting campaign slogan for Federico Peña's hotly contested mayoral reelection bid in 1987—summarizes his impact on Denver politics. Despite first-term frustrations as he and his advisers mastered the bruising art of city politics, Peña offered his city, well aware of its national reputation as a cultural backwater and minor regional center, a vision of itself as a major industrial, economic, transportation, and cultural hub. Peña thought big: His megaprojects included a revitalization of Denver's downtown and its infrastructure, at a cost of nearly $330 million; Coors Field, a state-of-the-art sports facility for the Colorado Rockies; the sprawling Colorado Convention Center, which opened in 1990 and is the tenth-largest such facility in the United States; and, most controversially, a major new international airport.

With his irrepressible optimism, his commitment to cutting-edge ecologically friendly technologies, his savvy way with potential investors, and his charismatic appeal to the city's growing minority communities, Peña enjoyed a landmark second term. His visionary energy had its critics, most notably in the form of entrenched resistance to the new international airport, which was the centerpiece of his vision for Denver. Initially, vested interests resisted his proposal, arguing that the existing Stapleton International Airport simply needed to be expanded. Peña, however, fought hard for the project. Construction of a new airport bogged down in nearly a decade of construction delays, labor disputes, rumors of insider contracts, and cost overruns, although by then Peña was no longer serving as mayor. When the new airport opened in 1995, however, it bore out Peña's vision. Its sweeping architecture, with a five-point white fiberglass roof made to simulate the snow-capped Rockies, dazzled visitors. The facility quickly became one of the busiest airports in the world, regularly selected by travel magazines and news outlets as one of the most efficient and traveler-friendly airports in the country. For his contributions to Denver's growth, Peña was inducted in 2001 into the state's Tourism Hall of Fame.

alternatives to choked highway systems, and to pursue often controversial government recalls to ensure safer cars and trucks.

Although Peña opted not to serve in Clinton's second term, the president asked him to stay on as the secretary of energy. Reluctantly, Peña remained in Washington, D.C., and for a year he advocated for alternative energy policies and brokered delicate negotiations about storing nuclear waste in the West.

Peña left office on April 6, 1998, and returned to Denver. He accepted a position as managing partner at the billion-dollar international equity firm of Vestar Capital Partners. In 2007, nearly a year before the national elections, Peña publicly endorsed U.S. senator Barack Obama for president, despite Peña's close political affiliation with Hillary Clinton, Obama's chief rival. Later, Peña served as the Obama campaign's national cochair. He also worked on the newly elected president's transition team and helped advise Obama on immigration reform.

Significance

Although Peña succeeded in reshaping the physical layout of Denver and transforming the city into a major commercial center, his success, as he readily acknowledged, was a joint effort, reflecting his ability to forge a coalition of business visionaries, technology wonks, and the city's minority leaders and voters. Peña's ambitious and activist agenda while serving in the Clinton administration often met with stiff political opposition. Peña, however, accomplished something far more important. He was one of the first high-profile Hispanic politicians and one of the first politicians to mobilize Hispanic voters, who would become one of the most sought-after voting blocs in American politics. Given Colorado's neglected Hispanic community in the late 1970's, Peña's electoral successes paved the way for the next generation of Latino candidates by demonstrating that voters were ready to accept, or reject, candidates based not on ethnicity but on their vision and their accomplishments.

Joseph Dewey

FURTHER READING

Dempsey, Paul Stephen, Andrew Goetz, and Joseph S. Szyliowicz. *Denver International Airport: Lessons Learned.* New York: McGraw-Hill, 1997. Detailed and balanced analysis of both the good and the bad aspects of the megaproject most associated with Peña's administration.

Maraniss, David. *First in His Class: A Biography of Bill Clinton.* New York: Simon & Schuster, 1995. Among the glut of biographies available on Clinton, this book, written by a Pulitzer Prize-winner, is one of the most helpful. Describes the initial logic behind the best-and-the-brightest cabinet initiative that included Peña.

Salazar, Kenneth, and Cindy Browsky. *Wellington Webb: The Man, the Mayor, and the Making of Modern Denver.* Golden, Colo.: Fulcrum, 2007. Laudatory biography of Peña's immediate successor. Defines the magnitude of Peña's vision and his accomplishments, many of them long-term and not completed until after he left office.

See also: Henry G. Cisneros; Alberto Gonzales; Edward Hidalgo; Manuel Luján, Jr.; Bill Richardson; Ken Salazar; Hilda L. Solis.

ALONSO PERALES

American lawyer, diplomat, and journalist

Perales was a civil rights attorney, diplomat to Latin American countries, and second president of the League of United Latin American Citizens (LULAC).

Latino heritage: Mexican
Born: October 17, 1898; Alice, Texas
Died: May 9, 1960; San Antonio, Texas
Also known as: Alonso S. Perales
Areas of achievement: Law; activism; journalism

EARLY LIFE

Alonso S. Perales (peh-RAH-lehs) was born on October 17, 1898, in Alice, Texas. Both parents died during his youth—first his mother, then his father. He was orphaned by the age of twelve and was therefore motivated to take care of himself. He worked various jobs during high school and college and used his earnings to pay for tuition and living expenses. However, his college days were cut short when he was drafted for military service during World War I.

Following his honorable discharge from the Army, Perales enrolled at George Washington University in Washington, D.C., where he eventually earned a bachelor of arts degree. Perales later enrolled at National University, where he earned a juris doctorate in 1926. While in college, he worked for the Commerce Department in Washington, D.C.

Soon thereafter, Perales married Marta Pérez y Peña. They adopted a daughter and two sons. In the 1920's, Perales was appointed to serve as a diplomat in Chile, Cuba, the Dominican Republic, Mexico, Nicaragua, and the West Indies. He remained in this role until the 1930's.

LIFE'S WORK

After the Mexican-American War ended, thousands of Mexican immigrants became U.S. citizens. However, they were not treated as citizens. Mexican Americans faced widespread discrimination. As a result, several civil rights organizations were founded. These organizations eventually merged to form the League of United Latin American Citizens (LULAC) in 1927. Perales played a major role in the unification; his goal was to merge all Hispanic organizations in a show of solidarity and to fight the overt discrimination that was prevalent in America. Perales, along with José Tomás Canales and Eduardo Idar, created the LULAC constitution. He was sworn in as the group's second president at its 1930 convention in Alice, Texas.

As president of LULAC, one of Perales's greatest accomplishments was the defeat of the Box Immigration Bill in 1930, which would have put a quota on Mexican immigration to the United States. His other civic activities included founding the Independent Voters Association, a Mexican American political club in San Antonio, introducing legislation outlawing racial discrimination, and membership in other religious and civil rights organizations. For his civic activities, Perales was honored by Spain with the Medal of Civil Merit, one of the nation's highest civil honors.

Perales also was a superb journalist. He published books, speeches, and essays. His book *Are We Good Neighbors?* (1948) documents cases of racial discrimination, and *En defensa de mi raza* (1937) includes his essays and speeches on racial discrimination as well as writings of other advocates. In addition, Perales was a columnist for the Spanish publication *La prensa.* He wrote numerous articles for other Spanish publications, reporting on issues in the Catholic Church and civil rights battles in the Mexican community. Perales died in 1960 in San Antonio, Texas.

SIGNIFICANCE

Perales's defeat of the Box Immigration Bill holds great historical significance. The bill would have placed a quota on the number of Mexican immigrants permitted to enter the United States. Accompanied by Canales and civil rights activist Ben Garza, Perales went to Washington, D.C., and testified in congressional hearings against the bill. Perales was honored by Mexican Americans for his faith and courage in the face of tremendous adversity.

Perales was elected to serve as LULAC's second president. Although he only served one term, his leadership was critical in the organization's early days. For several decades following its founding, LULAC has remained a vital and influential organization.

Sandra W. Leconte

FURTHER READING

Buitron, Richard A. *The Quest for Tejano Identity in San Antonio, Texas, 1913-2000.* New York: Routledge, 2004. Describes Perales's importance as an intellectual and activist leader.

Kaplowitz, Craig Allen. *LULAC, Mexican Americans, and National Policy.* College Station: Texas A&M University Press, 2005. Detailed history of LULAC that examines its influence on national policy over the years. Includes discussion of Perales's role.

Orozco, Cynthia. *No Mexicans, Women, or Dogs Allowed: The Rise of the Mexican American Civil Rights Movement.* Austin: University of Texas Press, 2009. Well-documented and thoroughly researched history of the drive for equal rights and treatment for Mexican Americans, including examination of Perales and LULAC.

See also: Gus C. Garcia; Reies López Tijerina.

JAMES PEREZ

Mexican-born physician

Perez, a physician in Burlington, Colorado, has encouraged doctors to pursue the difficult challenges and special opportunities of practicing rural medicine.

Latino heritage: Mexican
Born: 1968; Durango, Durango, Mexico
Also known as: Jesús James Perez
Area of achievement: Medicine

EARLY LIFE

Jesús James Perez (hay-SOOS jaymz PEHR-ehz) was born in Durango in the northwest Mexican state of the same name. His parents worked the cotton and wheat fields that surrounded the capital city until Perez was five, and the family, which included Perez's younger brother Raul, migrated to California, settling in North Hollywood in the San Fernando Valley. Unable to find steady work, the Perez family adopted the peripatetic life typical of migrant workers—following the crops, living at different times in Florida, then Michigan, then Ohio before settling in the remote rural farm community of Burlington, Colorado, along the Kansas border on the high plains. The town's population of around three thousand was more than 25 percent Hispanic, reflecting Burlington's agricultural economy. Perez's father found steady farmwork, and his mother, who spoke only Spanish, washed dishes at a local hotel's restaurant. Despite the community's high percentage of Hispanics, when Perez attended public schools there was only one other Latino in his class. Acutely aware that he and his family were different, Perez made few friends, but he excelled in school, particularly in science and math. His father, who had finished only the sixth grade, preached to both his sons that education was the key to success in their adopted country.

Perez's eventual decision to pursue medicine came when, at fifteen, his brother, who had long suffered from seizures, was diagnosed with a brain parasite by a white doctor in a Denver hospital. The doctor's recommendation was risky brain surgery. This news was terrifying to the family, and over the next several months Perez's father drained the family's savings by returning to California to get a second medical opinion. The California doctors, many of them Hispanic, found evidence in Raul of a brain disorder treatable with a relatively simple regimen of medication. The misdiagnosis in Denver,

the family suspected, came from the white doctors who treated minority patients with less concern. Perez was certain now that he wanted to attend medical school.

LIFE'S WORK

Although few of his Hispanic friends even aspired to college (at the time, fewer than 10 percent of Hispanics nationwide who matriculated in college completed the four-year program), Perez was determined. In 1988, he was accepted at Colorado State University in Fort Collins. Despite shuttling to Burlington on most weekends to help his family by picking up odd jobs, Perez dedicated himself to his studies and graduated four years later with a premedicine degree and Phi Beta Kappa honors. By now, Perez was married and had a son, and he faced the intimidating cost of paying for the medical school he had dreamed of attending since his brother's crisis. Burlington was a small town and news of his dilemma spread. In a fortuitous coincidence, the town was facing its own crisis, with two of its four longtime physicians on the verge of retirement. The fact that the town relied on only four doctors to help three thousand residents was difficult enough, but the prospect of dropping to two doctors compelled the town to take drastic action. Burlington had tried in vain to recruit city doctors to relocate to this remote town. Seeing an opportunity to help one of the town's most promising students and at the same time solve the town's doctor shortage, the mayor brokered a deal with a local businessman, who had made millions of dollars selling farm machinery. The deal was simple: Burlington would pay for Perez's medical school, a cost of more than $100,000, and in return Perez would agree to return to Burlington to practice for at least one full year. Perez enthusiastically agreed, and the deal was sealed with a simple handshake. Perez's childhood friend, Sacramento Pimentel, entered into a similar deal with Burlington.

Perez completed the curriculum at the School of Medicine at the University of Colorado in Denver and his three-year residency in family medicine at the Northern Colorado Medical Center in Greeley, just south of Fort Collins. Without hesitation, Perez returned to Burlington. The unique deal he had struck with the town was the subject of numerous local news features and a profile in *People* magazine. Although he was bound to stay in Burlington for only one year, Perez remained, accepting a position at Kit Carson County Memorial Hospital. Perez was committed to his original ambition of giving the community of Burlington a full-time resident family practitioner and, more specifically, of providing the community's growing Hispanic population with a reassuring medical presence. Perez tirelessly advocated the need for medical school graduates to make a similar commitment to small-town practice despite the appeal, and lucrative salaries, of urban practice. The School of Medicine at the University of Colorado featured Perez in a video extolling the importance of rural doctors, seeing in their commitment to small-town practice the satisfying reward of contributing an invaluable service to the life of the community.

SIGNIFICANCE

James Perez enjoyed a moment of celebrity by dint of the once-in-a-lifetime deal his small town offered him as a way to realize his dream of becoming a doctor, and Perez never forgot this lucky break. He has dedicated his professional life to promoting the often grueling regimen of being a "country doctor," that particularly nineteenth century-sounding phrase a reminder of a career choice whose importance is routinely overlooked by a progressively more urban-oriented twenty-first century culture. By bringing current expertise and cutting-edge technology to the rural health care system, Perez has served as a reminder for a new generation of doctors of the continuing importance of that commitment.

Joseph Dewey

FURTHER READING

O'Neill, Anne-Marie. "Homeward Bound." *People*. August 19, 1996. Early profile of Perez focusing on the deal he made with the town of Burlington.

Rabinowitz, Howard K. *Caring for the Country: Family Doctors in Small Rural Towns*. New York: Springer, 2004. Revealing anecdotal accounts of the lives of ten rural doctors. Addresses the special challenges of the profession and underscores the scarcity of country doctors. Intended for premedicine students.

University of Colorado, Denver, Anschutz Medical Campus. www.ucdenver.edu. Includes a link to resources on rural medicine and the program that first attracted Perez. Features Perez's testimonial video.

See also: John F. Alderete; Richard Henry Carmona; Norma Martinez-Rogers; Sacramento Pimentel.

ROSIE PÉREZ

American actor, dancer, and activist

Best known for her acting in films such as Do the Right Thing *(1989) and* White Men Can't Jump *(1992), Pérez also has made significant contributions as a dancer and choreographer and an activist on issues related to Puerto Rico.*

Latino heritage: Puerto Rican

Born: September 6, 1964; Bushwick, Brooklyn, New York

Also known as: Rosa María Pérez

Areas of achievement: Acting; filmmaking; dance; activism

EARLY LIFE

Rosa Maria Pérez (PEH-rehz) was born on September 6, 1964. She is a twin and one of eleven children—six girls and four boys. Although she would later develop a close relationship with him, Pérez's birth father, merchant marine Ismael Serrano, was absent early in her life, leaving her to be raised by Lydia Pérez, her biological mother, and Ventura Pérez, Lydia's husband. Lydia was a former singer, and both parents loved to dance salsa, so the Brooklyn home was alive with music. However, Ventura was a small-time racketeer who abused his wife, making it difficult for her to care for her ten children. After Lydia sent the children away, Pérez spent time in a group foster home and in the home of an aunt who worked three jobs to care for her charges.

LIFE'S WORK

Despite this turbulent early life, Pérez was a good student with varied interests. Her talent for science took her from Grover Cleveland High School in Queens, New York, to Los Angeles City College, where she began studies in marine biology as a biochemistry major. Her talent for performing, however, soon took her away from academics. One night, while Pérez was dancing at a Latin club in Los Angeles, a producer for television's *Soul Train* offered her a spot dancing on the weekly variety show. There she met Louis Silas, then senior vice president of black music at MCA Records, who offered

Rosie Pérez.
(Albert L. Ortega/PictureGroup.com via AP Images)

her a place in a recording group. She declined the offer, and stopped dancing on *Soul Train* after a few sessions.

Moving on to dance at various venues in the late 1980's, Pérez again was approached by Silas, who wanted her to recruit dancers and choreograph for singer Bobby Brown, at the time a young, rising star. The inexperienced Pérez at first declined, but upon listening to the music planned for Brown's third solo album (*Bobby*, 1992), she accepted. Her effort was a success, launching her career as a choreographer: the Bobby Brown project led to work for the Motown group the Boys; Pérez and her dance group, Heart and Soul, soon were choreographing for the Fly Girls, the dance troupe on the Wayans brothers' sketch-comedy show, *In Living Color* (1990-1994). Pérez also choreographed for stage and video productions featuring recording artists such as Al B. Sure, L. L. Cool J., and Diana Ross.

Pérez did not limit her talents to choreography. One night while dancing at the club Funky Reggae, Pérez again was singled out—this time by film director Spike Lee. Although she still was in college when she returned Lee's phone call to play the part of Tina in his fourth film, *Do the Right Thing* (1989), Pérez accepted the role that changed her life. She moved into film acting through the next two decades, then into directing and narrating such works as *Yo soy Boricua! Pa'que tu lo sepas!* (2006; *I'm Boricua, Just So You Know!*). She also performed onstage in *Frankie and Johnnie in the Clair de Lune* (1987) in 2002. Pérez has received or been nominated for several awards, including an Oscar nomination for Best Actress in a Supporting Role for *Fearless* (1993).

Pérez also actively supports research and education on acquired immune deficiency syndrome (AIDS) and has long been an activist for Puerto Rican rights, participating in such noted events as the protest in 2000 to stop the U.S. Navy from testing bombs on Vieques, a small island off the coast of Puerto Rico.

SIGNIFICANCE

Pérez made her first significant contributions as a choreographer of what she would later describe as lean, crisp, authentic hip-hop. A well-known character actor, she was known for her distinctive Puerto Rican-Brooklyn accent, and she built a career playing quirky, tough, yet relatable women. She later rejected her early role in *Do the Right Thing* as stereotypical and vowed to play characters not defined by ethnic clichés.

Roxanne McDonald

FURTHER READING

Lee, Spike, and Kaleem Aftab. *That's My Story and I'm Sticking to It*. New York: W. W. Norton, 2005. Lee's autobiography covers the making of *Do the Right Thing* and his discovery of Pérez. Pérez herself also offers her observations about the film and director.

Pérez, Rosie. "I, Latina." Interview by Mim Udovitch. *Vibe* 1, no. 4 (December, 1993-January, 1994): 65-68. Lengthy cover story and interview with Pérez early in her career, in which she discusses her youth in Brooklyn and personality.

Valdivia, Angharad N. "Stereotype or Transgression? Rosie Perez in Hollywood Film." *The Sociological Quarterly* 39, no. 3 (1998): 393-409. A thorough investigation into the creation and perception of Latinas in Hollywood film, by way of the application of interviews with Pérez, film reviews, and textual analysis of films.

See also: María Conchita Alonso; Catherine Bach; Lynda Carter; John Leguizamo; Eva Longoria; George Lopez.

Victor Perez-Mendez
Guatemalan-born scientist and inventor

Perez-Mendez was a medical physicist who created equipment for improving medical diagnostic procedures. His work with digital dental radiography was among the first to allow dentists to switch from conventional X-rays to digital images.

Latino heritage: Guatemalan
Born: August 8, 1923; Guatemala City, Guatemala
Died: November 1, 2005; Oakland, California
Areas of achievement: Science and technology; medicine

Early Life
Although Victor Perez-Mendez (PEH-rehs MEHN-dehs) was born in Guatemala, his family moved to Manchester, England, when he was eight years old. The family later relocated to Jerusalem, Israel, the birthplace of his parents. There Perez-Mendez earned his bachelor's degree from St. George's Academy and a master's degree from Hebrew University. Perez-Mendez moved to the United States in order to study physics at Columbia University in New York City. After receiving his doctorate degree in 1951, Perez-Mendez remained at the university to complete a two-year postdoctoral fellowship.

Life's Work
Upon completion of his education, Perez-Mendez accepted a position at the University of California as an investigator in the Lawrence Livermore National Laboratory (1953-1955). Perez-Mendez transferred to the Lawrence Berkeley Laboratory (LBL) in 1955, where he would stay for the remainder of his career (1955-1995).

Initially, Perez-Mendez was employed solely in the physics, computer science, and mathematics division of the University of California. During this time his work focused on nuclear physics. He studied particle detectors, which are devices used to detect high-energy particles such as those from nuclear reactions. However, Perez-Mendez changed career paths to focus on medical physics, which is the application of physics to medical imaging, after he received an additional appointment in the Radiology Department of the University of California at San Francisco (UCSF). He researched how physics played an important role in new medical diagnostic procedures, including computer tomography (CT) scans, magnetic resonance imaging (MRI), and ultrasounds. Perez-Mendez described the initial physical techniques of CT imaging and continually published updated research articles on methods to improve the nascent imaging tool, heavily relying on emerging computer hardware and mathematical programs becoming available. He additionally developed an imaging modality to view the thyroid after patients were given nuclear medicine.

Perez-Mendez's noteworthy accomplishment in the latter part of his career occurred when he developed a digital radiology technique to obtain dental images. These digital images provided much less radiation exposure than a typical dental X ray. The technology that Perez-Mendez, colleague John Drewery, and student Tao Jing marketed with the company Air Techniques, Inc., differed from competitors because the light-emitting material allowed greater X-ray sensitivity and resolution. Because the new technique required one-tenth of the radiation dose, provided dentists with larger images than traditional X-ray films to visualize teeth, and allowed storage of the films on the computer rather than in offices, this digital invention quickly gained popularity.

After forty years of service, Mendez-Perez retired from laboratory work in 1995. During his career Perez-Mendez wrote more than three hundred scientific journal articles and edited two books. He was awarded a patent for the creation of a magnetostrictive readout for wire spark chambers (1967). This technology determined the position of a wire carrying a current from a spark. He also obtained patents for creating an amorphous silicon radiation detector (1992) and for creating a method and apparatus that improved the spatial resolution of particle detectors (1992); both of these inventions were necessary for the creation of digital dental images.

Perez-Mendez was a member of the American Physical Society, the Institute of Electrical and Electronics Engineering, the New York Academy of Sciences, and the American Association for the Advancement of Sciences. He was married to his wife, Gladys Cobert, for fifty-six years. The couple had one son, David. Perez-Mendez died at Kaiser Hospital in Oakland, California, at the age of eighty-two.

Significance
Even though the field of medical physics is continually evolving, the basic science behind all of Perez-Mendez's patented work continues to serve as the foundation for current technology. The digital radiology techniques that Perez-Mendez and his laboratory team created have now evolved beyond dentistry to assist with many other

diagnostic procedures, including digital mammography and cardiology. The development has also allowed previous images to be easily compared to current examination studies, thereby improving patient care.

Janet Ober Berman

FURTHER READING

Drewery, J. S., et al. "Improvements to Amorphous Silicon Radiation Detectors by Doping Profile Changes." *Nuclear Science Symposium and Medical Imaging Conference* 1 (October, 1992): 76-78. Scientific article describing Perez-Mendez's original work on the technology and how it was continually adapted in order to improve performance.

Hollins, Martin. *Medical Physics.* 2d ed. Cheltenham, England: Nelson Thornes, 2001. Textbook explaining the basic scientific principles behind the field of medical physics necessary for understanding Perez-Mendez's complicated work.

Mills, Joshua. "Information Technology: Say Ah! A Dental Tool with a Widening Future." *The New York Times*, April 17, 1995. Article describing the initial development of digital dental technology and its potential applications.

Moore, W. S. "Dental Digital Radiology." *Texas Dental Journal* 119, no. 5 (May, 2002): 404-412. Review of the benefits and limitations of digital versus conventional dental radiology and how Perez-Mendez's work has allowed advancement in the industry.

Zuley, M. L. "The Basics and Implementation of Digital Mammography." *Radiologic Clinics of North America* 48, no. 5 (September, 2010): 893-901. Summary of the advances in mammography and the current technology available for digital mammography, a future goal of Perez-Mendez's initial digital work.

See also: Richard Henry Carmona; Fernando E. Rodríguez Vargas.

ÁSTOR PIAZZOLLA

Argentine-born tango musician and composer

Piazzolla is one of the major figures of tango music. In the 1950's and 1960's, he infused the tango with borrowings from other genres, such as jazz and classical music. His works initially met with mixed reviews, yet by the 1980's, he gained worldwide recognition.

Latino heritage: Argentinean
Born: March 11, 1921; Mar del Plata, Argentina
Died: July 4, 1992; Buenos Aires, Argentina
Also known as: Ástor Pantaleón Piazzolla
Area of achievement: Music

EARLY LIFE

Ástor Pantaleón Piazzolla (AH-stohr PAHN-tah-leh-OHN PEE-ah-TZOH-lah), the only child of Vicente "Nonino" Piazzolla and Asunta Manetti, was born March 11, 1921, in Mar del Plata, Argentina. His right leg was twisted at birth and required numerous surgeries to correct, leaving the leg two centimeters shorter than the left. Throughout his life, Piazzolla maintained an aversion to hospitals and hated when people commented on his limp. His parents, especially his father, felt that their only son was destined for greatness and fostered his interest in whatever he happened to enjoy, be it boxing or music.

The Piazzolla family left Mar del Plata in 1925 for New York City, hoping for better financial prospects. They moved into an apartment in the Lower East Side, a predominantly Jewish and Italian neighborhood. Piazzolla credits the music he heard at Jewish festivities as having an influence upon his rhythmic development. In 1929, he received a *bandoneón* (an instrument similar to a concertina or accordion), which he gradually grew to love more than baseball and boxing. In 1932, at age eleven, he performed his instrument at a small concert of Argentine music at Roerich Hall. Piazzolla's love for the excitement and applause cemented his desire to become a musician.

Also, while in New York, Piazzolla met Carlos Gardel, the most famous tango singer of the era. Gardel allowed the teenage Piazzolla to play *bandoneón* for him, as entertainment at the star's numerous parties. In 1937, the family returned to Mar del Plata, but Piazzolla, feeling more American than Argentinean, found the move aggravated his restlessness. He left Mar del Plata that same year for bustling Buenos Aires. After several short-lived stints in various cabarets, Piazzolla joined bandleader Aníbal Troilo's prestigious tango orchestra.

LIFE'S WORK

Piazzolla was uninspired by the standard repertoire played by Troilo and other tango orchestras. In 1941, he began taking composition lessons with the notable Argentinean composer Alberto Ginastera, studies that continued for six years. During this time, Piazzolla expanded his knowledge of harmony, counterpoint, rhythm, and orchestration. Eager to incorporate his new musical training into his beloved tango, he would try out his experiments with other band members after hours. Piazzolla's tangos, meant for listening instead of dancing, fared poorly among dance band musicians. He left the Troilo orchestra in 1944, determined to form an orchestra that was capable of and willing to play his music. He directed a series of bands throughout his life, most notably Octeto Buenos Aires (1955-1958), Quinteto (1960-1970, 1978-1988), and Octeto Electrónico (1974-1977).

In 1953, Piazzolla's composition *Buenos Aires, tres movimientos sinfónicos* won the Fabien Sevitzky Prize. The prize included a premiere of the work, conducted by Sevitzky, a small monetary award, and most importantly, a one-year French government scholarship. Piazzolla and his first wife, Dedé, spent 1954-1955 in Paris. There, he took composition lessons with the esteemed pedagogue Nadia Boulanger. Boulanger listened to Piazzolla's classical compositions with respect, yet insisted they were without feeling. When Piazzolla finally played his tango "Triunfal" for his teacher, Boulanger exclaimed that this music was the true Piazzolla.

Taking his teacher's advice, Piazzolla synthesized the tango with classical music, with emphasis on the *bandoneón* as a virtuosic instrument. In 1959, Piazzolla composed a tango, "Adiós Nonino," on the occasion of his father's death. This work was his first international success.

The 1960's, 1970's, and 1980's provided Piazzolla with opportunities for recordings and touring, performing concerts in the United States, Japan, England, France, Sweden, and numerous other countries. His most ambitious and controversial composition, the "tango-opera" *María de Buenos Aires* (1968), with a libretto by Horacio Ferrer, nearly bankrupted him. In true Piazzolla fashion, he remarked to journalist Alberto Speratti that it was "much more important to be broke with *María de Buenos Aires* than to have done some garbage and to be flush." The work continues to receive mixed reviews and was revived in 1987 and 2007. Piazzolla's collaboration with Ferrer constitutes one decidedly good outcome of the tango-opera. They continued their partnership for the next several decades, producing songs such as "Chiquilín de Bachín" and popular "Balada para un loco."

Although Piazzolla's stamina was legendary, he began to have heart problems in 1988. He underwent a quadruple bypass operation and resumed touring as soon as the doctors gave him a clean bill of health. By 1990, the strain of touring and recording had worn him down, and in August of that year, he suffered a stroke in his Paris apartment. He was eventually flown home on a special flight arranged by the president of Argentina. Piazzolla never recovered and spent his last twenty-three months unable to speak or write and fighting various complications from the stroke. He died on July 4, 1992.

SIGNIFICANCE

Some experts, such as cellist Yo-Yo Ma and journalist Don Heckman, have compared what Piazzolla did for the tango to what George Gershwin and Duke Ellington did for jazz. Indeed, Piazzolla took the tango to the height of artistry and introduced it to audiences worldwide. His music has only increased in popularity since his death and has secured his legacy as one of the finest and most original composers of the twentieth century.

Alyson Payne

Ástor Piazzolla. (Redferns/Getty Images)

FURTHER READING

Azzi, María Susana. "The Tango, Peronism, and Ástor Piazzolla During the 1940's and 1950's." In *From Tejano to Tango: Latin American Popular Music*, edited by Walter Aaron Clark. New York: Routledge, 2002. Azzi explores Piazzolla's politics in depth against the background of the creation of "new tango."

Azzi, María Susana, and Simon Collier. *Le Grand Tango: The Life and Music of Ástor Piazzolla*. New York: Oxford University Press, 2000. This is a definitive biography of Piazzolla, with useful appendices containing a listing of Piazzolla's recordings as well as a glossary of South American terms.

Cannata, David Butler. "Making It There: Piazzolla's New York Concerts." *Latin American Music Review* 26, no. 1 (Spring-Summer, 2005): 57-87. This article details Piazzolla's personal and professional ties to New York City from his youth until his death. Cannata pays particular attention to the reception history surrounding his live performances.

Gorin, Natalio, comp. *Ástor Piazzolla: A Memoir*. Portland, Ore.: Amadeus Press, 2001. Gorin compiled this book from interviews and tapes made in the last five years of Piazzolla's life. It also contains an essay by Horacio Ferrer on his friendship with Piazzolla.

See also: Claudio Arrau; Jorge Bolet; Justino Díaz; Eduardo Mata; Jesús María Sanromá; Juan Tizol.

Pío Pico

American entrepreneur and politician

One of early California's most colorful historical characters, Pico was born into poverty but rose to become a wealthy and influential landowner and rancher. Despite a disease that disfigured him for more than a decade in his middle age, he served in a variety of political offices, culminating in a term as California's last governor under Mexican rule.

Latino heritage: Spanish and Mexican

Born: May 5, 1801; Mission San Gabriel Arcángel, Alta California (now in California)

Died: September 11, 1894; Los Angeles, California

Also known as: Pío de Jesús Pico IV

Areas of achievement: Business; government and politics

EARLY LIFE

Pío de Jesús Pico IV (PEE-oh PEE-koh) was born at Mission San Gabriel Arcángel in Alta California, one of the original Spanish missions, in what is now San Gabriel, California. Pico grew up in a shack next to the mission. He was of mixed Spanish, Italian, African, and Native American heritage, the grandson of Santiago de la Cruz Pico, a solder who served under the Spanish Alta (Upper) California explorer Juan Bautista de Anza. His Mexican-born parents were José María Pico, a soldier and colonist, and María Eustaquia Gutiérrez. He was one of nine children (out of twelve born) who survived to adulthood, the second oldest son, and the fourth member of the Pico family since the early 1600's to be called Pío. The family moved to San Diego in 1805. Little is known about Pico's early life or education, beyond the fact that he never learned to speak, read, or write English.

In 1819, Pico's father died. Since his older brother José was away in military service, eighteen-year-old Pico took responsibility for the welfare of his family. He began several lucrative enterprises, possibly using the proceeds from various wagers (he was known all his adult life as an enthusiastic gambler at cards and horseracing). These included a hide tanning operation, a saloon—where he was alleged to have inserted false bottoms into ox-horn drinking vessels to reduce drink quantities and increase profits—and a store where he sold shoes, chairs, foodstuffs, and other basic provisions. By the early 1820's, after Mexico won independence from Spain, Pico had begun investing his profits in land and cattle. By the middle of the decade, he had become well known and had grown prosperous enough to enter politics.

LIFE'S WORK

In 1826, Pico became a member of the provincial governor's advisory council, and he served in that capacity periodically until the early 1840's. Within three years, Pico had acquired a nearly 9,000-acre ranch near San Diego, the first piece of what would become vast land holdings. By 1831, Pico had relocated to the village of Los Angeles. That same year, as president of the local

Pío Pico. (© Corbis)

assembly, he fomented a revolt against the dictatorial rule of Governor Manuel Victoria. Threatened with exile to Mexico, Pico and several fellow revolutionaries raised a small army that clashed with Victoria's troops at the Cahuenga Pass. The governor was wounded and relinquished his position. Pico was named interim governor and served a few weeks before he was replaced.

In 1834, Pico married María Ignacia Alvarado, niece of Juan Bautista Alvarado, a prominent citizen who served as governor from 1836 to 1842. That same year, Pico was appointed administrator of newly secularized San Luis Rey Mission (still standing in present-day Oceanside), where he served for six years, meanwhile operating a profitable cattle-slaughtering business. In 1836, he campaigned to become mayor of Los Angeles but had to settle for the role of Southern California's elector for Mexican elections. In 1838, Pico again revolted, this time against the rule of Governor Alvarado. He was briefly imprisoned but, as a relative by marriage, was quickly forgiven for his disloyalty. In the early 1840's, Alvarado granted huge tracts of land (Rancho Temecula and Rancho Santa Margarita y Las Flores—later the site of Camp Pendleton) to Pico and his brother Andres.

Another rebellion broke out in 1844, this time between the forces of sitting governor Manuel Micheltorena and ex-governor Alvarado; the Pico brothers supported Alvarado. After bloodless skirmishes, Micheltorena relinquished power. Pico, as senior member of the assembly, was named governor in 1845. When the Mexican-American War broke out the following year, Pico initially worked to raise forces to defend California but received little support. When American forces invaded, Pico, fearing execution, fled to Sonora, Mexico. After the signing of the Treaty of Guadalupe Hidalgo, in which California and other Mexican territories were ceded to the United States, Pico returned to Los Angeles—no longer governor, but as a private American citizen.

After the war, Pico engaged in the life of a wealthy rancher. He became one of California's largest and richest landowners, built a large adobe mansion, El Ranchito— where he lived for most of his remaining years— and bred racehorses. He gambled freely and fell in and out of debt.

Pico cut a dashing, if grotesque figure. From the late 1840's until at least the late 1850's, as contemporary photographs show, he was afflicted with a usually fatal disease of the pituitary gland, later termed acromegaly. The disease caused his features to swell, his eyes to become asymmetric, his hands to become enlarged, and his facial hair to disappear. He also was probably rendered infertile: his wife died childless in 1860. During the worst of the disease, Pico was subjected to great cruelty for his appearance, called "monster" and other unflattering names in print. He compensated by dressing flamboyantly, wearing jewelry and other decorations, sporting a top hat, and carrying a cane that resembled a woman's leg. At some point, the disease went into full remission, and in later images Pico appears normal, with a full beard. Although he never remarried, he took a common-law wife and reputedly fathered five children, whom he adopted.

Late in life, Pico suffered a series of setbacks. In 1870, he built Pico House, a luxury hotel with gas lighting and indoor plumbing (now a state historical landmark), but lost it ten years later because of financial difficulties. His mansion was severely damaged in several floods and earthquakes, and he had to sell some of his lands to raise money for repairs. Gambling losses depleted his fortune. As a final insult, he was defrauded: thinking he was signing a loan, he actually signed away ownership of El Ranchito. Subsequent unsuccessful lawsuits to regain his property exhausted his remaining

Pico's Political Legacy in California

Pío Pico played a pivotal role in California's government during the volatile years of the 1830's and 1840's as a vocal member of the state assembly. The rebellions he helped instigate toppled two Mexican governors, paving the way for his own ascent to the state's highest office.

Following the migration of significant numbers of Americans to California in the early 1840's, Pico foresaw the inevitability of U.S. invasion. During his tenure as governor, he worked covertly to persuade the British or the French to conquer the territory but was unsuccessful. As governor, he moved the territorial capital from Monterey to Los Angeles, establishing the latter's predominance in the state. Although laws were in place providing for deportation of immigrants who refused to take Mexican citizenship and convert to Catholicism, Pico did not enforce them as governor. An important role Pico did fulfill was completion of the secularization of the missions, whose lands were sold and whose power was greatly diminished. Perhaps the most lasting legacy of his brief term in office was the unlearned Pico's belief in the power of education: he proposed a tax to fund education, advocated mandatory attendance for schoolchildren, and earmarked public funds for teachers' salaries.

funds. Ill, aging, and as poor as he had been at birth, Pico spent his last days living in the home of a daughter, Joaquina Pico Moreno. He died on September 11, 1894.

SIGNIFICANCE

A key figure in California history, Pico spanned the dominions of Spain, Mexico, and the United States during almost a century of life. A shrewd investor, he negotiated the acquisition of large parcels of prime land totaling more than a half-million acres that incorporated the modern communities of Whittier, Encino, Canoga Park, North Hollywood, Reseda, Van Nuys, and other areas of Southern California. Several structures he erected, including El Ranchito and the Pico House, still exist. Numerous schools and other landmarks, such as the city of Pico Rivera and Pico Boulevard in Los Angeles, were named in his memory.

Jack Ewing

FURTHER READING

Hackel, Steven W., ed. *Alta California: Peoples in Motion, Identities in Formation*. San Marino, Calif.: Huntington Library Press, 2010. A collection of essays that explores the complex relationships among the various peoples and cultures that clashed during California's settlement.

Salomon, Carlos Manuel. *Pio Pico: The Last Governor of Mexican California*. Norman: University of Oklahoma Press, 2010. The first full-length biography of Pico, this well-researched work vividly depicts his rise and fall, complete with photographs.

Yenne, Bill. *The Missions of California*. San Diego, Calif.: Thunder Bay Press, 2004. A history of California's original missions, around which the state's major cities grew, this contains historic and contemporary photographs of the structures, all of which still exist.

See also: Juan Bautista Alvarado; Joseph Marion Hernández; José Antonio Navarro; Juan Seguin.

SACRAMENTO PIMENTEL

American physician

The son of Mexican immigrants, Pimentel became a doctor in rural Burlington, Colorado, and he is a compelling advocate for physicians committing to the difficult demands and particular challenges of practicing medicine in rural areas.

Latino heritage: Mexican

Born: 1969; Burlington, Colorado

Also known as: Sacramento Solorio Pimentel; Zach Pimentel

Area of achievement: Medicine

EARLY LIFE

Eight years before Sacramento Solorio Pimentel (sahkra-MEHN-toh soh-LOH-ree-oh pih-mehn-TEHL) was born, his parents migrated to America from the state of Michoacán, along the Pacific Coast in southwestern Mexico. Experienced as field hands in a Mexican state that was predominantly agricultural, the parents pursued migrant farmwork opportunities in the vast rural outback of western Colorado, settling in the remote town of Burlington along the Kansas border. With a population of only three thousand, Burlington was nevertheless the largest town in Kit Carson County, and because of the farmlands that surrounded the town, more than 25 percent of its residents were Hispanic. Pimentel was born in Burlington, the second of what would be five children. His father worked as a farmhand, while his mother was a dishwasher at a local restaurant. Although the family struggled to make ends meet, Pimentel enjoyed a relatively happy childhood, save that his father was a diabetic and required frequent medical attention. Young Pimentel loved the feel and majesty of the vast open Colorado countryside.

Although it would be too tidy to suggest that a single event determined that Pimentel would pursue medicine, he would recall years later that at the age of nine, he broke his wrist in a skateboarding accident and how, in the emergency room at the local hospital, the doctor worked to repair the damaged bone and also to reassure the scared child. During the summers, Pimentel worked in town at odd jobs, often with his mother at the restaurant, and on weekends he worked in the bean fields and cornfields alongside his father. He loved school, and in 1988, he became the first member of his family to graduate from high school. Few of his Hispanic classmates entertained ideas about college, and Pimentel was the only Hispanic student in his college preparatory classes. Convinced that education was his most viable opportunity for success in his adopted country, Pimentel was accepted at Colorado State University in distant Fort Collins along the Wyoming border. It was a cultural shock. Fort Collins had a much smaller Hispanic population, and everything about college, including choosing a course of study, was entirely strange to Pimentel. Thinking of his emergency room experience and the treatments that allowed his father to live a normal life, Pimentel elected to major in premedicine.

Life's Work

Pimentel was determined to succeed despite the hard reality that at the time less than 10 percent of Hispanics entering American universities graduated. For Pimentel, Colorado State was something of a suitcase college; he would attend classes during the week and then return home to Burlington to be with his family and to work when and where he could. He got married when he was a sophomore and, recognizing his obligations, as he approached graduation he considered the daunting responsibility of financing medical school. Burlington was a small town and news of Pimentel's dilemma spread. The

local newspaper editor was involved in Burlington's efforts to persuade doctors to move to their town. Of the town's four doctors, two were ready to retire. Desperate, the editor offered to broker a deal with the town's richest resident—a former mayor who had made millions of dollars selling farm machinery—to cover Pimentel's more than $100,000 worth of medical school expenses in return for Pimentel agreeing to return to Burlington to practice family medicine for at least one year. Pimentel readily agreed. Pimentel's childhood friend, James Perez, entered into a similar deal with Burlington.

Pimentel attended the University of Colorado School of Medicine in Denver. After a three-year residency at the Northern Colorado Medical Center in Greeley, Pimentel, then twenty-seven and determined to make good on his deal, headed back to Burlington. Although the agreement with the town had been sealed with only a handshake and was binding for only one year, Pimentel made a professional commitment to become one of the town's permanent doctors. News of the unusual deal was picked up by the news media, and Pimentel was profiled in *People* magazine. Despite lucrative employment offers from major city hospital systems and attempts to turn his story into a television film, Pimentel wanted only to practice medicine among the rural people with whom he had grown up, relishing the interaction with his patients and the certainty that he was part of his community's life. Although he established his family practice at the city's only hospital, Kit Carson County Memorial Hospital, Pimentel regularly visited homebound patients who could not get to town, driving miles into the high plains surrounding Burlington. Although he never sought celebrity, he was profiled on the University of Colorado School of Medicine's Web site, and his video promoting the rewards of being a rural doctor was part of the school's continuing campaign to bring doctors to Colorado's outback. More than fifteen years after the year he promised to work in Burlington, Pimentel continued his family practice in the town responsible for giving him his start in his medical career.

Significance

Although it is tempting to focus on Pimentel's singular deal with the town of Burlington when he was preparing for medical school, and Pimentel himself extols the town's faith in him as a once-in-a-lifetime chance, his larger significance comes from his decadelong advocacy of rural medicine. He has continued to promote the difficult demands of fourteen-hour workdays to ensure that rural communities have appropriate health care in an era when medical school graduates are more attracted by the glamor and more lucrative rewards of urban and suburban practice.

Joseph Dewey

FURTHER READING

O'Neill, Anne-Marie. "Homeward Bound." *People,* August 19, 1996. Early profile pf Pimentel describing the deal he made with the town of Burlington.

University of Colorado, Denver, Anschutz Medical Campus. www.ucdenver.edu. Includes a link to resources on rural medicine and the program that first attracted Pimentel. Features Pimentel's video.

Zink, Therese. *The Country Doctor Revisited: A Twenty-First Century Reader*. Kent, Ohio: Kent State University Press, 2010. A far-ranging collection of essays, stories, and even poems about and by health care professionals who have accepted the challenge of rural medicine.

See also: John F. Alderete; Richard Henry Carmona; Norma Martinez-Rogers; James Perez.

LAFFIT PINCAY, JR.

Panamanian-born jockey

Pincay was one of the leading jockeys of his generation, excelling in parts of five decades and riding some of the most legendary horses in racing history. At his retirement, Pincay had won every major stakes in which he had competed and made the greatest impact on horse racing in North America of any Latino jockey.

Latino heritage: Panamanian

Born: December 29, 1946; Panama City, Panama

Also known as: Laffit Alejandro Pincay, Jr.

Areas of achievement: Sports

EARLY LIFE

Laffit Alejandro Pincay, Jr. (lah-FEET pihn-KAY) was born on December 29, 1946, in Panama City, Panama. He grew up with more material comfort than most Panamanians but also experienced the divorce of his parents at a young age. Pincay, like many Panamanians, was a baseball fan and grew up wanting to play for the New York Yankees; his position, second base, utilized the agility and quick reflexes for which Pincay later became well-known.

Horse racing was not unfamiliar to Pincay, as his father, Laffit, Sr., was a jockey who had gone to Venezuela to race after the divorce. In 1962, Pincay got a job as a "hot walker," a worker who walks horses after races, at a racetrack in Panama City; in 1963, he began riding horses in practice runs. The next year, he began to race competitively, stunning the Panamanian horse-racing world with his win on the horse Huelen at the Hipódromo Presidente Remón on May 16, 1964. Mentored by the veteran jockey Bolivar Moreno, Pincay soon became the leading rider in Panama. Even in a far less globalized racing world than that of the twenty-first century, news traveled fast, and Pincay came to the attention of prominent American horse owner and breeder Fred Hooper, an early pioneer in bringing Latino jockeys to the United States.

With the assistance of the Cuban-born agent Camille Marin, Pincay immigrated to the United States, beginning his racing career in the Los Angeles area. At first, it was difficult for Pincay to adapt, particularly because of the language barrier. However, with the assistance of his American-born wife, Linda Radkovich, whom he married in 1967, Pincay soon became so proficient in the language that after his retirement he was sought out as a television commentator for English-language broadcasts. Pincay's mother also moved to the Los Angeles area, facilitating her son's adaptation to the new language and culture. Pincay also faced athletic challenges, as his frame (5 feet, 1 inch tall, 109 pounds) was unusually small even for jockeys, yet if he gained too much weight, his all-important agility would be diminished. He had to adhere to a grueling regimen of diet and training in order to stay at his best.

Soon, Pincay was dominating California racetracks such as Santa Anita and Hollywood Park and beginning to be a presence in Chicago and New York as well. In 1970, he won the Santa Anita track's prestigious George Woolf Award for unusually meritorious personal and professional conduct. By 1971, he had become one of the stars of the U.S. racing world and had run his first Triple Crown races, although his first Kentucky Derby mount, Unconscious, ran miserably in a race he had been favored to win.

LIFE'S WORK

Pincay became nationally famous in 1973—for races he did not win. That was the year of the greatest horse in American racing history, Secretariat, and Pincay was notable as the jockey whose mount, Sham, provided a serious contest for Secretariat. In the Wood Memorial, the spring race often seen in the racing industry as a preparation for the Kentucky Derby, Sham nosed out Secretariat for second place in a race Angle Light unexpectedly won. In the Kentucky Derby that year, Sham led at the head of the stretch only to succumb to Secretariat's dramatic surge on the outside. In the Preakness, Pincay took Sham to the outside and spurred his horse to maximum effort, but Secretariat withstood this challenge. (The Preakness was to be the only major U.S. stakes Pincay never won). In the Belmont Stakes, the culminating leg of the Triple Crown, Sham took the early lead, but Secretariat eventually took advantage of the course's length and overcame Pincay's horse.

Although Pincay's valiant effort made him a household name, he did not reap the publicity garnered by Secretariat's jockey, Ron Turcotte. Pincay and fellow Latino riders such as the Panamanians Jorge Velásquez and Jacinto Vásquez and the Puerto Rican Angel Cordero, Jr., were not particularly popular among certain segments of the white population, who overtly rooted for white jockeys such as Bill Shoemaker and Eddie Delahoussaye to prevail in key races. Nonetheless, Pincay began to pick up media endorsements and make more media appearances after he proved he could speak English well enough to do so. Pincay's earlier baseball experience even came to the fore in a bizarre sidelight when Oakland Athletics owner Charles O. Finley encouraged Pincay to try out for the Major League Baseball team's vacant second baseman position. Pincay was not distracted from his racing career, however, and went on to triumph on a series of iconic horses. In 1978, he took over Affirmed, the Triple Crown winner, from jockey Steve Cauthen and won that year's Travers Stakes and the following year's Hollywood Gold Cup. In 1982, Pincay won the Belmont Stakes for the first time, prevailing on Conquistador Cielo, whose commanding win was one of the great examples of poise under pressure on a racetrack. He also won the Belmont in 1983 with Caveat. Pincay won his sole Kentucky Derby in 1984 on Swale and then vaulted to an impressive Belmont win after finishing seventh in the Preakness. Eight days after his victory, Swale unexpectedly died on the way to his stall.

Pincay also was associated with horses that had long careers, wining more and more races as the newly instituted Breeders' Cup began showcasing older horses. The Argentine mare Bayakoa won several distaff races in the late 1980's and was ridden by Pincay in the vast majority of her wins. Another veteran horse, John Henry, ran until the age of ten. In the 1990's, Pincay kept running and winning regularly, now competing against a new generation of riders. One of his former competitors, Bill Shoemaker, retired with the record for racing wins, 8,833; Pincay surpassed the record in 1999 with his win on Irish Nip. Russell Baze later broke Pincay's record.

Pincay continued riding well into his fifties, surmounting obstacles such as the suicide of his wife Linda in 1985. He attracted even better mounts once he broke Shoemaker's record.

On March 1, 2003, Pincay was badly injured during a race at Santa Anita when he was rolled over by the horse Trampus Too. Although some thought he might return, on July 29, he officially announced his retirement. Neil Papiano represented Pincay in a lawsuit against the racetrack. In 2007, Pincay was awarded a $2.7 million judgment.

Laffit Pincay, Jr. (AP Photo)

Pincay's Racing Records
Laffit Pincay, Jr., set imposing records in his home racing region of Los Angeles, winning the Santa Anita Derby seven times, the Del Mar Derby five times, and the Rancho Bernardo Handicap nine times. He won the Kentucky Derby once (in 1984 with Swale) and the Belmont Stakes three consecutive years (1982, 1983, 1984). He also won seven Breeders' Cup races. Pincay was inducted into the National Museum of Racing and Hall of Fame in 1975 and was a five-time winner of the Eclipse Award for best jockey of the year. With 9,530 career wins, Pincay is one of the all-time winningest jockeys in the history of the sport. After his retirement, the Hollywood Gold Cup race created the Laffit Pincay, Jr. Award, which honors a person who has served the racing industry with integrity and distinction. Pincay won the Gold Cup a record nine times.

SIGNIFICANCE

Pincay's triumphs evinced not just skill or tactical cunning but also sheer athleticism. The legendary jockey defied odds with a career that spanned five decades. He was a pioneer for Latinos in the racing industry and also a major figure in the sport's transition to a media-dominated age. His son, Laffit III, also became a successful jockey.

Nicholas Birns

FURTHER READING

Cain, Maureen. *Laffit: Anatomy of a Winner.* Pasadena, Calif.: Affirmed Press, 2009. This award-winning biography is the definitive source for the story of Pincay's life and achievements.

Drape, Joe. *To The Swift: Classic Triple Crown Horses and Their Race for Glory.* New York: St. Martin's Press, 2008. Discusses Pincay in the context of the history of the signature events of the American racing industry

Finley, Bill. "Laffit to be King After Years of Battling Personal Demons." *The New York Daily News*, December 12, 1999, p. 110. Lengthy profile of Pincay, discussing his personal struggles as well as his professional achievements.

Gurnick, Ken. "Riding Perseverance to a Jockey's Record; Pincay Nears Shoemaker's Mark for Victories." *The New York Times*, December 3, 1999, p. D1. Detailed profile of Pincay as he approached Shoemaker's record.

Scanlan, Lawrence. *The Horse God Built: The Untold Story of Secretariat, the World's Greatest Racehorse.* New York: St. Martin's Press, 2007. Describes Pincay in relation to the career of the greatest horse in U.S. racing history.

See also: Angel Cordero, Jr.; Ismael Valenzuela.

MIGUEL PIÑERO

Puerto Rican-born playwright and poet

The first Puerto Rican playwright to break into the mainstream, Piñero was a heroin addict and convict whose unflinching, powerful, and surprisingly lyrical plays and poems reflect his troubled and violent life on the destitute Lower East Side streets of the 1960's and 1970's.

Latino heritage: Puerto Rican

Born: December 19, 1946; Gurabo, Puerto Rico

Died: June 18, 1988; New York, New York

Also kown as: Miguel Antonio Gómez Piñero

Areas of achievement: Theater; poetry; screenwriting

EARLY LIFE

Miguel Antonio Gómez Piñero (pih-NYEH-roh) was born on December 19, 1946, in Gurabo, Puerto Rico, the eldest child of Miguel Angel Gómez Ramos and Adelina Piñero. In 1950, he moved to New York City with his parents and younger sister. Like many Puerto Ricans who arrived during the Great Migration of the 1940's and 1950's, they settled in the area that was later dubbed *Loisaida*, Spanglish for "Lower East Side."

Piñero's father abandoned the family four years after they moved to New York. Cast adrift in the projects and slums of the Lower East Side and Brooklyn, Adelina found shelter for her family in latrines, basements, and stairwells before learning how to eke out a marginal living with the help of the welfare program. The young Piñero was a scrappy and precocious child who was affronted by the racism against Latino students at the three schools that he attended. To supplement his mother's welfare income, he turned to crime, stealing food for his family. The first of his many run-ins with the law came at the age of eleven, when he was arrested for theft and sent to a juvenile detention center in the Bronx.

Piñero dropped out of school in seventh grade and began associating with neighborhood gangs, participating in car thefts and armed robberies. After robbing a jewelry store, he was sentenced to three years in prison at Rikers Island, where he was introduced to heroin. Back on the streets, his drug habit made it difficult for him to find steady work. Relapsing into criminal activities, he received a second sentence at Rikers Island, which led to a drug rehabilitation program at Manhattan State Hospital, where he received his high school equivalency diploma. During this time, he also became affiliated with the Young Lords, a militant Puerto Rican civil rights group much like the Black Panther Party. Arrested again in 1971 for armed robbery of an East Village apartment, he was sentenced to five years in the Sing Sing Correctional Facility at Ossining.

LIFE'S WORK

At Sing Sing, facing his longest stretch in prison, Piñero began attending a drama workshop run by Clay Stephenson and Marvin Felix Camillo, two theater professionals who were part of a movement to reform prisoners through the arts. Piñero's participation in the theater workshops at Sing Sing was catalytic. Struck by his talent, Camillo submitted Piñero's poem "Black Lady with a Blonde Wig On" to a contest, where it won second prize and fifty dollars. Encouraged, Piñero wrote a short play and several more poems, which Camillo staged for a public event at Sing Sing that was attended by prominent theater critic Mel Gussow. His subsequent article in *The New York Times* inspired Arthur Bartow, the director of the Theatre at the Riverside Church, to invite Piñero to stage a full-length play. In response, Piñero began to write *Short Eyes*, a visceral account of a group of prisoners exacting justice on an alleged child molester. Upon his parole in 1973, he and Camillo further developed the play.

The premiere of *Short Eyes* in 1974 was an astounding success. Theater producer Joseph Papp brought it to the Public Theater and from there the production was transferred to the Vivian Beaumont Theater at Lincoln Center. The play was nominated for six Tony Awards, and it won an Obie Award and the New York Drama Critics' Circle Award for Best American Play. Piñero received a Drama Desk Award for Outstanding New Playwright and became a literary sensation, but he refused to be reformed by his success. On the night that he received the New York Drama Critics' Circle Award, he was arrested for urinating on the sidewalk and possession of heroin.

Miguel Piñero. (AP Photo)

Piñero's subsequent plays continued to examine the underbelly of urban street life. In *The Sun Always Shines for the Cool* (1976), a repentant drug addict attempts to save his daughter from the designs of the pimp whom she loves. In *Eulogy for a Small-Time Thief* (1977), a petty crook dreams of escaping his sordid life but is crushed by a visitor from his shady past. *A Midnight Moon at the Greasy Spoon* (1981) is set in a diner run by a retired vaudevillian that is frequented by a motley group of prostitutes, drug addicts, and pimps.

Success in theater led Piñero to work in television and film. In 1977, he adapted *Short Eyes* into a film directed by Robert M. Young, which featured a hit sound track by Curtis Mayfield. He wrote episodes for the television shows *Kojak* and *Baretta*. He also acted in films and television, playing a drug lord in the pilot episode of *Miami Vice* and a drug dealer in the film *Fort Apache, The Bronx* (1981).

Piñero also continued to write his incantatory poems, which freely borrowed from the social criticism of Beat poetry and the rhyming lyricism of Puerto Rican *décimas*. Slyly humorous and critical of materialism, capitalism, and the American Dream, his best-known poems include "The Book of Genesis According to St.

Miguelito," in which Piñero presents a god who creates poverty and the slums and then goes on vacation to Puerto Rico on his day of rest, and "A Lower East Side Poem," in which Piñero disparages the sordidness and violence of the Lower East Side that he paradoxically cannot exist without.

Unrepentant in his drug use and profligate lifestyle, Piñero was constantly in conflict with the law. When *Short Eyes* was being filmed in the Tombs (New York City's court and prison complex), he was being arraigned elsewhere in the building for heroin possession and grand larceny. He was notorious for stealing from the sets of the television shows that employed him. Hospitalized repeatedly for various ailments related to drug abuse, Piñero died of cirrhosis of the liver in 1988 at the age of forty-one.

SIGNIFICANCE

With the success of *Short Eyes*, Piñero became the leading voice of Puerto Rican street culture, a role he took seriously. He formed a short-lived theater group of Puerto Rican street kids called the Young Family, which eventually numbered thirty youths attempting to stay off the streets. He became friends with Miguel Algarín, a professor of English at Rutgers University, and participated in poetry readings at Algarín's home, which later developed into the Nuyorican Poets' Café. With Algarín, Piñero edited *Nuyorican Poetry: An Anthology of Puerto Rican Words and Feelings* (1975), which helped coalesce the Nuyorican literary movement. He briefly taught creative writing at Rutgers University and received a Guggenheim Fellowship in 1982.

Short Eyes opened the door to an urban reality that was unfamiliar to theater audiences in 1974, and in his subsequent plays and poems, Piñero continued to give voice for the marginalized, the dispossessed, and the destitute. His influence can be felt in the plays of Stephen Adly Guirgis, as well as in the work of hip-hop artists such as Tupac Shakur and Reg E. Gaines. With his unique use of Puerto Rican street slang and sense of absurdity, he humanized the criminals, addicts, and con artists that people his work, framing their anger and desperation in the powerlessness and social marginalization of racism and poverty.

Victoria Linchong

FURTHER READING

Piñero, Miguel. *Outlaw: The Collected Plays of Miguel Piñero*. Houston: Arte Público Press, 2010. The

---

Short Eyes

Miguel Piñero's most famous play, *Short Eyes* (1974), presents a segregated prison world of blacks, Latinos, and a white minority. The prisoners' society is upended by the arrival of Clark Davis, a young, white doctor who has been arrested for child molestation. Clark is despised by the guard and all the prisoners for being a "short eyes," prison slang for pedophile. The play recounts an escalating series of brutal acts that culminates in Clark's murder. Only the Latino petty thief Juan refuses to participate, although he is repulsed when Clark wretchedly and graphically confides to him his sexual transgressions with young Puerto Rican girls. Despite knowing the truth of the allegations, Juan argues for compassion and has to be physically restrained by the prisoners when they finally murder Clark. Later, when the prisoners learn that Clark was acquitted of his crime, they remorsefully turn to Juan to expiate their guilt but he refuses to, instead condemning them for their act of judgment and moral superiority.

Short Eyes is a searing account of retribution that presents the prison world as a highly concentrated microcosm of society, with all of its racial and sexual problems magnified. The play revealed Piñero's gift for translating street slang into lyrical dialogue and his talent for lucidly depicting the underbelly of society. Although the violence and sexual transgressions are graphically and unflinchingly depicted, Piñero shows a deep compassion for his imperfect characters, who evince both a higher and lower self.

---

definitive volume of Piñero's work, including ten plays and several poems.

_____. *Short Eyes*. New York: Hill and Wang, 1975. Piñero's masterwork with an introduction by his mentor Marvin Felix Camillo, who directed the original production.

Turan, Kenneth, and Joseph Papp. "Short Eyes." In *Free for All: Joseph Papp, the Public, and the Greatest Theater Story Ever Told*, edited by Kenneth Turan. New York: Doubleday, 2009. This work about the Public Theater includes a chapter on *Short Eyes* that provides an inside look on the creation and production of this seminal work.

See also: Oscar Zeta Acosta; Miguel Algarín; Jimmy Santiago Baca; Victor Hernández Cruz; Eduardo Machado; Piri Thomas; Luis Miguel Valdez.

JIM PLUNKETT

American football player

A gifted athlete with a never-say-die mentality, Plunkett overcame multiple challenges and hardships to taste athletic success on the highest levels.

Latino heritage: Mexican
Born: December 5, 1947; Santa Clara, California
Also known as: James William Plunkett
Areas of achievement: Football

EARLY LIFE

James William Plunkett was born in Santa Clara, Califor†na, on December 5, 1947, to William and Carmella Plunkett. He grew up in nearby San Jose and identifies himself as Latino, although his last name came from an Irish great-grandfather who immigrated to Mexico in the 1800's. Plunkett's parents struggled to make ends meet: His mother was born blind, and his father slowly lost his sight and was completed blind by the time Plunkett was in college. Although he was a gifted athlete, there was no extra money to help pay for athletics, and as one of three children, Plunkett was expected to help contribute to the family economically with part-time work during school.

By high school, Plunkett was developing into a talented quarterback in football. His throwing arm was powerful, and although he was not exceptionally quick, he was mobile enough to avoid most would-be tacklers. He attracted significant recruiting attention from colleges throughout the western United States.

LIFE'S WORK

In the summer before enrolling in Stanford University, Plunkett experienced one of the first serious setbacks to his athletic career. After experiencing weakness and other physical problems, he received a diagnosis of thyroid cancer. Although surgery to remove a walnut-sized tumor from his neck was entirely successful, Plunkett found it hard to catch up physically with his teammates; even though he remained on the team, it appeared unlikely that he would remain at quarterback.

Plunkett was determined to prove his doubters wrong, to show that his career as a quarterback was far from over. After two years of aggressive physical training, Plunkett was able to win the starting position at Stanford. For the next three years, from 1968 to 1971, Plunkett threw for almost 8,000 yards and 55 touchdown passes, setting multiple collegiate records in the process.

His accomplishments were reflected in multiple postseason awards, including the 1970 Heisman Trophy. Plunkett was the first Latino player to win the award.

Despite his collegiate success, Plunkett remained grounded, which he attributed to the humility and work ethic of his parents. He also recognized his responsibility to the Hispanic community, volunteering considerable time to Latino youths, mentoring them and encouraging them to pursue education.

In 1971, Plunkett was selected first in the National Football League (NFL) draft by the Boston Patriots. Although he won the league's rookie of the year award that year, it was one of the few successes Plunkett experienced in New England. While the Patriots had a few other good players, they were unable to build a successful team. To pass effectively, a quarterback needs good receivers and an offensive line that can protect him and give him time to complete passes. The Patriots provided Plunkett with neither. Constantly on the run and physically harassed, Plunkett endured several injuries to his legs and his throwing shoulder.

Jim Plunkett. (AP Photo)

In the mid-1970's, Plunkett was traded to the San Francisco 49ers and initially looked forward to returning to California. Playing just up the road from his hometown of San Jose, Plunkett received the warm support of his childhood community. Unfortunately, the injuries he sustained from his years with the Patriots limited his effectiveness. Over the course of several seasons with mediocre protection, Plunkett developed the bad habit of rushing his passes to avoid being sacked. While it meant he endured less physical punishment, the habit also increased his number of incomplete passes and interceptions.

It speaks to Plunkett's remarkable physical resilience that he was even able to walk, let alone play professional football. In the 1970's, Plunkett had multiple injuries to his knees and shoulders, most of which required extensive surgeries, and multiple severe injuries to his back and ribcage.

After two seasons in San Francisco, Plunkett's career appeared to be almost over. He signed a free-agent contract with the Oakland Raiders, mainly to mentor their inexperienced backup quarterbacks. During the early and mid-1970's, the Raiders were one of the more entertaining franchises in the NFL. While most other teams were happy to run the ball repeatedly for short gains, the Raiders' offense was built around long passes. This called for savvy, strong-armed quarterbacks who were capable of eluding defensive players during the time it took for the play to develop. For two years, Plunkett helped develop the other quarterbacks on the roster and trained constantly to recover from lingering injuries and bad playing habits.

By 1980, Plunkett was thrust into a starting role when the team's starting quarterback received a season-ending injury early in the year. At first he looked dreadful, but over the course of the season, Plunkett began to resemble the quarterback of a decade before. The Raiders' offensive line was much better than the Patriots' had been, and his receivers were among the most talented in football. In the play-offs, the Raiders defeated team after team, eventually winning Super Bowl XV over the Philadelphia Eagles. Plunkett threw three touchdown passes and was named most valuable player for the game.

For most of the 1980's, Plunkett enjoyed moderate success, including another Super Bowl victory in 1983, over the Washington Redskins. For several more seasons, as the Raiders' offensive philosophy became more run-oriented, Plunkett was able to provide a reasonable passing threat to keep opposing teams off balance.

Plunkett's Rescue from Oblivion by the Raiders

Parts of Jim Plunkett's story are familiar to many football fans, even if they know little of his career. Many Heisman Trophy-winning quarterbacks end up on bad professional teams, and their professional careers often end in injuries, losses, and benching. Most never recapture their collegiate success. For Plunkett, however, the most improbable of circumstances gave him another opportunity to achieve success. Signed in 1978 by the Oakland Raiders as a cheap, third-string tutor for their inexperienced second-string quarterback, Plunkett had few expectations placed on him. Plunkett was perhaps the only Raider who still thought he could contribute as a player. In mid-October, 1980, the team's record was 2-3; adding injury to insult, the starting quarterback broke his leg early in a game against the Kansas City Chiefs. The second-string quarterback, a rookie, was clearly not ready to take over, so Plunkett was put into the game. His performance was awful; three years away from the game had disrupted his timing, and Plunkett ended up throwing five interceptions.

A week later, Plunkett was named the starter against the San Diego Chargers. Not even those who had watched Plunkett at Stanford could have predicted what would come next: wins in nine of the Raiders next eleven games, including six straight wins. In the postseason, Plunkett guided the Raiders to four straight victories, capping the season with a Super Bowl championship.

SIGNIFICANCE

Besides his athletic accomplishments, the collegiate Plunkett was lauded for his volunteerism and for the considerable physical and economic obstacles he overcame. As a professional, Plunkett was honored for his endurance and his remarkable rise to Super Bowl hero.

Michael R. Meyers

FURTHER READING

Boyles, Bob, and Alan Guido. "Jim Plunkett." In *Fifty Years of College Football: A Modern History of America's Most Colorful Sport*. New York: Skyhorse, 2007. Provides an overview of Plunkett's college career.

Frisch, Aaron. *The History of the Oakland Raiders*. Mankato, Minn.: Creative Education, 2005. Aimed at young readers, this book provides a short overview of Plunkett's contribution to the franchise.

O'Keefe, John. "Jim Plunkett, Raiders Quarterback." *Sports Illustrated* 90, no. 2 (January 18, 1999). Provides details of Plunkett's amazing career resurrection with the Raiders.

See also: Tedy Bruschi; Manny Fernández; Jeff Garcia; Tony Gonzalez; Joe Kapp; Anthony Muñoz; Rich Rodriguez; Tony Romo; Eddie Saenz; Danny Villanueva.

MARY HELEN PONCE

American writer and educator

Ponce is an accomplished writer and professor whose works draw on her experiences and upbringing in California's San Fernando Valley.

Latino heritage: Mexican
Born: January 24, 1938; Pacoima, California
Also known as: Maria Elena Ponce; Merrihelen Ponce
Areas of achievement: Literature; education; journalism

EARLY LIFE
Mary Helen Ponce (POHN-say) was born Maria Elena Ponce on January 24, 1938, in Pacoima, California. She was the youngest of the eight children of Tranquilino and Vincenta (Solis) Ponce. The child of Mexican immigrants, Ponce's childhood was spent in the city Mexican American residents called "Pacas" in the San Fernando Valley of California. Although Ponce's girlhood was generally happy, she sometimes regretted being the youngest in a large family. The household bustled with constant noise and Ponce often sought peace and quiet by either locking herself into the bathroom or finding a tall tree to climb. Her sisters encouraged her love of literature, but the lack of pencils and paper forced her to write her first stories with a stick on the patches of earth surrounding the family home.

Ponce attended Pacoima Elementary School, which introduced her to classical literature and writing and, ironically, caused her to lose much of her fluency in Spanish—a loss she decried as much as her Anglicized name. She started reading and dreamed of the day when she could write stories about her life and the people who lived and worked on Hoyt Street—a dirt street without sidewalks.

LIFE'S WORK
Ponce graduated from high school, but a swift marriage and equally abrupt divorce left her with four children (Joseph, Ana, Mark, and Ralph) and little money. She remarried but stayed mostly at home; raising her children occupied much of her time. It was not until her youngest child was old enough to go to school that Ponce was able to enroll at California State University, Northridge (CSUN). In her classes, she discovered that she had a burning desire to commemorate her Mexican American heritage and her ancestors' presence in Southern California. She graduated with her bachelor's degree in 1978 and her first master's degree in 1980.

Ponce was gratified to find an early receptive audience for her work. Three articles she wrote for *El Popo*, the student newspaper for CSUN, were immediately accepted for publication in 1980. Much of her early writing was based on the people she remembered from her childhood and stories she had heard from her family. She was particularly gratified to accept an invitation by the Mexican American Women's National Association to read some of her first-person narratives at a meeting the group was holding in Washington, D.C. Academically, Ponce found steady work teaching: She worked as an instructor at the University of California at Los Angeles from 1982 to 1988. This work allowed her to spend time researching the background for her novel *Taking Control* (1987).

Ponce accepted an adjunct professorship in women's studies at the University of New Mexico at Albuquerque in 1988. During this time, she was inspired to write *The Wedding* (1989), a novel that tells the tale of Blanca, a young Mexican American woman preparing to marry her childhood sweetheart. In 1992, Ponce accepted a teaching position in the Chicano studies program at the University of California at Santa Barbara. She was steadily encouraged in her writing by her family and her readers—support that she found invaluable when she felt constrained by her many responsibilities. In 1993, she finally finished a project she had started as an undergraduate student at CSUN—*Hoyt Street: An Autobiography* (1993).

Between raising children, teaching, and writing, Ponce also found time to complete her Ph.D. at the University of New Mexico in 1995. She also has written articles for *The Los Angeles Times* on such issues as bilingual classrooms, women's issues in the immigrant community, and children's literacy programs. In 2008, Ponce reissued *The Wedding* with a new, updated introduction and extensive textual corrections. Her hope was to extend the work to a new generation of Latinas in search of their roots.

SIGNIFICANCE

Ponce has remarked that an awareness of culture and history is what drives her to write her fiction and her biographical writings. From her childhood, she carried an unshakable sense on herself as Latina even when her early education seemed set on stripping her Mexican heritage from her. Dialogue and descriptions in her works are liberally sprinkled with Latino slang and Spanish idiom—something she does to give readers the flavor and color of a Mexican-American immigrant community.

Julia M. Meyers

FURTHER READING

McCracken, Ellen. "Subculture, Parody, and the Carnivalesque: A Bakhtinian Reading of Mary Helen Ponce's *The Wedding*," *MELUS* 23, no. 1 (Spring, 1998): 117. An interesting critical study of *The Wedding* that suggests an intertextual reading of the novel causes the reader to question the traditional patterns of marriage and family.

Ponce, Merrihelen. "On Language: An Essay" *Women's Studies Quarterly* 26, nos. 1/2 (Spring/Summer, 1998): 197-201. Ponce's essay discusses the problems of bilingual literacy in the immigrant community. She touches on the lack of available books, the pressures to conform to an "English-only" school system, and the denigration of Mexican idiom in American culture.

Villarreal, Mary Ann. "Finding Our Place: Reconstructing Community Through Oral History." *The Oral History Review* 33, no. 2 (Summer/Autumn, 2006): 45-64. Villarreal refers to *The Wedding* and other writings in her discussion of the oral traditions of storytelling within the Mexican American community. Ponce's stories frequently are based on legends and stories.

See also: Isabel Allende; Gloria Anzaldúa; Marie Arana; Norma Elia Cantú; Ana Castillo; Denise Chávez; Martha P. Cotera; Alma Villanueva.

LILIANA PORTER

Argentine-born artist; educator

Porter is best known for her pictorial illusionistic collage work of drawings, screen prints, and intaglios. Her work provides a three-dimensional vision of objects, is grounded in the mixed media of photography and works on canvas, and has been featured in galleries around the world. She is cofounder and director of the New York Graphic Workshop.

Latino heritage: Argentinean
Born: October 6, 1941; Buenos Aires, Argentina
Also known as: Liliana Alicia Porter
Areas of achievement: Art; education

EARLY LIFE

Liliana Alicia Porter (LIH-lee-AN-ah) was born in 1941 in Buenos Aires, Argentina. As a child she displayed an indelible propensity toward the arts. She began her artistic endeavors in the medium of printmaking but expanded to include painting and drawing, photography and filmmaking. After graduating from Escuela Nacional de Bellas Artes, she left Argentina for Mexico, where she attended Universidad Iberoamericano and studied print making. In 1959, she displayed her first solo exhibit at the Galeria Proteo in Mexico City. Her exhibit was featured in the gallery until 1968, when the gallery became defunct. She returned to Argentina in 1961 and became critical of the Argentine government and the artistic restrictions under dictator Juan Carlos Ongania, which led her to leave Argentina and settle in New York.

LIFE'S WORK

When Porter moved to New York in 1964, her art was greeted with great anticipation and approval because her work had been recognized with good reviews from her exhibits in Argentina and Mexico. During this period, she exhibited at two important galleries: the Lirolay Gallery in 1966 and the Di Tella Institute in 1969, both of which solidified her position as a forerunner in visual artistry. She was able to escape many of the artistic labels of the era, such as postmodernist and minimalist, by consciously creating artwork that was a departure from the pervasive styles during the late 1960's and early

Liliana Porter. (© Ana Tiscornia)

1970's. Highly politically minded, Porter also sought to dispel the eroticist stereotypes of Latina artists through her work, while maintaining an apolitical position. She once said,

> Work with clear political intent and content, referring to concrete social injustices or to specific historical facts, are the most difficult to control. Once they enter the context of the market—exhibition, collections, and criticisms—the effectiveness of artworks is challenged by the institution of art. Things may get more complicated if there is the artist's need to serve as the main protagonist.

These factors, along with a critical sense of the incorporation of her international experiences, allowed her work to constantly evolve.

When Porter moved to the United States in 1964, she cofounded the New York Graphic Workshop, which became her workplace from 1965 until 1970. Four years later she cofounded the Camnitzer-Porter Studio in Lucca, Italy, with her husband Luis Camnitzer, whom she met and married in 1965. Through her position as an instructor of etching, she reformulated her techniques of art production, which resulted in the refining of her

visual and material artistry. In 1970, Porter and her husband were invited to display their reductionist works in the Museum of Modern Art. Porter's art was frequently compared to that of other minimalists of the time, but it could not be connected visually. She defied expectations by incorporating a figurative style. Porter taught at the State University of New York (SUNY) system of higher education as an adjunct lecturer from 1974 to 1976 and 1987, as an etching instructor from 1974 to 1976 and 1988, and as a full professor at Queens College beginning in 1991.

In addition to visual artistry, Porter enhances her three-dimensional figurations with cinematography. She is involved in what she calls "the natural next step" to still art, photography and film, which she combines with music to create a kind of staged play. Porter has continued to build upon her legacy of creative expression, forging a path through creative media, which includes print making, drawing, painting, collage, photography, and film. Her ever-evolving aesthetic sensibility has afforded her the ability to transcend the labels so often stamped on artists. When asked in an interview about the changes in the media she has used over the years and how she has been able to maintain her approach to her artistry, Porter responds that her,

> Work went through different stages and different contexts, but there is, as you say, a constant, unifying thread, which has to do with reality, illusion, words, objects. . . . In fact, I came to realize not only that everything is representation but also that the only reality lies in the abstractions, in the archetypes.

S<small>IGNIFICANCE</small>

Porter has been a trailblazer in the visual arts for the past fifty years. She has been featured in more than three hundred exhibits on five different continents. She is the recipient of more than twenty-five awards, spanning a fifty-year period and ranging from awards in digital print, animation, digital video, photography, and multimedia. She has published dozens of articles, and master's theses and doctoral dissertations have been written about her and her work. She has continued to create three-dimensional art that defies the concept of visual artistry, blurring the lines between reality and representation.

Derrick J. Jenkins, Sr.

F<small>URTHER</small> R<small>EADING</small>

Bazzano-Nelson, Florencia. *Liliana Porter and the Art of Simulation*. Burlington, Vt.: Ashgate,

2008. This book is a portrait of the life and works of Porter through three distinct eras in her artistic career.

Pindell, Howardina. "A Conversation with Liliana Porter." In *Liliana Porter: Arte Poética, a Selection of Works from 1968 to 1997*. Stony Brook, N.Y.: University Art Gallery, Staller Center for the Arts, 1998. This book is an intimate dialogue with Porter as she gives insight into the creative process behind her works spanning three decades.

Weber, Paolina. *"For You" by Liliana Porter*. New York: Annina Nosei Gallery, 1999. This book is a light-hearted take on the life and times of Porter and how these factors came together to influence her artistry.

See also: Olga Albizu; Tony Labat; María Martínez-Cañas.

ESTELA PORTILLO TRAMBLEY

American writer

Although primarily known for her outstanding plays, Portillo Trambley created a vast body of literature that also includes essays, poetry, novels, and short fiction. Her literary emphasis on women's experiences illuminates social inequities and gives voice to a group historically marginalized by a patriarchal culture.

Latino heritage: Mexican

Born: January 16, 1927; El Paso, Texas

Died: December 28, 1998; El Paso, Texas

Also known as: Estela Portillo

Area of achievement: Literature; theater; poetry

EARLY LIFE

Estela Portillo Trambley (pohr-TEE-yoh TRAM-blee) was born Estela Portillo on January 16, 1936, to Frank and Delfina Portillo. Frank was a diesel mechanic of Italian heritage, while Delfina was a homemaker of Mexican descent. Portillo Trambley spent much time with her maternal grandparents, who ran a grocery store named Amigo de la Pobres (Friend to the Poor). This early exposure to cultural and socioeconomic diversity would influence and inform Portillo Trambley's later literary works.

In 1947, Portillo Trambley married Robert D. Trambley, who worked in the automobile business. Together, they had six children. Throughout the 1950's and early 1960's, Portillo Trambley raised her young family while attending the University of Texas at El Paso for a degree in English. By 1957, Portillo Trambley had achieved a baccalaureate, after which she taught high school English. In addition, she served as the chairperson for the English Department at the El Paso Technical Institute.

In 1973, an event occurred that would place Portillo Trambley in the spotlight and change the trajectory of her literary career. As a guest editor of the influen-

tial periodical *El Grito*, Portillo Trambley provided a collection of literary works written by Chicana authors. The first anthology of its kind, the publication highlighted a previously unknown treasure trove of literature and shed light on the sociocultural experiences of contemporary Chicanas.

LIFE'S WORK

Portillo Trambley's literary career blossomed in the 1970's, and coincided with the Chicano movement of the 1960's and 1970's, during which an outpouring of literary and cultural efforts served to highlight the Mexican American cultural narrative throughout the United States. Portillo Trambley received her start in playwriting as a dramatist at El Paso Community College, where she directed and produced many plays. Not simply content with her own playwriting prowess, Portillo Trambley also hosted a radio program, *Estela Says*; furthermore, she created a cultural program for television named *Cumbres*.

In 1971, Portillo Trambley published her first play. Titled *The Day of the Swallows*, she won the Quinto Sol Literary Prize shortly after its publication, from an eponymous publishing company that sought to highlight Chicano literature. A subsequent play, written and published in 1973, won the 1985 New York Shakespeare Festival's Hispanic American Playwrights competition.

A storyteller at heart, Portillo Trambley did not limit herself to one literary convention. She wrote poetry, a collection of short fiction entitled *Rain of Scorpions, and Other Writings* (1975), and a novel called *Trini* (1986). The former was well received by the Chicana community, as it was one of the few works that addressed their own cultural narrative. The latter, a novel about a Mexican women entering the United States, also was critically acclaimed. Although the prolific Portillo Trambley produced a large body of literature throughout the 1970's, she did not received national acclaim until the collection *Sor Juana, and Other Plays* was published in 1983.

The themes and motifs throughout Portillo Trambley's literature focus on the sociocultural and political experiences of Chicanas (Mexican American women). Portillo Trambley describes her protagonists as "angry women" who undergo the cultural conflict of contrasting their own ideas of self and womanhood with that of Anglo-based patriarchal, and misogynistic stereotypes. In many of her plays and short stories, the female protagonists choose suicide or physical violence as means of self-expression, driven by the oppressive society that silences them. She died on December 28, 1998, in El Paso.

SIGNIFICANCE

Portillo Trambley's husband, Robert D. Trambley, remarked in an interview that his wife strove to alleviate the inequities that women suffered through her literature. Her literary emphasis on women's experiences illuminated the challenges and setbacks women face. Through her literature, Portillo Trambley gives voice to a group historically marginalized by a patriarchal culture.

Rebecca M. Marrall

FURTHER READING

Aldama, Arturo J., and Naomi Helena Quiñonez. *Decolonial Voices: Chicana and Chicano Cultural Studies in the 21st Century*. Bloomington: Indiana University Press, 2002. Examines her political, feminist, and literary legacy.

Herrera-Sobek, Maria. *Beyond Stereotypes: The Critical Analysis of Chicana Literature*. Binghamton, N.Y.: Bilingual Press, 1985. Examines Portillo Trambley's body of short fiction and its use of a literary device called "personal vision."

Portillo Trambley, Estela. "Estela Portillo Trambley." Intervyew by Karin Ikas. In *Chicana Ways: Conversations with Ten Chicana Writers*, by Karin Ikas. Reno: University of Nevada Press, 2002. Provides a brief biography of Portillo Trambley and an interview transcript in which she discusses her life and her literature.

Vento, Arnoldo C. *Mestizo: The History, Culture, and Politics of the Mexican and the Chicano—The Emerging Mestizo-Americans*. Lanham, Md.: University Press of America, 1998. Offers a chapter devoted to Portillo Trambley's literary legacy and its impact on the Chicano cultural narrative.

See also: Gloria Anzaldúa; Marie Arana; Norma Elia Cantú; Denise Chávez; Martha P. Cotera; Mary Helen Ponce; Alma Villanueva.

FREDDIE PRINZE

American comedian and actor

A brilliant but troubled stand-up comedian, Prinze became an overnight sensation as a teenager after appearing on late-night television talk shows. The star of a popular television series and a Las Vegas headliner, Prinze was overwhelmed by sudden success. He sank into depression and substance abuse before fatally shooting himself.

Latino heritage: Puerto Rican
Born: June 22, 1954; New York, New York
Died: January 29, 1977; Los Angeles, California
Also known as: Frederick Karl Pruetzel
Area of achievement: Entertainment; radio and television

EARLY LIFE

Freddie Prinze (FREHD-ee prihnz) was born Frederick Karl Pruetzel. His father, Edward Karl Preutzel, a German-born tool and die maker, had fled to the United States in 1934 at the rise of Nazism. Pruetzel married and fathered a daughter, Alice, who accidentally drowned at age five, an incident that drove him to drink and led to the breakup of his marriage. He later married a Puerto Rican woman, Maria Graniela, a factory worker who gave birth to Freddie. As a child, Freddie grew up in multicultural, Latino-dominated Washington Heights on Manhattan's Upper West Side. Raised in both Catholic and Protestant faiths, he attended a private Lutheran grade school on weekdays and went to Catholic Mass on Sundays.

A pudgy asthmatic, Prinze wore glasses as a child and was an easy target for bullies. His mother signed him up for ballet classes in order to help control his weight. To deflect the cruelties of classmates, he used his natural humor and quick wit to develop a talent for

Freddie Prinze. (AP Photo)

mimicry. He regularly entertained former tormenters with impressions of teachers or students. After junior high, Prinze was accepted into Fiorello H. LaGuardia High School of Music and Art and Performing Arts. He continued ballet classes and learned to play a variety of instruments, including piano, drums, and guitar. He also participated in dramatic productions in which he built his comedic repertoire, creating characters based on composites of people from his neighborhood. As a teen, Prinze began performing during amateur nights at New York City comedy clubs, where he perfected his persona of a strongly accented "Hungarican"(half Hungarian and half Puerto Rican) immigrant. He left high school during his senior year to work full time in stand-up comedy, specializing in Lenny Bruce-styled observational humor. He even briefly dated Bruce's daughter and contemplated suicide when they broke up.

LIFE'S WORK

Working in comedy clubs alongside such up-and-coming funny men as Robin Williams, Jay Leno, and David Brenner, Freddie used the stage name Prinze, reflecting his desire to become the prince of comedy (Alan King already had a patent on the title "the king of comedy").

Prinze began to get noticed. He first attracted national attention in 1973 with appearances on late-night television. Still in his teens, he performed on *The Jack Paar Show* and then on *The Tonight Show*. A television producer caught Prinze's routine and earmarked the comedian as a possibility for the lead role in a new situation comedy. Negotiations soon followed and Prinze was signed to star in *Chico and the Man*, which debuted the following year and shot to the top of the ratings.

In the wake of his success, further opportunities quickly blossomed for the young comedian. Prinze substituted as host several times for Johnny Carson on *The Tonight Show*. He was paid $25,000 a week to perform at clubs in Las Vegas, Lake Tahoe, and Miami. He was a popular participant on *The Dean Martin Celebrity Roasts*, firing off one-liners poking fun at honorees Sammy Davis, Jr., and Muhammad Ali. During the mid-1970's, he was in demand as a guest on such shows as *The Midnight Special*, *The Hollywood Squares*, *The Mike Douglas Show*, *Tony Orlando and Dawn,* and *Dinah!* In 1975, he released his only comedy album, *Looking Good*, a line he frequently delivered on his television show, which was recorded during a live performance in Chicago. In 1976, he was cast in the lead role in the made-for-television heist film *The Million-Dollar Rip-Off*, playing a former convict and electronics wizard who conspires with four women to steal one million dollars. Early in 1977, he performed at a preinauguration event for newly elected President Jimmy Carter.

To the world at large, it seemed that Freddie Prinze had everything anyone could desire. Beneath the surface, however, the young star was in turmoil. In 1975, he married Katherine "Kathy" Cochran, and in 1976 they had a son, future actor Freddie Prinze, Jr. By then, he was showing signs of chronic depression, perhaps brought on by his rags-to-riches rise to fame and fortune; having accomplished so much, so soon, there appeared to be nothing left to live for. Prinze underwent regular psychological counseling. He began drinking to excess—he was arrested in Hollywood for driving while intoxicated —and abusing drugs, particularly cocaine and Quaaludes. He took to carrying handguns, threatened suicide on more than one occasion, and often behaved erratically. His wife left him, and they ultimately divorced.

By late January, 1977, Prinze was living alone in a luxurious Los Angeles hotel apartment. *Chico and the Man* was still going strong, ranked in the top ten among prime-time television programs. Prinze had just

Chico and the Man

A situation comedy set in an East Los Angeles barrio, *Chico and the Man* debuted on NBC in September, 1974. Comedian Freddie Prinze starred as Chico, a young, brash Chicano who begins working at the rundown garage of a crusty, bigoted Caucasian named Ed Brown, whom Chico calls "the Man," played by veteran actor Jack Albertson. The supporting cast, reflecting the multicultural neighborhood in which the series was set, included Scatman Crothers, Bonnie Boland, Ronny Graham, Della Reese, and Isaac Ruiz. The plot of the show was simple, revolving around the contrast in attitudes as portrayed by the two principles: Chico's cheerful, optimistic nature, and Ed's pessimistic outlook on life. Though of vastly different temperaments, the two characters make compromises to achieve common goals, and over the course of time each grudgingly acknowledges the other's worth.

Chico and the Man struck a harmonious chord with viewers, and the series was consistently rated in the top ten during its first two seasons (1974-1976). The local Mexican American community protested that Prinze, a Puerto Rican American, was playing the part of a Chicano. The show's producers defused this objection with a plotline that revealed that Chico had both Mexican and Puerto Rican ancestry.

After Prinze's sudden death, the show's producers attempted to salvage *Chico and the Man* by writing episodes that explained his absence. Substitute characters were introduced, but it was all for naught. The show's ratings dropped precipitously without Prinze, and the show limped on until its eventual cancellation in July, 1978.

landed a lucrative deal to perform at Caesar's Palace in Las Vegas, and new opportunities in film loomed on the horizon with Universal and Warner Brothers Studios. Prinze, however, wanted out.

On the night of January 28, 1977, he phoned relatives, his former wife, his psychiatrist, friends, and business associates to say he intended to kill himself. His business manager rushed over, arriving in time to witness Prinze fire a bullet into his own head. The comedian clung to life for a day before dying at age twenty-two. His death was initially ruled a suicide. However, several years later his case was reexamined as the result of a civil lawsuit and, based on the testimony of numerous people who had seen Prinze pretending suicide for comedic effect, a jury ruled his death accidental. The decision made his widow and son beneficiaries of substantial insurance payouts.

SIGNIFICANCE

Freddie Prinze's meteoric rise and sudden crash made him an instant member of a dubious club: celebrities who died tragically young. He joined a long list of stars—Jean Harlow, Hank Williams, James Dean, River Phoenix, Sid Vicious, Kurt Cobain, Jimi Hendrix, Jim Morrison, Janis Joplin, Heath Ledger, and others—who will forever be linked in the public consciousness for having early success and early deaths.

In the year after his death, Prinze's mother published his biography, *The Freddie Prinze Story*. In 1979, a made-for-television film, *Can You Hear the Laughter? The Story of Freddie Prinze*, with Ira Angustain in the title role, commemorated his life. In 2004, Prinze, the first person of Puerto Rican heritage to star in a television show, was posthumously awarded a star on the Hollywood Walk of Fame. His son, Freddie Prinze, Jr., was present at the unveiling of his father's star, and he has become a celebrity in his own right as an actor.

Jack Ewing

FURTHER READING

Beltrán, Mary C. *Latino/a Stars in U.S. Eyes: The Making and Meanings of Film and TV Stardom*. Champaign: University of Illinois Press, 2009. A study of the impact of Hispanic actors on American film and television history, through the examples of stars like Freddie Prinze.

Pruetzel, Maria, and John A. Barbour. *The Freddie Prinze Story*. Kalamazoo, Mich.: Master's Press, 1978. A loving and reverent illustrated biography of Prinze, cowritten by his mother.

Snauffer, Douglas. *The Show Must Go On: How the Deaths of Lead Actors Have Affected Television Series*. Jefferson, N.C.: McFarland, 2008. An examination, through the recollections of associates, of television programs such as *Chico and the Man* that have been affected by the demise of their stars.

See also: María Conchita Alonso; Catherine Bach; Andy Garcia; George Lopez; Cheech Marín; Elizabeth Peña; Paul Rodríguez; Jimmy Smits.

TITO PUENTE

American musician

Puente is best known for his energetic timbales playing as well as his integration and fusion of jazz elements into his compositions for and arrangements of Latin band music. His musical innovations led to an entirely new style of sophisticated yet danceable Latin music. His musical acumen and electric style of playing led to the popularization of Cuban style dance music.

Latino heritage: Puerto Rican
Born: April 20, 1923; New York, New York
Died: May 31, 2000; New York, New York
Also known as: Ernesto Antonio Puente, Jr.; El Rey
Area of achievement: Music

EARLY LIFE

Ernesto Antonio Puente, Jr. (poo-EHN-tay) was born in New York on April 20, 1923, to Ernesto and Ercilla Puente. His parents were immigrants from Puerto Rico, and he grew up in Spanish Harlem.

Puente took piano, drum, and dance lessons as a child and, with the encouragement of his mother, both he and his sister Anna danced with a local group called Stars of the Future. Puente would later credit his early dance study and success with his ability to arrange and compose dance-based music, going so far as to encourage younger bandleaders to pursue similar courses of study. Early observers commented on Puente's obsession with music, which included playing boogie-woogie for classmates, singing in impromptu doo-wop groups in school stairwells and on street corners, and teaching himself to play the alto saxophone with the aid of a music teacher to whom his parents had rented a room.

Three major events that influenced Puente's musical development occurred when he was sixteen. The first was that he quit school to pursue music full time. That same year, he met another sixteen-year-old who was newly arrived from Puerto Rico. Pablo Rodríguez, who years later would become famous in the Latin music community as Tito Rodríguez, became close friends with Puente because of their mutual passion for music. Finally, Puente met the Cuban pianist José Curbelo, who would be integral to Puente's immediate development as a drummer and professional musician. Curbelo's musical mentorship of Puente, as well as Puente's introduction to the Cuban bandleader Frank Grillo (better known as Machito) represent the confluence of Puerto Rican and Cuban music and the merging of the two styles into a single unique New York City-based sound.

Prior to being drafted into the Navy in 1942, Puente traveled widely, played with a number of Latin orchestras including the Machito Orchestra, recorded with a group on Decca Records, appeared in several short films with Noro Morales, and even joined the Jack Cole Dancers for a time. Puente continued to compose and arrange during his tour of duty; upon his discharge from the Navy in 1945, he returned to New York, where he played with several major orchestras, including those of Curbelo, Frank Martí, Fernando Alvarez, and Pupi Campo. He also undertook a period of study at the Juilliard School with the assistance of the G.I. Bill. It was during this course of study that Puente familiarized himself with mathematician and theorist Joseph Schillinger's system of composition and arranging, which had become widely popular with jazz artists such as Stan Kenton, someone whom Puente admired greatly.

Puente formed his own group, the Picadilly Boys, in 1949. This early era was important in the development

Tito Puente. (AP Photo)

of Puente's sound. The Palladium Ballroom in New York became the center of a multicultural musical fusion movement with jazz and Latin music at its heart. The Picadilly Boys had a heavy brass sound that was influenced by Kenton's orchestra. Most of Puente's music was based on Afro-Cuban dance, but his forays into and understanding of jazz music set his style apart.

LIFE'S WORK

Puente's work in the early 1950's, especially in recordings and performances at the Palladium Ballroom, reflected the earlier collaborative innovations of musicians like Machito, who had worked with the idea of marrying Cuban dance music with bop. What made Puente's musical style unique was his ability to create percussion through his use of the entire orchestra as a percussive device. This is particularly apparent in his development of the mambo.

Puente's innovations are apparent as early as his 1949 recording of "Mambo Diablo." In this piece, he uses vibraphone, Puente's unique addition to the Latin orchestra sound, as well as fluid improvisations that integrate both mambo and bop. The rhythmic and melodic concepts Puente borrows directly from both traditions were so completely integrated that the music continued to spawn entirely different and new forms. Puente therefore was able to write instrumental mambos, such as "Mambo Diablo," which were highly sophisticated and yet still danceable.

Because of his wide ability, Puente's musical experiments were well-received, and he was able to evolve his own style. He recorded with the Cuban singer Celia Cruz, as well as jazz greats such as Buddy Morrow and Doc Severinsen. The 1950's and 1960's were the height of Puente's early popularity. The younger musicians of the salsa movement of 1970's, including Willie Colón, Sonny Bravo, Johnny Rodríguez, and Carlos Santana (who created a rock recording of Puente's "Oye como va") subsequently revived Puente's popularity.

Salsa music had developed out of the fusion style of Latin orchestra music that Puente had helped create, and younger musicians looked to him for leadership and inspiration. The salsa explosion of the late 1970's was, in part, a direct reflection of Puente's musical evolution and output. Puente won his first Grammy Award in 1978 for his album *Homenaje a Beny*, demonstrating the importance of older Latin musicians in the development of the newer style. Latin jazz had grown and evolved to a

---

Puente's Musical Compositions

Tito Puente often featured the instruments he played in his musical compositions. Although he was a world-renowned timbales player, he also was accomplished on the piano, vibraphone, marimba, conga, and saxophone. His ability to use all of the timbres of his orchestra to great percussive effect made his music unique in the world of Latin dance. He often would write in a clave rhythm at the bottom of the page on a piece he was composing or arranging in order to better match the figurations. Puente's time at the Juilliard School studying music taught him how to juxtapose these clave beat patterns seamlessly with the jazz melodies with which he also was enamored. The Latin rhythmic element gave Puente's music its danceable character and charismatic energy. His best-known compositions include "El rey del timbal," "Picadillo," "Mambo Diablo," "Machito Forever," "Ran Kan Kan," "I Like It (Like That)," "Sin amor," and "Oye como va."

---

point where Puente and a number of other Latin musical artists began to see it as a separate, specialized category. They lobbied to have it declared as such and their appeals were answered in 1993 when the Grammy Awards included it under the jazz field.

Into the 1980's and 1990's, Puente continued to record. His music continued to evolve as he disbanded and recreated his musical ensembles, and his popularity remained constant among fans of many cultures and generations. The children and grandchildren of those who listened to his music in the 1940's and 1950's continued to listen, and Latinos and non-Latinos alike found his musical sound and charismatic playing infectious. For non-Latinos, the Spanish lyrics to his songs became secondary in importance to Puente's musical language. From films such as 1992's *The Mambo Kings* to his 1995 guest appearances on the animated television series *The Simpsons*, Puente proved himself to be an important part of American popular culture. He died on May 31, 2000, in New York.

SIGNIFICANCE

Puente's influence as a musician can still be felt in the music of the younger generations of Latin artists, from Carlos Santana to Jennifer Lopez. His status as a symbol of New York Puerto Rican identity helped elevate countless younger artists and musicians and open the eyes of the larger public to what was once a niche market. During his career, he managed to play with, lead, or influence scores of important Latin and jazz musicians. There are few American composers or musicians who have not been influenced by Puente.

Teri A. Herron

FURTHER READING

Fernandez, Raul A. *From Afro-Cuban Rhythms to Latin Jazz*. Berkeley: University of Caifornia Press, 2006. Well-researched and thoughtfully written book on the fusion of Latin and jazz musical elements and how they were recreated into Latin jazz by Puente and others.

Loza, Steven. *Tito Puente and the Making of Latin Music*. Urbana: University of Illinois Press, 1999. Impressively researched biography with a large number of musical examples and interviews with Puente. This volume provides excellent explanations of the musical examples for non-musicians.

Morales, Ed. *The Latin Beat: The Rhythms and Roots of Latin Music from Bossa Nova to Salsa and Beyond.* Cambridge, Mass.: Da Capo Press, 2003. This history includes excellent explanations of the roots of modern Latin music (including salsa, rock, and hip-hop) from the styles of Puente and others.

Payne, Jim. *Tito Puente: King of Latin Music*. New York: Hudson Music, 2006. Accompanying a DVD by the same title, this book is a wonderful introduction to the artist for a younger audience. It includes a number of photographs and interviews with Puente, as well as a discography.

Salazar, Max. *Mambo Kingdom: Latin Music in New York*. New York: Schirmer, 2002. This book focuses on the development of Latin music in New York City beginning in the 1920's. It provides information on the important Latin musicians of the day.

See also: Ray Barretto; Rubén Blades; Willie Colón; Paquito D'Rivera; Flaco Jiménez; Noro Morales; Poncho Sánchez; Carlos Santana.

ALBERT PUJOLS

Dominican-born baseball player

After breaking into the major leagues with the St. Louis Cardinals in 2001, Pujols was one of the best and most consistent athletes in professional baseball during the 2000's. He received the National League most valuable player award three times in that decade and led the Cardinals to the 2006 World Series title.

Latino heritage: Dominican
Born: January 16, 1980; Santo Domingo, Dominican Republic
Also known as: José Alberto Pujols Alcántara; The Machine; Prince Albert; Phat Albert; Sir Albert; el Hombre
Area of achievement: Baseball

EARLY LIFE

José Alberto Pujols Alcántara, better known as Albert Pujols (POO-hohlz), was born in Santo Domingo, Dominican Republic, on January 16, 1980. His father, Bienvenido Pujols, was a painter and softball pitcher, and after his parents divorced when he was three years old, Pujols and his father moved in with his grandmother. During the summer of 1996, Pujols, his father, and his grandmother immigrated to New York City, but shortly after arriving moved to Independence, Missouri, a suburb of Kansas City.

Because of his inability to speak English, Pujols initially struggled adjusting to life in the United States but excelled as a shortshop for Fort Osage High School's baseball team. Pujols played two years for his high school team before graduating early, during the first semester of his senior year, in order to play an additional season for Maple Woods Community College against tougher competition. During high school and college, Pujols drew the attention of several Major League Baseball (MLB) scouts and was drafted by the St. Louis Cardinals in the thirteenth round of the 1999 MLB Draft. During the 2000 season, he rapidly progressed through the Cardinals' farm system, beginning in low-level Class A and ending the year with the Cardinals' Class-AAA club. In the minor leagues, Pujols was developed as a third baseman but also played left field.

LIFE'S WORK

Before the 2001 season, Pujols was invited to spring training but was expected to start the year in AAA. Because of his excellent performance while playing a variety of positions during spring training, Pujols made the major-league club and started for the Cardinals on opening day. He got off to a hot start and was named National League rookie of the month for both April and May, and,

Albert Pujols. (AP Photo)

after remaining productive throughout the season, was selected for the National League All-Star team. After batting .329 with 27 home runs and 130 runs batted in (RBI) during the 2001 season, Pujols was unanimously selected the National League rookie of the year and finished fourth in National League most valuable player (MVP) voting.

Pujols was originally expected to be a third baseman, but he played a number of different positions during his rookie season, including first base, third base, right field, and left field. Pujols continued the offensive success of his rookie season in 2002, even though he played the majority of his games in left field becuase the Cardinals had acquired third baseman Scott Rolen. During the 2003 season, Pujols split time between the outfield and first base, but continued his offensive consistency, winning the National League batting title with a .359 average while hitting 43 home runs. Pujols was made a full-time first baseman in 2004 and had one of his best offensive seasons, leading the Cardinals to the World Series, where they were swept by the Boston Red Sox.

After the 2005 season Pujols received his first National League MVP award; he later received the award again in 2006 and 2009. He next led the Cardinals to the 2006 World Series title. After the 2006 season, Pujols

received his first Gold Glove award, issued to the top fielders at every position in both leagues. Pujols continued to amass numerous awards throughout the remainder of the 2000's, including player of the decade awards from *Sports Illustrated*, *The Sporting News*, and ESPN.

SIGNIFICANCE

Pujols is one of the most consistent and well-rounded baseball players of his generation. Although he has dealt with several injuries, he has never missed significant time, appearing in more than 140 games in each of his major league seasons through 2010. He also has hit for both average and power, batting over .300 and hitting more than 30 home runs and 100 RBI from 2001 to 2010. In addition to his athletic achievements, Pujols is active in the community through his Pujols Family Foundation. The foundation was established in 2005 by Pujols and his wife, Deidre, to assist families and children with Down syndrome and support impoverished children in the Dominican Republic. For his humanitarian efforts, Pujols received the 2008 Roberto Clemente Award, which is given to one major league player each year for his activities both on and off the playing field.

Matthew Mihalka

FURTHER READING

Abrams, Dennis. *Baseball Superstars: Albert Pujols*. New York: Chelsea House, 2008. In addition to providing a biography of Pujols, this book also contains a time line of his career, his statistics through 2007, and a glossary of typical baseball terms.

Bissinger, Buzz. *3 Nights in August: Strategy, Heartbreak, and Joy, Inside the Mind of a Manager*. Boston: Houghton Mifflin, 2006. Focusing on Tony LaRussa, manager of the St. Louis Cardinals, this book chronicles a three-game series between the Cardinals and the Chicago Cubs during the 2003 season.

Rains, Rob. *Albert the Great: The Albert Pujols Story*. Champaign, Ill.: Sports Publishing, 2005. Chronicles Pujols's early life and the beginning of his baseball career. It also documents when and where Pujols hit all of his home runs and his career milestones through 2004.

_____. *Albert Pujols: Simply the Best*. Chicago: Triumph Books, 2009. Numerous full-page color photographs, especially of the 2009 All-Star game played in St. Louis, accompany Rains's biography of Pujols.

See also: Miguel Cabrera; David Ortiz; Manny Ramirez; Alex Rodriguez; Freddy Sanchez; Johan Santana; Miguel Tejada.

Q

ANTHONY QUINN

Mexican-born actor, artist, and writer

Quinn gained renown playing supporting roles and won two Academy Awards as a supporting actor. In addition to film, he acted on Broadway and in television and was cast in several international films.

Latino heritage: Mexican

Born: April 21, 1915; Chihuahua, Mexico

Died: June 3, 2001; Boston, Massachusetts

Also known as: Antonio Rudolph Oaxaca Quinn; Tony Quinn

Areas of achievement: Acting; theater; radio and television; art

EARLY LIFE

Anthony Quinn was the first of two children of Francesco Quinn, a soldier, railroad worker, and migrant worker, and Manuela Oaxaca, a laundress and migrant worker. Quinn's father was the son of an Irish railroad worker who had married a Mexican. His mother had an Indian mother and Mexican father. Both parents fought with Pancho Villa during the Mexican Revolution. Quinn was separated from his father as a baby, but the family reunited when Quinn was two years old. They relocated from Juarez, Mexico, to El Paso, Texas and later settled in East Los Angeles.

After his father died in 1926, Quinn worked a number of jobs to supplement the family income. His jobs included electrician's assistant, janitor at a meat-packing plant, and fruit picker. He also started boxing and had some success but left the sport once he realized he lacked a "killer instinct." Although he worked

Anthony Quinn. (AP Photo)

briefly at a dance hall, he had his heart set on becoming an architect. During eleventh grade at Polytechnic High School, Quinn won first prize for his plans for a supermarket. Part of the prize was an introduction to Frank Lloyd Wright. It was Wright who called Quinn's attention to his speech impediment, caused by a tight frenum, a piece of skin under the tongue.

Quinn had surgery to correct the problem but was left unable to speak properly. It was suggested he take voice lessons, to learn to control his now-freed tongue. He found a school run by former actor Katherine Hamil. Unable to pay tuition, Quinn traded work as a janitor for lessons. After Max Pollock, director of the school's production of Noël Coward's play *Hay Fever* (1925), watched Quinn reciting lines, he offered Quinn the part of Simon. Quinn received good notices, found he liked acting, and appeared in another play, Maxim Gorky's *The Lower Depths* (1912). Quinn began working with the Gateway Players and was noticed by Mae West, who was looking for "Latin types" to play gigolos in a new play she was producing. Subsequent roles did not materialize, and Quinn began to doubt acting as a career choice. He had one nonspeaking role in the film *Parole* (1936) but was ready to sign onto a fishing boat bound for the Orient when he saw a newspaper ad for a casting call for Native Americans for a Cecil B. De Mille film *The Plainsman* (1936), starring Gary Cooper. Quinn auditioned, representing himself as a full-blooded Cheyenne and pretended to speak only Cheyenne. His "ethnic" looks and tall, trim build impressed De Mille. Quinn got his first speaking part and signed a long-term contract with Paramount Studios.

LIFE'S WORK

Other roles followed for Quinn; however, most were in B-films. By 1940, he had acted in twenty films. Because he was dark and his looks were somewhat unusual, he lost roles to more conventional-looking actors. He played gangsters, Native Americans, and various ethnic roles. In 1941, he played a matador in *Blood and Sand*. After this role, Quinn thought he could escape from being typecast, but that was not the case. Most of his subsequent pictures were forgettable. He decided to return to the stage and in 1947 relocated to New York City to act in Emmet Lavery's new play *The Gentleman from Athens*. Quinn had the lead in the comedy about a Greek American gangster who is elected to the United States Senate; he was so confident of the play's success that he invested $25,000 in it. The play closed after six performances, but Quinn caught the attention of director Elia

---

Quinn's Multiethnic Film Roles

Anthony Quinn got his start in film because of his looks. When director Cecil B. De Mille needed a Native American for *The Plainsman* (1936), Quinn played up his unusual looks and got the part. Initially, ethnic roles suited Quinn as he built a career, but he quickly tired of playing to stereotypes. Roles ranged from Indian to Mexican to Pacific Islander. In 1952, he won an Academy Award for playing the Mexican Euremio Zapata. Although the award showed his acting talent, his looks continued to result in roles such as a Portuguese sailor in *The World in His Arms* (1952); a Madagascan pirate in *Against All Flags* (1952); a Seminole chief in *Seminole* (1953); and a Javanese in *East of Sumatra* (1953). Although Quinn starred on Broadway in a variety of roles, he usually is associated with ethnic types. In fact, he represented almost every ethnicity. He played a Philippine soldier in *Back to Bataan* (1945); an Arab leader in *Barabbas* (1961); a Mexican American mayor in the short-lived television series *The Man and the City* (1971-1972); and the Greek father of Aristotle Onassis in a television miniseries *Onassis: The Richest Man in the World* (1988).

Kazan, who offered him the role of Stanley Kowalski in the touring company of Tennessee Williams's *A Streetcar Named Desire* (1947). The show toured for two years and also played again on Broadway, with Quinn in the lead. Success in this role won Quinn a costarring role with Marlon Brando in Kazan's film about the Mexican Revolution, *Viva Zapata!* (1952). Playing Eufemio Zapata, brother of Emiliano, Quinn won his first Academy Award for Best Supporting Actor.

Quinn traveled to Rome to work with some important Italian film directors. He made several films, including *Ulysses* (1954) with Kirk Douglas, and starred as Attila the Hun in *Attila* (1954). His most outstanding role was as the circus strongman Zampano in Federico Fellini's *La Strada* (1954). The film won the Academy Award for Best Foreign-Language Film in 1956 and made Quinn an international star. Back in the United States, he had a number of good roles. Playing Paul Gauguin in *Lust for Life* (1956), he won a second Oscar for Best Supporting Actor. Quinn was in demand in Hollywood and on Broadway. In 1956 he appeared on Broadway in *Becket* as King Henry II; starred as Quasimodo in the film *The Hunchback of Notre Dame* (1956); and in 1962 returned to Broadway in the debut of *Tchin-Tchin*, a comedy by Sidney Michaels. The same year, he costarred in *Lawrence of Arabia* as an Arab warlord.

In 1964, Quinn played Alexis Zorba in *Zorba the Greek*, based on the Nikos Kazantzakis novel; it became his signature role, and his performance was nominated for an Oscar. When the musical *Zorba* (1968) flopped on Broadway, Quinn, neither a singer nor dancer, revived it. He played the part on tour in 1983 and in New York until August, 1986, never missing one of the 1,240 performances. During the 1990's, Quinn continued to make films and also starred in the made-for-television film *The Old Man and the Sea* (1990), playing Santiago. His final film was *Avenging Angelo* (2002) with Sylvester Stallone. Quinn played a Mafia chief.

Besides being a successful actor, Quinn also was a talented painter and sculptor. In 1982 his show of painting and sculpture in Honolulu sold out, earning $2 million. Quinn also wrote two autobiographies.

Quinn was married three times and fathered thirteen children. He first married Katherine De Mille, an actor, the adopted daughter of Cecil B. Mille, on October 3, 1937. They had five children and divorced on January 21, 1965. Quinn married Iolanda Addolori, a costume designer, on January 2, 1966; they had three children and divorced on August 19, 1997. His third marriage was to Kathy Benvin, his secretary, on December 7, 1997; they had two children. Quinn, who became a naturalized United States citizen in 1947, died from respiratory failure.

SIGNIFICANCE

In a career that spanned more than fifty years, Quinn appeared in more than one hundred films and a number of plays. From humble beginnings, he became an award-winning actor. In 1952, Quinn was the first Mexican American to win an Academy Award. He also was the recipient of the Cecil B. De Mille award in 1987 for his "outstanding contribution to the world of entertainment."

Marcia B. Dinneen

FURTHER READING

Gates, Anita. "Anthony Quinn Dies at Eighty-six." *The New York Times*, June 4, 2001, p. B6. The obituary includes an overview of Quinn's life and career.

Natale, Richard. "Quinn Defined by 'Zorba.'" *Daily Variety*, June 4, 2001, p. 6. A lengthy obituary, focusing on Quinn's career as an "ethnic" actor.

Quinn, Anthony. *The Original Sin: A Self-Portrait*. Boston: Little, Brown, 1972. An autobiography organized around visits to a psychiatrist in which Quinn looks back on events in his past.

Quinn, Anthony, and Daniel Paisner. *One Man Tango*. New York: HarperCollins, 1995. Quinn's second autobiography includes more information on his film roles than his first book.

See also: José Ferrer; Mel Ferrer; John Gavin; Fernando Lamas; Ricardo Montalbán; Ramón Novarro; César Romero.

Gregory Rabassa

American literary translator and critic

Rabassa, an American who is fluent in Spanish and Portuguese, has translated sixty works of fiction by forty writers in a dozen countries, including such Latin American authors as Gabriel García Márquez, Julio Cortázar, and Jorge Amado.

Latino heritage: Cuban
Born: March 9, 1922; Yonkers, New York
Area of achievement: Literature

Early Life

Gregory Rabassa (rah-BAH-sah) was born in 1922 in Yonkers, New York, to a Cuban sugar broker, Miguel Rabassa, and his American wife, Clara MacFarland Rabassa, a native of the Hell's Kitchen neighborhood of New York City. He was the second of three sons and the brother of Jerome and Bob. When their father's sugar job went sour, the family lost its large home on Park Hill in Yonkers, one of its two Cadillacs, and Charlie the chauffeur. Dispossessed though he was, Miguel "Mike" Rabassa was able to hang onto his thousand-acre farm in Hanover, New Hampshire, where Gregory and his brothers were raised.

Fortunately for Gregory, the linguist-to-be, both parents were "word" persons. "As a foreigner and especially as a Cuban, my father not only had become fluent in English but would fool around with it as only someone with an outside vantage could," Rabassa recalled in his memoir *If This Be Treason: Translation and Its Discontents* (2005). "My mother had brought with her the lingo of 'Hell's Kitchen,' in Manhattan, and also her mother's colorful parlance . . . mainly from an older New York." With all the diverse mannerisms of speech that infiltrated his consciousness, young Gregory developed an ear for sounds. Curiously, he did not pick up much Spanish at home, most likely because his father spoke English, except when he and a Cuban friend crossed paths. His father's most illustrious friend was artist José Clemente Orozco, who would visit the family for some *arroz con pollo* when he was painting his murals in the reserve reading room of the Dartmouth College library.

Rabassa began his formal language training in high school with classes in Latin and French, the only foreign languages that were offered. At Dartmouth College, he switched majors from chemistry and physics to Romance languages, starting to learn Spanish and continuing to learn French. His first professor of Portuguese had picked up the language early from fishermen in his native Nantucket, Massachusetts.

During World War II, Rabassa signed up as a volunteer with the Army's Enlisted Reserve Corps assigned to the Office of Strategic Services, the agency charged with obtaining information about Japan, Germany, and Italy and sabotaging these nations' war potential and morale. Rabassa eventually was sent to Algiers as a cryptographer, a type of work related to translation because in decoding messages into clear text the cryptographer has to paraphrase the messages in order to disguise the easily broken transposition ciphers.

Rabassa completed his M.A. degree at Columbia University in 1947, writing his thesis on "The Poetry of Miguel de Unamuno." He earned his Ph.D. from Columbia in 1954 with a dissertation on "The Negro in Brazilian Fiction Since 1888." After twenty-two years as a lecturer and associate professor of Spanish and Portuguese at Columbia, he left this university in 1968 for Queens College, City University of New York, where he became the distinguished professor of Romance languages and comparative literature.

LIFE'S WORK

Rabassa's career as a translator arose from his work at *Odyssey Review*. In 1960, he agreed to be the associate editor of this new literary journal, which was located at Columbia University, where he was then teaching. As associate editor, he was asked to help compile literary works for an issue on literature in translation. In 1963, he received a call from Sara Blackburn, an editor at Pantheon, who asked him to translate a new novel by a young Argentine writer, Julio Cortázar. The novel was *Rayuela* (1963). Although Rabassa was unfamiliar with Cortázar's oeuvre, he signed a contract and translated the novel as *Hopscotch* (1966). *Hopscotch* contains instructions on how to read the novel in two versions. Aware of this, Rabassa later realized that he had provided a third reading of the novel by translating it from the first page to the last. Reading the complete novel only as he translated it—"following my instincts by letting the words lead the way"—became a practice he would repeat in most of his efforts. *Hopscotch* won Rabassa the 1967 National Book Award for translation and led to his enduring friendship with Cortázar.

Rabassa departed from his usual practice for what has proved to be his most famous translation—that of Gabriel García Márquez's *Cien años de soledad* (1967; *One Hundred Years of Solitude*, 1970). "Because everyone was talking about it," he said he read the novel through before taking on its translation. A twelve-page chapter in Rabassa's memoir proves how inexact yet demanding literary translation can be. For Rabassa, the problems with *Cien años de soledad* began with the title. *Cien* (one hundred) in Spanish bears no article, while its English equivalent must be expressed as "one hundred" or "a hundred." He explained that, "I viewed the extent of time involved as something quite specific, as in a prophecy, something definite, a countdown, not just any old one hundred years . . . I am [still] convinced

that Gabo [García Márquez] meant it in the sense of *one* as this is closer to the feel of the novel. There was no cavil on his part." The word *soledad* (solitude) is similarly ambiguous, for it carries the meaning of its English kin—"solitude"—but also the sense of loneliness, thus bearing both the positive and the negative feelings associated with aloneness. Rabassa said, "I went for *solitude* because it's a touch more inclusive, also carrying the germ of *loneliness." One Hundred Years of Solitude*, his best-known translation, is virtually Rabassa's only instance in which he read a novel through in the original and then rewrote it in English. In a deft bit of self-justification, he concluded that being acquainted with *Cien años* prior to translating it may have been providential.

Despite these difficulties, García Márquez has said that he prefers Rabassa's English version to his own original Spanish text, adding that the plot "all came together in his mind [beforehand] and he just sat down and strung the words needed to express it." Thus, Rabassa consoles himself by declaring that he "simply translated in a way close to the way the book was composed."

In making a work by Cortázar his first translation, Rabassa assumed the proper frame of mind to take on subsequent projects. Spanish and Latino literary surrealism, from Miguel de Cervantes's *El ingenioso hidalgo don Quixote de la Mancha* (1605, 1615; *The History of the Valorous and Wittie Knight-Errant, Don Quixote of the Mancha*, 1612-1620; better known as *Don Quixote de la Mancha*), to *Hopscotch* more than 350 years later, seem to Rabassa to be unfinished. Successive translations cannot help but provide new readings and new endings. "In the sense or nonsense of it, every translation I have done since *Hopscotch* has in some way or another been its continuation," he has said. Near the end of Rabassa's memoir, in discussing Oswaldo Franca, Jr., a little-known Brazilian writer, and his novel *O Homem de Macacão* (1972; *The Man in the Monkey Suit*, 1986), Rabasso regrets that by letting a flat-talking auto mechanic narrate in first-person voice the story of ordinary people, Franca is unlikely to attract American readers. "It could be that for foreign books to be successful here there has to be some scent of the exotic or strange. . . . What if the mechanic had been the narrator of [F. Scott Fitzgerald's 1925 novel] *The Great Gatsby*?"

Rabassa maintains that, "The translator must always listen to the characters' voices as they come over into English and not his or her voices as they are being translated." He wonders what writer Fyodor Dostoevski would have sounded like had he walked the streets of Rio de Janeiro rather than those of St. Petersburg. Since Rabassa's auspicious debut as winner of the National Book Award for the translation of *Hopscotch* and the PEN American Center Translation Prize in 1977 for his English translation of García Márquez's *El otoño del patriarca* (1975; *Autumn of the Patriarch*, 1975), he has received more formal recognition than any translator before him.

SIGNIFICANCE

Whatever the meaning of the much debated term "Magical Realism," which began to be heard in the 1960's with the booming popularity of García Márquez, Cortázar, Mario Vargas Llosa, Jorge Amado, Miguel Ángel Asturias, and at least forty other Latin American writers of fiction, this literary style came at a time when postmodernists were proclaiming the death of narrative. However, the developing world to the south of the United States was just beginning to discover that it had its own tales to tell. The primary entry for North American readers to these fresh narratives was forged by the translations of Gregory Rabassa.

Richard Hauer Costa

FURTHER READING

Deresiewicz, William. *New York Times Book Review*, May 15, 2005, p.36. A good backgrounding of Rabassa's memoir. Deresiewicz notes seeming contradictions in the translator's aesthetic, but he concludes that Rabassa's combination of "literal rendering with imaginative transfiguration" constitutes art.

Hoeksema, Thomas, "The Translator's Voice: An Interview with Gregory Rabassa." *Translation Review* 1 (1978). Hoeksema's interview is characterized by candor. Rabassa acknowledges instances of "educated guesses." He says he never rereads his published translations "because I see all the changes I want to make." He finds bad writing harder to translate than good, commending García Márquez's *Autumn of the Patriarch*, for which the translation "was like a good, enjoyable reading."

Rabassa, Gregory, *If This Be Treason: Translations and Its Discontents, a Memoir.* New York: New Directions, 2005. A refreshing defense for his ideas. Rabassa's theories, while often containing a chip on the shoulder, are never solemn or pedantic. In describing his problems with a text such as *One Hundred Years of Solitude*, he provides fresh entries for novice readers.

See also: Raymond Barrio; Angela de Hoyos; Rolando Hinojosa; Felipe de Ortego y Gasca; Pedro Juan Soto; Piri Thomas.

MANNY RAMIREZ

Dominican-born baseball player

A star outfielder and power hitter, Ramirez was almost as well known for his eccentric behavior as for his play on the field. He led the long-suffering Boston Red Sox to two World Series championships, in 2004 and 2007, and his 28 career postseason home runs are more than any player in Major League Baseball history. However, his career ended amid controversy as he retired in early 2011 rather than serve a long suspension for a positive drug test.

Latino heritage: Dominican

Born: May 30, 1972; Santo Domingo, Dominican Republic

Also known as: Manuel Aristides Ramírez Onelcida

Areas of achievement: Sports

EARLY LIFE

Manuel Aristides Ramírez Onelcida (rah-MIH-rehz) was born in the Dominican Republic in 1972 in the capital city of Santo Domingo. His parents, Onelcida and Aristides, left the Dominican Republic when Ramirez was eleven years old and immigrated to New York to work. His mother became a seamstress and his father a cab driver. They lived and worked in New York City until they could afford to bring Ramirez and his siblings to the United States in 1985. Once the whole family was in the United States, they settled in the Washington Heights neighborhood of New York City.

As a young boy Ramirez enjoyed playing baseball. While attending George Washington High School he played baseball as an outfielder from 1989 to 1991. He was named an All-City selection three times, and in his senior year he was named New York City Public School Player of the Year.

LIFE'S WORK

In 1991, Ramirez was picked thirteenth in the Major League Baseball (MLB) draft by the Cleveland Indians.

Manny Ramirez. (AP Photo)

After starting his career in the minor leagues, in 1993, he was called up to the majors by the Indians. In his first full season in the major leagues, Ramirez batted .269 with 17 home runs and 60 runs batted in (RBI) in 91 games. He came in second in voting for rookie of the year. In 1995, he was selected for his first All-Star Game and won his first Silver Slugger Award, given to the best offensive player at each position by coaches and managers, in 1996.

While with the Indians, Ramirez had 236 home runs and 804 RBI in 967 games. He also appeared in the 1995 and 1997 World Series.

In 2000, Ramirez left Cleveland to play for the Boston Red Sox. He signed an eight-year, $160 million deal. In his first season with the Red Sox, he had a .306 batting average with 41 home runs and 125 RBI. In 2004, Ramirez was named the most valuable player of the World Series when the Red Sox won their first title since 1918, breaking the franchise's long streak of disappointments.

After winning the World Series, the Red Sox were rumored to be considering trading Ramirez to the New York Mets. After Boston lost in the first round of the play-offs in 2005, Ramirez asked to be traded and even

threatened to not attend the 2006 spring training. By the beginning of 2006, however, Ramirez decided to stay with the Red Sox. In the 2007 season, Ramirez helped take the Red Sox back to the World Series where they swept the Colorado Rockies.

Ramirez's 2008 season with the Red Sox was clouded by controversy. In May, Ramirez got into an altercation with teammate Kevin Youkilis and was caught on camera slapping Youkilis. Before the end of the season, Ramirez had been involved in a second altercation, this one with Red Sox traveling secretary Jack McCormick, in which Ramirez reportedly pushed McCormick to the ground. These incidents, in addition to other eccentric behavior, led coaches, fans and the media to question Ramirez's commitment to the team. During the season, Ramirez was traded to the Los Angeles Dodgers.

Ramirez received a hero's welcome in Los Angeles and got off to a hot start there. He was named the National League player of the month for August, 2008, his first month with the team. Ramirez finished the season with 37 home runs and 121 RBI. In the spring of 2009, Ramirez signed a two-year, $45 million contract with the Dodgers.

In May, 2009, Ramirez found himself in the headlines again when he was suspended 50 games for his use of a medication that was banned under the MLB's performance-enhancing drug policy. Later that year, an investigation by *The New York Times* revealed that Ramirez had tested positive for performance-enhancing drugs in 2003. The rest of Ramirez's time in Los Angeles was underwhelming; he spent much of 2010 on the disabled list, and the Dodgers waived him in August. Ramirez was acquired by the Chicago White Sox, with whom he finished the season. He signed a one-year contract with the Tampa Bay Rays in 2011 but played only five games before abruptly retiring in early April. It was reported that Ramirez had tested positive on another drug test and was facing a one-hundred-game suspension.

SIGNIFICANCE

Ramirez is considered one of the best hitters of his generation. He regularly ranked among the league's best in home runs, RBI, slugging percentage, and total bases, and was selected as an All-Star twelve times. He also was known for his eccentric personality; his antics typically were described as "Manny being Manny," a catchphrase attributed to Cleveland Indians manager Mike Hargrove. In 2004, Ramirez became a U.S. citizen, but he continued to embrace his Dominican heritage and the Spanish language.

Fawn-Amber Montoya

FURTHER READING

Rhodes, Jean E., and Shawn Boburg. *Becoming Manny: Inside the Life of Baseball's Most Enigmatic Slugger*. New York: Scribner, 2009. An in-depth look at Ramirez's life, based on interviews conducted over a period of time. The authors address how Ramirez views his life and his sport.

Sandler, Michael. *Manny Ramirez and the Boston Red Sox: 2004 World Series*. New York: Bearport, 2008. Aimed at younger readers, this source recaps the Red Sox's historic World Series win and Ramirez's role in it.

Verducci, Tom. "The Night the Lights Went Out in Mannywood." *Sports Illustrated* 110, no. 20 (May 18, 2009). Describes the implications of Ramirez's drug suspension.

See also: Miguel Cabrera; Pedro Martinez; Rafael Palmeiro; Albert Pujols; Alex Rodriguez; Freddy Sanchez; Johan Santana; Sammy Sosa; Miguel Tejada.

SAMUEL A. RAMIREZ, SR.

American entrepreneur and investment banker

Ramirez founded Samuel A. Ramirez and Company, a full-service securities firm and the first Hispanic investment bank in the United States, then developed his company into a major competitor on Wall Street. He also created the Ramirez Hispanic Index, the first index of U.S. Hispanic companies, and an accompanying investment portfolio.

Latino heritage: Puerto Rican
Born: September 20, 1940; New York, New York
Also known as: Samuel Alfred Ramirez, Sr.
Area of achievement: Business

EARLY LIFE

Samuel Alfred Ramirez, Sr. (rah-MIH-rehs) was born in New York City to parents who migrated to Spanish Harlem from Puerto Rico. His father, Regino, was employed at the Brooklyn Navy yard, and his mother, Amilia, was a seamstress. They taught Ramirez and his five siblings the value of education and the importance of hard work and loyalty. These lessons were invaluable assets for a young man who would later found a securities business.

Ramirez graduated from Boys' High School in 1958 and earned a bachelor of arts degree in economics at St. Francis College in 1965; both institutions are in Brooklyn, New York. While still a college student, Ramirez worked summers as an equity order clerk for Kidder, Peabody, and Company. Later, he became a top salesman at Stoever Glass and Company, an investment banking firm on Wall Street that specialized in municipal bond investment. Ramirez married Diane Marie Dolan on May 11, 1968.

LIFE'S WORK

In 1971, Ramirez risked his earnings to found Samuel A. Ramirez and Company. Two years later, on June 28, 1973, the company incorporated. As the owner of the first Hispanic investment bank, Ramirez worked diligently to avoid having it become typecast as merely a niche ethnic business. His efforts soon gained his company a reputation for being one that focused on preserving funds and avoided placing them at high risk. This would become a great asset during times of economic downturn.

Ramirez saw opportunity in the growing market of Hispanic-owned companies and created an equity research department to review the trading activities and capital base of numerous publicly traded companies. This ultimately led to the creation of a new stock index, the Ramirez Hispanic Index, which tracked the ten largest Hispanic companies by trading volume and market value. A couple of months after the index was published, a new investment trust, the Ramirez Index Equally Weighted Portfolio, formed to allow prospective investors to buy into the indexed companies. The department eventually employed many financial analysts who were devoted to Latin America.

In 2004, Ramirez's company won approval to build a new multimillion-dollar, nine-story corporate headquarters building near the historic district at the corners of Greenwich and Hubert streets in New York. The next year, expansion, diversification, and the formation of new business alliances took place in the comapny's Puerto Rico office. By 2006, Ramirez's company was managing more than $2 billion and had offices throughout the United States and in San Juan, Puerto Rico.

Ramirez's company rose to become the tenth largest U.S. underwriter of bonds and equities. The company grew to include six divisions: private client services, municipal bonds; equity capital markets; debt capital markets; and institutional equity and taxable fixed income. All of these divisions serve individuals, businesses, institutions, and government agencies. Ramirez's son, Samuel, Jr., joined the company and became senior vice president and managing director. His daughter Christa Ramirez Harpin and son-in-law Chris Harpin also have worked for the company. Ramirez has five grandchildren.

In addition to building and overseeing his company, Ramirez has served on several financial boards, including the Bond Market Association, the Municipal Forum, and the Municipal Bond Club of New York. His company has partnered with the Futures and Options Program, a New York-based program that helps underprivileged teenagers explore career options. His philanthropy included serving as a trustee of the Museum of the City of New York. He also has served as both president and director of the Catholic Big Brothers and Sisters of New York. Ramirez has been honored by the American Cancer Society, the Valerie Fund for children with cancer, and at the Celebrate Brooklyn Festival. He also received the Austin V. Koenen Award for his achievement in the municipal bond industry.

SIGNIFICANCE

As president and chief executive officer, founder, and owner of Samuel A. Ramirez and Company, Inc., Ramirez has created a success story. From rather humble beginnings, Ramirez has produced new investment opportunities and proven his ability on Wall Street. He recognized investment needs and founded his company at a time when the Hispanic population of the United States was increasing and gaining buying power.

Cynthia J. W. Svoboda

FURTHER READING

Dana, Paul Leo, ed. *Handbook of Research on Ethnic Minority Entrepreneurship: A Co-evolutionary View on Resource Management.* Northampton, Mass.: Edward Elgar, 2008. Discusses Ramirez's company and the index that he created to monitor ten large Hispanic companies.

Garcia, Kimberly. "It's All in the Family: For Samuel A. Ramirez and Co., Family Values Spell Success." *Hispanic Business* 18, no. 3 (March, 2005): 46. Overview of the growth Ramirez's company, the development of his Hispanic Index, and his dedication to family.

LeClaire, Jennifer. "Samuel Ramirez Making Wall Street History." *Hispanic Trends*, December 2005/ January 200, p. 30-34. Cover story on Ramirez and the development of his company.

Oliver-Mendez, Ken. "Samuel Ramirez Is in Expensive, Diversification Mode" *Caribbean Business*, March 23, 2006, p. 10. Discusses changes and alliances being made in the San Juan office of Ramirez's company.

See also: Linda Alvarado; Ralph Alvarez; Frank Lorenzo; Arte Moreno.

SARA ESTELA RAMÍREZ

Mexican-born playwright; activist; writer

Known as the Texan Muse, Ramírez tapped into the changing political and literary landscape of life along the Mexico-United States border. Her literary emphasis on women's experiences illuminated the social inequities inherent in a woman's lot at the dawn of the twentieth century. Ramírez's work gave voice to a group historically marginalized by a patriarchal culture, and her impact on Chicano literature is significant.

Latino heritage: Mexican

Born: 1881; Villa de Progreso, Coahuila, Mexico

Died: August 21, 1910; Laredo, Texas

Also known as: The Texan Muse; La Musa Tejana

Areas of achievement: Literature; theater; social issues; women's rights

EARLY LIFE

Sara Estela Ramírez (SAR-ah eh-STEHL-ah rah-MEER-ehz) was born in Villa de Progreso, within the state of Coahuila, Mexico, in 1881. Her mother died when Ramírez was in her adolescence, leaving Ramírez to care for her younger sister and father. While running the household, Ramírez found opportunities for education. She attended public school in Monterrey, Nuevo Leon, and then pursued her teacher's credentials from Ateneo Fuentes, a teaching institution located in Saltillo, Coahuila.

At the age of seventeen, Ramírez moved to Laredo, Texas, where she took a position as a Spanish teacher at the Seminario Laredo. Ramírez soon joined the Partido Liberal Mexicano, the most progressive political party of the time, and one that would eventually help foment the Mexican Revolution.

LIFE'S WORK

A prominent supporter of the Partido Liberal Mexicano, Ramírez was considered a leader within the party and a representative of the party to the public. The party was formed in 1906, by Ricardo Flores Magón (a self-identified anarchist), and welcomed women into its ranks. The party faced opposition from Porfirio Díaz, the president of Mexico from 1876 to 1911. Though Díaz's title was "president," with the implied executive limits and political responsibilities, most historians consider Díaz a dictator. His rule, which lasted more than two decades, did create national stability and economic growth. However, Díaz's continued leadership—under the well-known mandate "Pan, o Palo" ("Bread, or a Beating")—resulted in his unpopularity by the dawn of the twentieth century. It was in these times that Ramírez continued her activism on behalf of the Partido Liberal Mexicano.

However, politics were not the extent of Ramírez's activities. A writer, playwright, and poet, Ramírez enjoyed immense popularity with Mexican Americans throughout the region. She published the majority of her essays and poetry in the Spanish-language periodicals *El democrata fronterizo* and *La cronica*, both of which enjoyed large circulation numbers throughout southern Texas. In June, 1901, Ramirez began self-publishing two periodicals entitled *La corregidora* and *Aurora*. The former publication featured literature and poetry and, though published in Mexico City, was distributed to Laredo and San Antonio. The latter publication was prepared and published in Laredo.

In addition to her literary and publishing efforts, Ramírez collaborated with other Mexican American women through feminist organizations. Ramírez worked with Juana Gutiérrez B. de Mendoza on a newspaper for women and the Mexican working-class newspaper *Vesper: Justicia y libertad*. Ramírez's work on *Vesper* was part of her association with the feminist organization Regeneración y Concordia, which sought to raise awareness about women's issues and civil rights of the era. Because of her extensive work on *Vesper* and with Regeneración y Concordia, Ramírez is considered one of the founding mothers of the Mexican feminist movement.

Despite her extensive record of newspaper publication—none of which remain in publication today—Ramírez's collected literary works amount to twenty-one poems and essays and one play, *Noema*. The majority of these publications appeared in various venues between 1908 and 1910 and offered insights on women's experiences in Mexico and the United States. Indeed, the majority of Ramírez's literature focused on politics, female-male sociocultural dynamics, and sisterhood. In one of her well-known poems, entitled "Rise Up!" and published in *La Cronica* in 1910, she addresses Mexicana and Tejana (women of Mexican-Texan ethnic heritage) as queens and goddesses—defying the Anglo perception of women, regardless of cultural background, as passive figures, as mere vessels for men's needs. Ramírez's death from illness at the age of twenty-nine in 1910 cut short a rich legacy of literature and activism.

SIGNIFICANCE

In Ramírez's eulogy, published in the periodical *La cronica*, Jovita Idar praised Ramírez's efforts in every aspect of her life. Idar called Ramírez "La Musa Tejana": the Texan Muse, a name that remained with Ramírez. An appropriate title, the Texan Muse had tapped into the changing political and literary landscape of life along the Mexico-United States border. Her literary emphasis on women's experiences illuminated the social inequities inherent to a woman's lot at the dawn of the twentieth century. Indeed, Ramírez's work gave voice to a group historically marginalized by a patriarchal culture, and her impact on Chicano literature is significant.

Rebecca M. Marrall

FURTHER READING

Anderson, Greta. *More Than Petticoats: Remarkable Texas Women*. Guilford, Conn.: TwoDot, 2002. Text devotes a chapter to Ramírez's feminist, literary, and political legacy to Texas and to the United States.

Freedman, Estelle. *The Essential Feminist Reader*. New York: Modern Library, 2007. Text examines Ramírez's poetry through a feminist lens and offers commentary about her legacy.

Hernandez, Ines, and Sara Estela Ramírez. "Sara Estela Ramírez: Sembradora." *Legacy* 6, no. 1 (Spring, 1989): 13-26. Thoughtful and richly detailed overview of Ramírez's life and work.

Mendoza, Louis Gerard. *Historia: The Literary Making of Chicana and Chicano History.* College Station, Tex.: A and M University Press, 2001. Text devotes a chapter to Ramírez's literary legacy and its subsequent impact upon Chicano literature everywhere.

See also: Lorna Dee Cervantes; Lucha Corpi; Ernesto Galarza.

ÁNGEL RAMOS

Puerto Rican-born journalist and founder of Telemundo

Ramos is best known as the founder of Telemundo, the second-largest Spanish-language television network in the United States. Ramos also developed the telenovela, or Spanish-language soap opera.

Latino heritage: Puerto Rican

Born: October 3, 1902; Manati, Puerto Rico

Died: September 1, 1960; Harrison, New York

Also known as: Ángel Manuel Ramos Torres

Areas of achievement: Radio and television; business; journalism

EARLY LIFE

Ángel Manuel Ramos Torres (AHN-hehl RAH-mohs) was born in Manati on Puerto Rico's northern coast in 1902. The untimely death of his father forced Ramos to go to work at an early age to help support his family, but he continued his education in his spare time. When the family moved to San Juan to take advantage of better economic opportunities, Ramos landed a job in a print shop and continued his studies at Central High School in Santurce.

Ramos next was hired as a proofreader and sorter for *El mundo*, San Juan's largest daily newspaper. With a strong work ethic and motivation to succeed, he moved up through the ranks with amazing speed, working as a reporter, translator, classifieds manager, and then editor. In 1924, at the age of twenty-two, he was appointed publisher. In 1929, Ramos and journalist Jose Coll Vidal seized the opportunity to purchase the paper when the owner retired. Ramos and Vidal expanded the paper's circulation and became fixtures in the San Juan business community.

In 1944, Ramos became the sole owner of what was until the 1970's the largest daily circulation newspaper in Puerto Rico. On a business trip to New York City, he met and later married Argentina Schifano, who would be instrumental in leading the Ángel Ramos Foundation after his death.

LIFE'S WORK

Ramos's media empire began in 1947 with the founding of WEMB Radio El Mundo, a classical music station. Two years later, Ramos consolidated Puerto Rico's radio industry by purchasing WKAQ and WNEL, the first two stations established on the island. These acquisitions enabled him to dominate the communications market, but not everyone welcomed the change. A strike by the Newspaper and Radio Guild of Puerto Rico was the first of several labor disputes that would challenge Ramos's leadership. Nonetheless, his newspaper and radio ventures were financially successful, allowing him to amass capital for his next venture, television.

In 1954, the Federal Communications Commission granted Ramos a license to establish the first television station in Puerto Rico. In March, WKAQ Telemundo began regular broadcasts, beating a rival station, WAPA, by only two months. Early programming on Telemundo was generally produced in Mexico and consisted mostly of comedy, variety, and cooking shows, news programs, and films. That August, Telemundo began broadcasting the first telenovela, *Anita la ley*, which also has the distinction of being the first television series produced in Puerto Rico. Other popular radio shows then began moving to television. Ramos signed Ramon Rivero, a popular actor, comedian, and producer, whose *Tremendo Hotel* was the most listened-to radio show in Puerto Rico, to produce comedy-variety shows for Telemundo. His well-received programs *La taberna India* and *La farandula corona* helped Telemundo capture a large audience. In addition, Ramos established a separate company, Film and Dubbing, to provide Spanish-language versions of popular American shows such as *Superman*, *Wyatt Earp*, and *Hopalong Cassidy* to Telemundo and other stations. By 1960, Ramos's empire was complete and enjoying rapid growth as televisions became available to more households. At the time of his death, Ramos

Telenovelas

The *telenovela* often is compared to the American soap opera, and both employ over-the-top drama and serialized storylines to keep viewers engaged. However, there are important differences between the two genres. Spanish-language television stations usually air *telenovelas* for a prime-time audience that includes men and women of all ages, while soap operas typically air during daytime programming. Also, while successful soap operas can run for years—even decades—*telenovelas* usually run for about six months and then come to a dramatic close. They typically revolve around a romantic relationship rather than a family, and in many countries, *telenovela* writers have introduced such innovations as colloquial dialogue, real events, and even improvisation.

The first *telenovelas* aired in the 1950's on Ángel Ramos's Telemundo station in Puerto Rico and quickly spread to other countries in Latin America. The first series were based on radio programs with similar themes. American corporations helped spur the growth of the genre, because it offered an opportunity to target housewives, the purchasers of household products. During the 1960's, *telenovelas* tended to be adapted from romantic novels, but by the end of the decade broadcasters were producing their own stories, often with elements of local culture. The 1970's were a period of further growth, as the leading producers invested in enhanced production values. By the end of the century, *telenovelas* had evolved with different characteristics in each Latin American country, with Mexico, Brazil, and Venezuela as the leading producers. Mexico produced the most *telenovelas* aired in the growing Spanish-speaking market in the United States.

was in the process of constructing a massive $18 million building in San Juan to house his newspaper, radio, and television operations under one roof.

During the 1950's, a wave of nationalism swept Puerto Rico. A fervent advocate of statehood for Puerto Rico, Ramos used the editorial columns of his newspaper to challenge the pro-commonwealth stance of Governor Luis Muñoz Marín, even though the two were personal friends. A frequent traveler to the continental United States, Ramos built a second home in Harrison, New York, and began dividing his time between there and Puerto Rico.

Ramos was active in a number of organizations. He served as chairman of the executive committee of the Inter-American Press Society (IAPS), which he helped found. The IAPS worked diligently to safeguard freedom of the press throughout the Americas, often in the face of hostile governments. He also supported a variety of arts and cultural activities in Puerto Rico, including the Casals Festival. In 1950, Ramos received the prestigious Maria Moors Cabot award from Columbia University for his contributions to inter-American friendship and understanding. In 1957, the Institute of Puerto Rico of New York City named Ramos its citizen of the year.

Having risen from humble beginnings to a position of wealth and influence, Ramos wanted to give back to the people of the island he loved. In 1958, Ramos, along with his wife and mother, established the Ángel Ramos Foundation. The foundation is a trust fund controlled by nine directors who initially oversaw the Ramos media empire, with the income shared by employees and a number of educational and charitable organizations in Puerto Rico. Over the years, the foundation has been involved in numerous projects, including the Ángel Ramos Foundation Visitors Center at the Arecibo Observatory and the Puerto Rico Museum of Art.

Ramos died at his home in Harrison, New York, in 1960. His widow remarried but continued to take an active role in the Ángel Ramos Foundation.

SIGNIFICANCE

Ramos was a major figure in developing mass media in Puerto Rico, bringing news and entertainment to the citizens of the island. The media empire that Ramos founded continued to prosper after his death. Telemundo has gone through several changes of ownership, and by 2010 was the second-largest Spanish-language network in the world. One of its unique programming innovations, the *telenovela*, has proved to be immensely popular throughout the Spanish-speaking world. Aside from the economic benefits that Ramos's business success brought to the island, thousands of Puerto Ricans have been helped by the educational and charitable work of the Ángel Ramos Foundation.

Robert E. McFarland

FURTHER READING

Ayala, Czar J., and Rafael Bernabe. *Puerto Rico in the American Century: A History Since 1898*. Chapel Hill: University of North Carolina Press, 2007. A detailed and scholarly history of the island during this past century, this history provides context for the economic and political world that Ramos operated in, as well as some information on the rise of Telemundo.

Benavides, Hugo O. *Drugs, Thugs, and Divas: Telenovelas and Narco-Dramas in Latin America.* Austin: University of Texas Press, 2008. A cultural study of origins and popularity of the *telenovela* and related forms among Latin American television audiences.

Rogers, E., and L. Antola. "Telenovelas: A Latin American Success Story." *Journal of Communication* 1985. Details the history of the *telenovela* genre and Ramos's role in its development.

See also: Samuel A. Ramirez, Sr.; Roberto J. Suarez; Nina Tassler.

MANUEL RAMOS OTERO

Puerto Rican-born writer and poet

Known for his innovative and imaginative verse, short stories, and novels, Ramos Otero was the first Puerto Rican author to speak about his homosexuality openly and to discuss homosexuality directly in his literary works. Many of his works are compelling and sexually charged explorations of the meaning of being gay and being Puerto Rican. Through his complex, passionate, and challenging writings, Ramos Otero brought the anguish of living ambiguous identities and experiencing the suffocating American political and cultural hegemony over the Puerto Rican people to literary life.

Latino heritage: Puerto Rican

Born: July 20, 1948; Manatí, Puerto Rico

Died: October 7, 1990; San Juan, Puerto Rico

Also known as: Jesús Manuel Ramos Otero; Chu

Areas of achievement: Literature; education; gay and lesbian issues

EARLY LIFE

Born Jesús Manuel to José Ramos Robles and Carmen Ana Otero Campos in Manatí, Puerto Rico, Ramos Otero (RAH-mohs oh-TEH-roh) received his primary education at Immaculate Heart School in his native town. In 1955, the family moved to Río Piedras, where Ramos Otero attended various Catholic schools. Later that year the family moved to San Juan, and the boy enrolled in the Junior-Senior High School of the University of Puerto Rico (1960-1965). He graduated in 1965 and began undergraduate studies at the University of Puerto Rico. Ramos Otero was awarded his bachelor's degree from the Faculty of Social Sciences in 1968, with a major in sociology and a minor in political science.

LIFE'S WORK

Exasperated with the homophobia in Puerto Rico, Ramos Otero moved to New York City in 1968, where he hoped to study theater and film. A protégé of director Lee Strasberg at the Lee Strasberg Theatre Institute, Ramos Otero founded in 1970 his own experimental traveling theater company, Aspasguanza, which produced Puerto Rican dramatic works. Earning great critical acclaim for its innovative techniques, daring themes, and engaging personal style, the company toured the United States over the next three years. In 1971, Ramos Otero published one of his finest collections of short stories, *Concierto de metal para un recuerdo y otras orgías de soledad* (*Metal Concert for a Memory, and Other Orgies of Solitude*), which gathered together several award-winning short stories that he had written over several years, such as "Concierto de metal para un recuerdo" (1967), "Happy Birthday" (1969), "Alrededor del mundo con la Señorita Mambresí" (1970), and others. In this collection, for which he won the prize for best literary work of the year from the Puerto Rican Atheneum, Ramos Otero explores the themes of homoeroticism, loneliness, and sexual tension.

Anxious to share his ideas about literature and explore the dimensions of his identity more deeply, Ramos Otero began to publish more actively around the mid-1970's, and he was invited to edit two editions of the literary journal *Zona de carga y descarga* (*Zone for Loading and Unloading*). He founded a small press in 1976, the *Editorial Libro Viaje*, with the support of the Instituto de Cultura Puertorriqueña and the New York Foundation for the Arts and through which he published his highly creative and challenging work *La novelabingo* (*The Bingo Novel*) in that same year. His collection *El cuento de la Mujer del Mar* (1979) contains the controversial short story "La última plena que bailó Luberza" (1975), a provocative piece of fiction based on the life of Isabel Luberza, the famous owner of a brothel in Ponce.

Ramos Otero was awarded a master's degree in Spanish and Hispanic American literature from New York University in 1979, following which he served as an instructor of Spanish and Puerto Rican literature and history at various institutions of higher learning, including Rutgers University, LaGuardia Community College, John Jay College, and York College. Accepting a full-time position at Lehman College as a professor of Spanish and Puerto Rican literature and culture, Ramos Otero was soon named the director of the university's Center for Puerto Rican Studies. Two books of poetry, *El libro de la muerte* (1985) and *Invitación al polvo* (1991), take up the theme of death, as does his short-story collection *Página en blanco y staccato* (1987). Ramos Otero began doctoral studies at New York University but never finished, dying from complications of acquired immunodeficiency syndrome (AIDS) at the age of forty-two.

SIGNIFICANCE

Ramos Otero was the first gay Puerto Rican author to discuss his identity freely in public and to explore what had always been taboo themes: homoeroticism, the struggle to live an openly gay lifestyle, the anxieties of living and working as a marginalized member of society, the homophobia one experienced in Puerto Rico, and the racial prejudice suffered by Puerto Ricans in the United States.

Mark T. DeStephano

FURTHER READING

La Fountain-Stokes, Lawrence. *Queer Ricas: Cultures and Sexualities in the Diaspora*. Minneapolis: University of Minnesota Press, 2009. A fine consideration of Ramos Otero's significance as a gay Puerto Rican writer, this study situates him well within the life and work of other gay writers in the Hispanic tradition.

Padilla, José Torres, and Carmen Haydee Rivera, eds. *Writing off the Hyphen: New Critical Perspectives on the Literature of the Puerto Rican Diaspora*. Seattle: University of Washington Press, 2008. This study contains a brief but important discussion of Ramos Otero's work and his significance in the Puerto Rican literary canon.

Ríos Avila, Rubén. "Caribbean Dislocations: Arenas and Ramos Otero in New York." In *Hispanisms and Homosexualities*, edited by Sylvia Molloy and Robert McKee Irwin. Durham, N.C.: Duke University Press, 1998. One of the first important studies of the life and work of Ramos Otero, contrasting the significance of his time in New York City with that of the gay Cuban author Reinaldo Arenas.

See also: Gloria Anzaldúa; Reinaldo Arenas; Jimmy Santiago Baca; Rigoberto González.

IRMA RANGEL

American politician and educator

The first Latina to be elected to the Texas House of Representatives, Rangel remained in office for almost three decades, working tirelessly for equal rights and opportunities for Latinos, women, and the poor and for the improvement of education in the state of Texas.

Latino heritage: Mexican
Born: May 15, 1931; Kingsville, Texas
Died: March 17, 2003; Kingsville, Texas
Also known as: Irma Lerma Rangel
Areas of achievement: Government and politics; education

EARLY LIFE

Irma Lerma Rangel (rahn-HEHL) was born in Kingsville, near the famous King Ranch in south Texas, to Presciliano and Herminia Lerma Rangel in 1931. One of three daughters, Rangel grew up working alongside her sisters and parents in family-owned businesses, including a clothing shop and a furniture store. The Rangel family was the first Latino family to move into a prosperous middle-class neighborhood near the local college, Texas College of Arts and Industries (now part of the Texas A&M system), which Rangel later attended, earning a degree in education in 1952. She taught in schools in small towns in south Texas, Alice and Robstown, before deciding, along with her elder sister Olga, to teach in Venezuela, where she eventually became principal of a school in Caracas. After more than a decade in South America, Rangel returned to the United States to teach in Menlo Park, California.

In 1966, in her mid-thirties, Rangel moved to San Antonio, Texas, and attended St. Mary's University School of Law, graduating with a law degree in 1969.

She clerked for Chief Justice Adrian Spears in the U.S. District Court in West Texas before moving to Corpus Christi to become an assistant district attorney. In 1973, she returned to her hometown of Kingsville and practiced law, first as a partner with a local friend, Hector Garcia, and then in private practice. During the 1970's, she grew increasingly interested in politics and became active in the Democratic Party in her county, Kleberg, eventually becoming chairperson in 1974.

LIFE'S WORK

In the bicentennial year of 1976, Rangel ran for the office of state representative for the Forty-ninth Legislative District, which encompassed not only her home county of Kleberg but also those of the neighboring counties of Hidalgo, Willacy, and Kenedy. She won and held the position for the next twenty-six years.

As the first Latina ever elected to the Texas State House of Representatives, Rangel quickly established her political priorities, which clearly reflected her background, her concern for the plight of Hispanics, the poor, and women, and her earlier career in education. Her first act as a legislator was to devise and secure the

Irma Rangel. (AP Photo)

passage of Texas House Bill 1755, which sought to secure opportunities for education and jobs for single and working-class mothers.

Although Rangel worked tirelessly for her state and region throughout the late 1970's and 1980's, her greatest triumphs came in the 1990's and the first decade of the twenty-first century. In the early 1990's, she helped to ensure the passage of what was labeled the South Texas Border Initiative, a proposal that resulted in almost five hundred million dollars going to colleges and universities in the southern part of the state. Her work in regard to this initiative resulted in her being named a few years later chairperson of the Higher Education Committee of State House of Representatives, a leadership role that she maintained until 2005. She also was instrumental in the creation of the Texas Grant I and Grant II programs, which offered millions in scholarships to young people from working-class families throughout Texas. Rangel helped write the original proposals for these grants and was their primary sponsor in the legislature.

Perhaps her most controversial endeavor involved affirmative-action programs in the state of Texas. In 1996, a student filed a suit questioning the fairness and legality of affirmative-action programs of the law school at the University of Texas. When the state's Fifth Circuit Court ruled in favor of the student, Attorney General Dan Morales declared that the decision indicated that all considerations of race and ethnicity should be eliminated during the admission process to colleges and universities across the state. In order to circumvent what amounted to a ban on affirmative action, Rangel worked with a friend and colleague, state senator Gonzalo Barrientes. The two wrote House Bill 588, which set up what later came to be known as the Top 10 Percent Program, insuring automatic acceptance to any institution of higher learning for all applicants who were in the top 10 percent of their graduating class in high school. This ensured that many Latino students from predominantly Hispanic communities could attend college. It also helped students from rural areas and small towns, regardless of their ethnicity, get into the schools of their choice.

One of her greatest accomplishments on a personal level came in 2001, when she wrote House Bill 1601, which set up and provided funding for a school of pharmacy at Texas A&M, Kingsville, near which she had lived as a child and from which she had graduated in the 1950's. Upon her death from cancer two years later, the school was named in her honor: the Irma Rangel School of Pharmacy.

SIGNIFICANCE

By becoming the first Latina state representative in Texas, Rangel earned a place in the history of Latinas in the United States. However, by focusing on the concerns of her first career, education, in pursuing her second career as a politician, Rangel established a legacy for herself as a champion of higher education not only for the more than nine million Latinos in Texas but also for women and low-income students throughout the state, regardless of ethnicity.

Thomas Du Bose

FURTHER READING

Arreola, Daniel D. *Tejano South Texas*. Austin: University of Texas Press, 2002. Good, thorough description and analysis of Rangel's home region.

Briseno, Veronica. "In Recognition of Representative Irma L. Rangel: Legislator and Role Model." *Texas Hispanic Journal of Law and Policy* 4, no. 1 (1998): 3-5. Concise review of Rangel's life, career, and significance.

Guinier, Lani. "An Equal Chance." *The New York Times*, April 23, 1998. Commentary on affirmative action references the groundbreaking work of Rangel.

See also: Joe J. Bernal; Leticia Van de Putte.

JOHN RECHY

American novelist, educator, and activist

Best known for his groundbreaking semiautobiographical novels about the isolation felt by gay people in America, Rechy is a prolific novelist, playwright, essayist, and memoirist, as well as an educator. His works have been hailed as hallmarks of gay fiction, and some of his writings touch on various aspects of Chicano identity.

Latino heritage: Mexican

Born: March 10, 1931; El Paso, Texas

Also known as: John Francisco Rechy; Juan Francisco Rechy; Johnny Rechy

Areas of achievement: Literature; education; gay and lesbian issues

EARLY LIFE

John Francisco Rechy (REH-chee) was born Juan Francisco Rechy on March 10, 1931, in El Paso, Texas. He was the last of six children born to Roberto Sixto Rechy and Guadalupe Flores Rechy and was named after his famous Scottish grandfather, Juan Francisco Rechy, who was born in Spain and became the personal physician to Mexican president Porfirio Díaz. Rechy's father, an accomplished musician, rose to become a director of the Mexican Imperial Symphony. Because of the brutality of the Díaz regime and the Mexican Revolution of 1910, Roberto, along with his parents and his first wife, fled Mexico and eventually arrived in El Paso, Texas. After his divorce, Roberto fell in love with and married

Guadalupe. Roberto was an abusive father, and Rechy always felt that his older brother, Robert, was his true male role model.

John Rechy. (© Christopher Felver/Corbis)

As a child, Rechy's hobbies included drawing and writing. He was something of a recluse and had few friends. His personality drew the ire of his father, who wished the boy were more athletically inclined. Rechy was known as Juan until his kindergarten teacher started addressing him as "John" or "Johnny." He soared academically and won a journalism scholarship to Texas Western College (now the University of Texas at El Paso) and graduated in 1952, majoring in English with a minor in French.

In college, Rechy wrote an epic poem about Jesus judging God and wrote about the foolishness of college activities in a parody of T. S. Eliot's *The Waste Land* (1922). Upon graduation, Rechy enlisted in the U.S. Army, becoming a writing teacher at Dachau, near the infamous Nazi concentration camp. After his stint in the Army, he was accepted into the New School for Social Research for graduate work.

LIFE'S WORK

In 1958, Rechy had his essay "El Paso del Norte" published in *Evergreen Review*. This work detailed elements of Mexican American life. A few years later, in 1961, Rechy won the Longview Foundation fiction prize for his short story "The Fabulous Wedding of Miss Destiny," which eventually became a chapter in his novel *City of Night*.

In 1963, at the age of thirty-two, Rechy's seminal novel, *City of Night*, was published by Grove Press and became a best seller. The novel is considered by many to be his masterpiece. The nomadic protagonist in the novel embarks on a sexual odyssey through various "cities of the night," encountering the hidden milieu of the gay underground. Rechy's minimalist prose is sparse and electrifying. Writers such as James Baldwin and Christopher Isherwood praised the author's effort. However, *City of Night* is much more than a "gay novel." While the main character represents the homosexual man forced to go "underground" in a society that rejects him, he also subconsciously symbolizes the marginalization to which Mexican Americans are subjected as fellow unwanted creatures of the night. Rechy's book thus deserves equal standing among the great works of Chicano/Latino literature. In 1988, Rechy's novel *Marilyn's Daughter* was published. The main character's search for identity mirrors the quest of Latinas in America.

City of Night was nominated for the the International Publishers' Prix Formentor. In 1976, Rechy received a National Endowment for the Arts grant. The PEN USA-West Lifetime Achievement Award was presented to Rechy in 1997. *City of Night* was listed by the Publishing Triangle in 2000 as one of the twenty-five greatest novels ever written.

Rechy also is known as an inspiring educator who cares deeply for his students. He has taught writing at Yale University, Duke University, Occidental College, the University of California at Los Angeles, and the University of Southern California and is a nonpareil film scholar as well.

SIGNIFICANCE

Although Rechy's works are more closely identified with the gay and lesbian literature canon than as touchstones of Chicano literature, his characters often have backgrounds similar to his own. For example, in *City of Night*, the motifs of isolation and wandering are based on the experiences of Mexican Americans who are caught between two worlds with no clear home. In his works, Rechy gives voice to these important themes and to his people as a whole.

Gabriel Fernández

FURTHER READING

Casillo, Charles. *Outlaw: The Lives and Careers of John Rechy.* Los Angeles, Calif.: Advocate, 2002. Casillo's book is a well-organized, fluid biography of the life of Rechy and includes personal interviews with the author about his life and works.

Rechy, John. *About My Life and the Kept Woman: A Memoir.* New York: Grove Press, 2008. Rechy's telling memoir includes discussion of his relationships with his parents and siblings, his homosexuality, and his career as an educator.

_____. *City of Night.* New York: Grove Press, 1963. Rechy's seminal work depicts the seedy underworld of male prostitution and the alienation and isolation felt by the gay man in America.

_____. *The Miraculous Day of Amalia Gómez.* New York: Arcade, 1991. In this novel, Rechy questions the construction of *Latinidad*, or Latino cultural identity. The main character, a Latina, must confront her past, her spirituality, and her ethnicity.

See also: Luis Alfaro; Rudolfo Anaya; Gloria Anzaldúa; Raymond Barrio; Rigoberto González; Cherríe Moraga; Tomás Rivera.

EVARISTO RIBERA CHEVREMONT

Puerto Rican-born poet

Ribera Chevremont, known as the "Poet of the Sea," was one of the greatest Puerto Rican poets of the twentieth century. His verse, which is reflective and idealistic, was called "metaphysical" and "religious." Ribera Chevremont is noted for his poetic experimentation and his mastery of the sonnet as an effective medium to communicate both modernist and postmodernist ideas of the literary art.

Latino heritage: Puerto Rican
Born: February 16, 1890; San Juan, Puerto Rico
Died: March 1, 1976; San Juan, Puerto Rico
Area of achievement: Poetry

EARLY LIFE

Evaristo Ribera Chevremont (eh-vah-REES-toh rih-BEH-rah chehv-reh-MOHNT) was born in San Juan to Cesáreo Rivera Soto, of Santiago, Spain, and Mercedes Chevremont, a Puerto Rican. Ribera Chevremont attended Lincoln Elementary School, Moczó High School, and the Ibero-American Center in San Juan. At the age of fifteen, he went to work in a factory and, at night, engaged in intensive reading of the Ribadeneyra Collection of classic literature, especially the works of Antonio Machado, Charles Darwin, Plato, and the Spanish Generation of '98. Between 1912 and 1913, Ribera Chevremont published extensively in the form of poems, short stories, and literary criticism in journals such as *Puerto Rican Enlightenment*, *Puerto Rico Illustrated*, *Carnival*, and *Antilles Journal*. Ribera Chevremont garnered critical acclaim with the publication of his first collection of poems, *Romantic Parade* (1914).

He became the editor of *The Impartial* in 1918 and in the following year won a grant from the Spanish Cultural Center to go to Spain, where he would remain from 1920 to 1924. During this time Ribera Chevremont made many connections with literary figures and was exposed to the vanguard movements in European literatures. In 1919, he published *El templo de los albastros*, as well as other books of verse that remained unedited and unpublished for many decades, including *El hondero lanzó la piedra* (1975). Another collection of Ribera Chevremont's poems from this time, *La copa del Hebe* (1922), is one of the finest examples of the poet's verse, which shows some influence from the European modernists.

LIFE'S WORK

Ribera Chevremont returned to Puerto Rico in 1924, proclaiming the stagnancy of poetry in Europe and his home island and encouraging experimentation and a renovation of the poetic art. Through his inspiration, a number of avant-garde movements took root in Puerto Rico, including, in the opinion of most critics, two of the most influential: Noísmo, which sought to remove all limits from creative expression, and Atalayismo, which promoted experimentation. In 1926, began to publish *Poliedro*, a literary magazine that appeared every Saturday. In the next year, Ribera Chevremont began to write a weekly column, the "Vanguard Page," which appeared in the magazine *Democracy* and which was to become one of the great sites of cultural exchange between Europe and Puerto Rico. The column gave Ribera Chevremont a regular outlet to affect public thought and opinion in literary questions. These innovative and authoritative writings in the column came to exercise enormous influence in intellectual circles throughout the island. Ribera Chevremont was celebrated for his virtuosity in writing sonnets, many of them dealing with the themes of the Puerto Rican homeland, nature, love, and the sea. He scorned the elaborate and, in his opinion, overly fabricated verse forms of the European modernists and advocated the creation of a more personal and authentic poetry. His 1928 collection, *Los almendros del Paseo Covadonga*, in which the poet uses traditional poetic forms such as the *silva* (unlimited verses of seven and eleven syllables with consonantal rhyme) and the *romance* (unlimited verses of eight syllables with assonantal rhyme), shows the influence of Ribera Chevremont's time in Spain. His next two collections, *Pajarera* (1929) and *La hora del orifice* (1929), give evidence of modernist influence. In his 1930 elegy *Tierra y sombra*, written upon the death of his sister, Ribera Chevremont returned to more traditional forms. *Color*, his 1938 masterpiece, is a collection of highly creative verse in which the poet returns to his quest for originality by incorporating elements from the Parnassian school of nineteenth-century French poetry into his verse.

In *Tonos y formas* (1943), believed by many critics to be his finest collection, Ribera Chevremont explores the intimate relationship between the form of the Spanish language—its words—and their harmonious interplay in verse. Awarded "Best Work of the Year" by the Institute of Puerto Rican Literature, *Anclas de oro* (1945) is Ribera Chevremont's hymn to the beauty of nature: sea, sun, breeze, and hills. In all, his poetic collections number some twenty-nine books.

SIGNIFICANCE

Ribera Chevremont is considered by many critics to be Puerto Rico's greatest lyric poet of the twentieth century. Through his verse, his critical commentaries, and the literary publications he founded, he attracted several generations of Puerto Ricans to the cultivation of the lyric art. Ribera Chevremont has left a legacy of hundreds of creative and innovative poems that range from the deeply sentimental to the patriotic, the reflective, and the comic. His love of Puerto Rico's natural beauty frequently shines forth in his verses, which are intimate and endearing.

Mark T. DeStephano

FURTHER READING

Anderson Imbert, Enrique. *Spanish American Literature: A History (Vol. II, 1910-1963)*. Translated by John V. Falconieri. Detroit: Wayne State University Press, 1969. Anderson Imbert briefly studies Ribera Chevremont's life and work in this classic reference history of Spanish-American literature.

Márquez, Roberto, ed. *Puerto Rican Poetry: A Selection from Aboriginal to Contemporary Times*. Amherst: University of Massachusetts Press, 2007. Contains a selection of Ribera Chevremont's poems, translated into English.

Unruh, Vicky. *Latin American Vanguards: The Art of Contentious Encounters*. Berkeley: University of California Press, 1994. Unruh presents Ribera Chevremont briefly but captures the essential aspects of his project of poetic renovation.

See also: Román Baldorioty de Castro; Victor Hernández Cruz; Lola Rodríguez de Tió; Clemente Soto Vélez.

BILL RICHARDSON

American politician

Richardson has made his mark as a legislator, diplomat, and state executive. He served more than fourteen years in the United States House of Representatives, a year as ambassador to the United Nations, two years as secretary of the Department of Energy, and eight as governor of New Mexico.

Latino heritage: Mexican
Born: November 15, 1947; Pasadena, California
Also known as: William Blaine Richardson III; Pancho
Areas of achievement: Government and politics; diplomacy; social issues

EARLY LIFE

The childhood of William Blaine Richardson III depended on the employment of his father, William II, a manager of the Mexico City branch of an important American bank who was married to a Mexican woman, Maria Luisa Lopez-Collada. Before Richardson's birth in 1947, his father—who had been born on a boat heading to Nicaragua and thus had been questioned about his own citizenship—moved his wife to Pasadena, California, so there would be no question of the child's American citizenship. Immediately after giving birth, Maria Luisa returned to Mexico with her young son.

Richardson grew up in Mexico City, as did his younger sister, Vesta. His father was a strict disciplinarian and always insisted that he work and study to full capacity; Richardson came to appreciate his mother as a "mediator" between her husband and the children. Until the age of thirteen, he attended school in Mexico, and he became fluent in Spanish.

Richardson showed great talent as a baseball player. In 1960, he was sent to Concord, Massachusetts, to attend the Middlesex School. There he had some difficulties, partly because he was not as proficient in English as he was in Spanish, but also because he was not an outstanding student. As an athlete, however, he was much appreciated. At the age of eighteen, he met a Concord native named Barbara Flavin, and they quickly became inseparable. Again starring as a baseball pitcher, he considered a professional career, but his father insisted that he attend college.

Richardson enrolled in Tufts University in 1966. After his graduation, he earned a master's degree from the Fletcher School of Law and Diplomacy at Tufts. Hearing Hubert Humphrey, the former vice president, speak about public service on a school trip to Washington convinced Richardson of the type of career that he should enter. Upon completion of his studies, he joined

Bill Richardson. (AP Photo)

the staff of Frank Bradford Morse, a Republican congressman from Massachusetts. In 1972, his father, who had suffered from Alzheimer's disease, died a few days before Richardson's wedding to Barbara Flavin, but his mother encouraged them to keep the date, and his father was memorialized in English and Spanish at the wedding.

LIFE'S WORK

Richardson did research and wrote summaries for Morse during his time on the congressman's staff. In a later assignment with the Department of State, his work on human rights issues convinced him that he should become a Democrat. After serving on the staff of a Senate foreign relations subcommittee from 1975 to 1978, he and his wife moved to Santa Fe, where he became executive director of the Democratic Party in New Mexico. He ran for a House of Representatives seat in the state's First District in 1980 but was defeated by his Republican opponent. Two years later, he was elected to represent the state's new Third District.

Richardson was reelected seven times and was appointed to the House Energy and Commerce Committee. Later, he served on the Interior and Insular Affairs

Committee and the Select Intelligence Committee. He introduced many measures to assist the large Latino and Native American communities in his state, but his habit of adding amendments to bills often displeased his colleagues. He developed a strong relationship with President Bill Clinton in the 1990's and was rewarded with a number of international assignments. He negotiated the return of an American pilot captured in North Korea, Red Cross workers imprisoned in Sudan, and American contractors held by dictator Saddam Hussein in Iraq. In 1997, Clinton named Richardson ambassador to the United Nations, a position in which he felt hampered by the nation's refusal to pay its dues and by its policy of keeping to a minimum his opportunities to employ veto power. He traveled to Afghanistan, met with Taliban officials and those of the Northern Alliance, who were engaged in a civil war, and attempted unsuccessfully to negotiate a ceasefire.

In his next position, secretary of energy from 1998 to 2000, Richardson fired Wen Ho Lee, a scientist working at the Los Alamos National Laboratory, for suspected espionage. When Lee was cleared of all but one relatively minor charge against him, Richardson was the target of harsh criticism. Despite successes such as his efforts to contain nuclear proliferation, the Lee affair contributed to Al Gore's decision not to consider him as a vice presidential candidate at the time of Gore's presidential candidacy.

In 2002, Richardson was elected governor of New Mexico. At the time, he was the only Hispanic sitting governor in the United States. Although some of the bills he signed were controversial—including one that allowed illegal immigrants to obtain drivers' licenses and others that legalized medicinal marijuana and banned the death penalty in the state—he was a popular governor. In 2006, he received the highest percentage of votes of any gubernatorial candidate in the history of his state. Recognized by his peers, he served as chairman of the Democratic Governors Association.

New Mexico's constitution did not allow Richardson a third term. During his second term as governor, he launched an unsuccessful attempt to win the Democratic nomination for the presidency in 2008. Richardson declined President Barack Obama's nomination to the position of secretary of commerce in early 2009 amid charges that he had exercised favoritism toward a company.

SIGNIFICANCE

Richardson has demonstrated remarkable energy and enthusiasm for his work but has provoked strong

Richardson's 2008 Presidential Bid

The race for the 2008 Democatic nomination to the presidency involved a number of candidates, three of whom—Barack Obama, Hillary Clinton, and John Edwards—were early favorites. In this high-spending campaign, Bill Richardson raised a large sum of money but Clinton raised ten times as much and Obama twenty-six times as much as him. Less affluent candidates, however, could gain access to a national audience by participating in televised debates in 2007.

Of the major candidates, Richardson was the strongest opponent of the Iraq war. He called for complete withdrawal of American troops from Iraq and the redeployment of many of them to Afghanistan. He also opposed the "No Child Left Behind" educational policy of President George W. Bush. He sought to roll back most of the tax cuts that were scheduled to end in 2010 but retain them for the wealthiest 2 percent. He favored civil unions for same-sex partners. He advocated securing national borders with guards but providing legal status—although not full amnesty—to illegal immigrants already in the country. Despite vigorous efforts in Iowa and New Hampshire, Richardson trailed his top three opponents substantially in these key early races and withdrew after the January 8, 2008, New Hampshire primary. His decisive stands on the Iraq war and educational policy probably hurt his chances, but Obama's huge financial advantage also was an important factor in his defeat.

to significant positions in his administration. His interest in foreign policy and tough-minded diplomatic skills served his country in negotiations with foreign powers and earned him several nominations for the Nobel Prize in Peace. Convinced that his intercultural background helped him understand people of other cultures, he has been an inspiration to Americans of Latino ancestry.

Robert P. Ellis

FURTHER READING

Blumenthal, Ralph, and Dan Frosch. "Richardson Is Running on a Résumé Both Local and National." *The New York Times*, February 23, 2007. In-depth examination of Richardson's record as governor of New Mexico, congressman, and diplomat.

Carbajal, Frank, and Humberto Medina. *Building the Latino Future: Success Stories for the Next Generation.* Hoboken, N.J.: John Wiley & Sons, 2008. Includes a chapter on Richardson as a model for success in the field of government and politics.

Richardson, Bill. "A Presidential Candidate's View: Intelligence for the 21st Century." *SAIS Review* 28, no. 1 (Winter/Spring 2008): 145-146. Richardson states his qualifications for the presidency, emphasizing the need to strengthen American intelligence sources.

Richardson, Bill, and Michael Ruby. *Between Worlds: The Making of an American Life.* New York: G. B. Putnam's Sons, 2005. This autobiography is very useful for studying Richardson's early life.

See also: Toney Anaya; Jerry Apodaca; Dennis Chavez; Manuel Luján, Jr.; Joseph M. Montoya; Ken Salazar.

opposition on several occasions. He won reelection easily as a congressman and governor and, as governor, named many people of Hispanic and Native American descent

FELISA RINCÓN DE GAUTIER

Puerto Rican-born politician

The first female mayor of San Juan, Rincón de Gautier is best known for leading a number of city-wide social reforms and public works. In addition to transforming the city of San Juan, Rincón de Gautier dedicated her political career to social causes such as women's suffrage, child care programs, and services for the elderly.

Latino heritage: Puerto Rican
Born: January 9, 1897; Ceiba, Puerto Pico
Died: September 16, 1994; San Juan, Puerto Rico

Also known as: Felisa Rincón; Felisa Rincón Marrero; Doña Fela

Areas of achievement: Government and politics; women's rights

EARLY LIFE

Felisa Rincón de Gautier (feh-LEE-sah reen-COHN deh GOH-tee-ehr) was born on January 9, 1897, to Rita Marrero Rivera de Rincón, a teacher, and Enrique Rincón Plumey, a lawyer. When she was six years old, her mother gave up teaching to raise a growing family. However, her parents both stressed the importance of education and etiquette for women. As a lawyer and lover of philosophy, Enrique invited artists, politicians, and poets to stay in his home. As a result, Rincón de Gautier and her siblings were familiar with classic texts, which later informed her work in public affairs.

When Rincón de Gautier was eleven years old, her mother died while giving birth to a daughter, Rita. Unable to care for eight children on his own, Enrique asked Rincón de Gautier to drop out of school to care for her siblings and the family home. However, this setback did not hinder Rincón de Gautier's education. After graduating from high school at a later date, she went on to study pharmacy.

In her early twenties, Rincón de Gautier began to show an interest in politics. In 1917, the passage of the Jones Bill made Puerto Ricans citizens of the United States. This bill and the active women's suffrage movement in the United States brought an increased interest in women's suffrage in Puerto Rico. In 1921, when the Nineteenth Amendment granted U.S. women the right to vote, the women's suffrage movement in Puerto Rico began to gain momentum. Rincón de Gautier was

Felisa Rincón de Gautier. (AP Photo)

introduced to suffragist Ana Roque while unsure about openly supporting a woman's right to vote. Inspired by Roque's words, Rincón de Gautier's dedication to social reform and improving the status of Puerto Rican women was solidified.

In 1932, when Puerto Rican women were granted the right to vote, Rincón de Gautier not only defied her father by registering to vote but also by becoming actively involved in politics as a representative for the Liberal Party. Her first political action was registering women to vote and to join the party.

As Rincón de Gautier's involvement in politics taught her more about the hardships of women and the poor, she decided that she wanted to help. In 1934, she moved to New York City, where she learned the art of fashion design and mastered her sewing skills. Rincón de Gautier brought these skills back to Puerto Rico where she opened a dress shop called Rincón de Gautier's Style Shop and employed Puerto Rican women who otherwise would have worked in sweatshops.

Life's Work

While managing her dress shop, Rincón de Gautier continued her political activism by working for the Liberal Party. The party asked her to run for the senate in 1936, but because of her father's protests, she turned down the offer. In 1938, Rincón de Gautier and her political counterparts left the Liberal Party over their diverging perspectives and formed the Popular Democratic Party (PDP). The PDP was much more focused on mobilizing the working class and poor, which would later inform Rincón de Gautier's social reform projects during her twenty-two years as mayor of San Juan.

While working for the PDP, Rincón de Gautier met and fell in love with the party's secretary, Jenaro Gautier. In March of 1940, she and Jenaro were married and instead of taking a honeymoon they stayed in San Juan, moving into the PDP's offices to work on the upcoming elections. That same year, Rincón de Gautier was asked to be the president of the San Juan Committee of the Popular Democratic Party. In this position, she was able to gain political power that was rarely granted to women.

In 1944, Rincón de Gautier was asked to run for mayor of San Juan but declined because of Jenaro's disapproval. However, in 1946, after the resignation of the current mayor, Rincón de Gautier was asked again and this time she accepted the position. Her first act as mayor would lay the foundation for her many successful public works that would win San Juan the title of All-American City in 1959. Her first day as mayor, Rincón de Gautier visited the Public Works Department on a mission to clean up the slums of San Juan. In addition to cleaning up the city, she created a Public Housing Authority to decrease homelessness. In her twenty-two years as mayor, she initiated the construction of schools, hospitals, and sanitation facilities, and created new programs to help underprivileged people.

Rincón de Gautier was responsible for increasing government accessibility to the people. In her first term, Rincón de Gautier opened City Hall to the public on Wednesdays. During that time, any resident of San Juan could visit City Hall and share complaints in an open forum. Rincón de Gautier's openness with the public earned her the familiar title Doña Fela and did not stop with the forums. After two years in office, she hosted a large party with gifts for the underprivileged children of San Juan on the Feast of the Three Kings (January 6). Later, she would become widely known for flying in a planeload of snow each year for children's Christmas parties.

During her twenty-two years as mayor, Rincón de Gautier traveled widely on behalf of the U.S. Department of State. She was awarded many honors, including the Woman of the Americas award given by the United Women of America. Beginning in 1960, Rincón de Gautier's political opponents organized negative campaigns and accusations in order to oust her from office. Wearied by these campaigns and accusations that resulted in a politically charged court trial, she retired in 1968.

Rincón de Gautier's political work did not end when she retired. Until she was ninety-five years old, she remained a member of the U.S. Democratic National Committee, serving as a delegate at national conventions. In 1994, Rincón de Gautier suffered a heart attack and died in a San Juan nursing home.

SIGNIFICANCE

During a time when women around the world were discouraged and often banned from political leadership, Rincón de Gautier's successful political career paved the way for other female Puerto Rican political leaders. Beloved by her followers and the people of San Juan, Rincón de Gautier revolutionized city government and advanced the city of San Juan. In addition, her commitment to helping the underprivileged and reforming government resulted in the dedication of a Felisa Rincón de Gautier Museum and Foundation in San Juan and a

Rincón de Gautier's Work for Women's Rights

Felisa Rincón de Gautier was a pioneer for the rights of Puerto Rican women. Despite her father's strong opinions that women should not vote or participate in politics, Rincón de Gautier became a politician and champion of women's rights. While she was not active in the early movement to grant Puerto Rican women suffrage, Rincón de Gautier defied her father by being the fifth woman in line to register to vote once that right was granted. That same day, she became the official representative of the Liberal Party and not only worked to register women to vote but also encouraged them to advocate for themselves. Furthermore, as one of the first women to hold a political office, Rincón de Gautier established many programs that contributed to the liberation of Puerto Rican women. One such program was a preschool program called Escuelas Maternales, which eventfully became a model for Operation Head Start in the United States. This program not only provided women with jobs but also allowed women with small children to pursue employment. Rincón de Gautier's commitment to quality childcare would allow women to become self-sufficient, moving them toward liberation and empowerment. Programs such as these, as well as Rincón de Gautier's own success, provided Puerto Rican women with the tools and inspiration to seek leadership roles in their own lives and country.

Felisa Rincón de Gautier Institute for Law and Public Policy in New York City.

Erin E. Parrish

FURTHER READING

"Felisa Rincón de Gautier." In *Latinas in the United States: A Historical Encyclopedia*, edited by Vicki L. Ruíz and Virginia Sánchez Korrol. Bloomington: Indiana University Press, 2006. Succinct but thorough biography of Rincón de Gautier, covering her life and influence on Puerto Rican politics and women's rights.

Gruber, Ruth. *Felisa Rincón de Gautier: The Mayor of San Juan.* New York: Thomas Y. Crowell, 1972. The first extensive biography on Rincón de Gautier, this book includes details on her public and personal lives.

LaCossit, Henry. "The Mayor Wears Flowers in Her Hair." *Saturday Evening Post* 226, no. 47. (May,

1954): 38-169. While slightly dated, this article not only provides biographical details about Rincón de Gautier but also provides insight to her public works and social reforms as they were happening.

Norris, Marianna. *Dona Felisa: A Biography of the Mayor of San Juan*. New York: Donn, Mead, 1969.

While written for a juvenile audience, this book captures the influence Rincón de Gautier's social reform works had on the citizens of San Juan.

See also: Pedro Albizu Campos; José Celso Barbosa; Rubén Berríos; José de Diego; Luis A. Ferré; Lolita Lebrón.

ALBERTO RÍOS

American writer

In down-to-earth poetry with imagery that tests the border between the real and the fabulous, Ríos explores the extraordinarily ordinary realities, the joys and the heartaches surrounding the quest for self-identity among Hispanics living within the bicultural environment of the American Southwest.

Latino heritage: Mexican
Born: September 18, 1952; Nogales, Arizona
Also known as: Alberto Álvaro Ríos; Tito Ríos
Areas of achievement: Literature; education

EARLY LIFE

Alberto Álvaro Ríos (ahl-BEHR-toh ahl-VAH-roh REE-ohs) was born in Nogales, Arizona, a city that straddles the border with Mexico. His father was born in Mexico and his mother in Great Britain. Although public education at the time discouraged students from speaking Spanish, Ríos, like children from other families in his neighborhood, grew up speaking both English and Spanish. By his adolescence, however, Ríos had lost touch with Spanish.

Ríos was an inveterate daydreamer; he loved to read, especially fairy tales and his family's multivolume encyclopedia. Raised Catholic, he was fascinated by the natural world—the forbidding Arizona desert—as a manifestation of a powerful spirituality. His father was an amateur photographer, and as diabetes robbed him of his sight, Ríos would help him hold the camera, revealing the wonder of the world to the boy. Ríos was writing poems before he was ten. A high school teacher recognized his promise and introduced him to the Beats, a movement that was expanding American poetry into bold, expressive free verse, which played to the boy's love of music; Ríos played cornet in the band and sang in the chorus.

Although Ríos matriculated at the University of Arizona as a political science major, he soon transferred to English, completing his degree in 1974. He remained at the Tucson campus for another year to complete a second degree in psychology, seeing the study of human behavior as essential to any writer. After flirting with the idea of law school, he returned to Tucson and completed a master of fine arts degree, with a concentration in creative writing, in 1979.

While attending the university, Ríos published his poetry in small, reputable literary magazines and gathered a sampling in a chapbook, *Elk Heads on the Wall* (1979). He published his first book of poems, *Whispering to Fool the Wind* (1981), while he was teaching creative writing at Central Arizona College. This work won the Academy of American Poets' Walt Whitman Award and five hundred dollars as the best first book of poems. Later that year, Ríos was invited to teach creative writing at Arizona State University. He thrived in the classroom, relishing the opportunity to open young minds to both writing and literature. He remained at Arizona State and eventually was appointed to the regents' endowed chair in English.

LIFE'S WORK

In that time, Ríos emerged as one of the most prolific of the new generation of Southwestern writers, his dedication to place part of his interrogation of identity in the border world of Hispanics in American culture. Although he published several collections of well-regarded short stories and a memoir of growing up along the Mexican border and the struggle to define his identity as both a Mexican and an American, Ríos established a national reputation as a poet. His poetry was selected for numerous literary anthologies, and he published six collections of poems: *Five Indiscretions* (1985); *The Lime Orchard Woman* (1988); *Teodoro Luna's Two Kisses* (1990); *The*

Smallest Muscle in the Human Body (2001), which was shortlisted for the National Book Award for Poetry in 2002; *The Theater of Night* (2006), which shared the PEN/Beyond Margins Award, now known as the Open Book Award, presented annually for outstanding books by writers of color; and *The Dangerous Shirt* (2009).

Written in a plain style unadorned by pretentious ornamentation or intricate verbal play, in sinuous lines that move at their own duration without the confining demands of beat and rhythm (indeed, his work has been set to music), Ríos's poetry speaks to a populist audience. He celebrates the imperative of language to create community in a divided world. Reflecting his upbringing, Ríos's best work reflects his fascination with borders. He writes cusp poems that explore a wide range of borders: between Mexican and American heritages, the real and the fabulous, words and silence, memory and imagination, perception and reality, carnal and sacred, and life and death. His poems draw on the rich moments his own life—his schooling (he often assumes the voice of a child witness), his bicultural roots, his experiences in the classroom as student and teacher, and his deep love of the Arizona wilderness. In fact, his most accomplished and most ambitious work, *The Theater of Night*, is a cycle of poems that recounts nearly a century in the lives of his grandparents, deftly shifting narrative perspective from poem to poem, drawing on his interest in psychology to investigate the human moments of family, love, faith, and ultimately death. Although he is drawn to the collision of cultural identities inevitable in a multicultural environment—writing poetry about generations in a family, language, and bigotry—his poems speak to the wider community of humanity. The title poem of his 2001 collection, *The Smallest Muscle in the Human Body*, refers to a tiny muscle in the ear that prevents people from hearing their own hearts beating. Ríos reminds his readers that they must overcome indifference to realize the complex wonder of their existence.

SIGNIFICANCE

Although Ríos is recognized as the unofficial poet laureate of Arizona (there is no official designation) and is called on to present original work at august state occasions, and although he is a tireless advocate of Hispanic culture and the importance of defining the fullest cultural identity, Ríos's best work speaks to a much wider audience than the Southwest or Hispanic populations. Rather he excavates into his own experience to distill from it those moments of common ground that define ordinary life in imagery that is at once immediate and magical, arresting and fabulous.

Joseph Dewey

FURTHER READING

Anzaldúa, Gloria. *Borderlands. La Frontera: The New Mestiza*. 3d ed. San Francisco: Aunt Lute Books, 2007. Critical social and cultural study that, although specifically interested in women, explores and defines the position, the pressures, and the identity anxieties of artists who, like Ríos, draw from both American and Hispanic cultures.

Ferlinghetti, Lawrence. *These Are My Rivers: New and Selected Poems, 1955-1993*. New York: New Directions, 1994. Broad introduction to the poet who initially inspired Ríos to pursue the craft of free verse. Introduction provides helpful commentary on the poetics of free verse.

Ríos, Alberto Álvaro. *Capirotada: A Nogales Memoir*. Albuquerque: University of New Mexico Press, 1999. Coming-of-age autobiography about growing up literally on the border of Mexico and America. Best introduction to the writing and sensibility of Ríos.

See also: Gloria Anzaldúa; Jimmy Santiago Baca; Lorna Dee Cervantes; Martín Espada; Gary Soto; Luis Alberto Urrea.

MARIAN LUCY RIVAS

American scientist and educator

Rivas published extensively in the field of medical genetics, especially with respect to results of genetic linkage analysis studies. She cowrote the first scientific paper establishing genetic linkage for the condition myotonic dystrophy. Rivas also was influential in integrating computer databases and programs into genetics research and clinical work and in establishing the field of genetic counseling.

Born: May 6, 1943; New York, New York

Also known as: Marian L. Rivas

Areas of achievement: Science and technology; education; medicine

EARLY LIFE

Marian Lucy Rivas (MAR-ee-ehn LEW-see REE-vahs) was born on May 6, 1943, in New York City. Little information is available about her childhood years or the early influences that led to her pursuing a scientific career. She received a bachelor of science degree from Marian College, now known as Marian University, in Indianapolis, Indiana, in 1964. She then went to Indiana University for a master of science degree in medical genetics (1967) and a doctorate in the same subject (1969). Medical genetics, rather than human genetics, was a relatively new specialty in the field; it applied genetic knowledge and laboratory findings directly to patient care and management of heritable disorders.

LIFE'S WORK

Rivas completed a medical genetics fellowship at Johns Hopkins University in 1969 and 1971. While at Johns Hopkins University, Rivas cowrote a paper on the genetic disorder myotonic dystrophy. This study was groundbreaking because it found genetic linkage (markers) for a serious human disease caused by an autosomal gene mutation. Identification of the markers would allow prenatal diagnosis of myotonic dystrophy in an at-risk pregnancy and additionally provide accurate recurrence risk figures for counseling families.

After her genetics fellowship, Rivas was hired as an assistant professor at Rutgers University, Douglass Campus, in New Brunswick, New Jersey. She remained at Rutgers for four years (1971-1975). While at Rutgers, Rivas published several scientific articles on genetic linkage analysis, including several regarding the identification of potential genetic markers of human salivary amylase, an enzyme involved in food digestion. During this time Rivas also maintained a position as visiting assistant professor in the department of medical genetics at the School of Medicine, Indiana University (1973-1974). She was promoted from assistant professor to associate professor in 1975.

From Rutgers Rivas moved to the Division of Medical Genetics and Hematology at the University of Oregon Health Sciences Center, where she became a professor in 1982. Rivas additionally was made associate scientist at the Neurologic Science Institute of the Good Samaritan Hospital in Portland, Oregon. Rivas then moved to the Department of Pediatrics at the University of Tennessee, Memphis as a professor. She taught courses in medical genetics and published several human genetics papers on such topics as risks of increasing maternal age in pregnancy and chromosomal abnormalities. She also provided statistical calculations in order to elucidate the inheritance patterns of certain genetic disorders.

In addition to extensively publishing on linkage analysis, Rivas researched the possible underlying genetic etiologies of epilepsy. She also was specifically interested in how computer applications may aid in genetic risk assessment. Rivas helped create comprehensive computer databases for common genetic conditions, such as inborn errors of metabolism and X-linked recessive disorders in order to help with data collection and analysis. The programs help provide accurate risk assessment for individuals who may be carriers of a genetic condition and are useful educational tools for students learning how to perform risk calculations.

Rivas is a former member of the Board of Directors for the American Society for Human Genetics (ASHG). She established one of the first genetic counseling programs in the United States at Rutgers University, Douglass College. As a member of the Ad Hoc Committee on Genetic Counseling for ASHG, Rivas and colleagues created the first report establishing and defining the new field of genetic counseling. The ASHG Board approved the proposal in 1975.

Rivas has served on several committees and boards, including those at the National Institutes of Health and ASHG. Rivas and Victor McKusick wrote *Human Genetics: Loop and Learn Educational Program* (1972), which teaches about basic human genetic diseases and disorders and is available currently as an educational tool. Rivas settled in the Bronx, New York, and has remained a member of the ASHG.

SIGNIFICANCE

Rivas entered the nascent field of medical genetics when molecular diagnostic testing options and prenatal diagnosis were not routinely available. As such, she is one of the first medical geneticists to publish findings that paved the way for the current generation of geneticists to complete the Human Genome Project. Her vision of encompassing computers and technology into the genetics field was ahead of its time. Rivas also recognized the importance of communicating such genetic findings to the patient and public through trained genetic counselors. Although the definition of what genetic counseling is and encompasses has since been modified by the

757

National Society for Genetic Counselors, ASHG's Ad Hoc Committee's original paper has remained a pivotal and often-cited publication for the field. Today, the genetic counseling field has grown to have more than two thousand members nationwide.

Janet Ober Berman

FURTHER READING

Harper, Peter S., et al. "Genetic Linkage Confirmed Between the Locus for Myotonic Dystrophy and the ABH-Secretion and Lutheran Blood Group Loci." *American Journal of Human Genetics* 24 (1972): 310-316. Rivas and her colleagues' pioneering research, which allowed molecular rather than clinical diagnosis of myotonic dystrophy.

LeVine, Harry. "Genetic Engineering: A Reference Handbook." 2d ed. Santa Barbara, Calif.: ABC-CLIO, 2006. A brief outline of Rivas's academic and career accomplishments in medical genetics.

Rivas, Marian L., and Paula R Martens. "RISK-XLr: A Microcomputer-Based Genetic Risk Program for X-linked Recessive Traits." *Proceedings of the Annual Symposium on Computer Application in Medical Care.* (November 4, 1987): 193-198. Rivas's computer program to help medical geneticists, genetic counselors, and students calculate proper risk assessment for certain genetic disorders.

See also: Richard Henry Carmona; Jane L. Delgado; Jose Alberto Fernandez-Pol.

MAGGIE RIVAS-RODRIGUEZ

American journalist, educator, and activist

Rivas-Rodriguez, an accomplished journalist and academic, gained national prominence for her advocacy of the preservation of the Hispanic legacy through improved representation of U.S. Latinos in the media. She is well known for her efforts in promoting professional development and cultural understanding and recognition of Hispanic media professionals. Her interest in creating awareness and preserving the legacy of U.S. Hispanics who served in the armed forces during World War II spawned the Oral History Project at the University of Texas at Austin.

Latino heritage: Mexican

Born: 1955; San Antonio, Texas

Also known as: Maggie Rivas

Areas of achievement: Journalism; education; activism

EARLY LIFE

Maggie Rivas-Rodriguez (REE-vahs rah-DREE-gehz) was born Maggie Rivas in San Antonio, Texas, in 1955 to Ramón Rivas and Henrietta Lopez, both Mexican American. One of seven children—siblings Robert, Irma, Henri, Carmen, Connie, and Lupe being the others—Rivas-Rodriguez spent her adolescent years in the city of Devine, which is located in Medina County, Texas. After her marriage to Gil Rodriguez, her two children, Ramón and Agustín, were born.

Rivas-Rodriguez earned her bachelor's degree in journalism from the University of Texas, Austin in 1976, graduating with honors. Her next stop was Columbia University's Graduate School of Journalism, where she earned her master's degree in 1977. She then went on to earn a Ph.D. in mass communication from the University of North Carolina, Chapel Hill in 1998.

During her undergraduate studies, Rivas-Rodriguez's passion for journalism blossomed. Her jobs at *The Daily Texan* (the student newspaper at the University of Texas, Austin) and a Spanish-language radio station solidified this burgeoning interest. After graduating with her master's degree, she worked for two years as a copy editor and reporter for United Press International in Dallas, Texas. From 1979 to 1988, she worked as a reporter for WFAA-TV in Dallas, Texas, and *The Boston Globe*, a prominent newspaper. For the following eight years (1988 to 1996) she was employed as the chief of the border bureau for *The Dallas Morning News*. After completion of her Ph.D. in 1998, she accepted a faculty position at the University of Texas, Austin School of Journalism, where she became an associate professor.

LIFE'S WORK

Rivas-Rodriguez leveraged her journalistic prowess and her academic platform to advocate for the preservation of the Hispanic legacy through improved representation of U.S. Latinos in the media. Her desire to champion this cause, however, goes back to her early college years. She observed that even though news products were supposed to be a reflection of the community make-up, the Latino community conspicuously was omitted from news stories. She resolved immediately to engage in initiatives to bring diversity to the news media. Rivas-Rodriguez proceeded to serve on the committee that instituted the National Association of Hispanic Journalists (NAHJ) in April, 1984. The goal of this organization was to provide support to Hispanics involved in the media so that the manifest underrepresentation of Latinos in the newsroom would be remedied, thereby providing a voice for diversity in the news media. Broadly included in this definition of support were such goals as promoting career development and

---

Voces Oral History Project

Historical chronicles of World War II generally fail to acknowledge the specific contributions made by Latinos serving in the armed forces. To rectify this omission, Maggie Rivas-Rodriguez created the U.S. Latino and Latina WWII Oral History Project at the University of Texas at Austin in 1999. Her objective was to memorialize the contribution of Latino veterans through the compilation of videotaped interviews and other salient artifacts, and use this as a vehicle to enlighten society about the experiences of the World War II generation. Interviews were conducted in the United States, Mexico, and Puerto Rico. While the project was initially conceived around the contribution of Latinos in World War II, a grant of $428,000 from the Institute of Museum and Library Services facilitated an extension of the scope of the project in 2009 to include the Korean War and the Vietnam War. This warranted a name change to Voces Oral History Project. By 2011 the project had amassed in excess of 650 oral interviews and thousands of other artifacts that were prepared for preservation at the Nettie Lee Benson Latin American Collection and the Center for American History at the University of Texas, Austin.

In addition to the videotaped interviews and other artifacts from the wartime periods, the project has also generated publications. *Newspaper Narratives* was a journalism class initiative that produced a newspaper of the stories from the WWII Latino and Latina veterans. This was discontinued in 2004, to be replaced by the *Narratives Insider* newsletter that is published semiannually and includes, among other things, summaries of new interviews. Using the data collected from the oral interviews, Rivas-Rodriguez was involved in the publication of two books, *A Legacy Greater than Words* and *Mexican Americans and World War II.*

---

cultural understanding of Hispanic media professionals, fostering fair treatment and recognition, and encouraging Hispanics to engage in the study and the practice of journalism and communications. Rivas-Rodriguez specifically initiated two of the organization's most successful projects, one of which has been replicated by several journalism organizations engaged in training and mentorship programs.

In 1999, Rivas-Rodriguez established the U.S. Latino and Latina World War II Oral History Project at the University of Texas, Austin to preserve the legacy of Hispanics in the United States who served in the armed forces during World War II. The project subsequently broadened its scope to include the Korean and Vietnam Wars. Her devotion to this cause took her to the national stage in 2007, where she publicly protested Ken Burns's Public Broadcasting Service documentary *The War* because it failed to commemorate the contribution of Latinos during World War II. Her stand against this resulted in Burns incorporating the stories of Latino servicemen and women into the documentary.

Rivas-Rodriguez's advocacy and efforts to promote and preserve the Latino legacy have garnered her national recognition and numerous awards. In 2006, she was inducted into the Dallas-Fort Worth Network of Hispanic Communicators Hall of Fame. In 2007, she was awarded the Rubén Salazar Award for Communications from the National Council of La Raza. That same year she also received the Leadership Award from the National Association of Hispanic Journalists and the award for Outstanding Support of Hispanic Issues in Higher Education from the American Association of Hispanics in Higher Education (AAHHE). These awards acknowledge and bear testimony to the indelible role Rivas-Rodriguez has played in promoting, supporting, and advancing Hispanic issues in the United States.

SIGNIFICANCE

Rivas-Rodriguez's life's work has profoundly altered the lens through which society views the contributions of Latinos during U.S. wartime periods. Her creation of the Voces Oral History Project, in addition to providing a voice for the forgotten generations who faithfully served in the armed forces, cultivates universal awareness of the urgent need to create culturally authentic resources that foster a legacy for future generations. Her efforts to challenge the news media for failing to include the contribution of U.S. Latinos in World War II not only preserves the legacy of the Hispanic population but also ensures accuracy and validity in media representations of historical events. Her books, *A Legacy Greater than Words: Stories of U.S. Latinos and Latinas of the World War II Generation* (2006) and *Mexican Americans and World War II* (2005), are a permanent tribute and voice to the experiences of the Latinos who contributed to the aspirations of the American people.

Jeff Naidoo

FURTHER READING

Rivas-Rodriguez, Maggie. *A Legacy Greater than Words: Stories of U.S. Latinos and Latinas of the World War II Generation.* University of Texas at Austin: U.S. Latino and Latina World War II Oral History Project, 2006. This volume provides a glimpse into why Rivas-Rodriguez embarked on her journey of advocacy. The poignant stories provide a penetrating look into what motivated her to restore veracity to news reporting.

Rivas-Rodriguez, Maggie. *Mexican Americans and World War II.* Austin: University of Texas Press, 2005. While this book is a comprehensive exploration of the wartime Mexican American experience, it lays bare the soul of Rivas-Rodriguez, who is of Mexican American heritage. Through the stories of her forebears, she provides an insightful glance into an aspect of her cultural legacy that defines her person and her life's work.

Stuart, Reginald. "A Historical Omission." *Diverse: Issues in Higher Education* 24, no. 16 (September, 2007): 20-22. This article highlights the significant contribution Rivas-Rodriguez has made toward drawing attention to the Latino experience during wartime periods.

See also: Nicolás Kanellos; Roberto J. Suarez.

CHITA RIVERA

American dancer, actor, and singer

Rivera is a dancer, singer, and actor whose stellar career includes national and international stage performances and touring shows, film and television productions, and several albums. Her extraordinary talent and dedication led the 2009 Presidential Medal of Freedom honoree to be considered a legend of Broadway and American theater.

Latino heritage: Puerto Rican
Born: January 23, 1933; Washington, D.C.
Also known as: Dolores Conchita Figueroa del Rivero
Areas of achievement: Dance; theater; music

EARLY LIFE

Chita Rivera (CHEE-tah rih-VEH-rah) was born January 23, 1933, to Pedro Julio Figueroa del Rivero and Katherine Anderson del Rivero. Her Puerto Rican father was a musician who played clarinet and saxophone for the United States Navy band. He died when Rivera was only seven years old, and her widowed mother took a job with the Pentagon.

Rivera's mother enrolled her in the Jones Haywood School of Ballet with the hope that she would learn discipline and poise. She was allowed to take classes three times a week. Doris Jones and Claire Haywood founded their school of dance expressly to serve minority children because they believed all children deserved the opportunity to benefit from classical dance instruction. Rivera always expressed appreciation to Jones and Haywood.

Chita Rivera. (AP Photo)

In 1950, a teacher from George Balanchine's School of American Ballet in New York visited the Jones Haywood studio. Fifteen-year-old Rivera was one of two students selected to audition for Balanchine in New York City. In an action that has become legendary, Balanchine realized that the determined young ballerina was dancing even though her foot was bleeding through her toe shoe. He stopped the audition to bandage her foot himself. Rivera was accepted to Balanchine's School of American Ballet and given a scholarship, making it possible for her to study with such major twentieth-century American ballet dancers as Allegra Kent, Edward Villella, and Maria Tallchief. Two years later, intending only to encourage a friend's ambition, she attended the auditions for the national tour of *Call Me Madam* (1950) starring Elaine Stritch. She won the part, beating out her friend. This marked the end of her ballet aspirations and the beginning of her musical theater career. Rivera made her Broadway debut in 1950 as a dancer in the musical *Guys and Dolls*. In 1952, she danced in *Call Me Madam*, and in 1953, in *Can-Can*. In 1957, she was cast in her most famous role, that of fiery Anita in *West Side Story*.

LIFE'S WORK

In 1957, Rivera's dancing ability helped choreographer Jerome Robbins realize his groundbreaking vision for *West Side Story*. Playing her first major supporting role, that of the Puerto Rican sweetheart of the Shark gang leader, Rivera was introduced to an entirely new dimension of performing. She married Tony Mordente, a dancer in the *West Side Story* cast, in 1957, and continued to appear in the show on Broadway until 1959. By 1958, her presence had become so important to the show that when she made her London debut, the producers postponed the production until her daughter, Lisa, was born. She starred as Rosie Alvarez in *Bye Bye Birdie* on Broadway in 1960 and in the London production the following year. She played Anyanka in the play *Bajour* from 1964 to 1965. Rivera and Mordente were divorced in 1966. Whether she was performing on Broadway or touring the nation, Rivera consistently energized audiences. She starred in *Born Yesterday* (1946), *Flower Drum Song* (1958), *The Rose Tattoo* (1951), *Threepenny Opera* (1928), *Sweet Charity* (1966), and *Kiss Me, Kate* (1948). She traveled to Japan with the Radio City Music Hall Rockettes in an international tour of *Can-Can*. She performed in the 1973 revue *Sondheim: A Musical Tribute*. In 1975, she appeared as Velma Kelly in the original

Bringing a Classic Sensibility to Contemporary Dance

Chita Rivera's remarkable career brought her a number of accolades. While she is an exceptional singer and actor, she is best known for her achievements as a dancer. After studying dance with Doris Jones and Claire Haywood in Washington, D.C., and with such twentieth-century ballet superstars as Allegra Kent, Edward Villella, and Maria Tallchief at George Balanchine's School of American Ballet in New York City, traditional ballet exerted a profound influence on her life and her art. Her ballet training made it possible for her to bring the classical sensibility and pure athleticism of traditional ballet to contemporary dance. She proved that an unknown chorus dancer could take center stage and become a star. Her electric personality and dazzling dancing skills combined with professional discipline not only inspired but also made it possible for her to work with Broadway's greatest and strictest stage choreographers, including Bob Fosse and Gower Champion, Jerome Robbins, Jack Cole, and Peter Gennaro, whose original and groundbreaking choreographic vision transformed contemporary dance in the musical theater.

cast of *Chicago*. Rivera also made appearances on such television variety shows as *The Arthur Godfrey Show*, *The Sid Caesar Show, The Dinah Shore Show*, *The Judy Garland Show*, *The Ed Sullivan Show*, and *The Carol Burnett Show*. She played Nickie in the film version of *Sweet Charity* (1969) with Shirley MacLaine, and she played Fastrada for the 1981 television version of the musical *Pippin* (1972).

Disaster struck at the height of Rivera's career in 1986, when an automobile accident in New York broke her left leg in twelve places. Determined to prevail, she endured painful rehabilitation and returned to the stage in 1987, appearing in *Happy Birthday, Mr. Abbott! or Night of 100 Years*. In 1988, she appeared in *Can-Can*. Also in 1988, she and novelist Daniel Simone opened Chita's, a popular Forty-second Street restaurant. In 1993, Rivera won a Tony Award for Best Leading Actress in a Musical for her performance in *Kiss of the Spider Woman*, which ran in Toronto and New York City.

Rivera also is a recipient of the prestigious Kennedy Center Honor. She has won two Tony Awards as Best Leading Actress in a Musical, received six Tony nominations, and was honored with the 2009 Presidential Medal of Freedom. She starred in the 2006 Broadway biographical production *Chita Rivera: The Dancer's Life*, which told her life story.

SIGNIFICANCE

Rivera's remarkable dancing ability combined with her spectacular singing and acting skills made her a Broadway legend. Rivera was not limited to the stage but also performed in film and television productions. Her voice is heard on several original Broadway cast recordings. Her dedication and perseverance brought her countless awards and nominations. She was the first Hispanic recipient of a Kennedy Center honor, given in recognition of unique and valuable contributions to the cultural life of our nation.

Jan Statman

FURTHER READING

Gold, Sylviane. "On Broadway: What Becomes a Legend Most? Chita Rivera's New Show Revisits Her Struggles and Triumphs." *Dance* 79, no. 12 (December, 2005). Describes Rivera's experiences in dance, music, and acting en route to stardom on Broadway.

Rivera, Chita. "Chita Rivera." Interview by Wendy Perron. *Dance* 81, no. 4 (April, 2007): 16. Brief interview that provides insights into Rivera's life and work.

_____. "*West Side Story*." Interview by Robert Viagas. *The Sondheim Review* 9, no. 3 (Winter, 2003). In-depth interview with Rivera regarding her experiences with the staging and creation of *West Side Story* on the show's forty-fifth anniversary.

Trescott, Jacqueline. "For Chita Rivera, a Career with Legs," *The Washington Post*, December 8, 2002, pp. G01-G10. Extensive biography covering Rivera's life and career.

Viagas, Robert. *I'm the Greatest Star: Broadway's Top Musical Legends from 1900 to Today*. New York: Applause Books, 2009. Presents life stories of forty Broadway stars who fascinated audiences from 1900 to the present, including Rivera.

See also: Evelyn Cisneros; Miriam Colón; Linda Cristal; Rita Moreno; Olga San Juan; Raquel Welch; Carmen Zapata.

GERALDO RIVERA

American television broadcaster, journalist, lawyer, and author

In 2010, Rivera celebrated his fortieth anniversary as an extremely popular television broadcaster and talk show host. His fame was largely because of his flamboyant style, dynamic personality, and high-profile stories.

Latino heritage: Puerto Rican

Born: July 4, 1943; New York, New York

Also known as: Geraldo Michael Rivera; Gerald Michael Riviera; Gerry Riviera

Areas of achievement: Journalism; radio and television; social issues

EARLY LIFE

Geraldo Michael Rivera (huhr-AHLD-oh rih-VEHR-ah) was born in Manhattan, New York, and raised in West Babylon on Long Island. He was the son of Cruz Rivera, a restaurant owner of Puerto Rican descent, and Lillian Friedman Rivera, a waitress of Russian Jewish ancestry. In addition to his two sisters, the family adopted his uncle's son, with whom Rivera had several violent fights. Although never particularly religious, he

attended a synagogue with his mother and was given a Bar Mitzvah. He generally avoided anti-Latino prejudices by referring to his Jewish background and using the name "Riviera," which his mother put on his birth certificate. When in the presence of anti-Semites, he identified himself as a person of Puerto Rican ancestry.

During his youth, Rivera was not particularly interested in school and scholarly pursuits. While he was in high school, he belonged to a delinquent group that took pleasure in stealing hubcaps and tires, and on at least one occasion they stole an automobile, which they dumped after a fast joyride. Although Rivera was never caught for car theft, the police did discover some of his stolen tires, but the only consequence was an embarrassing lecture in the presence of his father.

Following graduation from high school, he was a student for two years at the New York State Maritime College, but he left because of his dislike of military regimentation. He then attended the University of Arizona, where he played on the lacrosse team as goalie. Endowed with a good memory, he earned money by taking exams for other students, but his own grades were

Geraldo Rivera. (AP Photo)

rather mediocre. Nevertheless, he was admitted to the Brooklyn Law School, graduating with a J.D. in 1969. For a short period he worked as an investigator for the New York Police Department, and he then became the attorney for a radical Puerto Rican group, called the Young Lords, whose goals he supported at the time.

In *Exposing Myself*, Rivera provides much information about his lifelong obsession with women and his numerous liaisons. In 1965, he married his first wife, Linda Coblentz, but after three years she left him because of his "relentless promiscuity." Soon after the divorce, one of Rivera's "several conquests," called "Sally" in his autobiography, became pregnant, and he arranged for an illegal and dangerous abortion. Two years later, another woman, "Julia," became pregnant, but this time he was able to arrange for a legal abortion. Between 1971 and 1975, Rivera was married to Edith Vonnegut, and thereafter he married three additional times. Between 1979 and 2005, he became the father of five children.

Life's Work

In 1970, the news director of New York station WABC-TV was hoping to find a competent Latino journalist in order to make the staff look more like the station's audience. While reporting on the Young Lords' occupation of a church, the director was impressed with Rivera's energetic personality and communication skills. Despite Rivera's lack of experience, he was hired as a reporter for *Eyewitness News*. That summer he obtained intensive training at Columbia University's School of Journalism. Reflecting the rebellious culture of the period, he helped invent television activism, and he quickly gained a reputation as an unusually talented person who specialized in dramatic and controversial stories.

His 1972 report on the abuse and neglect of mentally disabled patients at Staten Island's Willowbrook State School was awarded the Peabody Award and attracted national attention. After appearing on news programs for ABC, he served as host for *Good Morning America* from 1973 to 1976 and for *Goodnight, America* from 1974 to 1977. During the summer of 1977, he landed an exclusive interview with Cuban president Fidel Castro and produced a series on the Panama Canal controversy. In 1978, he became one of the core correspondents for the ABC newsmagazine *20/20*. His hour-long report, "The Elvis Cover-up," was *20/20*'s highest rated show for more than two decades. In 1985, nevertheless, he was fired after he publically questioned the integrity of the program's director for not running a controversial segment about Marilyn Monroe's relationships with President John F. Kennedy and Senator Robert F. Kennedy.

While unemployed, Rivera reluctantly agreed to host the sensationalistic opening of a vault that reportedly had belonged to Al Capone. The resulting publicity helped make it possible for him to produce and host the daytime talk show *Geraldo*, which ran from 1987 to 1998. Many critics disliked the show's theatrical tone and use of controversial, sometimes bizarre guests. In 1988, for instance, he featured an interview with cult leader Charles Manson. After he received a broken nose during a fight between white racists and their opponents, the cover of *Newsweek* carried his photograph next to a headline, "Trash TV: From the Lurid to the Loud, Anything Goes." In 1993, while continuing his daytime show, Rivera also began to host a nightly news talk show called *Rivera Live*, which helped him regain the image of a serious journalist. In 2000, he received his third Robert F. Kennedy Journalism Award for his National Broadcasting Company (NBC) News documentary *Women in Prison*.

In 2001, Rivera joined the Fox News Channel (FNC) as a war correspondent, and in that capacity he

---

Rivera and "The Mystery of Al Capone's Vault"

In 1986, Geraldo Rivera hosted a special two-hour television broadcast on the opening of a recently discovered vault that was underneath the Lexington Hotel in Chicago. Workers renovating the hotel had recently come across a series of secret tunnels thought to be part of Al Capone's business between 1928 and 1931, and one tunnel contained a large vault. A historian claimed that Capone had hidden great wealth in such a vault. At the time of the broadcast, Rivera had been fired from ABC, and he wanted to attract the attention of television producers and the public. The highly publicized program reached an audience of about thirty million curious viewers—considered the largest audience for any syndicated television special.

When the vault was opened, it was found to contain only dirt and a few empty bottles. Thereafter, the expression "Al Capone's vault" became a way of referring to an excessively hyped event with a disappointing outcome. Rivera wrote in his autobiography that hosting the program made him feel "small and humiliated," but it nevertheless succeeded in helping him return to the competitive world of television.

---

traveled with the military in Afghanistan and Iraq. In 2003, he discussed an upcoming operation in a FNC broadcast, which military authorities denounced as possibly endangering U.S. troops. The evening program *Geraldo at Large*, which debuted in October, 2005, concentrated on interesting people, featuring a combination of serious journalism and tabloid-type stories. Rivera continued to attract controversy. In his report on the aftermath of Hurricane Katrina, he became engaged in a feud with *The New York Times* over an article alleging that he pushed aside rescue workers to be filmed assisting a woman in a wheelchair. In 2008, while providing live coverage of Hurricane Ike in Galveston, Texas, he courageously stayed outside and was knocked over by the storm surge

SIGNIFICANCE

Soon after his entry into television in 1970, Rivera emerged as one of the most interesting, entertaining, and controversial personalities in the nation. By 2010, his work was recognized with more than 170 journalistic awards.

A veteran foreign correspondent, he covered numerous trouble spots, including Afghanistan, Lebanon, Bosnia, and Colombia. Although often criticized for his sensationalism, Rivera frequently called attention to serious social problems and stimulated debate about issues of public policy.

Thomas Tandy Lewis

FURTHER READING

Marvis, Barbara J. *Famous People of Hispanic Heritage: Geraldo Rivera, Melissa Gonzales, Federico Pena, Ellen Ochoa*. Child, Md.: Mitchell Lane., 1995. Biographical highlights and personal profiles aimed at young readers.

Rivera, Geraldo. *The Great Progression: How Hispanics Will Lead America to a New Era of Prosperity*. New York: Penguin, 2009. In a hopeful and prophetic book, Rivera argues that Latinos, both leaders and everyday people, are making a positive impact on the economic, social, and political conditions of the country.

_____. *His Panic: Why Americans Fear Hispanics in the U.S.* New York: Penguin, 2008. An account of the impact of Latino population growth on the changing face of America, with strong criticisms of the view that most of the country's problems are caused by illegal immigrants.

Rivera, Geraldo, with Daniel Paisner. *Exposing Myself*. New York: Bantam, 1991. An unusually frank autobiography that describes both Rivera's successes and imperfections, including his early fights and sexual exploitation of women.

See also: Ron Arias; Maria Hinojosa; Soledad O'Brien; Rubén Salazar; Roberto J. Suarez.

TOMÁS RIVERA

American author, educator, and activist

Rivera was a talented writer of poetry, novels, and short stories, as well as an accomplished professor and university administrator. His accomplishments have made him a role model in the Chicano community.

Latino heritage: Mexican

Born: December 22, 1935; Crystal City, Texas

Died: May 16, 1984; Fontana, California

Areas of achievement: Literature; poetry; education; activism

EARLY LIFE

Tomás Rivera (toh-MAHS rih-VEHR-ah) was born to Florencio and Josepha Rivera on December 22, 1935. As a child and through his teen years, Rivera worked with his family as a migrant farm laborer. His family traveled throughout the Midwest, including Michigan, Minnesota, North Dakota, and Wisconsin. During the years he worked as a field laborer, Rivera, with the support of his grandfather, decided to become a writer of essays and fiction.

Rivera graduated from Crystal City High School in 1954, and two years later he enrolled at Southwest Texas Junior College. While at college, he encountered some of the discrimination and injustice he would continually face as a lower-class Chicano. One of the difficulties he experienced was trying to get his work published. Rivera's work was primarily written in Spanish, which widely restricted its audience. However, Rivera used this setback as a motivation to continue writing and to obtain an education.

Rivera graduated from Southwest Texas State University (now Texas State University) in 1958 with a B.A. in English, while also minoring in Spanish, history, and education. After graduating, he taught English and Spanish at local secondary schools until 1965. While teaching, Rivera also earned a master's degree in educational administration from Southwest Texas State University in 1964. Still believing that an education was the only way for a Chicano to escape from migrant work, Rivera enrolled at the University of Oklahoma, from which he graduated with an M.A. in Spanish literature, as well as a Ph.D. in Romance languages and literature in 1969.

Immediately upon receiving his Ph.D., Rivera was hired at Sam Houston State University as an associate professor, a position he held until 1971. Over the next seven years, he held multiple academic positions, including some in administration, before becoming the executive vice president at the University of Texas at El Paso in 1978.

LIFE'S WORK

On November 27, 1958, Rivera married Concepción Garza, with whom he later had three children: Ileana, Irasema, and Javier. During the years of his flourishing career in education, Rivera managed to have an equally influential literary career. His drive to further his education and share his writings with the world can be attributed to his experiences as a migrant laborer—a part of his life he never forgot. Rivera used his memories of this time and wrote them into his works. It is said that Rivera's writings are the place in which he left much of what was the best of him.

In the world of literature, Rivera is remembered as a poet and short-story writer. One of his most accomplished works is his novel *. . . . y no se lo tragó la tierra* (*. . . And the Earth Did Not Part*), published in 1971. Rivera received the Quinto Sol Award for this book in 1971, an award created by a publishing company whose primary focus was to publish Chicano literature. With *. . . y no se lo tragó la tierra*, Rivera expressed his belief that one of the most important characteristics of Chicano literature is its ability to capture and remember the past.

In all, Rivera wrote more than eighty-five thousand works, including papers, essays, poems, and short fiction. Many of these works share a capacity for remembrance. Rivera's works are said to speak for themselves most of the time, with the exception of a few scenes and sections in which he seems to be directly commenting on his feelings and passions regarding the topic at hand. His works, employing dramatic language, multiple voices, and varying registers of emotions, convey the language and experience of the Chicano community.

In addition to his success in the academic and literary worlds, Rivera was also an activist in the many communities in which he lived. His activism was spurred by his belief that young people are the future of the nation. Over the years, Rivera served on numerous boards, committees, and councils, such as the American

Severo Peréz's Film . . . *And the Earth Did Not Swallow Him*

Severo Peréz, an independent Chicano film-maker and writer, achieved his dream of directing a film that was based on the novel . . . *y no se lo tragó la tierra* (1971), written by Tomás Rivera. Peréz became determined to film the book after he read it in 1973.

However, just as Rivera had trouble publishing his book, it took Peréz more than twenty years of tackling racist obstacles within the industry before he could finally release his film. . . *And the Earth Did Not Swallow Him* premiered at the Santa Barbara International Film Festival in 1995. The film closely follows the novel's events and depicts the coming-of-age of a young Chicano boy, Marcos, played by Jose Alcala, who faces racial oppression. The film is set in 1952 and follows Marcos's fight to overcome conflicts as a migrant worker in Texas and Minnesota. Throughout the film, Marcos's family experiences hardships that they must confront and overcome together. In the end, Marcos comes to realize his place in the world and the powerful importance of strong familial bonds. In order to stay true to the novel, the film, which is primarily in English, also features a great deal of Spanish dialect.

Association for Higher Education, the American Council on Education, and the National Commission on Secondary Schooling for Hispanics. His efforts on behalf of these organizations were influenced by his multiple trips to and from Mexico.

Rivera received numerous honors, including an award from the Chicano News Media Association recognizing his achievements within the Chicano community. He also obtained an award from the Riverside, California, chapter of the National Association of Colored People (NAACP) in recognition of his leadership as chancellor of the University of California at Riverside, a position he held from 1979 until his death on May 16, 1984.

SIGNIFICANCE

Rivera's legacy continued long after his death. Many communities and universities have dedicated buildings and awards in his honor. For example, the library and plaza at the University of California at Riverside, are named for him, as is a local elementary school; the tutoring center at the University of Texas at San Antonio is also named in his honor. The College of Education at Texas State University at San Marcos established the Tomás Rivera Mexican American Children's Book Award to honor authors and illustrators who create literature that depicts the Mexican American experience. Rivera's award-winning novel . . . *y no se lo tragó la tierra* was the inspiration for Severo Peréz's 1995 film . . . *And the Earth Did Not Swallow Him*.

After his death, Rivera's wife, Concepción Rivera, donated all of Rivera's papers and works to the Tomás Rivera Library at the University of California at Riverside. The success Rivera achieved in the academic world was indicative of his hard, selfless work and serves as a model to young Chicanos that an education and hard work can provide them with social mobility.

Macey M. Freudensprung

FURTHER READING

Lattin, Vernon E., Rolando Hinojosa, and Gary D. Keller, eds. *Tomás Rivera: The Man and His Work*. Tempe, Ariz.: Bilingual Review/Press, 1988. Compilation of some of Rivera's works, as well as photographs of him and other materials.

Olivares, Julián, ed. *International Studies in Honor of Tomás Rivera*. Houston: Arte Público Press, 1986. A collection of essays regarding Rivera's life and works. Includes brief biographical information and discussions of his life and writings.

Rivera, Tomás. *Tomás Rivera: The Complete Works*. Edited by Julián Olivares. Houston: Arte Público Press, 2008. Compilation of Rivera's works, as well as images from his original manuscripts and a lengthy introduction discussing the significance and meaning of his writings.

_____. . . . *y no se lo tragó la tierra*. Berkeley, Calif.: Quinto Sol, 1971. An English- and Spanish-language edition of Rivera's novel. Includes a biography of Rivera and an introduction discussing his significance.

See also: Oscar Zeta Acosta; Rudolfo Anaya; Martha P. Cotera; José Montoya; Raúl R. Salinas; Luis Rafael Sánchez; Bernice Zamora.

HORACIO RIVERO, JR.

Puerto Rican-born military leader and ambassador to Spain

After graduating third in his class from the U.S. Naval Academy in 1931, Rivero had a distinguished career in the Navy until his retirement in 1972. The second Latino to become a four-star admiral, Rivero played an important role in the 1962 blockade of Cuba, and he oversaw the daily operations of the Navy during the Vietnam War.

Latino heritage: Puerto Rican

Born: May 16, 1910; Ponce, Puerto Rico

Died: September 24, 2000; Coronado, California

Also known as: Rivets

Areas of achievement: Military; government and politics; diplomacy

EARLY LIFE

Horacio Rivero, Jr. (oh-RAHS-see-oh rih-VEHR-oh) was born on May 16, 1910, to Horacio Rivero and Margarita DeLucca Rivero, who also had two daughters, Sara and Lydia. The family lived in Ponce, located along the southern coast of Puerto Rico. Rivero attended public school in Ponce before graduating from Central High School in San Juan. Growing up along the coast, Rivero always wanted to join the Navy. He was the second alternate in line for the appointment to the U.S. Naval Academy given by Puerto Rico's commissioner Felix Cordova Davila. After the principal and first alternate appointees failed the academy's entrance exam, Rivero was given the spot on June 20, 1927, when he was seventeen years old.

The Navy waived its height requirement to accept Rivero, who was just over five feet tall. While attending the naval academy, an officer had difficulty reading Rivero's name patch on his uniform, asking, "What's your name? Rivets?" The nickname Rivets stuck with Rivero throughout his career with the Navy. On June 4, 1931, Rivero graduated from the academy, third in his class of 441 students.

He first served as a junior gunnery officer aboard the USS *Northampton* before becoming the communications watch officer on the USS *Chicago*, USS *New Mexico,* and USS *California.* He was promoted to first lieutenant and served as assistant fleet communications officer until June, 1936. For the next two years, Rivero worked as an assistant gunnery officer on the USS *Porter.* In 1938, he studied ordnance engineering at the Naval Postgraduate School in Annapolis, Maryland,

and he earned a M.S. in electrical engineering from the Massachusetts Institute of Technology in 1940. Rivero married Hazel Hooper in 1941.

LIFE'S WORK

Shortly after the United States entered World War II, Rivero was assigned to the newly commissioned USS *San Juan* as the assistant gunnery officer. During the next few months aboard, Rivero participated in the landings at Guadalcanal and Tulagi, a raid of the Gilbert Islands, and the battle of the Santa Cruz Islands. For his service in the Pacific Theater, Rivero received the Bronze Star with Combat "V." He served as the *San Juan*'s gunnery officer until the middle of 1944. He then became the gunnery officer and later the executive officer on the USS *Pittsburgh.* In June, 1945, the *Pittsburgh* was struck by a typhoon, severing its bow. Rivero's swift action, leadership, and damage control allowed the ship to safely make it to port without any casualties. He was awarded the Legion of Merit for his role in saving the ship.

In August, 1945, Rivero returned to the United States, working for the Special Weapons Division of the Office of the Chief of Naval Operations. By 1946, he had been promoted to captain, and he received the Navy Commendation Medal for "outstanding performance" while a technical assistant to the deputy commander of Operation Crossroads. Rivero's science and technical knowledge was key to his appointment to the staff of the joint task force commander during nuclear weapons testing on Eniwetok and the Bikini Islands in 1948. He commanded the USS *William C. Lawe* until the spring of 1949, when he was assigned to the Weapons Systems Evaluation Group, Office of the Secretary of Defense, a position he held until August, 1951. Rivero then received command of the USS *Noble,* transporting troops and equipment to and from the Korean war zone.

After almost a year aboard the *Noble,* Rivero attended the National War College, completing a course in nuclear weapons in June, 1953. In October, 1955, he was promoted to rear admiral, and he became deputy chief of the Armed Forces Special Weapons Project in Washington, D.C. Rivero continued to move up the ranks over the next few years, both commanding ships and holding positions in Washington. By 1961, he was the deputy chief of staff and deputy chief of staff for plans and operations to the commander in chief of the Atlantic Fleet. He also held other staff positions under other commanders in chief at this time.

In October, 1962, during the Cuban Missile Crisis, Rivero was in command of the Atlantic Fleet's amphibious force. He was awarded a Gold Star, in place of the Second Legion of Merit, for his exemplary conduct during the crisis and blockade of Cuba. In October of the following year, Rivero served as director of Navy program planning in the Office of the Chief of Naval Operations. On July 31, 1964, he was promoted from vice admiral, making him the second Latino four-star admiral in American history.

Admiral Rivero served as vice chief of naval operations, the second-highest position in the U.S. Navy, until 1968. In this position, he oversaw the day-to-day planning of the Navy during the Vietnam War, and he was a strong supporter of developing the "brown-water navy," or riverine force, that patrolled the shallow rivers and deltas of Vietnam. In early 1968, Rivero became the commander in chief of the Allied forces in Southern Europe; he held this position until his retirement from the Navy in 1972. While serving in Europe, Rivero had visited Spain's dictator Francisco Franco, which Rivero believed lead to his being appointed ambassador to Spain by President Richard Nixon. Rivero was ambassador for two years.

During his retirement, Rivero served as an adviser to the chief of naval operations, the U.S. Naval Academy, and the National War College. He also occasionally reviewed books on naval history for the San Diego *Union-Tribune*. Rivero died in his home in Coronado California, on September 24, 2000, at the age of ninety. He was survived by his sisters, daughter, grandchildren, and great-grandchildren.

SIGNIFICANCE

Rivero was the second Latino four-star admiral in U.S. Navy history. He had a distinguished forty-one year career, earning a number of medals, including the Bronze Star with Combat "V," Distinguished Service Medal with two Gold Stars, Legion of Merit with Gold Star, Navy Commendation Medal, National Defense Service Medal with Bronze Star, and the American Defense Service Medal. Rivero also received awards from several foreign countries. By his retirement in 1972, he was vice chief of naval operations, the Navy's second-highest ranking position. He was then appointed ambassador to Spain by President Nixon. In retirement, Rivero held positions on several advisory boards, and he was honorary

Rivero and the Blockade of Cuba

In 1962, the Cuban Missile Crisis accelerated the Cold War between the United States and the Soviet Union. By September, an increasing number of Soviet cargo ships were arriving in Cuba every month. Photographs taken by Navy reconnaissance aircraft and intelligence reports showed increasing numbers of Soviet personnel and the construction of launch complexes. The information strongly suggested the building of surface-to-air missile sites capable of attacking the United States.

On October 15, Horacio Rivero, Jr., was placed in command of the Navy's amphibious forces in the Atlantic. On October 20, the secretary of defense had the Navy prepare plans for a limited blockade or quarantine of Cuba. On October, 22, Rivero was in the Caribbean preparing for a training operation that was canceled, and the naval forces headed to Cuba. All of the amphibious forces were in place by November 2.

On October 24, the Navy implemented phase one of the quarantine: identifying, trailing, and intercepting ships going in and out of Cuba. The second phase, November 5-11, covered the removal of missiles by Soviet ships. Rivero authorized an amphibious landing exercise in North Carolina on November 16. It was the largest exercise of its type in almost twenty years. The landing was remarkably successful and demonstrated the readiness of the Navy's amphibious forces. The final phase continued the monitoring of ships and ended the blockade on November 21. Rivero received a Gold Star in place of a second Legion of Merit for his "exceptionally meritorious conduct" during the Cuban Missile Crisis.

chairman of the American Veterans' Committee for Puerto Rico Self-Determination.

Jennifer L. Campbell

FURTHER READING

Mason, John T. *The Atlantic War Remembered.* Annapolis, Md.: Naval Institute Press, 1991. A collection of oral histories, including Rivero's, dealing with the Atlantic and Mediterranean theaters of World War II. Provides personal, first-hand accounts of both famous and unknown events that lead to victory in Europe.

United States Naval Institute. *Reminiscences of Admiral Horacio Rivero, Jr., U.S. Navy (Retired).* Annapolis, Md.: Naval Institute Press, 1978. An oral history interview with Rivero, in which he discusses his childhood in Puerto Rico, his time at the U.S. Naval Academy, his extensive career with the Navy, his retirement, and his years spent as ambassador to Spain.

Utz, Curtis. *Cordon of Steel.* Washington, D.C.: Naval Historical Center, 1994. Reprint. Honolulu: University Press of the Pacific, 2005. A detailed history of the U.S. Navy's involvement with the blockade and Cuban missile crisis. Shows how efficient and effective the Navy was while under the growing threat of war. Includes several pictures of armed ships and aircraft. Available for free download from the Naval Historical Center.

See also: Roy Benavidez; Richard E. Cavazos; Guy Gabaldon.

FRANCISCO RODÓN

Puerto Rican-born artist

Puerto Rico's best known and most highly respected artist, Rodón studied abroad but was largely self-taught. He began painting still lifes and landscapes before moving to figurative work and portraiture, and he became famous for imaginatively capturing the essence of many Latin American personages.

Latino heritage: Puerto Rican

Born: June 6, 1934; San Sebastián, Puerto Rico

Also known as: Francisco Rodón Elizalde

Area of achievement: Art

EARLY LIFE
Francisco Rodón Elizalde (fran-SEES-coh roh-DON ehl-ihs-AL-day) was born to Victor Rodón Cabrero and Inés Elizalde Arocena. He attended elementary school in his hometown of San Sebastián, Puerto Rico, and in 1949 he moved with his parents to San Juan, where he completed high school. An excellent student, Rodón won a scholarship to participate in a cultural exchange program, and in 1952 he traveled to several Latin American countries. In Mexico City he was captivated by the numerous murals to be found there and decided to study art.

In 1953, Rodón left for Paris, France, and registered for courses at the Julien Academy. The following year, he enrolled at the San Fernando Academy in Madrid, Spain. Rodón was frequently absent from classes at both locations; he preferred to visit museums, where he could closely examine the paintings of fine artists and discover their techniques for himself in order to develop his own style. In 1955, he returned to Puerto Rico and found a patron in Inés, the wife of Luis Muñoz Marín, the first democratically elected governor of Puerto Rico. Under Inés's sponsorship, Rodón was granted a scholarship to study at La Esmeralda Academy of the National Institute of Fine Arts in Mexico City. However, his mother died soon after his arrival, and he returned grief-stricken to Puerto Rico. In 1958, he ventured forth again, taking classes in composition and drawing at the Art Students League in New York. In 1959, he took courses at the Graphic Arts Workshop at the Institute of Puerto Rican Culture.

LIFE'S WORK
Despite the multitude of brief educational opportunities, Rodón learned more on his own than in classrooms. He

Francisco Rodón. (AP Photo)

burst into public consciousness in 1960, winning first prize for an oil painting and honorable mention for an engraving at the Puerto Rican Athenaeum Christmas contest. In 1961, he held his first solo exhibition at the Institute of Puerto Rican Culture, showing an assortment of landscapes, portraits, and still lives. These early works were characterized by his use of thick black borders surrounding areas of color that forced the viewer's eye to perceive individual objects as part of an encompassing composition. In 1961, he won two prizes for oil paintings in local artistic competitions. Throughout the rest of the decade, while serving as director of the museum at the University of Puerto Rico and as a teacher at the university, he continued to produce landscapes and still lives, building up an impressive body of work.

Beginning in the late 1960's, Rodón concentrated on figurative studies, working in large-scale formats and experimenting more freely with the use of color. His portraits became expressionistic, incorporating not only realistic likenesses but also capturing the psychological moods of artist and subject. Rodón's work won critical approval, and his first show outside Puerto Rico, at the 1972 Biennial Art Exhibition in Colombia, was particularly well received. In 1973, he was selected to paint an Argentine icon, writer Jorge Luis Borges. Rodón lived in Buenos Aires for a time while completing a series of paintings featuring Borges.

On the strength of these portraits, during the 1970's and 1980's Rodón was frequently commissioned to portray other celebrities and prominent individuals. These included Puerto Rican governor Muñoz Marín, Venezuelan president Rómulo Betancourt, Mexican author-photographer Juan Rulfo, Cuban prima ballerina Alicia Alonso, Russian ballet dancer and choreographer Vaslav Nijinsky, Peruvian writer Mario Vargas Llosa, Nicaraguan poet Rubén Darío, and Mexican writer Octavio Paz. Because of the psychological elements in his renderings, many of Rodón's sometimes disturbing—yet strangely compelling—portraits caused controversy when they were displayed. Betancourt, for example, was depicted with the scars from an assassination attempt shown prominently. Puerto Rican actor Mona Marti was painted in the nude in a pose duplicating Francisco de Goya's *The Naked Maja*.

Rodón was one of the founders of the Museum of Contemporary Art in San Juan, Puerto Rico, and he established the Francisco Rodón Foundation. His work has been shown in numerous exhibitions from Chile to New York and from Spain to Harvard University. His paintings, which command prices in the six-figure range, are included in collections in Venezuela, Mexico, Argentina, the United States, Puerto Rico, and elsewhere.

SIGNIFICANCE

Francisco Rodón has received many awards for his work. Named painter in residence at the University of Puerto Rico in 1968, he won the United Nations Educational, Scientific, and Cultural Organization's (UNESCO) Hall of Paintings Prize in 1975 and garnered the Francisco Oller Medal at Puerto Rico's Sixth Biennial of Latin American Engravings in 1983. Perhaps his greatest honor was being selected as Puerto Rico's most important painter of the twentieth century, joining compatriots Francisco Oller, representing the nineteenth century, and José Campeche, representing the eighteenth century. The three artists were featured in the Plaza of the Americas at the 1992 World's Fair in Seville, Spain, which celebrated the five-hundredth anniversary of Christopher Columbus's discovery of the New World and which drew more than fifteen million visitors. Later that year, the same three artists were highlighted at a Sotheby's exhibition in New York. Sotheby's in 2009 sold a Rodón painting for more than $300,000, setting a record for a work by a Puerto Rican artist.

Jack Ewing

FURTHER READING

Brotherhood of Graphic Artists of Puerto Rico. *Puerto Rico Art and Identity*. San Juan: University of Puerto Rico Press, 2004. An illustrated bilingual work that examines the unique character of the island and its inhabitants through artworks.

Tannenbaum, Judith, and Rene Morales. *Island Nations: New Art from Cuba, the Dominican Republic, Puerto Rico, and the Diaspora*. Providence: Rhode Island School of Design, 2004. A brief, illustrated glimpse at contemporary art originating from the Spanish-speaking islands of the Caribbean.

Worth, Richard. *Puerto Rico in American History*. Berkeley Heights, N.J.: Enslow, 2008. An overview of the more than century-long relationship between the United States and Puerto Rico.

See also: Alfredo M. Arreguín; Lorenzo Homar; Francisco Oller.

ALEX RODRIGUEZ

American baseball player

Rodriguez was one of the top players in Major League Baseball during the 1990's and 2000's and is one of the most prolific home-run hitters of all time. Throughout his career he has received numerous awards and has signed two of the largest contracts for a professional athlete.

Latino heritage: Dominican

Born: July 27, 1975; New York, New York

Also known as: Alexander Emmanuel Rodriguez; A-Rod

Area of achievement: Baseball

EARLY LIFE

Alex Rodriguez (rahd-REE-gehs) was born Alexander Emmanuel Rodriguez to Dominicans Victor and Lourdes Rodriguez in New York City on July 27, 1975. His father ran a shoe store and his mother worked at a car factory. Having saved enough money, the family soon moved back to the Dominican Republic, though the family business quickly faltered, necessitating a move back to the United States, this time to Miami, Florida, when Rodriguez was eight years old. His father abandoned the family a year later, and Rodriguez's parents ultimately divorced. Soon thereafter, Rodriguez began playing organized baseball. While attending Westminster Christian High School, he played for the school's baseball, basketball, and football teams.

Rodriguez was selected first overall by the Seattle Mariners in the 1993 Major League Baseball draft. He quickly rose through the minor leagues and made his major league debut at shortstop on July 8, 1994, at the age of eighteen. Rodriguez initially struggled while playing with the Seattle Mariners and was eventually sent back down to the minors. During the 1995 season, he split his time between the Mariners and their Class AAA minor league team before returning to the majors for good that August.

LIFE'S WORK

Rodriguez was named the Mariners' starting shortstop before the 1996 season. In his first full year in the majors, he led the American League in batting with a .358 average, 36 home run hits, and 231 runs-batted-in (RBI). Ineligible for Rookie of the Year honors because of his previous major league experience, Rodriguez finished a close second in voting for the American League's Most Valuable Player (MVP), and he garnered Player of the Year honors from *Sporting News* and Associated Press.

His offensive production dropped slightly during the 1997 season, but the following year he became the third player in baseball history to hit forty home runs and steal forty bases in the same season. Rodriguez suffered his first major injury during the first week of the 1999 season when he tore cartilage in his left knee, but he still managed to hit 42 home runs and 111 RBI despite playing in only 129 games. In 2000, Rodriguez led the Mariners to the American League Championship Series, batting .316 with 41 home runs and 132 RBI.

After the 2000 season, Rodriguez left the Mariners to sign a lucrative ten-year deal with the Texas Rangers, who were in last place in the American League West Division during the 2000 season. Even with the addition of Rodriguez, however, this team continued to struggle, due in large part to a lack of effective pitching. The Rangers finished last in each of Rodriguez's three seasons with the team, even though his power numbers improved in the Rangers' hitter-friendly home park. In 2001, his first season with the Rangers, Rodriguez hit 52 home runs, the most ever by a shortstop, which he improved upon the

Alex Rodriguez. (AP Photo)

next season by hitting a major league best of 57 home runs. Rodriguez received his first American League MVP Award following the 2003 season after hitting 47 home runs and 118 RBI.

Rodriguez's last season with the Rangers was 2003. The Rangers, as a business, were losing money and as a baseball team were not expected to contend for a championship. The Rangers and the Boston Red Sox agreed to trade Rodriguez. but the deal was vetoed by the Major League Baseball Players Association, since it required a voluntary reduction in Rodriguez's salary. Rodriguez was eventually traded to the New York Yankees for fellow offensive star Alfonso Soriano. The Yankees already had an established shortstop in Derek Jeter, so Rodriguez shifted positions and became the Yankees' starting third baseman.

With the change of position and increased media scrutiny of New York, Rodriguez struggled slightly in his first season with the Yankees but still posted respectable offensive statistics. He rebounded during the 2005 regular season, winning his second American League MVP Award, but he struggled during the play-offs, batting .133 with no runs-batted-in. In 2006, Rodriguez again posted good regular season numbers but struggled during the play-offs. During the 2007 season, Rodriguez hit his five hundredth home run and won yet another MVP award, but the Yankees again exited the play-offs early.

Rodriguez missed the first month of the 2009 season because of a torn labrum, but after returning in May he provided many timely hits that resulted in victories for the Yankees. His clutch hitting continued in the play-offs, in which he hit several late-inning, game-tying home runs during the first two rounds of the play-offs en route to leading the Yankees to the World Series. He continued his offensive productivity as the Yankees won the World Series title by four games to two against the Philadelphia Phillies.

Like many other baseball players active during the 1990's and 2000's, Rodriguez has been accused of steroid use. In a 2007 book, former major leaguer José Canseco accused Rodriguez of steroid use, which Rodriguez denied. Two years later, it was reported that Rodriguez had tested positive for steroids during the 2003 season while playing for the Texas Rangers. The results of the exploratory tests conducted in 2003 were supposed to remain private, but they were seized during a federal raid and later revealed. Rodriguez soon admitted that he took performance-enhancing drugs from 2001 to 2003 because of the pressure to perform after signing his lucrative contract with the Rangers.

Rodriguez's Lucrative Contracts

During his career, Alex Rodriguez has signed two of the largest contracts in professional sports, both in the total amount paid and in yearly salary. Rodriguez became a free agent after the 2000 season and signed a ten-year deal with the Texas Rangers for $252 million, at that time the largest contract in sports history. He only played three seasons for the Rangers before being traded to the New York Yankees, though the Rangers continued to pay a large portion of the remainder of his contract. Rodriguez opted out of this contract after the 2007 season, forfeiting the remainder left on the contract in order to pursue an even more lucrative deal: He ultimately re-signed with the Yankees for $275 million during ten years.

Rodriguez could make an extra $30 million for reaching various home- run milestones, $6 million each for tying the career home run totals of Willie Mays (660), Babe Ruth (714), Hank Aaron (755), and Barry Bonds (762) and an additional $6 million for breaking Bonds's career home-run record.

He expressed regret for his actions and stated that he had not taken any illegal substances since he joined the Yankees.

SIGNIFICANCE

Since breaking into the major leagues during the mid-1990's, Rodriguez has been one of the best, and most well-compensated, players in baseball. He is also one of baseball's most polarizing figures, frequently criticized because of his lack of clutch performances and his off-the-field behavior. Early in his career, Rodriguez helped redefine the role of the shortstop, adding offensive prowess and power to the traditional defensive capabilities valued at the position. He posted several of the top statistical seasons ever recorded for a shortstop and continued his offensive production after switching to third base with the Yankees.

One of the best all-around players in baseball, Rodriguez has received numerous offensive and defensive awards. In addition to his three American League MVP Awards, he has also received four Hank Aaron Awards (given to the top hitter in each league), been selected to play in the All-Star Game twelve times, and collected two Golden Gloves (given to the top fielders in each league at every position) while playing shortstop for the Texas Rangers. He is also one of the most prolific home-run hitters in major league history, having hit 612 through the 2010 season, the most ever by a player of Latino decent and the sixth highest number in baseball history.

Matthew Mihalka

FURTHER READING

Canseco, José. *Vindicated: Big Names, Big Liars, and the Battle to Save Baseball.* New York: Simon Spotlight Entertainment, 2008. In this second book on steroids by former baseball player Canseco, he claims to have introduced Rodriguez to a steroid dealer in the late 1990's.

Roberts, Selena. *A-Rod: The Many Lives of Alex Rodriguez.* New York: Harper, 2009. Roberts contends that Rodriguez may have used steroids as early as high school, and that his use of performance-enhancing drugs may extend into his career as a Yankee. Roberts also explores the circumstances that resulted in the end of Rodriguez's marriage and his inner conflicts and insecurities.

Stewart, Wayne. *Alex Rodriguez: A Biography.* London: Greenwood Press, 2007. This biography, published before Rodriguez's steroid use was revealed, contains a time line of his career and a short photo essay.

See also: José Canseco; Pedro Martinez; David Ortiz; Albert Pujols; Manny Ramirez; Freddy Sanchez; Johan Santana; Miguel Tejada.

CHI CHI RODRIGUEZ

Puerto Rican-born golfer

Rodriguez, along with Lee Trevino, were the golfers who led the way in the 1960's and 1970's for subsequent Latino professional golfers. Rodriguez's crowd-pleasing style established him as a fan favorite well into the 1990's.

Latino heritage: Puerto Rican
Born: October 23 1935; Río Piedras, Puerto Rico
Also known as: Juan Rodriguez
Areas of achievement: Sports; philanthropy

EARLY LIFE

Chi Chi Rodriguez (rahd-REE-gehs) was born Juan Rodriguez in Rio Pedras, Puerto Rico, on October 23, 1935, and he endured a childhood of poverty that never crushed his spirit. His father encouraged his son to develop his athletic abilities, and Chi Chi turned to baseball as a young boy. At the age of either seven or eight, according to differing accounts, he got a job as a fore caddie at a local golf resort. When he was bigger he began carrying golf bags, and a member eventually loaned him a set of clubs so he could play golf on the days that caddies were allowed to do so. By the age of twelve, he had gained a reputation as one of the top youth golfers on the island.

In 1954, he enlisted in the U.S. Army. He was stationed at Fort Sill, Oklahoma, home of the Field Artillery, and he had the opportunity to play in golf competitions regularly, winning the championship at Fort Sill before his discharge in 1957.

LIFE'S WORK

Rodriguez returned to Puerto Rico after his military service and worked for three years as an assistant golf professional at the Dorado Beach Resort. He enlisted

Chi Chi Rodriguez. (AP Photo)

the services of a golf instructor named Pete Cooper to coach him in the finer points of the game. Cooper remained Rodriguez's only coach throughout his long playing career, including his noteworthy years spent on the Senior Tour, later renamed the Champions Tour, on which he began playing when he reached the age of fifty in 1985.

Rodriguez left Puerto Rico for the mainland United States and joined the Professional Golfers' Association (PGA) tour in 1960. His earnings for the first three years were meager, but his big breakthrough came when he won the Denver Open at the age of twenty-eight, a victory he maintains was the greatest thrill of his playing career. The following year he notched two PGA tour victories, one of which was the most prestigious triumph of his regular tour career. The Western Open, held at the Tam O'Shanter Country Club in Niles, Illinois, at the time was widely regarded as an unofficial "major" tournament, ranking alongside the U.S. Open, the PGA championship, and the Master's tournament held every year in Augusta, Georgia. Other winners of the Western Open in the 1960's included Jack Nicklaus, Billy Casper, and Arnold Palmer, all eventual members of the World Golf Hall of Fame. In 1964, Rodriguez bested the legendary Palmer by one stroke to claim his victory in the Western Open.

Rodriguez's other tour victories were strung out over a period of sixteen years. His longest drought between first-place finishes was between 1973 and 1979. Most of his wins after the Western Open occurred at tournaments that appeared either late or early on the annual tour schedule. These were tournaments that the top professionals frequently skipped, which meant Rodriguez got to compete against a less talented group of players.

Win or lose, Rodriguez was still a prominent personality on the tour schedule. He frequently made side bets with other professional golfers, and he enjoyed keeping up a constant banter with the fans in the gallery, who were delighted by his lighthearted approach to the game, a stark contrast to the dour, businesslike approach of so many tour professionals. Early in his career he would cover the hole with his hat when he sank a putt. Later on he replaced that trick with the toreador dance, holding his putter as if it were a sword in a sheath, twirling it in the air in a very dramatic manner, then replacing it in the imaginary sheath while flashing a huge grin. These antics created a demand for his appearances at corporate events and exhibitions usually held on Mondays and Tuesdays before tournaments, which were

Popularity with Fans

Golf is commonly viewed as a stodgy and silent sport, and the very notion of a "golf clap" testifies to this. Chi Chi Rodriguez, however, believed that he was on the golf course not only to win money but also to have fun, and he wanted golf fans to share his good time. His nonstop banter with fans became legendary. While waiting to hit a shot, standing on the tee, or strolling down the fairway, he always had something to say, and he reacted to comments from the crowd with undisguised glee. His attitude made him a favorite at weekday golf exhibitions, where he would hit his driver while on his knees, or hit a hook and a slice in rapid succession that crossed paths in midair and then announce with a huge grin, " I know someone who can make those balls collide! His name is Jesus!" Golf fans expect two things from professional golfers: superhuman golfing feats and a human side to which they can relate. Few tour golfers have ever combined these two traits as successfully as Rodriguez.

held from Thursdays through Saturdays. Rodriguez also played in tournaments outside the United States, attaining victories at the 1963 Colombian Open and the Bahamas Open and Panama Open in 1979.

In 1980, the Senior Tour began its inaugural season. The founders hoped there was a market for tournaments featuring older golfers who made up with personality what they had lost in physical skills. The new tour succeeded beyond the wildest dreams of everyone involved. Lee Trevino, a Senior Tour star, asserted that he much preferred competing against the round bellies of the Senior Tour players instead of the flat bodies of the regular tour. Rodriguez blossomed on the Senior Tour, winning sixteen events in his first five years. Along with his victories came lucrative endorsement deals with Toyota and a major golf company. He won two senior major tournaments, and as of 2010 he was tied for sixth with most wins on the Senior Tour, trailing only Bob Charles and Miller Barber from his age group.

Rodriguez rose out of poverty, and he never forgot his roots or the need to lend a hand to young people who faced poverty. In the 1980's, he established the Chi Chi Rodriguez Golf Foundation in Clearwater, Florida. The foundation, located on the grounds of a public golf club, provides character development for youths by teaching them the rules and etiquette of golf. The impressive board of directors has included business executives like Robert Basham, the founder of the Outback Steakhouse restaurant chain. Despite a heart attack in 1998, Rodriguez remained one of the most popular ambassadors for the sport of golf and an excellent role model for aspiring Latinos.

SIGNIFICANCE

Rodriguez, along with Lee Elder and Lee Trevino, were significant for showing that professional golf was not the exclusive domain of Caucasians. Rodriguez chose never to openly comment on discrimination the way Trevino did, perhaps because he learned the game in Puerto Rico, while Trevino grew up facing more blatant discrimination in New Mexico. Despite Rodriguez's silence on ethnic issues and golf, his success and the dignity and humor he displayed at all times were a valuable contribution to the Latino legacy.

Michael Polley

FURTHER READING

Friedman, Ian. *Latino Athletes*. New York: Facts On File, 2007. A solid survey of the life and career of Rodriguez, especially detailed about his youth and early adult years.

Novas, Himilce. *The Hispanic 100*. New York: Citadel Press, 1995. Only nine athletes are included, with most of them baseball players, proving that Rodriguez was truly outstanding.

Rodriguez, Chi Chi, with Chuck Fit. *Everybody's Golf Book*. New York: Viking, 1975. Offers commonplace golf tips, but is also a tribute to the belief that anyone who works hard at it can improve his or her golf game.

See also: Nancy Lopez; Lee Trevino.

JOSÉ POLICARPO RODRÍGUEZ

Mexican-born explorer, minister, and writer

Rodríguez was an important figure in Texas history as a scout for the U.S. government's exploration missions. His many skills and experiences as a hunter, a surveyor, an interpreter, and a Methodist minister were freely given in community service. On his ranch, he built Polly's Chapel, a Texas historic landmark, and a one-room schoolhouse.

Latino heritage: Mexican
Born: January 26, 1829; Zaragoza, Coahuila, Mexico
Died: March 22, 1914; Poteet, Texas
Also known as: Polly; Policarpo
Areas of achievement: Religion and theology; exploration

EARLY LIFE

José Policarpo Rodriguez (hoh-ZAY pah-lih-CAR-poh rahd-REE-gehz) was born in Zaragoza, Coahuila, Mexico, west of the present Eagle Pass, Texas. He was one of ten sons born to parents José Antonio Rodríguez and Encarnación Sánchez, who were well educated with suitable financial means. José Policarpo Rodríguez was named after his father José and Saint Policarpo, an early apostolic father in the Catholic Church. His father wanted Rodríguez to be a priest. At age six, Rodríguez attended school at Nadadores, Coahuila, and then at Cuatro Cienegas for a total of fourteen months. After that, young Rodríguez, known as Polly, was home-schooled by his father. In 1841, when Rodríguez was twelve, his family moved to San Antonio, where he became an apprentice gunsmith for three years. At the end of this apprenticeship, Rodríguez joined a team of surveyors. At just fifteen years old, he received the pay and responsibility of an adult. During this time, Rodríguez learned more about hunting and trailing. The surveyor team lived on wild meat, such as deer, turkey, and bear. Another valued food was honey from beehives inside trees. Rodríguez became acquainted with the Indians in the area and learned how to avoid them.

LIFE'S WORK

At age twenty, Rodríguez was hired as a scout by the Whiting and Smith expedition, led by Army engineers Lieutenant William H. C. Whiting and Lieutenant William F. Smith. The mission of this group was to establish a road from San Antonio to El Paso, Texas. Rodríguez faced known and unknown threats as the scout for this team for some three months. The work was difficult, with dangerous confrontations with Indians and natural challenges, such as bears, drought, and rattlesnakes. Whiting, the commander of the expedition, wrote in his diary rave reviews about "this boy Policarpo," describing Rodríguez as one of the most valued members of the team. Indeed, Rodríguez's experience with hunting and trailing, combined with his skill as a surveyor, handler of animals, and interpreter, made him a perfect scout. His success in this role gave him additional employment opportunities with the government for twelve years.

On one of his last trips as a scout, Rodríguez camped on Privilege Creek in Bandera County. He decided to buy 360 acres of land and build a home and ranch. During this time, Texas seceded from the Union, which disappointed Rodríguez. He would have to leave his home and family to continue in service to the U.S. troops, so he resigned. Though offered a commission as a captain in the Civil War, he declined and instead worked with the Bandera Home Guards. Their role was to protect the community from Indians and dismiss disorderly conduct. Rodríguez served the four years of the Civil War in this role.

Although Rodríguez was reared Catholic, he detailed his conversion experience to the Protestant faith in his autobiography. He became licensed to preach as a Methodist minister in 1878. His family thought he had gone crazy when he began to pray for others to convert them to Protestantism. He served as the minister at the limestone Polly's Chapel, a Texas historical landmark built with his own hands on his land in 1882. Rodriguez also helped build a small one-room school on his land.

Three of the women Rodríguez intended to marry died from cholera or other complications. In his autobiography *The Old Guide* (1898), he explained that he wanted to be married, so he prayed for a wife. Rodríguez revealed a touching story about how he believed his wife was given to him; he knew Nicholasa Arocha was to be his wife when he saw her; they had five children. When she died, he married a second time at age seventy-four and had four more children. His last child was born when he was eighty-four, a year before his death at eighty-five. Rodríguez was buried within view of Polly's Peak, not far from Polly's Chapel.

SIGNIFICANCE

Rodríguez wrote in his autobiography that he had lived in Texas through its many changes, from its being part of Mexico, to being an independent state, to becoming part of the Confederate states. He was directly responsible for the success of much of the exploration in Texas that occurred during his lifetime. He excelled as a hunter, a surveyor, a scout, a gunsmith, a marksman, an interpreter, a pioneer, a rancher, and a Methodist preacher. The U.S. government employed him as a scout on many expeditions where his skills and experience made the difference between life and death for his team members and the success of the mission. He spent his later years in service to his faith as a Methodist minister. His diverse accomplishments and the stories he recorded in his autobiography leave a legacy for Texans and Mexican Americans.

Marylane Wade Koch

FURTHER READING

Hunter, John Marvin. *Pioneer History of Bandera County: Seventy-Five Years of Intrepid History*. Bandera, Tex.: Hunter's Printing House, 1922. Brief description of key events in the life of Rodríguez.

Rodriguez, José Policarpo. *The Old Guide.* Nashville, Tenn.: Publishing House of the Methodist Episcopal Church, 1898. An autobiography of Rodríguez, in which he details his life and adventures.

Wooster, Robert. *Frontier Crossroads: Fort Davis and the West*. College Station, Tex.: TAMU Press, 2006. Discusses the history of Fort Davis, which included the services of Mexican civilian and scout Rodriguez.

See also: Joaquín Murieta; Esteban Ochoa.

LUIS J. RODRÍGUEZ

American writer and activist

Rodríguez came through the gang culture of the East Los Angeles barrios and wrote a best-selling book about his experiences, Always Running: La Vida Loca, Gang Days in L.A.

Latino heritage: Mexican

Born: July 9, 1954; El Paso, Texas

Also known as: Luis Javier Rodríguez

Areas of achievement: Literature; journalism; activism

EARLY LIFE

Luis Javier Rodríguez (lew-EHS hahv-YEHR rahd-REE-gehs) was born by design in El Paso, Texas, on the American side of the Mexican border. His parents had lived in Cuidad Juarez, Mexico, across the Rio Grande from El Paso. His father, a high school principal, and his mother, a school secretary, wanted their children to grow up in the economic promise of America and away from the violent street life of Juarez. The family initially relocated to El Paso but moved to Los Angeles when Luis was two, settling in the barrios of East Los Angeles. Young Luis loved the stories his mother would tell, some drawn from Walt Disney films the boy had never seen, others from the folk tales of her Raramuri people. She would recite long ballads from memory, and Luis would be mesmerized by the music of language. He loved to escape into books; facing punishment in school for speaking Spanish, he used books to teach himself English. As he adjusted to the hard reality of poverty, the routine indignities of bigotry, the oppressive presence of the police, and the omnipresence of warring street gangs, he sought the refuge of the public library where he would read until the building closed. As he read, however, he noticed that, save for minor characters in John Steinbeck's novels, few Chicanos were depicted.

LIFE'S WORK

Although he never lost his love of books, by the age of eleven Rodríguez had been recruited into a gang. He began stealing and, within a year, was using drugs. He participated in gang battles, witnessing friends knifed and shot. Friends died of drug overdoses or committed suicide. As his street life—or la vida loca (the crazy life)—became more criminal, Rodríguez drifted from school, dropping out at fifteen. In and out of juvenile detention centers for offenses ranging from hitting a police officer to attempted murder, he was kicked out of his home a year later and forced to live on the streets until his parents relented and he moved into the garage. By then he was a heroin addict and a hardcore gang member.

Despite such activities, by the late 1960's Rodríguez was politically active in the radical Chicano movement, becoming involved in a civil rights organization that promoted Hispanic pride and culture. He also took part in the movement that opposed the American military presence in Vietnam. In addition, as he sat in jail cells, Rodríguez began to write stories and free-verse poems about gang life and the barrio. Years later he claimed that by then violence and drugs had rendered him invisible and that writing reclaimed his identity.

Indeed, creativity became a viable alternative. Rodríguez loved to paint, and he designed a series of street murals for his neighborhood. At the encouragement of a counselor, he entered some of his jailhouse vignettes in a regional writing contest, and his work won honorable mention. However, he was still an addict and still in his gang. When he was arrested at eighteen for participating in a killing as part of a gang initiation, he was

given a lighter sentence of six years largely because of the intervention of counselors and neighborhood leaders who saw promise in him. Determined to validate their confidence and now convinced that the street life was a dead end, Rodríguez got off drugs and alcohol and, once released, found regular work at a steel mill. He finished high school and took night courses at East Los Angeles Community College. He began writing for local newspapers and was hired as a crime reporter and photographer for the *San Bernardino Sun*.

In 1985, he moved to Chicago to write about cultural and political issues for an underground newspaper. Believing that writing had been crucial to his own reclamation, he promoted poetry readings in some of Chicago's poorest neighborhoods and helped start the Guild Complex, a multimedia arts center. Rodríguez also spoke at schools and prisons, youth facilities and churches, and he secured financial investors to start Tia Chucha Press. Named for his beloved aunt, the press published activist poetry by minority writers.

Although by 1991 he had published two volumes of poetry, Rodríguez had never returned to his jailhouse notes. When his fifteen-year-old son professed ambitions to join a Chicago street gang, Rodríguez shaped these notes into a memoir, *Always Running: La Vida Loca, Gang Days in L.A.*, published in 1993. Rodríguez's narrative of the street life marked the first time that a Chicano gang member had come out so publicly to describe the gang experience. The book became a national best seller; critics praised its documentary-like realism and its unflinching account of the violence, drug use, promiscuous and often violent sex, and criminal activity of the gang culture. For Rodríguez, however, the book was solely intended to ensure that his son did not pursue gang life. Despite Rodríguez's intention to protect high school students and the book's enthusiastic endorsement by both parents and teacher groups, *Always Running* became one of the most challenged, and most censored, works in the contemporary canon.

Now a national celebrity, a frequent guest on radio and television, and a much-sought-after speaker for schools, Rodríguez turned to numerous writing projects, and in the next decade he published volumes of poetry, award-winning children's books, short story collections, and a novel. In addition, his nonfiction writings appeared in prominent newspapers and news magazines. More important, he used his celebrity to spearhead community action projects, including Youths Struggling for Survival, an organization that aims to expose low-income urban youth to the power of creativity.

Always Running: La Vida Loca, Gang Days in L.A.

At the time he wrote *Always Running: La Vida Loca, Gang Days in L.A.* (1993), Rodríguez had completed only a year of college and brought to writing only raw talent, a love of storytelling, and an ear for the harsh music of his adopted language. His coming-of-age narrative is much more than yet another scared-straight strategy to pressure impressionable teens away from hardcore criminal behavior. Although the book was hailed for its chiseled, raw prose and its deadpan narration that reveals the depth of the gang's activities—vicious rapes, brutal fights, random killings, rampant drug use, and countless burglaries—without intrusive emotional counternarrative, *Always Running* refused to simply pander to the public's prurient fascination with violence. The book is more than a searing documentary of life on the mean streets of the barrios of East Los Angeles. Rodríguez deftly moves his narrative toward the generous and entirely convincing offer of a way out of the street life. It is not an easy or quick solution; indeed, the title refers to Rodríguez's lifelong movement away from his dissolute youth and, by extension, his fears of his own son's flirtation with gang culture in Chicago. Rodríguez shapes his own experiences into a cautionary tale that seeks to actually change teens' lives. With the publication of this book, Rodríguez joined Kurt Vonnegut, Toni Morrison, and John Updike, among others, to win the prestigious Carl Sandburg Literary Award, presented annually by the Chicago Public Library Foundation for a work that most enhances the power of the written word to impact lives.

Rodríguez returned to Los Angeles in 2000. There, he was instrumental in establishing the Tia Chucha's Centro Cultural, an arts complex that provided a forum for the paintings, poetry, performance recitations, music, and writings of artists that represented the full range of Los Angeles's rich multicultural community. Since then, Rodríguez has tirelessly promoted cultural activities that transcend the city's racial and ethnic divisions, which he argues have made inevitable the city's violent streets. He maintains that gang culture can be eradicated only by addressing the economic and cultural conditions that created this culture.

SIGNIFICANCE

Luis J. Rodríguez understood that hope was a tough sell to the teens in the barrios. Without relying on extravagant promises or quick-fix solutions, without peddling some program or touting his credentials in counseling or psychology, Rodríguez had immense impact because he drew on his own experience, his own reclamation from the streets. His very presence offered hope. His writings and his advocacy of teen intervention programs designed to show at-risk, disillusioned youth creative alternatives to self-destructive criminal activity and drug and alcohol dependence have shaped a heal-yourself therapy in which teens recognize the dangers and embrace productive alternatives. In a vision that grew increasingly spiritual as Rodríguez matured, he challenged the younger generation to expand its vision beyond the radical isolation of the street and the narrow concerns of turf warfare to engage a broader sense of compassion and shared humanity.

Joseph Dewey

FURTHER READING

Rodríguez, Luis J. *Always Running: La Vida Loca, Gang Days in L.A.* 1993. Reprint. Clearwater, Fla.: Touchstone Books, 2005. Reprint of Rodríguez's gang memoir. Includes a poignant introduction that discusses his dedication to his son and the proliferation of gang violence in a post-September 11, 2011, urban world.

_____. *Hearts and Hands: Creating Community in Violent Times.* New York: Seven Stories Press, 2003. Rodríguez's careful analysis of the spiritual isolation of gang life and his prescription for remedying its causes: intercity violence, poverty, and drug use.

Vigil, Diego James. *A Rainbow of Gangs: Street Cultures in the Mega-City.* Austin: University of Texas Press, 2002. Wide-ranging look at the broad influence of gangs on the contemporary city. Introduces the cultural context that explains the appeal of gangs for disillusioned, disenfranchised urban youth.

See also: Jimmy Santiago Baca; Martha P. Cotera; Nicky Cruz; Tomás Rivera; Gary Soto.

NARCISO RODRIGUEZ

American fashion designer

A graduate of the prestigious Parsons School in New York City, Rodriguez gained experience working at Anne Klein and later Calvin Klein. His coveted wedding gown designed for Carolyn Bessette in 1996 propelled him to instant stardom in the fashion world.

Latino heritage: Cuban
Born: January 27, 1961; Newark, New Jersey
Also known as: Narciso Rodriguez III
Areas of achievement: Fashion; business

EARLY LIFE

Narciso Rodriguez (nahr-SEE-soh rahd-REE-gehz) was born Narciso Rodriguez III to Cuban immigrant parents Narciso Rodriguez II and Rawedia Maria Rodriguez on January 27, 1961. Before leaving Cuba, his parents worked as sugar refiners; after moving to New Jersey, his father took work as a longshoreman and his mother stayed at home to care for the young Rodriguez and his two sisters. Rodriguez grew up in Newark, New Jersey, in a neighborhood that contained many families of Cuban, Brazilian, and African American descent. Rodriguez was often surrounded by other neighborhood mothers who, like his own, took on seamstress work to make extra income. Eventually the Rodriguez family moved to a predominantly Caucasian suburb called Kearney. From the earliest years, Rodriguez showed an interest in the arts, especially drawing and working with textiles. In high school, he found work as an apprentice for a local tailor. He was later accepted at the renowned Parsons New School for Design in New York, which helped launch the careers of other famous designers such as Donna Karan, Mark Jacobs, Tom Ford, and others. After graduating from Parsons in 1982, Rodriguez worked as a freelance designer in Manhattan's Garment District until 1985, when he was hired by fashion label Anne Klein. Rodriguez studied under fellow Parsons alumna and Anne Klein design director Donna Karan. Under Karan, Rodriguez gained invaluable experience in the industry, and he was responsible for designing women's wear and accessories.

After six years at Anne Klein, Rodriguez left in 1991 for the position of design assistant at Calvin Klein. He struck an important friendship with the label's publicist, Carolyn Bessette. The two remained close until Bessette's death in 1999.

LIFE'S WORK

Rodriguez left Calvin Klein in 1994. He went on to work for a variety of labels, including TSE, a company specializing in cashmere, and Nino Cerutti, a Parisian design house where Rodriguez oversaw the women's line. During this time he also began designing wedding dresses under his own name, and his first break came in 1996 when he designed the gown for actor Dina Ruiz for her wedding to Clint Eastwood. Later that year, Rodriguez also designed the gown worn by Bessette for her wedding to John F. Kennedy, Jr. The wedding was highly publicized, and Bessette's gown was an immediate sensation; overnight, Rodriguez became a coveted name in the industry and to consumers.

Rodriguez created his own label the following year, and his debut collection in Milan in October, 1997, was well received. In 1998, he won the Perry Ellis Award for Best New Designer for Women's Wear. During this

Narciso Rodríguez.
(MPI13/MPI/PictureGroup via AP Images)

time, Rodriguez began designing collections for other companies, including Louis Vuitton, and a Spanish brand of leather luxury goods called Loewe. His pieces also appeared in luxury department stores, including Neiman Marcus and Barneys New York. In 1999, he was named Best New Designer at the Vogue Fashion Awards. In 2002, he won the Womenswear Designer of the Year Award from the Council of Fashion Designers of America; the following year, he won the award again, becoming the first person ever to win the award two consecutive years running. By 2003, Rodriguez's sales were grossing $20 million per annum. His popularity among celebrities also grew, as he developed relationships with actors Claire Danes, Salma Hayek, and Anna Paquin, among others, who have worn his gowns for red-carpet events. His pieces also became regular wardrobe features of the fictitious fashionista Carrie Bradshaw of HBO's series *Sex and the City*. He also began a design relationship with the actor who portrayed her, Sarah Jessica Parker.

Rodriguez's profile rose even further when First Lady Michelle Obama wore a dress from his spring, 2009, collection. The dress was a black chiffon shift with a graphic red detail across the front and was generally disliked by the majority of the American public. However, some fashion critics praised Obama for her edgy choice, and she continued consulting Rodriguez on her style choices.

SIGNIFICANCE

Rodriguez rose from an economically depressed childhood to become one of the most renowned American fashion designers in the world. As a child of immigrant parents who spoke little English, he often experienced racial abuse in the white suburb in which he was raised. He later had to combat homophobia; his parents forbade him to study clothing design, which they equated with homosexuality. Despite these obstacles, Rodriguez pursued his interest in fashion and is today considered an American fashion icon. He has worked with some of the most esteemed fashion houses in the world and dressed high-profile celebrities. He has continued to win acclaim for his effortless, streamlined designs.

Shannon Oxley

FURTHER READING

Marsh, Lisa. *The House of Klein: Fashion, Controversy, and a Business Obsession*. Indianapolis, Ind.: John Wiley & Sons, 2003. An in-depth look at the history of the Calvin Klein fashion house, with special focus on the years that Rodriguez worked there.

Perez, Daniel Enrique. *Rethinking Chicana/o and Latina/o Popular Culture*. New York: Palgrave MacMillan, 2009. A topic that infuses the life of Rodriguez. This text looks at the stereotypes of homophobia that exist in Latino culture.

Ramirez, Catherine. "Crimes of Fashion: The Pachuca and Chicana Style Politics." *Meridians* 2, no. 2 (2002): 1-35. This article examines homosexual politics relating to the fashion world in Latino culture.

Rodriguez, Narciso, and Betsey Berne. *Narciso Rodriguez*. New York: Rizzoli International, 2008. This book showcases the designer in his New York studio and also focuses on inspirational photographs taken by Rodriguez.

See also: Jessica Alba; Oscar de la Renta; Carolina Herrera; Eva Longoria.

PAUL RODRÍGUEZ

Mexican-born comedian and actor

Rodríguez was the first Mexican-born stand-up comedian to appear as a guest on The Tonight Show. *He was also the star of* a.k.a. Pablo, *the first situation comedy about a Mexican American family to appear on mainstream American television.*

Latino heritage: Mexican
Born: January 19, 1955; Mazatlán, Mexico
Also known as: Pablo Leobardo Castro Rodríguez

Areas of achievement: Entertainment; acting; radio and television; activism

EARLY LIFE

Paul Rodríguez (rahd-REE-gehs) was born Pablo Leobardo Castro Rodríguez on January 19, 1955, to migrant farm workers in Mazatlán, Mexico. In 1957, Rodríguez's parents relocated to California, where his father found work in a factory. After Rodríguez's father suffered an injury, breaking his back, the family was once again forced to make a living as migrant farm workers. Rodríguez, the youngest of five children, was required to travel from state to state as a child, picking fruit with his family. While working in Texas, one of Rodríguez's earliest childhood memories was that of a Crystal City restaurant refusing to serve his family because they were Latinos.

Eventually, Rodríguez's family was able to work as farm laborers in San Pedro, California, where he attended Barton Hills Elementary School. The Rodríguezes later moved to Compton, California, in 1965, one month before the Watts riots. Known as the class clown, Rodríguez attended Dominguez High School and joined the Compton Varrio Setentas street gang. After transferring to Roosevelt High School, Rodríguez dropped out of school and spent time on the streets of East Los Angeles before changing his name from Pablo to Paul. Drafted into the military, Rodríguez specialized in Air Force communications. Transferred to Duluth, Minnesota, the Philippines, and Iceland, Rodríguez was trained to monitor the location of Soviet submarines.

After leaving the Air Force, Rodríguez entered college in 1977 on the G.I. Bill, aspiring to become a lawyer.

Paul Rodríguez. (AP Photo)

An elective class in theater piqued his fascination with comedy, however, and he graduated from Long Beach Community College with an associate of arts degree. While working as a valet and doorman at The Comedy Store in Los Angeles in 1979, he watched performances by world-famous comedians, like Richard Pryor and George Carlin, and Rodríguez studied the art of comedy, gradually perfecting his own comedic talent. While performing stand-up comedy routines at concerts and college campuses throughout California, in 1982 Rodríguez broke into show business when he won a role doing comedy warm-ups for the television situation comedy *Gloria*, starring Sally Struthers. The show was canceled after only one season, but Rodríguez's exposure led to successive roles in television and films.

LIFE'S WORK
Rodríguez's film debut was playing cab driver Xavier in *D.C. Cab* (1983). Producer Norman Lear was so impressed with Rodríguez's performance in *Gloria* and *D.C. Cab* that in 1984 Lear wrote and produced a new television situation comedy for Rodríguez, *a.k.a. Pablo,* starring Rodríguez as an up-and-coming Chicano comedian. The American Broadcasting Company (ABC) canceled the show after only six episodes because of low ratings. Rodríguez's role in *a.k.a. Pablo* established his reputation as a comic, however, and in 1986 he appeared as Juan in the film *Miracles*, starring Teri Garr. That role led to Rodríguez's big film breakthrough playing Javier, Rudy Robles's Mexican-born factory worker cousin in Cheech Marín's hugely successful *Born in East L.A.*

In 1988, Rodríguez became the first Mexican American to host a game show on television when he replaced Bob Eubanks as the host of the *The Newlywed Game*. Rodríguez went on to star in two subsequent comedy television series on CBS, *Trial and Error* (1988) and *Grand Slam* (1990), both of which were canceled after one season. From 1990 to1994, Rodríguez became comedy host of Unavision's *El show de Paul Rodríguez*, the first bilingual international skit and comedy talk show, broadcast in seventeen countries. Beginning in 1991, Rodríguez produced and starred in the enormously popular HBO television series, *Paul Rodríguez, Behind Bars*, stand-up comedy concerts from San Quentin State Prison, culminating in a live show in 2004.

Appearing in more than forty films, Rodríguez's other memorable roles include his appearance as Jose in *Made in America* (1993), along with Whoopie Goldberg and Ted Danson, and as Frank in *Mambo Cafe* (1999). In

a.k.a. *Pablo* and Mexican American Stereotypes

In an episode of *a.k.a. Pablo*, the 1984 television situation comedy starring Paul Rodríguez, struggling Chicano comedian Paul Rivera, known as Pablo to his family, is seen performing a stand-up comedy routine live on stage in front of producer Merv Griffin and an Anglo audience, while Rivera's Mexican American family is watching the performance at home on television. Although Griffin and his live Anglo audience are laughing uproariously at Rivera's routine, replete with derogatory Latino characterizations and negative Mexican American stereotypes, in stark contrast Rivera's relatives at home are silent and somber, transfixed in solemn disbelief. Likewise, Mexican American audiences reacted with anger, frustration, and disappointment when they witnessed the much-touted first Chicano family to be displayed on a mainstream situation comedy show.

Instead of viewing an accurate portrayal of unique individuals with diverse talents and complexities, Latino audiences watching *a.k.a. Pablo* encountered many Mexican American stereotypes under which they had unjustly labored for centuries. Critics charged that the show negatively portrayed Mexican Americans as one-dimensional cardboard figures, depicting illegal immigrants, criminals, gang members, low riders, and Don Juans who were illiterate, lazy, dishonest, and hot-blooded. These characterizations outraged the Latino community. Mexican Americans were deeply proud of Rodríguez's national success in a public arena which had previously been largely inaccessible to Latinos. However, they profoundly resented and rejected Rodríguez for finding favor and acceptance with Anglo audiences at the expense of Mexican Americans by perpetuating offensive Latino stereotypes.

2001, Rodríguez played Diego in *Crocodile Dundee in Los Angeles*, and in 2002, Rodríguez starred alongside his idol, Clint Eastwood, as Detective Arrango in the thriller *Blood Work*. Also in 2002, Rodríguez produced and starred in *The Original Latin Kings of Comedy*, along with Cheech Marín, George Lopez, Alex Reymundo, Joey Medina, and Nayib Estefan. In 2005, Rodríguez appeared as Fernando with Sir Anthony Hopkins in *The World's Fastest Indian*, and in 2008, Rodríguez starred as the voice of the iguana Chico in Walt Disney's blockbuster *Beverly Hills Chihuahua*. In 2010, Rodríguez voiced the character of Crazy Carlito for *Cats and Dogs: The Revenge of Kitty Galore*.

Rodríguez is the first Mexican American to own a comedy club, co-owning the Laugh Factory in Los Angeles. He has traveled for many years with the United Services Organization (USO) to entertain American troops in the Middle East. Ever since the state of California shut off the water in has mother's orange groves, he has been chairman of the California Latino Water Coalition , advocating for needed water for the agriculture industry, which many Latinos in the state depend upon for their livelihood.

Married and divorced twice, Rodríguez is the father of two sons, Lucas and professional skateboard champion Paul Rodríguez, Jr.

SIGNIFICANCE

As the first Mexican American comedian to write, direct, and star in his own film, *A Million to Juan* (1994), loosely based on Mark Twain's *The £1 Million Bank Note*, Rodríguez's influence in the film industry has been considerable, paving the way for other Latino comedians to follow in his footsteps. The film, which cost only $165,000, was highly successful at the box office, earning millions of dollars. Although *A Million to Juan* was the first film Rodríguez directed, his ability to make it appeal to a crossover audience of both Anglos and Latinos is the secret to his success as a comedian, whether acting, directing, or performing stand-up. While Rodríguez uses his Latino background as a source and inspiration for his comedic writing, his true gift lies in his ability to create characters, situations, and truisms which speak universally to people of all races and cultures about the absurdities of life.

Mary E. Markland

FURTHER READING

Bender, Steve. *Greasers and Gringos: Latinos, Law, and the American Imagination.* New York: New York University Press, 2003. Rodríguez recounts his experience as child working as a migrant worker in the California fields with his family; crop dusting planes flew over spraying pesticides on them, while his mother covered him with her shawl and said not to breathe the chemicals.

Glennon, Robert. *Unquenchable: America's Water Crisis and What to Do About It.* Washington, D.C.: Island Press, 2009. Discusses Rodríguez's role as the chairman of the California Latino Water Coalition and his efforts to ensure water for the $37 billion state culture industry.

Mellado, Carmela. "Hispanic Engineer National Achievement Awards, 1991 Co-Hosts and Award Presenters." *Hispanic Engineer* 7, no. 4 (October, 1991): 83. In this profile of Rodríguez as a successful Hispanic comedian and television and film star, he recalls that his migrant-worker parents never thought that becoming an actor or comedian was possible, so their ambition for him was merely to find a regular job.

See also: María Conchita Alonso; Catherine Bach; Andy Garcia; John Leguizamo; George Lopez; Cheech Marín; Elizabeth Peña; Freddie Prinze; Jimmy Smits.

RICH RODRIGUEZ

American football coach

Rodriguez, a prominent college football coach, is considered one of the godfathers of a revolutionary offensive philosophy in American football: the spread. While he was not alone in the spread's development, many regard him as the master at coaching this offensive technique.

Latino heritage: Mexican
Born: May 24, 1963; Chicago, Illinois
Also known as: Richard A. Rodriguez; Rich Rod
Area of achievement: Football

EARLY LIFE

Richard A. Rodriguez, better known as Rich Rodriguez, (rahd-REE-gehs), was born on May 24, 1963, in Chicago, Illinois. He grew up in Grant Town, West Virginia, the son of a coal miner. Raised on a farm outside the small town, Rodriguez developed a sense of feistiness combined with a strong physique while growing up. As he went through school he showed proficiency playing four different sports. By the end of his high school career, he had earned All State honors in both football and basketball. With his parent's encouragement and his own desire to avoid working in the mines of West Virginia, Rodriguez graduated from high school and enrolled at West Virginia University (WVU), where he became a "walk-on," a player without a scholarship, on the football team. As a freshman defensive back, he stood out because of the many fights he had with teammates during practice. His intensity eventually proved useful and he honed his skills, enabling him to earn a scholarship. However, a professional career was not in the offing, and Rodriguez began to focus on coaching.

LIFE'S WORK

During the 1985-1986 college football season, Rodriguez served as a student assistant for coach Don Nehlen at WVU, and he followed that by becoming the special teams coordinator at Salem College (now Salem International University) in Salem, West Virginia. The following year, Rodriguez became defensive coordinator, and in 1988, he accepted the position of head coach, becoming the youngest coach in the country at age twenty-five.

After suffering through a year when his team earned a two-win eight-loss record, Rodriguez was informed that Salem was dropping its football program. He returned to WVU, where he took the position of linebackers' coach. The following year, 1990, Rodriguez

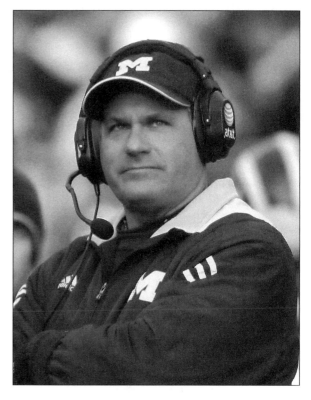

Rich Rodriguez. (AP Photo)

assumed the position of head coach at Glanville State College, also in West Virginia. Though his first two years showed little sign of promise, his third season as coach brought a winning record, which was followed by a season with ten wins and three losses. That year proved not to be an aberration, and he continued to lead Glanville to success. His team's results gained him attention as a coach on the rise, and he was hired to be offensive coordinator at Tulane University in New Orleans.

At Tulane, Rodriguez helped cultivate the spread offense, using an offensive innovation that opened the field so his quarterback had more space to make plays. During Rodriguez's tenure at Tulane, the team scored a twelve-win season that resulted in the head coach, Tommy Bowden, becoming head coach at Clemson University. Bowden brought Rodriguez with him and the Clemson Tigers enjoyed two winning seasons, reaching the Peach and the Gator Bowls, respectively.

In late 2000, Nehlen, the WVU coach, announced his retirement and the university hired Rodriguez as his replacement. Rodriguez's first season as head coach seemed to be a relative disaster, with only three wins. However, the next season he coached the Mountaineers to nine wins. The next five seasons demonstrated Rodriguez's acumen as a coach, as the team continued to have winning seasons, including a Sugar Bowl victory over the Georgia Bulldogs and a Gator Bowl win over Georgia Tech. In his last season as head coach at WVU, the team rose to as high as number one in the national rankings before losing its last game of the season.

Though he had spurned previous offers to coach elsewhere, after the 2007 season Rodriguez agreed to become the coach at the University of Michigan. The contentious move brought lawsuits from WVU, which was coupled by a lukewarm reception for Rodriguez by Michigan fans. Many of the fans' fears were proven correct, as the Michigan team won just three games in Rodriguez's first season and five in his second. The third season showed more promise, as the team opened with five straight wins but would finish with a record of seven wins and six losses. During Rodriguez's tenure at Michigan, the National Collegiate Athletic Association (NCAA) charged the football team with committing four major violations. These allegations, combined with the team's lackluster performance, led to Rodriguez's dismissal on January 5, 2011.

SIGNIFICANCE

Though Rodriguez's move to the University of Michigan ultimately proved to be problematic, his career in coaching has generally been a success. His work at WVU showcased his ability to introduce and use the spread—a dynamic offensive system that produced remarkable results. Even after his firing from Michigan, many pundits still believed that Rodriguez had many winning seasons ahead of him.

P. Huston Ladner

FURTHER READING

Evans, Thayer, and Pete Thamel. "West Virginia's Coach Is Now Michigan's Man." *The New York Times*, December, 17, 2007, p. 5. While there was substantial media coverage on Rodriguez's move to the University of Michigan, this article offers one of the best overviews of this development.

Lemire, Joe. "Making It, Rich." *Sports Illustrated*, August 20, 2008, 60-65. Details Rodriguez's move to the University of Michigan and the hope of his ability to build a championship-winning football program.

Rodriguez, Rich. "The Spread Offense: Four Receivers, Part1." *Coach and Athletic Director* 77, no. 1 (August, 2007): 16-22.

_____. "The Spread Offense: Four Receivers, Part 2. *Coach and Athletic Director* 77, no. 2 (September, 2007): 24-28. Rodriguez details the fundamentals of the spread offense and how to make it effective.

See also: Tedy Bruschi; Jeff Garcia; Tony Gonzalez; Anthony Muñoz; Tony Romo.

RICHARD RODRIGUEZ

American writer and journalist

Best known for his poignant autobiographical work Hunger of Memory, *a memoir about his coming-of-age linguistically as a Latino schoolboy in California, Rodriguez emerged in the late twentieth century as one of the United States' most respected prose stylists and essayists. His eclectic philosophy, which blends linguistic conservatism with passionate sympathy for Mexican Americans' ties to Mexico, has made him both widely read and at times highly controversial.*

Latino heritage: Mexican

Born: July 31, 1944; San Francisco, California

Also known as: Ricardo Rodriguez

Areas of achievement: Literature; journalism; education; activism

EARLY LIFE

Richard Rodriguez (rahd-REE-gehs) was born Ricardo Rodriguez in San Francisco, the third of four children of Mexican immigrants who, when Rodriguez was only a few years old, moved into a middle-class suburb of Sacramento, California, where the boy was enrolled in a private Catholic school. When the nuns who taught at the school realized that Rodriguez spoke almost no English, they visited his parents and persuaded them to adopt an English-only policy at home for their children. Even at this early age, Rodriguez became keenly aware of the changes this shift from Spanish to English caused in his household, as his father, Leopoldo, who had always clearly been the head of the family but who was not very fluent in English, was eclipsed in authority and decision making by his mother, Victoria, and the couple's older children, who were much more adept at English than Leopoldo.

The transition from Spanish to English as the home language of the Rodriguez family also made young Richard keenly aware of language differences and inspired in him a fascination with words, sounds, writing, and reading. At Don Bosco High School, he excelled in English and upon graduation enrolled at Stanford University, where he earned a B.A. degree in English. He then completed a M.A. degree in English from Columbia University. Soon after leaving Columbia, Rodriguez entered a doctoral program in literature of the English Renaissance at the University of California at Berkeley. His experiences in these various degree programs at American universities, however, led him to become disenchanted with the affirmative-action guidelines adhered to by most institutions of higher education in the United States. As a result, he withdrew from academia and began to write and publish a number of essays attacking affirmative-action policies as inherently unfair and bilingual education as counterproductive for Latino pupils in American school systems. Although these essays angered many Latino activists and educational authorities, Rodriguez persisted, and the controversial nature of his views and the eloquence of his writing style drew much attention. He soon decided to coalesce these essays into a memoir.

LIFE'S WORK

When *Hunger of Memory: The Education of Richard Rodriguez, an Autobiography* was published in 1982, it elicited much praise for the author's style and evocation of mood and memory, but the book also drew scornful rebuke from some Latino activists who saw Rodriguez as an "assimilationist" and a *pocho,* that is, a betrayer of the cause of the Latino people because he seemed to be championing mainstream Anglo culture and values. Affirmative action and bilingual education were mainstays of Latino activist ideology since the 1960's, and many politically active Latinos were infuriated that Rodriguez, a first-generation Mexican American who had managed to succeed academically in some of the most prestigious institutes of higher education in the United States, would not only reject these programs but also repeatedly denounce them in this autobiographical work and in subsequent interviews and articles. The controversy was in many ways a prototypal American conflict pitting the understandable pride of immigrants and their descendants in their ethnicity against the cherished classic American virtues of self-sufficiency and individualism in the mode of Ralph Waldo Emerson and Henry David Thoreau.

Richard Rodriguez. (© Roger Ressmeyer/Corbis)

Hunger of Memory and *Days of Obligation*

When *Hunger of Memory: The Education of Richard Rodriguez, an Autobiograpy* appeared in 1982, it at once sparked two extreme reactions: one from critics rapturously praising its sumptuous prose style. and another, angry and often vituperative, from activists who were upset about Richard Rodriguez's views on affirmative action and bilingual education. *Hunger of Memory* is composed of a prologue and six chapters, the latter of which are for the most part revisions of previously published essays. In the prologue, "Middle-Class Pastoral," Rodriguez identifies his intent—telling the story of his life, describing in the opening scene the pathways that led him to be what he is: a cultured man at a Bel Air cocktail party who stands out among the other sophisticates because of his complexion.

The essays that follow each tend to focus on one or two aspects of his life. For example, the first essay, "Aria," recounts his experiences as a little boy and describes the dramatic effects wrought on his household by the nun-imposed English-only policy enacted by his parents. The second essay, "The Achievement of

Desire," details his education, drawing heavily on the theories of English academician Richard Hoggart. The fifth, "Profession," is especially important in that it offers a rationale for his controversial opinions about bilingual education and affirmative action.

Appearing a decade later, *Days of Obligation: An Argument with My Mexican Father* (1992) is similar in structure but more diverse in thematic content. Like *Hunger of Memory*, it is a collection of essays, this time dealing with the complex, intricately interwoven histories of northern Mexico and the Southwestern United States. The best of these essays are "In Athens Once," a meditation on the relationship between Tijuana, Mexico, and San Diego, California," and "The Missions," a literal and spiritual travelogue in which Rodriguez visits every Catholic mission site in California. *Days of Obligation* also explores Rodriguez's feelings and experiences as a gay man in the midst of the acquired immune deficiency syndrome (AIDS) epidemic, and it examines similarities and differences between Latinos and other minorities in the United States, such as Asians.

Hunger of Memory garnered Rodriguez an impressive array of honors, including the International Journalism Award and the Frankel Medal from the National Endowment for the Humanities. *Hunger of Memory* also won Rodriguez a Gold Medal from the Commonwealth Club of California and the Christopher Prize for Autobiography. Despite the controversy engendered by the book among Latino activists, *Hunger of Memory* also resulted in Rodriguez being given the Anisfeld-Wolf Prize for Civil Rights.

Ten years later, Rodriguez published what many readers and critics saw as a sequel to *Hunger of Memory*, *Days of Obligation*: *An Argument with My Mexican Father* (1992). This work was nominated for a Pulitzer Prize. In 2002, a third, somewhat similar volume appeared, *Brown: The Last Discovery of America*, which was nominated for the National Book Critics Award. Although reviewers sometimes refer to these books as a trilogy, Rodriguez does not seem to have conceived of the books as such. *Brown* deals primarily with the impact of Americanization on Latinos and the influence of Latinos on the cultural, intellectual, and emotional life of the United States.

In addition to his writing, Rodriguez has served as an editor for the Pacific News Service and as a contributing editor for *U.S. News and World Report* and *Harper's*

Magazine. In the 1990's, he appeared regularly as a commentator on Public Broadcasting Service's (PBS) nightly *NewsHour*; in 1997, he won a George Foster Peabody Award for his work on this program. He has also published numerous magazine articles in periodicals, such as *Time* and *Mother Jones*.

SIGNIFICANCE

Richard Rodriguez represents fundamental ironies of the immigrant experience in the United States. His eloquent expressions of palpable nostalgia for the Mexican and Indian/Native American part of his experience and heritage refute much of the criticism from some activists who see him as a sell-out. At the same time, however, he has never wavered in his opposition to bilingual education and affirmative action for minorities, which many Latino activists see as ideologically axiomatic.

By embracing both of the words in the phrase "Mexican American," Rodriguez, a first-generation American, embodies traditional American individualism. Furthermore, his graceful, elegant prose style has made him one of the preeminent essayists in the English language in the late twentieth and early twenty-first centuries. *Hunger of Memory* is frequently taught in high school English classes, and his essays and articles routinely appear in freshman English textbooks assigned in American college and university courses.

Thomas Du Bose

FURTHER READING

Challener, Daniel. *Stories of Resilience: The Narratives of Maya Angelou, Maxine Hong Kingston, Richard Rodriguez, and Tobias Wolff.* New York: Routledge, 1997. Provides an interesting and worthwhile assessment of Rodriguez's autobiographical writings in the context of other well-known memoirists of his generation.

Guajardo, Paul. *Chicano Controversy: Oscar Acosta and Richard Rodriguez.* New York: Peter Lang, 2002. Explains the controversy generated by Rodriguez's stance on affirmative action and bilingual education.

Rodriguez, Richard. *Brown: The Last Discovery of America.* New York: Viking, 2002. A poetic reverie on the meaning of the word "brown" in North American parlance and on the interrelationship of Latino and Anglo peoples and cultures.

_____. *Days of Obligation: An Argument with My Mexican Father.* New York: Viking, 1992. Branches out into areas unexplored in *Hunger of Memory*, especially Rodriguez's homosexuality.

_____. "Family Values." In *The McGraw-Hill Reader*, edited by Gilbert H. Muller. 10th ed. New York: McGraw-Hill, 2008. Although basically a narrative about Rodriguez's coming out to his parents about his gayness, this essay is also an insightful meditation on Americans' attitudes toward family and family life.

_____. *Hunger of Memory: The Education of Richard Rodriguez, an Autobiography.* New York: Bantam-Dell, 1982. A potent example of a well-constructed and well-phrased autobiography that remains controversial.

See also: Linda Chavez; Maria Hinojosa; Soledad O'Brien.

ROBERT RODRIGUEZ

American entertainer and writer

Rodriguez learned almost everything necessary for filmmaking on his own. Caught between extreme ambition and poverty, Rodriguez made a film with a one-man crew, graduating from film school to become a successful and popular director.

Latino heritage: Mexican

Born: June 20, 1968; San Antonio, Texas

Also known as: Robert Anthony Rodriguez

Areas of achievement: Filmmaking; screenwriting

EARLY LIFE

Robert Anthony Rodriguez (rahd-REE-gehz) was born on June 20, 1968, in San Antonio, Texas, the third of ten children born to Cecilio, a cookware sales manager, and Rebecca, a nurse. At an early age, Rodriguez demonstrated an interest in making pictures by creating animated flip films in the margins of books. By age twelve, Rodriguez used his father's camera for sales presentations to make home films recording the escapades of his siblings.

By the time he was in high school in San Antonio, Rodriguez realized his life's goals were to become a cartoonist and a filmmaker. Studies were largely ignored in his pursuit of his craft and in the study of music. He learned to play the guitar, saxophone, and piano, which he later used in scoring his films. Denied entrance to the University of Texas Film School, Rodriguez created a comic strip about his siblings. One of his short films won an award, allowing him to enter the film school.

To secure the money to make his first film, *El Mariachi* (1992), Rodriguez became a laboratory test subject, participating in a clinical research trial for cholesterol-reducing drugs, while using the mandated hospital time to write the film's script. Essentially a film of mistaken identities, the narrative follows the adventures of a Mexican guitar player looking for work who becomes confused with an assassin carrying a similar guitar case packed with weapons. Using a silent 16-millimeter camera and then dubbing in from a recording the actor's lines, Rodriguez, along with his friend and cowriter, Carlos Gallardo, shot the film in fourteen days. By using local actors who worked free, Rodriguez managed to keep the total cost of the film under seven thousand dollars.

Rodriguez had hoped to sell the film as a learning experiment to the Spanish-language video market, but it won the Audience Award at Sundance Film Festival in 1992, whereupon he was approached by an agent from International Creative Management, who brokered a

Robert Rodríguez. (AP Photo)

two-year, two-picture deal with Columbia Pictures. The studio subtitled *El Mariachi*, improved the sound, and expanded it to 35-millimeter. Upon its release, the film earned six million dollars, most of which went to recoup production costs.

LIFE'S WORK

Working briefly in Los Angeles during the mid-1990's, Rodriguez remade a 1959 film into *Roadracers* (1994) for Showtime. Despite the fact that it was an homage to 1950's drive-in film theaters, the film's only apparent value was in providing a training ground for Rodriguez, who worked as director, screenwriter, editor, songwriter on the thirty-five-millmeter film.

In 1995, Rodriguez filmed a sequel to *El Mariachi*, titled *Desperado*, made in the same border town as the earlier film, but with a seven-million-dollar budget. In the sequel, the mariachi ventures into the underworld as he chases after a Mexican drug lord, and the film ends in a huge, bloody showdown. Rodriguez's cartoonish, humorous violence in his first film achieves new levels of overkill in the second film, which required enormous amounts of ammunition, weapons, and blood substitute for massive explosions. Hoping to dispel the notion that

Mexicans are "bad guys" in films, Rodriguez includes an honorable character and a beautiful, strong female lead to redefine role models for Mexican Americans.

Rodriguez's next film, *From Dusk Till Dawn* (1996), based on a script by Quentin Tarantino, follows two psychotic brothers, played by Rodriguez and Tarantino, across the Southwest and into Mexico, where they capture a former preacher and his two children. The film is divided into two parts: the first half, an action film that seems influenced by Tarantino, and the second half, which, once the pair reaches Mexico, becomes a vampire film relying on Rodriguez's cartoonish violence, special effects, and dizzying editing for its lurid effects.

Once Upon a Time in Mexico (2003), Rodriguez's second sequel to *El Mariachi* and *Desperado*, is a series of comedic episodes that relate to plot elements in the earlier two films. They also allow opportunities for impressive actors, specifically, Antonio Banderas, as El Mariachi, who is searching for the killer of his wife (Salma Hayek), and Johnny Depp, Willem Dafoe, Mickey Rourke, Eva Mendes, and Cheech Marín to shine in the individual sequences. Alluding to the titles of Italian director Sergio Leone's films, *Once Upon a Time in the West* (1969) and *Once Upon a Time in America* (1989), and the manner of Hong Kong action films, Rodriguez creates the complicated excesses that have become his trademark.

In *Sin City* (2005), Frank Miller's graphic novel became the basis and setting for Rodriguez's film written by Miller and Rodriguez and directed by Rodriguez, Tarantino, and Miller. Three stories focus on three male leads— Bruce Willis, Rourke, and Clive Owen— who find themselves in violent circumstances that lead to fateful ends. As a modern noir film—one that plunges to the depths of the corruption of circumstances and of character—the film is black and white, with splashes of color, namely blood. The film was quite successful at the box office.

Two years later, in 2007, Rodriguez again teamed with Tarantino for *Grindhouse*, a tribute to exploitation films of the 1960's and 1970's that, despite containing a healthy helping of sleaze and gore and exhibiting poor production values, amassed a cult following. Clearly, both Rodriguez and Tarantino were members of that cult. Presented as a double-feature film with some fake trailers, *Grindhouse* fared somewhat poorly at the box office.

SIGNIFICANCE

The earliest influences upon Rodriguez's film development—his siblings and their inventiveness—proved

Spy Kids Films

In 2001, Robert Rodriguez forsook his trademark film violence to create a perfect vehicle for family viewing. *Spy Kids* tells the story of two children, whose parents, once exceptional spies, fell in love and gave up spying to raise a family. When the parents disappear, the children realize that they must also become high-tech spies in order to rescue their parents and save the world. Rodriguez's use of special effects, fast-paced action, and an amazingly imaginative script made this an entertaining, family-oriented film. The success of the first film continued in the second film, *Spy Kids Two: Island of Lost Dreams* (2002), also featuring Rodriguez's wit, ingenuity, and fun with gadgets. The children become junior spies, who, in their efforts to save the president's daughter, end up on a mysterious island matching wits with a mad scientist and his bizarre characters. Rodriguez's *Spy Kids 3D: Game Over* (2003) initiated a change by showing about two-thirds of the film in 3D. The interesting storyline followed a character who becomes lost in a video game, but the frustration arising from the glasses to be worn for the film quite possibly drowned out the enjoyment of the film.

to be the strongest and most enduring ones. He practiced making home films of their antics; one of his short comedies, *Bedhead* (1991), told from the perspective of his nine-year-old sister, but featuring all of his nine siblings, won awards at fourteen festivals, including one in Australia.

Rodriguez's first films, echoing his home films, are filled with rapid-fire actions, with few connecting or transitional devices, and with his own taste for lurid, absurd violence. Audiences were amazed by Rodriguez's indifference to background, character building or development, and any hint of morality. As his popu-

larity grew and his budgets soared into the millions, audiences came to expect the cartoonish, yet stylish violence and no serious impediments to the nonstop special effects, explosions, mishaps, and carnage that contribute to the sheer juvenile enjoyment of comic-book fun with film. Rodriguez's collaboration with other directors seems to encourage an appraisal of his techniques alongside theirs. Whereas Tarantino's scenes of violence are grotesque and gory, Rodriguez's humorous violence suggests a youthful appreciation of the excesses in his films.

Mary Hurd

FURTHER READING

Kanellos, Nicolas, and Tamra Orr, eds. *Great Hispanic Americans*. Lincolnwood, Ill.: Publications International, 2005. Written for nine- to twelve-year-olds, this collection of biographies of successful and notable Hispanic individuals includes a profile of Rodriguez, with photographs and background information.

Miller, Frank, and Robert Rodriguez. *Frank Miller's "Sin City": The Making of the Movie*. Austin, Tex.: Troublemaker, 2005. Guide to the filming of Miller's graphic novel, showing Rodriguez's faithful adaptation of Miller's images. Includes discussions by Miller and Rodriguez, cast, and crew.

Rodriguez, Robert. *Rebel Without a Crew: Or, How a Twenty-Three-Year-Old Filmmaker With Seven Thousand Dollars Became a Hollywood Player*. Berkeley, Calif.: Plume, 1996. Detailed account of Rodriguez's innovative making of *El Mariachi* on a tiny budget and its award at Sundance Film Festival, which led to a contract with Columbia Pictures.

See also: Luis Alfaro; Elizabeth Avellán; Hector Elizondo; Cheech Marín; George Romero; Danny Trejo.

LOLA RODRÍGUEZ DE TIÓ

Puerto Rican-born poet and activist

Rodríguez de Tió, a revered figure in Cuban and Puerto Rican history, was a nineteenth-century lyric poet who fought for the independence of both countries. As a member of the ruling elite, her work on behalf of opportunities for women made her one of Latin America's most influential early feminists.

Latino heritage: Puerto Rican
Born: September 14, 1843; San Germán, Puerto Rico
Died: November 10, 1924; Havana, Cuba
Also known as: María de los Dolores Rodríguez de Tió; Dolores Rodríguez de Astudillo y Ponce de León

Areas of achievement: Poetry; activism; women's rights

EARLY LIFE

Lola Rodríguez de Tió (TEE-oh) was born Dolores Rodríguez de Astudillo y Ponce de León in San Germán, into a family belonging to Puerto Rico's ruling class. Her father was Don Sebastian Rodríguez de Astudillo, one of the founders of the Puerto Rican Bar Association and holder of a magisterial deanship; her mother was Doña Carmen Ponce de León, a descendant of Ponce de León, the famous explorer and first colonial governor. Rodríguez de Tió attended religious schools and studied with private tutors in her home, often present for the nearby gatherings of the assorted intellectuals and politicians meeting with her father. Her well-educated mother managed the child's education, and though it was rare at the time for a woman to be an intellectual, Rodríguez de Tió, as a comfortable member of Puerto Rico's ruling elite, also found support and encouragement in her literary endeavors from the poet Ursula Cardona de Quinones.

Bonacio Tío Segarra, journalist and also a poet, married Rodríguez de Tió when she was twenty. Sources suggest that the two had a modern relationship as partners in life and politics, and politically the couple worked against the corruption and brutality in Puerto Rico under Spain's colonial government. Tío Segarra recognized and supported Rodríguez de Tió's gift for lyricism and wrote the preface to her first published poetry collection. As advocates of radical nationalist beliefs, the two together experienced harassment and tribulation once the Spanish authorities became aware of their work.

LIFE'S WORK

Rodríguez de Tió published her first book of poetry, *Mis cantares*, in 1876. The book sold 2,500 copies. Prior to that, the fiery lyric piece "La Borinquena," composed for a traditional melody, established Rodríguez de Tió's reputation and caused her to be deported after she read it out loud at a literary gathering in her own home. The song's development as the national anthem happened gradually from its original form as a song of romantic love, into the resulting chant to liberty and a symbol of patriotism.

Because of their rebellious stance against tyranny, Rodríguez de Tió and her husband were forced to live in exile at various times over the years, first in Venezuela, then Cuba, then New York City. Wherever they went, they worked for Puerto Rican and also Cuban independence and formed alliances with the artistic and intellectual communities in each city. In Venezuela, for example, they met Eugenio María de Hostos, a brilliant patriot who became an important influence on Rodríguez de Tió. While in New York City, Rodríguez de Tió began intense political contact with José Martí and other Cuban political exiles, creating the Cuban Revolutionary Party in 1895. Rodríguez de Tió served in the leadership of the clubs Rius Rivera in 1896 and Caridad in 1897. When she returned to Cuba in 1899, she spent the rest of her life working for social justice and the improvement of the situation of Cuban women.

Rodríguez de Tió published three books: *Mis cantares* (*My Songs*) in 1876, *Claros y nieblas* (*Bright Intervals and Mist*) in 1885, and *Mi libro de Cuba* (*My Book on Cuba*) in 1893. Some sources have recounted that Fidel Castro quoted from one of her well-known poems, "Cuba and Puerto Rico," in a 1966 speech, but that he attributed the poem to Martí. Still, Rodríguez de Tió's poetry expresses her affection for both Puerto Rico and her adopted homeland. She died on November 10, 1924, in Havana, Cuba, at the age of eighty-one.

SIGNIFICANCE

Considered a leading literary figure and a national hero, Rodríguez de Tió was named to the Cuban Academy of Arts and Letters in 1910 and Patron of the Galician Beneficent Society in 1911. She has been called Puerto Rico's most distinguished nineteenth-century lyric poet, and as the most prominent female Puerto Rican Romantic poet she certainly stands tall. However, Rodríguez de Tió's activism and political engagement truly set her apart from other patriots of her generation. With her stalwart dedication to Romanticism in tandem with her fierce militancy, Rodríguez de Tió embodied the tension between the legacy of Spain's Golden Age and Spanish authoritarian colonialism.

Jan Voogd

FURTHER READING

Babin, Maria Teresa, and Stan Steiner, eds. *Borinquen: An Anthology of Puerto Rican Literature.* New York: Knopf, 1974. Discusses the process and impact of Rodríguez de Tió's "Song of Borinquen" and its relationship to the national anthem of Puerto Rico.

Rodríguez de Tió, Lola. *Mis cantares.* Reprint. Alexandria, Va.: Alexander Street Press, 2005. An example of poetry originally published in the 1880's but recently more available as new editions of her work have been produced in electronic format and print-on-demand.

_____. *Obras completas*. 4 vols. San Juan: Instituto de Cultura Puertorriquena, 1968-1971. Difficult to find but forms the cornerstone of understanding Rodríguez de Tió's artistry.

_____. *Poesías patrióticas, poesías religiosa; Cantares, nieblas y congojas; and Mi libro de Cuba*. Barcelona: Ediciones Rumbos, 1967, 1968. Originally published in the 1800's, these are ex-amples of work republished in Spain during the 1960's.

Ruiz, Vicki, and Virginia Sanchez Korrol. *Latina Legacies: Identity, Biography, and Community*. New York: Oxford University Press, 2005. Includes an entire chapter on Rodríguez de Tió and the struggle for freedom in Puerto Rico.

See also: Victor Hernández Cruz; Judith Ortiz Cofer; Pedro Juan Soto; Clemente Soto Vélez.

FERNANDO E. RODRÍGUEZ VARGAS

Puerto Rican-born dentist and military leader

Rodríguez Vargas is best known for the groundbreaking research he performed as a military dentist. He was the first individual to discover the types of bacteria that cause dental cavities and to demonstrate oral disinfectants for possible use in dental procedures.

Latino heritage: Puerto Rican

Born: February 24, 1888; Adjuntas, Puerto Rico

Died: October 21, 1932; Washington, D.C.

Also known as: Fernando Emilio Rodríguez Vargas

Areas of achievement: Medicine; science and technology; military

EARLY LIFE

Fernando Emilio Rodríguez Vargas (fuhr-NAHN-doh rahd-REE-gehs VAHR-gahs) was born to Luciano Rodríguez and Dolores Vargas in Adjuntas, Puerto Rico. He attended the University of Puerto Rico in Rio Piedras, San Juan, for undergraduate studies. Rodríguez Vargas showed an interest in the medical field from an early age when he attended paramedic courses at the university. He graduated from the university with a teaching certificate. After college, Rodríguez Vargas held several positions, including an inspector for the U.S. Internal Revenue Service and a Spanish translator for the U.S. War Department.

LIFE'S WORK

Rodríguez Vargas left Puerto Rico to further his education. In 1913, he received a doctorate in dental surgery from Georgetown University in Washington, D.C. He remained in Washington, D.C., after completing school in order to enter into private practice. After two years, Rodríguez Vargas relocated to Tuc-son, Arizona, to perform dental research for the U.S. Indian Medical Services, a federal health program for American Indians and Alaskan Natives. Here he studied the Pima Indian tribe, which developed dental cavities at a greater frequency than the general population. His initial work with the tribe led him to suspect that the substantial rotting of dental enamel was caused by a poor drinking water supply. His later research on dental cavities would reveal other causes for this condition.

In 1917, Rodríguez Vargas entered the military as a first lieutenant in the Army Dental Reserve Corps of the U.S. Army. He was first stationed in England, then at Camp Las Casas in San Juan, Puerto Rico, during World War I. Rodríguez Vargas would eventually be promoted to captain (1919) and finally major (1929). While serving in the Army in San Juan, Rodríguez Vargas met his wife, Maria Anita Padilla. The couple had one son, Roberto.

After his service in World War I, Rodríguez Vargas returned to Washington, D.C., to continue research on dental diseases, specifically dental cavities, through the Army Dental Corps. The breakthrough that Rodríguez Vargas is best known for occurred when he discovered the bacteria that are responsible for dental cavities. His landmark research was published in 1922 in the *Military Dental Journal* and was entitled, "The Specific Study of the Bacteriology of Dental Cavities." Rodríguez Vargas was the first to describe the three types of *Lactobacillus* species, which, when broken down, cause cavities. In 1928, Rodríguez Vargas demonstrated the use of chemical disinfectants, such as iodine, that could be used to clean the mouth for dental procedures. Rodríguez Vargas became associate professor of bacteriology at Georgetown

University's dental school while concurrently receiving a B.S. degree from the university in 1924. While he remained in the military, he was reassigned to the Army's general dispensary in Boston, Massachusetts, where he worked from 1925 through 1926, and he was then sent to the Holabird Quartermaster Depot in Baltimore, Maryland.

Rodríguez Vargas died from complications associated with pneumonia at Walter Reed Hospital on October 21, 1932, at the age of forty-four. He was buried at Arlington National Cemetery.

Rodríguez Vargas was a member of several professional dental organizations, including the American College of Dentists, International Association of Dental Research, and District of Columbia Dental Society. He posthumously earned a number of awards and honors in recognition of his significant contributions to the field of dentistry. Among these honors, he received a plaque from the American College of Dentists in 1940; seven years later, the U.S. War Department renamed the Army General Hospital at Fort Brooke in San Juan, Puerto Rico, the Rodríguez General Hospital in his honor. After Fort Brooke closed in 1949, an outpatient clinic at Fort Buchanan was renamed the Rodríguez Army Health Clinic. The Puerto Rico College of Dental Surgeons established the Dr. Fernando E. Rodríguez Scientific Contest in his name in 1950.

SIGNIFICANCE

As the first individual to document the underlying biological cause of dental cavities, Rodríguez Vargas helped transform the field of dental medicine. Establishing this etiology allowed others to develop methods of treating this problem. Current hygienic dental practice still focuses upon the elimination of bacteria from the mouth in order to prevent the development of tooth and gum disease. Rodríguez Vargas is a substantial figure in the Latino scientific and military community, as evidenced by the fact that he is the only individual of Puerto Rican ancestry to have a plaque and bust honoring his work at the Walter Reed Army Institute of Research in Washington, D.C.

Janet Ober Berman

FURTHER READING

Kanasi, E., et al. "Microbial Risk Markers for Childhood Caries in Pediatricians' Offices." *Journal of Dental Research* 89, no. 4 (February, 2010): 378-383. Study showing how the *Lactobacillus* species of bacteria is a risk factor for children developing cavities, which Rodríguez Vargas first documented.

Snyer, Lynne Page. "Celebrating Seventy-Five Years of the Dental Corps: Origins and Early Years of Service." *Public Health Reports* 109, no. 5 (September-October, 1994): 710-712. A history of the significant contributions of key individuals in the Army Dental Corps, including Rodríguez Vargas.

Srinivasa Rao, K., et al. "Trace Elemental Analysis of Dental Caries in Human Teeth by External Pixe." *International Journal of Applied Biology and Pharmaceutical Technology* 1, no. 1 (May-July, 2010): 68-78. Describes the pioneering work of Rodríguez Vargas in the field of dental disease and the newer literature now available.

See also: Aristídes Agramonte; Teresa Urrea.

GILBERT ROLAND

Mexican-born actor

Known primarily for playing the Cisco Kid, Roland had leading roles in films from the silent era to the 1980's. He was nominated twice for Golden Globe Awards for his roles in The Bad and the Beautiful (1952) and Cheyenne Autumn (1964).

Latino heritage: Mexican
Born: December 11, 1905; Juárez, Chihuahua, Mexico
Died: May 15, 1994; Beverly Hills, California
Also known as: Luis Antonio Dámaso de Alonso
Area of achievement: Acting

EARLY LIFE

Gilbert Roland was born Luis Antonio Dámaso de Alonso. He moved from Mexico with his family to Texas in 1910 at the onset of the Mexican Revolution. As a child, he wanted to become a bullfighter, like his father. However, in the 1920's, Roland left his family for Los Angeles, where he would become a film star instead. He changed his name to Gilbert Roland, combining the last names of film actors John Gilbert and Ruth Roland, whom he admired greatly.

It was during the 1920's, the silent film era, that Roland came to know actor Rudolph Valentino. Roland's knowledge of bullfighting resulted in his landing the job of preparing Valentino for the bullring scenes in *Blood and Sand* (1922). Legend has it that when a fight broke out among assistants to the stars, Valentino himself tended to the superficial stab wound that Roland endured by using a monogrammed handkerchief for a bandage. Valentino liked Roland and helped create many opportunities for him, not the least of which was the role in the silent film that introduced Roland to actor Clara Bow, *The Plastic Age* (1925). When Valentino suddenly died of peritonitis, Roland could have been Valentino's successor as a "Latin lover," but while Roland would have a lengthy acting career, he would never attain the popularity of his legendary friend.

LIFE'S WORK

As a young man, Roland looked mature beyond his years, but as an older man he seemed to look younger. He was almost 6 feet tall, with hazel eyes and a hairy chest, on which he wore a gold medallion. Not surprisingly, this good-looking young man had numerous romantic encounters. He fell in love with Bow and later with actor Norma Talmadge, with whom he began an

affair on the set of *Camille* (1926). So serious was the relationship between Roland and Talmadge that her husband would not agree to a divorce and made his threats stick when the studios would hire neither actor. Roland and Talmadge never married.

Roland made his first appearance as the Cisco Kid in the 1946 film *The Gay Cavalier*, and he was the only person of Mexican descent to play the role of the Mexican cowboy. Some of Roland's films in the Cisco Kid series credited him with "additional dialogue." Indeed, much of the series's banter was highly personalized, as when an actor reminded Roland of an uncle, and Roland commented on this in the film. This demonstrativeness was characteristic of Roland, who hugged everyone he knew and was not ashamed to cry when appropriate.

Roland served in the Army Air Corps as a lieutenant during World War II. While he was in the service he received many letters, including two from actor Greta Garbo, who described him as "my little soldier" and hoped that the "ladies don't bother you too much." In

Gilbert Roland. (Hulton Archive/Getty Images)

From the Cisco Kid to *Barbarosa*

Gilbert Roland made his first appearance as the Cisco Kid in *The Gay Cavalier* (1946). Many people who initially thought he was a non-Hispanic actor playing a Mexican role soon realized that he really was Mexican. As the Cisco Kid, Roland displays a certain energy when his character gets into the thick of things, as well as a cool way of drawing on a cigarette, placing it behind his ear, and slowly explaining what he is planning to do about his predicament. Roland made six Cisco Kid films, replacing Warner Baxter and César Romero, and in turn being replaced by Duncan Renaldo.

Over the years, Roland was to play many leading and supporting parts. He had major roles in *Camille* (1926), *The Sea Hawk* (1940), *Bullfighter and the Lady* (1951), *The Bad and the Beautiful* (1952), *Thunder Bay* (1953), *Underwater!* (1955), *Guns of the Timberland* (1960), *Cheyenne Autumn* (1964), and the spaghetti Western *Any Gun Can Play* (1967). In *Barbarosa* (1982), his last film, there is a scene in which his character, an elderly, crippled man, looks over the young guns who have agreed to kill Barbarosa after others have died trying. He must pick one of the young men for the job, and the expressions on his face as he sizes up each man are priceless.

1946, Roland divorced actor Constance Bennett, with who he had two daughters, Lorinda and Gyl. He later met Guillermina Cantú, whom he married in 1954 in Yuma, Arizona, and with whom he would spend the remaining forty years of his life. Roland remained interested in bullfighting all his life. In 1951, he starred in the film *The Bullfighter and the Lady*. Roland became a fan of Manolete, the famed Spanish bullfighter, after he watched him perform in the bullring in Mexico, and Roland enjoyed Barnaby Conrad's book *The Death of Manolete* (1958).

In his later years, Roland appeared in small parts in films and made guest appearances on television programs, including *Hart to Hart*, *Barnaby Jones*, *Combat*, and *Zorro*. He played Zorro's father in the television film *The Mark of Zorro* (1974), which gave him the chance to sword fight, proving that the sixty-eight-year-old actor had retained his athletic ability. His last film was *Barbarosa* (1982). Roland died of cancer in 1994 at the age of eighty-eight.

SIGNIFICANCE

At a time when there were few film roles for Latinos, Roland carved a niche for himself in the film industry and later in television. He was nominated for Golden Globe Awards for his roles in *The Bad and the Beautiful* (1952) and *Cheyenne Autumn* (1964), and he has a star on the Hollywood Walk of Fame.

Ernesto M. Bernal

FURTHER READING

Flint, Peter B. "Gilbert Roland Is Dead at 88: Actor from Silent Films to TV." *The New York Times*, May 18, 1994, p. 8. An obituary tracing Roland's career.

Roland, Gilbert. "Valentino Smiled, Shook My Hand, and I Trembled." *TV Guide*, November 22, 1975. Roland recalls the magnetism of the legendary Valentino.

See also: Leo Carrillo; Dolores del Río; Beatriz Noloesca; Ramón Novarro; César Romero; Lupe Velez.

CÉSAR ROMERO

American actor and entertainer

Known for his tall, good looks, suave demeanor, and skill in ballroom dancing, Romero had a long career in film, playing secondary roles. Wearing clown makeup and a green fright wig, he gave a manic and memorable portrayal of the Joker on the television series Batman.

Latino heritage: Cuban
Born: February 15, 1907; New York, New York
Died: January 1, 1994; Santa Monica, California
Also known as: César Julio Romero, Jr.

Areas of achievement: Acting; dance; theater

EARLY LIFE

César Julio Romero (SAY-zahr HOO-lee-oh roh-MAR-oh), Jr., was born and raised in New York City. Both his father, César Julio Romero, who exported sugar refining machinery to Cuba, and his mother, María Mantilla Romero, who was a singer and concert pianist, emigrated from Cuba. Romero's maternal grandfather was the Cuban revolutionary leader José Martí, often called

César Romero. (Time Life Pictures/Getty Images)

"the liberator of Cuba." Growing up, Romero and his three siblings enjoyed an affluent lifestyle. However, he favored a career in the arts rather than joining the family business.

Romero's first acting experience was as a student at the Collegiate School in New York City, where he played four roles in the school production of *The Merchant of Venice*. His good looks made him a popular escort for New York debutantes, but the failure of his father's business resulted in Romero taking a job in a Wall Street bank. In 1927, he was offered an opportunity when heiress Elizabeth Higgins asked him to form a dance team. Romero had never had formal dance lessons, but his years of escorting debutantes to various balls made him a good dancer, and he jumped at the chance. Romero and Higgins appeared at some of New York's most exclusive dinner clubs; their act was a hit, and they were asked to appear in the Broadway revue *Lady Do*. The show opened on April 18, 1927, and Romero and Higgins did the foxtrot, waltz, and tango for fifty-six performances. He and Higgins continued to dance at dinner clubs until 1929.

When Romero injured his shoulder while lifting Nita Vernille, his new dance partner, he turned to the theater. He opened in *The Street Singer* in September, 1929, costarring with Andrew Tombes. During his 191 performances, Romero caught the eye of producer Brock Pemberton, who was looking for a replacement for the romantic lead in *Strictly Dishonorable* (1929). Playing the Count Di Ruvo in this play, Romero starred on Broadway, toured with the road company during the summer, and returned to the Broadway production. He appeared in *The Social Register* during the first half of 1932, and played the role of Ricci, the chauffeur, in the hit show *Dinner at Eight* (1932).

LIFE'S WORK

Romero made his film debut in 1933 in *The Shadow Lights*, and the next year he had a bit part in the hit film *The Thin Man* (1934). At this point he was being touted as the next Rudolph Valentino, but Romero never became a leading actor. Loaned to Universal Studios, Romero had a role in *British Agent* (1934). Universal signed him to a three-year contract, and his role as the sexy gigolo in the comedy *The Good Fairy* (1935) was highly regarded. Subsequently, he was typecast in parts that stressed his image as the "Latin lover." Several films followed for Universal; he was also loaned out to Twentieth Century-Fox studios for a number of films, including *Clive of India* (1935) and *Cardinal Richelieu* (1935). He won the leading role in *The Devil Is a Woman* (1935), but the film was a commercial and critical failure. Its portrayal of the Spanish military so incensed the government of Spain that the film was pulled from theaters after seven months, in effect ending Romero's opportunity to a become leading actor. In 1937, Romero left Universal and contracted with Twentieth Century Fox. He stayed with the company for fifteen years, making as many as five films a year. During the late 1930's and early 1940's he worked with Shirley Temple in *Wee Willie Winkie* (1937) and *The Little Princess* (1939) and skater Sonja Henie in *Happy Landing* (1938). Romero was the first Latino actor to portray the Cisco Kid, which he did in six films, beginning with *The Return of the Cisco Kid* (1939). Not the cowboy type, he played the legendary hero as more of a dandy and rogue than a fighter for justice.

His talent in dance also led to roles in many musicals, including *Weekend in Havana* (1941), *Tall, Dark, and Handsome* (1941), and *Springtime in the Rockies* (1943). Romero enlisted in the U.S. Coast Guard in 1942, serving in various capacities for three years. He rose to the rank of chief boatswain's mate and made frequent public appearances aimed at supporting the troops during World War II. After the war ended, he costarred with Tyrone

Power in *Captain from Castile* (1947); Romero played Spanish explorer Hernán Cortés and considered this his favorite role. Between 1947 and 1949 he made seven films for Twentieth Century-Fox, including the popular romantic musicals *Carnival in Costa Rica* (1947) and *That Lady in Ermine* (1948). In 1950, Romero left Fox to work as an independent actor. He continued to make an average of two films a year for the next thirty years, appearing with big-name actors, such as Gary Cooper and Burt Lancaster in *Vera Cruz* (1954), Frank Sinatra and Dean Martin in the original *Ocean's Eleven* (1960), and John Wayne in *Donovan's Reef* (1963). He also appeared in three Disney studio films, including *The Computer Wore Tennis Shoes* (1969). Romero's final film was a black comedy, *Mortuary Academy* (1988).

Film, however, was not Romero's only venue. Beginning in the 1950's, he regularly appeared on television in a number of variety shows, Westerns, comedies, and dramas. He played the mysterious diplomatic courier Steve McQuinn in the television series *Passport to Danger* (1954-1956). His most well-known television role was the Joker on the television series *Batman* during its 1966-1967 season. As the Joker, he covered his handsome face with white clown makeup, but he refused to shave his mustache, which had to be covered in white greasepaint. He played Batman's enemy with over-the-top comedy and repeated the part in the 1966 film *Batman*. During the 1980's, at age seventy-eight, he began

Musicals with Carmen Miranda

Over the years, César Romero had a number of dancing partners. Perhaps the most flamboyant of them was Carmen Miranda, known as the "Brazilian bombshell." With her exotic good looks, colorful costumes, and tall, fruit-covered headwear, Miranda was a showstopper; she was also a skillful dancer. She and Romero teamed in two musical films: *Weekend in Havana* (1941) and *Springtime in the Rockies* (1942).

In *Weekend in Havana*, Romero plays Monte Blanca, a gambler and the worthless manager and boyfriend of Rosita Rivas, a nightclub star, played by Miranda. When Romero's character romances the leading lady, played by Alice Faye, the fireworks begin when Rosita tries to recapture her boyfriend. In *Springtime in the Rockies*, Romero plays Victor Price, a former dance partner and old flame of the female lead Vicky Lane, played by Betty Grable. Romero dances with both Grable and Miranda, who plays Rosita Murphy, the secretary of the male lead.

playing Peter Stravos, the love interest of Jane Wyman on *Falcon Crest*, appearing in fifty episodes from 1985 through 1988. In 1990, still handsome and debonair, Romero appeared as Tony Delveccio, Sophia's boyfriend in the situation comedy *The Golden Girls*.

Romero never married and continued to appear in dinner theaters, at Hollywood social events, and for charity functions until his death on January 1, 1994. He died at St John's Hospital in Santa Monica, California, from a blood clot, a complication of a severe case of pneumonia.

SIGNIFICANCE

Nicknamed the "Latin from Manhattan," Romero's handsome face, height, and dancer's grace made him a popular actor in film and television. In a career that spanned more than sixty years, he appeared in more than one hundred films and numerous television shows. Romero had roles in Westerns and musicals, as well as dramas and comedies, showing his range as an actor. Although never a leading man, his strength as a character actor kept him before the cameras. In addition, his charm and reliability made him a sought-after actor for numerous television shows. Romero won several awards, including the Imagen Hispanic Media Award for Lifetime Achievement in 1991.

Marcia B. Dinneen

FURTHER READING

Lindgren, Laura. *Legends en Español: The 100 Most Iconic Hispanic Entertainers of All Time*. New York: Penguin, 2008. This bilingual publication includes a biography and color portrait of Romero.

Natale, Richard. "Obituary." *Variety*, January 10, 1994, 68. Discusses Romero's career and what made him the ideal romantic foil in various films.

The New York Times. "César Romero, Actor, Dies at 86." January 3, 1994: A24. An obituary that includes biographical information.

Reyes, Luis, and Peter Rubie. *Hispanics in Hollywood, an Encyclopedia of Film and Television*. New York: Garland, 1994. Describes how Romero portrayed stereotypes of Hispanic characters in films. Includes biographical information and background on specific Romero films.

See also: Leo Carrillo; Dolores del Río; Beatriz Noloesca; Ramón Novarro; Gilbert Roland; Lupe Velez.

GEORGE ROMERO

American film director and screenwriter

Romero has been one of the most influential Latinos in the American film industry. As a young, struggling director of independent films, he managed in Night of the Living Dead *(1968), for which he directed and collaborated on the script, to revolutionize horror films, redefine the mythic monsters frequently depicted in such films, and restructure the tropes of the genre.*

Latino heritage: Cuban
Born: February 4, 1940; New York, New York
Also known as: George Andrew Romero
Areas of achievement: Filmmaking; screenwriting

EARLY LIFE

George Andrew Romero (jorg AN-drew roh-MAR-oh) was born in New York City to a father of Cuban descent and a mother of Lithuanian background. While still a small boy, he was given an eight-millimeter film camera for his birthday. Soon he was writing and directing short films which were shown to relatives and neighbors. Upon graduating from high school in New

George Romero. (AP Photo)

York, he moved to Pittsburgh, Pennsylvania, which would long be the center of his creative activities, to attend Carnegie Mellon University. Upon graduating from college in 1960, Romero returned briefly to New York City, where he obtained work making short industrial films and commercials. These jobs led to his first significant employment as a member of the staff of the popular children's television program, *Mr. Rogers' Neighborhood.* Reputedly, Romero was first drawn to the horror genre after filming an episode of this program in which Mr. Rogers has to have his tonsils removed.

Eager to work on feature-length films, Romero banded together with several like-minded friends, especially John Russo, to form a production company, Image Ten Productions. The company's first production was *Night of the Living Dead* (1968), based on a screenplay by Romero and Russo and produced by two other members of the Image Ten team, Russell Streiner and Karl Hardman, both of whom also acted in the low-budget film. *Night of the Living Dead* was financed with money from the writers, the producers, and various friends and associates of theirs. It soon became one of the most popular and influential horror films of all time.

LIFE'S WORK

When *Night of the Living Dead* premiered in Pittsburgh in early October, 1968, it drew little critical reception, and most of the reaction was negative, criticizing the film's ghoulishness, literally and figuratively, and its graphic gore, which was remarkably intense for the time. Soon, however, in large part because of word of mouth among young people, the film began to draw huge crowds. By the end of the 1970's, it had earned about $15 million dollars in the United States and twice that in foreign countries. By the early 1970's, it was considered a classic and analyzed repeatedly in articles in cinema journals and in discussions in college film studies classes.

Romero filmed fairly consistently throughout the rest of the twentieth and early twenty-first centuries, but his first few films after the breakthrough success of *Night of the Living Dead* were not as successful critically or financially. The first, *There's Always Vanilla* (1971), followed the attempts of a typical young couple of the era as they experiment with drugs, free sex, and revolutionary politics. His next film, *Jack's Wife*, which in later

---

Night of the Living Dead

The first film in what would eventually become one of the most successful and influential franchises in American film history, *Night of the Living Dead* was truly groundbreaking. Although the popular Hammer horror films from England that began in the 1950's had been more direct in their use of blood and sexuality on screen than had their older Universal studio counterparts, nothing prepared the first audiences of *Night* for George Romero's spectacle of the bloody, maimed, sometimes naked undead consuming human entrails and chewing on the bones of their victims. Thereafter, graphic gore quickly became a staple of horror films, not only in the United States but also in Europe.

Most American horror films had heretofore been fairly apolitical. However, once critics regained their senses after their initial negative reactions to Romero's use of gore and *Night of the Living Dead*'s downbeat ending, they quickly reassessed the film, in which a microcosm of Americans (young and old, black and white, male and female) confined in a small farmhouse try to survive a night of attacks by mysteriously reanimated corpses who feed upon the living, as a political allegory of late-1960's America. Pundits quickly saw the film as reflecting race relations, gender inequities, youthful revolution, rampant consumerism, and Cold War fears.

In an interview in 2010, Romero freely admitted that he used his zombies to explore social and political issues metaphorically—but without being explicit about the issues he was addressing. *Night* also revamped the traditional image of the cinematic zombie, who was usually a shambling, ambling, blank-eyed automaton in early horror films; Romero's film added to his zombies the predatory cannibalism of another folkloric creature, the ghoul, traditionally an undead monster who feeds on human corpses.

Despite Romero's impressive innovations in *Night of the Living Dead*, his influences should not be overlooked, especially that of the veteran director of thrillers, Alfred Hitchcock. The basic storyline of *Night of the Living Dead*, which begins when Barbara, ostensibly the film's protagonist, enters the countryside, where she is soon attacked and besieged in claustrophobic surroundings by inexplicable aggressors, mirrors the plots of two of Hitchcock classics, *Psycho* (1960) and *The Birds* (1963). Both of these works feature an attractive young blond woman much like Barbara traveling to remote rural areas, where they fall victim to inexplicable attacks in confined spaces, leading either to their death (Marion in the shower stall in *Psycho*) or to their retreat into near-comatose silence (Melanie in *The Birds*).

---

release was called *Season of the Witch* (1972), dealt with social issues of the time, but with a return of supernatural elements similar to those of *Night of the Living Dead*. The title character, angered by her abusive husband and disrespectful daughter, experiments with witchcraft as a means of empowerment. Romero's next two films, however, earned a modicum of success. *The Crazies* (1973), which was thematically similar to *Night of the Living Dead*, depicts a neighborhood in which suburbanites become violently homicidal as a result of environmental pollution, and *Martin* (1978) is about a murderous young sociopath who imagines himself to be—or pretends to be—a vampire. *Martin* became popular on the arthouse/independent film circuit and drew critical acclaim.

Nevertheless, major success eluded Romero until he returned to the genre he had all but created, the contemporary zombie film, with the immensely popular sequels to *Night of the Living Dead*, *Dawn of the Dead* (1978) and *Day of the Dead* (1985). Further sequels followed over the next few decades: *Document of the Dead* (1985), *Land of the Dead* (2005), *Diary of the Dead* (2008), and *Survival of the Dead* (2010). More-

over, he wrote, but did not direct, two remakes of his first two zombie films, *Night of the Living Dead* (1990) and *Dawn of the Dead* (2004).

Other than the zombie films, Romero's most successful work commercially has involved collaboration with horror writer Stephen King: the anthology film *Creepshow* (1992), directed by Romero from a screenplay by King based on some of his own stories that he and Romero felt reflected the lurid horror comics of the 1950's that both men had loved as boys, and *The Dark Half* (1993), directed by Romero from his own screenplay based on King's best-selling novel of that title.

SIGNIFICANCE

With *Night of the Living Dead*, George Romero rewrote popular folklore and thereby revised the tropes and conventions of the horror film, creating inadvertently a new subgenre, one which was quickly emulated by other directors, as in the Return of the Evil Dead series, and spoofed in seriocomic films, such as *Shaun of the Dead* (2004) and *Zombieland* (2009). This reinvigorated zombie genre as redefined by Romero spread to horror fiction as well, inspiring the novel *Cell* (2006) by Stephen King, the most popular and well-established horror writer in American history. Romero also demonstrated how the horror film not only could offer its viewers the traditional chills and thrills but also could treat political and social issues effectively.

Thomas Du Bose

FURTHER READING

Gagne, Paul R. *The Zombies That Ate Pittsburgh: The Films of George Romero.* New York: Dodd, Mead, 1987. Entertaining, popularly oriented history of Romero's career through the late 1980's.

Romero, George. "10 Questions" (Interview). *Time,* June 7, 2010, 4. Brief but meaty interview in which Romero addresses the relationship between his zombie films and sociopolitical concerns.

Russell, Jamie. *Book of the Dead: The Complete History of Zombie Cinema.* Surrey, England: Fab Press, 2005. Detailed overview of zombie films before and after *Night of the Living Dead.*

Twitchell, James B. *Dreadful Pleasures: An Anatomy of Modern Horror.* New York: Oxford University Press, 1985. Pages 266 through 271 contain concise analyses of *Night of the Living Dead* and *Martin,* including a pithy assessment of how Romero combined elements of various folkloric creatures to reinvent and reinvigorate the zombie film genre.

Williams, Tony. *Knight of the Living Dead: The Cinema of George A. Romero.* London: Wallflower Press, 2003. Similar to Gagne (see above) but a bit deeper and more scholarly.

See also: Raúl Juliá; Sylvia Morales; Robert Rodriguez; Martin Sheen.

OSCAR I. ROMO

American religious leader, theologian, and social reformer

Romo served as the first Hispanic in an executive position in a Southern Baptist Convention program. During his twenty-five years as director of the Language Church Extension Division of the North American Mission Board (originally known as the Home Mission Board) in Atlanta, Georgia, Romo led the denomination to minister to 103 ethnic groups and 97 Native American Indian tribes with 98 languages represented. Under his guidance, the number of congregations ministering to non-English-speaking groups grew from less than a thousand to nine thousand. Romo also provided leadership to Baptists in Panama, Cuba, and American Samoa.

Latino heritage: Mexican

Born: January 29, 1929; Lockhart, Texas

Died: January 16, 2009; Cumming, Georgia

Also known as: Oscar Ishmael Romo; Ismael Romo, Jr.; Oscar Ismael Romo

Areas of achievement: Religion and theology; social issues

EARLY LIFE

Oscar Ishmael Romo (AHS-kahr IHSH-may-ehl ROH-moh), the youngest of five siblings and the only son, was born to Concepción Ortega and Ismael Romo in Lockhart, Texas, on January 29, 1929. Romo's father was a blacksmith and grocer in the Mexican American community of Lockhart; his mother stayed at home, although she had been educated as a teacher in Mexico. The family included Romo's maiden aunt, who had accompanied his mother from Mexico when the two sisters fled the Mexican Revolution. Romo's parents had both been raised as Protestants.

In 1940, at the age of ten, Romo was invited to attend Vacation Bible School at the First Baptist Church in Lockhart and became the first Hispanic Baptist in Lockhart. The following year, the family moved to San Antonio, because Romo's father had been taken to a hospital there after being kicked by a mule. As a young boy, Romo thought that the best way he could fight social injustice was to become a lawyer. However, it was during his junior high school years, while working in a grocery store that was visited repeatedly by his pastor, D. H. Roberts, that Romo realized he wanted to make the church his life. With Roberts's help, Romo obtained a music scholarship and attended Howard Payne University in Brownwood, Texas. Romo had to work three jobs in Brownwood to make ends meet and send money home, but he was ordained as a Baptist minister in 1949.

After graduating with a B.A. in 1951, Romo studied at Southwestern Baptist Theological Seminary in Fort Worth, Texas, receiving his master's of divinity in 1956. Eventually, Romo earned his doctor of ministries, multicultural and multilingual studies, from Austin Presbyterian Theological Seminary in Austin, Texas, in 1982. Romo also was awarded many honorary doctoral degrees from universities in California, Missouri, and Texas. In June, 1956, Romo married Zoe Harmon, whom he had met while studying at the seminary. They adopted two children, Nelson and Miriam.

LIFE'S WORK

While in Brownwood, Romo began pastoring churches and continued during his time at the seminary. As the pastor of a growing church, Romo knew the difficulties faced by a Mexican congregation trying to establish itself. When he requested a loan from the Baptist General Convention of Texas for his church and was turned down, it made him all the more determined to show the church leadership that Mexican Americans were worthy of the church's trust and financial assistance. He eventually prevailed upon the leaders to grant a ninety-day loan, and the congregation repaid it in sixty-five days. This and other similar demonstrations of skill in bridging the gap between Hispanic congregants and the church leadership led to the establishment of the Latin American Loan Fund.

When he graduated from the seminary Romo was offered the position of associate in the Language Missions Department of the Texas Baptist Convention, and he moved to Dallas with his new bride. He served there until 1965. With his success in planting and growing Hispanic Baptist congregations in Texas, Romo became the first ethnic American to be asked to join the staff of the Home Mission Board in Atlanta, Georgia. He moved his family to Atlanta in 1965. Romo was an assistant secretary in the Language Missions Department of the Home Mission Board from 1965 to 1970. In 1971, he became the director of the Language Missions Division (formerly Department) and served in that capacity until 1989, when the scope of the program changed and he continued as director of the Language Church Extension Division until his retirement in 1994. After his first wife died, he married Merry Purvis, who had worked with him at the Home Mission Board. Upon retirement, he founded Mosaic Ministries, a nonprofit organization to assist evangelical denominations in their evangelization of ethnic America. Romo died of complications from Parkinson's disease in 2009.

SIGNIFICANCE

Romo directed the first statewide Latin American Kindergarten Workshop, the first Latin American Baptist Youth Congress in 1965, and the first Catalytic Church Growth Conference in 1966. Romo contributed to several denominational publications, serving as editor of *El Boletín Bautista, El Estandarte Bautista* (Spanish edition of *The Baptist Standard*). He led in the establishment of theological training in Puerto Rico and the Ethnic Branch of the New Orleans Baptist Theological Seminary in Miami. He worked with Australia and New Zealand to establish a ministry to ethnics. Romo initiated work among international seamen in fifty ports and founded the Southern Baptist Refugee Resettlement Office in 1975. He established Christian Ministries to the United Nations in New York in 1980 and worked with diplomats in Washington, D.C. A major focus of his work overseas was in the Baptist Church in Cuba from 1970 through 1990, when congregations grew in number from 68 to 105. Romo was honored by the Southern Baptist Hispanic Pastors Conference as Hispanic Baptist Statesman of the Century in August, 1992.

Norma A. Mouton

FURTHER READING

Romo, Oscar I. *American Mosaic: Church Planting in Ethnic America*. Nashville, Tenn.: Broadman Press, 1993. Outlines the multitude of ethnic groups in the United States and how to meet their spiritual needs through the founding of churches specific to those needs.

_____. "Ministering with Hispanic Americans." In *Missions in the Mosaic*, edited by M. Wendell Belew. Atlanta, Ga.: Home Mission Board of the Southern Baptist Convention, 1974. Describes challenges in evangelizing Hispanic Americans.

See also: Fray Angélico Chávez; Virgilio Elizondo.

TONY ROMO

American football player

Romo is best known as an undrafted free agent who became an all-pro quarterback for the Dallas Cowboys of the National Football League. He also has had success as a golfer on the Celebrity Players Tour and has attempted to qualify for the U.S. Open golf tournament.

Latino heritage: Mexican
Born: April 21, 1980; San Diego, California
Also known as: Antonio Ramiro Romo
Area of achievement: Football

EARLY LIFE

Antonio Ramiro Romo (ROH-moh) is a third-generation Mexican American, who was born in San Diego, California, to Ramiro and Joan Romo. He is the youngest of three children and has two older sisters, Danielle and Jossalyn. After Ramiro got out of the Navy in 1982, the family moved to Burlington, Wisconsin, known as Chocolate City, U.S.A., because of the Nestlé Chocolate and Confection Company located there.

Growing up, Romo played all sports and had such success in basketball, golf, and football that he earned all-state honors in all three sports. Interestingly, he rarely played football until he was in high school and did not become the starting quarterback until he was a junior. Romo would eventually throw for nearly 4,000 yards and 42 touchdowns in two seasons at Burlington High School and earn honorable-mention status on the Wisconsin Football Coaches Association All-State Team his junior years and first team honors his senior year. Additionally, he was named the 1997 Player of the Year by the *Racine Journal Times*.

Nevertheless, he was not recruited heavily out of high school and wound up getting only a partial scholarship to attend Eastern Illinois University, a Division 1-AA school in Charleston. However, he continued to have success at Eastern, becoming a starter in his sophomore year and ultimately setting both school and conference records with 8,212 passing yards and 85 touchdowns on his way to being named All-Ohio Valley Conference and Ohio Valley Conference Player of the Year three years in a row and earning All-American status for three consecutive years. To top it all off, in his senior year he became the first Eastern Illinois and Ohio Valley Conference player to win the Walter Payton Award, given to the top offensive player in Division 1-AA football and the equivalent to the Heisman Trophy for players in Division 1-A. In 2009, he was inducted into Eastern Illinois University's Hall of Fame and was the first player to have his number retired.

LIFE'S WORK

In February, 2003, Romo attended the National Football League (NFL) Combine in Indianapolis, an event at which NFL prospects are evaluated. He did nothing to distinguish himself and did not get drafted; instead, he entered the NFL in 2003 as a free agent with the Dallas Cowboys.

After three seasons as a backup, Romo began the 2006 season as a backup to starter Drew Bledsoe, but Romo took his first regular-season snap against the Houston Texans. He made the most of it by going 2-2 passing for 35 yards, with his first NFL completion going to Sam Hurd for 33 yards. Later in the game Romo threw his first regular-season touchdown pass to Terrell Owens. Two games later Romo got his first start against the Carolina Panthers and guided the Cowboys to a win. He ultimately would help lead the Cowboys to

Tony Romo. (AP Photo)

second place in the National Football Conference East Division and a Wild Card spot in the play-offs, and he was selected to the Pro Bowl after the season ended. He has established a number of Cowboys' records, including most games passing over 300 yards, most passing touchdowns in a season, most passing yards in a season, and most completions in a season.

Off the field, Romo has contributed his time and money to Burlington High School, Eastern Illinois University, the Make-A-Wish Foundation, the Salvation Army, and the United Way. After his father was diagnosed with prostate cancer, Romo began participating in events to help raise money to help find cures and treatments for cancer. In May, 2011, Romo married Candice Crawford in a ceremony in Dallas.

SIGNIFICANCE

Burlington's motto is "The Town with Tall Tales" because of its association with a long-standing community group called the Burlington Liars Club. Romo's story might sound like one of those tall tales, as he has risen from a small, Midwestern town to the heights of professional success. He was not heavily recruited coming out of high school and not drafted coming out of college from a Division 1-AA school. He had to battle perceptions about his height, speed, and background but would eventually make it to the top of his profession as an All-Pro quarterback with a multimillion-dollar contract with the Cowboys and a multimillion-dollar endorsement deal with Starter.

He also would become the focus of media attention for dating celebrities such as Carrie Underwood and Jessica Simpson, and he became the number-one-ranked player in the Golf Digest 2009 rating of athlete golfers. In addition, he was the winner of the 2010 Brodie Award, named for former NFL quarterback and Senior Professional Golf Association Tour member John Brodie, being recognized for his accomplishments in both a chosen profession and the sport of golf.

Paul Finnicum

FURTHER READING

Bednar, Chuck. *Tony Romo*. Broomall, Pa.: Mason Crest, 2008. This was written for nine-to-twelve-year-olds but provides great pictures and numerous statistics that paint the picture of Romo's career.

Engel, Mac. *America's Next Quarterback: Tony Romo*. Chicago: Triumph Books, 2007. This book is written with the Dallas Cowboys fans in mind, using extensive illustrations that follow Romo from high school to his all-pro career in the National football League.

Sandler, Michael. *Tony Romo*. New York: Bearport, 2010. A brief look at Romo's development from star high school quarterback to all-pro quarterback in the NFL.

See also: Tedy Bruschi; Manny Fernández; Tom Flores; Jeff Garcia; Tony Gonzalez; Anthony Muñoz.

LINDA RONSTADT

American singer

Best known for her reign as the "Queen of Rock" in the 1970's and 1980's, Ronstadt has enjoyed one of the most successful careers of any American singer, and she managed for decades to maintain a large fan base while experimenting with a wide array of musical genres, including rock, jazz, folk, opera, and mariachi.

Latino heritage: Mexican
Born: July 15, 1946; Tucson, Arizona
Also known as: Linda Marie Ronstadt
Areas of achievement: Music; theater

EARLY LIFE

Linda Marie Ronstadt (LIHN-dah MAH-ree RON-stat) was born in Tucson, Arizona, to Gilbert Ronstadt and

Ruth Mary Copeman Ronstadt. Ronstadt's father's family was descended from a German engineer who had immigrated to Mexico in the middle of the nineteenth century; the family eventually moved to Tucson. Gilbert met Ruth Mary, the daughter of a prominent inventor, in college when both were attending the University of Arizona in Tucson.

Linda Ronstadt and her brothers and sister, Peter, Michael, and Suzi, were brought up in a close-knit family and exposed by their father to a wide variety of music. Among the many singers the siblings grew up listening to were Frank Sinatra, Ella Fitzgerald, Billie Holiday, Peggy Lee, Hank Williams, Edith Piaf, Elvis Presley, and Mexican music icon Lola Beltrán. Gilbert Ronstadt sang semiprofessionally, both in concert and on local radio, and his sister Luisa toured with a band singing Mexican songs. Michael, Linda, and Suzi formed a singing group while they were still quite young that performed around Tucson for a number of years, calling themselves, among other names, the Three Ronstadts and the Union City Ramblers. Another young musician with whom Linda sometimes performed at the time was Bob Kimmel, who soon moved to California to pursue a career in music.

After a single semester at the University of Arizona, Ronstadt found herself following her friend Kimmel to the West Coast to see if she could also find work in the recording industry. Ronstadt arrived in Los Angeles in 1964 during a time of great growth and experimentation within the popular music community there, and she quickly became acquainted with a host of soon-to-be famous singers, musicians, and songwriters, including, among others, Bonnie Raitt, Frank Zappa, Jackson Browne, and the members of the Eagles, the Turtles, and the Beach Boys.

With Kimmel and a singer-songwriter named Kenny Edwards, Ronstadt formed a folk-pop trio called The Stone Poneys, the name of which was taken from the title of a song by blues musician Charlie Patton. The group resembled two leading folk-rock bands of the

Linda Ronstadt. (AP Photo)

time, Peter, Paul, and Mary and the Seekers, both of which performed blends of traditional folk music and modern folk-inflected pop songs, and both of which featured charismatic female lead singers. The Stone Poneys released three albums that synthesized folk, country, and rock, but the group met with little critical and popular success except for one single, "Different Drum," a song written by Michael Nesmith of the Monkees. "Different Drum" became a Top 20 hit in 1968, but the three band members had become thoroughly disenchanted, and they broke up soon after the release of their third and final album later that year.

LIFE'S WORK

Soon after the break-up of the Stone Poneys, Ronstadt began work on her first solo album, *Hand Sown . . . Home Grown*, produced by Chip Douglas, who had worked with the Monkees. The record contained a number of songs written by Nesmith, as well as compositions by Randy Newman, Bob Dylan, and former bandmate Edwards. Released in 1969, the album drew little attention, but her next ablum, *Silk Purse*, yielded her first Top 30 hit, "Long, Long Time," which also won her a Grammy Award nomination for best country vocal performance. Like her first album, *Silk Purse* consisted primarily of rock, pop, folk, and country songs, as did her third, *Linda Ronstadt* (1972). Her back-up band for this album included Glenn Frey, Don Henley, and Bernie Leadon, who later became the Eagles.

For her next album, Ronstadt hired as her manager and producer former English pop star Peter Asher, and with his assistance she embarked on her most productive period. Their first collaboration, *Don't Cry Now* (1973), reached the Top 50 of the album charts. Their next project, *Heart like a Wheel* (1974), was Ronstadt's breakthrough, regarded as one of the best pop albums of the 1970's. It yielded several hugely popular singles, especially "You're No Good" and "When Will I Be Loved?" and established a paradigm for her subsequent albums of the 1970's: *Prisoner in Disguise* (1975), *Hasten Down the Wind* (1976), *Simple Dreams* (1977), and *Living in the U.S.A.* (1978). All these best-selling albums feature an appealing mixture of cover versions of classic pop hits from a variety of genres, including early rock and roll, country, soul, and folk, and new songs written by up-and-coming young contemporary songwriters, such as Karla Bonoff and Warren Zevon. In 1987, Ronstadt collaborated with her close friends Emmylou Harris and Dolly Parton on a much-delayed joint project, the album *Trio*.

Ronstadt and Mariachi Music

Linda Ronstadt's two albums of Spanish-language songs, recorded in 1987 and 1993, seem to be both a labor of love and an evocation of childhood experiences involving her family in Tucson, Arizona. She had mentioned in various interviews how she had grown up listening to mariachi music. Her father Gilbert often played Spanish-language records in their home and performed it professionally, and her Aunt Luisa toured the United States in the 1920's and 1930's, performing traditional dances, singing Mexican songs, and telling Mexican folktales.

The title of Ronstadt's first Spanish-language album, *Canciones de Mi Padre,* was taken from an anthology of Mexican songs that Luisa Ronstadt had assembled and published in honor of her father, Linda's grandfather. By borrowing her aunt's title and including some of her father's favorite songs, Linda honored her grandfather, her father, and her aunt simultaneously. The songs themselves represent many types of mariachi songs—*corridos* (stories in song format); *rancheras* (rural folk songs); dance numbers such as *huapangos* and *habaneras;* and Mexican cowboy songs. Two of the songs on the album were favorites of her father's—"La Barca de Guaymas" and "Dos Arbolitos"—and on the drinking song "Y Andale," she sings with her niece, Mindy Ronstadt. The second album, *Mas Canciones,* is also a family affair. Several songs are sung by Ronstadt and her two brothers, and her father drew some of the artwork.

A superstar for much of the 1970's, Ronstadt saw her career falter somewhat in the 1980's, as she experimented briefly with trends of the time, such as New Wave and synthesizer-laden pop. However, she found success exploring musical venues other than rock and mainstream pop. She joined the cast of producer Joseph Papp's revival of Gilbert and Sullivan's *The Pirates of Penzance* in 1980 and drew positive reviews. After recording the cast album and appearing in a film of the production, she moved from operetta to opera, singing the role of Mimi in a New York production of *La Boheme.* She then worked with famed bandleader Nelson Riddle on a trio of albums of prerock popular music classics, *What's New?* (1983), *Lush Life* (1984), and *For Sentimental Reasons* (1986), featuring such songs as "What'll I Do?" and "Am I Blue?" Her most expansive musical statement about her Latino heritage came in a pair of albums, *Canciones de mi Padre* (1987) and *Mas Canciones* (1993), which were collections of Mexican folk and pop songs sung in Spanish. The first of these went double-platinum, selling more than two million copies, and both won Grammy Awards. After her success with mariachi albums, Ronstadt continued to record in diverse styles: children's music, jazz, Cajun songs, Caribbean music, and collaborations with minimalist composer Philip Glass.

SIGNIFICANCE

Although the terms "icon" and "superstar" are often overused, they are probably not hyperbolic in reference to Linda Ronstadt. She dominated the American pop music scene for almost two decades, made a record amount of money, and was nominated for almost thirty Grammy Awards, winning eleven of them. Her eclectic musical tastes introduced many young Americans to musical genres that they might not otherwise have encountered, and her phenomenal success paved the way for other women in rock and pop, not only those of Latina heritage, such as Christina Aguilera and Shakira, but also other women, like Madonna and Lady Gaga.

Thomas Du Bose

FURTHER READING

Bego, Mark. *Linda Ronstadt: It's So Easy!* Austin, Tex.: Eakin Press, 1990. Perhaps too adulatory of, even star-struck by, its subject, but a good overview of the singer's career and source of direct quotations from Ronstadt.

Berman, Connie. *Linda Ronstadt.* Proteus, 1983. An insightful look at Ronstadt just as her career was moving from its "Rock Queen" phase to a more experimental era.

Hoskyns, Barney. *Hotel California.* Hoboken, N.J.: John Wiley and Sons, 2006. Colorful evocation of the California milieu in which Ronstadt moved early in her career.

O'Brien, Lucy. *She-Bop: The Definitive History of Women in Rock, Pop, and Soul.* New York: Penguin, 1996. Provides a good context for Ronstadt's long career in various styles of popular music.

See also: Joan Baez; Rubén Blades; Vikki Carr; Mimi Fariña; José Feliciano; Julio Iglesias; Carlos Santana; Ritchie Valens.

ILEANA ROS-LEHTINEN

Cuban-born politician

Ros-Lehtinen was elected to the Florida House of Representatives in 1982 and the state senate in 1986, making her the first Latina to serve in either office. She was elected to the U.S. House of Representatives in 1989, making her the first Latina to serve in Congress.

Latino heritage: Cuban

Born: July 15,1952; Havana, Cuba

Also known as: Ileana Ros y Adato Lehtinen; Ileana Ros y Adato; Lily

Area of achievement: Government and politics

EARLY LIFE

Ileana Ros y Adato Lehtinen, better known as Ileana Ros-Lehtinen (IHL-ee-AHN-ah rahs-LAY-tih-nehn), was born in Havana, Cuba, on July 15, 1952. Her family immigrated to the United States when she was eight years old after they were forced to leave Cuba to escape the oppressive communist regime of Fidel Castro. Her family, which included a brother, settled in the Miami area. Ros-Lehtinen is the daughter of Amanda Adato Ros and Enrique Emilio Ros, who became a Florida-based Cuban businessman. Ros-Lehtinen's parents, along with fellow Cubans who had escaped to America, were involved in plotting the downfall of the Castro regime. After the failed invasion at the Bay of Pigs in 1961, the possibility of the family's returning to Cuba became remote and Enrique Ros vowed to raise his children with ethnic pride in their Cuban roots, as well as patriotism for the country to which they had relocated. Ros-Lehtinen's maternal grandparents were Sephardic Jews from Turkey, active in Cuba's Jewish community. Her mother eventually converted to Catholicism and Ros-Lehtinen became an Episcopalian.

Ros-Lehtinen attended Southside Elementary School in Miami's Little Havana neighborhood, West Miami Junior High, and Southwest High School. She received her A.A. degree from Miami-Dade Community College in 1972. She then attended Florida International University, receiving her B.A. in 1975 and a M.S. in English in 1985. She also earned a Ph.D. in education at the University of Miami in 2004. Before entering politics, Ros-Lehtinen was an educator and administrator at Eastern Academy, a private bilingual elementary school she founded in Hialeah, Florida.

LIFE'S WORK

Ros-Lehtinen was led into politics by the values and national pride her father Enrique instilled in her and by the parents and students of Eastern Academy, who urged her to fight on their behalf for lower taxes, improvement of the educational system, and a more promising economic future. When Ros-Lehtinen was elected in 1982 to the Florida State House of Representatives and in 1986 to the state senate, she became the first Latino woman to serve in either office. She was a member of the Florida House of Representatives from 1982 through 1986 and served in the state senate from 1986 through 1989.

On June 9, 1984, she married Dexter Lehtinen. She is the stepmother of Douglas and Katherine Lehtinen, and she and Lehtinen had two children together, Dexter Rodrigo and Patricia Marie Lehtinen.

In a special election held in 1989, Ros-Lehtinen, a Republican, was chosen to fill the vacancy created by the death of U.S. Representative Claude Pepper, and she was subsequently reelected ten times. In 2011, she

Ileana Ros-Lethinen. (AFP/Getty Images)

Ros-Lehtinen's Anti-Castro Efforts

True to her ethnic heritage and upbringing, Ileana Ros-Lehtinen remains a fierce adversary of Fidel Castro's dictatorship and an advocate for a free Cuba. In 2011, she chaired the House Committee on Foreign Affairs, and she has this committee as a platform to denounce Castro's oppressive regime, as well as express her support of Israel and human rights. She works with other members of the Cuban-American Lobby to put pressure on the Cuban government in order to promote political change. She organized the Cuba Democracy Group in 2004 to prevent U.S. banks from doing business with the Cuban government and to curtail American agricultural exports to this nation.

Ros-Lehtinen was outspoken against South African leader Nelson Mandela's visit to Florida because of his support of Palestine Liberation Organization leader Yasir Arafat, Libyan leader Muammar al-Qaddafi, and the Castro regime. She stated that Cuban Americans who wanted to return to a democracy in their country of origin could not overlook the fact that members of Mandela's African National Congress had received military training on Cuban soil. She voted against holding the Pan American Games in Cuba in August, 1991, believing that any boost to the failing Cuban economy is an effort by Castro to strengthen his power. As a native Cuban who escaped to America as a child, she not only strives to end the oppression in Castro's communist regime, but also works to end terrorism and persecution by corrupt governments throughout the world.

chaired the House Committee on Foreign Affairs, and she has served on the Subcommittee on Western Hemisphere Affairs and the Subcommittee on Employment and Housing.

True to her political affiliation with the conservative Republican Party, Ros-Lehtinen opposes abortion unless it is necessary to save the mother's life and favors a constitutional amendment to ban flag burning. She also supports tax cuts, the elimination of unnecessary government spending, and increasing tax incentives for small businesses and middle-class families.

Ros-Lehtinen, who founded a school that provided bilingual education, is a proponent of bilingual instruction. While in the Florida legislature, she passed a bill in 1986 creating the Florida Prepaid College Plan, which became the largest prepaid college tuition program in the nation. More than one million students have used the program to go to college. As a congresswoman,

Ros-Lehtinen has worked to improve the Federal Application For Student Aid by making the process easier and available to more students.

Ros-Lehtinen is a strong advocate for women, and she has voted to reinstate the Violence Against Women Act, which increases resources for women seeking help as the result of domestic abuse, sexual assault, or dating assault. She also supports legislation to increase criminal penalties for people who commit Medicare fraud.

The wife of a Vietnam War veteran and the stepmother of U.S. Marine aviators, Ros-Lehtinen works to improve the military and to provide health care and education for veterans. She voted to authorize military force in Iraq and for solidarity with Israel in its fight against terrorism. She has been a leader in foreign policy issues, such as the fight against Islamist extremism, and she is against free trade agreements with Columbia, Panama, and South Korea. She promotes war only when necessary as means of protection for people oppressed by corrupt governments. Ros-Lehtinen was also a proponent of the Iran Sanction Act, which aimed to end that nation's nuclear development program.

Ros-Lehtinen voted in favor of the Water Resources Development Act, which will environmentally restore and develop South Florida's coral reefs and the Miami River. She participated in a scuba dive to the Aquarius Habitat, where she appeared on a live underwater broadcast shown to third- to sixth-graders at the Islamorada Montessori School who were learning about coral reefs in the Florida Keys.

SIGNIFICANCE

Ileana Ros-Lehtinen has made an impact on the Latino Cuban community as the first Latina to serve in the U.S. Congress. As a representative of Florida's Eighteenth Congressional District, which includes Miami, Miami Beach, Little Havana, Pinecrest, Coral Gables, Westchester, and the Florida Keys, she is an advocate for the diverse social issues and needs of the people she represents. Being a representative for Florida and for Latinos, as well as a Latina, is something she takes seriously. As a political pioneer, she has opened the doors for the success of other Latinos, and she encourages the empowerment of other Latinas.

Crystal Wolfe

FURTHER READING

Black, Chris. "Miami Voices." *Boston Globe*, August 31, 1989, 3. Discusses Ros-Lehtinen's election to

Congress, providing biographical information and explaining why she became involved in politics.

Parker, Laura. "Cuban Americans Lead in Races for House Seat: Pepper Long Represented Miami District." *The Washington Post*, July 30, 1989, p. A3. Covers Ros-Lehtinen's bid for U.S. Congress.

Ros-Lehtinen, Ileana. Congresswoman Ileana Ros-Lehtinen: Representing the 18th District of Florida. http://ros-lehtinen.house.gov. The congresswoman's official Web site, providing information on her biography, positions, and activities.

Telgen, Diane, and Jim Kamp, eds. *Notable Hispanic American Woman*. Detroit: Gale Research, 1993.

Includes a profile listing Ros-Lehtinen's accomplishments in the Latino community.

Time. "Miami: End of a Bitter Race." September 11, 1989, 31. Discusses the election in which Ros-Lehtinen became the first Latina to be elected to Congress.

Wait, Marianne. "Women of the House." *Ladies' Home Journal*, November, 1991, 180. Ros-Lehtinen and two other congresswomen discuss how they make their homes "vote-winning."

See also: Luis Gutiérrez; Joseph Marion Hernández; Edward R. Roybal; Loretta Sánchez; Leticia Van de Putte.

EDWARD R. ROYBAL

American politician

Roybal was one of the most successful Latino politicians of his generation, serving both as a member of the Los Angeles City Council and for thirty years in the U.S. House of Representatives. His career symbolizes the gains made by Latino Americans in the second half of the twentieth century.

Latino heritage: Mexican
Born: February 10, 1916; Albuquerque, New Mexico
Died: October 24, 2005; Pasadena, California
Also known as: Edward Ross Roybal; Ed Roybal
Area of achievement: Government and politics

EARLY LIFE

Edward Ross Roybal (ROY-bahl) was born in Albuquerque, New Mexico, on February 10, 1916.The Roybal family traced its roots back many generations in New Mexico. In 1922, a rail strike caused his unemployed father to move the family to the Boyle Heights neighborhood of East Los Angeles, where Roybal attended public school, receiving his high school diploma in 1934. Following a stint in the Civilian Conservation Corps, he pursued studies in business administration at the University of California at Los Angeles and law at Southwestern University. In the early 1940's, he gained employment with the California Tuberculosis Association. Following military service in World War II, from 1944 through 1945, he returned to his former job, eventually becoming the director of health education at the Los Angeles County Tuberculosis and Health Association.

As a child Roybal learned at first hand the effects of racial discrimination. One example from his early years occurred when Latinos were banned from using a local swimming pool, except for a brief period of time before it was cleaned and disinfected. In 1947, his feelings regarding discrimination, as well as a growing interest in politics, led him to run for the Los Angeles City Council. Running in a district whose population was 34 percent Latino, he was unable to gain broader support and lost to longtime incumbent Parley P. Christensen. Following the election, Roybal helped organize the Community Service Organization, a group that sought to bring together activists from a variety of religious, ethnic, and labor backgrounds. The group's achievements, especially its work in registering minority voters, contributed to the success of Roybal's second city council campaign in 1949. This victory served to bring about a new direction in city politics, with Roybal becoming the first Latino member of the Los Angeles City Council since the nineteenth century and, in the process, providing a voice for a host of newly enfranchised voters. He would retain the seat for the next twelve years until his successful campaign for a seat in the U.S. House of Representatives in 1962.

LIFE'S WORK

As a member of the city council, Roybal waged a frequently uphill battle for the rights of his constituents. Many of his proposals, including his support of fair employment practices, rent control, and public housing, were defeated. He was also unsuccessful in his opposition to

Edward R. Roybal. (AP Photo)

the city's decision to designate Chavez Ravine, a Latino neighborhood, as the site for a new Dodger baseball stadium in the 1950's. During the same period, he also gained attention for his stand against the politics of the Joseph McCarthy era, casting the only vote opposing a new city subversive registration ordinance. Despite the failure of many of his legislative efforts, Roybal retained the support of his constituents, gaining reelection in 1951, 1953, 1957, and 1961.

During his years on the city council, Roybal made two attempts to gain higher office, running for lieutenant governor as a Democrat in 1954 and for a nonpartisan seat on the Los Angeles County Board of Supervisors in 1958. In both instances he lost, meeting behind-the-scenes resistance from the California Democratic Party organization. In 1962, however, he defeated the Anglo Democratic candidate, William Fitzgerald, to gain the party's nomination to run for U.S. Congress representing California's 30th district, a part of which included the city council district he had represented for the previous twelve years. In the November general election he easily defeated his Republican opponent to move onto the national political scene.

As a member of Congress from 1963 until his retirement in 1993, Roybal fought hard for legislation to improve the conditions of Latino Americans. In the 1960's, he sponsored a bill to provide bilingual instruction in schools, and in the decade that followed he introduced similar legislation to bring bilingualism into court proceedings. He also voiced strong opposition to the Simpson-Mazzoli Immigration and Control Act during the course of its early debate in the 1980's. Extending his political focus to a broader base, Roybal was a dedicated supporter of programs for Vietnam War veterans and the rights of the elderly. In the latter regard, as a member of the House Select Committee on Aging, he contributed to the passage of legislation to fund low-cost public housing for seniors, to assure the continuance of the Meals on Wheels program, and to reverse a 1989 U.S. Supreme Court decision permitting age-based discrimination in the allocation of employment benefits. He was also a strong supporter of the Equal Rights Amendment, the establishment of the U.S. Department of Education, and funding for acquired immunodeficiency syndrome (AIDS) research.

In 1974, Roybal shifted from the 30th congressional district to the 25th as a result of redistricting. Four years later, in 1978, controversy briefly entered his career when he and two other California representatives received reprimands for their involvement in the "Koreagate" voting scandal, but he was able to put the misstep behind him and was reelected by a strong majority later that year.

After thirty years in Congress, Roybal retired in 1993. He spent his last years engaged in the work of the Edward R. Roybal Foundation, which is dedicated to providing college scholarships to individuals pursing public health careers, and the Edward R. Roybal Institute of Applied Gerontology. In January, 2001, he was awarded the Presidential Citizens Medal by President Bill Clinton. He died on October 25, 2005, survived by his wife of sixty-five years, Lucille Beserra-Roybal, and three children, one of whom, Lucille Roybal-Allard, succeeded him as a member of Congress, first elected from California's 33rd congressional district in 1993.

SIGNIFICANCE

The career of Edward R. Roybal serves to demonstrate the gains made by Latino people in the United States in the second half of the twentieth century. His election to the Los Angeles City Council in 1949,

The National Association of Latino Elected and Appointed Officials and the Congressional Hispanic Caucus

In 1976, after having served for thirteen years as a Latino member of the U.S. House of Representatives, Edward R. Roybal participated in the formation of two important groups intended to strengthen Latinos' voice in politics. In September of that year, he was involved in the founding of what would become the National Association of Latino Elected and Appointed Officials (NALEO). The stated purpose of the group continues to be the development and implementation of "programs promoting the integration of Latino immigrants into American society, developing future leaders among Latino youth, providing assistance and training to Latino elected and appointed officials and . . . conducting research on issues important to the Latino population." Roybal's strong commitment to the organization also extended to his service as its president from 1976 to 1992. In December, 1976, Roybal also participated in the formation of the Congressional Hispanic Caucus and served as its chair from 1978 to 1980.

becoming the first Latino to serve on that body since the nineteenth century, was a landmark event, as was his election to the U.S. House of Representatives thirteen years later. In both positions he served with distinction, helping to give Latinos a new voice in the political process. He is also remembered as an individual who supported legislation not only to improve conditions for his Latino constituents but also for the greater good of the nation.

Scott Wright

FURTHER READING

Burt, Kenneth C. "The Power of a Mobilized Citizenry and Coalition Politics: The 1949 Election of Edward R. Roybal to the Los Angeles City Council." *Southern California Quarterly* 85, no. 4 (December 2003): 413-438. Focuses on the organizational techniques used by Roybal and his supporters to bring about his election to the city council in 1949.

Ramos, George. "Edward R. Roybal, 1916-2005; Pioneer in Latino Politics in Los Angeles." *Los Angeles Times,* October 26, 2005, p. A.1. An obituary rich in details regarding Roybal's career and accomplishments both on the Los Angeles City Council and in the U.S. House of Representatives.

Sanchez, George. "Edward R. Roybal and the Politics of Multiracialism." *Southern California Quarterly* 92, no. 1 (Spring 2010): 51-73. Examines Roybal's 1949 election to the Los Angeles City Council and his years of service that followed, with a special emphasis on racial and ethnic issues. Includes discussion of the changing ethnic character of his district following his departure and his own views on these changes.

Underwood, Katherine. "Pioneering Minority Representation: Edward Roybal and the Los Angeles City Council, 1949-1962." *Pacific Historical Review* 66, no. 3 (August 1997): 399-425. Looks at Roybal's election to and twelve years of service on the city council, focusing on the difficulties he faced with racial prejudice and in seeking to implement his political agenda.

See also: Luis Gutiérrez; Joseph Marion Hernández; Ileana Ros-Lehtinen; Loretta Sánchez; Leticia Van de Putte.

David Domingo Sabatini

Argentine-born scientist and educator

Sabatini made fundamental contributions to the techniques and tools of cell biology and provided new insights into cellular interactions at the level of organelles and proteins.

Latino heritage: Argentinean
Born: May 10, 1931; San Carlos de Bolivar, Argentina
Areas of achievement: Science and technology; education

EARLY LIFE

David Domingo Sabatini (DAY-vihd DOH-mihng-goh SAH-bah-tee-nee) was born in San Carlos de Bolivar, a small city in the province of Buenos Aires, Argentina. His family moved when he was very young to the city of Rosario, where he completed primary and secondary school. Sabatini graduated in 1954 with a doctorate in medicine from the Universidad del Litoral in Rosario. After attempting to conduct research in Rosario, he joined the Department of Histology within the medical school at the University of Buenos Aires, which was headed by the pioneer electron microscopist Eduardo de Robertis. De Robertis became his mentor and had Sabatini work on studies of the endoplastic reticulum membrane. De Robertis also helped Sabatini successfully apply for a Rockefeller Foundation Fellowship in order to attend Rockefeller University for postdoctoral training. However, laboratory space at Rockefeller University was not available for six months, so Sabatini's

mentor at the university, George E. Palade, arranged for Sabatini to spend this time as a researcher at Yale University's school of medicine, working in the laboratory of histochemist Russell Barrnett. Sabatini returned to Rockefeller University in the summer of 1961. While conducting his research there over the next several years, he also pursued and received his Ph.D. in cell biology in 1966.

LIFE'S WORK

While at Rockefeller University as a doctoral student, Sabatini was investigating cellular structures, but he kept being stymied by the fact that the tissues would be affected by the necessary use of the electron microscope. He devised a way to fix the tissues using glutaraldehyde, a disinfectant commonly used in medicine and dentistry, which for the first time allowed tissues to be examined without alteration under the electron microscope. This discovery was the first of several such innovations he would introduce to instrumentation and technique within the field of cell biology.

Working with Rockefeller University Professor Günter Blobel, Sabatini achieved a major scientific breakthrough by developing what became known as the "signal hypothesis." The two men formulated and published in 1971 a hypothesis that each protein within a cell carries within it a biochemical signal that determines its destination and routing within the cell. Their theory was later proven by César Milstein, and Blobel was awarded the 1999 Nobel Prize in Physiology or Medicine. Sabatini and Blobel were jointly awarded the 1986 E. W. Wilson Award from the American Society for Cell Biology for their lifetime contributions to cell biology. During his time at Rockefeller University, Sabatini eventually was promoted to associate professor.

In September, 1972, Sabatini moved to New York University (NYU) to become the Frederick L. Ehrman Professor of Cell Biology and chair of the Department of Cell Biology at the NYU Langone Medical Center. He rapidly expanded the department's faculty and researchers and made it a leading center for cell biology. At NYU, he conducted fundamental research and taught various programs in the medical school. His major research interest has been the study of how proteins are sorted within eukaryotic cells. To this end, his laboratory has investigated how newly synthesized proteins are targeted to their respective relevant functions in different membranes and organelles within the cell. The rough endoplasmic reticulum is of particular interest because it is a key site in which polypeptides are altered.

Sabatini has pioneered new applications of modern technology for the study of cell biology, especially in regard to preserving tissues for electron microscopy and isolating microsomes for study within the cell. These techniques have enabled scientists to more precisely study the control of protein traffic within cells. His team has also created a way to study cellular systems outside of cells in artificial environments, which has greatly advanced the understanding of the functions and mechanisms employed by organelles within cells.

Sabatini's research achievements include hundreds of publications dating back to 1957. His work has been recognized internationally by his election to the American Academy of Arts and Sciences in 1980, America's National Academy of Sciences in 1985, and the French Academy of Sciences in 1992. He was awarded the Gold Medal of the French Academy of Sciences in 2003

and the senate of Argentina awarded him an Honorable Mention Domingo Faustino Sarmiento prize in August, 2004. Sabatini has been a Howard Hughes Medical Investigator and a member of the International Scientific Committee of the Institute Leloir, and he has served as a board member of the Richard Lounsbery Foundation. He has been active in chairing the American Society of Cell Biology and the Electron Microscopy Section of New York, and for many years he edited the cell biology section of the *Proceedings of the National Academy of Sciences*. He has served on many editorial boards of research journals, including *Cell Biology* and the *Journal of Cellular Biochemistry*. In 2010, he became a member of the board of directors of the American Association for the Advancement of Science.

SIGNIFICANCE

Sabatini has furthered the understanding of cell function and the intricate biochemical activities that occur in cells by his ingenious creation of new techniques and physical methods to study the organelles that make up eukaryotic cells.

Dennis W. Cheek

FURTHER READING

Sabatini, David D. "In Awe of Subcellular Complexity: Fifty Years of Trespassing Boundaries Within the Cell." *Annual Review of Cell and Developmental Biology* 21, no. 1 (2005): 1-33. A memoir of Sabatini's life and scientific career.

Young, John K. *Introduction to Cell Biology*. New York: World Scientific, 2010. A thorough introduction that highlights many of the central procedures of what occurs within cells; many of these processes were made possible by Sabatini's innovations.

See also: Anne Maino Alvarez; Francisco Dallmeier; Elma González; Diana Montes de Oca Lopez; Severo Ochoa.

EDDIE SAENZ

American football player and actor

Saenz was the first Hispanic American to win an individual statistical championship in the National Football League (NFL), leading in kickoff return yardage, while playing for the Washington Redskins in 1947 and repeating that in 1949. Following his football career, he became

involved in the television and film industry, playing a variety of secondary roles in noted films and television series.

Latino heritage: Mexican

Born: September 21, 1922; Los Angeles, California

Died: April 28, 1971; Los Angeles, California

Also known as: Edwin Matthew Saenz; Tortilla

Area of achievement: Football; acting

EARLY LIFE

Eddie Saenz (sinz) was born Edwin Matthew Saenz, the fifth and youngest child of Manuel and Rosa Saenz, on September 21, 1922. His father was a boxing promoter, and his grandfather emigrated from Mexico in 1852; both of Eddie Saenz's parents were born in the United States. He attended high school in Venice, California, and distinguished himself as an outstanding athlete, eventually attending Loyola Marymount University in Los Angeles. During World War II, male enrollments of colleges and universities across the country were decimated, and Saenz transferred across town to the University of Southern California (USC) for the completion of his college years. He competed as a fullback and receiver and often played defense. His five-foot, eleven-inch frame carried about 170 pounds.

As was the burden of most Mexican Americans, Saenz endured being called "Tortilla," but he soon earned the attention and respect of players and fans. He played a supporting role in USC's 1944 Rose Bowl upset of the previously undefeated Washington Huskies, 29-0. This was the first Rose Bowl broadcast to servicemen. Saenz enlisted in the Navy as World War II ended and competed for the famed Great Lakes Naval Team in 1944, coached by the legendary Paul Brown. In a schedule against primarily Big Nine (forerunner of the Big Ten Conference) and service teams, Saenz was a starter; against Wisconsin he ran for 112 yards on 11 carries, including a 40-yard score. That team finished 9-2-1, losing only to Ohio State and Notre Dame while tying Illinois. Saenz married Helen Haneman in 1943.

LIFE'S WORK

Saenz was drafted by the National Football League's Washington Redskins in 1945, the 150th player chosen in the 13th round. The Redskins had experienced successful teams in the preceding years, winning five of the previous nine NFL championships. However, they were beginning a period of competitive drought, and Saenz played for four coaches in his six-year career with the team. As a twenty-four-year-old rookie, Saenz started three of the team's eleven games in the 1946 season, finishing as the second leading receiver (232 yards and 1 touchdown on 12 catches), third leading rusher (213 yards and 3 touchdowns on 55 attempts),

and tied for third in points scored (24). His three touchdown catches placed him tenth in the league in that category, but he began to be used on kickoff and punt returns, which would become his expertise. However, the 1947 season was his best. Though the team slipped to 4-8, Saenz started six games and was responsible for gaining 741 yards rushing and receiving. However, his proficiency in returning kicks and punts kept the Redskins from suffering more losses as he became the first Hispanic and Mexican American to lead the NFL in an individual statistical category, which he did in eight categories that season. Saenz led the league in nonoffensive touchdowns (2), all-purpose yards (1,846), yards per touch (13.4), kick returns (29), kick return yards (797), kick returns for touchdown (2), kick and punt returns (53), and kick and punt return yards (1,105). An injury-shortened 1948 season gave way to more success in 1949 as Saenz again led the NFL in kick returns (240), second in kick and punt returns (41), and finished sixth in all-purpose yards (1,105) in twelve games. Saenz would still contribute in the Redskins' 1950 season, though he retired because of injury after a shortened 1951 season, finishing with 4,780 all-purpose yards, 12 touchdowns, and 2 interceptions in his 50-game career as halfback, defensive back, and return specialist.

Following his professional football career, Saenz became involved in television and films. Building on a film debut in 1949's *House of Strangers* with Edward G. Robinson and Susan Hayward, he performed in *The Buccaneer* (1958), directed by Anthony Quinn, and various television episodes of *Mike Hammer*, *Peter Gunn*, and *Batman*, among others. He died in Los Angeles on April 28, 1971.

SIGNIFICANCE

As the third player of Mexican heritage to be drafted by the National Football League, Saenz became the first Hispanic American to lead the NFL in an individual statistical category when, playing for the Washington Redskins in 1947, he led the league in eight statistical categories: nonoffensive touchdowns, all-purpose yards, yards per touch, kick returns, kick return yardage, kick returns for touchdowns, kick and punt returns, and kick and punt return yardage. Saenz was a Navy veteran; following his football career, he played support roles as a stuntman and an extra in a variety of television series and films from 1949 to 1967, including several episodes of the 1960's series *Batman*.

P. Graham Hatcher

FURTHER READING

Longoria, Mario. *Athletes Remembered: Mexicano/ Latino Professional Football Players, 1929-1970.* Tempe, Ariz.: Bilingual Press, 1997. Comprehensive compilation of many players' lives and careers, which provides an overview of Saenz's impact on the game of professional football.

Richman, Michael. *The Redskins Encyclopedia.* Philadelphia: Temple University Press, 2008. This work includes a history of the team during the era Saenz played and summarizes his records and accomplishments.

See also: Manny Fernández; Joe Kapp; Anthony Muñoz; Danny Villanueva.

KEN SALAZAR

American politician

Salazar was confirmed as the fiftieth secretary of the U.S. Department of the Interior in 2009. Prior to his appointment to President Barack Obama's cabinet, Salazar had served in numerous government positions, including Colorado state attorney general and U.S. senator.

Latino heritage: Spanish and Mexican
Born: March 2, 1955; Alamosa, Colorado
Also known as: Kenneth Lee Salazar
Area of achievement: Government and politics

EARLY LIFE

Kenneth Lee Salazar (KEHN-ehth lee sahl-leh-ZAR) was born in Alamosa, Colorado, to Henry and Emma Salazar. Both parents served in World War II, his father as a staff sergeant in the Army and his mother as a clerk for the War Department. The Salazars' main livelihood, however, came from farming the lands of the family's ranch in the small town of Los Rincones in the San Luis Valley of Colorado.

Although Salazar refers to himself as Mexican American, his family history can be traced back to the Southwest as early as the sixteenth century, long before the states of Colorado or New Mexico belonged to either Mexico or the United States. His Spanish ancestors helped to establish the city of Santa Fe in New Mexico. His family later settled in southern Colorado.

Salazar, along with his seven siblings, grew up on a ranch owned by his family for five generations. Without electricity, running water, or telephone service, Salazar grew up with very little material resources. He and his siblings often had to sit around a kerosene lamp in order to finish their schoolwork. His family placed a high value on education and reminded him of the many opportunities an education could offer him. His parents' educational aspirations instilled in Salazar and his four brothers and three sisters the importance of attaining a higher education. Salazar and his siblings became the first generation in his family to graduate from college.

Living in the vastness of rural Colorado inspired in Salazar a great appreciation for nature and the environment. Working and tending to the land taught him the meaning of hard work. Multiple generations of his family had labored the same lands, working to provide him and his siblings with greater opportunities.

Salazar earned a degree in political science from Colorado College in 1977. He received his law degree

Ken Salazar. (AP Photo)

from the University of Michigan Law School in 1981. In 1985, he married Esperanza (also known as Hope) Hernandez. The couple had two daughters, Melinda and Andrea.

LIFE'S WORK

After graduating from law school, Salazar worked in the private sector, focusing primarily on water and environmental law. He also owned a variety of business ventures with his wife, including a Dairy Queen and two radio stations, one in Pueblo, Colorado, and another one in Denver.

In 1986, Salazar served on the cabinet of Colorado governor Roy Romer. He worked as chief legal counsel to the governor. From 1990 through 1994, he served as executive director of Colorado's Department of Natural Resources. In this position, he fought to protect the environment by reforming oil, mining, and gas operations. Great Outdoors Colorado, created under his leadership, is a major portion of a constitutional amendment authored by Salazar that aims to protect and preserve Colorado's open spaces.

In 1999, Salazar was elected attorney general of Colorado, becoming the first Latino to hold statewide office in Colorado's history. He was reelected in 2002 but left the position in 2004 to serve as a U.S. senator.

In 2004, Salazar ran as a Democrat and won election to the U.S. Senate. He defeated the Republican candidate Pete Coors, the heir to the Coors Brewing Company founded by his great-grandfather. Salazar's election was a significant and historic accomplishment on many levels. Coors, fairly new to politics, was recruited as the Republican candidate mostly for his name recognition and his wealth. Latinos were the largest ethnic group in the state of Colorado but before the 2004 race, they had not had a significant influence on statewide elections. Campaigning in a predominantly Republican and conservative state, Salazar had to assiduously reach Latino voters, as well as moderate Republicans and independents. That same year, his brother John Salazar won his bid for the U.S. Congress. Ken Salazar and Mel Martínez, a Cuban American from Florida, were sworn into the U.S. Senate in 2005, the first Latinos elected to the Senate since 1977.

As a senator, Salazar served on numerous committees, including the Agriculture, Ethics, and Veterans Affairs Committee, and he continued his conservation efforts on the Energy and Natural Resource Committee. Along with Senator John McCain, a Republican from Arizona, Salazar took on the difficult task of drafting an

Attorney General of the State of Colorado

From 1999 through 2004, Ken Salazar served as Colorado's thirty-sixth attorney general. His duties included working on behalf of the people of the state of Colorado on legal issues pertaining to water, the environment, criminal justice, and consumer protection. During his tenure, Salazar was well known for his efforts to protect consumers against fraud. In 1999, he published "Respecting Our Elders: A Statewide Action Plan to Combat Senior Fraud." The state assembly adopted many of the recommendations from this report. Subsequently, the nonprofit organization AARP (American Association of Retired Persons) Colorado Elderwatch was established to continue the work outlined in the report in order to protect older Americans from exploitation.

In response to the Columbine school shootings in 1999, Attorney General Salazar partnered with law enforcement, social service organizations, and schools to negotiate and streamline communication strategies to ensure school safety. Salazar also met with school and community leaders to discuss the effects of bullying and harassment in schools and develop a series of prevention efforts around these issues.

In addition, Salazar established various law enforcement units in the office of attorney general, including the office's first gang prosecution unit, an environmental crimes unit to investigate cases involving air and water quality and hazardous substance spills, and the fugitive prosecutions unit to catch and arrest persons accused of murder who have fled the state. In recognition of his achievements, Salazar received the Profile in Courage in Public Service Award from the Conference of Western Attorneys General for his efforts to uphold the law in the state of Colorado.

immigration bill aimed at reforming the country's immigration system.

In 2009, Salazar was confirmed unanimously as the fiftieth secretary of the U.S. Department of the Interior, appointed by President Barack Obama to be one of two Latinos to serve on his presidential cabinet. (The other Latino is Secretary of Labor Hilda L. Solis). As secretary of the interior, Salazar oversees the Bureaus of Reclamation; Indian Affairs; Land Management; and Ocean Energy, Management, Regulation and Enforcement, as well as the National Park Service; the Office of Surface Mining, Reclamation and Enforcement; the U.S. Fish and Wildlife Service; and the U.S. Geological Survey. Under the administration of President George W. Bush, the Department of the Interior had been plagued by scandal. Touted for his years as an advocate for environmental conservation, Salazar was brought in to overhaul the department.

SIGNIFICANCE

Ken Salazar has had a significant impact on the Latino community, transforming the public perception of Latinos' relationship to the environment. His humble beginnings have served as the foundation for his political career. Growing up in rural Colorado as a landowner and rancher, he has been at the forefront of land conservation efforts at the state and national levels. As secretary of the interior, Salazar has expanded the Youth Conservation Corps, providing the opportunity to foster a commitment to the environment among young people through education and recreational programming. Remembering his family's heritage in the United States and the limited perspective of history he received in school, he continues to advocate for the discovery and discussion of the impact of Latinos on the United States, most recently by serving on the Commission for the National Museum of the American Latino. As of 2010, Salazar became one of the highest-ranking Latinos in national government.

Karina Cervantes and Aída Hurtado

FURTHER READING

Aledo, Milagros "Mimi," Rafael J. Lopez, and Liz Montoya. "The Joy in the Journey: An American Dream Realized." *Harvard Journal of Hispanic Policy* 17 (2004/2005): 5-11. An interview with Senator Salazar about the impact Latinos have had on the United States and his top priorities during his first term in the senate.

Juenke, Eric Gonzalez, and Anna Christina Sampaio. "Deracialization and Latino Politics: The Case of the Salazar Brothers in Colorado." *Political Research Quarterly* 1 (March, 2010): 43-54. Focuses on the strategies used by Ken and John Salazar in their respective political campaigns in a traditionally conservative region of the United States.

"The New Law of the Land." *Hispanic Magazine* 22, no. 1(February/March, 2009): 38-41. Highlights Salazar's upbringing in rural Colorado on his family's ranch and how his early appreciation for the outdoors shaped his political career.

See also: Henry G. Cisneros; Mel Martínez; Joseph M. Montoya; Bill Richardson; Hilda L. Solis.

RUBÉN SALAZAR

Mexican-born journalist and writer

An investigative reporter, Salazar was highly respected for his fearlessness in tackling tough subjects, the quality of his writing, and his advocacy of the rights of Mexican Americans. Simultaneously a broadcast newsman and a newspaper columnist, he was killed on the job, and his death remains shrouded in controversy.

Latino heritage: Mexican

Born: March 3, 1928; Ciudad Juárez, Chihuahua, Mexico

Died: August 29, 1970; Los Angeles, California

Areas of achievement: Journalism; literature

EARLY LIFE

Rubén Salazar (rew-BEHN SAL-ah-zar) was born in the Mexican border town of Ciudad Juárez, the son of timepiece repairman Salvador Salazar and Luz Chavez Salazar. While still in infancy, he moved with his parents across the Rio Grande to El Paso, Texas. He attended Lamar Elementary School before graduating

from El Paso High School. After graduation, he enlisted in the U.S. Army and served two years between the end of World War II and the beginning of the Korean War. After leaving the military, Salazar became a naturalized American citizen. He enrolled at Texas Western College (now the University of Texas at El Paso) on the G.I. Bill and graduated with a bachelor's degree in journalism in 1954.

During his time in college, Salazar wrote for the student newspaper, *The Prospector*. In his junior and senior years, he worked as an investigative reporter at the *El Paso Herald-Post*, and he went undercover to explore stories that particularly affected the Chicano community. Seeking the truth about reports of prison brutality directed at minorities, he dressed in rags and was arrested as a vagrant. He crossed the border into Juárez and went undercover again to file some of the earliest articles about drug trafficking.

After graduation, Salazar was hired as a reporter at the *Press Democrat* in Santa Rosa, California. In 1957,

Rubén Salazar. (© Bettmann/Corbis)

he moved south to become a reporter for the *San Francisco News*. Two years later, he joined the staff of the *Los Angeles Times*.

LIFE'S WORK

In Los Angeles, Salazar married Sally, a non-Hispanic woman, by whom he would father three children. Salazar wrote a regular column for the *Los Angeles Times*, which focused on the Latino community, then centered in East Los Angeles, and he exposed injustices in education, employment, and civil rights. For his objective, thorough writing, Salazar twice won the Greater Los Angeles Press Club Award, and in 1965 he received an award from the Equal Opportunity Foundation for serving as a minority spokesperson.

In 1965, the *Los Angeles Times* sent Salazar as a foreign correspondent to Vietnam to document the growing American presence in the war. He was one of the first to report on the disproportionately large number of minorities—especially Latinos—serving in the U.S. military and on the alarming percentage of Latinos among combat casualties. Two years later, Salazar was named the *Los Angeles Times*' bureau chief in Mexico City, the first Chicano at a major American newspaper

to rise to such a responsible position. Salazar traveled to the Dominican Republic to report on the American invasion. In Mexico City, he covered the massacre of students at Tlatelolco before the start of the 1968 Olympics. While Salazar was reporting from Panama, revolutionaries captured and held him for a time as a suspected Central Intelligence Agency (CIA) undercover spy before releasing him unharmed.

Late in 1968, Salazar returned to the *Los Angeles Times* as a special assignment reporter, covering the increasingly active Mexican American community in Los Angeles. He filed reports on migrant farmworkers' fight for equal pay, walkouts, and the rise of the Brown Berets, and he renewed his coverage of the injustices inherent in the high percentage of minorities serving—and dying—in Vietnam. In 1969, he was offered and accepted a position as news director at a Los Angeles Spanish-language television station, KMEX-TV. The *Times* asked him to continue writing his Chicano-oriented weekly column, and Salazar used both print and broadcast media to campaign against stereotyping, racism, prejudice, segregation, underrepresentation, and inequality.

In his dual capacities, Salazar ultimately fell afoul of law enforcement. In investigating allegations of beatings, the planting of evidence on Latino felony suspects, and other abuses, he accused the Los Angeles Police Department and the Los Angeles County Sheriff's Department of treating Chicanos unfairly. The authorities, including the Federal Bureau of Investigation (FBI), began to investigate him. His movements were closely monitored, and he was followed wherever he went.

Salazar did not retreat in the face of intimidation. In 1970, he and his camera crew were a highly visible presence at the third, and to that date the largest, National Chicano Moratorium march against the Vietnam War, which brought out a sizable crowd of protestors, with estimates ranging from seven thousand to thirty thousand. Though the march in East Los Angeles along Whittier Avenue from Belvedere Park to Laguna Park was peaceful, confrontations between the marchers and law officers broke out, and a full-scale riot ensued. In the melee, dozens of protestors and police officers were injured, stores were burned and looted, scores of people were arrested, and three people—including Salazar—were killed.

Salazar and his camera crew were relaxing over beers in the Silver Dollar Café, more than twenty blocks from the heart of the riot. Suddenly, a deputy sheriff, acting on an alleged report of a gunman on the

Salazar as a Chicano Martyr

More than forty years after the death of Rubén Salazar, many in the Latino community still believe he was a victim of assassination at the hands of Los Angeles law enforcement. Law enforcement officials, however, maintain his death was a tragic mishap.

In the wake of the fatal shooting, a sixteen-day coroner's inquest was conducted. The inquest concluded that Salazar's death was a homicide by accident, and no one was ever charged with any crime in the incident. The inquest, and a subsequent independent investigation in 2010 based on withheld evidence obtained through the Freedom of Information Act, revealed facts that supported conspiracy theorists and apologists alike. There is no question, for example, that Salazar suspected he was being watched and followed, and he feared for his life, as numerous witnesses attested. There is also no question that law enforcement officials were highly annoyed at Salazar, as multiple internal memos proved.

Whether accidental or intentional, the shooting was shown to be the result of numerous embarrassing law enforcement blunders. The tear gas canister that killed Salazar (an unreliable, atypical choice of weapon for an assassination) was not the cardboard-enclosed type used to disperse crowds. Instead, it was a high-velocity, metal-encased canister used to penetrate walls, which was fired through a curtain drawn across the entrance of the Silver Dollar Café. The café was not surrounded to prevent the escape of hypothetical "gunmen." The sheriff's deputies at the café did not bring gas masks and had to wait hours until the gas dissipated to discover Salazar's body. (The deputy who fired the tear gas, Tom Wilson, was later promoted to sergeant and ultimately left the Sheriff's Department.)

Though it is unlikely that the whole truth will ever be known, one fact is particularly telling. Salazar's widow, Sally, filed a wrongful death lawsuit, and Los Angeles County, while admitting no wrongdoing, settled out of court for $700,000.

premises, fired a tear gas canister into the café. The projectile struck Salazar in the temple. He died instantly, at the age of forty-two.

SIGNIFICANCE

In death, as in life, Rubén Salazar served as an inspiration. One of only a handful of Hispanics in the era to be elevated to foreign correspondent, bureau chief, and columnist for a major mainstream publication, he became an icon, particularly for a new wave of Latino journalists that emerged during the 1970's and who made significant contributions to the craft of reporting.

Salazar received many posthumous honors for his courage as an investigative journalist and his excellence as a writer. In 1971, he was the recipient of a special Robert F. Kennedy Journalism Award. Laguna Park, site of the 1970 riot, was renamed Salazar Park. Buildings at Sonoma State University and California State University were named in his honor. A public housing complex in his former hometown of El Paso was also named in his memory, and the city commissioned several murals depicting the reporter. The first inductee into the Hispanic Journalists Hall of Fame, Salazar was the subject of a singular Mexican American tribute—a *corrido*, or ballad, about his life. In 2008, he received worldwide recognition as part of a United States Postal Service series commemorating outstanding journalists, taking his place alongside John Hersey, Martha Gellhorn, George Polk, and Eric Sevareid.

Jack Ewing

FURTHER READING

Chavez, Ernesto. *Mi Raza Primero! (My People First!): Nationalism, Identity, and Insurgency in the Chicano Movement in Los Angeles, 1966-1978*. Berkeley: University of California Press, 2002. A study of the period during Salazar's heyday, when Mexican Americans in Southern California began to be empowered.

Mariscal, George. *Aztlan and Viet Nam: Chicano and Chicana Experiences of the War*. Berkeley: University of California Press, 1999. An anthology of stories, articles, and recollections that reflect the high rate of participation, injury, and death among Mexican Americans during the Vietnam War.

Salazar, Rubén. *Rubén Salazar, Border Correspondent: Selected Writings, 1955-1970*. Edited by Mario T. Garcia. Berkeley: University of California Press, 1998. A representative collection of Salazar's articles and columns.

See also: Soledad O'Brien; Roberto J. Suarez.

ZOË SALDANA

American actor

Trained as a dancer, Saldana parlayed her first film role, as ballet student Eva Rodríguez in Center Stage *(2000), into a series of increasingly high-profile roles, including the 2009 science-fiction blockbuster films* Star Trek *and* Avatar.

Latino heritage: Puerto Rican and Dominican

Born: June 19, 1978; Passaic, New Jersey

Also known as: Zoë Yadira Zaldaña Nazario; Zoe Saldana; Zoe Saldaña; Zoë Saldaña

Area of achievement: Acting

EARLY LIFE

Zoë Saldana (ZOH-ee sahl-DAHN-ah) was born Zoë Yadira Zaldaña Nazario in New Jersey to a Puerto Rican mother and a Dominican father. The second of three sisters very close in age, Saldana spent the first part of her childhood in New York City, speaking both English and Spanish. Her father died when she was ten, and her mother relocated the family to the Dominican Republic. It was during this time that Saldana studied ballet seriously. Her experience performing led her to join an acting troupe called Faces upon her return to New York at age seventeen; this troupe specialized in performing skits on social issues, such as rape and drugs, in order to convey positive messages to teens.

Upon graduation from high school, Saldana decided to pursue acting full time. After signing with a talent agency, she was awarded a small guest role on the television show *Law & Order* in 1999. In 2000, Saldana received her first big break when she was cast as the talented but disagreeable ballet dancer Eva Rodríguez in the film *Center Stage*, about a group of aspiring dancers attending a prestigious ballet academy in New York City.

LIFE'S WORK

In 2002, Saldana won supporting roles in *Drumline* and *Crossroads*, the latter of which garnered a great deal of attention because it was singer Britney Spears's film debut. Saldana's consistently strong onscreen performances led to more high-profile roles in *Pirates of the Caribbean: The Curse of the Black Pearl* (2003) and *The Terminal* (2004), opposite Johnny Depp and Tom Hanks, respectively. In 2004, Saldana completed *Haven*, in which she played the teenage daughter of a prominent Caribbean businessman who objects to her romance with a poor fisherman played by Orlando Bloom. In 2005, Saldana had her first leading role in a mainstream romantic comedy, starring opposite Ashton Kuchner in *Guess Who*, a remake of the classic *Guess Who's Coming to Dinner* (1967), which starred Sidney Poitier and Katharine Hepburn. The ethnicity is flipped in the remake; instead of a young white woman bringing a black man home to meet her family, Saldana played a young black woman bringing a white man home to meet her family, including a disapproving father humorously played by Bernie Mac.

Additional parts followed during the next few years, but it was not until 2009 that Saldana truly became a household name. That year saw the release of the first new *Star Trek* film in which the story line from the 1960's television series was rebooted and the original characters were recast with young up-and-coming actors. Saldana played Uhura, the communications officer whose role was originated by actor Nichelle Nichols, and she was complimented by critics for staying true to the original material while simultaneously making the role her own.

Zoë Saldana. (AP Photo)

Also in 2009, Saldana starred in director James Cameron's groundbreaking three-dimensional science-fiction blockbuster *Avatar*. Rather than appearing onscreen in the traditional sense, Saldana's performance was recorded with motion-capture technology, then digitally altered to portray her as a ten-foot tall, blue-skinned alien princess named Neytiri. To prepare for this challenging role, Saldana studied martial arts, archery, and horseback riding, and she worked to master the language created for the film's fictional Na'vi people. She even trekked through rainforest terrain to ensure that her recorded movements would be authentic when translated to the digitally created alien world. Both *Star Trek* and *Avatar* were extremely successful worldwide, and sequels for both were quickly proposed.

In addition to acting, Saldana's increasing public exposure has led to a number of endorsements for companies, such as Calvin Klein and Avon, and she is often photographed and praised in popular magazines for her taste in fashion. She has expressed an interest in directing and producing, as well as acting, in part because she wants to promote high quality projects that may be overlooked by more commercial producers. In 2010, Saldana announced her engagement to longtime boyfriend Keith Britton.

SIGNIFICANCE

Zoë Saldana's talent and versatility as an actor have led to increasingly prominent leading roles in a wide variety of commercially and critically successful films. Although she has expressed an interest in acting in Spanish-language, as well as English-language, films, she does not wish to be typecast based on her ethnic background, noting that she has portrayed both black and Latino characters. She has also played roles that were originally written for Anglo actors, helping to break the barriers of Hollywood stereotypes.

Amy Sisson

FURTHER READING

Bowles, Scott. "*Avatar* Stars Radically Transform Their Careers." *USA Today*, January 5, 2010, p. 2D. Focusing on Saldana and her *Avatar* costar Sam Worthington, this article discusses Saldana's admiration for the strong heroines in director James Cameron's films, as well as her extensive physical and mental preparation for her *Avatar* role.

Gdula, Kimberly. "Star Turns." *Dance Spirit* 6, no.6 (July/August 2002): 120. Focuses on the adjustment Saldana had to make in transitioning from ballet in the 2000 film *Center Stage* to hip-hop and stepping choreography for the 2002 film *Drumline*.

Hernández, Ambar. "Zoë Saldana." *Hispanic* 17, no. 6 (June 2004): 72. Interview in which Saldana discusses her name change, early career, and Hispanic roots.

Weitzman, Elizabeth. "Zoë Saldana." *Interview* 34, no. 6 (July 2004): 72. This interview focuses on Saldana's role in the Caribbean-centered film *Haven*. as well as her desire to transcend ethnic labels in her career.

See also: Jessica Alba; Cameron Diaz; America Ferrera; Eva Longoria.

RAÚL R. SALINAS

American poet, activist, and social reformer

Mainly self-educated in numerous penitentiaries, Salinas—a Xicanindio (Mexicano, Chicano, Indio) poet and indigenous activist in the forefront of the 1960's pinto prison poetry movement of the United States—transformed self-alienation and prison indignation into political awareness, civil and human rights struggles, and antineocolonialism resistance. As a revolutionary icon, Salinas not only promoted the cultural underpinnings between Mexican and Indian cultures but also advocated globally for human rights and indigenous movements of the Americas.

Latino heritage: Mexican

Born: March 17, 1934; San Antonio, Texas

Died: February 13, 2008; Austin, Texas

Also known as: Raúl Roy Salinas; Tapón; El Maestro; Autumn Sun

Areas of achievement: Poetry; activism; social issues

EARLY LIFE

Even though he was born in the city of San Antonio, Raúl Roy Salinas (rah-EWL roy sah-LEE-nahs), who styled his name as raúlrsalinas, grew up in an eastside barrio of Austin, Texas. Abandoned by his father and growing up in a single-parent household, Salinas attended Catholic elementary schools, and Tapón, as his friends called him, was an average student. In eleventh grade, he dropped out of public high school; however, his mom and grandmother instilled in him a penchant for literary expression. Without a high school diploma and no motivation, in his early twenties, Salinas moved to California in search of labor as a migrant farmworker; after a drug conviction, though, he landed at Soledad State Prison in 1957.

In jail, Salinas began an arduous process of self-instruction during a twelve-year span in both state and federal penal institutions, including Huntsville (Texas), Leavenworth (Kansas), and Marion (Illinois). Many years later, Salinas came to regret deserting his own family and not growing up with his children, repeating a similar, familial pattern of paternal dereliction. However, prison gave him plenty of time for self-reflection and a new perspective on life: He embraced a revolutionary intellect, experienced renewed spirituality, and, most of all, cultivated political passion.

LIFE'S WORK

During one stint at the Leavenworth Federal Prison in 1969, Salinas began printing an in-house literary journal, *Aztlán de Leavenworth*, wherein he showcased his most famous poem, "Un Trip Through the Mind Jail y Otras Excursions." Titled by the same name, a collection of his early verse was eventually published by the Editorial Pocho-Ché underground press in 1980, giving him a major boost as a Chicano literary figure. Beat poetry and jazz music were also major influences on Salinas as writer and spoken-word performer.

His years of imprisonment from 1957 to 1972, furthermore, helped to shape his role as an advocate for inmates' rights during the prison rebellion years, directly impacted by the Chicano and Black Power movements of the late 1960's and early 1970's. His activism made him, to fellow inmates, a jailhouse reformer and to guards an unabashed agitator. This inevitably landed him at Marion, where he became one of the so-called "Marion Brothers," prisoner agitators transferred from numerous federal lockups into Marion's control units and subjected to notorious behavior modifications. Setting a legal precedent, Salinas was one of four plaintiffs in the successful landmark case *Adams v. Carlson* (1973), involving prisoner rights and penal reform.

In prison settings, Salinas interacted with Puerto Rican *Independistas*, Black Muslims, Native Americans, and even politicized, working-class whites, who introduced him to various militant authors, radical ideas, and perspectives of anticolonialism and anti-imperialism. At a time when jails were divided by prison gangs, proliferating along racial and ethnic lines, Salinas bonded instead with prisoners of all colors and promulgated political alliances to challenge legally—in Salinas's own rhetoric—the status quo of "prisons of empire," which are maintained by the state as "backyard colonialism."

Going into exile in Washington State (to avoid Texas and California law enforcement) after jail release in the early 1970's, Salinas became a community activist in the Seattle area, supporting Native American fishing rights, assisting the American Indian Movement (AIM), and joining the Leonard Peltier Defense Committee. In the 1980's, he moved back to East Austin and set up Resistencia Books, a space for grassroots organizing, and Red Salmon Arts, a Native American Chicano cultural arts group. For almost the next three decades, Salinas proceeded to promote the *indio* ancestry of Chicanos, using the term *Xicanindio* to describe himself as indigenous. In the Nahuatl tongue, the Aztecs' native

---

Raúl Salinas and Pinto Poetry: Spear Against the State

During the late 1960's prison rebellion years in U.S. penitentiaries, pinto poets (prison authors) wrote about their experiences behind bars. Pinto is the adjective modifier for *la pinta*, Spanish slang for "the pen"; and as a subgenre of Chicano poetry, pinto verse attracted such writers as Raúl R. Salinas, Judy Lucero, Ricardo Sánchez, Reymundo "Tigre" Pérez, Abelardo Delgado, and Jimmy Santiago Baca, to name a few. Pinto poetry not only embraces autobiography and critical self-examination but also vitriol against a penal system that regularly brutalizes them—physically and mentally—thus providing emotional and expressive outlets, to channel fears, frustrations and loneliness, that pintos suffer while incarcerated. In *la pinta*, Salinas's poesy became his weapon of choice to critique the prison industrial complex, or the "jail machine," as he referred to it. Salinas's "pen" thus became the spear against the U.S. prison system. In most cases, pinto poets—usually high school dropouts like Salinas—refashion themselves: first by reading and self-learning, then by transcending alienation and self-despair, and finally by expressing something positive and constructive.

language, the "Chi" syllable in Chicano is spelled as "Xi," and since *indio* is the Spanish word for Indian, *Xicanindio* thus emphasizes the mixed-blood, indigenous roots of Chicanos.

As exemplar of the pinto poetry movement, Salinas published three collections of poems: *Un Trip Through the Mind Jail y Otras Excursions* (1999), *East of the Freeway: Reflections de mi pueblo* (1995), and *Indio Trails: A Xicano Odyssey thru Indian Country* (2006). His last book, *Raul Salinas and the Jail Machine: My Weapon Is My Pen* (2006), edited by Louis G. Mendoza, is a compilation of his personal letters and journal articles from his jail years and his subsequent release. As a spoken-word artist, Salinas also recorded three compact discs: *Los Many Mundos of raúlrsalinas: Un Poetic Jazz Viaje con Friends* (2000), *Beyond the BEATen Path* (2002), *Red Arc: A Call for Liberación con Salsa y Cool* (2005), a collaboration with a baritone saxophonist Fred Ho.

His literary awards include the Louis Reyes Rivera Lifetime Achievement Award in 2002, the Martin Luther King, Jr., César Chávez, Rosa Parks Visiting Professorship Award in 2003, and the Alfredo Cisneros Del Moral Foundation Award in 2007. Distinctions on his behalf also included the Raul Salinas Literary Media Lab in the Mexican American Cultural Center (MACC) of Austin, Texas. In 1994, Stanford University acquired Salinas's personal and literary archives, from the 1950's to the 1990's. Salinas died of liver disease in 2008.

SIGNIFICANCE

From the rough streets of East Austin to state and federal prisons, Salinas transcended economic disadvantages of birth, transformed into a celebrated poet, sued the federal government, and morphed into an advocate for human rights. Salinas also devoted much effort to help at-risk youths in detention centers. He provided a community space to advocate for the arts, especially encouraging artistic creativity in public schools. In the international arena, he was an unrelenting spokesperson for social justice, resisting oppression everywhere. A humanist artist activist, Salinas was the *Xicanindio* bard of the barrio and a protector of the global masses, not unlike the icon of *La Virgen de Guadalupe*, the patron saint of the Americas, which he had tattooed across his sternum.

Itzcóatl Tlaloc Meztli

FURTHER READING

Beltran, Raymond R. "Out of the Ashes, the Pínto Poet Arises." *La Prensa San Diego* 26, no. 46 (November 15, 2002). A newspaper account of Salinas' visit to San Diego for a poetry performance. It discusses the Coahiltecan influence on his work, from his grandmother's indigenous heritage.

Gomez, Alan Eladio. "Resisting Living Death at Marion Federal Penitentiary, 1972." *Radical History Review* 96 (Fall, 2006): 58-86. Because of their political activism during the convict upheaval years, more than a hundred so-called "problem inmates" from various federal penitentaries were transferred to Marion's control units, and the mental "torture" techniques used for behavioral rehabilitation are discussed.

_____. "Troubadour of Justice: An Interview with raúlrsalinas." In *Behind Bars: Latino/as and Prison in the United States*, edited by Suzanne Oboler. New York: Palgrave MacMillan, 2009. This interview reveals Salinas's participation in the prison agitation years, his years locked up, and how he became one of the plaintiffs in a prison landmark case.

Mendoza, Louis. "The Re-education of a Xicanindio: Raúl Salinas and the Poetics of Pinto Transformation." *MELUS* 28, no. 1 (Spring, 2003): 39-60. Salinas's development from "social criminal" to political prisoner is tracked, resulting in his transfer to Marion Federal Penitentiary in 1972.

Olguín, B. V. *La Pinta: Chicana/o Prisoner Literature, Culture, and Politics.* Austin: University of Texas Press, 2010. This is a study based on research about Chicano/Chicana "pintos/pintas," including Salinas and other writers. Olguín also critiques prisoner tattoo and handkerchief art and gang exploitation films.

West, Phil. "Poetry as Activism: Raúl Salinas's Passion for Literature and Life." *The Austin Chronicle* (March 21, 1997). A newspaper article on Salinas that mentions his work on behalf of two so-called "political prisoners": Leonard Peltier and Mumia Abu-Jamal. Also a discussion of Salinas's visit with the Zapatistas in Chiapas, Mexico, and author commentary and critique of his poetry by English professors.

See also: Gloria Anzaldúa; Lola Rodríguez de Tió.

Julian Samora

American sociologist, educator, and activist

A prominent Mexican American researcher, scholar, and activist, Samora overcame personal hardship and became one of the first Mexican American sociologists in the United States. His research made significant contributions on issues directly affecting the Latino population. His advocacy benefited many, and his research and scholarship continues through the Julian Samora Research Institute.

Latino heritage: Mexican

Born: March 1, 1920; Pagosa Springs, Colorado

Died: February 2, 1996; Albuquerque, New Mexico

Areas of achievement: Sociology; scholarship; education; activism

Early Life

Julian Samora (HOO-lee-ahn sah-MOR-ah) was born in the ranching town of Pagosa Springs, Colorado, on March 1, 1920. Despite pervasive prejudice and discrimination against Mexican Americans, he distinguished himself academically. In 1938, he earned the Frederick G. Bonfils Foundation scholarship, which allowed him to go to college. He obtained a bachelor's degree in history and political science from Adams State Teacher's College in Alamosa, Colorado, in 1942. He then worked as a school teacher from 1942 to 1943. In 1947, he received a master's of science degree in sociology from Colorado State University at Fort Collins, Colorado. In 1953, he was the first Mexican American to earn a Ph.D. in sociology and anthropology at Washington University in St. Louis.

Immediately after his doctoral training, Samora taught at the University of Colorado School of Medicine, where he was an assistant professor of preventive medicine and public health from 1955 to 1957. During this time, he was also a visiting professor at the University of New Mexico in Albuquerque. From 1957 to 1959, he was an associate professor of sociology and anthropology at Michigan State University. He was a professor of sociology and anthropology at Notre Dame University from 1959 until his retirement in 1985.

Life's Work

Samora's doctoral dissertation was titled "Minority Leadership in a Bilingual Community." He investigated perceptions and styles of leadership in a Mexican American community that operated within a European-American environment. During his academic career, he conducted research in medical sociology, immigration, border studies, rural poverty, and Chicano studies. His research had the consistent focus of elucidating the cultural, political, economic, and medical experiences of Mexicans and Mexican Americans. He researched the medical delivery systems of Mexican Americans during his academic tenure at Colorado State University. Samora was particularly interested in studying indigenous conceptions of health and disease as perceived by Mexican Americans. His writings in this area provide a comprehensive framework of information on disease prevention, causation, diagnosis, and treatment from the perspective of Mexican American folk healing.

Samora was a prolific author, and the following coauthored publications are widely known in the area of Chicano studies: *Conceptions of Health and Disease Among Spanish-Americans*, published in 1961 in the *American Catholic Sociological Journal*; *La Raza: Forgotten Americans* (1966); *Mexican-Americans in the Southwest* (1969); *Los Mojados: The Wetback Story* (1971); *A History of the Mexican-American People* (1977); and *Gunpowder Justice: A Reassessment of the Texas Rangers* (1979). He was a frequent reviewer of scholarly writings as a member of several editorial boards of prestigious journals, including *Ethnicity: An Interdisciplinary Journal of the Study of Ethnic Relations*, *Migration Today*, and the *Latin American Research Review*.

In *A History of the Mexican-American People*, Samora and coauthor Patricia Vandel Simon emphasized the historical and cultural linkages between Mexican Americans and their ancestry in Latin America at a time when other historians often omitted this Latin American heritage. *Los Mojados: The Weback Story* is a study of illegal immigration from Mexico to the United States conducted by the United States-Mexico Border Studies Project at the University of Notre Dame and funded by the Ford Foundation. Considered a classic in Chicano studies based on its sociological methodology, the study surveyed undocumented Mexicans at several detention centers in the Southwest. One of Samora's graduate students at Notre Dame University assumed the identity of an undocumented Mexican citizen in order to experience the pathos and hardship of these detainees. *Gunpowder Justice: A Reassessment of the Texas Rangers*, coauthored with Joe Bernal and Albert

Peña, critically discusses the popular image of the Texas Rangers and analyses the reasons why the Texas Ranger is a popular figure and often a folk hero among many Anglos, while the Ranger is a dreaded symbol of oppression among a large number of Mexican Americans.

In addition to his scholarly pursuits, Samora was also an advocate for social justice. He was one of the founders of the National Council of La Raza, a civil rights organization dedicated to improving opportunities for Hispanic Americans. He played a crucial role in the founding of the Mexican American Legal Defense and Educational Fund. His activism was acknowledged by his receipt of multiple awards. He was the recipient of the La Raza Award in 1979 presented by the National Council of La Raza. In 1985, the White House recognized his contributions to the U.S. Latino population with the White House Hispanic Heritage Award. In 1990, the Mexican government presented him the prestigious national award of the Order of the Aztec Eagle in recognition of his scholarly contributions for a better understanding of Mexicans and Mexican Americans.

Samora died in Albuquerque, New Mexico, on February 2, 1996, at the age of seventy-five from medical complications related to progressive supranuclear palsy.

SIGNIFICANCE

Samora's research topics and findings made important scholarly breakthroughs and continue to have important implications, and his work increased the understanding of Chicanos and Mexicans. His nationally respected writings and scholarly reputation attracted a large group of Mexican American students to Notre Dame University, where he became a mentor for a new generation of future Chicano scholars, researchers, writers, and

activists. Samora's research and academic legacy continues through the Julian Samora Research Institute, which was established in 1989 at Michigan State University and conducts extensive research on Hispanic Americans.

He was also distinguished for this advocacy and involvement in the promotion of social justice.

Fernando A. Ortiz

FURTHER READING

Blea, Irene Isabel. *Toward a Chicano Social Science.* Westport, Conn.: Praeger, 1988. Provides an in-depth discussion of Chicano social science and the primary Chicano social scientists working with Samora.

López Pulido, Alberto, Barbara Driscoll de Alvarado, and Carmen Samora, eds. *Moving Beyond Borders: Julian Samora and the Establishment of Latino Studies.* Champaign: University of Illinois, 2009. Details the life of Samora, citing original sources. Researchers who knew him personally provide a comprehensive overview of his academic and activist career.

Samora, Julian. *Julian Samora Papers, 1934-1989.* Austin: University of Texas. A comprehensive scholarly and biographical collection of Samora's correspondence, written works, and personal and biographical materials. The repository can be accessed at the Texas Archival Resources Online at http://www.lib.utexas.edu/taro/utlac/00117/lac-00117p1.html.

See also: María Herrera-Sobek; Margarita Bradford Melville; George I. Sánchez.

OLGA SAN JUAN

American actor, singer, and dancer

San Juan, whose studio publicized her as "The Puerto Rican Pepperpot," appeared in a number of films that highlighted her dancing and singing. She also starred in a Broadway musical.

Latino heritage: Puerto Rican

Born: March 16, 1927; Brooklyn, New York

Died: January 3, 2009; Burbank, California

Also known as: The Puerto Rican Pepperpot

Areas of achievement: Acting; theater; dance

EARLY LIFE

Olga San Juan (OHL-gah san wahn) was born in Brooklyn, New York, to Puerto Rican parents Mercedes and Luis San Juan. The family moved back to Puerto Rico, living in Santurce, when San Juan was three years old. They returned to New York City after three years. San Juan started dancing when she was four. By age seven she was a member of the Latino dance ensemble

Olga San Juan. (AP Photo)

Infantile Ballet Valencia and danced the fandango for President Franklin D. Roosevelt at the White House. By age ten she was singing and dancing with the Hispanic Theater in the Bronx. As she grew older, San Juan began dancing and singing at New York nightclubs, including El Morocco and the Copacabana. She worked with Tito Puente, the famed jazz and mambo musician. She also appeared on radio and formed a nightclub act, Olga San Juan and Her Rumba Band. With her tiny frame and fiery Latin temperament, San Juan was an eye-catching entertainer.

San Juan was "discovered" by a talent scout for Paramount Studios and signed to a contract in 1943. Her first film was a tropical musical short, *Caribbean Romance* (1943); her second short film was *Bombalera* (1945), where she was billed as "the Cuban Cyclone." Hollywood did not differentiate between Latin types, as far as geography was concerned. In her third short film, *The Little Witch* (1945), she played a nightclub singer.

LIFE'S WORK

San Juan's first feature-length film was *Rainbow Island* (1944), in which she played a supporting role to

leading lady Dorothy Lamour. Other roles followed for San Juan, who was publicized by the studio as "The Puerto Rican Pepperpot." She was in *Duffy's Tavern* (1945) and had an important role, although not the lead, in *Blue Skies* (1946). Featuring the music of Irving Berlin, *Blue Skies* was one of the top-grossing films of the year and introduced San Juan to a number of future fans. In this film she danced with Fred Astaire and sang with Bing Crosby; she sang a duet "I'll See You in C-U-B-A" with Crosby, and her torrid dance number "Heat Wave" with Astaire has become a film classic. She also illustrated her comic timing, deftly exchanging lines with star comedian Billy De Wolfe. San Juan appeared in a number of "B" films, such as *Variety Girl* (1947); her number "He Can Waltz" was a highlight of this film. She moved to Universal Studios and appeared in *Are You with It?* (1948), dancing with Donald O'Connor.

She was also in *One Touch of Venus* (1948), singing with stars Ava Gardner and Eve Arden. In *The Countess of Monte Cristo* (1948), starring ice skating phenomena Sonja Henie, San Juan played a film extra trying to pass herself off as an aristocrat. In the Western musical *The Beautiful Blonde from Bashful Bend* (1949), she played Conchita, actor Betty Grable's sidekick. San Juan generally had roles that stressed her cute looks and spunky nature. With her heavy accent, San Juan was not perceived as leading lady material.

San Juan left Hollywood for Broadway. She had been singing at a Hollywood party and caught the attention of party guests Alan Jay Lerner and Frederick Loewe. They were currently looking for a young woman to play the part of Jennifer Rumson in their new musical *Paint Your Wagon*. San Juan was invited to New York to audition and immediately got the part. In the show, which opened on Broadway on November 12, 1951, San Juan played the leading role and sang two showstoppers, "What's Going on Here?" and "How Can I Wait." *New York Times* critic Brooks Atkinson praised her performance, and San Juan won the Donaldson Award for Best Debut Performance by an Actress. *Paint Your Wagon* ran only eight months, but before it closed, San Juan had already left the show to focus on her family.

In 1948, she met actor Edmund O'Brien at a publicity function; they were married the same year. They had three children, and San Juan essentially retired from performing, although she did some work on television and radio. One of her appearances was on the radio program *Musical Comedy Theater*, starring in *The Kissing Bandit* with John Conte in 1952. She had small parts in two films starring her husband, *The Barefoot Contessa* (1954) and *The Third Voice* (1960). San Juan and O'Brien divorced in 1976. After years of failing health, she died of kidney failure on January 3, 2009.

SIGNIFICANCE

Despite her small stature and heavy accent, San Juan found a niche in film, playing roles that highlighted her dancing, singing, and comic appeal. During her career, she appeared with a number of top box office favorites and held her own. She was also a success in her one and only Broadway play. San Juan was honored for her contributions in entertainment and received the Screen Actors Guild Latino Legacy Award.

Marcia B. Dinneen

FURTHER READING

Lerner, Alan Jay. "Painting the Wagon." *The New York Times,* November 11, 1951, p. X1. Lerner describes the musical and tells how he discovered San Juan for the lead.

The New York Times. "Olga San Juan, 81, 'Puerto Rican Pepperpot' Actress." January 7, 2009, p. A20. An obituary, providing an overview of San Juan's life and career.

Otfinoski, Steven. *Latinos in the Arts.* New York: Facts on File, 2007. A brief article, including biographical material on her early life.

Vallance, Tom. "Olga San Juan." *Independent*, February 20, 2009, p. 40. A lengthy obituary with a focus on her career.

See also: John Gavin; Rita Hayworth; Katy Jurado; Ricardo Montalbán; María Montez; Elena Verdugo; Carmen Zapata.

FÉLIX SÁNCHEZ

American Olympic hurdler

Revered for his ability to finish races in record times, Sánchez has represented the Dominican Republic impressively, particularly as a four-hundred-meter hurdler. He has been a trailblazer, nabbing the Dominican Republic's first gold medals in various hurdles events and popularizing track and field in that country.

Latino heritage: Dominican

Born: August 30, 1977; New York, New York

Also known as: The Dictator; El Super Sánchez; Superman; Super Félix; The Invincible

Area of achievement: Sports

EARLY LIFE

Félix Sánchez (FAY-lihx SAHN-chehz) was born in the Washington Heights neighborhood of Manhattan, New York, to parents from the Dominican Republic. Sánchez briefly lived with both parents in New York until his mother and father separated and moved to different places.

Young Sánchez headed off with his mother to San Diego, California. His youth was far from ordinary since he lived hundreds of miles away from his father, who had moved back to the Dominican Republic. Fortunately, Sánchez maintained some ties to his Dominican culture through his mother and through other Dominican relatives who lived in California.

While growing up in San Diego, Sánchez engaged in sports. Early on, he played baseball, an immensely popular sport among Dominicans. He pursued athletics while attending San Diego's University City High School. Sánchez's mind was first set on other high school sports, such as baseball, football, and wrestling, yet his attention soon turned to track and field after he injured his wrist during a wrestling exercise. With encouragement from the school's track coach, Sánchez decided to go for a sport he could still pursue despite having an injured wrist. During team tryouts, other runners, including a female runner, outran Sánchez. However, this moment of defeat did not discourage him, and he made efforts to improve his performance in the sport.

Eventually, he went on to pursue track and field at San Diego Mesa College and later at the University of Southern California, where he earned a degree in psychology. Sánchez continued to show potential, particularly as a 400-meter hurdles athlete, and he earned numerous athletic honors, such as junior college championship titles and the National Collegiate Athletic Association (NCAA) title.

LIFE'S WORK

Sánchez held his Dominican heritage dear to his heart and was motivated to compete in track and field on

Félix Sánchez. (AP Photo)

Sánchez's track-and-field journey was filled with glorious moments as well as setbacks and defeats, yet he endured. After his unwelcome loss at the 2000 Sydney Olympics, he won an astonishing forty-three races, one after another, between 2001 and 2004. His accomplishments during this time include victories at the 2001 Super Grand Prix event in Switzerland and the 2002 IAAF Golden League competition. In 2003, Sánchez was honored as Track and Field Athlete of the Year by *Track and Field News* magazine.

Following 2004, injuries hurt his ability to compete. Still, he bounced back in 2007, winning a silver medal during the world championships 400-meter hurdles event. After his defeat in the 2008 Beijing Olympics, he continued to diligently train, compete, and enjoy successes, such as his victory in the 2010 University of California, San Diego Triton Invitational. His dedication to track and field is further evident in his role as hurdles coach at California's Harvard-Westlake School, where he has trained students in the sport.

SIGNIFICANCE

By choosing to compete in track and field for the Dominican Republic, Sánchez demonstrated initiative and commitment to his Dominican culture. The Dominican Republic had been a country noted for baseball, but Sánchez put the spotlight on track and field and paved the way for other Dominican athletes to follow in his fleet footsteps. By tapping into opportunities few have pursued and by venturing down paths few have trod, Sánchez showed incredible ambition and leadership qualities, which other Latinos can emulate. Sánchez did not abandon his Dominican roots, despite being pressured to be a track-and-field athlete for the United States, and he has inspired others to stay connected to their heritage.

Brooke Posley

the Dominican Republic's behalf. Although technically he could compete for either the United States or the Dominican Republic, since he was a citizen of both countries, Sánchez wished to be a Dominican athlete. Prior to 1999, Sánchez faced obstacles in becoming a Dominican track-and-field athlete since this sport was not as well established as baseball was in this country. However, a series of events in 1999 enabled Sánchez to compete in track and field for the Dominican Republic.

Sánchez made Dominicans proud to call him their track-and-field athlete. By 2004, he had achieved milestones for the Dominican Republic. Among his most impressive accomplishments are his gold medals earned in various 400-meter hurdles events. In 2001, he beat his competitors in 47.49 seconds and won the Dominican Republic's first world championships's gold medal in the 400-meter hurdles event. He won a second one in 2003, finishing his race in 47.25 seconds. In a quick 48.19 seconds, he nabbed the Dominican Republic's first Pan American Games gold medal in the 400-meter hurdles 2003 event. Then in just 47.63 seconds, he won the 400-meter hurdles event at the 2004 Olympics in Athens, Greece, attaining the Dominican Republic's very first Olympic gold medal.

FURTHER READING

Gonzalez, David. "Pan American Games: Games Lift Spirits in Santo Domingo." *The New York Times*, August 8, 2003. Sheds light on life in the Dominican Republic and the positive impact of the Pan American Games and of Sánchez on the country.

Jenkins, Chris. "Sánchez's Gold Medal a First for His Country." *The San Diego Union-Tribune*, August 27, 2004. Reveals Sánchez's motivations for representing the Dominican Republic and lists his running times for track-and-field events.

Turnbull, Simon. "Felix Hurdles Out of the Blue and Into Glittering Contention." *The Independent*, July 29, 2001. Discusses Sánchez's early athletic experiences and the significance of his quest to win the world championships for the Dominican Republic.

Zeigler, Mark. "Morning Glory: Sanchez's 5:30 a.m. Workouts Paid Off." *The San Diego Union-Tribune*, August 26, 2004. Reveals how Sánchez has diligently prepared for track-and-field events

See also: Joaquín Andújar; César Cedeño; Tony Fernandez.

FREDDY SANCHEZ

American baseball player

Although he was born with a clubbed right foot and a seriously pigeon-toed left foot, Sanchez overcame his disability to became a Major League Baseball player. He helped the San Francisco Giants win the 2010 World Series, becoming the first player in league history to amass three doubles in his first three times at bat.

Latino heritage: Mexican
Born: December 21, 1977; Hollywood, California
Also known as: Frederick Phillip Sanchez, Jr.
Area of achievement: Baseball

EARLY LIFE

Frederick Phillip Sanchez, Jr., better known as Freddy Sanchez (SAHN-chez), was born on December 21, 1977, in Hollywood, California. Doctors told his parents that he might never walk because he was born with a clubbed right foot and a seriously pigeon-toed left foot. Sanchez underwent foot surgery when he was thirteen, followed by years of physical therapy, and eventually was able to walk properly.

In 1996, Sanchez graduated from Burbank High School in Burbank, California, where he was a three-year varsity baseball player. He then attended Glendale Community College for two years, leading the baseball team to a cochampionship in the Western State Conference, the college's first play-off appearance since 1981. In his junior year, he transferred to Dallas Baptist University, for which he played in the National Association of Intercollegiate Athletics (NAIA) College World Series. He attended Oklahoma City University in his senior year and was named a NAIA All-Star.

LIFE'S WORK

In 2000, Sanchez was signed by the Boston Red Sox after he was selected in the eleventh round of that year's draft. He initially played with the Triple-A Pawtucket Red Sox, and on September 10, 2002, he made his major league debut with the Red Sox. He played for both Pawtucket and Boston in 2003, and the following year began playing for the Pittsburgh Pirates. When Pirates' third baseman Joe Randa suffered an injury on May 6, 2006, Sanchez assumed this position.

One baseball writer described 2006 as Sanchez's "storybook season," because he rose from a low-profile player to the player who attained the most votes for that year's All-Star team. In that year he also became the first Pirate to be named the National League batting

Freddy Sanchez. (AP Photo)

champion since Bill Madlock in 1983; Sanchez beat out Florida Marlins third baseman Miguel Cabrera on the last day of the 2006 season.

In 2007, Sanchez was moved to second base. He was the only Pirate on that year's All-Star team, and he ended that season with a batting average above .300 and a career-high 11 home runs. On February 5, 2007, he signed a multiyear contract with the Pirates, guaranteeing him two seasons with the team and an option to remain with the team in 2010 if he met certain performance criteria in 2009. Under the terms of the contract, Sanchez would receive a maximum of $18.9 million.

Sanchez's performance was lackluster during the first half of 2008, but it improved in the second half, and his batting average was .271, with 9 home runs. On July 29, 2009, Sanchez was traded to the San Francisco Giants. Three months later, it was announced that Sanchez had signed a two-year contract with the Giants.

During 2010, his first full season with the Giants, Sanchez's batting average was .292 with 7 home runs and 47 runs batted in . That year, the Giants won the World Series, and Sanchez helped lead the team to victory when he amassed three doubles in his first three times at bat.

SIGNIFICANCE

In more than a decade with the major leagues, Sanchez has proved to be an award-winning batter. In 2006, in addition to being named the National League batting champion, he was the league's doubles champion and the winner of the Tony Conigliaro Award for having overcome his physical adversities. In 2010, he helped the San Francisco Giants win its first World Series since the team left New York in the late-1950's.

Michael J. Bennett

FURTHER READING

Baggarly, Andrew. *A Band of Misfits: Tales of the 2010 San Francisco Giants*. Chicago: Triumph Books, 2011. Detailed chronicle of the Giants' unlikely run to the World Series that covers Sanchez's key role in their success.

ESPN. Freddy Sanchez. http://espn.go.com/mlb/player/_/id/5315/freddy-sanchez. Provides a profile of Sanchez, career statistics, a game log, photographs, and videos.

Fost, Dan. *Giants Past and Present*. 2d ed. Minneapolis: MBI, 2011. A history of the team that includes information on Sanchez.

See also: Pedro Martinez; David Ortiz; Manny Ramirez; Alex Rodriguez; Johan Santana; Miguel Tejada.

GEORGE I. SÁNCHEZ

American educator, scholar, and activist

Sánchez was nationally and internationally recognized as a pioneer critic of the use of psychological assessment tools on ethnic minorities in the United States. His findings have been cited in key U.S. Supreme Court decisions addressing the improper use of intelligence assessment on children from ethnic minority populations.

Latino heritage: Mexican

Born: October 4, 1906; Albuquerque, New Mexico

Died: April 5, 1972; Austin, Texas

Also known as: George Isidore Sánchez; Jorge Isidoro Sánchez y Sánchez

Areas of achievement: Education; activism; scholarship

EARLY LIFE

George Isidore Sánchez (SAHN-chez) was born on April 5, 1906, in the neighborhood of Barelas in Al-

buquerque, New Mexico, where his parents, Telésforo Sánchez and Juliana Sánchez, traced their Mexican American ancestry to early colonial times. He completed elementary school and most of his early education in the small mining town of Jerome, Arizona, and high school in Albuquerque, New Mexico. In 1922, he gained his first teaching experience as an instructor in the small town of Yrrisarri, near Albuquerque. From 1926 to 1930, he worked as a teacher and eventually became a principal in Bernalillo County, New Mexico. These formative years of professional experience in rural schools provided him with an influential exposure to the educational practices affecting Mexican Americans.

LIFE'S WORK

Working full time as a teacher and administrator, it took Sánchez eight years to complete his bachelor's degree in education in 1930 at the University of New Mexico by taking courses on weekends and in the summer. A year later he obtained a master's degree in educational psychology and Spanish at the University of Texas with a thesis titled "A Study of the Scores of Spanish-Speaking Children on Repeated Tests." He continued to study and research education among Mexican Americans and bilingual populations. From 1931 through 1934, he was the director of the Division of Information and Statistics of the New Mexico State Department of Education. In this position of leadership he actively worked to improve the funding of public education, while concurrently completing his doctoral training in education. He earned a doctorate in education degree in 1934 at the University of California at Berkeley, and his doctoral dissertation, "The Education of Bilinguals in a State School System," examined the academic performance of bilingual students.

Throughout Sánchez's career, his research focused on how bilingual children learn and how they are psychologically evaluated through the use of often unfair and biased intelligence evaluation instruments. In many of his publications, Sánchez criticized the use of Intellectual Quotient (IQ) tests, maintaining they were unreliable and invalid tools to assess the intelligence and educational abilities of Mexican Americans. He questioned the psychometrics of standardized assessment tools and voiced criticism against educators who worshipped the infallibility of IQ evaluation results. He also advocated for children born in other countries

A Class Apart: The *Hernandez v. Texas* Decision

Hernandez v. Texas 347 U.S. 475 (1954) is a landmark U.S. Supreme Court decision that ruled that Mexican Americans have equal protection under the Fourteenth Amendment of the U.S. Constitution. For the first time in American history, on January 11, 1954, two Mexican American attorneys, Carlos Cadena and Gus García, argued a case in front of the nine Supreme Court justices and successfully defended Pedro Hernandez, a worker accused of murdering his employer in the town of Edna, Texas. The attorneys argued that Mexican Americans were a "class apart" and did not really fit into the current U.S. legal structure that strictly recognized only black and white Americans. To bolster their legal strategy, the lawyers relied on the extensive theoretical and empirical findings regarding the educational and legal status of Mexican Americans conceptualized by George I. Sánchez.

who studied in American schools. In the journal articles "Bilingualism and Mental Measures: A Word of Caution," "The Implications of a Basal Vocabulary to Measurement of the Abilities of Bilingual Children," and "Group Differences and Spanish-Speaking Children," Sánchez conclusively stated that bilingualism should never be considered a detriment to a child's education. His conclusions made him an early pioneer and advocate for educational justice and equality. His activist tone is clearly visible in many of his writings not only in his advocacy for Mexicans and Mexican Americans but also for Navajos, which is articulated in his book *The People: A Study of the Navajos* (1948).

Sánchez's academic and research work was not limited to ethnic minorities in the United States, and he expanded his scholarship to include Latin American countries. From 1935 through 1936, with a grant from the Julius Rosenwald Fund, Sánchez spent several months in Mexico researching the education of the Mexican population. He focused on the educational methods used by the revolutionary "cultural missions" inspired by socialist agendas. He visited elementary schools in rural areas, normal schools, agricultural schools, regional training schools, and schools for downtrodden Mexican indigenous groups. Research findings from this project resulted in the publication of his well-known book *Mexico: A Revolution by Education* (1936).

With additional funding from the Julius Rosenwald Fund, he extended his research from Mexico to the American South, where he studied the rural educational systems serving primarily Mexican and black students. From 1937 through 1938, he served as a technical adviser for the national department of education in Venezuela. In 1940, with funding assistance by the Carnegie Foundation, he published his book *Forgotten People: A Study of New Mexicans,* which provides a study of the state's residents, focusing on Taos County. In this comprehensive historical analysis, Sánchez maintains that New Mexicans have been economically and politically victimized and culturally and geographically forgotten. He concludes that New Mexicans lack education and that their salvation will come through literacy.

Sánchez distinguished himself as a rigorous and dedicated professor. From 1938 to 1940, he taught at the University of New Mexico, but after encountering opposition and criticism based on his outspoken approach to research and instruction, he moved to Texas and began teaching at the University of Texas, where he was a professor until his death. During his long academic tenure at this university, he held several prominent national positions in educational leadership and advocacy. From 1941 to 1942, he was the president of the League of United Latin American Citizens, and from 1945 to 1950 he was the president of the Southwest Council on the Education of Spanish-Speaking People. He also served as the director of the American Council of Spanish Speaking People.

Sánchez died on April 5, 1972, in Austin, Texas. On June 16, 1972, the Texas senate adopted a concurrent resolution honoring Sánchez for being a "distinguished educator, father of Mexican American studies and intellectual leader of the Mexican American movement in Texas and the Southwest."

SIGNIFICANCE

Sánchez led many political and educational battles in New Mexico and Texas aimed at improving educational opportunities for Spanish-speaking children. He participated in many court cases dealing with the segregation of Spanish-speaking people. The most famous case concerned his development of the "class apart" theory used by the plaintiffs in the U.S. Supreme Court decision *Hernandez v. Texas* 347 U.S. 475 (1954) . Sánchez received recognition from Presidents John F. Kennedy and Lyndon B. Johnson, who appointed him to national and international commissions dealing with the problems of Latino people.

Fernando A. Ortiz

FURTHER READING

Blanton, Carlos. "George I. Sánchez, Ideology, and Whiteness in the Making of the Mexican American Civil Rights Movement, 1930-1960." *The Journal of Southern History* 72 (August, 2006): 569- 604. Sánchez advocated for assimilation and integration of Mexican Americans into the U.S. culture through citizenship and language. This article explains how he approached the concept of "whiteness" in the 1930's, a time of bigotry, eugenic movements, and pseudoscientific theories of racial superiority.

Paredes, Américo, ed. *Humanidad: Essays in Honor of George I. Sánchez*. Los Angeles: Chicano Studies Center Publications, University of California, 1977. Includes a biography of Sánchez, as well as essays providing an overview of his work, discussing his views on testing, and examining other aspects of bilingual education and the lives of Chicanos in the Southwest.

Welsh, Michael. "A Prophet Without Honor: George I. Sánchez and Bilingualism in New Mexico." *New Mexico Historical Review* 69 (January, 1994): 29-32. Details Sánchez's perspective on bilingualism among bicultural Mexican Americans and his advocacy for bilingual education.

See also: Lauro Cavazos; Julian Nava; Julian Samora.

LORETTA SÁNCHEZ

American politician

Sánchez entered political office in 1996 when she defeated Bob Dornan, becoming the first Latina from Orange County, California, to serve in Congress. Representative Sánchez has worked on a variety of issues ranging from national defense to women's rights, as well as issues pertaining to commerce, the economy, and small business.

Latino heritage: Mexican
Born: January 7, 1960; Lynwood, California
Areas of achievement: Government and politics; women's rights; business

EARLY LIFE

Loretta Sánchez (law-REHT-ah SAHN-chehz) was born in Lynwood, California, to parents who had immigrated from Mexico in search of more opportunity for their children. The family initially settled in El Monte, a city in Los Angeles County. Concerned about their children's access to better education, her parents moved to the city of Anaheim in Orange County. In Anaheim, Sánchez grew up in a neighborhood with few Latino families, and, as a result, she came to appreciate the cultural values instilled by her family, particularly her parents, who taught her the value of persistence, hard work, and education as a way of achieving success in one's professional and public life.

Sánchez credits her parents, as well as the Head Start program, with helping her to succeed in school. Throughout her school years, her parents supported and encouraged her to study diligently and earn high grades. She describes her parents as role models who cultivated in her a love of learning, as well as an appreciation for how hard other immigrant families had to work in the United States. Sánchez was an exemplary student who excelled in school and at learning about her family's cultural heritage. Her father was instrumental in this regard, guiding her in reading Spanish literature at home, and his efforts provided her with a cultural knowledge of Latin America and enabled her to be bilingual.

At Katella High School, Sánchez scored well on her Scholastic Aptitude Test (SAT) and qualified as a National Merit Scholar. After graduating from high school, she was offered scholarships at several prestigious schools and decided to attend Chapman College, a private college in the city of Orange. Upon finishing college, she entered graduate school, and after earning her MBA at American University she embarked on a successful business career.

Sánchez worked as a financial analyst in the 1980's and early 1990's before she decided to enter politics.

In 1994, she campaigned for city council, and although she did not win the election, this did not deter her from politics. In the 1996 election, Sánchez, a Democrat, challenged Republican Bob Dornan, who represented California's Forty-seventh District in the House of Representatives, an area that traditionally had been Republican and politically conservative. However, during Dornan's more than ten years in office, the demographics of the 47th district and much of Orange County had changed considerably, gradually shifting to a more Democratic constituency because of the growth of the Latino community. This change, as well as her well-run grassroots campaign, resulted in Sánchez's victory. Dornan contested the results, but the voting count was upheld, and Sánchez took her seat in the House of Representatives. By 2011, Sánchez had represented the district for almost fifteen years.

LIFE'S WORK

Sánchez characterizes herself as a "blue dog Democrat" who advocates for a variety of social and economic issues, while at the same time supporting responsible fiscal management. As of 2010, Sánchez had worked on many important issues reflecting the diversity of her district's constituency. These issues include greater equality for women in the military, more resources for all levels of public education, strong national security, effective health care, support for small businesses, and international human rights.

Sánchez has promoted women's rights and worked to advance and empower women in all walks of life.

Loretta Sánchez. (AP Photo)

In 2005, she began investigating cases of sexual assault in the military and succeeded in amending the Uniform Code of Military Justice in order to provide greater protection for victims of sexual assault. Sánchez has also sponsored legislation aimed at providing equal wages for women and ensuring reproductive rights.

Sánchez believes strongly in the power of education to empower individuals to achieve their dreams. She explains in her autobiography that not only does America's economic well-being rely on access to strong public education, but also its national security depends on the quality of the nation's educational institutions and their ability to serve students. Without resources and support systems for schools and students, particularly minority students, Sánchez notes, the United States runs the risk of losing its economic competitiveness in the world economy. She advocates for more counseling and academic and financial support services for students in underserved school districts.

Sánchez has also advocated for a strong national defense. She has served on the House Committee on Armed Services, including the Subcommittees on Strategic Forces and Military Personnel. After the terrorist attacks on September 11, 2001, she became vice chair of the House Committee on Homeland Security and chair of the Subcommittee on Terrorism, Unconventional Threats and Capabilities. In 2006, she supported the Security and Accountability for Every Port Act, which increases both port security and shipping commerce in the Los Angeles and Long Beach areas.

Sánchez has brought her previous business experience to bear as a member of the Joint Economic Committee, which studies and provides research data to Congress on matters relating to the economic health of the United States. She supports legislation to stimulate small business in Orange County and throughout California, including access to business loans, lower taxes, and the development of mass transit to improve the flow of goods and services. Sánchez's congressional district includes not only large portions of the Latino community but also the largest Vietnamese community outside of Vietnam. In 2008, she became cochair of the Congressional Caucus on Vietnam, and in this position she called for greater religious freedom and civil rights in Vietnam.

SIGNIFICANCE

Loretta Sánchez made history when she was elected in 1996 as the first Latina representative of Orange County in the U.S. Congress. During her tenure in office,

Sánchez has served on the Congressional Caucus on Women's Issues and has been a strong advocate for public education, national defense, and greater equality for women in civilian life, as well as for women serving in the military. She has also worked to increase access to public and higher education for all students.

William A. Teipe

FURTHER READING

Sánchez, Loretta. Congresswoman Loretta Sanchez Representing California's 47th District. http://www.lorettasanchez.house.gov. The congresswoman's official Web site, providing information on her biography, positions, and activities.

Sánchez, Linda, and Loretta Sánchez, with Richard Buskin. *Dream in Color: How the Sánchez Sisters Are Making History in Congress*. New York: Grand Central, 2008. Loretta Sánchez and her sister Linda, who also serves in Congress, recount their life stories, recalling their parents and their childhood with five other siblings, as well as their political experiences.

See also: Luis Gutiérrez; Joseph Marion Hernández; Ileana Ros-Lehtinen; Edward R. Roybal; Leticia Van de Putte.

LUIS RAFAEL SÁNCHEZ

Puerto Rican-born playwright, writer, and educator

One of the most prominent Puerto Rican authors of the late twentieth and early twenty-first centuries, Sánchez has published celebrated works in every major genre. Noted for his humor, his earthy themes, and his closeness to the common person, Sánchez has enjoyed extraordinary success with his readers and with critics. His work as both an educator and a writer has contributed to a renovation of the novel, the drama, and the short story, all written in a Spanish with distinctly Puerto Rican vocabulary and syntax.

Latino heritage: Puerto Rican

Born: November 17, 1936; Humacao, Puerto Rico

Also known as: Wico

Areas of achievement: Theater; literature; education

EARLY LIFE

Born to Luis Sánchez and Agueda Ortiz in Humacao, Puerto Rico, Luis Rafael Sánchez (lew-EES rah-fee-

EHL SAHN-chez) attended the José Celso Barbosa Elementary School. At the age of twelve he moved with his family to Calle Sol (Sun Street) in Old San Juan, and he attended Central High School. In 1955, he went to Mexico to participate in a theater competition and was awarded a medal by the National Institute for Mexican Youth as best young actor of the year. In 1956, he began his undergraduate work at the University of Puerto Rico, from which he received a B.A. degree in theater in 1960. During his years as a college student, Sánchez actively participated in the university's theater program, the Commedietta Universitaria, as well as in the programming of the university's radio station.

By 1957, Sánchez had already begun to write for prestigious publications, such as the newspaper *El Mundo*, and literary journals, such as *Asomante* and the *Revista del Instituto de Cultura Puertorriqueña*. Sánchez was awarded a special scholarship for the summer of 1959 in order to study drama and theater technique at

Luis Rafael Sánchez. (AP Photo)

Columbia University. With the publication of his first dramatic work, *The Waiting* (1960), he had begun what was to be a long and distinguished literary career. Sánchez earned a master's degree from New York University in 1963 and a doctoral degree in Spanish from the University of Madrid in 1976.

LIFE'S WORK

Sánchez had already begun to work as a professor of Spanish in the School of General Studies at the University of Puerto Rico in 1969. After receiving his doctoral degree, he returned to the faculty to teach Puerto Rican, Hispanic American, and Spanish literature full time, frequently traveling and lecturing the world over. Nonetheless, he has been able to balance both a successful academic career and a literary career of staggering proportions. One of his first dramatic works to garner the praise of critics was his play *Our Daily Bile* (1962), which presents the reality of two Puerto Rican mainstays: *espiritismo* (a local form of spiritualism) and the lottery, which the protagonist is offering a sacrifice to win. *In Shirt Sleeves* (1966), perhaps Sánchez's finest collection of short stories, is an outstanding example of his ability to write in a popular form

of Spanish rather than the correct Spanish of the upper and educated classes.

Sánchez's 1968 masterpiece *The Passion According to Antígona Pérez* is a political drama based on the life of Olga Viscal Garriga, a member of the Puerto Rican Nationalist Party who was imprisoned for eight years for failing to recognize American sovereignty over Puerto Rico. The comparison between the moral dilemmas presented in Sophocles' *Antigone* (441 B.C.E.; English translation, 1729) and the conundrum of the island's political status was not lost on the audience when the work was presented at the 1968 Puerto Rican Theater Festival in the celebrated Tapia Theater of San Juan.

Another of Sánchez's works, his novel *Macho Camacho's Beat* (1976), also caused a sensation in the Hispanic American literary world. A tale set in the humdrum boredom of a massive traffic jam, the novel is a collection of voices that echoes the beat of the pulsating and diverse urban landscape. Sánchez's focus in this novel is to present the modern, Americanized Puerto Rico, whose chaotic streets and seemingly mass confusion reflect the political disarray of the island under United States hegemony. This same theme of Puerto Rico's irregular and disconcerting cultural condition under American rule is also the subject of Sánchez's essay *The Flying Bus* (1994), which explores the confusion provoked by attempts to assimilate the two cultures. His 1998 novel *Don't Cry for Us Puerto Rico* continues to examine the problems of Puerto Rico's cultural dichotomies. In 2005, Sánchez published *Devour Me Again*, an additional collection of reflections on the cultural and political situation of the island. His 2007 novel *Indiscretions of Clinton's Dog* is a trenchant, humorous, and highly innovative work in which the "First Dog" of the Bill Clinton White House divulges embarrassing secrets.

SIGNIFICANCE

One of the greatest Puerto Rican writers of his time, Luis Rafael Sánchez has excelled in producing excellent literary works in virtually every genre. His signature works in the essay, drama, the short story, and the novel are all numbered among the finest in contemporary Puerto Rican literature. What is more, Sánchez has had a distinguished career as a university professor and spokesman for the cultural hegemony of Puerto Rico and its Hispanic traditions. His literary virtuosity has made him one of the few Puerto Rican authors to have an international recognition and reputation for excellence.

Mark T. DeStephano

FURTHER READING

Perivolaris, John. *Puerto Rican Cultural Identity and the Work of Luis Rafael Sánchez.* Chapel Hill: University of North Carolina Department of Romance Languages, 2000. An excellent study of Sánchez's literary skill and the cultural significance of his works in the search for Puerto Rican identity.

Reyes, Israel. *Humor and the Eccentric Text in Puerto Rican Literature.* Gainesville: University Press of Florida, 2005. Sánchez's artistic ability is considered in various sections of this fascinating analysis of the role of humor and irony in the construction of Puerto Rican identity and the resistance to external cultural influences.

See also: Miguel Algarín; Giannina Braschi; Victor Hernández Cruz; Judith Ortiz Cofer; Lola Rodríguez de Tió; Esmeralda Santiago; Clemente Soto Vélez.

PONCHO SÁNCHEZ

American musician

Sánchez has been a prominent band leader, singer, and percussionist. He has released dozens of recordings, received Grammy Awards, and is widely regarded as one of the leading figures in Latin jazz.

Latino heritage: Mexican
Born: October 30, 1951; Laredo, Texas
Also known as: Ildefonso Sánchez; Papa Gato
Area of achievement: Music

EARLY LIFE

Poncho Sánchez (POON-choh SAHN-chehz), the youngest of eleven children, was born Ildefonso Sánchez in Laredo, Texas. His parents immigrated to the United States from the northern Mexican state of Vallecillo. The family moved to Los Angeles, where Sánchez grew up in the Norwalk barrio from the age of three and attended the Grayland Avenue Elementary School. From an early age, Sánchez was exposed to a wide range of musical styles in his home through the radio selections of his parents, which included Latin music, doo-wop, soul, and *bugalú* styles.

At home, Sánchez's siblings sang and danced to the Afro-Cuban music of Tito Puente, Machito, and Cal Tjader, which focused his listening on the mambo, mariachi, and *cumbia* styles. This early exposure to recordings of Latin music would later define much of his mature performing career. Sánchez also developed an interest in mainstream jazz performers, including Charlie Parker, Dizzy Gillespie, Clifford Brown, Thelonious Monk, and the Jazz Crusaders. He taught himself to sing and play the guitar, flute, and drums. From 1966 to 1971, he was the vocalist for a local teen rhythm and blues band called the Halos. During high school he was a jazz drummer in a group called Midnight Set. Inspired by famed Cuban conga player Mongo Santamaria, Sánchez began playing percussion instruments, including the timbales and congas. Sánchez continued to play in local bands, particularly with a Latin rock band called Sabor, in the Los Angeles area and to work in an aluminum foundry before he was hired to play in Tjader's band in 1975.

Poncho Sánchez. (Redferns/Getty Images)

LIFE'S WORK

Sánchez's mature career began with his seven-year membership in Tjader's band, in which he remained until Tjader's death in 1982, producing fourteen recordings during this period. Tjader's *La onda va bien* album launched the Concord Picante label in 1980, and it also won that year's Grammy Award for Best Latin Album. During his last years with Tjader's group, Sánchez was also performing with his own Latin Octet, which issued their first recordings *Poncho* in 1979 and *Straight Ahead* in 1980 on the Discovery recording label. After working with pianist Clare Fischer in Tjader's group, Sánchez performed on Fischer's recordings *Salsa picante* (1978) and *Macacha* (1979), both on the Discovery record label.

Carl Johnson, the founder of the Concord Picante record label, signed Sánchez to a contract for annual recordings starting in 1982 with *Sonando*. This contract and the numerous recordings issued in the 1980's and 1990's made Sánchez one of the leading Latin jazz recording artists in the world. In 1999, Sánchez was awarded a Grammy Award for Best Latin Recording for his album *Latin Soul*.

Sánchez has been among the primary proponents of Latin jazz music through his recordings and live performances. The instrumentation of his Latin Octet typically includes one reed player (playing flute or saxophone); one high-brass player (trumpet or flugelhorn); one low-brass player (trombone); three percussionists playing timbales, congas, bongos, and chekere; a bassist; and keyboard players on piano and organ. The band's repertoire has been a mixture of Latin jazz tunes, Afro-Cuban music, and jazz standards. Guests on recordings have included many of the most famous Latin jazz performers and composers, including Mongo Santamaria, Chick Corea, and Freddie Hubbard.

Although he has been known exclusively as a performer, Sánchez published an instructional book for conga players in 2002. *Poncho Sánchez' Conga Cookbook: Develop Your Conga Playing by Learning Afro-Cuban Rhythms from the Master* offers a new vehicle for Sánchez to educate a new generation of young musicians about Latin jazz..

SIGNIFICANCE

For decades, Sánchez consistently sought an accessible style that has had broad appeal to fans of Latin music. He has maintained a singular commitment to the highest quality performances and recordings of Latin jazz blended with traditional jazz melodies. In doing so, Sánchez continued the style of his mentor Tjader. Through numerous recordings and extensive international touring, Sánchez has also been among the most prominent individuals developing the Latin jazz performance tradition in the United States and internationally. As a Mexican American, Sánchez initially found himself shut out of the salsa music tradition, which had been dominated by Cuban Americans and Puerto Rican Americans. However, his perseverance and steadfast commitment to quality have removed the barriers to Chicano performers playing salsa music.

David Steffens

FURTHER READING

Berendt, Joachim-Ernest. *The Jazz Book*: *From Rag-Time to Fusion and Beyond*. 6th ed. Brooklyn, N.Y.: Lawrence Hill Books, 1992. Includes a brief mention of Sánchez and his place in jazz history.

Larkin, Colin, ed. *Encyclopedia of Popular Music*. Vol. 7. New York: Oxford University Press, 1992. Includes a brief biography of Sánchez and a listing of recordings, including compilation recordings and video recordings.

Sanchez, Pablo. The Official Poncho Sanchez Website. www.ponchosanchez.com. Includes an extensive biography, discography, photo gallery, performance schedule, merchandise, equipment endorsements, and contact information.

Sánchez, Poncho, with Chuck Silverman. *Poncho Sánchez' Conga Cookbook: Develop Your Conga Playing by Learning Afro-Cuban Rhythms from the Master*. New York: Cherry Lane Music, 2002. Includes an introductory biography, instruction in traditional conga techniques and rhythms, and a listing of recommended recordings.

Snodgrass, Mary Ellen. "Poncho Sánchez: Classic Conguero." In *Contemporary Hispanic Biography*, edited by Ashyia Henderson. Vol. 2. Detroit: Gale Press, 2003. This article includes an extensive biography, selected discography from 1982 through 2001, and a listing of sources.

Varela, Jesse. "Poncho Sánchez: Straight Up." *Jazz Times*, November, 2001, p. 41. This brief article was written after an interview with Sánchez at the Fujitsu-Concord Jazz Festival in July, 2001.

See also: Rubén Blades; Willie Colón; Paquito D'Rivera; Charlie Palmieri; Tito Puente; Carlos Santana.

JESÚS MARÍA SANROMÁ

Puerto Rican-born classical pianist

Internationally recognized as a one of the foremost concert pianists of the twentieth century, Sanromá also championed and advocated for Puerto Rican art music. In addition to giving concerts, he made numerous significant recordings. He also taught piano and founded the piano department of the Puerto Rico Conservatory of Music.

Latino heritage: Puerto Rican

Born: November 7, 1902; Carolina, Puerto Rico

Died: October 12, 1984; Guaynabo, Puerto Rico

Also known as: Chuchú

Area of achievement: Music

EARLY LIFE

Jesús María Sanromá (sahn-roh-MAH) was born on November 7, 1902, in Carolina, Puerto Rico. Three years later, he moved to the town of Fajardo when his father accepted a position as an organist there. At home, the young Sanromá corrected mistakes his father made while he practiced at the keyboard, poking at him for every wrong note. In early piano lessons, his first piano teacher complained that he progressed too quickly.

At an early age, Sanromá displayed promise as a professional musician, mastering the piano sonatas of Wolfgang Amadeus Mozart and Ludwig van Beethoven, and at age twelve, he debuted as a concert pianist in Fajardo. In 1915, his family moved to Santurce, a city outside of the capital San Juan. Sanromá quickly gained recognition in Puerto Rico for his talent, receiving a scholarship in 1916 from the government to study at the New England Conservatory of Music. Shortly afterward, father and son moved to Boston. The fourteen-year-old Sanromá studied at the conservatory with Nicaraguan pianist David Sequeira. Under his piano teacher, he trained in classical and Romantic piano repertory as well as the music of Claude Debussy and Maurice Ravel. Graduating in 1920, Sanromá won the annual piano competition, which included a new piano. His next teacher was the Polish pianist Antoinette Szumowska-Adamowska, newly appointed to the New England Conservatory of Music. Following his success in Boston, Sanromá traveled to Europe and studied piano with Alfred Cortot in Paris and Artur Schnabel in Berlin.

LIFE'S WORK

Beginning in 1926, Sanromá embarked on his long-lasting collaboration as a solo pianist with the Boston Symphony Orchestra under Serge Koussevitzky. The relationship lasted until 1944 and produced numerous recordings. Sanromá returned to his alma mater, the New England Conservatory of Music, where he taught piano from 1930 to 1941. Sought out by many contemporary composers because of his abilities, he gave numerous premieres as a pianist. In 1939, he gave the world premiere of Walter Piston's concertino for piano along with the Boston Symphony Orchestra. Sanromá met the celebrated German composer Paul Hindemith in 1940 at the prestigious Berkshire Music Center (now Tanglewood Music Center), and the two formed a long-term friendship. In 1945, the Puerto Rican pianist commissioned Hindemith to compose a concerto that highlighted the piano in a virtuosic and modern manner. The world premiere of the piano concerto took place in 1947 with the Cleveland Orchestra under conductor George Szell.

Sanromá signed with the talent agency Columbia Concerts Corporation in 1943, leading to numerous tours in both North America and South America. His repertoire remained immense and diverse; the public, in particular, recognized his talents at playing George Gershwin's *Rhapsody in Blue* (1924). During the 1940's, he frequently returned to his native Puerto Rico, and he moved back there permanently in 1950.

In Puerto Rico, Sanromá served as an important musical figure, assisting in the development of the island's emerging musical culture. He played a vital role in the improvement of the Puerto Rico Conservatory of Music, Puerto Rico Symphony Orchestra, Institute of Puerto Rican Culture, and the Pablo Casals Festival. In addition to the classical canon and the works of modern European composers, Sanromá performed, recorded, and advanced the importance of music by Puerto Rican composers such as Rafael Balseiro Dávila, Héctor Campos-Parsi, Rafael Hernández Marín, José Enrique Pedreira, Manuel Gregorio Tavárez, and Amaury Veray. Sanromá served as the head of the music department at the University of Puerto Rico in 1951 and later as the chair of the piano department at the Puerto Rico Conservatory of Music. He died on October 12, 1984, in Guaynabo.

SIGNIFICANCE

One of the leading pianists of the Western Hemisphere, Sanromá excelled as a concert pianist, recording artist, and teacher. He gave more than three thousand concerts, performed in more than twenty countries, and was featured as a soloist with hundreds of the top orchestras in the world. He masterfully performed works belonging to the classical and Romantic piano repertory; however, he also was a leading promoter of modern music, giving world premieres of works by Walter Piston and Paul Hindemith and U.S. premieres of works by Igor Stravinsky, Maurice Ravel, Francis Poulenc, and Arthur Honegger. He served as one of the most important interpreters and advocates of Puerto Rican music.

Mark E. Perry

FURTHER READING

Hernández, Alberto. *Jesús María Sanromá: An American Twentieth-Century Pianist*. Lanham, Md.: Scarecrow Press, 2008. A comprehensive work, this is the essential biography of Sanromá.

Noss, Luther. *Paul Hindemith in the United States*. Urbana: University of Illinois Press, 1989. Chronicles the musical activities in the United States of the celebrated European composer who collaborated with Sanromá.

Thompson, Donald. "Sanromá." In *Concert Life in Puerto Rico, 1957-1992*, edited by Donald Thompson and Francis Schwartz. San Juan: University of Puerto Rico Press, 1998. A chapter on the life and works of the celebrated Puerto Rican pianist.

See also: Claudio Arrau; Jorge Bolet; Justino Díaz; Eduardo Mata; Noro Morales; Lalo Schifrin.

CARLOS SANTANA

Mexican-born musician

The music of Santana, a legendary rock guitarist, is a testament to the ideals of a multicultural society, demonstrating that multiple races, ethnic groups, and musical styles can coexist harmoniously.

Latino heritage: Mexican
Born: July 20, 1947; Autlán de Navarro, Jalisco, Mexico
Also known as: Carlos Augusto Alves Santana
Areas of achievement: Music; activism

EARLY LIFE

Carlos Santana (KAHR-lohs sahn-TAHN-ah) was born Carlos Augusto Alves Santana on July 20, 1947, in Autlán de Navarro, Mexico, the son of José and Josefina Santana. Santana came from a musical family, and as a child he learned violin from his father. In addition to being trained in the works of Ludwig von Beethoven and other classical composers, Santana learned about music through his live performances, which ranged from accompanying his father on traditional mariachi music to playing blues guitar at Tijuana cabarets patronized by American tourists.

In 1963, Santana's family immigrated to the United States, settling in San Francisco. The move created a threefold sense of displacement in Santana. As a student he faced a language barrier that adversely affected his academic performance in core subjects. He also was unable to line up steady musical gigs, and his preference for African American blues fused with Mexican-influenced music was incompatible with the "surf-rock" sound embraced by his peers. Despite the struggle of readjusting to a radically different environment, Santana

Carlos Santana. (AP Photo)

graduated from Mission High School in 1965. The following year, he organized a group of musicians originally named the Santana Blues Band and later simply named Santana. Over the years, the members of Santana changed, but the composition of its musicians remained multiracial, multiethnic, and occasionally multigendered.

LIFE'S WORK

Concert promoter Bill Graham played an important role in Santana's early career. Through Graham's efforts, the band made its live debut at the Fillmore West theater in San Francisco on June 16, 1968. Graham also persuaded organizers of the 1969 Woodstock Music and Arts Festival to include Santana on the program. The band performed a seven-song set on August 16, the second day of the festival. This appearance gave a significant boost to the careers of both the band and Carlos Santana himself, as they were introduced to an audience of about half a million people. At this time, the band's members were a mix of Anglo, Latino, and African American musicians, including drummer Michael Shrieve; organist and lead vocalist Greg Rolie; bass player David Brown; conga players Mike Carabello, a Puerto Rican; conga and timbale player José Chepitó Areas, from Nicaragua; as well as lead guitarist Carlos Santana. The band's music was a unique blend of Mississippi Delta blues, San Francisco Bay Area rock, Memphis soul, and Latin jazz.

This early incarnation of Santana produced three classic albums: *Santana* (1969), *Abraxas* (1970), and *Santana III* (1971). The self-titled debut album *Santana* received a boost from a tour and the high-profile Woodstock performance. Early success, however, created friction among band's members, some of whom left the group. Carlos Santana had the rights to use the name "Santana," and he changed personnel and musical direction, abandoning a Top Forty format for more serene Latin jazz, with traces of soft rock and middle-of-the-road soul.

In his life, Carlos Santana embarked upon many spiritual quests, ranging from the Roman Catholic heritage of his family to the idealism of the 1960's counterculture, ancient Indian philosophy, and Christianity. In 1972, Carlos, through musician John McLaughlin, was introduced to guru Sri Chinmoy. As a disciple of the guru, Carlos embraced a lifestyle of spiritual disciplines, including meditation and alternative dietary practices. Chinmoy gave Carlos an honorary name, Devadip, which means "the eye, the lamp, and the light of God." Carlos's spiritual quest became evident in the musical direction of his second trilogy of recordings:

Abraxas

During the fall of 1970, the band Santana released its second album, *Abraxas*, whose tracks included such classic rock staples as "Black Magic Woman/Gypsy Queen," "Oye Como Va," and "Samba Pa Ti." The album featured a mix of blues, rock, and refined Latin American musical genres, which was a break from the raw and free-form styles and arrangements of Santana's debut album, *Santana* (1969). Although Carlos Santana's guitar played a leading role in most of the songs, percussionist José Chepitó Areas was influential in the evolution of the album's sound. Areas introduced the band to the classic Latin rhythms of the cha cha, as evident in Santana's cover version of the Fleetwood Mac song "Black Magic Woman"; Santana's version reached number four on the *Billboard* singles chart. Latin influences are also heard in the band's cover version of Tito Puente's "Oye Como Va" and the more up-tempo *guaracha* style of "Gypsy Queen."

Although *Santana* provided a foundation for the band's sound, *Abraxas* established Santana's signature musical style for years to come. The album cover of *Abraxas*, which Carlos Santana chose after seeing a reproduction of a painting in a periodical, also made a significant contribution. The visual appeal of the album cover can be attributed to the artwork, *Annunciation*, by Mati Klarwein. *Abraxas* also benefited because its release coincided with the release of the film *Woodstock* (1970), which featured a performance by Santana and exposed the band to a broader audience, elevating it from moderate visibility to superstardom.

Caravansari (1972), *Welcome* (1973), and *Borboletta* (1974). The release of these albums coincided with the official end of the 1960's, the closing of the Fillmore East, and major shifts in the band's musical direction and personnel.

In 1973, Carlos established the Milagro Foundation, a nonprofit organization that provides financial assistance for the education and medical needs of children. That same year, he married Deborah King. The couple had three children, Salvador, Stella, and Angelica, before they divorced in 2008.

From the late 1970's to the late 1990's, the band Santana received favorable reviews, but it enjoyed only a few modest hits. Changing tastes in popular music resulted in waning popularity and declining record sales. During these years Carlos became increasingly active in political causes for peace and social justice and was an advocate for human rights, fighting world hunger, and world peace.

In 1982, Carlos parted ways with Chinmoy because the musician could not reconcile his guru's teachings with Carlos's personal life. Carlos viewed Chinmoy's rules, such as being forbidden to reproduce and to have children within the context of marriage, as irrational.

With some help from Graham, Santana was one of the featured acts at the 1985 Live Aid concert, which raised funds for famine relief in East Africa. Carlos also performed at the Amnesty International Concert in 1986. Carlos Santana and several of his former bandmates were inducted into the Rock and Roll Hall of Fame in 1998.

After consistently declining record sales over a twenty-year period, the 1999 release of *Supernatural* was a breakthrough in Carlos's musical career. The album sold twenty-five million copies to attain multiplatinum-sales status, and it received two Grammy Awards for Album of the Year and Best Rock Album. Several of the songs on the album also were honored, with "Smooth" receiving three Grammys, including Best Record of the Year, and the songs "Maria, Maria," "The Calling," and "El Farol" each obtaining a Grammy. Ironically, the success Carlos enjoyed in his fifties far exceeded that of his post-Woodstock period. Along with the triumph of *Supernatural* came an expanded fan base across both racial barriers and generational lines.

SIGNIFICANCE

Contrary to most of his contemporaries, whose successes peaked early in their careers and then waned, Carlos

Santana's greatest achievement occurred with the album *Supernatural*, which was released thirty years after his band's debut album. *Supernatural* ranks among the best-selling recordings of all time in all musical genres. At the beginning of the twenty-first century, Santana had become a "household name," and his popularity transcended cultures and generations. In 2003, *Rolling Stone* magazine ranked him at number fifteen in its list of the One Hundred Greatest Guitarists of All Time. He became one of the few Latin Americans in the music industry to reach the pinnacle of success, and he has served as a role model for many younger musicians of all races and ethnicities.

Michael D. Royster

FURTHER READING

Leng, Simon. *Soul Sacrifice: The Santana Story*. London: Firefly, 2000. Provides a comprehensive account of Carlos Santana's struggles and triumphs in both his musical career and personal life.

Santana, Deborah. *Space Between the Stars: My Journey to an Open Heart*. One World/Ballantine, 2006. Deborah, Carlos Santana's wife for more than thirty years, provides an autobiographical account of the couple's life.

Shapiro, Marc. *Carlos Santana: Back on Top*. New York: St. Martin's Press, 2000. Biography that discusses how Santana's musical comeback occurred at an unpredictable time in his career.

See also: Sheila E.; José Feliciano; Jerry Garcia; Tito Puente; Jon Secada.

JOHAN SANTANA

Venezuelan-born baseball player

One of baseball's dominating pitchers, the two-time Cy Young Award winner has used his success to create the Johan Santana Foundation, which supports youth baseball and other children's charities in his native Venezuela.

Latino heritage: Venezuelan
Born: March 13, 1979; Tovar, Mérida State, Venezuela
Also known as: Johan Alexander Santana Araque
Areas of achievement: Baseball; philanthropy

EARLY LIFE

Johan Santana (YOH-hahn san-TAN-ah) was born Johan Alexander Santana Araque, the second of five

children, on March 13, 1979, in Tovar, Venezuela. Although the region is best known for soccer players and artists, several quality baseball players called it home, including Santana's father, Jesus, a part-time semipro shortstop, and Santana's older brother, Franklin. Early on, most believed it was Franklin who showed the most potential playing baseball.

Growing up, Santana exhibited overwhelming enthusiasm for the game. As a youngster, emulating his father, he strove to play shortstop. However, as a natural lefty, he soon learned that left-handers traditionally did not play shortstop. Santana didn't allow this to stop him and taught himself how to play the position right-handed

Johan Santana. (AP Photo)

However, while playing the outfield, he would revert to his natural left-handed play, highlighting his natural throwing ability.

Santana eventually moved away from shortstop and settled in as the center fielder for his local team, the Chiquilines. Each year, when the Chiquilines competed in the Venezuelan national baseball tournament, their success was more than expected, and the team gradually drew the attention of major league scouts. This is where, in 1994, Santana was first noticed by Houston Astros scout Andrés Reiner.

Reiner was so taken by Santana that Reiner decided to spend his own money to visit Santana at his home in Tovar. Although other teams were also interested in Santana, his family was impressed with Reiner's effort and convinced Santana to sign with the Astros. Reiner insisted that Santana possessed major league pitching talent, and the Astros agreed. By the summer of 1996 Santana was pitching for the Astros' team in the Dominican summer league.

The following summer Santana played in both the Gulf Coast League and the New York-Penn league. Then in 1998, Santana was given the opportunity to play most of the season as a starter for the Auburn Doubledays of the New York-Penn League. His success propelled him to the next level.

LIFE'S WORK

After spending the entire 1999 season with the Michigan Battle Cats of the Class-A Midwestern League, Santana was still not the pitcher the Astros had hoped for and they chose to leave him unprotected in the upcoming draft. He ultimately found himself on the Minnesota Twins roster for the 2000 season. With a roster full of developing young players, the Twins had more time to develop Santana and planned to use him as a relief pitcher and spot starter that season. Although Santana struggled throughout the summer of 2000, the Twins awarded him with a roster spot for the 2001 season. Unfortunately, he spent much of that season nursing an elbow injury.

The following season Santana impressed the Twins by posting an 8-6 record, a 2.99 earned-run average (ERA), and 137 strikeouts in 108 innings. Looking to give him more opportunities to pitch, the Twins had Santana begin the 2002 season with its Class-AAA affiliate in Edmonton. Nine starts later he was back on the Twins roster. Santana now had developed three pitches: a blistering fastball, a slider, and a change-up that would keep hitters off balance for years to come.

After starting the 2003 campaign in the Twins' bullpen, Santana joined the starting rotation in July and was soon on his way to becoming the staff's ace. He completed the season with a 12-3 record, a 3.07 ERA, and 169 strikeouts in just over 158 innings. In 2004, Santana overcame a slow start to have one of his best seasons. He completed the campaign with 20 wins, 265 strikeouts, and a 2.61 ERA, and he earned his first Cy Young Award. The following three years Santana continued his dominance in Minnesota, winning a second Cy Young Award in 2006 and baseball's Triple Crown, leading the league in wins, strikeouts, and ERA.

Following the 2007 season, Santana was traded to the New York Mets. He was quickly signed to what was then the largest contract ever given a pitcher in major league baseball history, six years and $137.5 million. He established himself as the ace of the Mets staff, finishing his first season in New York as the league leader in ERA (2.35). Although somewhat slowed by injuries the following two seasons, Santana was still the leader of the Mets staff and regarded as one of the top pitchers in the game.

SIGNIFICANCE

At the conclusion of the 2010 season, Santana had established himself as one of his generation's greatest pitchers. A two-time Cy Young Award winner, he also has won baseball's Triple Crown in pitching, played on three All-Star teams, and received the American League Gold Glove Award in 2007. Santana's baseball achievements are perhaps second only to the charity work he does through the Johan Santana Foundation, created in 2006 to support youth baseball and other children's charities near his hometown in Venezuela. In the summer of 2007, Santana held his first annual Celebrity Bowl-A-Thon as a tribute to a friend who had died from melanoma. Santana also is Major League Baseball's spokesman for the "Play It Smart When It Comes to the Sun" Program, raising awareness about skin cancer.

Michael D. Cummings, Jr.

FURTHER READING

Curry, Jack. "Scout Listens to His Instincts, Not to His Boss, and Uncovers a Star." *The New York Times*, January 31, 2008. Story about how Reiner spotted Santana at the age of fifteen.

Jenkins, L. "The Savior of Port St. Lucie." *Sports Illustrated*, 108, no. 8 (February 25, 2008): 30. This article provides details about the Mets' acquisition of Santana and the importance of his arrival in New York.

Price, S. L. "Sweet Sound of Santana: His Clubhouse Style, Like His Pregame Preparation, Is All Music, Fun, and Games, but on the Mound Johan Santana of the Twins Has Become the Game's Most Dominant Performer." *Sports Illustrated*, May 23, 2005, 42. Price provides an in-depth look at Santana's rise from Venezuelan school kid to major league superstar.

See also: Joaquín Andújar; Willie Hernández; Pedro Martinez; Luis Tiant; Fernando Valenzuela.

GEORGE SANTAYANA

Spanish-born philosopher, writer, and poet

Santayana was a prolific essayist, poet, novelist, and philosopher. His thought is difficult to classify, but his writing is characterized by an easy grace and subtle reflections on the beauty and pathos of everyday life.

Latino heritage: Spanish

Born: December 16, 1863; Madrid, Spain

Died: September 26, 1952; Rome, Italy

Also known as: Jorge Agustín Nicolás Ruiz de Santayana y Borrás; Jorge Santayana

Areas of achievement: Philosophy; literature; poetry; education

EARLY LIFE

George Santayana (SAHN-tah-YAHN-ah) was born Jorge Agustín Nicolás Ruiz de Santayana y Borrás in Madrid, the only child of a Spanish couple, Agustín Ruiz de Santayana, a career diplomat, and his new bride, Josefina Borr Sturgis, the Scottish-Catalan widow of George Sturgis, an American from Boston. Santayana's parents were never emotionally close and their marriage was troubled from the start. Santayana's mother took his three older half-siblings with her to Boston in 1869, while he remained with his father in Spain. In 1872, his father brought him to Boston in an attempt to reconcile with his mother, but when this attempt failed, his father left him behind and returned to Spain. Santayana later wrote in his autobiography that being abandoned at age nine by his father was traumatic.

Speaking mainly Spanish at home and having worked hard to become bilingual in Spanish and English, Santayana entered the Boston Latin School in 1874, won its poetry prize in 1880, and graduated in 1882. He then matriculated at Harvard University, where he earned his B.A. in 1886 and his Ph.D. in 1889 with a dissertation on the German philosopher Hermann Lotze. Among his professors were William James and Josiah Royce, from whom he learned much about critical thinking and the history of philosophy, even though his later philosophy shows little in common with theirs.

Santayana joined the Harvard philosophy faculty in 1889 but never relished teaching. Even as early as 1892 he was tired of academic life. However, he remained at Harvard until 1912, when he took early retirement to follow his preferred career—writing. His first two books of poetry were *Sonnets and Other Verses* (1894) and *A Hermit of Carmel, and Other Poems* (1901). His first major philosophical work was a treatise on aesthetics, *The Sense of Beauty* (1896), which is sometimes regarded as the beginning of American philosophy of art. His first published play was

Lucifer: A Theological Tragedy (1899), whose characters included figures from Christian, Greek, and Semitic mythology. Also in this period he began to publish literary criticism: *Interpretations of Poetry and Religion* (1900) and *Three Philosophical Poets: Lucretius, Dante, and Goethe* (1910). In each of these genres his works were immediately popular and, aided by a substantial inheritance from his mother, he soon became able to earn a living from them.

LIFE'S WORK

Upon leaving Harvard, Santayana lived in Paris and then in England, Spain, and southern France before settling in Italy in the 1920's, dividing his time thereafter between Rome and Cortina d'Ampezzo. He never returned to the United States, even for a visit. In Europe, where he plainly felt more comfortable, he continued his prolific career as a writer with *Winds of Doctrine: Studies in Contemporary Opinion* (1913), a general evaluation of Western culture. Similarly, *Character and Opinion in the United States, with Reminiscences of William James and Josiah Royce and Academic Life in America* (1920) is a series of critical essays on American civilization from a sometimes condescending, but never unkind, European point of view.

Santayana wrote *Egotism in German Philosophy* (1915) as World War I Allied propaganda with a deliberate anti-German bias. He knew German philosophy very well and could have written about it more objectively, but this book, a product of its time, has little philosophical merit. Another result of Santayana's experiences in World War I was *Soliloquies in England and Later Soliloquies* (1922), a collection of miscellaneous essays, including "On My Friendly Critics," which he wrote while living in Oxford and Cambridge to avoid the devastation and danger on the Continent.

Scepticism and Animal Faith (1923) is the central piece of Santayana's philosophy. In it, with uncharacteristic bluntness, he calls himself a materialist, but the book is not an exposition of materialism, because rather than clarify, as one would expect a philosopher to do, he meanders, as befits a poet or essayist. Nevertheless, it is a good place to start for students who eventually wish to read the five volumes of *The Life of Reason* (1905-1906), a critique of pragmatism, and the four volumes of *The Realms of Being* (1927-1940), which present his entire philosophy in detail. Among these four realms—essence, matter, spirit, and truth—the most important is essence because of its depth, naturalness, and beauty.

George Santayana. (Library of Congress)

His skepticism is not of the hypothetical Cartesian kind, which is resolved by the certain knowledge that man exists as a thinking thing. Rather, Santayana directs his skepticism at metaphysics, which he sees as an unnecessary superstructure on the bedrock of nature. The remedy for this skepticism is the solipsism of the present moment, the unique, naturalistic viewpoint of each particular individual at each particular instant of life, which makes life beautiful and worth living. This viewpoint is sometimes called "critical realism."

Dialogues in Limbo (1925) and its expanded edition (1948) provide gentle philosophical criticism in conversational form. Similar literary and philosophical themes, from Plotinus to William Shakespeare to John Dewey, characterize Santayana's *Obiter Scripta: Lectures, Essays and Reviews*, edited by Justus Buchler and Benjamin Schwartz (1936). This book's title is a pun on *obiter dicta*, an incidental remark by a judge that has no bearing on the case. Santayana's other works from his mature period include *Little Essays* (1920), *Platonism and the Spiritual Life* (1927), *The Genteel Tradition at Bay* (1931), *Some Turns of Thought in Modern Philosophy* (1933), *The Idea of Christ in the Gospels* (1946), and *Dominations and Powers: Reflections on Liberty, Society, and Government* (1951).

Santayana's most popular work in his lifetime and the most enduring after his death was his ostensibly fictitious but rather autobiographical *The Last Puritan: A Memoir in the Form of a Novel* (1935). Its main character, Oliver Alden, wrestled for decades with the cultural traditions of his native New England until finally coming to terms with them. Thus the book is in the lineage of the bildungsroman, a lengthy work of fiction or semi-fiction, such as Daniel Defoe's *Moll Flanders* (1722), Johann Wolfgang von Goethe's *Wilhelm Meister Apprenticeship* (1795-1796), or James Joyce *A Portrait of the Artist as a Young Man* (1916), which recounts how an individual person develops a complex relationship with the world. Santayana's actual autobiography appeared later in three volumes: *Persons and Places* (1944), *The Middle Span* (1945), and, posthumously, *My Host the World* (1953).

Santayana retained his Spanish citizenship, never married, and refused several lucrative offers from prestigious universities. In 1941, he moved into a convent in Rome, the Clinica della Piccola Compagna di Maria, where he spent the rest of his life, more as a refuge from Benito Mussolini's fascist Italy than because of religious conviction. He died in Rome on September 26, 1952.

SIGNIFICANCE

Santayana's reputation as a philosopher dwindled after his death but remained strong as a novelist, literary stylist, and social critic. His philosophical writings are impressionistic rather than systematic. He was an exception to the rule that philosophers crave precision. He seldom defined his terms or identified a technical vocabulary. This tendency has frustrated readers, who expect definitions to help them through difficult philosophical arguments, even if these definitions are written, as Santayana's are, in mellifluous prose.

Santayana was conservative, aristocratic, and urbane, yet in many ways paradoxical. Born Catholic, he turned atheist, but he always admired the aesthetics and culture of Catholicism. Aloof, yet generous, he was always willing to provide financial help for writers and scholars with whom he disagreed if he perceived genius in them.

Eric v. d. Luft

Santayana's Aphorisms

Philosophy is usually built upon precise definitions of terms and the rigorous exposition and interrelation of concepts. George Santayana, however, seemed reluctant to define much and would explain his concepts in vague, allusive, almost antiphilosophical ways. Accordingly, he is better remembered for pithy sayings than for the actual content of his work. In this regard, he somewhat resembles Friedrich Nietzsche, which is ironic, since Santayana despised Nietzsche.

Among the famous aphorisms extracted from Santayana's philosophical prose is his remark in *The Life of Reason* (1905-1906) concerning the importance of education for progress in history: Whoever cannot remember the past is doomed to repeat it. In *The Sense of Beauty* (1896), he wrote that beauty is objectified pleasure, yet he kept characteristically ambiguous about whether beauty is an objective quality of things that give pleasure or a subjective perception which individuals then impart to things as if it were a quality. "Nothing Given Exists" is a chapter title in *Scepticism and Animal Faith* (1923) in which he oscillates between solipsism and an almost Spinozistic belief in universal substance. He admired philosopher Baruch Spinoza, whose pantheism he likened in "On My Friendly Critics" to his own pious atheism.

FURTHER READING

Butler, Richard. *The Mind of Santayana*. Chicago: Regnery, 1955. A clear exposition of Santayana's method, philosophical background, and doctrine of essence, concluding that he should be considered a critical neorealist.

Jeffers, Thomas L. *Apprenticeships: The Bildungsroman from Goethe to Santayana*. New York: Palgrave Macmillan, 2005. Sets *The Last Puritan* within its literary context of works by Henry James, E. M. Forster, Charles Dickens, D. H. Lawrence, and Johann Wolfgang von Goethe.

Kirby-Smith, Henry Tompkins. *A Philosophical Novelist: George Santayana and The Last Puritan*. Carbondale: Southern Illinois University Press, 1997. An interpretation of Santayana's fiction and literature in view of his philosophical ideas of essence, matter, and detachment, especially as derived from philosopher Baruch Spinoza.

Lachs, John. *On Santayana*. Belmont, Calif.: Thomson Wadsworth, 2006. Sees Santayana as a pragmatist in the American tradition and emphasizes the practical aspects of his unsystematic philosophy as a guide for living in the modern world.

McCormick, John. *George Santayana: A Biography*. New Brunswick, N.J.: Transaction, 2006. A monumental, meticulous, but readable work, likely to remain the standard biography for many years.

Schilpp, Paul Arthur, ed. *The Philosophy of George Santayana*. Vol. 2 in *The Library of Living Philosophers*. New York: Tudor, 1951. Contains essays on Santayana's thought by George Boas, Charles Hartshorne, Milton Munitz, Stephen Pepper, Bertrand Russell, Eliseo Vivas, and several other prominent philosophers. Also features Santayana's own responses to these critiques and an extensive bibliography.

Sprigge, Timothy L. S. *Santayana: An Examination of His Philosophy*. London: Routledge, 1995. A worthy attempt to come to grips with essence, being, beauty, spiritual life, natural intuition, animal faith, the solipsism of the present moment, and other major but elusive components of Santayana's thought.

See also: Ignacio Manuel Altamirano; Julio Arce; Eugenio María de Hostos; Cleofas Martinez Jaramillo.

ESMERALDA SANTIAGO

Puerto Rican-born novelist, journalist, and feminist

Best known for her emotionally charged memoirs, Santiago has led a successful career as a journalist and award-winning novelist. Drawing upon her experiences as an immigrant from Puerto Rico, her writing deftly captures the borderland perspective of negotiating a bilingual, bicultural world.

Latino heritage: Puerto Rican
Born: May 17, 1948; Santurce, Puerto Rico
Areas of achievement: Literature; journalism

EARLY LIFE

Esmeralda Santiago (ehz-meh-RAHL-dah sahn-TEE-ah-goh) was born on Calle Linda Vista in Villa Palmeras, Santurce (suburb of San Juan), Puerto Rico, to poet and carpenter Pablo Santiago Díaz and factory worker Ramona Santiago. During Esmeralda Santiago's childhood in Puerto Rico, she and her younger siblings moved often, living near paternal and maternal relatives. Her parents' tumultuous relationship prompted many of these moves, and in 1961 Santiago relocated to New York City with her mother and siblings (which eventually would include ten brothers and sisters) to live with her maternal grandmother.

Throughout this time, Santiago began to understand the hybrid experience of an immigrant teenager negotiating dual cultures, languages, and worlds. Her dark skin, hair, and eyes along with her accented English set her apart from her American counterparts, and her fading Spanish and assertiveness indicated to her family and friends in Puerto Rico that she was becoming Americanized. This borderland reality is one that Santiago would later recount in her writing and published memoirs.

Although she struggled to assimilate into the U.S. education system, Santiago excelled in her coursework and was supported by her teachers to enroll at the prestigious New York City Performing Arts High School, where she studied drama and dance. Upon graduation, she attended various community colleges part time before receiving a full scholarship to Harvard University, where she graduated magna cum laude in 1976 with a bachelor of arts degree. In June, 1978, she married filmmaker Frank Cantor, with whom she founded the film and media production company CANTOMEDIA the previous year. In the 1980's, after the births of her two children, Lucas David and Ila, Santiago enrolled in the fiction-writing program at Sarah Lawrence College in Bronxville, New York, where she graduated in 1992 with a master of fine arts degree.

LIFE'S WORK

Santiago's writing is rooted in her experiences as an immigrant and a bicultural, bilingual American. Puerto Rican culture, strong familial ties, feminism, and self-exploration are examined in her works, which include essays, short stories, documentaries, memoirs, and novels for adolescents and adults.

Santiago began her writing career with the educational documentaries that she and her husband created for CANTOMEDIA. In 1984, she participated in a writing workshop that boosted her confidence to begin writing essays for periodicals such as *Sports Illustrated*, *House and Garden*, *The Boston Globe*, *The New York Times*, and *Radcliffe Quarterly*. One of these essays caught the attention of book editor Merloyd Lawrence, who encouraged Santiago to pen her childhood

Esmeralda Santiago. (Getty Images)

memories as a book. The result was Santiago's first published memoir, *When I Was Puerto Rican* (1993), which vividly captures the author's transient childhood experiences throughout the rural and urban areas of Puerto Rico and her subsequent traumatic move to New York City. Immediately the book received praise from literary review sources that applauded her authentic storytelling.

A few years later, Santiago published *América's Dream* (1996), her first work of fiction, which follows América, a Puerto Rican woman living in an abusive relationship, and her struggle to gain independence for herself and to provide a better life for her daughter in the United States. Based upon the experiences of abused women living in a shelter that Santiago founded in Norfolk County, Massachusetts, the novel received literary acclaim and positioned Santiago in the growing league of Latina authors, such as Julia Alvarez, Denise Chávez, Cherríe Moraga, and Ana Castillo.

In 1998, Santiago published her second memoir, *Almost a Woman*, which received considerable positive attention from critics and was named one of the American Library Association's Alex Award Winners. This emotionally charged sequel to *When I Was Puerto*

Rican describes Santiago's struggles to find her place in a hybrid world of dual cultures and languages and follows her coming-of-age experiences navigating high school, first jobs, and community college. Santiago wrote the screen adaptation of the memoir, which was produced by the Public Broadcasting Service (PBS) *Masterpiece Theatre* in 2001 and received multiple broadcasting awards, including the George Foster Peabody Award and the Imagen Foundation Award for Best Actress and Best Miniseries.

Santiago's third memoir, *The Turkish Lover*, was published in 2004, enjoying an immediate flurry of literary praise. This sequel to *Almost a Woman* candidly paints the rocky and abusive relationship that Santiago endured with Turkish filmmaker Ulvi Dogan. Spanning a period of seven years, the novel follows Santiago from the time she left New York City in 1969 to her graduation from Harvard in 1976 and deftly explores sex roles in Puerto Rican, Turkish, and American cultures.

In addition to her writing for adults, Santiago has published works for adolescents and children. Two of her coedited anthologies with Joie Davidow—*Las Christmas: Favorite Latino Authors Share Their Holiday Memories* (1998) and *Las Mamis: Favorite Latino Authors Remember Their Mothers* (2000)—include collections of stories from diverse Latino authors recounting memories of holidays past and of their mothers. In 2005, Santiago published her first picture book, *A Doll for Navidades*, which describes her childhood memory about learning the true meaning of giving. She also created her documentary *Writing a Life: The Esmeralda Santiago Story*, which details the hardships she experienced as an impoverished immigrant and serves as an inspirational video to encourage immigrant and marginalized adolescents and their educators.

Santiago has received numerous honors for her literary works and humanitarian efforts, working with battered women and children. Some of these awards include Honorary Doctor of Letters from Trinity College, Pace University, Metropolitan College, and Universidad de Puerto Rico, Recinto de Mayagüez; *Latina* magazine's Latina of the Year in literature (1999); a Girl Scouts of America National Woman of Distinction Award (2002); and All-Star Award for Women in Communications (2002).

SIGNIFICANCE

Living a life that epitomizes the "rags to riches" American Dream, Santiago emerged from her humble Puerto Rican roots to become one of the most well-known

Latina authors in the twentieth century. Her evocative memoirs detail the daily hardships and prejudice experienced by waves of immigrants and provides inspiration to those struggling to find their voice. Santiago's work has continued to challenge the social constructions of feminism while exploring the roles of strong Latinas in the current U.S. culture.

Jamie Campbell Naidoo

FURTHER READING

Barszewska Marshall, Joanna. "'Boast Now, Chicken, Tomorrow You'll Be Stew': Pride, Shame, Food, and Hunger in the Memoirs of Esmeralda Santiago." *MELUS* 32, no. 4 (2007): 47-69. Critically examines three of Santiago's memoirs to determine how food and proverbs about food relate to her construction of "Puertoricanness."

Morales-Díaz, Enrique. "Catching Glimpses: Appropriating the Female Gaze in Esmeralda Santiago's Autobiographical Writing.*" Centro Journal* 14, no. 2 (2002): 131-147. Critical analysis of Santiago's memoirs, which deconstructs her representation of females in both Puerto Rican and U.S. societies.

Santiago, Esmeralda. *Almost a Woman*. Reading, Mass.: Addison-Wesley, 1998. Santiago's second memoir, which describes her struggles to assimilate into American life in New York at high school and various community colleges.

_____. *The Turkish Lover*. Cambridge, Mass.: Perseus, 2004. Santiago's third memoir, which describes her turbulent relationship with Turkish filmmaker Dogan.

_____. *When I Was Puerto Rican*. Reading, Mass.: Addison-Wesley, 1993. Santiago's first memoir, which describes her childhood in Puerto Rico and her jarring transition to America at the age of thirteen.

Stephens, Gregory. "*When I Was Puerto Rican* as Borderland Narrative: Bridging Caribbean and U.S. Latino Literature." *Confluencia* 25, no. 1 (Fall, 2009): 30-45. Stephens suggests that Santiago's memoir effectively creates a bridge between Caribbean and Latino literature through her references to jíbaro culture in Puerto Rico.

See also: Julia Alvarez; Ana Castillo; Denise Chávez; Cherríe Moraga; Judith Ortiz Cofer.

JOHN PHILLIP SANTOS

American writer, journalist, and teacher

Santos has worked as a journalist for various media organizations and as an educator, teaching creative-writing courses at the University of Texas, San Antonio. He is best known for researching and writing about his mother's and his father's family histories and stories in Places Left Unfinished at the Time of Creation *(1999) and* The Farthest Home Is in an Empire of Fire *(2010) and for producing numerous award-winning documentaries.*

Latino heritage: Mexican
Born: 1957; San Antonio, Texas
Areas of achievement: Literature; journalism; education

EARLY LIFE

John Phillip Santos (SAHN-tohs) was born in San Antonio, Texas, in 1957 to Juan Jose, Jr. and Lucille Santos. John Phillip Santos and his two siblings, George David and Charles Daniel, attended Roman Catholic elementary schools and public high schools. Santos attended Churchill High School, where he was placed in a remedial English class and was encouraged to enroll in a vocational track because of prejudice against Hispanics. Santos's examination of his education further allowed him to realize that in school there were no stories about the great migration of Mexicans to the United States or about the Indians who had lived in San Antonio long before anyone else. Despite the prejudice he experienced in school, Santos nevertheless decided to attend college. After his high school graduation, Santos attended the University of Notre Dame, where he obtained his undergraduate degree in English. While a sophomore at Notre Dame, Santos organized a literary festival that included notable writers such as Tennessee Williams and William Burroughs. He then continued his education at Oxford University, where he was the first Mexican American Rhodes scholar. Shortly after receiving his master's degree, Santos returned to the United States to pursue a Ph.D. in English at Yale University. In 1983, he dropped out of the Ph.D. program to pursue a career in journalism. For a short period, Santos worked as an arts critic for the *San Antonio Express-News*. The following year, he moved to New York, where he worked as a producer.

LIFE'S WORK

While living in New York, Santos worked as a freelance filmmaker, producer, journalist, and writer. Specifically he produced for television networks, including the Columbia Broadcasting System (CBS) and Public Broadcasting Service (PBS). He also produced documentary films, including *From the AIDS Experience: Part I, Our Spirits to Heal, Part II, Our Humanity to Heal* (1981) and *Exiles Who Never Leave Home* (1985). His work also includes articles in *The New York Times* and *Los Angeles Times*. In 1997, he joined the Ford Foundation, where he worked on the Media Projects Fund and new media technologies, especially those pertaining to developing countries.

Santos's interest in his own family's history and stories initially emerged as he reflected on the absence of his culture in school. Santos began writing down his family's stories to fill the void and to demonstrate how other Latinos could do the same by remembering. His first book, *Places Left Unfinished at the Time of Creation* (1999), explores his father's family and his grandfather's suicide; the book received high praise, including a National Book Award nomination. The memoir examines Santos's childhood experiences growing up in San Antonio and his family's history. It is in this text that he examines his own mestizo identity and acknowledges that many Latinos from Texas share similar experiences.

Santos's second memoir, *The Farthest Home Is an Empire of Fire: A Tejano Elegy* (2010), chronicles the Lopez and Vela families on his mother's side. Santos's investigation of these two families leads him to recover the history of Spanish colonial immigrants to south Texas in the eighteenth century. As he traces his family's roots to Spain, Santos yet again recognizes that his mestizo heritage existed long before his family migrated to the United States. While these genealogies are personal to Santos, he demonstrates that his family's stories, identity, and history are shared by all Latinos and mestizos. Santos won the Academy of American Poets' Prize at Notre Dame, the Oxford Prize for fiction, and

Berlin Prize Fellow at the America Academy in Berlin, Germany. He also won two Emmy nominations for his television work.

SIGNIFICANCE

At the age of seventeen, Santos discovered the story of his paternal grandfather's supposed suicide, which encouraged him to research the story. As Santos attempted to uncover his origins, he reflected on his family's history and their links to both Mexico and the United States. Of particular importance has been Santos's ability to convey the fluidity of the physical and spiritual borders between Mexico and the United States. The understanding of this fluidity has allowed Santos to embrace his mestizo heritage. Santos moved to San Antonio with his wife, the poet and teacher Frances Treviño, and their daughter, Francesca. Santos was appointed by the Honors College of University of Texas, San Antonio, as a University Distinguished Scholar in Mestizo Cultural Studies. In this new position, Santos has examined the concept of mestizaje, as it pertains to the Southwestern United States and Mexico.

Margaret E. Cantú-Sánchez

FURTHER READING

Colloff, Pamela. "The Literature of Family." *Texas Monthly* (September, 2000): 161. Colloff observes that Santos's *Places Left Unfinished at the Time of Creation* examines the stories of his identity and that of Mexican Americans by tracing his family's heritage and stories.

Santos, John Phillip. *Places Left Unfinished at the Time of Creation.* New York: Viking, 1999. Santos researches and examines the supposed suicide of his paternal grandfather, which leads him to a better understanding of his Mexican, Mestizo, and American roots.

_____. *The Farthest Home Is an Empire of Fire: A Tejano Elegy.* New York: Penguin, 2010. Santos traces and explores his mother's origins back to the Iberian Peninsula, while also examining his first days at Oxford and his twenty-two years in Manhattan.

See also: Oscar Zeta Acosta; Jimmy Santiago Baca; Carolina Monsivaís.

JOSÉ SARRIA

American gay activist and entertainer

Although initially making a name for himself as a flamboyant drag entertainer in nightclubs in the gay districts of postwar San Francisco, Sarria turned to political activism and pioneered gay rights initiatives. In 1961, he became the first openly gay candidate to run for office in the political history of the United States.

Latino heritage: Colombian and Nicaraguan

Born: December 12, 1922; San Francisco, California

Also known as: José Julio Sarria; Her Royal Majesty, Empress of San Francisco José I, the Widow Norton

Areas of achievement: Activism; entertainment; gay and lesbian issues

EARLY LIFE

José Julio Sarria (hoh-ZAY HEW-lee-oh sah-REE-ah) was born in San Francisco. His mother was a Colombian immigrant who had met his father, a Nicaraguan, on the boat to California. The two never married; Sarria's father abandoned responsibility for raising the child and returned to Central America when Sarria was in his teens. At the height of the Depression, Sarria's mother, working as a maid, shared the financial responsibility for raising her child with his godparents. Early on, Sarria showed a flair for outrageous entertaining. He dressed up in girl's clothing; he took classes in ballet and tap dance and studied voice with a retired opera tenor. Although Sarria struggled in school, he showed a felicity for languages. By the time he graduated from high school, he commanded Spanish, English, French, and German. While still in high school and tutoring a married Austrian baron, Sarria had his first homosexual relationship.

Upon graduating from high school, Sarria planned to study home economics in college, but with the advent of World War II he decided to enlist in the Army. He entered basic training with the Army Signal Corps and, given his remarkable proficiency in language, was being considered for admission to the Intelligence Service, when, inexplicably, his application was rejected. Years later, Sarria became convinced that the Army had suspicions of his homosexuality. He served out his enlistment as a cook and as a staff sergeant running an officers' mess in postwar Germany.

Returning to San Francisco with ambitions of being a teacher, Sarria was arrested in a police sweep of a reputed gay hotel. He was convicted of what was then considered illegal behavior, which meant he could never be certified as a teacher. Sarria turned to what he loved: singing. He took a job waiting tables at the Black Cat, a nightclub that was one of the epicenters of the city's Beat culture and of its burgeoning gay community. In full drag regalia, Sarria waited tables while singing campy parodies of popular songs and demanding arias from repertoire operas.

LIFE'S WORK

Although he was a natural entertainer with a flair for the flamboyant, Sarria used his performances to encourage bar patrons to celebrate their homosexuality at a time when gays were routinely targeted for police harassment through raids of gay bars and drag clubs. Because there was seldom admissible evidence, the patrons would be released but only after their employers and families had been notified. Sarria saw that political activism was the only way to address such institutionalized persecution. To prove his point, in 1961, Sarria filed papers to run for a seat on the city's powerful eleven-member board of supervisors. His campaign made headlines across the country as it was the first time an openly gay candidate had run for any office in American political history. That Sarria lost was not a surprise; that he got 5,600 votes, however, sent a message not only to the city's political establishment but also to the gay community, then largely in the closet, to reconsider questions of its identity in political terms.

Perhaps coincidentally, after more than a decade of police pressure, in 1963 the Black Cat lost its liquor license. The following year, Sarria was invited to become a financial partner in a restaurant, an investment that proved over the next decade to be quite lucrative, most notably running lavish food pavilions at a succession of world fairs. Sarria, however, never abandoned his activism. In 1963, he helped found the Society for Individual Rights, whose mission was to work the streets of the Castro District, San Francisco's growing gay neighborhood, and organize the area as a political bloc. Sarria used the organization particularly to spearhead voting registration initiatives and to canvas potential citywide candidates for their stands on gay rights.

Sarria never entirely abandoned his love of the spectacular. He loved the spotlight and he became a fixture on the city's drag scene. In 1964, he was elected queen of the city's Beaux Arts Ball. Proclaiming that he was already a queen, Sarria dubbed himself Her Royal Majesty, Empress of San Francisco José I, the Widow Norton, the last word a reference to a much-celebrated local eccentric, a commodities entrepreneur who a century earlier had declared himself Emperor of the United States. Sarria's elaborate name stuck. Under the auspices of that pretend title, Sarria founded the Imperial Court System, eventually an international alliance of nonprofit fund-raising organizations and grassroots political groups geared specifically to gay rights initiatives. The Imperial Court System took the lead in projects related to acquired immunodeficiency syndrome (AIDS) starting in the 1980's. Sarria retired from the Imperial Court in 2007.

SIGNIFICANCE

It is not hyperbole to assert that gay pride and gay rights were largely the invention of a flamboyant drag queen. A decade before the demonstrations at New York's Stonewall Inn and more than a generation before the political ascendancy of San Francisco's first successful gay politician, Harvey Milk (whose candidacy for the board of supervisors Sarria endorsed), Sarria unapologetically articulated a then radical premise: Gays and lesbians should not be marginalized, and only collectively in organized grassroots efforts could their rights be protected from harassment by the police and their agenda be recognized by the political establishment.

Joseph Dewey

FURTHER READING

Boyd, Nan Alamilla. *Wide-Open Town: A History of Queer San Francisco to 1965.* Berkeley: University of California Press, 2003. Important look at the context of Sarria's historic political campaign. Argues that gay rights were part of San Francisco culture for nearly a century before Sarria's political challenge.
Dececco, John, and Michael Gorman. *The Empress Is a Man: Stories from the Life of José Sarria.* New York: Routledge, 1998. Seminal look at Sarria's career. Anecdotes from Sarria himself make vivid his crusade for gay rights.
Shilts, Randy. *The Mayor of Castro Street: The Life and Times of Harvey Milk.* Reprint. New York: St. Martin's Griffin Press, 2008. Landmark study of the political world of gay San Francisco. Includes Sarria's legacy.

See also: Corky Gonzáles; José Ángel Gutiérrez; Reies López Tijerina.

LALO SCHIFRIN

Argentine-born musician

Schifrin produced some of the best-known scores for television and films made in Hollywood over a forty-year period. At the same time, he pursued the goal of trying to bring the audiences for jazz and classical music together, based on his early classical training and his experience working with many of the great names in the jazz world.

Latino heritage: Argentinean
Born: June 21, 1932; Buenos Aires, Argentina
Also known as: Boris Claudio Schifrin
Areas of achievement: Music; entertainment

EARLY LIFE

Lalo Schifrin (LAH-loh SHIHF-rihn) was born Boris Claudio Schifrin on June 21, 1932, in Buenos Aires, Argentina. He was born into a musical family; his father Luis was concertmaster of the orchestra that became the Buenos Aires Philharmonic, and his mother Clara Ester met her husband-to-be when he was giving violin lessons. Their Jewish and Russian origins were not conspicuous among Argentina's many immigrants, although the subsequent political atmosphere under dictator Juan Peron made any sort of liberalism dangerous. Lalo (the name was a diminutive of his middle name) started taking music lessons at the age of six from the father of noted conductor and pianist Daniel Barenboim, and he rapidly acquired technical mastery of the piano. He did not initially think of music as a career and spent some time at the University of Buenos Aires studying social sciences and law. In addition, he also took a course on film that was to play a role in his subsequent career. He also kept up with his musical studies outside the university.

Even more influential was Schifrin's discovery of jazz, thanks to recordings that often had to be smuggled

Lalo Schifrin. (AP Photo)

composing, and arranging. In addition to Gillespie, he also arranged for musician Stan Getz and a variety of vocalists. Schifrin toured with the Gillespie ensemble from 1960 to 1962, and he worked some of his classical training into their repertoire, as evident in the concerto *Gillespiana.*

After a few years of touring, however, Schifrin decided that he would rather travel less and headed west to Hollywood. He had already written two film scores, originally in Argentina and then in the United States. The television industry appreciated his ability to range over genres and promptly gave him the chance to write music for popular series. Few television viewers of the 1960's would have been unfamiliar with his imaginative mixture of sounds and musical instruments, especially on series like *Mannix, The Man from UNCLE,* and, most conspicuously, *Mission Impossible.* He won two Grammy Awards for the *Mission Impossible* theme, a mixture of contemporary sound and tempo.

Schifrin also made his mark as a composer for film, a responsibility he took seriously. From his perspective, the composer had to make sure that the score was an ingredient in the audience's appreciation of what was on the screen rather than just music capable of being detached from the visual element. His earliest major score was for *Cincinnati Kid* in 1965, but subsequent scores for *Bullitt* (1968) and *Dirty Harry* (1971) were even better known. He developed a particular relationship with actor Clint Eastwood, the star of *Dirty Harry.* In the course of his career, Schifrin wrote music for more than 160 films, starting from a spare, minimalist style but working in themes from a variety of traditions.

After a number of years of composing at a rapid rate, Schifrin took on more conducting roles around the world. In 1987, a group of French musicians came together to form the Paris Philharmonic Orchestra, and Schifrin became its first music director, a position he held for five years. The orchestra specialized in the performance of music from film scores, but not exclusively Schifrin's. He conducted and arranged for the Three Tenors and for the series of concerts on television *Christmas in Vienna.* He continued to compose for commissions and brought his musical style to small communities, as well as large concert halls. In 1995, he conducted the London Philharmonic Orchestra in *Jazz Meets the Symphony.*

Schifrin taught film composition at the University of California at Los Angeles from 1968 through 1971. His first marriage was breaking up, and he married his second wife, Donna, during this time period. He had

into the country during the repressive Peronist atmosphere. He had felt somewhat stifled with the study of classical music, since that was expected of him by his father. Jazz he felt to be his own discovery. When he was given the opportunity to pursue musical study at the Conservatoire in Paris on the strength of a scholarship, Schifrin gladly took the opportunity to escape from Argentina in 1950. While he was in Paris, he continued his formal musical training but also spent time listening to music and playing in jazz clubs. This sort of moonlighting was frowned on by some of his instructors at the Conservatoire. After the end of the Peronist regime in Argentina, Schifrin returned to Buenos Aires and introduced jazz by establishing the first big band in the country in 1956.

LIFE'S WORK
Schifrin's life and career took a decisive turn with the visit by jazz musician Dizzy Gillespie to Argentina with the support of the U.S. State Department in 1957. Gillespie was so impressed with Schifrin that he invited Schifrin to perform with him in New York. When Schifrin arrived in New York in 1958, his talents were soon put to use at a variety of tasks, including performing,

Schifrin's Classical Compositions

In the early part of his career, Lalo Schifrin tried to put a distance between his classical training and his jazz performances and compositions. In the course of time, however, he recognized that there was no way to fully appreciate jazz without recognizing the classical roots out of which it arose. As a result, he spent much of his life as a composer bringing jazz and classical music together. One way in which he did this was to create jazz compositions in a classical form, such as his ballet *Jazz Faust* and *Jazz Suite on the Mass Texts*. He also produced versions of his film scores for classical ensembles, such as his *Rise and Fall of the Third Reich*, first performed at the Hollywood Bowl in 1967. He went beyond classical practice by including the magnified sound of Adolf Hitler's voice, but other composers for opera and other classical settings followed Schifrin in broadening the tools for performance. In addition to the twelve-tone compositional style of the twentieth century, Schifrin included aleatory elements, where chance is allowed to dictate the notes actually performed, in his classical works. Schifrin probably was able to broaden the classical toolkit because of the reputation he had already acquired in the domains of jazz and film scores.

three children, none of them exposed to the pressure he had felt as a child to pursue a musical career.

SIGNIFICANCE

Schifrin's first musical contribution was to bring jazz to Argentina, a liberating musical form after the fall of the Peronist regime. More conspicuous was his lifelong dedication to the task of making jazz more welcome in classical music settings, as well as his bringing contemporary classical musical ideas to the motion picture theater and television screen. While recognizing the musical accomplishments of the previous generation of Hollywood composers, he knew that films and television programs aimed at capturing the grit and anxiety of daily life needed to be accompanied by the sounds of that life rather than the violins of the past. His use of instrumentation, tempi, and compositional styles that were products of the twentieth century guaranteed that viewers would place what they were watching in the right decade. He took music for the screen from the comfortable to the age of anxiety.

Thomas Drucker

FURTHER READING

Brown, Royal S. *Overtones and Undertones: Reading Film Music.* Berkeley: University of California Press, 1994. Includes a lengthy interview with Schifrin, as well as analysis of his musical development and those who most influenced him.

Donnelly, K.J. *The Spectre of Sound.* London: The British Film Institute, 2005. Detailed analysis of the reasons for the success of Schifrin's scores for well-known films, including scenes where there was no music at all.

Schifrin, Lalo. *Mission Impossible: My Life in Music.* Lanham, Md.: Scarecrow Press, 2008. Schifrin's autobiography is arranged thematically rather than strictly chronologically and is especially helpful for the Argentinean periods of his life.

Thomas, Tony. *Music for the Movies.* South Brunswick, N.J.: A. S. Barnes, 1973. Helpful guide to what distinguished Schifrin's scores from those of his contemporaries before his techniques and ideas had become widespread.

See also: Ray Barretto; Paquito D'Rivera; Paul Gonsalves; Eduardo Mata; Ástor Piazzolla; Claudio Spies; Juan Tizol.

ARTURO ALFONSO SCHOMBURG

Puerto Rican-born bibliophile, collector, and curator

Schomburg, a native Puerto Rican of African and German descent, saw it as his mission to collect and rescue from the hidden recesses of historiography the artistic contributions of people of African descent, including people from Latin America.

Latino heritage: Puerto Rican
Born: January 24, 1874; Santurce, Puerto Rico

Died: June 10, 1938; Brooklyn, New York
Also known as: Arthur Schomburg; Guarionex (pen name)
Areas of achievement: Education; scholarship; literature

EARLY LIFE

The parentage of Arturo Alfonso Schomburg (ahr-TOW-roh al-FON-soh SHOM-behrg) is uncertain. His mother was Mary Joseph, an unmarried, mulatto washerwoman from the Virgin Islands; it is believed that his father was a white German-born merchant named Carlos Federico Schomburg. Mary Joseph's father was black and worked as a butcher; her mother was a mulatto. Schomburg's maternal relatives nurtured him, while his paternal relatives had little if anything to do with him. At a young age he became well acquainted with the operations of race. He observed that those darker in hue were cast as lesser human beings. He would later write that when, on occasion, a dark-complexioned person accomplished some degree of success, he was set apart from the group. As a youth, Schomburg also observed how whites spoke with pride about their heritage. It is said that a fifth-grade teacher told him that black people lacked a history. This observation, along with questions about his mixed-race ancestry and olive brown complexion, appears to have set him on a course to uncover contributions made by people of African descent.

Months before his birth, Spain had abolished slavery in Puerto Rico, but the far-reaching tentacles of racial prejudice and the subjugation of Puerto Rico as a colonial acquisition of Spain affected the trajectory of Schomburg's life. Education was not free, and although Schomburg was highly intelligent, he received a minimal classroom Education. When he moved to New York City in 1891 at the age of seventeen, he became a part of the Puerto Rican and Cuban community, but his lack of acceptable credentials from an educational institution erected a barrier that waylaid his aspirations to gain validity in the larger society. He compensated for his lack of credentials by teaching himself. He was an avid reader, and he had an almost encyclopedic memory for recalling bibliographic references. This ability would stun many and endear him to students, common people, artists, intellectuals, and the Hispanic and black communities.

In 1895, he married his first wife, an African American named Bessie Hatcher. The couple had three sons—Maximo Gomez, Arthur Alfonso, Jr., and Kingsley Guarionex—between 1897 and 1900. Bessie died unexpectedly in 1900, and the couple's boys were cared for by their maternal grandparents. It is around this time that Schomburg began identifying more with the black community and began using Arthur, the anglicized pronunciation of his first name. In 1902, Schomburg married Elizabeth Morrow Taylor, another fair-skinned African American woman. Together they had two sons, Reginald Stanfield and Nathaniel José. Upon the untimely death of Elizabeth, these boys were raised by their maternal relatives. Schomburg and his last wife, Elizabeth Green, another African American, had three children: Fernando, Dolores Marie, and Placido Carlos. These children were raised in the home with Schomburg, but it appears that his work and many activities left him little time to spend with his family.

LIFE'S WORK

Schomburg's collecting, research, and writing activities; his political, civic, and social affiliations; and his regular jobs left little time for leisure. From 1901 to 1906, he worked as a clerk-messenger for the law firm of Pryor, Mellis and Harris. He then began working for Bankers Trust Company, where he was employed for the next twenty-three years. Both jobs supplied him with the money to purchase rare books and other items and helped him establish networks with book dealers, artists, and suppliers of rare objects around the world.

During his early adult life, Schomburg joined a number of organizations. When he came to the United States he was already involved in the Puerto Rican and Cuban national independence movements. After arriving in New York, he immersed himself in the life of the Harlem community and over time connected with a host of organizations, totaling well over thirty during his lifetime. The Masons, the Negro Society of the American Negro Academy, and the American Negro Academy are a few of these groups.

Around 1904, he began writing essays about people of African origin from various countries in Latin America and around the world. Although his Spanish was impeccable, intellectuals often had problems translating his works into clear English because his writings in English could sometimes be disjointed. This did not stop him from contributing essays to many publications, *Crisis* and *Opportunity* among them. The problems with his writing were not reflected in his speeches, for he lectured extensively. Schomburg's easy and approachable manner and his effective ability to communicate with all people enabled him to create linkages with those who spoke different languages.

Later in life, from 1930 to 1932, he was the curator of the collection of resources in black history and culture at Fisk University in Nashville, Tennessee. After leaving Fisk, he worked at the New York Public Library on 135th Street, where he presided over the massive collection of materials on black culture that the Carnegie Corporation had purchased from him for the library in 1926.

SIGNIFICANCE

Schomburg saw it as his mission to cull out from obscurity the African historical past that demonstrated the achievement of people of African descent, a past that harkened well beyond the nascent slavery era of the seventeenth and eighteenth centuries. He believed that a restoration of the African past would minimize prejudice. Schomburg sought after rare documents that gave proof of an obscured past in which people of African descent composed poetry, wrote of their travails and aspirations, and painted and sculpted works of art in homage to members of their race. Schomburg spent his adult life committed to collecting books, prints, paintings, engravings, busts, ephemera, and other materials. He maintained and freely shared materials with those eager to learn more about black history. He lectured at libraries, churches, and other forums and planned exhibits that educated the public about different aspects of black world history. His treasure trove of historical and cultural data formed the core of the Schomburg Center for Research in Black Culture. Located in New York City, the center is one of the leading repositories in the United States, and possibly the world, containing materials on almost every aspect of black history and culture.

Alesia McFadden

FURTHER READING

Ortiz, Victoria. *The Legacy of Arthur Alfonso Schomburg: A Celebration of the Past, a Vision for the Future.* New York: Schomburg Exhibition Curatorial Committee, The New York Public Library, 1986. A well-researched essay in both Spanish and English that details Schomburg's life and explains what he attempted to accomplish during his lifetime.

Schomburg, Arthur A. "From 'Racial Integrity': A Plea for the Establishment of a Chair of Negro History." In *Negro: An Anthology*, edited by Nancy Cunard. New York: Frederick Ungar, 1970. Schomburg discusses a number of writers of African descent from Latin America, Africa, Europe, and elsewhere who have created important works. He calls for a historian or philosopher to take the lead in detailing the African record of accomplishment.

_____. "The Negro Digs Up His Past." *Survey Graphic* (March, 1925): 670-672. Schomburg argues that blacks whose roots can be traced to Africa can be proud of their lineage because there is an impressive record of achievement when one looks beyond the surface.

Sinnett, Elinor Des Verney. *Arthur Alfonso Schomburg: Black Bibliophile and Collector.* Detroit: Wayne State University Press and The New York Public Library, 1989. Using the personal papers of Schomburg, as well as interviews with his children and close associates, Sinnett, a librarian whose dissertation was on Schomburg, crafts an engaging and thorough biography on this bibliophile of black works.

See also: Pura Belpré; Carlos E. Castañeda.

JON SECADA

Cuban-born singer and actor

Secada was one of the most successful pop stars of the 1990's. By 2010, he had won two Grammy Awards and sold more than twenty million albums worldwide. Widely appealing to both Latino and white audiences, Secada was a pioneer of the Latino invasion in modern pop music.

Latino heritage: Cuban

Born: October 4, 1962; Havana, Cuba

Also known as: Jon Francisco Secada Martínez; Juan Francisco Secada Martínez

Areas of achievement: Music; theater; radio and television

EARLY LIFE

Jon Francisco Secada (jon frahn-SEES-koh seh-KAH-dah), an only child, was born October 4, 1962, in Havana, Cuba, to Jose and Victoria Secada. His African father and Hispanic mother struggled under Fidel Castro's repressive regime, and Secada's father was imprisoned from 1966 to 1971 for attempting to leave Cuba. Secada's mother ran a coffee shop to support the family during the time his father was imprisoned. In 1971, Secada's father was finally released from prison, and the family immigrated to Miami, but they were forced to leave everything they owned behind in Cuba.

Secada's parents opened a Cuban coffee shop in Miami, where Secada worked after school. An excellent student, Secada grew up speaking both Spanish and English fluently. Although his aunt, Moraima Secada, became a famous bolero singer in Cuba, Secada never realized his own musical talent until he sang in a musical Christmas play during his junior year in high school. Upon hearing Secada's beautiful voice for the first time, his teachers and classmates convinced him to pursue a musical career.

After graduating from Hialeah High School in 1979, Secada attended the University of Miami, where he studied African American jazz, eventually earning bachelor's and master's degrees in jazz vocal performance. After graduate school, Secada taught voice at Miami-Dade Community College, and at night he was a working musician, playing with various groups in Miami and continually refining his songwriting skills.

LIFE'S WORK
Between 1985 and 1990, Secada worked as a songwriter and backup singer for the Miami Sound Machine, an extremely successful pop group. In 1990, Secada legally changed the spelling of his first name from "Juan" to "Jon." Secada cowrote six songs on the Miami Sound Machine's multiplatinum album *Into the Light*, including "Coming Out of the Dark," an international number-one hit. While touring with the Miami Sound Machine in 1991, Secada was given the opportunity to perform a solo at each concert; exposed to millions of fans worldwide, Secada became an instant success, and he earned his first recording contract with SBK Records.

In 1992, Secada released his debut album, *Jon Secada*, and the album sold six million copies worldwide, going triple-platinum in the United States. Secada simultaneously released *Otro dia mas sin verte*, a Spanish-language version of *Jon Secada*, which became the number-one Latin album of 1992. Secada received a Grammy Award for Best Latin Pop Album in 1992 for *Otro dia mas sin verte*. In 1994, Secada's follow-up album, *Heart, Soul, & a Voice*, sold more than one million copies. Secada's second Spanish-language album, *Amor*, won Secada his second Grammy Award in 1995 for Best Latin Pop Performance. Secada also recorded "If I Never Knew You" in 1995 for the soundtrack of the Disney animated film *Pocahontas*. His third album, *Secada*, released in 1997, was a commercial disappointment, but *Better Part of Me*, released in 2000, achieved moderate success. Secada's 2005 album, *Same Dream*, attained critical acclaim, and *A Christmas Fiesta* became the number-one contemporary Christmas album

Jon Secada.
(Michal Czerwonka/PictureGroup via AP Images)

of 2007. *Expressions*, a collection of jazz songs released in 2009, was a radical departure from Secada's earlier albums, but it further expanded his diverse audience. He returned to his roots with *Classics*, a compilation of Latin ballads, released in 2010.

Secada was honored to perform live at a charity concert in Italy with famed opera signer Luciano Pavarotti; in addition, Secada was invited by Frank Sinatra to record "The Best Is Yet to Come" for Sinatra's *Duets II* album. Secada considers these two events to be the pinnacles of his career. Secada also has performed three times on Broadway. In 1995, he played the lead role of Danny Zuko in the musical *Grease*. In a 2003 production of *Cabaret*, Secada played the role of the nightclub emcee, and he starred as Joseph in *Joseph and the Amazing Technicolor Dreamcoat* in 2004. Two years later, Secada became a regular on television, signing a contract for several seasons to appear as a judge on *Latin American Idol*.

Secada's first marriage to makeup artist Jo Pat Cafaro ended after five years in 1993. Secada married publicist Maritere Vilar in 1997, with whom he had two children, Mikaela and Jon Henri.

SIGNIFICANCE

Secada's most profound contribution is as a songwriter, having written hundreds of songs since the 1980's that appear on albums ranging from Disney studio soundtracks to recordings by Mandy Moore, Jennifer Lopez, Ricky Martin, Enrique Iglesias, and Gloria Estefan. Secada's musical influences were diverse and eclectic, and although steeped in Latin and merengue music, he also loved Stevie Wonder, Elton John, and Earth Wind and Fire. Encompassing the passion of salsa and Latin ballads, Secada's music is also infused with African blues, soul, jazz, and rock. Secada's 1992 album *Otro dia mas sin vert*e was the first Latin album to contain four consecutive number-one hits. Bridging the gap between Miami Latin music and Southwestern "cowboy" Latin music, Secada's music crossed over to large numbers of white audiences. Lush, rich, and full in sound, Secada's songs have a wide audience appeal because of their intricate and diverse musical components.

Mary E. Markland

FURTHER READING

Cobo, Leila. "Acting Life Is a 'Cabaret' for Secada," *Billboard,* 115, no. 26, (June, 2003): 41. Secada discusses his acting career and his preparation for the role of Emcee in director Sam Mendes's production of *Cabaret*.

Marvis, Barbara, and Barbara Tidman. "Jon Secada," In *Famous People of Hispanic Heritage*. Childs, Md.: Mitchell Lane, 1995. Focuses on Secada's success as a bilingual singer and expounds upon his Afro-Cuban American heritage, and his musical influences.

Otfinoski, Steven. *Latinos in the Arts*. New York: Facts on File, 2007. Secada discusses songwriting and his first return to Cuba in 2005 for his concert at Guantanamo Bay.

See also: Gloria Estefan; Julio Iglesias; Jennifer Lopez; Ricky Martin.

JUAN SEGUIN

American military leader and politician

Seguin was a politician who opposed Antonio López de Santa Anna's plan to centralize the Mexican state and replace the constitution of 1824. A supporter of states' rights, Seguin joined forces with Texas independence leaders and participated in the Battles of the Alamo and San Jacinto.

Latino heritage: Mexican
Born: October 27, 1806; San Fernando de Béxar, New Spain (now San Antonio, Texas)
Died: August 27, 1890; Nuevo Laredo, Mexico
Also known as: Juan Nepomuceno Seguin
Areas of achievement: Military; government and politics

EARLY LIFE

Juan Nepomuceno Seguin, better known as Juan Seguin (wahn SAY-geen), was born in 1806 into a prominent landowning family at San Fernando de Béxar, New Spain (now San Antonio, Texas). His father, Erasmo Seguin, a merchant and postmaster, was a delegate to the Mexican congress that drafted the republican constitution of 1824. His mother was María Josefa Becerra.

Seguin became a successful rancher and a land speculator. In 1826, he married María Gertrudis Flores de Abrego, the daughter of a prominent Texas ranching family, and the couple had nine children who survived infancy. Seguin embarked upon a political career, serving as an alderman for San Antonio in 1929. He was a member of the district electoral assembly, and in 1834 was both the mayor of San Antonio and lieutenant governor for the San Antonio district .

The Seguin family opposed Mexican president Antonio López de Santa Anna's plan to scrap the constitution of 1824 and centralize power in Mexico City. Santa Anna's proposal forced Juan Seguin to form an alliance with the Americans in the Texas portion of the Mexican state who sought complete independence from Mexico.

LIFE'S WORK

During the 1820's and early 1830's, Seguin became friends with the future leaders of the Texas Revolution: James Bowie, William Barrett Travis, David Crockett, Stephen Fuller Austin, and Sam Houston. Seguin was one of the first to organize opposition to Santa Anna. Austin appointed Seguin the captain of a unit of native-born Texans who opposed the Mexican president. Seguin saw action at the Battle of Gonzales (1835), fought with Bowie at the Battle of Concepcion (1835), and he and General Edward Burleson successfully took control of the Alamo (a fort) and San Antonio in the Siege of Bejar (1835). The Alamo was rebuilt, strengthening the structure against a possible Mexican assault, although the Alamo's defenders knew they could not win against the larger army of Santa Anna. For this reason, Travis sent Seguin and Pablo Gomez to seek help from Colonel James Fannin at Goliad. Seguin and Gomez were chosen because they spoke Spanish and could more easily slip out of the Alamo and away from San Antonio without arousing Mexican suspicions.

Seguin was dealt a double blow in 1836, when he simultaneously learned that the Alamo had fallen to the Mexican soldiers and that Fannin had rejected his request for assistance. Seguin proceeded to contact Houston, who told Seguin that he had instructed Travis to blow up the Alamo and Fannin to leave Goliad, rather than surrender. Both Travis and Fannin were to merge their fighters with Houston's army, but neither man obeyed Houston's directives.

At the 1836 Battle of San Jacinto, Seguin commanded the Second Regiment Cavalry of native-borns and ordered his men to place white cards on their hats with the words "Remember the Alamo" in order to distinguish themselves from Santa Anna's troops. After Santa Anna's forces were defeated in this battle, Seguin persuaded Houston not to burn San Antonio in retaliation for the Texans' defeat at the Alamo. Houston instructed Seguin to return to San Antonio and find the remains of Travis, Bowie, and Crockett for proper burial. These remains were interred in San Antonio's historic St. Fernando's Roman Catholic Church.

Seguin's military and political career continued after the Battle of San Jacinto. He was promoted to lieutenant colonel in the Texas army; he served in the congress of the Texas Republic until 1840, representing Houston and Austin; and he was mayor of San Antonio from 1841 through 1842. Seguin was also on the Texas congressional committee that selected Austin as the new republic's capital. Unfortunately, Seguin's later career was ruined by American squatters in San Antonio, who questioned his patriotism to the Texas Republic. He fled to Mexico, where he was forced to join the Mexican army or serve a prison sentence.

With the end the Mexican-American War in 1848, Seguin no longer feared for his safety and returned to San Antonio to resume his ranching operations. He served

Bexar County as justice of the peace from 1852 through 1856 and founded this county's Democratic Party. He was named a judge for Wilson County, Texas, in 1869. Five years later, Seguin was declared a hero of the Texas war for independence and granted a lifetime pension. He ultimately returned to Mexico, where he had business interests and lived with his eldest son, the mayor of Nuevo Laredo. Seguin died there on August 27, 1890. He was reburied in Seguin, Texas, on July 4, 1976.

SIGNIFICANCE

It took tremendous courage for Juan Sequin to collaborate with the Americans, but his commitment to political ideals forced him to begin a rebellion against his own country. His recruitment of native-borns, his strengthening of the Alamo's defenses, his service as a courier for the Alamo's defenders, and his leadership at the Battle of San Jacinto, enshrine Seguin as a major figure in the successful outcome of the Texas Revolution.

William A. Paquette

FURTHER READING

Davis, William C. *Three Roads to the Alamo.* New York: HarperCollins, 1998. Regarded as the definitive study on the Alamo. Recounts the contributions of Crockett, Bowie, Travis, and the other major figures of the war of Texas independence.

Hollmann, Robert. *Juan Seguin.* Dallas, Tex.: Durban House, 2007. This narrative interview with Sequin's friend Pablo Gomez describes Seguin's role in Texas becoming independent from Mexico.

Reimers, Peggy A. *Lone Star Legends.* n.p.: P.A. Reimers, 2006. Focuses on Seguin's life during the Texas Revolution.

Sequin, Juan Nepomuceno. *A Revolution Remembered: The Memoirs and Selected Correspondence of Juan Seguin.* Austin, Tex.: Texas State Historical Association, 2002. The best resource for primary source documents on Seguin.

Thompson, Frank. *The Alamo.* New York: New Market Press, 2004. An illustrated history about the making of the film *The Alamo* includes a brief narrative about Seguin's role in achieving independence for Texas.

See also: Juan Bautista Alvarado; Joseph Marion Hernández; Pío Pico.

SELENA

American singer

Hailed as the "Queen of Tejano music," Selena was among the first female performers to succeed in the male-dominated genre by conquering the hearts of Tejano and Latin American audiences. A successful singer, fashion designer, and entrepreneur, she was preparing to make her debut in the English-language pop market at the time of her death.

Latino heritage: Mexican
Born: April 16, 1971; Lake Jackson, Texas
Died: March 31, 1995; Corpus Christi, Texas
Also known as: Selena Quintanilla-Pérez; Selena Quintanilla; Queen of Tejano music
Areas of achievement: Music; fashion; business

EARLY LIFE

Selena Quintanilla-Pérez (seh-LEE-nuh KEEN-tah-NEE-yah-PEH-rehz) was born on April 16, 1971, in Lake Jackson, Texas, to Abraham Quintanilla and Marcella Ofelia Samora. Her father performed with the Tejano group Los Dinos in his youth but eventually

Selena. (AP Photo/Houston Chronicle, Dave Einsel)

retired from music to work at the Dow Chemical plant in Lake Jackson. He provided his children with instruments and taught them to play as a family activity and they became Selena y Los Dinos: her brother A. B. played bass, sister Suzette played drums, and Selena acted as lead singer. The band started performing regularly at the family restaurant, Papagayo's, in 1980, as well as in clubs, local restaurants, and outdoor festivals, making a series of independent recordings starting with *Selena y Los Dinos* (1984). An excellent student, Selena had to be home schooled because of the demands and time commitment of touring throughout the Southwest when the band became the family's main source of income. After winning awards for female vocalist of the year and performer of the year at the 1987 Tejano music Awards, Selena was signed to EMI Records and released her first major-label album, *Selena*, in 1989.

Guitarist Chris Pérez joined the band in 1989, and he and Selena began dating two years later. They were married in 1992. Major-label albums and music videos allowed Selena to reach greater popularity, and her biggest success came with the 1994 release of *Amor prohibido*. Her appeal rested on the combination of her humble personality, powerful voice, spirited dance moves, and provocative outfits. Even at the peak of her career, the band remained a family affair, with her father acting as manager, brother A. B. writing and producing songs, and her sister and husband playing in the band. Selena designed the band's costumes. Her strong family ties coupled with her loyalty to her Texan working-class roots made her relatable to fans and earned her their devoted admiration.

LIFE'S WORK

Despite having grown up speaking only English, Selena worked on her Spanish and managed to gain the acceptance of Mexican audiences, who often were unforgiving of Mexican Americans' Anglo backgrounds. Her popularity spread throughout Latin America and led her to tour Mexico and Central and South America. After the success of *Amor prohibido*, Selena started branching out into other projects, which included appearances in the Mexican *telenovela Dos mujeres, un camino* and the film *Don Juan de Marco* (1994), as well as musical collaborations with the group Barrio Boyzz and singer Alvaro Torres. She also began designing a clothing line and distributing it at her Selena Etc.boutiques throughout Texas. Her star

Selena and the Evolution of Tejano Music

Texas-Mexican music, or *música Tejana*, developed in the regions along the Rio Grande border. Sung in Spanish and rooted in traditional Mexican music, the polka beat emerged as the backbone of Texas-Mexican dance music in the early twentieth century. Grupo Tejano appeared in the 1970's and became the dominant form of Tejano music; its main difference from previous types of ensemble Tejano was the inclusion of keyboards instead of the accordion. Tejano music evolved rapidly throughout the 1990's with the addition of new instruments, such as the keyboard and the conga, an expanded repertoire that included *cumbias* and ballads, and the involvement of the major record labels, which transformed the previously niche genre into an international musical style.

A major trend in Tejano music in the 1990's was the increased participation of female performers, which was largely propelled by Selena's success. Her triumph in a genre dominated by male performers and sexist attitudes opened the door for later female performers. Selena promoted a new Tejano aesthetic begun by earlier groups such as La Mafia and Mazz, which gave prominence to *cumbias* and ballads. Her biggest hits "Amor prohibido," "Como la flor" and "Techno-cumbia," are a testament to the popularity of the *cumbia* genre. On the other hand, in her ballads, such as "Si una vez" and the ranchera "No me queda Mas," Selena presented lyrics grounded in a female perspective that was assertive and independent and often critical of men's mistreatment of women. Lauded for her dynamic performances, she introduced intricately choreographed dance moves into her shows. Finally, her songs served to further modernize the Tejano genre by introducing elements of mariachi, pop, rap, rock and dance to the music.

status was clear when she performed at the Houston Astrodome for more than sixty-five thousand people.

Selena met Yolanda Saldivar in 1990 when Saldivar approached her with the idea of starting a fan club. Selena agreed, and Saldivar became the fan club's president, as well as manager of the Selena Etc. boutiques. In March, 1995, Selena's father discovered that Saldivar had been embezzling money from the boutiques. While Saldivar denied the accusations, the family decided to fire her. On March 31, Selena met with Saldivar at a Corpus Christi hotel to break the news to her and retrieve important documents that Saldivar had taken; the two argued, and as Selena was leaving, Saldivar shot her in the back. She died later at the hospital. Meanwhile, Saldivar locked herself in her truck in the hotel parking lot for nine hours before surrendering to police. She was convicted of first-degree murder and sentenced to life in prison.

At the time of her death, Selena had been working on songs for her English-language debut album, set to be released that summer. The album, titled *Dreaming of You* (1995), included songs in both Spanish and English and debuted at number one on the Billboard charts. The album sold well, making Selena a crossover success in the mainstream U.S. market.

Selena's memory is kept alive through myriad commemorations; the events of her life have been the subject of the musical *Selena Forever* (2000) and the film *Selena* (1997) starring Jennifer Lopez. Immediately after her death, *People* magazine produced a commemorative issue dedicated to her, only the third of its kind after issues devoted to Audrey Hepburn and Jacqueline Kennedy Onassis. George W. Bush, then governor of Texas, declared Selena's birthday, April 16, Selena Day. The family recording studios in Corpus Christi have been converted into a museum and a life-size statue of the singer was erected at the Mirador de la Flor memorial in Corpus Christi. The iconic outfit she wore at her Astrodome performance has even toured the country as part of the Smithsonian traveling exhibit America's Smithsonian.

SIGNIFICANCE

Selena reached millions of people with her music, many of them Latinas who saw her as a role model. By effectively melding her Anglo American upbringing and Mexican background, without renouncing her Texan working-class roots, she was seen as exemplary of what Latinas could accomplish. Likewise, musically she was able to bridge her two heritages by performing songs steeped in the traditional music of Mexico, yet also infused by elements of Anglo American rock and roll and pop. The public display of her fans' mourning brought visibility to Hispanic groups in the United States, and her success has been heralded as the beginning of the musical Latin invasion of the late 1990's.

Georgina Chinchilla-Gonzalez

FURTHER READING

Koegel, John. "Crossing Borders: Mexicana, Tejana and Chicana musicians in the United States and

Mexico." In *From Tejano to Tango*, edited by Walter Aaron Clark. New York: Routledge, 2002. Considers the contributions of female performers to the Tejano genre and Selena's unique role in the genre's development.

Novas, Himilce, and Rosemary Silva. *Remembering Selena: A Tribute in Pictures and Words/Recordando Selena: Un tributo en palabras y fotos*. New York: St. Martin's Press, 1995. Bilingual account of Selena's life and career featuring photos and stories from Selena's family.

Paredez, Deborah. *Selenidad: Selena, Latinos, and the Performance of Memory*. Durham, N.C.: Duke University Press, 2009. A scholarly exploration of the emergence of Selena as a Latina icon as seen through diverse practices of memorialization.

Patoski, Joe. *Selena: Como la flor*. Boston: Little, Brown, 1996. This detailed biography based on personal interviews and newspaper articles recounts Selena's life and career and remains an authoritative source.

Richmond, Clint. *Selena! The Phenomenal Life and Tragic Death of the Tejano Music Queen*. New York: Pocket Books, 1995. Bilingual biography that provides the English and Spanish translation side by side and contains previously unreleased photographs.

See also: Mariah Carey; Gloria Estefan; Jennifer Lopez; Ricky Martin; Jon Secada; Jaci Velasquez.

CHARLIE SHEEN

American actor

Well-known for tabloid scandals involving substance abuse and failed relationships, Sheen nevertheless has proved himself a more than capable actor in serious dramatic films and a gifted comedian, especially in his television roles.

Latino heritage: Spanish
Born: September 3, 1965; New York, New York
Also known as: Carlos Irwin Estevez
Areas of achievement: Radio and television; acting

EARLY LIFE

Charlie Sheen was born Carlos Irwin Estevez on September 3, 1965, in New York. He is the son of highly respected American film and stage actor Martin Sheen and artist Janet Templeton. When his father, the Spanish American Ramon Estevez, decided to become an actor, he chose the stage name "Sheen" in honor of the popular American cleric Bishop Fulton Sheen. Later, Charlie elected to Anglicize his name as well.

At birth, Sheen was a sickly child, and it was feared that he would not survive. A Dr. Irwin was integral in saving the boy, and so the grateful parents gave him the middle name "Irwin" in the medic's honor.

Sheen attended high school in Santa Monica, California, where he was a gifted baseball player and a budding actor and director, making and appearing in several amateur films with his brother Emilio Estevez and other schoolmates, including Rob Lowe. However, he was a lackluster and inattentive student and was expelled in his senior year. He immediately began to pursue an acting career, appearing in several bit parts before landing his first important part in a major film, playing a soldier in Vietnam in Oliver Stone's 1986 hit film *Platoon*, based in part on Stone's own experiences. The film won the Oscar for Best Picture that year and made Sheen a star. He quickly lined up more roles in important films, including Stone's *Wall Street* (1987), which again was popular with the public and critics. Sheen's partnership with Stone ended unpleasantly, however, in 1989, when Stone refused to cast Sheen in the starring role in *Born on the Fourth of July*.

LIFE'S WORK

Sheen rebounded from the professional break with Stone by appearing in a film by another major American director, John Sayles, about a subject dear to Sheen's heart: baseball. The film was *Eight Men Out* (1988), a historical sports drama about the 1919 World Series scandal, when members of the Chicago White Sox accepted bribes to throw games. Sheen played one of the eight men involved, Oscar Felsch. Later that year and early the next, he starred in two other hit films: *Young Guns* (1988), a Western drawing on legends of Billy the Kid, and *Major League* (1989), a baseball comedy.

After the success of *Major League*, Sheen starred in action films *The Rookie* and *Navy SEALS* (both 1990) and then in a pair of satires of such films, the popular

Charlie Sheen. (AP Photo)

Hot Shots! (1991) and *Hot Shots! Part Deux* (1993). This duo of spoofs revealed Sheen's flair for flippant humor, a talent that became the focus of his career from the mid-1990's onward. The rest of the 1990's and the 2000's saw Sheen experiment with diverse genres such as science fiction and documentaries and taking on numerous cameo roles, often as himself, most notably in *Being John Malkovich* (1999). He wrote the script for the television film *No Code of Conduct* (1998), in which he also starred, and appeared in the spoofs *Scary Movie 3* (2003) and *Scary Movie 4* (2006).

When Michael J. Fox left his CBS situation comedy *Spin City* in 2000 because of Parkinson's disease, the producers tapped Sheen to replace him as a wry assistant to a big-city mayor. He appeared in the series for two years, winning a Golden Globe for the role. The year after the series ended, Sheen began a long run in another CBS sitcom, *Two and a Half Men*, in which he played a shallow, womanizing playboy whose lifestyle is challenged when his brother and nephew move in with him. His cynical exchanges with Jon Cryer as his brother made the show a top-ten hit in a decade in which sitcoms tended not to fare well in the ratings. Sheen's portrayal of Charlie Harper

earned him two Golden Globe nominations and three Emmy nominations.

Off-screen, Sheen has found himself at the center of much scandal. One girlfriend, actor Kelly Preston, broke up with him after he accidentally shot her. In the 1990's, he was revealed to be a patron of "Hollywood Madam" Heidi Fleiss. His first marriage to model Donna Peele lasted barely one year; his second, to actor Denise Richards, lasted from 2002 to 2006. His third, to real-estate investor Brooke Mueller from 2008 to 2010, ended in part because of a violent episode on Christmas Day in 2009 during which Sheen was arrested for allegedly threatening Mueller with a knife. He later pleaded guilty to a misdemeanor assault charge. Another scandal erupted in October, 2010, when Sheen, under the influence of drugs and alcohol, vandalized a New York hotel room that he shared with former pornography star Capri Anderson.

In January, 2011, Sheen was hospitalized with abdominal pains and began a drug rehabilitation program in his home. Production of *Two and a Half Men* was suspended, and after Sheen made comments in an interview critical of series creator Chuck Lorre, he was fired from the show. Over the following months, Sheen attracted constant publicity for his erratic behavior and outrageous comments to the media and on social-networking site Twitter. He used his notoriety to launch a one-man stage show, *My Violent Torpedo of Truth/Defeat Is Not an Option*, and toured major cities throughout the United States, receiving mixed reviews.

SIGNIFICANCE

Despite Sheen's controversial public image, his record as an actor remains impressive: praiseworthy performances in celebrated films such as *Platoon* and *Wall Street* and a long and successful stint as a comedic actor on television. These facets of his career earned him accolades from the Latino community in the form of three nominations (including one win) for the American Latino Media Arts (ALMA) Awards.

Thomas Du Bose

FURTHER READING

Maerz, Melissa, and Scott Collins. "Charlie Sheen: 'I'm Tired of Pretending Like I'm Not Special.'" *The Los Angeles Times*, March 1, 2011. Chronicles Sheen's erratic behavior and dispute with producers of his hit show, *Two and a Half Men.*
Parish, James Robert. *Hollywood Bad Boys: Loud, Fast, and Out of Control.* New York: McGraw-Hill,

2002. Gossipy but entertaining compendium of scandals involving Sheen and other actors of his generation.

Shumacher, Lee, and David Riley. *The Sheens: Martin, Charlie, and Emilio Estevez.* New York: St. Martin's, 1989. Interesting collective biography of the three most famous of the Latino acting dynasty.

Tresniowski, Alex, et al. "Charlie Sheen's Troubled World." *People* 73, no. 2 (January 18, 2010): 64-67. A detailed examination of one of Sheen's most notorious scandals.

See also: Emilio Estevez; John Leguizamo; Cheech Marín; Freddie Prinze; Martin Sheen.

M<small>ARTIN</small> S<small>HEEN</small>

American actor and activist

Sheen is an accomplished actor who has appeared in major roles in scores of feature films, documentaries, and television programs. Recognized for his portrayal of the fictional liberal president on the acclaimed television series The West Wing *(1999-2006), Sheen is also known as a committed political activist.*

Latino heritage: Spanish
Born: August 3, 1930; Dayton, Ohio
Also known as: Ramón Antonio Gerard Estévez; Ramón Estévez
Areas of achievement: Acting; radio and television; activism

E<small>ARLY</small> L<small>IFE</small>

The actor known as Martin Sheen was born Ramón Antonio Gerard Estévez, the seventh of ten (surviving) children, of the immigrant couple Francisco Estévez and Mary Ann Phelan, who had met at a citizenship school in Dayton, Ohio. Estévez was originally from Spain, but he had entered the United States from Cuba, where he had worked for several years. Sheen had a difficult birth; the forceps used in his delivery broke bones in his left shoulder, which caused permanent damage in his left arm.

One of nine boys, Sheen grew up in the South Park neighborhood of Dayton, where his father worked as a machine inspector at the National Cash Register Company. The family had close ties to their Roman Catholic parish and local Catholic schools. From a young age, Sheen yearned to become an actor, despite his father's objections. After graduating from Chaminade High School, Sheen borrowed money to journey to New York. The young would-be actor found that he did not fit the physical type that producers expected from his Latino name. He adopted the stage name Martin Sheen, in tribute to Archbishop Fulton Sheen, an influential Catholic

theologian and television personality. It was a decision that disappointed the actor's father and that Sheen later regretted, never changing his name legally and using his given name of Ramón Estévez on all identification and legal documents.

Sheen has described his first years in New York and meeting Julian Beck and Judith Malina of the Living Theater as his university education. While supporting himself doing odd jobs, Sheen took acting lessons at the Living Theater and attended its diverse productions. Being in an environment rich in political and artistic ideas

Martin Sheen. (AP Photo)

shaped the attitudes of the naïve midwesterner. After an eye-opening trip to Europe with the Living Theater, the young actor found occasional work in television series, such as *The Defenders*, *Naked City*, and *Route 66*, and steady employment on the soap opera *As the World Turns*. He made his Broadway debut in 1964 in a short-lived production of *Never Live over a Pretzel Factory*.

LIFE'S WORK

Sheen's breakthrough as an actor came when he was cast as a returning veteran, the son, in a three-person Broadway drama set in 1946, *The Subject Was Roses* (1964). The play won a Pulitzer Prize for its author, Frank Gilroy, and a Tony nomination for Sheen, who again played Timmy Cleary in a 1968 film version. Several small film roles followed, and then Sheen costarred in *That Certain Summer* (1972), a made-for-television film. The Emmy Award-winning drama portrayed a homosexual couple sympathetically, a rare and controversial stance for the time. Like many actors of his generation, James Dean was an icon to Sheen, who played a Dean look-alike in Terrence Malick's brilliant debut film *Badlands* (1973). As the banal yet personable serial killer Kit Carruthers, Sheen is remarkable, creating a complex character, full of vigor and unpredictability. Decades later, the actor and many critics still consider it Sheen's best performance. A powerful portrayal of a World War II solider who was executed for desertion in the television docudrama *The Execution of Private Slovik* (1974) won Sheen a Emmy nomination, but it was as Captain Benjamin Willard in *Apocalypse Now* (1979) that Sheen achieved worldwide notoriety. In this famously difficult production, set during the Vietnam War, Sheen plays an assassin sent by the U.S. military to kill a rogue Green Beret colonel. Willard's journey into Cambodia becomes a metaphor for entry into the darkness of the human soul. Sheen suffered a life-threatening heart attack while filming; during his convalescence his brother Joe Estévez became his stand-in. The experience changed Sheen, who had been drinking heavily and using drugs. He returned to work a more disciplined actor and a more committed pacifist.

The hard-working, versatile Sheen has appeared in scores of films, sometimes as many as nine released in a single year (1995). In 1974, he played Robert Kennedy in the docudrama *The Missiles of October* and would subsequently appear in many fictional films and docudramas set in political contexts: as John Kennedy in the television miniseries *Kennedy: The Presidential Years* (1983); as the narrator in *JFK* (1991); as Confederate

---

Sheen's Political Activism

Martin Sheen might be said to have political commitment in his blood, for his mother's family was connected to the Irish Republican Army. His activism was first triggered in the mid-1960's by César Chávez, who led the farmworker movement in California. Sheen has endorsed the civil rights group By Any Means Necessary (BAMN) in its goal of forcing the state of California to honor the César Chávez holiday. A pacifist, Sheen is aligned with the Consistent Life Ethic, an organization that opposes capital punishment, war, and abortion. By 2010, Sheen had been arrested more than seventy times for his involvement in various protests and civil-disobedience actions (typically trespassing on military property).

As an off-screen narrator, Sheen has lent his rich baritone voice to numerous documentaries espousing political causes with which the actor has been associated, including *In the Name of the People* (1985), *Tibet: Cry of the Snow Lion* (2002), and *Return to El Salvador* (2010). He has appeared as an interviewee in another series of politically committed documentaries, including *SOA: Guns and Greed* (2001) and *On the Line: Dissent in an Age of Terrorism* (2005). He played Judge Samuel Salus II in the experimental documentary *In the King of Prussia* (1983), in which director Emile de Antonio had members of an antiwar activist group play themselves (voicing their own statements from the trial transcript). Paradoxically, it is Sheen who is the most convincing.

General Robert E. Lee in Gettysburg; as the chief of staff in *The American President* (1994); as a wealthy contributor in his son Emilio Estevez's *Bobby* (2006); and, memorably, as Josiah Bartlet, the liberal, strong-willed Yankee president in the television series *The West Wing*. Over seven award-winning seasons, Sheen became so associated with the part of the admirable president that he was often urged to run for public office.

Amid the turbulence of a demanding acting schedule and the risks of his involvement in protests, Sheen has maintained a long and stable marriage. He and art student Janet Templeton married in 1961; they had three sons and a daughter, all of them actors, the most well-known of whom are Emilio Estevez and Carlos (who goes by the stage name Charlie Sheen). Martin Sheen has played the fictional father of his sons numerous times, pairing with Charlie in two episodes of the television series *Spin City* and in the films *Wall Street* (1987), *Hot Shots Part Deux* (1993), and *No Code of Conduct*

(1998) and with Emilio in *In the Custody of Strangers* (1982) and *The War at Home* (1995).

In the mid-1980's, Sheen formed a production company and began directing, starting with an award-winning Columbia Broadcasting Service *After-school Special*. He has returned to his first love, the theater, on rare occasions, including for a limited run in London in *The Normal Heart* (1987) and as the father in a 2010 revival of *The Subject Was Roses*, the play for which he received his first national fame forty-five years before, when playing the son.

SIGNIFICANCE

In a career that has included major roles in scores of theatrical films, dozens of made-for-television films, a cluster of important documentaries, a long-running and critically acclaimed series, and occasional theater appearances, Sheen has established himself as a actor of technical skill with considerable audience appeal. From early parts that emphasized his youthful charm and rebellious attitude to portrayals of mature men, often with great responsibilities, Sheen has earned a reputation as a versatile and creative performer and has won numerous acting awards.

His off-screen life has been one of political activism, often to the point of arrest for civil disobedience. Frequently Sheen combines his political commitments with his acting skills, serving as an off-screen narrator in documentaries that support causes to which the actor is committed. More than any other American performer of his generation, Sheen has demonstrated the possibility of having a commercially viable acting career in the midst of a robust, sometimes confrontational, political life.

Carolyn Anderson

FURTHER READING

Coppola, Eleanor. *Notes*. New York: Simon & Schuster, 1979. Director Francis Ford Coppola's wife Eleanor's thirty-two-month diary of the tumultuous creation of *Apocalypse Now*. Charts how the exhausting production changed its participants, including Sheen.

Gilroy, Frank D. *About Those Roses: Or, How Not to Do a Play and Succeed*. New York: Random House, 1965. Playwright's nineteenth-month diary provides a production history of *The Subject Was Roses*. Notes reveal Sheen's working style and responsiveness to direction. Includes text of play and reviews from New York dailies praising Sheen's performance.

Orosco, José-Antonio. *César Chávez and the Common Sense of Nonviolence*. Albuquerque: University of New Mexico Press, 2008. A thoughtful study of the man and the philosophy that have greatly influenced Sheen's political life.

Oumano, Ellen. "Martin Sheen." In *Movies for a Desert Isle*. New York: St. Martin's Press, 1987. Sheen's recollections on his early career, influences on his work, and thoughts on the responsibilities of actors.

See also: Emilio Estevez; Raúl Juliá; Charlie Sheen; Jimmy Smits.

JIMMY SMITS

American actor

Smits is best known for his roles in television dramas in the 1980's and 1990's. His multifaceted acting career has been complemented by activist work in the U.S. Latino community.

Latino heritage: Puerto Rican and Surinamese

Born: July 9, 1955; Brooklyn, New York

Also known as: Jimmy L. Smits

Areas of achievement: Acting; radio and television; activism

EARLY LIFE

Born in Brooklyn, New York, on July 9, 1955, Jimmy L. Smits is the son of a working-class Dutch-Surinamese immigrant father, Cornelius Smits, and a Puerto Rican mother, Emilina. He has two sisters, Diana and Yvonne. Smits grew up in New York and his childhood was deeply influenced by his frequent visits to Puerto Rico.

As a high school student, Smits participated in several theater productions that inspired him to earn a bachelor of arts degree in theater from Brooklyn College (1980) and a master of fine arts degree from Cornell

Jimmy Smits. (AP Photo)

University in 1982. During his years as an undergraduate student, Smits worked as union labor organizer.

In June 10, 1980, Smits married his girlfriend Barbara; their marriage ended in 1987. From this relationship, he has two children, Taina and Joaquin. In 1986, he began living with Latina actor Wanda De Jesus in Los Angeles, California.

In 1984, after appearing in several Off-Broadway productions, Smits won a role in the pilot for the television series *Miami Vice*. This role launched Smits's career as a screen actor. Most of his acting roles have capitalized on his ethnic background as a Puerto Rican, and he often has played good men with profound ethical values.

LIFE'S WORK

Smits's first major mainstream role came in 1984 when he appeared as Eddie Rivera in the pilot episode of *Miami Vice*. Rivera, the original partner of police detective Sonny Crockett (Don Johnson), is killed by a drug dealer shortly after the beginning of the episode. In 1986, Smits landed a leading role as Victor Sifuentes in the long-running television legal drama *L.A. Law*, a role that he played for the first five seasons of the show. He

earned an Emmy as Outstanding Supporting Actor in a Drama Series in 1990.

Two years later, in 1992, Smits left the show to explore other projects. In 1994, he worked with director Luis Miguel Valdez in the cable series *The Cisco Kid*. This remake of the 1950 western television series explores the adventures of two Mexican post-revolution "bandidos." Thereafter, Smits worked with director Robert M. Young on the Showtime film *Solomon and Sheba* (1995). During the filming in Morocco, Smits was asked to replace David Caruso in the television drama *NYPD Blue*. His role as Detective Bobby Simone led Smits to win a 1996 Golden Globe Award. In 1995, under the direction of Gregory Nava, Smits starred in the film *My Family*, playing the role of Jimmy Sanchez. This critically acclaimed film follows a Mexican American family over three generations, from their departure from Mexico to their settlement and challenges in East Los Angeles.

In 1998, after four years on the show, Smits left *NYPD Blue*. Over the next few years, Smits made occasional appearances in film and on television. In 2002, he landed a role as Senator Bail Organa in *Star Wars: Episode II—Attack of the Clones* and *Star Wars: Episode III—Revenge of the Sith* in 2005. His participation in this venerable science-fiction franchise proved to be a smart move garnering him the attention of a large base of new fans. In 2004-2005, Smits returned to television on NBC's political drama *The West Wing*. His character, Matthew Santos, eventually became the U.S. president in the show.

During the fall of 2007, Smits played Alex Vega in the short-lived CBS series *Cane*. The show was eventually canceled as a result of the Writers Guild of America strike, which halted production for several months. In 2008, Smits joined the cast of Showtime thriller series *Dexter* as Miguel Prado, a troubled assistant district attorney. This complex role garnered Smits an Emmy Award nomination.

In addition to his work as an actor, Smits cofounded the National Hispanic Foundation for the Arts, a nonprofit organization recognizing Latinos in the arts, entertainment, and media. He took part in protests against U.S. Navy bomb testing in Vieques, Puerto Rico. In 2010, Smits became a co-owner of the club the Congo Room in Los Angeles with fellow actors Jennifer Lopez, Paul Rodriguez, and Brad Gluckstein.

SIGNIFICANCE

Smits is a well-respected actor who has been a part of many popular and highly regarded television series and films. His social and political involvement has given him distinction within the Latino community. In 1997, the Congressional Award Committee in Washington, D.C., presented Smits with the Horizon Award for his contribution in expanding the opportunities for all Americans, especially youths, through his example and activism.

William Calvo and Aída Hurtado

FURTHER READING

Cole, Melanie. *Jimmy Smits: A Real-Life Reader Biography*. Hockessin, Del.: Mitchell Lane, 1997. A biography aimed at a young audience.

Limón, José E. Foreword to *Brown Gumshoes: Detective Fiction and the Search for Chicana/o Identity*, by Ralph E. Rodriguez. Austin: University of Texas Press, 2005. Discusses Smits's role on *NYPD Blue* in the context of Latino identity in popular culture and the media.

Otfinoski, Steven. "Jimmy Smits." In *Latinos in the Arts*. New York: Facts On File, 2007. Brief profile offering biographical details and a career summary.

See also: Benjamin Bratt; Hector Elizondo; Andy Garcia; Esai Morales; Edward James Olmos.

HILDA L. SOLIS

American politician

As a state legislator, congresswoman, and federal secretary of labor, Solis has worked to improve conditions for the nation's workers, to roll back environmental damage, and to insure that low-income and minority communities are not shortchanged.

Latino heritage: Nicaraguan and Mexican
Born: October 20, 1957; Los Angeles, California
Also known as: Hilda Lucia Solis
Area of achievement: Government and politics

EARLY LIFE

Hilda Lucia Solis (SOH-lihs) was the middle child of seven born to immigrant parents. Her mother, Juana Sequeira, was from Nicaragua. Her father, Raul Solis, was born in the United States but grew up in Mexico. He was a shop steward there with the Teamsters as a young adult. Solis grew up in a solidly union household; her father worked at a battery recycling plant, where he again served as a Teamster shop steward. Her mother, a member of the United Rubber Workers, was employed for many years at a Mattel factory. The family lived in La Puente, California, which had eight landfills and a Superfund site (a site that has been federally designated as contaminated by toxic waste). The concentration of these sites in a working-class suburb turned the young Solis into a lifelong environmental activist.

Upon graduating from La Puente High School, Solis enrolled in California State Polytechnic University at Pomona. She earned a B.A. degree in political science in 1979, and a master's degree in public administration

from the University of Southern California two years later. As part of her master's program, she spent a semester as an intern in the White House's Office of Hispanic Affairs. It was during this time that she met her future husband, Sam Sayyad.

Hilda Solis. (AP Photo)

LIFE'S WORK

Back in California, Solis became director of a state program providing preparation for and access to college for low-income students. Her experience in this job led, in 1985, to a run for the board of trustees of Rio Hondo Community College. This was a hotly contested seat, but through relentless campaigning, Solis defeated both the incumbent and another candidate. Once elected, she was an activist trustee, trying to bring more women and minorities on board as faculty.

In 1992, Solis ran for the California State Assembly, representing the Fifty-seventh District. This was the first election after redistricting, and she had two serious opponents in the Democratic primary. In the general election, seven new candidates, including Solis, were elected to the assembly.

Two years later, a state senate seat opened in Solis's district, the Twenty-fourth, and she decided to try for it. Once again, she won over multiple primary opponents and drew more than 63 percent of the vote in November. She became the first Latina to enter the state senate, as well as the first woman elected from the San Gabriel Valley. Her six-year service in the senate was notable for several achievements. When then-governor Pete Wilson vetoed a bill that would have raised the state minimum wage, she funded an initiative with her own campaign money and managed to get the minimum wage increased through a direct vote. Solis also sponsored a bill to prevent further concentration of environmental waste sites in low-income communities. After an initial veto, she reworked it, and after it passed, the next governor, Gray Davis, signed the bill into law. It was the first such law in the nation.

Having compiled an impressive record, Solis decided to take on an incumbent U.S. congressman in 2000. Mel Martínez had represented her district for eighteen years but had an undistinguished record and opposed abortion rights, labor protection, and other measures important to most Democrats. Solis defeated him in the primary by a wide margin and sailed to victory in November.

Once in Congress, Solis joined the Progressive Caucus and the Congressional Hispanic Caucus. She was chosen as freshman class whip, the member responsible for securing the votes of newly elected Democratic representatives. Among the issues she personally worked on were green jobs measures. Solis opposed George W. Bush administration's trade agreements, concerned about their lack of labor and environmental protections. She was passionately pro-labor and in favor of comprehensive immigration reform, neither of which causes went very far during her eight years as a congresswoman. More successful were measures she supported to decrease teenage pregnancy in minority communities. Her immigrants' rights bills were successful inasmuch as one bill, granting citizenship after one year of honorable service in the U.S. armed forces, became law in 2003.

Within the Democratic party, Solis proved especially effective at raising funds for congressional candidates and scouting potential candidates from Hispanic communities. During the 2008 presidential primaries she supported Senator Hillary Rodham Clinton. However, after the general election, President Barack Obama picked Solis to head the Department of Labor. This was

---

Solis and the Congressional Hispanic Caucus

The Congressional Hispanic Caucus was organized in 1976 to further the shared goals of Hispanic congressional members and their constituents. Upon Hilda L. Solis's election to Congress, joining this caucus was a logical move. Some of its projects—including awarding scholarships to Hispanic students and supporting first-time Hispanic candidates for national office—paralleled programs with which she had already worked. However, the caucus also has experienced more than its share of controversy. Its Republican members left in 1999 largely because of differences over U.S. policy toward Cuba. Other issues also gave rise to dissension, because not all Hispanic legislators' districts share the same economic or demographic makeup. Other disputes seem based more on personality clashes than on politics. In 2007, Representative Loretta Sánchez resigned from the caucus, claiming its chairman, Joe Baca, had used a vulgar term about her in speaking to the California State Assembly speaker. Baca denied the charge, but by that time, other Latina members—including Solis—had protested Baca's lack of respect for the caucus's female members. Indeed, Baca had once called Solis a "kiss-up" to House Speaker Nancy Pelosi. Baca eventually apologized. Solis stayed in the caucus, but she and other female members already had resigned from its political action committee in protest of its gift of $3,000 to Baca's sons for their campaigns for California state offices. Eventually, Baca was replaced as chairman. Before her selection for President Barack Obama's cabinet, Solis was highly regarded enough that she was elected as the Caucus's second vice chairperson.

among the executive departments he considered most in need of a turnaround, and Solis supplied it.

Although Solis's attempt to enact the Employee Free Choice Act—a top priority for organized labor—was deemed politically unfeasible, the Labor Department began using existing labor laws to aggressively crack down on firms that ignored safety regulations, fraudulently classified employees as independent contractors, and dodged minimum-wage requirements. She also refocused some faith-based and community programs into support for workers' rights and economic whistleblowing. While several other departments and their officials drew much public criticism for their actions in the Great Recession, Solis's Labor Department did not, which is perhaps a measure of its success.

SIGNIFICANCE

On a personal level, Solis's career is an affirmation of American values. The daughter of immigrants, she disproved a high school counselor's warning that she was not "college material" and went on to not only earn two degrees herself but also help other disadvantaged young people do so. Starting in a low-profile elective office, she worked to bring attention to a cluster of causes in which she fervently believed: environmental justice, worker protection from exploitation, and immigrants' and women's rights. At the same time, she learned to be a skilled practitioner of legislative tactics—compromising when it was necessary to get a bill passed, building a network of mentors and like-minded colleagues, and using available laws to get results when other efforts were blocked. Solis's accomplishments also exemplify the political coming of age of Hispanic citizens. Without slighting the traditional constituent services, she has seen her role in a larger perspective, as concerned with issues that affect all citizens.

Emily Alward

FURTHER READING

Garcia, F. Chris, and Gabriel R. Sanchez. *Hispanics and the U.S. Political System.* Upper Saddle River, N.J.: Pearson Prentice-Hall, 2008. Offering a context for Solis's career, this work includes an overview of the work of the Congressional Hispanic Caucus.

Hunt, Albert R. "Hilda Solis." in *Profiles in Courage for Our Time*, edited by Caroline Kennedy. New York: Hyperion, 2002. Essay traces Solis's career to that point and praises her determination in pressing for the first "environmental justice" law in the nation.

Kaplan, Esther. "A Rump Group at Labor." *The Nation* 290, no. 14 (April 12, 2010): 18-22. Surveys the changes Solis has brought to the U.S. Department of Labor and her priorities there.

See also: Cruz Bustamante; Alberto Gonzales; Gloria Molina; Edward R. Roybal; Loretta Sánchez.

LIONEL SOSA

American advertising executive

Sosa is known for his quality graphic advertising and effective political advertising. His success as a graphic artist served as the anchor for his career. His management of Sosa, Bromley, Aguilar, and Associates launched a successful career in advertising that spanned more than thirty years.

Latino heritage: Mexican
Born: May 27, 1939; San Antonio, Texas
Areas of achievement: Business; art

EARLY LIFE

Lionel Sosa (LI-oh-nehl SOH-sah) grew up in western San Antonio, Texas, home to many Mexican families. Sosa's father owned a laundry, and Sosa started working in his father's laundry at an early age, learning excellent work ethics and the appreciation of living wages. Sosa's mother encouraged him to appreciate and be proud of his Mexican heritage. She told him that he could become anything that he wanted, even though he was Mexican.

In 1963, Sosa was married with two children, expecting a third child, and working a desk job designing neon signs at Texas Neon, a small business, earning $1.10 an hour at a time when minimum wage was $1 an hour. Sally Pond, a customer, walked into the office and requested a specialty sign for her business, the School of Personal Achievement. This chance meeting changed Sosa's outlook on life and motivated him to launch his vision as a successful artist. He painted the commissioned sign for Pond, enrolled in the school for seventeen weeks, and eagerly learned the seventeen principles of getting rich that were outlined by millionaire

Napoleon Hill and taught by Pond. Sosa believed if he applied the seventeen principles to his life, he could become wealthy. Sosa studied the lives of successful individuals and began to align his goals for prosperous outcomes.

LIFE'S WORK

Sosa founded Sosa, Bromley, Aguilar, Noble, and Associates, an advertising firm. By 2010, the company was known as Bromley Communications, the largest Hispanic advertising agency in the United States. During the 1980's Sosa served as chief advertiser for Garcia KS. In the 1990's, Sosa served as chairman of the board for D'Arcy Masius Benton and Bowles/Américas. His clients included Procter and Gamble and Coca-Cola.

In addition to launching product advertising, Sosa managed media campaigns as a consultant for six Republican presidential candidates and significantly impacted the careers of many notable politicians. He worked as an adviser for President Ronald Reagan and President George W. Bush, in 2000 and 2006. His track record in political advertising resulted in more wins and than losses. Corporate America promoted his standing to more than one hundred million dollars in income during the 1980's. Sosa is recognized as an authority on Latino accomplishment, culture, voting, and shopping trends.

On November 13, 2006, Sosa was the featured speaker at the College of Business Frost Lecture Series at the University of Texas, San Antonio (UTSA). The College of Business at UTSA is a major institution for Hispanic scholars. The lecture series are a networking forum for students and prominent business leaders.

By 2010 Sosa's work as a portrait painter included commissioned portrait paintings starting at twenty-five hundred dollars and ranging as high as ten thousand dollars. Sosa and his wife Kathy host art exhibits throughout the United States. Kathy readily admits that Sosa's portraits are obvious real-life productions of subjects. In contrast, her artistic expression, called *mestizaje*, incorporates period textiles into her oil paintings, giving the appearance of collages. It is often difficult to identify the subjects in her paintings. She modifies the appearance and a multicolored portrait emerges. Kathy began her painting career at age forty-five. She and Sosa converted a traditional Texas farm house into an innovative art studio to facilitate painting and entertainment with family and friends.

Sosa has served on the American College Testing (ACT) Board of Directors, the Texas A&M University Board of Regents, and the Sesame Street Workshop Board. He also chaired the San Antonio Symphony Board of Directors and the United Way Campaign of San Antonio, Texas. In 2010, Sosa served on the Board of Directors for the Public Broadcasting Service and on Eastman Kodak's Diversity Advisory Panel. Sosa was inducted into the Texas Business Hall of Fame.

SIGNIFICANCE

Sosa became one of the most valued voices in America for Latino messaging through his robust advertising campaigns. His advertising firms defined Latino trends in America. *Time* listed Sosa as one of the twenty-five most influential Hispanics in America in 2005. In 2006, Sosa wrote *Think and Grow Rich: A Latino Choice.* He included positive writings on the lives of successful individuals, including that of Latina construction mogul Linda Alvarado.

Sandra W. Leconte

FURTHER READING

Campo-Flores, Arian. "Immigration: The MATT Movement." *Newsweek*, May 22, 2006. A detailed beginning of the organization Mexicans and Americans Thinking Together, founded by Sosa for the purpose of public illumination of the plights of Mexican Americans and the issue of immigration and other social concerns.

Martinez, Miriam. "Lionel Sosa, Marketing Visionary Who Changed Political History: Head of Garcia, KS." *The National Magazine of the Successful American Latino,* April/May, 2004. The history of how momentous advertising in the Latino media market changed the course of major political elections in America.

Sosa, Lionel. *The Americano Dream: How Latinos Can Achieve Success in Business and in Life*. New York: Penguin Putnam, 1998. A sociological perspective on the plight of Hispanic Americans and advice on how to move past discrimination and the formation of stereotypes to advance education, careers, and the pursuit of the American dream.

_____. *Think and Grow Rich: A Latino Choice.* New York: Random House, 2006. Self-help publication that offers detailed life philosophies and meaningful advice from successful Latinos.

See also: Linda Alvarado; Ralph Alvarez.

SAMMY SOSA

Dominican-born baseball player

While playing for the Chicago Cubs during the 1990's and early 2000's, Sosa was one of the best and most popular players in professional baseball. He is one of the top home run hitters in baseball history, but reports that he used performance-enhancing drugs have cast doubt on the legitimacy of his achievements.

Latino heritage: Dominican

Born: November 12, 1968; Consuelo, San Pedro de
    Macorís, Dominican Republic

Also known as: Samuel Peralta Sosa; Slammin' Sammy

Area of achievement: Baseball

EARLY LIFE

Samuel Peralta Sosa (SOH-sah) was born in the Dominican Republic in the town of Consuelo, found in the San Pedro de Macorís Province. Sosa's father, Juan Bautista Montero, worked in the sugarcane fields, while his mother, Lucrecia Sosa, worked as a maid and cook. After Juan Bautista died when Sosa was only six years old, the family struggled in poverty. Sosa and his siblings began working at an early age, with Sosa washing cars, selling oranges, and shining shoes. The family moved around a lot during those years in search of a better life and wages, before settling in San Pedro de Marcorís when Sosa was twelve.

Because Sosa was constantly working during his childhood, he did not have the time or financial means to play organized baseball, instead playing in the streets with balled-up rags and sticks for bats. He originally wanted to be a boxer but focused on baseball once his talent for the sport became apparent when he was fourteen.

Despite his limited experience, Sosa quickly drew the attention of several Major League Baseball (MLB) teams. Initially Francisco Acevedo, a scout for the Philadelphia Phillies, attempted to sign Sosa at the age of fifteen, but the contract was never finalized. The next year, Omar Minaya, a scout for the Texas Rangers, signed Sosa to his first contract with the team. After several years in the minor leagues, Sosa made his major league debut with the Rangers on June 16, 1989. Sosa's time with the Rangers was short, as he was traded to the Chicago White Sox on July 29. He spent the following two seasons playing for the White Sox and their minor league affiliates before being traded again before the 1992 season to the Chicago Cubs.

LIFE'S WORK

Sosa started the 1992 season as the Cubs' centerfielder but was plagued by injuries throughout the year. He missed thirty-four games with a broken metacarpal bone in his right hand after being hit by a pitch on June 12 and, ten days after he returned, had his season ended when a foul ball broke his left ankle. In 1993, Sosa emerged as a power hitter, hitting 33 home runs while playing mostly in right field. From 1993 to 1997, he averaged 34 home runs a year, with a high of 40 in 1996.

Sosa saw an exponential increase in power during the 1998 season, when he was involved in a home run race with Mark McGwire to see who would be the first to surpass Roger Maris's single-season home run record of 61. The chase came to a climax when McGwire became the first to reach 62 home runs in a game against the Cubs and, in a display of sportsmanship, Sosa ran in from the outfield and greeted McGwire after he finished rounding the bases. McGwire finished the season with 70 home runs, but Sosa also surpassed Maris's record with 66 home runs. The chase drew

Sammy Sosa. (AP Photo)

Sosa and Doping Scandal

Throughout his career, Sammy Sosa was dogged by insinuations that he used performance-enhancing drugs, but he never was revealed to have failed a drug test during his playing career. Before steroid testing was implemented for professional baseball, Sosa stated that he would willingly be tested, but when columnist Rick Reilly of *Sports Illustrated* challenged Sosa to a drug test in 2002 to demonstrate that he was clean, Sosa refused. Major League Baseball first tested for steroids during the 2003 season, although the purpose of the test was to determine the extent of steroid use in baseball and the results were to remain anonymous. In 2005, Sosa was accused by former major leaguer José Canseco, although Canseco said that he had no firsthand knowledge to support this claim. That same year, Sosa, along with several other prominent baseball players, took part in a congressional hearing on the use of performance-enhancing drugs in baseball. During these hearings, Sosa's attorney read a statement in which Sosa declared that he had never taken any illegal performance-enhancing drugs. In 2009, *The New York Times* revealed that Sosa was one of 104 baseball players who tested positive for performance-enhancing drugs during the survey tests conducted in 2003.

controversially left before its conclusion. After the 2004 season, he was traded to the Baltimore Orioles.

Sosa had one of his worst seasons in 2005, batting only .221 with 14 home runs. He became a free agent after the season and, not finding any potential offers satisfactory, declined to sign with any major league team. For the 2007 season Sosa signed a minor-league deal with the Texas Rangers and made the team's opening-day roster. Used primarily as a designated hitter, Sosa performed well, recording 21 home runs and 92 runs batted in. He also hit his 600th home run, becoming the fifth player to reach that mark, on June 20. After the 2007 season, Sosa did not sign with a major league team. He announced his retirement in May, 2008, but later declared his intent to play in the World Baseball Classic and the 2009 Major League Baseball season. Sosa was not selected for the Dominican Republic's team and again announced his retirement from professional baseball on June 3, 2009. That year, it was revealed that Sosa had tested positive for performance-enhancing drugs in 2003.

SIGNIFICANCE

Although his career has been tarnished by steroid allegations, Sosa remains one of the most prolific home run hitters of all time and one of the top players during the 1990's and early 2000's. Sosa retired with a career total of 609 home runs, and he was the first player to hit 60 or more home runs in three different seasons. The 1998 pursuit of Maris's single-season home run record by both Sosa and McGwire drew national attention and helped reinvigorate baseball after the 1994 players' strike. As the Cubs' top hitter, Sosa led the team to play-off berths in 1998 and 2003. He garnered a number of individual awards, including the 1998 National League most valuable player award, six Silver Slugger Awards (given to the top hitter at each position in both leagues), and seven All-Star selections. In 1998, in recognition of his humanitarian efforts, he received the Roberto Clemente Award.

Matthew Mihalka

national attention and dramatically increased Sosa's popularity. Sosa's offensive prowess that season helped power the Cubs to a play-off berth and garnered him the National League most valuable player award. The next season, Sosa again surpassed 60 home runs by hitting 63, but so did McGwire, who hit 65. Sosa led the National League in home runs during the 2000 season and hit 64 the year after.

Sosa started to fall out of favor with the Cubs' fans and organization during the 2003 season, even though the team won the National League Central Division title that year. On June 3, 2003, Sosa was ejected from a game when it was discovered that he had been using a corked bat. Sosa claimed that his use of the bat was accidental, as the corked bat was intended for use during batting practice. Several of Sosa's other bats were tested, but none were found to be corked. After an appeal, Sosa was suspended for seven games.

The next season, Sosa sneezed violently before a game in San Diego, triggering severe back spasms that resulted in his being placed on the disabled list. Sosa also asked to sit out the last game of that season and

FURTHER READING

Canseco, José. *Juiced: Wild Times, Rampant 'Roids, Smash Hits, and How Baseball Got Big*. New York: Regan Books, 2005. Written by a former major league player, this book accuses Sosa, among others, of taking steroids.

Sosa, Sammy, and Marcos Bretón. *Sammy Sosa: An Autobiography*. New York: Warner Books, 2000.

Published at the height of Sosa's popularity and prominence, this autobiography chronicles Sosa's rise from meager beginnings to his peak during his 1998 pursuit of the single-season home run record.

Westcott, Rich. *Great Home Runs of the Twentieth Century*. Philadelphia: Temple University Press, 2001. Westcott's book, which chronicles promi-

nent home runs and the individuals who hit them, includes a chapter on Sosa hitting his 60th home run for the second season in a row on September 18, 1999.

See also: José Canseco; David Ortiz; Albert Pujols; Manny Ramirez; Miguel Tejada.

GARY SOTO

American writer

Soto has had a varied career as a poet and writer of nonfiction, fiction, and children's literature. His writings incorporate his working-class, Mexican American heritage and culture, exploring the issues of poverty, social injustice, alienation, and violence.

Latino heritage: Mexican

Born: April 12, 1952; Fresno, California

Areas of achievement: Literature; poetry

EARLY LIFE

Gary Soto (SOH-toh) was born April 12, 1952, in Fresno, California, to working-class Mexican parents. His parents, Manuel Soto and Angie (Trevino) Soto, left high school to get married at the age of eighteen. Without an education, Manuel and Angie were trapped in poverty, lived in dangerous neighborhoods, and were forced to work menial jobs as laborers in the San Joaquin Valley just to survive. Even as a child, Soto joined his parents and grandparents in mind-numbing, physically exhausting work for very little pay and sometimes under dangerous conditions.

When Soto was five, his twenty-seven-year-old father was killed in an industrial accident. Manuel's death devastated the family both emotionally and financially. The grief and hardships surrounding his death became subjects Soto explored extensively in his later poetry.

When Soto was able to attend school, he was not academically motivated. Survival, not education, was his main priority. In 1970, he graduated from high school; however, unlike most of his peers who took low-paying jobs or entered the military, Soto enrolled in Fresno City College.

After enrolling in college, Soto discovered an anthology of poems titled *The New American Poetry* (1960) while browsing through the library. This discovery

proved to be life-altering. After reading several poems by such writers as Edward Field, Allen Ginsburg, and Lawrence Ferlinghetti, Soto knew instinctively he wanted to write poetry.

To pursue his dream, Soto transferred to California State University at Fresno and began taking writing workshops. He enrolled in Philip Levine's writing class, a decision that would have a profound effect on his future writing career. From 1972 to 1973, Levine encouraged Soto to explore his talent and taught him the importance of substance as well as craft. Under Levine's

Gary Soto. (AP Photo)

tutelage, Soto began a spiritual and emotional journey toward self-discovery by confronting his repressed feelings of grief over his father's death, his poverty, and his sense of alienation.

In 1975, Soto began postgraduate studies at the University of California at Irvine and married Carolyn Oda, the daughter of Japanese American farmers who were imprisoned in internment camps in World War II. Five years after they married, their daughter Mariko was born.

In 1976, Soto earned his master of fine arts degree and accepted a faculty position as an assistant professor at the University of California at Berkeley. He chose to leave this position in order to devote his time to writing.

Life's Work

Soto's Latino heritage has figured prominently in his varied, versatile, and prolific career and in his life as a teacher and advocate for equal rights and fair wages for Latinos. Critics laud not only his poetry but also his nonfiction and fiction for children and young adults. Between 1977 and 1999, Soto wrote ten collections of poetry. In 1977, he published his first book of poetry, *The Elements of San Joaquin.* In this collection, Soto gave voice to his anguish and despair over his father's death and the impoverished and sometimes violent world of his childhood—the result of his family's poverty and inability to achieve upward social mobility. This book won the United States Award of the International Poetry Forum.

In 1978, Soto's second book of poetry, *The Tale of Sunlight,* was published and nominated for a Pulitzer Prize. He was one of the first Latino Americans to achieve such an honor. In this book, Soto leaves behind the grimness of his first book of poetry and focuses on universal concepts such as love and death. His next book, *Where Sparrows Work Hard* (1991), once again delves into themes of poverty, survival, and the hardships Latinos face as a result of their economic and social status.

In 1985, Soto's third book of poetry, *Black Hair*, was published. It dealt with more philosophical themes, such as love, death, childhood events, and the importance of friendship. His later poetry collections, including *New and Selected Poems,* published in 1995, are mainly composed of selections from previously published works. *New and Selected Poems* was selected as a finalist for the National Book Award. In two of Soto's later books, *Junior College* (1997) and *A Natural Man* (1999), Soto mixes serious, somber subjects such as the self-doubt and alienation he experienced as a child with humorous recollections of his introduction to college life.

While still writing poetry, Soto ventured into a new genre, autobiographical prose. From 1985 to 2000, Soto published four books of nonfiction prose. His first book, published in 1985, *Living Up the Street*: *Narrative Recollections*, earned him an American Book Award. This book and his next one, *Small Faces,* published in 1986, vividly depict the working-class, racially mixed neighborhood in which he was raised, the hardships his family faced trying to survive, and the angst he experienced as a child and adolescent.

In 1990, Soto began writing fiction and nonfiction for young readers. His motivation for doing so was two-fold: He wanted to venture into a new genre, and he wanted to feature Mexican Americans and aspects of their culture to inspire young Mexican Americans to read. His first book, *Baseball in April, and Other Stories,* earned two awards: the American Library Association's Best Books for Young Adult Literature and the Beatty Award in 1990. In this novel and others, Soto depicts real-life situations and the fraught emotions of adolescence in an understated, humorous, and empathetic tone.

Soto remained a prolific writer throughout the 1990's and 2000's, publishing works including, *Buried Onions* (2006), *Accidental Love* (2008), and *Partly Cloudy: Poems of Love and Longing* (2009). In addition to his writings, Soto often visits schools and libraries as a young people's ambassador for the United Farm Workers of America, exposing young people to the life-threatening, harmful conditions and low-paying jobs farmworkers face in the United States.

Significance

Whatever the genre, Soto is a masterful storyteller. His constant attention to his craft has earned him the respect of readers and critics. His numerous awards attest to his literary genius and his versatility. He is a gifted writer whose work transcends ethnicity to universalize the human condition.

Sharon K. Wilson

Further Reading

Bruce-Novoa, Juan. *Chicano Poetry: A Response to Chaos.* Austin: University of Texas Press, 1982. This critical work examines Soto's ability to transcend issues of ethnicity.

Ganz, Robin. "Gary Soto." In *Updating the Literary West*, by the Western Literature Association. Fort Worth: Texas Christian University Press, 1997. This essay discusses Soto's treatment of the Mexican American experience in both his poetry and prose.

Olivares, Julian. "The Streets of Gary Soto." *Latin America Literary Review* 18, no. 35 (January-June, 1990): 32-49. Olivares discusses Soto's ability to transcend ethnicity and universalize the experiences his characters face.

Orr, Tamara. *Gary Soto*. New York: Rosen, 2005. Basic biography aimed at high school students.

See also: Jimmy Santiago Baca; Luis J. Rodríguez; Luis Alberto Urrea.

PEDRO JUAN SOTO

Puerto Rican-born writer and educator

A member of the Puerto Rican Generation of 1950 writers, Soto addressed in his novels and short stories the harsh realities of assimilation, focusing his lens carefully on the reality of Puerto Ricans who had gone to New York City to make a new life for themselves. His sense of irony compounded his criticisms of what he perceived to be the colonial status of Puerto Rico under American rule and of Puerto Ricans who were treated as second-class citizens in the United States and on their own island.

Latino heritage: Puerto Rican
Born: July 11, 1928; Cataño, Puerto Rico
Died: November 7, 2002; San Juan, Puerto Rico
Areas of achievement: Literature; education

EARLY LIFE

Born to Juan Soto and Elena Suárez on July 11, 1928, in Cataño, Puerto Rico, Pedro Juan Soto (PEH-droh hwahn SOH-toh) attended primary and secondary schools in nearby Bayamón. At the age of eighteen, he moved to the United States to begin premedical studies at Long Island University. He quickly became interested in literary studies, abandoned his preparation for medicine, and graduated with a bachelor of arts degree in English in 1950. During his undergraduate years, Soto began to write for local newspapers. He was drafted into the U.S. Army and served for one year, an experience that had a profound influence on his writings. After his discharge from the Army, Soto married Rosiña Arriví and wrote his first novel, *Los perros anónimos* (1950), which describes the experiences of a Puerto Rican soldier who is plunged into the suffering and chaos of the Korean War—a theme he would take up again in his short story "Garabatos" (1953).

Soto was awarded his master's degree in English from Columbia University in 1953. Working in New York as a courier, postman, and busboy, he eventually became a literary correspondent for the magazine *Visión*. During the years 1953-1954, he contributed to the prestigious Puerto Rican literary journal *Revista Asomante* and to *El Mundo*, *Diario de Nueva York*, and *Ecos de Nueva York*. Soto explored the life of a young, differently abled Nuyorican whose best friends are pigeons in his short story "The Innocent" (1954), which was awarded Best Prize by the Puerto Rico Atheneum. Soto returned to Puerto Rico in 1955 and began to work for the Division of Publications of the Puerto Rico Department of Education, where he would remain until 1966. The Puerto Rican Atheneum once again honored him in 1955, this time for his experimental play *The Guest*.

Among Soto's most celebrated works is *Spiks* (1957), a collection of short stories and vignettes that addresses the mistreatment of Puerto Ricans in New York City. In this collection, Soto demonstrates his virtuosity as a stylist of the Spanish language through his ability to imitate, in writing, the natural sounds and speech patterns of Spanish as it was spoken by Puerto Ricans living in New York. Soto's stories are fresh and current, capturing the harsh feel of the poverty on the Puerto Rican streets and the trenchant prejudice against them in the workplace.

The evils of American oppression are also the theme of his 1959 novel *Usmaíl*. Named for a mailbox his mother saw on their island of Vieques, the protagonist, "Usmaíl," is mocked for years by sailors from the U.S. naval base. When he witnesses the sailors' abuse of a local prostitute, however, Usmaíl fights them and eventually kills one of them. The novel concludes with Usmaíl denouncing the American presence on Vieques and declaring his pride in his homeland. Soto explores a similar theme in his next novel, *Hot Land, Cold Season* (1961), which deals with the confusion of identity that is experienced by the protagonist, who is called "Yankee" in Puerto Rico and "spik" in the United States. Soto continued to discuss the quest for liberation from colonial oppression in his novel *The Sniper* (1969), which many critics believe to be his best and which describes the Cuban Revolution, shifting back and forth from the Cuban to the Puerto Rican perspective.

Soto taught at the University of Puerto Rico from 1969 to 1988, earning his doctoral degree from the University of Toulouse, France, in 1976. Two years later, his son was tragically murdered by members of the Puerto Rican National Police in the notorious Cerro Maravilla incident. Known for his use of innovative techniques, Soto published a comic novel about high-rolling Americans living in Puerto Rico entitled *A Dark Smiling People* (1987). Soto was active in the Puerto Rican independence movement and continued to write until his death.

SIGNIFICANCE

One of the great literary figures of the Generation of 1950, Soto used his creativity and experimental techniques to transform Puerto Rican fiction in terms of theme and form. He was an outspoken voice in decrying American discrimination against Puerto Ricans and in advocating for Puerto Rican independence, especially after the murder of his son at Cerro Maravilla in 1978. Soto was especially gifted in the transcription of vernacular Spanish into his works, giving them life, realism, and humor.

Mark T. DeStephano

FURTHER READING

Sandoval Sánchez, Alberto. "Puerto Rican Identity Up in the Air: Air Migration, Its Cultural Representations, and Me, Cruzando el Charco." In *Puerto Rican Jam: Rethinking Colonialism and Nationalism*, edited by Frances Negron-Muntaner. Minneapolis: University of Minnesota Press, 2008. Several of Soto's works are briefly analyzed as works.

Seda Bonilla, Eduardo. "On the Vicissitudes of Being 'Puerto Rican': An Exploration of Pedro Juan Soto's *Hot Land, Cold Season*." In *Hispanic American Writers*, edited by Harold Bloom. Philadelphia: Chelsea House, 1998. A fine analysis of one of Soto's lesser works, but which discusses the primary theme of the search for Puerto Rican identity.

Simpson, Victor C. *Colonialism and Narrative in Puerto Rico: A Study of Characterization in the Novels of Pedro Juan Soto*. New York: Peter Lang, 2004. A comprehensive study of Soto's literary art and thematic preoccupations, which situates him within the contemporary Puerto Rican literary canon.

See also: Victor Hernández Cruz; Lola Rodríguez de Tió; Luis Rafael Sánchez; Clemente Soto Vélez.

SONIA SOTOMAYOR

American Supreme Court justice

Sotomayor is the first Hispanic American Supreme Court justice. She started her life in the housing projects of New York City but went on to attend Yale Law School and become a federal district and circuit court judge, before being nominated to the nation's highest court.

Latino heritage: Puerto Rican
Born: June 25, 1954; Bronx, New York
Also known as: Sonia Maria Sotomayor
Areas of achievement: Law; social issues

EARLY LIFE

Sonia Maria Sotomayor (SOH-toh-mah-YOHR) was born into a working-class household to her Puerto Rican-born parents. Her father died at a young age, and her mother greatly stressed the importance of education. Sotomayor's mother pushed both her and her brother Juan to do well in school, and both did, with Juan becoming a doctor. Sotomayor went to parochial schools for her elementary days and then attended the well-known high school Cardinal Spellman. She finished there as the valedictorian and was accepted into Princeton University.

Sotomayor struggled at Princeton, in part because she felt out of her element and in part because she had not been exposed to some of the things that Princeton took for granted, such as discussion of ancient literature. It did not help that Sotomayor found the whole experience overwhelming. Overcoming her anxiety, she asked for extra help and challenged the marginalization of Latin American culture at the university. She soon began to improve and ultimately won an award as the top undergraduate. Sotomayor had been interested in the law since an early age, and so she turned her attention to law school.

Sotomayor decided to attend Yale Law School and was awarded a scholarship. She was mentored by Yale's general counsel (who also taught at the law school), which was very beneficial. She graduated in 1979 and then moved to New York City, joining the bar in 1980.

Sotomayor joined the New York County District Attorney's Office and moved up the ladder to prosecute felonies. In 1983, she left that office, formed her own law firm, and finally joined a corporate law firm to gain experience in civil law.

Sotomayor had made quite an impression upon her boss at the New York County's District Attorney's Office and he recommended her to be on several public agencies and panels. From this background, she came to the attention of New York's Democratic senator at the time, Daniel Patrick Moynihan, who had an agreement with his Republican colleague allowing Moynihan to select some of the district judgeships even though there was a Republican in the White House. Unlike Sotomayor's later confirmation hearings, these early hearings were without controversy, and she was unanimously approved.

LIFE'S WORK

Sotomayor's real work began once she was a district court judge. She was a bit unusual on the district court bench for a number of reasons. She was one of only a handful of women in her judicial circuit, and she was the first Puerto Rican woman to serve on the federal

Sonia Sotomayor. (AP Photo)

district bench at all. She did not want to gain attention for the wrong reasons, but did have some well-known cases come through her courtroom. Those included the 1994 Major League Baseball strike, in which she issued a preliminary injunction that had the effect of ending the strike. She also ruled to allow *The Wall Street Journal* to print White House counsel Vince Foster's suicide note in 1993.

After five years on the district court bench, President Bill Clinton selected Sotomayor for the Second Circuit Court of Appeals. While little in her background caused controversy, even in 1997 some observers thought that Sotomayor was being groomed for the Supreme Court. Thus, certain senators were quite probing of the judge in her confirmation hearings. The vote on her nomination was delayed and did not occur until sixteen months after her nomination.

After joining the Second Circuit, Sotomayor wrote nearly four hundred majority opinions and was widely viewed as a centrist judge. Several of her opinions and some opinions in which she joined the majority drew attention either at the time or later during her Supreme Court confirmation hearings. These include a case in which the court upheld a state ban on nunchucks and another concerning affirmative action, in which Sotomayor voted with the majority to allow a city to retry a promotion board when not enough minorities were promoted. She drew the notice of football fans in 2004 when she overturned a lower court ruling and held that the National Football League was allowed to ban college running back Maurice Clarett from the draft because he did not meet the league's age requirement.

Besides serving as a district and circuit court of appeals judge, Sotomayor also taught at New York University School of law and Columbia Law School. Her decade of service on the circuit court of appeals, while shorter than that of some justices, is comparable to that of Justice Clarence Thomas and longer than the circuit court tenures of some other current justices, including Antonin Scalia.

Sotomayor was nominated for the Supreme Court when Justice David Souter stepped down in 2009. She was confirmed after a somewhat testy confirmation hearing. While on the court, she generally has voted with its liberal wing and thus has not varied much from her predecessor. She has, however, been very active in asking questions from the bench, something that other newly appointed justices sometimes have avoided early in their tenures.

Sotomayor's Supreme Court Confirmation Hearings

Sonia Sotomayor was nominated for the Supreme Court in May, 2009, and her confirmation hearings began in July. Some of the delay was attributed to scheduling issues and the fact that Sotomayor met a number of the senators in one-on-one meetings. Ideological lines formed somewhat predictably. Democrats favored her (Sotomayor was nominated by a Democratic president, Barack Obama), while Republicans argued that she was an "activist judge." In the hearings, the Republicans focused on a comment Sotomayor had made after a 2001 speech in which she suggested that a "wise Latina woman" had a distinct advantage in deciding a case over a white man who lacked similar life experiences. Sotomayor defended her comment as an attempt to inspire her audience (she was giving a lecture on diversity at the University of California at Berkeley) and as a rhetorical device, and linked her words to a quote by Sandra Day O'Connor, the first female Supreme Court justice.

Sotomayor also was questioned about several cases, including one in which she ruled against white firefighters in a reverse discrimination case; her decision was notable, as it had been overruled by the Supreme Court just days before her hearings. Sotomayor defended her decision as being correct based on the precedents in effect at the time. The full Senate ultimately confirmed her appointment by a vote of 68-31.

her the third woman on the court and one of the relatively few modern-era justices who have served in all three levels of the federal judiciary (district court, circuit court of appeals, and Supreme Court). None of the justices she joined on the high court has that distinction.

Scott A. Merriman

FURTHER READING

Felix, Antonia. *Sonia Sotomayor: The True American Dream*. New York: Berkley, 2010. Relates how Sotomayor became a Supreme Court justice and discusses her background, including her childhood in poverty in New York City.

McElroy, Lisa Tucker. *Sonia Sotomayor: First Hispanic U.S. Supreme Court Justice*. Minneapolis, Minn.: Lerner, 2010. Although aimed at a relatively young audience, this biography covers all the pertinent topics. Very readable and accessible.

Salkin, Patricia E., ed. *Pioneering Women Lawyers: From Kate Stoneman to the Present*. Chicago: American Bar Association, 2009. Stoneman was the first female lawyer in New York in 1886 and Albany Law School hosts a symposium in her honor. This work collects speeches given there on a wide variety of female pioneers in law, including some judges.

Terris, Daniel, Cesare Roman, and Leigh Swigart. *The International Judge: An Introduction to the Men and Women Who Decide the World's Cases*. Foreword by Sonio Sotomayor. Waltham, Mass.: Brandeis, 2007. This introduction to those who try the world's cases includes a foreword by Sotomayor and profiles of some of the judges.

See also: Joaquín G. Avila; Lourdes G. Baird; Norma V. Cantú; José Ángel Gutiérrez; Antonia Hernández; Vilma Socorro Martínez.

SIGNIFICANCE

Sotomayor is significant as the first Hispanic justice on the Supreme Court and one of the few justices who rose from poverty to the high court. Her appointment makes

CLEMENTE SOTO VÉLEZ

Puerto Rican-born writer and activist

Poet and journalist Soto Vélez is best known for cofounding the avant-garde literary movement La Atalaya de los Dioses and his radical activities on behalf of Puerto Rican independence. A lifelong innovator of language, he was dedicated to both literary and political revolution, searching for a socialist promised land in both his poetry and his political commitment.

Latino heritage: Puerto Rican
Born: January 4, 1905; Lares, Puerto Rico
Died: April 15, 1993; San Juan, Puerto Rico
Areas of achievement: Literature; journalism; activism

EARLY LIFE

Clemente Soto Vélez was born in Lares, a small town in western Puerto Rico known for being the seat of a revolt for independence from Spanish rule in 1868. Orphaned at the age of seven, he was taken in by his godfather, Francisco Mercano, who had escaped from his native Dominican Republic in disguise after being imprisoned for rebelling against the dictator Ulises Heureaux.

At the end of World War I, Soto Vélez's brother returned from the battlefields and suggested that he apprentice himself to a painter in Arecibo. Soto Vélez lived with the painter for more than a year, but soon Soto Vélez realized that his true talent was in writing.

In 1918, Soto Vélez moved to San Juan, where he lived with his sister and studied electrical engineering. After graduation, he found a position at the American Colonial Bank but preferred frequenting the literary and political gatherings at the Ateneo Puertorriqueño (Puerto Rican Athenaeum) and the Carnegie Library, one of the few free libraries in the city.

Life's Work

In the late 1920's, Soto Vélez and his friends created an avant-garde literary group called La Atalaya de los Dioses (*Watchtower of the Gods*), which spearheaded a literary movement known as Atalayismo. Much like Dadaism in Europe, Atalayismo attempted to break from traditional Puerto Rican poetry with unusual rhythms, themes, and imagery. The Atalayistas polarized Puerto Rican intellectual society in the 1930's by disparaging the work of traditional poets, wearing their hair long, using strange pseudonyms, and dressing in outlandish clothing.

La Atalaya was also firmly grounded in Puerto Rican nationalism and the overthrow of U.S. colonial rule. One of the most militant members of La Atalaya and the Nationalist Party, Soto Vélez was arrested several times throughout the 1930's for his revolutionary activities, including an attempted takeover of the capital building in San Juan in 1932 and the instigation of a sugar workers' strike in 1934.

In the meantime, his Atalayismo poems were published in numerous Puerto Rican periodicals, among them *Índice, Alma Latina*, and *El Nacionalista*, the official paper of the Nationalist Party. In 1928, Soto Vélez was hired as a journalist and later editor-in-chief of the newspaper *El Tiempo* but was dismissed after writing an editorial that favored laborers over sugar-company interests. He also founded *Armas*, a weekly pro-independence newspaper, which he edited until 1936.

That year, in the aftermath of the assassination of U.S.-appointed police chief Colonel E. Francis Riggs, Soto Vélez was arrested for seditious conspiracy with seven other prominent members of the nationalist movement, including fellow poet Juan Antonio Corretjer and party leader Pedro Albizu Campos. A local jury found them innocent, but the verdict was overturned by a second jury handpicked by the notorious Governor Blandon Winship. Soto Vélez was sentenced to seven years in federal prison. *Escalio* (fallow land), a series of philosophical essays that he wrote while awaiting retrial, was published by his friends in 1937, when he was shipped to the federal prison in Atlanta, Georgia.

In 1940, Soto Vélez was released and, upon returning to Puerto Rico, immediately violated the conditions of his parole by delivering four fiery speeches for the Nationalist Party. He was arrested again and served the remainder of his sentence in Lewisville, Pennsylvania.

Released in 1942, Soto Vélez was not allowed to return to Puerto Rico. Moving to New York City, he quickly became immersed in radical politics. He was an organizer for radical politician Vito Marcantonio and founded a Puerto Rican wing for the American Labor Party. The many Puerto Rican political, economic, and social groups that he organized included the Puerto Rican Merchants' Association, Casa Borinquén, and Casa Cultural del Bronx.

Soto Vélez also returned to journalism, working as an editor for the important literary weekly *Pueblos Hispanos* from 1943 to 1944 and contributing to the progressive journal *Liberación* from 1946 to 1949. In the 1950's, he founded and edited a magazine called *La Voz de Puerto Rico en Estados Unidos*.

Soto Vélez was most prolific as a poet in the 1950's. His first book of poetry, *Abrazo interno* (*Inner Embraces*), was published in 1954, and was followed by *Árboles* (*Trees*) in 1955. Considered his masterwork, his 1959 book of poems *Caballo de palo* (*Wooden Horse*) is an aching search for Puerto Rican identity. The paradoxes and dreamlike imagery in these works is interspersed with invented words and uniquely coupled with a socialist vision. In his epic work *La tierra prometida* (*The Promised Land*), published in 1979, the promised land is not only an independent Puerto Rico but also an egalitarian socialist society.

In the late 1980's, Soto Vélez returned to Puerto Rico and joined the Committee in Defense of Culture, which opposed the political movement to make Puerto Rico the fifty-first state. He died in 1993 at the age of eighty-nine.

Significance

Soto Vélez's poems are considered some of the best examples of the Puerto Rican literary movement

Atalayismo. He lived his life serving the Atalayista belief that literary revolution went hand in hand with political revolution. In both his writing and activities on behalf of Puerto Rican independence, Soto Vélez attempted to bring about a promised land that was free of oppression and injustice. He was an innovator of language, who admired the use of Spanglish and searched for a way to spell words so they would always be pronounced correctly. Forced to relocate to New York City, he became the bridge between the independence movement in Puerto Rico and the Puerto Rican community in the United States.

Victoria Linchong

FURTHER READING
Espada, Martín. *Zapata's Disciple*. Cambridge, Mass.: South End Press, 1998. This book includes several references to Soto Vélez in this book of essays by Espada.
_____. "The Lover of a Subversive Is Also a Subversive: Colonialism and the poetry of Rebellion on Puerto Rico." In *The Lover of a Subversive Is Also a Subversive: Essays and Commentaries*, edited by Annie Finch and Marilyn Hacker. Ann Arbor: University of Michigan Press, 2010. Essay on Soto Vélez's life and work by poet Espada.
Soto Vélez, Clemente. *The Blood that Keeps Singing/La Sangre Que Sigue Canta*. Willamantic, Conn.: Curbstone Press, 1991. The only collection of Soto Vélez's poetry translated into English, with a foreword by poet Martín Espada.

See also: Pedro Albizu Campos; Martín Espada; Nicholasa Mohr; Lola Rodríguez de Tió; Pedro Juan Soto.

CLAUDIO SPIES

Chilean-born composer

Spies is a well-known composer in the neoclassical and serialist styles. He also is a renowned educator and scholar who has taught composition and analysis since the early 1950's and wrote numerous articles about the music of modern composers, such as Igor Stravinsky and Arnold Schoenberg.

Latino heritage: Chilean
Born: March 26, 1925; Santiago, Chile
Also known as: Carlos Claudio Spies
Area of achievement: Music

EARLY LIFE
Carlos Claudio Spies (spees) was born on March 26, 1925, in Santiago, Chile, to parents of German-Jewish origin. He received an early education in Santiago. When Spies was a teenager, he became acquainted with Erich Kleiber and Fritz Busch, who regularly visited Santiago to conduct concerts. They allowed Spies to attend rehearsals, and he sat backstage with his scores, learning to conduct by observing their performances.

In 1942, when Spies was seventeen, he moved to America to study conducting with Boris Goldovsky at the New England Conservatory. There, he also studied cello with Alfred Zighera and bassoon with Raymond Allard. Several months later, Spies started to study music theory and composition with Nadia Boulanger at the Longy School of Music, in Cambridge, Massachusetts.

In 1943, Boulanger took Spies to New York to attend a concert at the Metropolitan Opera House, where Igor Stravinsky's *Apollo* (1928) was performed. Boulanger introduced Spies to Stravinsky, and the two soon became friends. Spies attended rehearsals and premieres of Stravinsky works, such as *The Rake's Progress* (1951), which premiered in the United States in 1953 at the Metropolitan Opera.

Spies entered Harvard College in 1947 and studied music theory with Irving Fine, Walter Piston, and Harold Shapero. He also took a theory course from Paul Hindemith. Spies graduated magna cum laude in 1950 and spent the following year in Paris as a recipient of J. K. Paine Fellowship. He returned to Harvard for graduate school and received his M.A. degree in composition in 1954.

LIFE'S WORK
Spies's first composition, *Descanso en jardin* for tenor, baritone, and woodwind quartet, was written in 1957 under the influence of Stravinsky's neoclassical style. After writing several neoclassical works, Spies wrote his first twelve-tone piece, *Five Psalms* (1959) for soprano, tenor, flute, bassoon, horn, mandolin, viola, and cello. His stylistic change corresponded to that of

Stravinsky, who began composing twelve-tone music shortly after Schoenberg's death in 1954. Despite the correspondence, Spies serial techniques were unique and differed from Stravinsky. For example, Spies employed various tempos along with the twelve-tone technique in *Tempi* (1962) for fourteen instruments. In his *Viopiacem* (1965) for viola, pianoforte, and harpsichord, Spies employed different instrumental combinations from section to section.

In 1968, Spice conducted Stravinsky's *Les noces* (1923) at a Harvard summer school concert in Sanders Theatre. On this occasion, he performed four preliminary versions (1914, 1915, 1916, and 1919) as well as the final version of the work. By presenting these different versions, Spies showed Stravinsky's compositional process, in which he tried various instrumental combinations. As shown in this scholarly approach, Spies has been active as a researcher. He published numerous articles on music theory and analysis while also teaching composition and analysis.

Spies taught at Harvard University as an instructor from 1953 to 1957, then spent one year as a visiting lecturer at Vassar College. Starting in 1958, Spies taught at Swarthmore College and conducted the college orchestra. In 1970, he became professor of music at Princeton University. In 1999, he joined the faculty at the Juilliard School. Spies received the Lili Boulanger Memorial Award in 1956, a National Institute of Arts and Letters Award in 1969, and a National Endowment for the Arts Fellowship in 1975. He became a U.S. citizen in 1966.

Significance

Spies is fluent in English, Spanish, German, Italian and French. His linguistic skills play an important role in his compositions: About half of his works include vocal music, and their texts cover all of these languages except French. His multilingual background also helped Spies to establish himself as a scholar. For instance, he transcribed Schoenberg's handwritten lecture notes about his twelve-tone method and translated them into English. The resulting article, published in the *Perspectives of New Music* in 1974, became an important piece of literature in the study of Schoenberg's twelve-tone method.

Fusako Hamao

Further Reading

Lansky, Paul. "The Music of Claudio Spies: An Introduction." *Tempo* 103 (1972): 38-44. Analyzes Spies's *Viopiacem* in terms of the instrumentation, use of twelve-tone technique, and rhythmic language.

Martino, Donald. "Claudio Spies: *Tempi.*" *Perspectives of New Music* 2, no. 2 (1964): 112-24. Martino, a Pulitzer Prize-winning composer, offers a detailed analysis of Spies's *Tempi.*

Pollock, Robert. "Claudio Spies." In *The New Grove Dictionary of Music and Musicians,* edited by Stanley Sadie. 2d ed. New York: Grove Dictionaries, 2001. This entry offers a brief biography of Spies with a selected list of his works and bibliography.

Spies, Claudio. "Conversation with Claudio Spies." Interview by Stephen Peles. *Perspectives of New Music* 32, no. 1 (Winter, 1994): 292-325. This interview covers many issues about Spies such as his early education in Santiago and the United States, his acquaintance with Stravinsky, and his development as a composer.

Vander Weg, John. *Serial Music and Serialism: A Research and Information Guide.* New York: Routledge, 2001. Offers an annotated bibliography of the studies on serial and twelve-tone music.

See also: Claudio Arrau; Jorge Bolet; Justino Díaz; Eduardo Mata; Ástor Piazzolla; Jesús María Sanromá; Lalo Schifrin.

Virgil Suárez

Cuban-born poet, novelist, and writer

In poetry and prose focusing on his separation from his birthplace, Cuba, Suárez has become the voice of the exile in an America of anonymity and alienation. Through his spare and poignant poems, novels, and memoirs, he reinterpreted the life of the refugee whose lamented world is lost in the past.

Latino heritage: Cuban

Born: January 29, 1962; Havana, Cuba

Also known as: Virgilio Suárez

Areas of achievement: Poetry; literature

EARLY LIFE

Virgil Suárez (VUR-jihl SWAHR-es) was born in Havana, Cuba, on January 29, 1962, to Virgilio Suárez and Oneida Rodríguez and spent his first years in Arroyo Naranja. A policeman under Cuban president Fulgencio Batista, his father worked as a pattern-cutter in a factory during Suárez's early childhood. An outspoken opponent to the Fidel Castro regime, Suárez's father was arrested several times in the mid-1960's. After a long period of work in a slaughterhouse and the sugarcane fields, the father managed to take his wife and Suárez, then eight years old, from Havana to Madrid, Spain, in 1970. The family feared that Suárez would be drafted into the Cuban military and sent to die in Angola in a few years. Suárez wrote of this in his first memoir, *Spared Angola: Memories from a Cuban American Childhood* (1997). His emotionally fraught relationship with his father informed his work, especially his memoirs, *Spared Angola* and *Infinite Refuge* (2002); his novel *The Cutter* (1998); and his book of poetry, *Banyan* (2001).

The family lived in Spain before immigrating in 1974 to Los Angeles, where Suárez grew up among Chicanos and Mexicans. This time of isolation from the community of Cuban exiles would leave Suárez with a wider outlook and definition of Latino *communidad* than many Cuban writers. After graduating from high school in 1980, Suárez earned his B.A. from California State University at Long Beach and an M.F.A. in creative writing from Louisiana State University in 1987, studying with Vance Bourjaily after a year at the University of Houston under Sir Angus Wilson.

LIFE'S WORK

By 2011, Suárez had published more than twenty books of prose, poetry, and major anthologies of Latino writers. He became a professor of creative writing at Florida State University, living in Tallahasee and Miami with his wife and daughters. Although he began his career publishing novels with *Latin Jazz* in 1989, by the early twenty-first century he had given up writing novels in favor of poetry. Suárez's first poetry collection, *You Come Singing*, was published in 1998, but he had been writing poetry since 1978, and, as he has said, "the poems just keep coming." He began editing anthologies in 1992 with *Iguana Dreams: New Latino Fiction*, the first of two anthologies he coedited with his wife, Delia Poey.

His four novels, *Latin Jazz*, *The Cutter*, *Havana Thursdays* (1995), *Going Under* (1996), and his col-

lection of short stories, *Welcome to the Oasis, and Other Stories* (1992), set out the themes that he would return to over and over in his memoirs and poetry: paternal strength and obstinacy; the loneliness of exile; the need for connection and roots; obsessive nostalgia for a semimythical past; bridging the gulf between two cultures; and the dangers of losing one's soul to the American Dream. Suárez turns directly to his past and his thematic obsessions in the memoirs, *Spared* and *Infinite Refuge*. His books of poetry, *You Come Singing*, *Garabato Poems* (1999), *In the Republic of Longing* (1999), *Palm Crows* (2001), *Shakespeare in Havana* (2001), *Banyan*, *Guide to the Blue Tongue* (2002), *Greatest Hits,1983-2002* (2003), *Landscapes and Dreams* (2003), *Ninety Miles: Selected and New Poems* (2005), deal with all of his themes, especially displacement and exile. His anthologies, *Iguana Dreams*, *Paper Dance: Fifty-five Latino Poets* (1995; with Victor Hernández Cruz and Leroy Quintana), *Little Havana Blues* (with Poey, 1996), and the later ones coedited with Ryan Van Cleave, *American Diaspora: Poetry of Displacement* (2001), *Like Thunder: Poets Respond to Violence in America* (2002), *Vespers: Contemporary American Poems of Religion and Spirituality* (2003), and *Red, White, and Blues: Poets on the Promise of America* (2004), have all been acclaimed as valuable teaching tools.

Suárez has received many honors and awards, including Best American Poetry, the Book Expo America/ Latino Literature Hall of Fame Poetry Prize, *The Daily News*/The Caribbean Writer/University of The Virgin Islands Poetry Prize, the Florida State Individual Artist Grant, a G. MacCarthur Poetry Prize, and a National Endowment for the Arts Fellowship. His work also has been published in Argentina, Australia, Canada, Chile, Colombia, Cuba, England, France, India, Israel, Spain, Venezuela, and New Zealand.

SIGNIFICANCE

One of the leading Latino writers of his time, Suárez has used his energy and his creative abundance to fuel an influential career, manifesting craftsmanship of the highest standards. His fiction has been praised for its tight, powerful narrative. His poetry mixes everyday language and vivid imagery to evoke the emotional displacements of the exile. In his impressive anthologies, he has brought Latino writers to the attention of the mainstream literary community. With his feet firmly planted in the United States, his memories back in Cuba, and his heart divided evenly between the two countries, he writes eloquently of the quintessentially American trait of always being from somewhere else.

Linda Rodriguez

FURTHER READING

Álvarez-Borland, Isabel. *Cuban-American Literature of Exile: From Person to Persona*. Charlottesville: University of Virginia Press, 1998. Suárez' s work is discussed throughout, and one chapter focuses on his memoir-writing.

Del Rio, Eduardo R. *One Island, Many Voices: Conversations with Cuban American Writers*. Tucson: University of Arizona Press, 2008. In this collection of interviews with Cuban American writers, Suárez's interview provides an intimate look into his creative process and personal history.

Suárez, Virgil. "In Praise of Mentors or How I Became a Cuban American Writer." *MultiCultural Review* 6, no. 1 (March, 1997): 30-37. Suárez writes of his path to becoming a writer and those who encouraged and helped him along the way.

_____. *Spared Angola: Memories from a Cuban American Childhood*. Houston, Tex.: Arte Público Press, 1997. Short essays and poems evoke the divide between Suárez's two places of the heart, the Florida where he now lives and the Cuba he left behind.

See also: Jimmy Santiago Baca; Ruth Behar; Lourdes Casal; Oscar Hijuelos.

CARMEN TAFOLLA

American writer, poet, and educator

Tafolla, a prolific writer and poet, transformed her life experiences growing up Mexican American and bilingual in San Antonio, Texas, into powerful literature. She has also been a consultant, keynote speaker, and presenter on cultural diversity, multicultural education, dual-language education, poetry, and creative writing.

Latino heritage: Mexican
Born: July 29, 1951; San Antonio, Texas
Also known as: Mary Carmen Tafolla
Areas of achievement: Poetry; literature; education

EARLY LIFE

Mary Carmen Tafolla (tah-FOY-yah) was born in San Antonio, Texas, to Mariano Tafolla and Mary Duarte. Her childhood within a large extended family in a Mexican American barrio, full of close-knit relationships and surrounded by storytellers, laid the foundation for her work as a poet and writer. In the 1960's, she attended barrio public schools, where school personnel sought to erase the extant culture and language of their pupils while emphasizing the low expectations held for Mexican American children. This experience defined Tafolla's future mission as an educator. An unexpected scholarship to Keystone, a private, academically accelerated high school, provided the impetus to pursue higher education. By 1973, Tafolla had earned a M.A. degree in multicultural education, and in 1982 she received her Ph.D. from the University of Texas at Austin.

Beginning with her first position as assistant professor of Spanish and director of the Mexican-American Studies Center at Texas Lutheran College in 1973,

Carmen Tafolla. (Courtesy of Carmen Tafolla)

Tafolla held faculty positions at colleges and universities in Texas, Arizona, and California for more than thirty years. Her appointment as director of the Mexican-American Studies Center, Tafolla writes in her autobiographical notes, brought her back in delight to the "denied areas" of her childhood and set the course for her future writing, as she taught courses in Chicano literature, bilingual education, Mexican American history, and conversational Spanish of the Southwest.

LIFE'S WORK

The 1970's saw the emergence of Tafolla as poet and writer with the publication, in 1976, of *Get Your Tortillas Together*, a book of poetry she coauthored with Reyes Cardenas and Cecilio Garcia-Camarillo. Some of her other poems were included in anthologies and journals. Her prose work, *To Split a Human: Mitos, Machos, y la Mujer Chicana*, came out in 1975. During those years, she also wrote scholarly articles and training and school texts, and she made significant contributions as head writer of *Sonrisas*, an innovative bilingual educational television series.

Tafolla's command of both English and Spanish is emblematic of her poems and stories, whether she uses each alone in crisp precision or makes the words flow and weave into each other while playing on occasion with south Texas vernacular in both languages. In 1983, *Curandera*, her second book of poetry, was published. *Sonnets to Human Beings, and Other Selected Works* appeared in 1992 and contains poetry, short stories, works for children, the author's autobiographical notes, and a selection of critical essays. That same year, this book was published in Germany as *Sonnets to Human Beings (Sonnette an Menschen)*. Her collection of short fiction, *The Holy Tortilla and a Pot of Beans: A Feast of Short Fiction*, came out in 2008. In these stories, Tafolla again draws on memories of *la familia* and her cultural community to create such characters as "La Santísima María Pilar, the Queen of Mean." A note about the author in *The Holy Tortilla* indicates that in 2008, Tafolla was living and working in San Antonio with her husband, Ernesto Bernal, a son and daughter, her mother, and several pets in a one-hundred-year-old house called Casa del Angel.

Since 1982, Tafolla has produced numerous children's books, many of them bilingual, such as *What Can You Do with a Rebozo?* (*¿Qué Puedes Hacer con Un Rebozo?*, 2009). One of her publications that has drawn critical praise and awards is *That's Not Fair: Emma Tenayuca's Struggle for Justice* (*No es Justo: La Lucha de Emma Tenayuca por la Justicia*, 2008), possibly the first book ever written on the Latina civil rights leader.

Starting in 1990, Tafolla began presenting a dramatic one-woman show, *With Our Very Own Names*, to audiences across the United States, Europe, and Mexico. By 2010, she had given more than two hundred performances at conferences, universities, school districts, and institutes. Tafolla's performances bring to life her poetry and stories in bilingual fluidity, reflecting the voices and themes of the people who inhabit her work.

Tafolla has received many awards and much recognition as an author and poet, as well as an educator and community activist. In 2010 alone, she received the Charlotte Zolotow Award for Best Children's Picture Book Writing, the International Latino Book Award, the Americas Award for Best Children's Book, and the Tomás Rivera Mexican American Book Award for Best Children's Book. In 2009, she was inducted into the Texas Institute of Letters and named to the San Antonio Women's Hall of Fame.

SIGNIFICANCE

Through all her writing, poetry and prose, Tafolla has evoked and preserved her ethnic heritage, her remembered language, and her cultural riches with a literary skill that set the standard for an emerging Chicano literature. In addition, Tafolla actively reached out to all venues and audiences through her teaching and performing, giving her work a life and continuity that endures.

Pilar Cotera Herrera

FURTHER READING

Tafolla, Carmen. *Carmen Tafolla*. www.carmentafolla.com. This exhaustive Web site was created and is maintained by Tafolla. It includes her resume, containing a complete listing of her scholarly and literary writing, as well as her lectures, presentations, and performances. Other sections focus on her prose and poetry, her dramatic performances, and her works for children.

_____. *The Holy Tortilla and a Pot of Beans: A Feast of Short Fiction*. San Antonio, Tex.: Wings Press, 2008. Contains stories that reach back to the wealth of Tafolla's cultural experience growing up in a bilingual barrio community. A glossary of Spanish terms and phrases is an interesting addendum.

_____. *Sonnets to Human Beings and Other Selected Works*. 2d ed. New York: McGraw-Hill, 1995. This volume contains a generous selection of some of

Tafolla's best poems and selected short stories, plus her autobiographical notes. The ten critical and interpretive essays are a good fit with the poetry and prose.

See also: Julia Alvarez; Jimmy Santiago Baca; Lorna Dee Cervantes; Sandra Cisneros; Oscar Hijuelos; Judith Ortiz Cofer; Luis J. Rodríguez; Gary Soto; Helena María Viramontes.

LEO TANGUMA

American artist

With numerous exhibits and permanent installations to his credit, Tanguma is respected both for his art and civic leadership. His murals and community art projects follow the tradition of great Mexican muralists like David Alfaro Siqueiros and Diego Rivera, whose narrative art inspired and educated international audiences.

Latino heritage: Mexican
Born: November 5, 1941; Beeville, Texas
Areas of achievement: Art; activism

EARLY LIFE

Leo Tanguma (tahn-GEW-mah) was born on November 5, 1941, to Ramón and Anita Tanguma in Beeville, Texas, where he grew up and attended public schools. In interviews he has credited his farmworker parents for giving him strong spiritual values and community roots. He himself worked the fields in Texas until he was fourteen. He has also credited a twelve-year-old sister for sparking his artistic interest with her gift of a paint set when he was eight. Joining the U.S. Army in 1958, he completed high school by passing the General Education Development (GED) test and received certificates in electronics and radio communication training. The Army also provided art opportunities by appointing him to paint murals in the Conn Barracks Service Club at Schweinfurt, Germany, in 1960 and the Mess Hall at Fort Ord, California, in 1961, for which he received official U.S. Army letters of commendation.

After honorable military discharge, Tanguma returned home to study liberal arts at Lee Junior College in Baytown, Texas, from 1963 to 1967. He attended Texas Southern University in Houston, an historically black institution, majoring in art from 1973 to 1974. At Texas Southern, he met his first professional mentor, John Biggers, an African American artist and professor celebrated for his portrayal of African American life and the Civil Rights movement. Tanguma was also profoundly affected by personal meetings with the renowned Mexican muralist David Alfaro Siqueiros and

some of his Mexican apprentices. These formative experiences nurtured a moral conscience keenly sensitive to such social justice issues as peace, poverty, racism, sexism, war, and heritage preservation.

LIFE'S WORK

Tanguma has acknowledged that his vision was shaped by his early family bonds, his military service, Texas Southern University's cultural pride, and Biggers's aesthetic guidance; it was further sharpened by the Chicano movement of the 1960's-1970's, a sociopolitical movement that grew out of the United Farm Workers' union-organizing activities and the student antiwar and civil rights movements. In the early 1970's, Tanguma painted Chicano-themed murals in El Paso, Texas, and was asked to participate in the 1971 La Raza Art Festival at Houston's Ripley House Community Center. The Contemporary Arts Museum of Houston in 1974 invited him to paint solo panels for *We the People,* a sculptural mural commemorating America's Bicentennial.

For these efforts he was honored in 1973 with a plaque of appreciation from the Houston Chamber of Commerce and named Hispanic Artist of the Year in 1974 by Houston's Institute of Hispanic Culture. Securing his importance in Texas art history, the Texas Sesquicentennial Commission recognized Tanguma's *Mural Rebirth of Our Nationality* as a Houston Historical Landmark in 1986.

As the Chicano movement spread geographically, artists and writers helped raise social consciousness by presenting their works at conferences, festivals, and other local and national venues. Concerned about the fragility of many outdoor murals, Tanguma experimented with alternative large-scale formats. He began creating freestanding mural sculptures on monumental wood frames. Invited by the Arvada (Colorado) Center for the Arts and Humanities to exhibit in a group show in 1985, his mural sculpture *Imagenes* took the First Place award.

Thus began the artist's connection to Denver, Colorado, his base for more than two decades. In 1987,

Tanguma received an individual artist fellowship from the Denver Commission on Cultural Affairs; that same year Denver North High School honored him for his mural painting and youth mentoring with a plaque of appreciation, an honor that was reprised by the University of Southern Colorado (1999), Overland High School in Aurora, Colorado (2002), and other recipients of his civic service. His artwork has been recognized twice by *Westword* magazine's annual The Best of Everything in Denver Award (1989 and 1997).

Tanguma's many artistic commissions include permanent installations in Colorado at the state capitol in Denver (1991), the state fairgrounds in Pueblo (1993),and the Denver International Airport (1995). The airport artwork, *In Peace and Harmony with Nature*, is on permanent display and consists of two monumental murals depicting interrelated aspects of humanity represented by children in the folk costumes of thirty-two countries. Tanguma has described this work as expressing his concern with the preservation of the natural environment, and his vision is viewed by thousands of international travelers every day.

Among his other works are *La Antorcha de Quetzacoátl*, a solo sculptural mural that was viewed by more than 100,000 people between 1988 and 1990 at multiple sites in Colorado, as well as in New Mexico. A related piece, *We Are All Children of Quetzal*, was exhibited in 1987 at the University of Oregon in Eugene and El Centro, a community center in Cornelius, Oregon. Tanguma's keen concern for education and community outreach are also captured in such sculptural murals as *The Teacher as Liberator* (1995), installed at the North Carolina Center for the Advancement of Teaching, as well as *Too Long In Darkness, Reaching for the Light* (1990), created for Bayaud Industries of Denver, Colorado.

Tanguma describes his community murals as planned and executed with the help and hopes of people who care about their neighbors. The artistic techniques he employs to project his vision are powerful images of bold colors, dynamic shapes, epic symbols, and engaging narrative illustrations. Always paying homage to mentors Siqueiros and Biggers, he acknowledges that his experiments with three-dimensional forms led him to the mural sculptures he developed as an alternative to traditional wall paintings and for which he is paid tribute.

Tanguma's integration of aesthetics and social justice has earned him widespread recognition from artists, including the Alliance for Contemporary Art, which honored him with its 1993 AFKEYAward. Elected officials have also paid him tribute, as in 1994, when he received the Mayor's Award for Excellence in the Arts from the city of Denver. In 1995, the Rocky Mountain Conference of the United Methodist Church gave him its Peacemaker Award, and he also received the 2003 Cinco de Mayo Civil Rights Award, among numerous other honors.

SIGNIFICANCE

Leo Tanguma has had an enormous impact as an artist, innovative muralist, community organizer, civic leader, and teacher. Fulfilling these roles with outstanding ability, beauty, courage, integrity, and persistence, he is also admired for his modesty and soft-spoken humility. As a maestro of harmony and peace he enhances American discourse while simultaneously broadening the range and texture of art and life themselves.

Cordelia Chávez Candelaria

FURTHER READING

Candelaria, Cordelia Chávez, ed. *Encyclopedia of Latino Popular Culture.* Vol. 2 Westport, Conn.: Greenwood Press, 2004. Includes an entry about Tanguma.

Goldman, Shifra. "Chicano Art Alive and Well in Texas: A 1991 Update." *Revista Chicanoriqueña* 9 (Winter, 1981): 34-40. This overview of Chicano art includes information about Tanguma's work.

Griswold del Castillo, Richard, Teresa McKenna, and Yvonne Yarbro-Bejarano, eds. *Chicano Art: Resistance and Affirmation, 1965-1985.* Los Angeles: Wight Art Gallery, University of California, 1991. Catalog accompanying an exhibition of that was mounted at several museums from 1990 to 1993. Places Tanguma's work within the broader context of contemporary Chicano art.

Keller, Gary D., et al. *Contemporary Chicana and Chicano Art.* 2 vols. Tempe, Ariz.: Bilingual Review Press, 2002. Provides biographies and discusses the work of about two hundred artists throughout the United States.

See also: Judith F. Baca; José Antonio Burciaga; Barbara Carrasco; Daniel DeSiga; Jesse Treviño.

YOLANDA TARANGO

American religious leader and social activist

As a member of the Sisters of Charity of the Incarnate Word, Tarango has been a key figure in the articulation of a mujerista theology which focuses on the struggle for justice faced by Latinas and other minorities.

Latino heritage: Mexican

Born: September 26, 1948; El Paso, Texas

Also known as: Sister Yolanda Tarango, CCVI

Areas of achievement: Religion and theology; women's rights; activism

EARLY LIFE

Yolanda Tarango (yoh-LAHN-dah tar-AN-goh), the daughter of Mexican American parents, was born in El Paso, Texas, into a Spanish-speaking family of seven children. In 1966, at the age of seventeen, Tarango joined the Sisters of Charity of the Incarnate Word, which accounts for the initials after her name, CCVI, the Latin acronym for Congregatio Caritatis a Verbo Incarnato. When she entered the convent, Tarango originally thought she would experiment with the monastic life for a semester and then continue her education as a lay student. Instead she decided to stay in the congregation and made vows as a religious sister. She earned a bachelor's degree from Incarnate Word College in San Antonio, Texas, in 1973, a master of divinity degree from Catholic Theological Union in Chicago in 1983, and a doctor of ministry degree from Austin Presbyterian Theological Seminary in 2004. In 1986, Tarango was instrumental in the founding of a transitional home for women, children, and victims of domestic violence. She also was a founding member of Las Hermanas, a national organization of Latinas originally founded by Chicana religious sisters.

LIFE'S WORK

The Sisters of Charity of the Incarnate Word came to San Antonio from France in 1869 to minister to the needs of people who had been injured in the Civil War. They opened the city's first hospital and in 1881 founded the University of the Incarnate Word. In the late twentieth and twenty-first centuries, the sisters cared for the homeless and immigrants and worked as teachers, administrators, attorneys, and engineers. As a member of the congregation and an adjunct professor at the University of Incarnate Word in San Antonio, Tarango taught Latino spirituality and theology classes.

On July 13, 2008, Tarango was installed as the congregational coordinator of her religious order, a title previously known as general superior. As congregational coordinator, Tarango led the largest Catholic religious order in Texas, a community of 420 members; she was the first Latino to assume this leadership position. The Sisters of Charity of the Incarnate Word work in Mexico, Guatemala, Peru, Zambia, and Ireland, as well as in the United States.

Tarango is best known for her efforts to articulate what is known as a *mujerista* theology. *Mujer* is the Spanish word for woman, and *mujerista* theology refers to Latinas' struggles for justice and liberation. The largest percentage of U.S. Latinas are of Mexican descent; others come from the Caribbean countries and Central and South America, where they have suffered under dictatorships, repressive governments, and exile. In the United States, many Latinas continue to live in poverty and are often disadvantaged because of their lack of English-language skills. Instead of teaching Latinas to resign themselves to poverty in this world and be content to receive their reward in heaven, *mujerista* theology emphasizes that it is not right to be passive in the face of humiliation and injustice.

In 1971, a group of religious sisters formed Las Hermanas, an organization of Catholic Latinas. Their goal was to make justice for Latinas a reality by actually embracing and identifying with these women's struggle. Las Hermanas challenged a traditional theology that had ignored the experiences of women, particularly women of color. A book by Tarango and Ada María Issai-Díaz, *Hispanic Women/Mujer Hispana: Prophetic Voice in the Church/Voz profetica en la iglesia* (1988), was inspired by Las Hermanas. In their book, the authors transcribe in-depth interviews with Latinas, which they then extrapolate into theological language.

SIGNIFICANCE

As she matured, Yolanda Tarango, a woman raised in a Latino culture, became increasingly aware of the discrimination and lack of opportunities experienced by the majority of Latinas. She began to write and teach about this situation, and she eventually became general coordinator of her religious congregation, whose mission was to work with the poor. She also espoused the *mujerista* theology, which worked to attain justice and liberation for Latinas.

Winifred Whelan

FURTHER READING

Deck, Allan Figueroa. "Hispanic Women: Prophetic Voice in the Church." *America* 159, no.12 (October 29, 1988): 322-323. Reviews the book *Hispanic Women,* which is coauthored by Tarango. Deck praises the book as a groundbreaking work that demonstrates how the Latino community creates theology by working for justice, reflecting on its actions, and reemerging with a new perspective.

Medina, Lara. "Transformative Struggle: The Spirituality of Las Hermanas." *Journal of Feminist Studies in Religion*, 17, no.2 (Fall, 2001): 107-126. Focuses on the founding and history of Las Hermanas, including an interview with Tarango.

Ramirez, Alice. "First Latina Leads Oldest Order." *Logos: Weekly Newsletter of the University of the In-* *carnate Word* 109, no. 1 (August, 2008). Gives an account of Tarango's installation as congregational coordinator of the Sisters of Charity of the Incarnate Word.

Tarango, Yolanda, and Ada María Isasi-Díaz. *Hispanic Women/Mujer Hispana: Prophetic Voice in the Church/Voz Profetica en la iglesia* . Scranton, Pa.: University of Scranton Press, 1988. Isasi-Díaz and Tarango offer extensive interviews with Latinas, demonstrating how the women themselves are theologizing their lives. Though the book is written in English, a summary of each chapter follows in Spanish.

See also: Fray Angélico Chávez; Virgilio Elizondo; Oscar I. Romo.

NINA TASSLER

American television executive

When Tassler was named president of CBS in 2004, she became the first Latina to hold such a high-ranking position at a major broadcast network.

Latino heritage: Puerto Rican

Born: June 19, 1957; New York, New York

Also known as: Nina C. Tassler

Area of achievement: Radio and television

EARLY LIFE

Nina C. Tassler (TAS-lur) was born into a diverse family (a Puerto Rican mother and a Jewish father) on June 19, 1957, in upstate New York, allowing Tassler at an early age to view the world as a multihued palette. She has stated that her family is comparable to the United Nations, one of the most inherently diverse organizations in the world. Her father's family is from Russia. Her mother converted to Judaism, and her mother's sister's husband is Mexican. In addition, Tassler has uncles and cousins who married Cuban Americans, Mexican Americans, Australians, and an Italian.

Tassler attended primary school in upstate New York. As a child, she was aware of her mixed heritage, as the only student in her school with a diverse legacy. She experienced both racism and anti-Semitism. To combat this negativity, her parents explained her uniqueness in a manner that instilled pride. Tassler had to face challenges when she was young, and she credits those lessons taught by her parents as anchors for building the confidence she has exhibited for many years of her life.

Tassler's admiration for theater and entertainment was formed in elementary school. Elementary school plays served as catalysts for her life-long entertainment goals. Tassler considered her transition into television programming a natural progression from her theater beginnings.

LIFE'S WORK

After graduating from Boston University, Tassler moved to New York City, where she worked at the Roundabout Theatre Company. A few years later, Tassler moved to Los Angeles, further building on her career in the entertainment business. Tassler worked five years as a talent agent at Triad Artists before moving to Warner Bros. Television (formerly known as Lorimar Television), where she worked in script development for such popular programs as *E.R.* and *Lois and Clark.* Tassler played several key roles at Warner Bros. in the 1990's, including director of films and miniseries, vice president of drama development, vice president of drama, CBS Productions, senior vice president of drama development, and executive vice president of drama series development.

In the 2009-2010 ratings war, Tassler was credited with making CBS "America's most watched network"

Nina Tassler. (AP Photo)

for the seventh time in eight seasons. In 2010, Tassler oversaw the CBS Network's entertainment programming for prime time, late night, and daytime, and she helmed program development for all genres, including comedy, drama, reality, specials, films, and miniseries. In 2010, she reported directly to Leslie Moonves, the president and chief executive officer of CBS Corporation.

By 2010, Tassler had become a programming expert. She added a Tuesday comedy line-up to link continuity of programming with the highly rated Monday comedy line-up.. She had introduced two critically acclaimed comedies, *The Big Bang Theory* and *How I Met Your Mother.* Tassler had increased drama programming with intriguing series, including *The Good Wife*, *NCIS: Los Angeles*, *The Mentalist*, and *Criminal Minds*. She also spearheaded the new reality series *Undercover*

Boss, which showed strong ratings following the Super Bowl. It emerged as the number-one new program of the 2010 television season. As executive vice president of drama series development, Tassler helped to create many of the commercially successful dramas on network television, including the highly successful *CSI* franchise and *NCIS.*

SIGNIFICANCE

In 2004, when Tassler became CBS programming chief, she had the authority to approve new shows or cancel existing programs. By 2010, CBS had experienced a ratings surge that enhanced prime-time ratings, scoring higher than Fox Television. In 2010, Tassler served on the board of directors at Boston University. Calling her most important position that of being a wife and mother, Tassler says family first is her operational plan.

Sandra W. Leconte

FURTHER READING

De Moraes, Lisa. "CBS Entertainment Chief: She Could've Danced All Night." *The Washington Post*, July 20, 2005. Article describes Tassler's ability to handle critics' questions with poise.

Hibberd, James. "Nina Tassler: Riding a Ratings Wave." *Hollywood Reporter*, November, 2010. The CBS Entertainment president has a few ideas about how to stay on top. An assessment of Tassler's leadership style.

James, Meg. "How I Made It: CBS Programming Chief Takes a Lot of Pitches in Search of a Hit." *Los Angeles Times*, July 25, 2010. Tassler talks about how she rose to her significant position in show business.

Rice, Lynette. "CBS Entertainment President Nina Tassler on Jay Leno: 'It Was Misguided.'" *Entertainment Weekly*, January 9, 2010. Tassler comments on a rival network's actions and her dealings with the troubled Charlie Sheen, who starred in her network's situation comedy *Two and a Half Men.*

See also: Linda Alvarado; Laura Contreras-Rowe; Ángel Ramos.

DIANA TAURASI

American basketball player

Taurasi's most important contribution was her devotion to a sport that demanded the best she had to give, but bestowed honors upon her in return. Her natural talent, once it had an opportunity to develop, made her into an all-round athlete whose maneuvers on court are seen as models of perfection.

Latino heritage: Argentinean
Born: June 11, 1982; Chino, California
Also known as: Diana Lurena Taurasi
Area of achievement: Basketball

EARLY LIFE

Diana Lurena Taurasi (tah-RAH-see) was born June 11, 1982, the second of two daughters born to Mario, an Italian native raised in Argentina, and Liliana Taurasi, who was born in Argentina. The family spoke Spanish at home. Mario, a machinist in Chino, had been a professional soccer player in Italy. Tall and gangly Taurasi, a natural athlete, was encouraged not to be ashamed of her height.

Taurasi modeled much of her basketball playing style after Magic Johnson, the Los Angeles Lakers' star point guard. Understanding that the game required much more than just shooting the ball, Taurasi became a dominant passer and defender. Most of what she knew about basketball she learned in pickup games in the neighborhood; her first organized basketball games were in the sixth grade.

Taurasi attended Don Antonio Lugo High School in Chino, scoring more than 3,000 points and becoming a basketball standout. Throughout high school, she set records, and in her senior year she averaged 28.8 points, 12.9 rebounds and 4.2 assists, catapulting her school into competition for the state title. She received *The Los Angeles Times*'s Cheryl Miller Award, given to the top high school player in Southern California. She also was named an All-American by *Parade* magazine and Nike.

Pursued by countless colleges, Taurasi chose University of Connecticut, a women's basketball powerhouse coached by Geno Auriemma, whose disciplinarian approach would mold her into a superb ballplayer. In her sophomore year, Taurasi became a dominating scorer and quickly joined the ranks of the national elite. That season, Connecticut defeated Tennessee for the national championship.

With Taurasi leading the way, Connecticut went on to win two more national titles, in 2003 and 2004.

Taurasi won the Naismith Award for player of the year and was named most outstanding player of the National Collegiate Athletic Association Tournament in both seasons.

LIFE'S WORK

After graduating from Connecticut, Taurasi was named to the United States Olympic team for the 2004 Summer Games in Athens, Greece. Despite being the youngest member of the team, Taurasi scored 13 points in the first game to defeat Japan. The U.S. team ultimately claimed the gold medal in Athens.

Next, Taurasi became the first overall selection in the Women's National Basketball Association (WNBA) draft. Signed by the Phoenix Mercury, she was named rookie of the year and earned a spot on the All-WNBA first team. However, the Mercury did not make the playoffs that year or the next.

At the beginning of Taurasi's third season in the WNBA, former National Basketball Association coach Paul Westhead took over as the Mercury's coach. Taurasi continued to break records, but the team was unable

Diana Taurasi. (AP Photo)

to make the play-offs. In 2007, the Mercury finally reached the postseason, and Taurasi and Cappie Pondexter led the team to a championship.

In 2009, Taurasi received the WNBA most valuable player (MVP) award and played a key role in defeating the Indiana Fever for the Mercury's second championship. She also was named the WNBA Finals MVP. In 2009, Taurasi was was arrested for driving under the influence of alcohol and suspended for two games. She later entered a guilty plea and served one day of a ten-day sentence.

In August, 2010, Taurasi signed a multiyear extension with the Phoenix Mercury. During the offseason, she agreed to play in Turkey for the Fenerbahçe team. In January, 2011, Taurasi was suspended from the team after reportedly testing positive for modafinil, a banned stimulant. Taurasi denied ever using performance-enhancing drugs and was vindicated a month later when the laboratory announced that her test had been a false positive.

SIGNIFICANCE

Taurasi is one of the most dominant women's basketball players of her generation and has excelled in the highest levels of her sport. A prolific scorer and well-rounded player, she has inspired a new generation of basketball players to emulate her.

Mary Hurd

FURTHER READING

Auriemma, Geno, and Jackie MacMullen. *Geno: In Pursuit of Perfection.* Foreword by Diana Taurasi. New York: Grand Central, 2009. One of college basketball's most successful coaches provides an interesting discussion of his strategies, philosophies, and the growth of women's basketball.

Baker, Christine A. *Why She Plays: The World of Women's Basketball.* Lincoln: University of Nebraska Press, 2008. Well-written account describing the experiences and perspectives of notable coaches and basketball players who have devoted their lives to the game.

Deford, Frank. "UConn's Flashy Finish." *Sports Illustrated* 100, no. 16 (April 19, 2004): 64. Looks back on Connecticut's championship season—its third straight—and Taurasi's importance as a new national women's basketball star.

Grundy, Pamela, and Susan Shackelford. *Shattering the Glass: The Remarkable History of Women's Basketball.* Chapel Hill: University of North Carolina Press, 2007. Excellently detailed overview of women's basketball in the United States.

See also: Carlos Arroyo; Rolando Blackman; Manu Ginóbili; Eduardo Nájera.

MIGUEL TEJADA

Dominican-born baseball player

Tejada became a star while playing shortstop for the Oakland A's and was named the American League's Most Valuable Player in 2002. However, his reputation was damaged by his involvement in the steroids scandal.

Latino heritage: Dominican
Born: May 25, 1974; Baní, Dominican Republic
Also known as: Miguel Odalis Tejada Martinez; La Gua Gua; the Bus
Area of achievement: Baseball

EARLY LIFE

Miguel Odalis Tejada Martinez, better known as Miguel Tejada (mee-GHEL tee-HAHD-ah), grew up in extreme poverty in Baní, Domincan Republic. As a child, he idolized Baltimore Orioles' shortstop Cal Ripken, Jr.

LIFE'S WORK

Like his idol, Tejada would pursue a career in Major League Baseball (MLB). A power hitter and a home-run producer with speed, Tejada joined the Oakland Athletics (A's) at the end of the 1997 season, and the next year became the team's starting shortstop. Tejada's breakout year was 2002, when his batting average was .308, and he made thirty-four home runs, leading the A's to their second Western Division title in three years. His performance earned him that year's American League Most Valuable Player (MVP) award. By the end of 2003 season, Tejada established himself as one of baseball's premier shortstops. Despite these accomplishments, the A's declined to retain him, and Tejada signed a six-year, $72 million dollar contract with the Baltimore Orioles.

On arrival in Baltimore in 2004, Tejada continued to rack up impressive numbers, leading the league with

150 runs batted in (RBI). He grew frustrated, however, with the Orioles' lackluster performance. On December 8, 2005, the Associated Press reported that Tejada had asked the Orioles to trade him to another team. He remained an Oriole through the 2007 season. Like his hero Ripken, Tejada proved durable at shortstop and played in his one thousandth consecutive game on July 1, 2006. His streak of 1,152 consecutive games is the fifth-longest in Major League history, behind Ripken (2,632), Lou Gehrig (2,130), Everett Scott (1,307), and Steve Garvey (1,217).

Tejada's durability may have been artificially enhanced. In 2005, Orioles player Rafael Palmeiro tested positive for steroids and, under MLB's steroid policy, was suspended for ten games. Palmeiro later told a baseball arbitration panel that Tejada gave him a supplement, which caused the steroids to enter his body. The House Committee on Oversight and Government Reform questioned Tejada about Palmeiro's statement, and Tejada denied the allegation. He maintained he had given Palmeiro vitamin B12, a legal substance under MLB policy.

On August 26, 2005, congressional staffers met with Tejada at a Baltimore hotel. A staffer asked him if "there [had] been discussions among other players about steroids?" Tejada, speaking through a Spanish interpreter, responded, "No, I never heard." Later in the meeting, Tejada was asked if he knew of any other player using steroids, and he replied that he did not.

Tejada's denials would later conflict with the Mitchell Report, an investigation of steroid use in baseball that was compiled by former U.S. Senator George J. Mitchell. The report, released on December 13, 2007, alleged that Tejada had discussed performance-enhancing drugs with a teammate, Adam Piatt, and purchased $6,300 of these drugs from him in 2003. According to Piatt, Tejada had approached him in the Oakland A's clubhouse in 2003, when Tejada noticed Piatt's physique. Tejada "mentioned that [Piatt] looked in great shape physically and asked [Piatt] what he was doing to help him be in such good physical shape." Tejada then bought human growth hormone from Piatt.

On January 15, 2008, Congressman Henry A. Waxman asked the U.S. Justice Department to investigate whether Tejada was truthful when he met with the congressional staffers in 2005. On February 10, 2009, Tejada was charged with one misdemeanor count of making a misrepresentation to Congress. The following day, Tejada pleaded guilty to charges that he lied to Congress. Although he could have been sentenced to a maximum

Miguel Tejada. (AP Photo)

of one year in federal prison and deported, on March 26, 2009, he received a sentence of one year of probation.

The Orioles had traded Tejada to the Houston Astros on December 12, 2007, the day before the release of the Mitchell Report. Tejada's 2008 and 2009 seasons with the Astros were, statistically, his worst since his rookie season of 1998. He returned to the Orioles in the 2010 season after signing a one-year, $6 million contract with the team on January 23, 2010. On July 29, 2010, however, the Orioles traded him to the San Diego Padres; and in December 2010, Tejada signed a one-year, $6.5 million contract with the world champion San Francisco Giants.

SIGNIFICANCE

Miguel Tejada began his career in Major League Baseball with great promise, and at the beginning of the twenty-first century, he lived up to his potential. In addition to being named the Most Valuable Player in the American League in 2002, he was the 2004 Home Run Derby winner, the MLB's Most Valuable Player in the 2005 All-Star Game, and the winner of two Silver Slugger Awards in 2004 and 2005. He also was selected to play in the All-Star games in 2002, 2004, 2005, 2006, 2008, and 2009. However, his career and reputation suffered after he became embroiled in the steroids scandal and was convicted of lying to Congress.

Michael J. Bennett

FURTHER READING

Bretón, Marcos, and José Luis Villegas. *Away Games: The Life and Times of a Latin Baseball Player*. New York : Simon & Schuster, 1999. Written fairly early in Tejada's Major League career, this book uses his life and career to demonstrate the difficulties that Latin American players encounter in their efforts to enter and remain in Major League Baseball.

Curry, Jack. "Rodriguez May Be Best, but Tejada Is MVP." *The New York Times*, November 13, 2002, p.5. Discusses the reasons why Tejada was named the American League's MVP.

Jenkins, Lee. "Out of the Basement." *Sports Illustrated*, August 30, 2010, 38. A cover story focusing on Tejada, when he was a shortstop for the San Diego Padres. Discusses how his batting and defensive play have improved since joining this team.

Mattern, Joanne. *Miguel Tejada*. Hockessin, Del.: Mitchell Lane, 2007. Biography of Tejada aimed at high school students.

Wilber, Del Quentin, and Dave Sheinin, "Tejada to Plead He Lied in Inquiry," *The Washington Post,* February 11, 2009. Covers the steroid scandal and how Tejada responded to his conviction.

See also: Tony Fernandez; Pedro Martinez; David Ortiz; Manny Ramirez; Alex Rodriguez; Freddy Sanchez; Johan Santana.

PIRI THOMAS

American writer and activist

One of the most powerful and creative voices of the Nuyorican community, Thomas was among the first to speak openly about the struggles of everyday New York Puerto Rican Americans to survive on the city's unfriendly and violent streets. Thomas's autobiographical trilogy was an especially poignant cry for help from a Nuyorican youth who had experienced the ills of drugs, crime, culture shock, and prejudice.

Latino heritage: Puerto Rican
Born: September 30, 1928; New York, New York
Also known as: Juan Pedro Tomás
Areas of achievement: Literature; activism; social issues

EARLY LIFE

Piri Thomas (PEE-ree) was born Juan Pedro Tomás on September 30, 1928, in New York City. He was born to Juan Tomás de Cruz and Dolores Montañez of Spanish Harlem (often referred to as "El Barrio") and was the eldest of seven children, only four of whom survived. Thomas was nicknamed "Piri" by his mother. He attended local primary and secondary schools but never pursued higher education. Being the only dark-skinned member of his family, young Thomas experienced racial prejudice both for being Puerto Rican and for being African American. Often insulted by local youths of different races, the boy frequently was forced to fight his way out of threatening situations.

In 1950, Thomas participated in an attempted robbery in New York's Greenwich Village, and he and a

Piri Thomas. (© Christopher Felver/Corbis)

police officer both were wounded in a shootout. Convicted of attempted armed robbery and felonious assault, Thomas was sentenced to a prison term of five to fifteen years.

LIFE'S WORK

Paroled at the age of twenty-eight, Thomas attempted to reconstruct his life by converting to Pentecostal Christianity, counseling troubled young men and gang members, and eventually working with Dr. Efrén Ramírez of the Hospital for Psychiatry in Río Piedras, Puerto Rico, to develop a rehabilitation program for troubled youths called Nueva Raza.

Thomas returned to New York and devoted himself to working with gang members full time, as well as collaborating in the production of the film *Petey and Johnny* (1961), which highlights rehabilitation work in East Harlem. Receiving a grant from the Louis M. Rabinowitz Foundation (1961-1962), Thomas spent five years writing his autobiographical work *Down These Mean Streets* (1967), which was followed by two other works in the trilogy, *Savior, Savior, Hold My Hand* (1972) and *Seven Long Times* (1974). The Puerto Rican Traveling Theatre produced his two-act play *Las calles de oro*, a drama about life in a slum, in 1972.

Down These Mean Streets explores the anguish of growing up in a base environment in which drugs abounded, theft was a commonplace, sex was a commodity, and life was cheap. Thomas describes his love of family, his inability to please his father, his crude initiation into the world of relationships and sex, his tremendous racial confusion because of his skin color, and his seemingly endless failures in attempting to be honest and to find acceptance in the broader society. Thomas also describes the many perils that lurk within the walls of the prison and his search for hope with the aid of inmates who encourage him to reach out to God for redemption. The second and third parts of his autobiographical trilogy describe his return to society after his prison sentence and his desire to help youths choose better paths than he did. He reflects on his prison term with a critical eye and uses his experiences to examine ways the justice system could aid in reforming and reintegrating convicts into society.

In *Stories from El Barrio* (1978), a collection of eight short stories, Thomas speaks directly to Latino youths and encourages them to believe in themselves and their ability to create beauty. The collection is an appeal for young people to dream big and to be generous with others. A lecturer and inspirational speaker,

Thomas frequently presents dramatic readings from his works.

SIGNIFICANCE

Thomas is one of the most influential voices of the Nuyorican community and one of the most prominent Latino writers in the United States. One of the first authors to discuss the difficulties of growing up black and Puerto Rican in New York City, Thomas employed a style that was piercing, compelling, and exciting, and that captured the plight of Hispanic immigrants in the large urban centers of the United States. Thomas also opened the eyes of the American public to the corruption, prejudice, and violence that often ensnared the

Thomas's Autobiographical Trilogy

Piri Thomas is the author of one of the most celebrated autobiographical trilogies in American literature: *Down These Mean Streets* (1967), *Savior, Savior, Hold My Hand* (1972), and *Seven Long Times* (1974). Taken together, these autobiographical works chronicle Thomas's troubled youth, personal and spiritual conversion, and mature reflection on his time spent in prison. In *Down These Mean Streets*, Thomas describes the many forces that created a sense of rage within him as a young Puerto Rican American. The book's abundant dialogue, dialect, transliteration of the sounds of the language of the streets, and smattering of Spanish bring the text to life, virtually allowing the reader to experience the hatred and discrimination that Thomas faced wherever he looked. The final part of the book describes Thomas's involvement in a robbery gone wrong and his imprisonment. *Down These Mean Streets* is a towering masterpiece among the contemporary works of American literature that seeks to describe the social ills of the city and the terrible effect these have on the nation's young people.

The second work of Thomas's trilogy, *Savior, Savior, Hold My Hand*, is an account of his rehabilitation after his parole. It describes how Thomas returned to his Christian faith, devoted himself to helping troubled youths, found love, married, and started a family. In *Seven Long Times*, the final work of the trilogy, Thomas takes a mature look at his years in Comstock Prison in Upper New York State. Considered by critics to be a prison journal, the book is far more controlled than *Down These Mean Streets*. Thomas describes the inner workings of the prison system and advocates that changes be made so that inmates can be effectively reintegrated into society.

poor, the uneducated, and the inexperienced. His works shocked middle-class and privileged Americans by revealing the horrors of the prison system that awaited outwardly tough but unsuspecting youths who had run afoul of the law. Thomas has become one of the most widely studied authors in contemporary ethnic American literature.

Mark T. DeStephano

FURTHER READING

Haney López, Ian F. "Chance, Context, and Choice in the Social Construction of Race." In *The Latino Condition: A Critical Reader*, edited by Richard Delgado and Jean Stefancic. New York: New York University Press, 1998. This article is an excellent study of the theme of race in *Down These Mean Streets*.

Pérez, Richard. "Racial Spills and Disfigured Faces in Piri Thomas's *Down These Mean Streets* and Junot Díaz's 'Ysrael.'" In *Contemporary U.S. Latino/a Literary Criticism*, edited by Lyn Di Iorio Sandín and Richard Perez. New York: Palgrave Macmillan, 2007. Pérez offers an insightful analysis of the role of race in two of the most important literary works of contemporary Latino literature.

Rodríguez de Laguna, Asela. "Piri Thomas' *Down These Mean Streets*: Writing As a Nuyorican/Puerto Rican Strategy for Survival." In *U.S. Latino Literature: A Critical Guide for Students and Teachers*, edited by Harold Augenbraum and Margarite Fernández Olmos. Westport, Conn.: Greenwood Press, 2000. A teaching guide that provides a concise study of Thomas's life, literary works, and major themes.

Sánchez González, Lisa. "The Boricua Novel: Civil Rights and 'New School' Nuyorican Narratives." In *Boricua Literature: A Literary History of the Puerto Rican Diaspora*. New York: New York University Press, 2001. A fine study of Thomas's works and a reflection on his place in the "Boricua" literary canon of the Puerto Rican diaspora.

Thomas, Piri. *Puerto Rican Voices in English*. Interview by Carmen Dolores Hernández. Westport, Conn.: Praeger, 1997. A fascinating interview in which Thomas discusses his family, growing up in New York, his prison experiences, and his thoughts on literature and the art of writing.

See also: Oscar Zeta Acosta; Miguel Algarín; Raymond Barrio; Junot Díaz; Judith Ortiz Cofer.

LUIS TIANT

Cuban-born baseball player

Tiant excelled as a pitcher on various teams. Following in the footsteps of his father, a legendary baseball player in both Cuba and the United States, Tiant likewise earned a reputation as one of the best pitchers of his era and one of the most beloved pitchers of all time.

Latino heritage: Cuban

Born: November 23, 1940; Marianao, Cuba

Also known as: Luis Clemente Tiant Vega; Luis Tiant, Jr.; El Tiante; Louie

Area of achievement: Baseball

EARLY LIFE

Luis Clemente Tiant Vega (TEE-ahnt) was born in Marianao, Cuba, the only child of Luis and Isabel Tiant. The elder Luis was a celebrated pitcher with legions of fans throughout Cuba. Once in the United States, he found himself a victim of Major League Baseball's segregation in the years before Jackie Robinson signed with the Booklyn Dodgers.

Tiant inherited his father's passion for baseball and played in juvenile leagues throughout Cuba in the late 1950's. He demonstrated impressive prowess on the pitcher's mound at a very early age. A scout for the Cleveland Indians, Bobby Avila, spotted him and signed Tiant to the Mexico City Tigers. This would be his gateway to the major leagues in the United States. After a stint in the minor leagues in 1961, Tiant was poised to be called up to the Indians' major-league squad. What should have been a jubilant occasion for Tiant was bittersweet, however, as it coincided with tumultuous events in his home country. The rise of Fidel Castro's communist regime meant that Tiant could not visit his family in Cuba. He would not see his father for fourteen more years.

In spite of this setback, Tiant progressed quickly through the Indians' farm system. On July 17, 1964, in his first major-league start, he defeated future Hall of Famer Whitey Ford and his New York Yankees in Yankee Stadium. The shutout victory by a rookie pitcher gained Tiant the attention of the baseball world.

Luis Tiant. (AP Photo)

LIFE'S WORK

After his impressive start in the majors, Tiant continued to wow baseball fans. He finished his rookie season with a 10-4 record, 105 strikeouts and a 2.83 earned run average (ERA) in nineteen games. Just two years later, Tiant tied a major league record when he pitched four straight shutouts.

He set franchise records and led the league in ERA, shutouts, and hits per nine innings while with the Indians. Tiant was known for a distinctive style of pitching in which he altered his delivery of the ball by turning away from home plate, thereby creating a kind of hesitation pitch. Tiant said that the new motion was his way of compensating for decreased pitch velocity that resulted from an early arm injury. His motion was nothing short of a contortion, as he twisted his body to face second base before releasing the ball.

Tiant's reign as the league's best pitcher ended in 1969. Plagued by injuries, Tiant was traded to the Minnesota Twins. He began his tenure in Minnesota with an impressive six wins but then suffered a fractured scapula. The injury ended his season, and some observers feared it would end his career. Tiant was sent back to the minor leagues. He managed to pitch well and was signed to the Boston Red Sox farm system.

Before long, Tiant was called up to the major leagues again. Although he struggled to regain the dominance of his earlier years, he continued to be a fan favorite. Tiant managed to hold his own, once again earning impressive stats despite being plagued by more injuries. He went on to play briefly for several other teams, including the Pittsburgh Pirates and California Angels (now the Los Angeles Angels).

After nineteen seasons, Tiant retired at the end of the 1982 season. He was inducted into the Boston Red Sox Hall of Fame in 1997. In 2002, he was inducted into the Hispanic Heritage Baseball Museum Hall of Fame. In 2009, Tiant was the subject of a documentary film, *The Lost Son of Havana.*

SIGNIFICANCE

Not surprisingly, Tiant did not fully leave the game after his retirement. He went on to become head coach for a college baseball team, and in 2007, he was named a pitching adviser by the Red Sox. Although induction into the Baseball Hall of Fame eluded him, Tiant's prodigious talent and charismatic personality endeared him to a generation of fans.

Yvette D. Benavides

FURTHER READING

González Echevarría, Roberto. *The Pride of Havana: A History of Cuban Baseball.* New York: Oxford University Press, 2001. An important and well-researched work about the many influential baseball players from Cuba that examines how politics and culture influence the game.

Hornig, Doug. *The Boys of October: How the 1975 Boston Red Sox Embodied Baseball's Ideals and Restored Our Spirits.* New York: McGraw Hill, 2004. This tribute to the 1975 team includes a chapter on Tiant and his unique pitching style and charisma.

Tiant, Luis, and Joe Fitzgerald. *El Tiante: The Luis Tiant Story.* New York: Doubleday, 1976. Tiant describes his Cuban upbringing and rise to baseball glory.

See also: Joaquín Andújar; Willie Hernández; Juan Marichal; Pedro Martinez; Johan Santana; Fernando Valenzuela.

Reies López Tijerina

American activist

During the 1960's and 1970's, Tijerina led a militant struggle to restore Spanish colonial land grants in New Mexico to the grantees' descendants.

Latino heritage: Mexican

Born: September 21, 1926; near Falls City, Texas

Also known as: King Tiger

Areas of achievement: Activism; social issues

Early Life

Reies López Tijerina (RAY-ehz LOH-pehz TEE-heh-REE-nah) was born on September 21, 1926, near Falls City, Texas. His father, Antonio, was a cotton sharecropper; his mother, Herlinda, was a strong-willed woman accustomed to carrying heavy cotton sacks on her back. Tijerina had three brothers and three sisters.

The Great Depression was particularly hard on cotton producers, forcing the Tijerina family to join the massive stream of migrant farmworkers who moved almost constantly in search of employment. During summers, the family usually worked in Michigan, then scraped out a living in San Antonio during the winter months. Like other Mexican Americans, Tijerina experienced a great deal of prejudice and discrimination. By the age of fifteen, he had begun talking back to white employers, and he resented his father's subservient behavior. As he matured, Tijerina became increasingly convinced that most Anglos were fundamentally unjust and hypocritical.

Like many children of migrant workers, Tijerina had limited opportunities for formal schooling and never graduated from high school. Influenced by his pious mother, however, he took a keen interest in religion, often reading the Bible during breaks in the field. Particularly attracted to the practical ethics of Jesus Christ, he had little concern for "otherworldly" doctrines such as the Trinity and the afterlife. Deciding to become a Protestant minister, Tijerina enrolled in 1944 at the Assembly of God Bible Institute in El Paso, Texas. His theological ideas were considered unorthodox at the school, and he withdrew in 1947 without graduating. Shortly thereafter, he married a fellow student, Mary Escobar, and for most of the next ten years, he traveled around the country as an itinerant minister. During this period, he developed close ties to many Mexican American communities and perfected his skills in public speaking and persuasion.

Life's Work

Tijerina became convinced that Christian churches were either unwilling or unable to promote social justice, and he decided to leave the ministry. In 1956, he led a group of seventeen families to southern Arizona with the goal of establishing a utopian commune. After a flood destroyed most of the commune, Tijerina experienced a vision in which three "interplanetary messengers or angels" informed him that he had been chosen for a special mission. He wrote in his autobiography: "I believed in what I saw and planned on obeying, fulfilling the mission."

In early 1957, Tijerina was accused of theft, and that July, he was formally charged with participating in a failed jailbreak scheme to free one of his brothers. Hearing rumors of an Anglo conspiracy to have him killed, he fled Arizona and was a fugitive for the next four years. By moving frequently, he successfully evaded law enforcement officers until the statute of limitations expired. The resulting stress, however, was particularly difficult on his wife, and the couple formally divorced in 1963.

Reies López Tijerina. (© Bettmann/Corbis)

While in northern New Mexico, Tijerina learned about the century-old grievance of poor Mexican American farmers in the region. In the Treaty of Guadalupe Hidalgo (1848), which ended the Mexican-American War, the U.S. government had agreed to respect property ownership based on Spanish and Mexican grants but refused to recognize communal lands (*ejido*) assigned to groups of farmers. Some of the land had been annexed as national forests, and thousands of acres were purchased by speculators. Infuriated by these accounts of Anglo greed and theft, Tijerina promised to try to help the farmers to regain possession of their ancestral lands. In order to learn more about the grants, he spent several months in Mexico examining archives and discussing the matter with legal scholars.

In 1963, Tijerina founded the Federal Alliance of Land Grants (La Alianza Federal de Mercedes), which grew to about fourteen thousand members in two years. He explained that its purpose "was to give the Indo-Hispanic people of the Southwest pride in their heritage, and to force the Anglo to respect him, just like we respect them." For a number of months in 1965, Tijerina publicized the land issue with a daily radio program, *The Voice of Justice*. On July 2, 1966, he mobilized a nonviolent march from Albuquerque to Santa Fe with the goal of drawing attention to the issue of land grants. Although the governor and media expressed sympathy for the farmers, the march failed to prompt any change.

Tijerina decided that a more militant strategy was necessary. On October 15, 1966, three hundred alliance members occupied the Echo Amphitheater portion of the Kit Carson National Park, arguing that a section of the park had been included in the San Joaquín land grant. The occupiers made citizens' arrests of two park rangers for trespassing. After five days, the occupation ended when government authorities moved in and arrested Tijerina and four others. The five men were charged with assault but released on bond. When the alliance held a meeting in Coyote on June 3, 1967, district attorney Alfonso Sánchez alleged communist influence and ordered that the meeting be disbanded. Although Tijerina escaped, eleven members were arrested and then jailed in Tierra Amarilla.

On June 5, 1967, Tijerina led three carloads of armed supporters to the courthouse in Tierra Amarilla. Their intent was to free their comrades and to make a citizens' arrest of Sánchez, who was not in the courthouse at the time. During the raid, a prison guard, Eulogio Salazar, and a sheriff's deputy were wounded. Tijerina and several followers escaped into the mountains.

Tijerina and the "Valley of Peace" Experiment

After becoming disillusioned with organized Christianity, Reies López Tijerina persuaded seventeen Mexican American cotton-picking families to join him in creating a utopian community. His goal was to share labor and resources while escaping the immorality, selfishness, and materialistic values of mainstream U.S. culture. He and his followers purchased 160 acres of desert land in southern Arizona, where they settled in June, 1956. The settlers called themselves the "brave ones" (*los bravos*) and named their community Valle de la Paz (Valley of Peace). They built subterranean shelters covered with materials found in garbage dumps. Although relations with their Caucasian neighbors were tense, the settlers got along well with other groups, especially the Pima Indians.

Because of a series of setbacks, the experiment lasted only about a year. When a jet crashed on the property, causing considerable damage, government officials did not provide any compensation. Soon thereafter, a group of Anglo youths damaged their subterranean dwellings by riding horses over them. Fires destroyed two of the residences, and the local sheriff refused to investigate the possibile arson. Next, a flood devastated the valley. The Valle de la Paz settlers also were dismayed that the Arizona government refused their request for home schooling and required that their children attend public schools. When Tijerina was accused of participating in a jailbreak in July, 1957, he and most of the settlers left the Valley of Peace and moved to northern New Mexico.

The National Guard, state police, and local officers conducted the largest manhunt in New Mexico's history. Five days after the raid, Tijerina was taken into custody when he was recognized by a gas station attendant. Salazar, who swore in a hearing that Tijerina was the one who shot him, was brutally murdered on January 2, 1968, but the crime was never solved. While awaiting trial, Tijerina was elected to lead the Chicano delegation of the Poor People's Campaign, and he helped plan many of the demonstrations. In May and June, he marched with major civil rights leaders in Albuquerque, Denver, Kansas City, Louisville, and Washington, D.C

Tijerina's first trial for the Tierra Amarilla shootout was held in Albuquerque in late 1968. He was allowed to defend himself with the help of two court-appointed lawyers. The judge was sympathetic, instructing the jury that a citizens' arrest included the right to use reasonable force. Acquitted of all charges relating to the raid, Tijerina was at the height of his popularity and held several large rallies.

Tijerina's problems with the law, however, continued. In March, 1969, his second wife, Patsy, with his encouragement, protested by burning a large federal sign at the Santa Fe National Forest. When armed forest rangers suddenly appeared, Tijerina threatened a ranger with his M-1 rifle, claiming the right of self defense. He was arrested and released on bail. A few months later, he traveled to Washington with the intention of placing Warren Burger, nominee for chief justice of the Supreme Court, under citizens' arrest; however, as Tijerina waited outside the Senate chamber, Burger dodged the arrest by exiting through a back door. Tried in federal court in September, 1969, for the Tierra Amarilla courthouse raid, Tijerina was found guilty and sentenced to nine years in prison. In October, New Mexico prosecuted him a second time for various charges relating to the Tierra Amarilla shootout, and this time the jury found him guilty of assaulting Salazar.

Tijerina's prison sentences added up to a combined twenty-six years. On July 26, 1971, however, the federal government released him on the condition that he not hold any leadership position in the Federal Alliance of Land Grants. Although he still faced prison time from his New Mexico convictions, the state kept him imprisoned for only six months in 1974. After his final release, Tijerina retained symbolic importance but no longer was a major activist leader with a large following. In 1994, he moved to Mexico, only to return to the United States in 2006. As he aged, Tijerina became less confrontational and emphasized the need for Anglo-Latino reconciliation.

Significance

During the 1960's, Tijerina was a militant spokesman and skillful organizer in the struggle for Latino pride and civil rights. Although he did not achieve his goal of winning legal recognition for preconquest communal land grants, his crusade promoted awareness of a historical injustice that affected thousands of poor farmers and ranchers. His extremist and violent tactics, however, detracted from his effectiveness, causing most of mainstream society to disregard the idealist ends that he espoused.

Thomas Tandy Lewis

Further Reading

Acuña, Rodolfo. *Occupied America: A History of Chicanos*. New York: Pearson Longman, 2004. A standard work in the Chicano studies field that emphasizes anti-Latino discrimination in the Southwestern U.S.

Blawis, Patricia Bell. *Tijerina and the Land Grants: Mexican Americans in Struggle for Their Heritage*. New York: International Publishers, 1971. Clearly written and well organized, this history casts Tijerina and his actions in a positive light.

Ebright, Malcolm. *Land Grants and Lawsuits in Northern New Mexico*. 3d ed. Santa Fe, N. Mex.: Center for Land Grant Studies, 2008. Scholarly historical study of Spanish and Mexican land grants in New Mexico.

Nabokov, Peter. *Tijerina and the Courthouse Raid*. Berkeley: Ramparts Press, 1970. Interesting and balanced account by a journalist who interviewed Tijerina, but its organization is rather confusing.

Rosales, F. Arturo. *Chicano: The History of the Mexican American Civil Rights Movement*. Houston, Tex.: Arte Público Press, 1997. Provides a historical context for Tijerina's life and career.

Tijerina, Reies. *They Called Me "King Tiger."* Translated by José Angel Gutiérrez. Houston, Tex.: Arte Público Press, 2000. Fascinating memoir in which Tijerina clearly and frankly describes his ideology and version of events.

See also: César Chávez; Corky Gonzáles; José Ángel Gutiérrez; Dolores Huerta; Antonio Orendain.

Juan Tizol

Puerto Rican-born jazz musician

As a valve trombonist, and as the composer of the major jazz standards "Perdido" and "Caravan," Tizol was an important participant in the music of the swing era and an early emissary of Puerto Rican musicianship to the United States.

Latino heritage: Puerto Rican

Born: January 22, 1900; Vega Baja, near San Juan, Puerto Rico

Died: April 23, 1984; Inglewood, California

Also known as: Juan Vicente Tizol Martínez

Area of achievement: Music

EARLY LIFE

Juan Vicente Tizol Martínez (wahn TEE-zohl) was born in a village not far from San Juan, Puerto Rico. His father died when Juan Tizol was ten, and he was raised by his uncle, Manuel Tizol, a well-known musician and bandleader in San Juan. Juan Tizol's uncle taught him violin and then euphonium and instilled in him the importance of punctuality and good money management.

By his teens, young Tizol had switched to the valve trombone and was playing in a local symphony orchestra. By the twentieth century, the valve trombone had lost favor among serious musicians because of its poor intonation, but its valve mechanism made it a handy instrument for performance of faster notes. The San Juan of his youth proved to be an excellent training ground for learning musicianship, because Puerto Rico enjoyed much cross-cultural fertilization. The Andalusian "tinge" that could be heard there later inspired Tizol's compositions of "exotica," such as "Caravan."

In 1920, Tizol immigrated to the United States. He remembered arriving in New York broke, and even his

Juan Tizol. (Library of Congress)

trombone had been lost on the way. He found his way to Washington, D.C., and was spotted by jazz bassist and fellow Puerto Rican Rafael "Ralph" Escudero, who gave him a job. Puerto Rican musicians were prized in orchestras for their musicianship and their ability to read music. In Washington, around 1920, he fell in love with an African American woman, Rosebud Browne. He wooed her successfully, and their marriage would last until her death in 1982.

During this period Tizol met Duke Ellington, who was playing with a small five-piece combo in the area. Ellington remembered Tizol some years later, in summer, 1929, when Ellington had landed a gig in a Ziegfeld musical, *Show Girl*; Ellington recruited Tizol because of his ability to quickly master the score.

LIFE'S WORK

Upon his hire with Ellington, Tizol immediately proved his worth to the bandleader in his ability to read music and to prepare it. Tizol quickly became Ellington's copyist and would remain on that task for Ellington until Tizon's departure from the band in 1944. Ellington's compositional brilliance materialized at the level of the sketch, and it was Tizol who fleshed out these musical ideas into parts for the band. Trumpeter Rex Stewart would declare that Tizol "truly was a very important cog in the Duke's wheel." Stewart is unambiguous in his estimation of Tizol's contribution to the Ellington sound: Tizol was able to create genuinely playable components from the fanciful musical motifs imagined by Ellington.

During his time in Ellington's orchestra, Tizol developed tremendously as a composer. During the swing era of the 1930's and early 1940's, the style of jazz composition known as "swing" was hugely popular, and one of Tizol's most beloved compositions, "Perdido," is in this style. Ballads—slow, romantic pieces—were also compositions that Tizol excelled in writing, and he wrote a number of such tunes for the Ellington band, such as "A Gypsy Without a Song" and "Have a Heart." Later, after his time with Ellington, Tizol wrote more ballads of great popularity, such as "You Can't Have Your Cake and Eat It Too" and "Escapade."

The most popular of Tizol's compositions are regarded as "exotica," tunes that evoke Asian or Middle Eastern impressions, reflecting the fact that Tizol had grown up in a musical atmosphere in which Moorish melodies were a common component of song. Certainly his single most famous tune, "Caravan," which has been played and recorded by many jazz acts, has an unmistakable Middle Eastern flavor, and from its first recording

Tizol's Work with Duke Ellington

While the creative peak of Juan Tizol's work as a trombonist, composer, and arranger was devoted to his years with Duke Ellington, and little of his career can be told without reference to Ellington, interesting details about Tizol's years with the Ellington orchestra have emerged. A religious nondrinker, the light-skinned Puerto Rican managing the rehearsals in a band of hard-living African Americans became a target and a source of practical jokes. According to some sources, itching powder was a favorite retaliation of Tizol, and he often sprinkled traces of the powder on band members' seats, sat back, and observed their obvious discomfort in trying to conduct themselves properly during performances. The band decided one night to take revenge on Tizol by distributing a substantial amount of itching powder in his trousers and shoes just before a performance, and they watched Tizol work while "red as a beet" and then rushing off to take a shower when intermission was called.

In the notorious "Mingus incident," Charles Mingus, who had joined Ellington's band for three days in 1953, argued with Tizol about which register in which to play a passage. Mingus threatened Tizol with an iron bar. When Ellington heard about the threatened assault of Tizol, a critical member of the band, Ellington fired Mingus on the spot.

recording in 1936 it stayed in the Ellington songbook, with several recorded versions by that band alone. A sizable number of other Tizol compositions could be categorized as "exotica," including other tunes written for the Ellington band, such as "Pyramid," "Bagdad," and "Bakiff."

A significant number of Tizol's compositions were Latin-flavored works. From the first Latin-styled piece, "Porto Rican Chaos" of 1935, Tizol went on to write major pieces such as "Moon Over Cuba" and the popular "Conga Brava." In this, Tizol pioneered a fusion of jazz and Latin musics that would prove tremendously popular for decades. Tizol's origination of the sound and idea of Latin jazz is often overlooked, but of American jazz artists, he was there first.

His importance as a trombonist merits mention. He was known as a band trombonist, and the valve trombone's precision, that is, its inability to "smear" notes, was favored by Ellington. Tizol's ability on the instrument gave the valve trombone a model that younger jazz trombonists would follow in later decades.

Tizol left the Ellington band in 1944, preferring to stay in California where his wife wanted to live. He went to work for trumpeter Harry James, and for the next twenty years would often alternate between playing for James and Ellington. He also played for Louis Bellson in the 1950's and was a vital member of the Nelson Riddle Orchestra when recordings were made featuring Frank Sinatra. During the 1956-1957 season, Tizol played for Nat "King" Cole at the height of the singer's popularity. In the 1960's, Tizol retired from the music business and spent his last years in the Los Angeles area, dying in 1984 of a heart attack.

SIGNIFICANCE

Tizol was an important voice in establishing Latin American cultural sensibilities in the mid-twentieth century United States, a time when Latinos were often thought of disparagingly. His performance abilities were first-rate, his compositional powers shined brightly even under the huge shadow of Ellington, and his theoretical and transcription work helped make the Ellington band the musical titan it became. As the one "white" face in an otherwise "black" orchestra, Tizol was an early transgressor of racial barriers that would defeat others for many years. His importance as being the founder of Latin jazz fusion cannot be overstated. Nonetheless, what may be the single most important part of Tizol's legacy may be his tune "Caravan," which remains one of the most beautiful and most frequently played jazz standards of all time. "Caravan" alone makes him a musical immortal.

Jeffrey Daniel Jones

FURTHER READING

Sarrano, Basilio. "Juan Tizol: His Talents, His Collaborators, His Legacy." *CENTRO Journal* 18, no. 11 (Fall, 2006): 82-99. Extensive and informative writing on Tizol, which discusses Tizol's biography at length and gives a detailed estimation of Tizol's compositional activities. This is a good source of information on Tizol's Puerto Rican background and the "Mingus incident," in which Tizol clashed with bass player Charles Mingus.

Dietrich, Kurt. "The Unique Juan Tizol." In *Duke's Bones: Ellington's Great Trombonists*. Rottenburg, Germany: Advance Music, 1995. A fascinating chapter on Tizol in this book, which concentrates upon the specific musical components of Tizol's playing for Ellington. Also, a discussion about Tizol's uncertainty in being a "legitimate" musician in a "jazz" orchestra.

Stewart, Rex. *Boy Meets Horn*. Ann Arbor: University of Michigan Press, 1991. This autobiography of

Stewart, a cornetist for Ellington, includes anecdotes about Tizol's contributions to the band.

See also: Ray Barretto; Paul Gonsalves; Tito Puente; Poncho Sánchez.

Danny Trejo

American actor

Trejo is one of the most visible and popular Latino actors in Hollywood. He began his career playing stereotypical "bandito" roles and later became an unlikely hero in the films of director Robert Rodriguez.

Latino heritage: Mexican
Born: May 16, 1944; Los Angeles, California
Also known as: Dan Trejo; The Mayor
Area of achievement: Acting

Early Life

The early life of Danny Trejo (TRAY-hoh) was complicated by his heroin addiction and a long stint in prison that derailed his aspirations of pursuing a career as a boxer. Ironically, his personal experiences with crime during his youth gave him an advantage in the Hollywood casting process, because he brought a certain authenticity to the criminal roles in which he was cast. When a director praised Trejo for his performance in a heist scene and asked him where he learned to act, Trejo responded: "Vons, Safeway, Thrifty Mart," names of stores he had robbed in his youth. His early career was linked to B-film fare in action-crime film star vehicles such as Charles Bronson's *Death Wish 4* (1987) and Steven Seagal's *Marked for Death* (1990). However, he began to have more sympathetic roles with his minor role in the independent film *Mi vida loca/My Crazy Life* (1994), in which his character was a junkie with "a heart of gold."

Life's Work

Trejo's "lowlife" characters began to appear in high-profile Hollywood films that made his presence more relevant in American popular culture. He had a small but significant role in Michael Mann's classic heist film *Heat* (1995) with a cast that included Robert De Niro, Al Pacino, Val Kilmer, and others. He also played a villainous role in *Con Air* (1997), a high-profile action film starring Nicolas Cage; in *Anaconda* (1997), which featured Jennifer Lopez's first starring role; and in *Six Days, Seven Nights* (1998), with Harrison Ford.

Trejo's career has been built around playing criminals. However, it acquired a different aspect when he began to collaborate with Latino director Robert Rodriguez. Trejo had antagonistic roles in Rodriguez's first two films (*Desperado*, 1995, and *From Dusk Till Dawn*, 1996), but this changed with his portrayal of two different characters named Machete, first in Rodríguez's *Spy Kids* trilogy (2001-2003) and then in the director's *Grindhouse* (2007) spinoff *Machete* (2010). In the *Spy Kids* series, Trejo played against type, his character being the child protagonist's charming uncle and scientist who designed gadgets for them. This series was popular with American children, and it made Trejo an iconic hero for a new generation. In *Machete*, he plays a Mexican "federale" banished to the United States, where he organizes illegal immigrants to fight a supremacist group. This film began as a mock trailer in Rodríguez and Quentin Tarantino's *Grindhouse*, but it gained so

Danny Trejo. (AP Photo)

much popularity, based on Trejo's charisma and the trailer's B-film irony, that it was expanded into a feature film with a cast full of stars, including Michelle Rodríguez, Jessica Alba, Don Johnson, Robert De Niro, and Steven Seagal. What is interesting about this project is that these actors have supporting roles to Trejo's hero, which shows how he has risen in stature in Hollywood. The film gained even more popularity when Rodriguez promoted it with another fake trailer, in which Trejo dedicates the short ad to the state of Arizona, which had just passed new legislation regarding enforcement of immigration laws.

Many examples can be provided of Trejo's transformed image that deviates from petty-criminal roles. In the animated series *King of the Hill* (2003-2010), he provided the voice for Enrique, a Latino middle-class coworker of the Caucasian protagonist Hank. Trejo also made guest appearances in popular television series such as *Desperate Housewives* and began to appear in the work of filmmaker Rob Zombie. In Zombie's horror classic *The Devil's Rejects* (2005), Trejo plays a bounty hunter who captures the murderous Firefly family. He is portrayed as a "bad guy," yet he is certainly more honorable than the Firefly family and the corrupt sheriff Wydell. In Zombie's *Halloween* (2007) remake, Trejo plays a janitor who tries to befriend psychotic killer Michael Myers. When Myers murders him, it is seen as the end of the protagonist's last connection to humanity. In the animated feature *The Haunted World of El Superbeasto* (2009), Zombie cast him as a gang member who helps the protagonist throughout the film. By 2010, Trejo had appeared in about two hundred films, keeping his schedule filled with major Hollywood films, straight-to-video films, and voice work for high-profile videogames such as *Grand Theft Auto IV* and *Fallout: New Vegas.*

SIGNIFICANCE

Trejo created a career in Hollywood by playing the "bandito" Latino stereotype that has been promoted in U.S. entertainment since the beginning of the film industry. However, thanks to his collaboration with director Rodriguez, Trejo was able to transform his "tough guy" persona into more positive roles that teach the American audience that Latinos with his physical appearance can also be good persons and attractive in a different way to the upper-class "Latin lover" stereotypes. Trejo's 2010 film *Machete* is an example of this type of role, through which he provides one of the most significant illegal immigrant characters captured on film.

Enrique García

FURTHER READING

Alson, Stuart. "Danny Trejo: From Convict to A-List." *IFQ Magazine* 14. An interview with Trejo, exploring his rise in Hollywood.

Barlow, Helen. "Robert Rodriguez and Danny Trejo Cutting a Short Story Long." *New Zealand Herald*, November 11, 2010. Article describes the happy working collaboration between Rodriguez and Trejo.

Beale, Lewis. "He Ain't That Bad." *New York Daily News*, May 9, 2007. Interesting article in which the author interviews Trejo about his early life problems.

See also: Ricardo Montalbán; Anthony Quinn; Robert Rodriguez; Martin Sheen.

JESSE TREVIÑO

Mexican-born artist

Treviño is known for his photorealistic paintings and his impressive religious and secular murals, which adorn much of San Antonio, Texas. He is the first Mexican American painter to have his work included in the collection of the Smithsonian Institution.

Latino heritage: Mexican
Born: December 24, 1946; Monterrey, Mexico
Area of achievement: Art

EARLY LIFE

Jesse Treviño (JEH-see truh-VEEN-nyoh) was born in Monterrey, Mexico, in 1946, one of twelve children (although in a 2004 interview, Treviño reported the number as thirteen). His father Juan was a truck driver and milkman; his mother, Delores Campos Treviño, was a homemaker. When Jesse was four, the Treviños moved to San Antonio, Texas, and his ability to draw became apparent at an early age. He won his first art contest, sponsored by San Antonio's Witte Museum, at age six, with a drawing of two doves. After graduating from Fox Technical High School, he won two scholarships, one to the Chicago Art Institute and the other to the Art Students League in New York City. Because he had family in New York, he moved there in 1965 to study under portrait artist William Franklin Draper. Treviño lived in Greenwich Village, earning money by painting portraits, but after a year he was drafted into the Army at age eighteen. Although he was not required to serve, as he was not at that time a U.S. citizen, he was sent to the Mekong Delta to serve in the Vietnam War. After a few months, however, an explosion shattered the right side of his body and cost him his right hand. As a result, he spent a total of two years in the hospital, and he received the Purple Heart medal for his military service.

Treviño became a naturalized citizen in 1970. He enrolled at San Antonio College in order to take a drawing course. He transferred to Our Lady of the Lake University, from which he earned a B.A. in fine arts. While there, he painted his first mural with his left hand. He subsequently earned his master's degree in studio art at the University of Texas at San Antonio.

LIFE'S WORK

Treviño's first big commission came from Kelly Field National Bank. *Imagenes de Mi Pueblo* was completed in 1982 and sold for $12,500. His early style of painting is termed photorealism, but he became more expressionistic in his murals and later portraits.

His most famous work is a veritable masterpiece: a 90-by-40-foot, nine-story ceramic tile mural titled *Spirit of Healing*. The funding for this project has been estimated at more than $1 million, as more than 150,000 tiles in more than fifty colors had to be imported from Germany for its creation. The mural began as a partnership between San Antonio businessman George Cortez, Santa Rosa Children's Hospital liaison Patty Elizondo, and Treviño. It took Treviño three years to construct this artwork. The tiles were mounted on 530 panels, which he and his assistants then affixed to a brick wall. *Spirit of Healing* was unveiled in 1997 and is located on the hospital's south wall, overlooking Milam Park. The mural depicts a child holding a dove, with a guardian angel and crucifix in the background. Treviño's ten-year-old son served as the model for the child, and his older daughter Eva is represented by the angel, who has a broken wing signifying Treviño's loss of his right hand. Treviño's other outdoor mural masterpiece is the forty-foot high, three-dimensional *La Veladora of Our Lady of Guadalupe*, completed in 2006 and located on one side of the Our Lady of Guadalupe Cultural Arts Center. This mural is made to look like a glass-contained prayer candle.

Treviño also has created indoor murals, such as *La Historia Chicana*, which he painted while he was a student and completed in 1974. This mural is located at the Sueltenfuss Library of Our Lady of the Lake University. Other indoor murals include *La Curandera*, completed in 1989, located at the Texas Diabetes Institute, and featuring a portrait of his brother George; and an untitled mural, normally referred to as "San Antonio World War II," located at the San Antonio Public Library's central building.

Treviño is one of the most honored Mexican American artists. In 1987, he won the National Hispanic Heritage Award for Arts, and his work was exhibited at the Smithsonian Institution in 1994. The following year, he was the first Mexican American awarded a one-man show at the San Antonio Museum of Art.

SIGNIFICANCE

Treviño is the first Mexican American artist to be shown at the Smithsonian, as his photorealistic paintings *Mis Hermanos* and *Tienda de Elizondo* were added to the collection in 1994. Treviño stated in an October, 2009, interview with the San Antonio Office of Cultural Affairs that in his work he wanted to find beauty in and bring attention to San Antonio's Chicano culture and to put a realistic face on that culture and its neighborhoods. His paintings attest to that drive. However, he will likely be remembered for the awesome scale and comprehensive scope of his murals, which adorn much of San Antonio.

Anthony J. Fonseca

FURTHER READING

Gerem, Yves. *A Marmac Guide to San Antonio*. Gretna, La.: Pelican, 2001. An extensive guide to the city, including verified information on Treviño's murals and paintings.

McDonnell, Sharon. "Treviño Creates a Vision of Hope." *Hispanic* 16, no.12 (December, 2003): 64-65. Discusses Treviño's *Spirit of Healing*.

"Mural Masterpiece Is San Antonio Treasure." *Hispanic Times Magazine* 19, no.4 (August-September, 1998): 53. An early interview with Treviño, following the completion of his nine-story mural.

Salas, Abel. "Arts Veteran." *Hispanic* 10, no.9 (September, 1997): 30-32. An early interview with Treviño, offering biographical information.

Treviño, Jesse. Oral History Interview with Jesse Treviño, July 15-16, 2004. Conducted by Cary Cordova. Archives of American Art, Smithsonian Institution. http://www.aaa.si.edu/collections/or-

alhistories/transcripts/trevin04.htm. The most extensive interview with the artist, transcribed from five hours of tape.

See also: Judith F. Baca; José Antonio Burciaga; Barbara Carrasco; Gaspar Enríquez; Carmen Lomas Garza; Leo Tanguma.

LEE TREVINO

American golfer

Trevino is famous both for his contributions to Mexican American golfers and for his success as a golfer in the 1970's. After moving to the Champions (Senior) tour, he enjoyed a good deal of success, winning the second-highest number of games as of December 2010.

Latino heritage: Mexican

Born: December 1, 1939; Dallas, Texas

Also known as: Lee Buck Trevino

Area of achievement: Sports

EARLY LIFE

Lee Buck Trevino (treh-VEE-noh) was born on December 1, 1939, in Dallas, Texas. His family was very poor, and he sometimes worked in the fields as a youth. He started working as a caddy at the Dallas Athletic Club while he was young. This job allowed him to make money and learn how to play golf, as there were some holes set aside for caddies.

Trevino started working full time as a caddy before the age of fifteen and shined shoes to supplement his income. He also earned money by hustling golfers, setting up absurd matches that he went on to win. Trevino served for a time in the U.S. Marine Corps, then worked as a golf professional before joining the Professional Golfers' Association (PGA) Tour in 1967.

LIFE'S WORK

Trevino had great success as a golfer, beginning in the late 1960's. Even though he did not win a tournament in 1967, he was named rookie of the year. The next year, he continued to improve. His first career win on the PGA Tour came in 1968, when he won the U.S. Open. He defeated the legendary Jack Nicklaus by four strokes and was one of Nicklaus's main competitors early in his career. Trevino won again in 1968 and once more in 1969. In 1969, he also was selected for the U.S. Ryder Cup team.

Trevino's best years were in the early 1970's. In 1970 and 1971, he had the lowest stroke average on the PGA Tour. In 1971, he also shined in the major tournaments, winning the U.S. Open and the British Open. He defeated Nicklaus again in the U.S. Open and defeated Lu Liang-Huan to take the British Open. The next year, Trevino repeated as champion of the British Open, defeating Nicklaus by one stroke. He then turned his attention to the two major championships he had not won yet, the Masters and the PGA Championship. He triumphed in the latter in 1974, beating Nicklaus again

Lee Trevino. (AP Photo)

by one stroke. His final major championship came some
eight years later in 1982, when he won the PGA Championship again. Trevino's success was limited only by
his inability to win at the Masters, a victory that would
have completed a rare career golf grand slam. Trevino's
top finish at the Masters was tenth, which he achieved
twice. Nonetheless, in terms of major tournaments won,
he ranks among the most successful golfers of all time.

Besides winning six majors, Trevino did well in
other PGA Tour events. Starting in 1969, he won at least
one tournament a year for thirteen straight years. In all,
he won twenty times on the PGA Tour. He also played
in other professional golf tours; like many other golfers of the time, he did not make enough between PGA
winnings and endorsements to play only the PGA Tour.
Trevino participated in the European Tour and the Japan
Golf Tour as well as other events and won eighteen tournaments as a professional.

By the time his career on the PGA Tour ended, Trevino trailed only Nicklaus in career earnings. Throughout his career, he was known for his sunny disposition
and humor. He once joked that the only person he was
afraid of was his wife. His play declined somewhat in
the 1980's, and he played less often. He served as a golf
analyst on television broadcasts from 1983 to 1989.

In addition to his solo victories, Trevino was successful in international play as part of the Ryder Cup
team. He served on the U.S. delegation for twelve straight

years, from 1969 to 1981, and won almost three-fourths
of his matches (excluding ties). After his playing days
were over, he was U.S. team captain in 1985. Trevino
also served as both a personal and financial role model
for Mexican Americans, especially golfers. He has established a number of scholarships for Mexican American students.

When Trevino turned fifty in 1989, he joined the
Senior Tour (now called the Champions Tour). Trevino
was one of the first major stars to play the senior circuit regularly, and he helped establish and popularize
it. Just as he had on the PGA Tour, Trevino won the Senior Tour's rookie of the year award. He also quickly
established his dominance of the majors, winning four
within his first five years on the senior circuit. Trevino
won numerous regular tournaments as well and has
frequently ranked among the top money winners on
that circuit.

During Trevino's career, he has received much
recognition for his success, including being named the
Sportsman of the Year in 1971 by *Sports Illustrated*.
Many lists produced in the 1990's listed him among the
top golfers of all time.

SIGNIFICANCE

Trevino's accessibility and humor put him at the forefront of golf's movement from a country club sport
to a sport with a broad and diverse fan base. He was
noted as a role model for Latino golfers, whose ranks
have grown in the years since he joined the PGA
Tour. Trevino also is widely respected for his humility and grace.

Scott A. Merriman

Opening the Door for Mexican American Golfers

Although Lee Trevino was born in the United
States, he was seen as a role model for Mexican and
Mexican American golfers. Jack Nicklaus, when Trevino was tormenting him or defeating him, would
sometimes jokingly tell Trevino to "go back to Mexico." Many of the Latino and especially Mexican
American golfers who followed him consider him a
role model. Trevino also increased opportunities for
Mexican American golfers in other ways, such as by
establishing himself as a likeable and marketable
celebrity. Professional golf is a business, and he
showed that a Mexican American star could appeal
to the American general public. Finally, Trevino also
funds numerous charities, some of which support
Mexican American golfers. Thus, both personally
and by example, Trevino paved the way for Mexican
Americans to find success at a game once dominated
by whites in country clubs.

FURTHER READING

Mackintosh, David. *Golf's Greatest Eighteen*. New York: McGraw-Hill, 2004. Trevino is profiled in this work on the game's top players.

Trevino, Lee, and Sam Blair. *The Snake in the Sandtrap (and Other Misadventures on the Golf Tour)*. New York: Henry Holt, 1987. Chronicles some of Trevino's experiences from throughout his career.

_____. *They Call Me SuperMex: The Autobiography of Lee Trevino*. New York: Random House, 1982. Although a bit dated, this autobiography is a useful source for information on Trevino's early life and career.

See also: Pancho Gonzales; Nancy Lopez; Chi Chi Rodriguez.

FÉLIX TRINIDAD

Puerto Rican-born boxer

Born in Puerto Rico, Trinidad became one of the world's greatest boxers. He moved up in weight classes to find better opponents and bigger paydays, and by 2000, Ring *magazine named him the fighter of the year.*

Latino heritage: Puerto Rican

Born: January 10, 1973; Fajardo, Puerto Rico

Also known as: Félix Juan Trinidad García; Tito; Félix Trinidad, Jr.

Area of achievement: Boxing

EARLY LIFE

Félix Juan Trinidad García, better known as Félix Trinidad (FEE-lihx TREE-neh-dahd), was born on January 10, 1973, in the small city of Fajardo, on the eastern side of Puerto Rico. One of six children born to Irma García and Félix Trinidad, Sr., he grew up in Cupey Alto, a part of San Juan, Puerto Rico. His father, a former featherweight national champion, began training him at age twelve. The younger Trinidad took to the sport with a seeming ease and began compiling an impressive

Félix Trinidad. (AP Photo)

amateur record. His determined focus on boxing combined with his father's tutelage and his talents brought about a high level of hopes for Trinidad.

Trinidad hoped to gain a place on Puerto Rico's boxing team for the 1992 Summer Olympics. However, the organization that oversaw the team was pushing for another fighter in Trinidad's weight class, despite Trinidad's record. The result was that Trinidad declined all offers to box in the Olympics and instead turned professional, making his debut on March 10, 1990, at age seventeen.

LIFE'S WORK

Trinidad entered boxing in a relatively easy fashion by knocking out his first opponent, Angel Romero, in the second round. In fact, Trinidad knocked out nine of the first ten fighters he faced. The only foe that seemed to be problematic for him was the injury he suffered to his right hand while winning a unanimous decision against Jake Rodriguez in late 1991. After recuperating, Trinidad resumed boxing and maintained his status as a rising fighter.

By 1993, Trinidad had achieved a level of success that prompted him to fight the International Boxing Federation's (IBF) champion, Michael Booker. Their fight took place in San Diego, California, on June 19, 1993, and in what was considered a stunning upset, Trinidad knocked out Booker in the second round, making him the IBF welterweight champion at age twenty. The fight had been broadcast on the Showtime television network, and this coverage helped garner Trinidad more fans and, just as important, brought about a working relationship with boxing promoter Don King.

King, well known in the boxing community, was able to get Trinidad high-profile fights, which brought both exposure and money. Over the next six years, Trinidad successfully defended his title sixteen times with notable fights against Hector "Macho" Camacho, Luis Ramon "Yory Boy" Campas, Oba "Motor City" Carr, and Freddie Pendleton. Each of these opponents was able to land impressive blows to Trinidad, but each time he came back to show a champion's resolve and win the fight.

On September 18, 1999, Trinidad fought one of the most publicized bouts in boxing history against Oscar "Golden Boy" De La Hoya. The bout would unite the IBF and World Boxing Council welterweight belts. The hype around this fight was significant and the public's interest high, and the bout met the expectations, going the full twelve rounds. The judges awarded Trinidad the win with a majority decision, 115-113, 115-114, and 114-114.

Seeking a new challenge, Trinidad then vacated the welterweight titles and sought to win the World Boxing Association's belt in the junior middleweight division. After winning it and defending it against Fernando Vargas, he again chose to move up in weight class, this time to middleweight. After two fights in the division, he met the renowned fighter Bernard Hopkins. Their bout on September 29, 2001, lasted until the twelfth round, when Trinidad's father stopped the fight, and the victory was awarded to Hopkins. It was Trinidad's first loss.

Following his loss to Hopkins, Trinidad fought once more in May, 2002, and then surprisingly announced his retirement. His retirement lasted about two years, and in March, 2004, he fought again, winning against Ricardo Mayorga. This fight would be his last victory, as Trinidad then lost to Winky Wright and Roy Jones, Jr., before again announcing his retirement. With a professional career that spanned eighteen years, and in which he won titles in three different weight divisions, it is no surprise that Trinidad is considered the best fighter that Puerto Rico has produced.

SIGNIFICANCE

Trinidad's boxing career shows a spectacular single-minded purpose to be the best fighter in the world. His drive, work ethic, and talent took him to the apex of the sport and left Trinidad with new challenges to attack. Since retiring from boxing, his focus has shifted to working with the Children with AIDS Foundation, helping children around the world afflicted with acquired immunodeficiency syndrome. In addition, he has had more time to spend with his wife and five children.

P. Huston Ladner

FURTHER READING

Hoffer, Richard. "Class Dismissed." *Sports Illustrated*, September 27, 1999, 56. This article is important for its discussion of Trinidad's fight with Oscar De La Hoya, describing how it affected both of their careers.

_____. "Spurred to Greatness." *Sports Illustrated*, May 14, 2001, 54. Provides one of the best insights into Trinidad's life, discussing his upbringing, his relationship with his father, and his personality that mistakenly keeps him at a distance from the press.

Nack, William. "Star Power." *Sports Illustrated*, February 19, 1996, 30. Focuses on Trinidad's rise to national prominence as he gained recognition for his win over Rodney Moore. The fight was one of the first in which Trinidad received top billing.

See also: Art Aragon; Wilfred Benitez; Oscar de La Hoya; Sixto Escobar; Aurelio Herrera.

JOSEPH A. UNANUE

American entrepreneur and philanthropist

Unanue grew a regional business into the largest Latino-owned company in the nation, diversifying American table foods, dishes, and desires as a consequence.

Latino heritage: Puerto Rican and Spanish
Born: March 14, 1925; Brooklyn, New York
Also known as: Joseph Andrés Unanue
Areas of achievement: Business; philanthropy

EARLY LIFE

Prudencio Unanue from Spain married Carolina Casal in Puerto Rico and then moved to Brooklyn, New York, where Joseph Andrés Unanue (YOH-sehf AHN-drehz yew-NAHN-yew-ah) was born, the second of four children. He attended St. Joseph's Grammar School and St. Celia's High School, learning early the workings of his parents' Goya Foods distribution business, where he began by bottling olives. After graduating from high school in 1943, Unanue was drafted into the U.S. Army, where after brief stationing at the College of Puget Sound in Tacoma, Washington, he landed in 1944 in France and joined General George S. Patton's Third Army in time for the Battle of the Bulge. As a private at nineteen years of age, he saw his sergeant killed during the battle and was immediately named sergeant and platoon leader. He distinguished himself on the field that day and was awarded a Bronze Star and later a Victory Medal.

Returning home in 1946, Unanue entered Catholic University of America in Washington, D.C., where he graduated with a degree in mechanical engineering. He married Carmen Ana Casal, with whom he would have six children and sixteen grandchildren. With degree in hand, he returned full-time to Goya Foods and spent the next twenty-five years working in diverse divisions of the company along with his two brothers, Tony and Frank. Unanue put his mechanical engineering knowledge to good use by leading and supervising the design and construction of new and better manufacturing and distribution facilities. As the years went by, Goya Foods provided ever more diverse products from the Caribbean, Latin America, and Spain to small stores and supermarkets, seeking to cater to the growing Latino populations across the United States and building increasing demand among non-Latinos for such products.

LIFE'S WORK

Upon his father's death in 1976, Unanue became chairman, president, and chief executive officer of the small regional company, with annual sales of about eight million dollars, then based in New Jersey. Frank and Unanue bought out brother Tony's share at this point. Frank then ran Goya de Puerto Rico, Inc., in Bayamon, Puerto Rico. Unanue, after a series of successful marketing efforts, grew the company until annual sales topped eight hundred million dollars a year, with more than two thousand employees and facilities in fifteen locations worldwide. He saw the wisdom of providing philanthropic backing to a variety of cultural organizations, including the Puerto Rican Traveling Theater, Repertorio Español, El Museo del Barrio, and the Metropolitan Museum of Art. The company's sustained patronage created an even more loyal customer base and further spread its name and wares into new non-Hispanic markets. His other two major innovations were recognizing the burgeoning Mexican American food market opportunities across America and convincing nonethnic buyers that Latino foods were healthier alternatives to their regular staples.

Unanue's sons, Joseph F. and Andy, also worked in the company. Joseph F. Unanue became the executive vice president of operations in 1985, a position he held until his death in 1998 at age forty-one, when his younger brother Andy was named to the role. In 1999, Goya Foods reached position 353 in the *Forbes 500* list. A bitter family dispute developed in the early twenty-first century over Joseph A. Unanue's plans to further diversify and grow the company by selling to national retailers, which father and son reckoned would double the size of the company in three to four years. This strategy found only limited support beyond his son Andy within the family-held company and board. Led by two of his nephews, Robert and Francisco, the family board voted to remove Unanue as president and chief executive officer in February, 2004, at which point Unanue and Andy filed a legal challenge. The Delaware Chancery Court in a widely watched decision ruled in November of that year that the ouster was legal.

The Unanues' philanthropic efforts have included numerous programs in the arts at major museums and galleries; support for Unanue's alma mater, on whose Board of Trustees he served for many years and where a campus house is named in his honor; Carmen's service on the Board of Trustees of WNET in New York City for many years; her prominent role in papal committees, and work for the American Bible Society. In 2005, they jointly established through their C and J Foundation the Joseph A. Unanue Latino Institute at Seton Hall University, which provides academic programs, internships, and study-abroad experiences. Unanue received honorary doctorates from Mercy College, Long Island University, and Felician College and numerous civic awards, including twice being named Man of the Year by the National Conference of Christians and Jews

and winning the National Minority Suppliers' Leadership Award, the 1994 Ellis Island Medal of Honor, the Knighthood of the Sovereign Order of Knights of Malta, and the National Hispanic Achievement Award in 1991 by *Hispanic Magazine.*

SIGNIFICANCE

By further diversifying into a product line of more than one thousand different items, developing strategic marketing and community-welcomed philanthropy, and reaching out beyond the Latino community, Goya Foods has grown to be the largest Latino food products company in the United States, with operations in several countries. Unanue also helped diversify the American palate and changed the culinary fare served in diverse households across the nation.

Dennis W. Cheek

FURTHER READING

De Lollis, Barbara. "At Goya, It's All in la Familia." *USA Today*, March 24, 2008. Profile of Bob Unanue gives a penetrating look at the development of Goya Foods and the family struggle that resulted in the ouster of Joseph A. Unanue.

Denker, Joel. *The World on a Plate: A Tour Through the History of America's Ethnic Cuisine.* Lincoln: University of Nebraska Press, 2003. A scholarly look at the ways in which ethnic foods, including those deriving from Latino cultures, have changed plates and palates in America. The frequent appearance of Latino foods on American tables is largely because of the influence of Goya Foods for past several decades and a lasting tribute to the business acumen of Unanue.

Deutsch, Claudia. "Goya Braces for a Challenge from the Food Giants." *The New York Times*, February 24, 1991. Unanue reveals his marketing strategies.

Dumaine, Brian, et al. "Does Race Still Matter? Ten Great Minority Entrepreneurs Weigh in on Affirmative Action, the Old Boys' Network, and Whether to Sell Out." *Fortune*, December 1, 2003. Comments from Unanue on embracing other ethnicities.

See also: Ralph Alvarez; Frank Lorenzo; Arte Moreno.

LUIS ALBERTO URREA

Mexican-born writer

Urrea, a Tijuana-born novelist, poet, essayist, and creative-writing professor, is perhaps best known for his nonfiction and investigative journalism about U.S.-Mexico border issues. Much of his fiction, as well as his nonfiction, focuses on border identity based on his own experiences and on painstaking research.

Latino heritage: Mexican

Born: August 20, 1955; Tijuana, Mexico

Also known as: Luis Urrea

Areas of achievement: Literature; poetry

EARLY LIFE

Luis Alberto Urrea (lew-EES ahl-BEHR-toh oo-RAY-ah) was born in Tijuana, Mexico, to Alberto Urrea Murray and Phyllis Dashiell. The son of a Mexican father and an American mother, he spent his early childhood in the barrios of Tijuana. By the age of four he suffered from tuberculosis, and his family moved just over the border to San Diego, California, in search of a healthier environment for their son. It was in a San Diego barrio that he first became aware of racism and cultural identity after being called "greaser" and other racial epithets. At school he was picked on by some for being Mexican, and by others for being white, while at home, the blond, blue-eyed youth's awareness of his hybrid identity developed further as his father insisted that he use Spanish, while his mother only addressed him in English.

Reading a broad range of authors, including John Steinbeck and Charles Dickens, and eventually writing provided an escape from the neighborhood hostilities, and with the joyful discovery of his mother's typewriter, Urrea took his first steps toward what would eventually become his career. As an adolescent he discovered poetry, and by age eighteen he had already found himself mesmerized by Latin American writers, such as Gabriel García Márquez, Jorge Luis Borges, Gabriela Mistral, Pablo Neruda, Mario Vargas Llosa, and Julio Cortázar. Two life-changing events in his senior year of college played an important role in his future career. The first was the traumatic death of his father in an automobile accident in Mexico, where he had gone to retrieve his savings as a gift for his son's upcoming graduation. Urrea was forced to bribe Mexican officials for the release of his father's body. The second event was a writing workshop with visiting novelist Ursula K. Le Guin. Le Guin was so impressed with the story that Urrea had written about his father's death that she published it in an anthology.

LIFE'S WORK

Urrea's literary work spans several genres, including poetry, short stories, novels, essays, and investigative journalism. It was Tijuana, however, that directly and indirectly launched his career in border studies, as well as his academic career. After graduating from the University of California at San Diego with a B.A. in writing in 1977, Urrea worked as a bilingual tutor and teaching assistant at San Diego Mesa College from 1978 to 1982, and he spent increasing amounts of time doing translation and field work with missionaries in the Tijuana garbage dumps. Overcome with the tragic realities of Tijuana, he contacted his former professor in search of janitorial work in Boston. Instead, the professor, Lowry Pei, found him employment teaching expository writing and fiction at Harvard University, a position Urrea held until 1987.

Luis Alberto Urrea. (Getty Images)

From 1987 to 1999, Urrea published extensively while teaching writing at universities in Massachusetts, Arizona, Colorado, and Louisiana, and he earned his M.A. in creative writing from the University of Colorado at Boulder in 1997. Among his many publications from that period are two poetry collections: *The Fever of Being* (1994) and *Ghost Sickness* (1996). His first novel, *In Search of Snow* (1994), was a coming-of-age tale set in the Southwest. Urrea's earlier work in the Tijuana garbage dumps eventually lead to two of his most compelling nonfiction books: *Across the Wire* (1993) and *By the Lake of Sleeping Children* (1996). Other notable nonfiction projects are his memoir, *Nobody's Son* (1998), and a collection of travel essays, *Wandering Time* (1999).

In 1999, Urrea joined the faculty at the University of Chicago as a professor of English and creative writing. *Vatos*, a book of Urrea's poetry with images from Pulitzer Prize-winning photographer José Galvez, was released in 2000. Two years later, he published *Six Kinds of Sky*, a collection of short fiction that includes "Father Returns from the Mountain," a dreamlike rendition of his father's death. His acclaimed first foray into investigative journalism, *The Devil's Highway* (2004), tackles the subject of immigration, centering on the case of fourteen undocumented immigrants who died in the Arizona desert in 2001. Family stories about Urrea's great-aunt "Saint" Teresita inspired his historical novel, *The Hummingbird's Daughter* (2005), while *Into the Beautiful North* (2009) presented one Mexican village's creative solution to the dearth of men caused by extensive immigration to the United States. By 2010, Urrea had settled in Naperville, Illinois, with his second wife, Cindy, and their children.

SIGNIFICANCE

Widely praised for his novels, poetry, short stories, and nonfiction, Urrea was inducted into the Latino Literary Hall of Fame in 2001. Known in particular for his work around the theme of border studies because of his nonfiction border trilogy (*Across the Wire*, *By the Lake of Sleeping Children*, and *Nobody's Son*), Urrea was a Pulitzer Prize finalist in 2005 for *The Devil's Highway*, and *The Hummingbird's Daughter* was the first book by a Latino author to win the Kiriyama Pacific Rim Prize for Fiction (2006). Urrea and his work exemplify the complex relationship between "whiteness" and "latinidad," as well as the duality implicit in Chicano identity.

Yolanda A. Doub

FURTHER READING

Heide, Markus. "Learning from Fossils: Transcultural Space in Luis Alberto Urrea's *In Search of Snow*." In *Literature and Ethnicity in the Cultural Borderlands*, edited by Jesús Benito and Ana María Manzanas. Amsterdam: Rodopi, 2002. Analyzes key themes of transculturation and intercultural spaces as presented in Urrea's coming-of-age novel *In Search of Snow*.

Urrea, Luis Alberto. *Nobody's Son*. Tucson: University of Arizona Press, 1998. The third book in the border trilogy, Urrea's memoir showcases his engaging style and humor as it offers the reader a thought-provoking window into the dual identity inherent in being a border child.

Villalobos, José Pablo. "Up Against the Border: A Literary Response." In *Border Transits: Literature and Culture Across the Line*, edited by Ana María Manzanas. Amsterdam: Rodopi, 2007. Provides lucid examples of the polemic surrounding representations of the U.S.-Mexico border. Addresses the significance of Urrea's role in the literary field of border studies.

See also: Julia Alvarez; Jimmy Santiago Baca; Ana Castillo; Lorna Dee Cervantes; Sandra Cisneros; Cristina García; Gary Soto; Helena María Viramontes.

TERESA URREA

Mexican-born activist and social reformer

In the 1890's, Urrea generated both a spiritual revival and political unrest among the indigenous and mestizo populations of northern Mexico by means of her charismatic personality, her healing powers, and her inspirational sermons. She has since become a celebrated folk heroine in northern Mexico and the U.S.-Mexico borderlands.

Latino heritage: Mexican

Born: October 15, 1873; Rancho de Santana, Sinaloa, Mexico

Died: January 11, 1906; Clifton, Arizona

Also known as: Niña García Noña María Rebecca Chávez; La Santa de Cabora; the Saint of Cabora;

Niña de Cabora; Teresita; Santa Teresa; the Queen of the Yaquis

Areas of achievement: Activism; religion and theology

Early Life

Teresa Urrea (tuh-RAY-suh oo-RAY-ah), born Niña García Noña María Rebecca Chávez, was the illegitimate child of Don Tomás Urrea, a wealthy landowner; her mother was Cayetana Chávez, a Tehueco Indian who worked on his ranch. Teresa Urrea was neglected and abused by the aunt who took charge of her after her mother abandoned her, but when Don Tomás relocated to the town of Cabora in 1880, the existence of Urrea was brought to his attention. He brought her into his hacienda, where she was established as a member of the Urrea family, and educated by Lauro Aguirre, a crusading journalist who shared Don Tomas's liberal politics. An equally formative influence in Urrea's young life was an old Indian woman, Maria Sonora, known as "La Huila," a *curandera*, or healer, who combined herbs and prayer to successfully treat a variety of illnesses.

Another major turning point in Urrea's life occurred at the age of sixteen, when she was sexually assaulted by a ranch hand. Lapsing into a coma, Urrea appeared to have died, but she revived while in her coffin and lived in a semitrance for some time afterward. After fully recovering, she demonstrated miraculous prophetic and healing powers, which she said had been given to her by God while she was in her coma, and for which she was told to refuse to accept payment. Her powers were such that she attracted poverty-stricken Indians and Mexicans from the entire area and some Americans.

Life's Work

Working as a *curandera*, Urrea also demonstrated increasing sympathy for the plight of the area's downtrodden indigenous tribes and began to preach sermons on the importance of equality, social justice, and human rights. Her fiery sermons defending the rights of local tribes against an increasingly genocidal government impressed and inspired the Yaquis, the Mayos, and especially the local Indian farmers from the village of Tomóchic, who made her their patron saint. Throughout the region Urrea came to be known as La Santa de Cabora, or the Saint of Cabora.

Throughout the first half of the 1890's, Urrea's sermons were thought to have inspired significant insurgency against the government of Porfirio Díaz. Although Urrea advocated nonviolence, in 1892 a group of Yaqui, Tarahumara, and Mayo Indians in Tomóchic engaged the government army with the battle cry "Viva la Santa de Cabora." After she was repudiated as a heretic by the Catholic Church, President Diaz denounced her as "the most dangerous girl in Mexico" and arrested her as the source of the uprisings. Instead of executing her, however, in 1895 Diaz deported Urrea and her father to Nogales, Arizona. All along the train route, Indian warriors raised their weapons to honor the charismatic Urrea as she rode with her father to sanctuary in the United States.

While distancing herself from involvement in Aguirre's plans for a revolution, Urrea did write for the newspaper he published in Texas, allowed her photograph to be sold to support the insurgency, and signed a revolutionary constitution drafted by Aguirre. Rebellion in her name continued in Mexico, and a number of her followers were massacred; many in the armed resistance wore a picture of Urrea over their hearts. Although Urrea advocated nonviolence, various tribes, calling themselves Teresitas, persisted in taking up arms against the government.

While she continued to support the insurgency, Urrea carried on her healing practice in the United States, treating the poor and the desperate, political insurrectionists from Mexico, and patients from as far away as Europe. Because the Mexican government attempted to assassinate her more than once, Urrea and her father relocated to Clifton, Arizona, where she opened a small clinic and became both a local favorite and increasingly an international celebrity. For a time, she toured the country as a near-miraculous healer and along the way bore two children. As she had predicted, Urrea died of tuberculosis at the age of thirty-three.

Significance

Sometimes known as the Mexican Joan of Arc, Urrea played an important part in the development of the unrest that led to the Mexican Revolution of 1910; her identity as La Santa de Cabora refers to her social activism as well as to her healing powers. In Mexico and the border states, her political and spiritual impact is such that graffiti that reads "Viva Teresita" or "Teresitia Vive" still appears. She remains an influence in communities that practice alternative medicine and is considered a folk saint among *curanderas*, Chicanos, Native Americans, and New Age thinkers in the U.S.-Mexico borderland culture. She continues to be commemorated in ceremonies, songs, books, and films.

Margaret Boe Birns

FURTHER READING

Dyck, Reginald and Cheli Reutter, eds. *Crisscrossing Borders in Literature of the American West.* New York: Palgrave Macmillan, 2009. Investigation of the literature of the borderlands includes discussion of two novels about Urrea, which demonstrate sacred, human, and transnational aspects of her identity.

Romo, David Dorado. *Ringside Seat to a Revolution: An Underground Cultural History of El Paso and Juarez, 1893-1923.* El Paso, Tex.: Cinco Puntos Press, 2005. Lively study of a variety of "fronterizos" in the borderlands between Mexico and the United States during the Mexican Revolution. Includes chapter on Urrea as "the woman who stirred things up" and a chapter on Aguirre.

Ruiz, Vicki L., and Virginia Sánchez Korrol. *Latina Legacies: Identity, Biography, and Community.* New York: Oxford University Press, 2005. Study of fifteen important Latinas of the nineteenth and twentieth centuries. Includes chapter on Urrea as *curandera* and folk saint, with special attention to her social justice activism.

Urrea, Luis Alberto. *The Hummingbird's Daughter.* New York: Back Bay Books, 2006. Noted Mexican American author's brilliant, prize-winning novel about his great aunt Teresa Urrea; distinguished by its extensive research and masterful storytelling.

Vanderwood, Paul J. *The Power of God Against the Guns of Government: Religious Upheaval in Mexico at the Turn of the Nineteenth Century.* Palo Alto, Calif.: Stanford University Press, 1998. Includes analysis of Urrea in the context of the Tomóchic rebellion's nexus of religious fervor and social protest.

See also: Luisa Capetillo; Ricardo Flores Magón; Luis Alberto Urrea.

ALISA VALDES-RODRIGUEZ

American novelist and journalist

An outspoken advocate for social justice and a former journalist, Valdes-Rodriguez is an emerging voice in contemporary U.S. Latino literature. Dubbed "The Godmother of Chica Lit," her groundbreaking novels defy gender and cultural stereotypes and highlight the vast diversity within the Latino population.

Latino heritage: Cuban
Born: February 28, 1969; Albuquerque, New Mexico
Also known as: Alisa Lynn Valdés; Alisa L. Valdés
Areas of achievement: Literature; journalism

EARLY LIFE

Alisa Valdes-Rodriguez (ah-LEE-sah val-DEHS rod-REE-gehs) was born Alisa Lynn Valdés in Albuquerque, New Mexico, to Nelson P. Valdés, a Cuban sociology professor, and Maxine Conant, a poet and novelist. As a child she had a passion for writing, spending hours keeping a journal of her deepest thoughts and daily experiences.

Her parents divorced when she was eleven years old, and Valdes-Rodriguez spent her childhood raised by a single father whose views on female sex roles were steeped in traditional Cuban values that often dictated what she was not allowed to do. Valdes-Rodriguez attended Del Norte High School, where she was actively involved in the school band. She moved to Boston in 1988, majoring in saxophone jazz performance at Berklee College of Music.

While attending Berklee, Valdes-Rodriguez became incensed that women were treated as second-class citizens in the music program. She wrote a piece in 1992

Alisa Valdes-Rodriguez. (WireImage/Getty Images)

for the *Boston Globe* about the unfair treatment of female students at the college, which resulted in sensitivity training for college faculty and a new course on women in music. That same year, Valdes-Rodriguez graduated from Berklee and worked full time as an aerobics instructor, a job she had been doing for some years to work her way through college. In 1993, she moved to New York City, where she continued to be an aerobics instructor, began writing for the *Village Voice*, and worked unsuccessfully as a musician. Soon she became disillusioned with the life she was living and yearned to return to her childhood dream of being a writer. Subsequently, she enrolled at the Graduate School of Journalism at Columbia University, from which she graduated in 1994.

Valdes-Rodriguez began her journalism career that same year as a staff writer for the Living/Arts section of the *Boston Globe* newspaper, for which she was often assigned to cover stories representing her perceived ethnic group: Spanish-speaking Latinos. After five years, Valdes-Rodriguez quit the newspaper, citing the institution as racist. She married journalist Patrick Jason Rodriguez in 1999 and they moved to Los Angeles, where she was hired by the *Los Angeles Times* to cover the Spanish-language music industry. While working for this newspaper, she became dissatisfied with the institution's understanding of race and ethnicity, as well as what she perceived as its general cultural incompetence. In 2000, she wrote a letter of resignation to her supervisors in which she accused the newspaper of perpetuating genocide on indigenous people from the Americas by using the term "Latino" to represent all brown-skinned, Spanish-speaking individuals. Her letter was widely circulated on the Internet and essentially ended Valdes-Rodriguez's journalism career.

She and her husband moved to Albuquerque, and her son, Alexander, was born in 2001. Although her stint as a journalist was over, Valdes-Rodriguez's career as a novelist was about to begin.

LIFE'S WORK

After the birth of her son, Valdes-Rodriguez submitted a proposal to a publishing house for a nonfiction book about Latina musicians. Although the idea was rejected, the publisher asked her for a fiction manuscript. During the next few weeks, she selected portions from her previous unpublished work to create the manuscript *The Dirty Girls Social Club*. Several publishers waged a bidding war for the rights to the book. Many of the publishing houses were looking for an author who would be the Latina version of Terry McMillan and amass a lucrative

following of Latina readers. St. Martin's Press was the winning bidder, advancing Valdes-Rodriguez $475,000 on the book's royalties.

In 2003, the book was published amid a flurry of positive reviews from readers and literary critics alike. Following the experiences of five Latinas from vastly diverse ethnic and cultural backgrounds, the groundbreaking novel presented white-collar, self-sufficient modern women who resembled the life of Valdes-Rodriguez more closely than Latinas in the works of literary giants such as Julia Alvarez, Sandra Cisneros, or Esmeralda Santiago. The book, deemed a "Latina *Sex in the City*," became a *New York Times* best seller, and film rights were secured by multiple studios. Virtually overnight *Dirty Girls* launched Valdes-Rodriquez into the public eye and led to the creation of the new literary genre of Chica Lit—literature written about successful Latino women who often describe shopping, fashion, and love affairs in a lighthearted manner that attracts both Latino and non-Latino readers.

A year after the publication of her first novel, Valdes-Rodriquez continued writing in her Chica Lit style, publishing *Playing with Boys* (2004), which also describes the high-powered lives of successful Latinas from diverse backgrounds in a dry, witty style that attracted a huge fan base and secured the author's position in the publishing industry. In 2006, she published her first young adult crossover novel, *Haters*, along with her next installment of Chica Lit, *Make Him Look Good*. Her fan base continued to grow in the years that followed as she published additional novels: *Dirty Girls on Top* (2008), the sequel to *The Dirty Girls Social Club; The Husband Habit* (2009); and *The Three Kings* (2010). In January, 2011, Valdes-Rodriquez published *All That Glitters*, her first e-book released exclusively and independently online and marketed solely through her Web site and through Facebook, Twitter, and other social-media sites.

Her work as a journalist and fiction writer have earned Valdes-Rodriguez numerous honors. In August, 2005, *Time* magazine named her "The Godmother of Chica Lit," and she was listed as one of the twenty-five most influential Hispanics in America. She also was named Woman of the Year by *Latina* magazine and was listed as one of the one hundred most influential Hispanics in the nation by *Hispanic Business* magazine.

SIGNIFICANCE

Inspired by a fiery passion for social justice and equality, Valdes-Rodriguez has created a genre of literature that highlights the diversity of Latino cultures while intro-ducing readers to strong, empowered females who break Latino literary stereotypes. Her work is widely read and addresses topics such as alternative religions and ho-mosexuality not covered in the broader body of Latin American literature. Valdes-Rodriguez's work attempts to portray Latinos as mainstream American citizens de-fined by their worth rather than their race or ethnicity.

Jamie Campbell Naidoo

FURTHER READING

Castillo, Debra. "Impossible Indian." *Chasqui* 35, no. 2 (2006): 42-57. Examines *The Dirty Girls Social Club* along with two vastly different literary works to determine Valdes-Rodriguez's conceptualization of indigenous people with Latin American roots.

Hurt, Erin. "Trading Cultural Baggage for Gucci Lug-gage: The Ambivalent Latinidad of Alisa Valdes-Rodriguez's *The Dirty Girls Social Club*." *MELUS* 34, no. 3 (2009): 133-153. Critically examines *The Dirty Girls Social Club* to determine how it breaks cultural stereotypes of Latinos and represents the diversity of Latino cultures while also propagating American consumerism.

Morrison, Amanda Maria. "Chicanas and 'Chick Lit': Contested Latinidad in the Novels of Alisa Valdes-Rodriguez." *The Journal of Popular Culture* 43, no. 2 (2010): 309-329. Critical discourse on how Valdes-Rodriguez brings Latina culture to the mainstream while also examining the constructions of ethnicity and race within the U.S. publishing industry.

See also: Julia Alvarez; Monica Brown; Denise Chávez; Sandra Cisneros; Cristina García; Esmeralda Santiago; Helena María Viramontes.

LUIS MIGUEL VALDEZ

American playwright and director

Valdez founded El Teatro Campesino (The Farmwork-ers' Theater) in 1965 and pioneered a new vision of Chicano theater that inspired dozens of other drama groups across the country. Fusing European theater traditions, pre-Colombian myth, and traditional Mexi-can music and dance, Valdez's raucous plays and films reexamine American popular history through a Chicano lens. With the phenomenal success of the play Zoot Suit *(1978) and the film* La Bamba *(1987), he paved the way for the mainstreaming of Latinos in theater and film.*

Latino heritage: Mexican

Born: June 26, 1940; Delano, California

Areas of achievement: Theater; screenwriting

EARLY LIFE

Luis Miguel Valdez (vahl-DEHZ) was born in Delano, California, the second of ten children of migrant farm-workers Francisco and Almida Valdez. He began work-ing in the fields with his family at the age of six, and although his education was frequently interrupted be-cause of his family's itinerancy, he finished high school and entered San Jose State University on a scholarship for math and physics.

Valdez's true interest was in theater, however, and after a year, he switched his major to English with an emphasis on playwriting. Valdez's first play, a one-act called *The Theft*, won a writing contest in 1961. It was followed in 1965 by his first full-length play, *The Shrunken Head of Pancho Villa*, a zany absurdist com-edy that skewers Mexican American stereotypes.

After graduating in 1964, Valdez joined the San Francisco Mime Troupe, one of the many guerrilla the-ater groups formed in the early 1960's that were crystal-lizing a new type of people's theater combining music, mask, movement, and commedia dell'arte. Performing for free in parks around the Bay Area, Valdez realized that the immediacy and accessibility of this type of the-ater would appeal to migrant farm laborers who had very little exposure to theater.

LIFE'S WORK

In 1965, the National Farm Workers Association, led by César Chávez and Dolores Huerta, joined a strike begun by Filipino farm workers against California grape com-panies. Hearing of this, Valdez returned to Delano and approached Chávez about forming a theater group to support the strike. Within a few weeks, he had founded El Teatro Campesino (The Farmworkers' Theater) with a handful of laborers who volunteered as actors.

In need of material that would be accessible to mi-grant workers while directly challenging the scare

Luis Miguel Valdez. (AP Photo)

East Coast for the first time, performing in New York City and before the Senate Subcommittee on Migratory Labor in Washington, D.C.

With the growth of interest in El Teatro Campesino, Valdez decided to leave the union to work on plays that addressed Mexican American issues beyond the fields. El Teatro Campesino moved to Del Rey, California, and debuted *Los vendidos* (1967; *The Sellouts*), an *acto* that has come to be one of the group's signature works. Going beyond agitprop, Valdez began to delve into the pre-Colombian indigenous heritage of Mexico. He started to write what he called *mitos* (myths), among them *Bernabé* (1970), in which a village idiot yearns to marry La Tierra (the Earth), and the antiwar play *Soldado razo* (1971). After El Teatro Campesino moved to Fresno, Valdez founded El Teatro Nacional de Aztlán (TENAZ), a nonprofit organization that spearheaded a Chicano theater movement throughout the United States.

In 1971, El Teatro Campesino moved to San Juan Bautista as Valdez began experimenting with *corridos*, traditional Mexican ballads. His 1973 epic play *La gran carpa de los rasquachis* (*The Big Tent of the Underdogs*) was acclaimed for its unique synthesis of music, stylized movement, Mayan myth, and early-twentieth-century Mexican tent shows.

Valdez's experiments with theatrical form reached fruition with *Zoot Suit* (1978), which fused *actos*, *mitos*, and *corridos* in a striking documentary play with music based on the Sleepy Lagoon murder of 1942. A phenomenal success when it opened in 1978, *Zoot Suit* ran for eleven months in Los Angeles and transferred to Broadway. In 1981, it was adapted by Valdez into a major motion picture that was nominated for a Golden Globe Award. *Zoot Suit* catapulted Valdez into mainstream Hollywood and he cemented his reputation in 1987 with *La Bamba*, an unexpected box office hit about Ritchie Valens, a Chicano pioneer of rock and roll.

Valdez turned to television in the 1990's, adapting the Mexican nativity story *La pastorela* for public television in 1991. It quickly became a holiday staple for the Spanish-language television channel Telemundo. He also cowrote and directed a remake of *The Cisco Kid* for Turner Network Television in 1994.

In the 2000's, Valdez's plays *Mummified Deer* (2000) and *Earthquake Sun* (2004) recall his earlier work examining pre-Colombian myth. He has also returned to Mexican *corridos* with the musical play *Corridos Remix*, which he staged for San Diego Repertory with his son Kinan Valdez in 2005. El Teatro Campesino celebrated its fortieth anniversary in 2005.

tactics of the grape corporations, Valdez developed a series of short plays from improvisations that often were derived from the experiences of his actor-laborers. Deliberately rustic and over-the-top, with the use of masks or placards that emphasized the archetypal nature of the characters, the *actos*, as he called them, were designed to speak directly to the people—La Raza—raising their political consciousness, discrediting oppressive power structures, and urging them to participate in social action. The *actos* were also unique for their use of stock characters of striker, replacement worker, contractor, and landowner, which not only were instantly recognizable to farmworker audiences but also recalled the stock characters and allegorical figures found in commedia dell'arte, and European morality plays.

El Teatro Campesino traveled to migrant camps throughout the San Joaquin Valley from 1965 to 1967, performing in the fields on a flatbed truck, in union meeting halls, and directly on picket lines. In 1967, they were invited to perform at Stanford University. The success of the performance led to a tour of colleges, churches, and community centers throughout California. That summer, El Teatro Campesino traveled to the

Zoot Suit

Luis Valdez's groundbreaking play *Zoot Suit* (1978) examines the anti-Mexican hysteria of the World War II era, which culminated in the so-called zoot-suit riots that rocked Los Angeles in the summer of 1943. Through this play, Valdez not only illuminates an event that had a major effect on the Mexican American community, but he also delves into Chicano identity with his examination of "pachuco" subculture.

Young Chicano men in the 1940's donned zoot suits—which had extra-long jackets, wide lapels, and padded shoulders—that signified their resistance to assimilation and subjugation. In the play, gang leader Henry Reyna has decided to enlist in the Navy, but the night before beginning his service, he is arrested for killing a rival gang member. Despite a lack of evidence, he and seven other pachucos are convicted by a racist judge. The press uses the case to stoke racial tensions in Los Angeles, which escalate into the zoot-suit riots. As

the war winds to an end, the conviction is overturned. *Zoot Suit* is an innovative blend of musical theater and agitprop and also features a narrator much like the allegorical figures in Valdez's *actos*. Named El Pachuco, he embodies defiance against the system and the *nahual*, or Aztec concept of the shadow self. The dialogue and lyrics in *Zoot Suit* are a lively blend of Spanish and English, peppered by the unique colloquialisms of pachuco subculture.

Zoot Suit was commissioned by the Mark Taper Forum and was Valdez's first play developed for a mainstream audience. The play opened in July, 1978, and wildly exceeded expectations. The success of the play led to a Broadway production and a 1982 film adaptation, which Valdez also wrote and directed. *Zoot Suit* was not only the first Chicano play to open on Broadway, but also the first major Hollywood film written and directed by a Chicano, starring Chicano actors as Chicano characters.

Valdez continues to lead the company and mentor a new generation of theater and film artists.

SIGNIFICANCE

Valdez's vision defined Chicano theater and gave birth to a Chicano theater movement. His broad and raucous plays mine pre-Colombian myth, Chicano history, and traditional Mexican music to examine sociopolitical issues affecting the Chicano community. He pioneered the use of Spanglish in plays with dialogue that switches between English and Spanish with striking authenticity and ease. The theater style that he created inspired a movement, at the peak of which as many as one hundred Chicano theater groups were active throughout the United States. His work places Chicanos within the popular history of America, and his success did much to change perceptions of Latinos in mainstream theater and film.

Victoria Linchong

FURTHER READING

Broyles-Gonzalez, Yolanda. *El Teatro Campesino*. Austin: University of Texas Press, 1994. A comprehensive history and critique of El Teatro Campesino, from its inception through the success of *Zoot Suit* and beyond.

Huerta, Jorge A., ed. *Necessary Theater: Six Plays About the Chicano Experience*. Houston: Arte Público Press, 1989. Collection of Chicano plays that includes Luis Valdez's earliest play, *The Shrunken Head of Pancho Villa*, with a biography of Valdez and an astute analysis of the play by Huerta.

Valdez, Luis. *Luis Valdez—Early Works: Actos, Bernabé, and Pensamiento Serpentino*. Houston: Arte Público Press, 1990. Volume of Valdez's *actos* and his allegorical play *Bernabé*, along with a poem and several essays.

_____. *Mummified Deer, and Other Plays*. Houston: Arte Público Press, 2005. Valdez's first play, *The Shrunken Head of Pancho Villa*, is published with *Mundo Mata*, another early play that was unfinished until 2001, and *Mummified Deer*.

_____. *Zoot Suit, and Other Plays*. Houston: Arte Público Press, 1992. Contains Valdez's most famous play, *Zoot Suit*, and two other plays that toy with historical fact and fiction: *Bandido!* and *I Don't Have To Show You No Stinking Badges!*

See also: Reinaldo Arenas; Denise Chávez; Maria Irene Fornes; Eduardo Machado; Robert Rodriguez.

RITCHIE VALENS

American musician

Although killed in an airplane accident in 1959 before he had even turned eighteen, Valens in a matter of months had become the first Chicano rock-and-roll star, his popularity on the rise with three influential hits and a following that transcended race and class barriers.

Latino heritage: Mexican

Born: May 13, 1941; Pacoima, California

Died: February 3, 1959; Near Mason City, Iowa

Also known as: Richard Steven Valenzuela; The Little Richard of the Valley, Ricardo Esteban Valenzuela Reyes

Area of achievement: Music

EARLY LIFE

Raised in the San Fernando Valley of Southern California, Ritchie Valens (RIHT-chee VAL-ehnz) was born Richard Steven Valenzuela, the son of Joseph Stephen "Steve" Valenzuela, a tree surgeon, horse trainer, and munitions factory worker, and his wife Concepcion "Connie" Reyes, who also worked at that factory. Valens's mother had an older son, Robert Morales, from a previous marriage. Valens's parents divorced when he was three years old, and in 1951 his father died from diabetes. At this time his mother moved into his father's former house with her two sons and Valens's two younger sisters, Connie and Irma; because the house was so small and crowded, Valens was sent to live with a series of nearby relatives, spending a lot of time at the home of his uncle and aunt, Lelo and Ernestine Reyes. From an early age Valens demonstrated a love for music, and, as an urban Chicano in the post-World War II period, he had grown up exposed to traditional Mexican music, rhythm and blues, Hollywood singing cowboy performances at Saturday matinees, and country music on the radio.

Valens took up the guitar at the age of eleven, and at the age of sixteen he joined the Silhouettes, a multiracial rhythm-and-blues band from his San Fernando High School. They played many local public and private parties, and with Valens taking on the responsibility of singing lead, they developed a following that included both white and Latino car clubs.

LIFE'S WORK

The stage charisma and innovative stylings of the young performer were brought to the attention of Del-Fi Records producer Bob Keane, who caught a Saturday-afternoon performance by Valens in May, 1958, and promptly invited him to Keane's home studio to make some demonstration tapes. Valens signed a contract with Keane's company, and Keane would use Gold Star Studios in Hollywood to make Valens's marketed recordings. As a promotional strategy, at Keane's suggestion, the musician anglicized his stage name to Ritchie Valens.

Valens only made two records that were released before his death, but both were innovative and influential. His first single, "Come On, Let's Go," was recorded in July, 1958, and released locally. It became a hit in Los Angeles, and its popularity spread throughout the Southwest, so it was released nationally in August, eventually rising to number forty-two on the *Billboard* singles chart and selling a half million copies. Rather than return for senior year, Valens decided to drop out of school to concentrate on his musical career, but he recorded a doo-wop tribute to his high school girlfriend Donna Ludwig as the A side of his next record: "Donna."

Ritchie Valens. (AP Photo)

The song went to number two nationally. Valens made personal promotional appearances in Los Angeles, New York, and Hawaii; performed on the televised popular music show *American Bandstand* twice; and appeared in Alan Freed's rock-and-roll film *Go, Johnny, Go!* (1959). Planning for the future, Valens was recording more tracks in the studio, too.

However, his next hit turned out to be the B side of "Donna." Taking a traditional Mexican song, speeding it up, and giving it a raucous rock-and-roll flair while maintaining the traditional lyrics in Spanish and a distinctively Latino sound at the same time, Valens had another hit with "La Bamba." Regardless of their ethnicity, young people responded positively to the rhythms and vivaciousness of the song, whether they understood the words or not. Since he had grown up speaking English, Valens had to learn the words to the song phonetically; his Aunt Ernestine helped him master the lyrics.

In early 1959, Valens was one of the hottest young stars in the United States, doing a Winter Dance Party Tour through the Midwest with Buddy Holly, Jiles Perry Richardson, Jr. (also known as "the Big Bopper"), Dion and the Belmonts, and Holly's new back-up band. After their tour bus broke down, Holly arranged for a small four-seater private plane to deliver some of their entourage to their next destination in Fargo, North Dakota. Valens won his seat on a coin toss. On February 3, 1959, the plane took off in a terrible snowstorm, crashed, and killed all aboard: the pilot, Holly, the Big Bopper, and seventeen-year-old Valens. This came to be known as "The Day the Music Died."

Significance

Valens was the first Latino rock-and-roll star. He came out of a multiethnic urban background and demonstrated great crossover appeal while integrating across musical traditions. With "La Bamba," he was the first to adapt traditional Mexican music and successfully remarket it through rock and roll to a large audience, and he paved the way for all Latino rock-and-roll musicians to come. Like Linda Ronstadt, who would record an album in Spanish in 1987, Valens did not speak fluent Spanish, yet he made Spanish-language music with Mexican roots accessible to and popular with millions of English-speaking Americans. The 1987 biopic *La Bamba*, directed by Luis Miguel Valdez and starring Lou Diamond Phillips as Valens, brought his life story to a new generation of Americans, and the sound track album that accompanied that film went to number one in the country in September, 1987, suggesting the

"La Bamba"

The song "La Bamba" originated in the Veracruz region of Mexico as a *huapango*, a type of traditional folk song with accompanying dance. It was often performed at weddings, and Ritchie Valens learned to play the song on the guitar from his cousin. With studio musicians working in Hollywood, however, he sped up the tempo, added some rock-and-roll riffs, and, releasing it as the B side of his second single in 1958, changed the future of Latin music forever, introducing the fusion of traditional Mexican music with rock and roll. The song would reach number twenty-two on the *Billboard* singles chart, but its legacy would go far beyond that. Some have called it the beginning of Latino rock and roll. Many music scholars suggest that both garage rock and later punk rock look back to this song as an antecedent, too. *La Bamba* was also ultimately the title selected for the film Luis Miguel Valdez made in 1987 about the story of Valens's life. The band Los Lobos performed "La Bamba" in the film, and that sound track went to number one album in the country in September, 1987. Harry Belafonte recorded an earlier version of the folk song than Valens, but Valens performed the version that has now become embraced internationally. Among the many who have since covered Valens's "La Bamba" are such diverse performers as the Kingston Trio, Trini López, Selena, the Ventures, and the Japanese hip-hop group Dragon Ash.

broadening acceptance of Latino music in the dominant culture at that time. He was inducted into the Rock and Roll Hall of Fame in 2001.

Scot M. Guenter

Further Reading

Lehmer, Larry. *The Day the Music Died: The Last Tour of Buddy Holly, the "Big Bopper," and Ritchie Valens*. New York: Music Sales, 2003. In-depth review of Winter Parade concert tour and the ill-fated flight.

Macias, Anthony F. "Bringing Music to the People: Race, Urban Culture, and Municipal Politics in Postwar Los Angeles." *American Quarterly* 56, no. 3 (2004): 693-717. The rise of Valens in rock and roll is contextualized within the multicultural musical and political world in which he lived.

_____. *Mexican American Mojo: Popular Music, Dance, and Urban Culture in Los Angeles,*

1935-1968. Durham, N.C.: Duke University Press, 2008. Racial and ethnic identity evaluated through the creation and evolution of Chicano music in this period.

Mendheim, Beverly. *Ritchie Valens: The First Latino Rocker.* Tempe, Ariz.: Bilingual Press, 1987. Background biography that explores Valens's life through emphasis on his songs: their origins, stylings, and recordings.

Reyes, David, and Tom Waldman. *Land of a Thousand Dances: Chicano Rock 'n Roll from Southern California.* Albuquerque: University of New Mexico Press, 2009. Revised and expanded edition. Traces the roots and development of Mexican American rock and roll.

See also: Joan Baez; Mariah Carey; Vikki Carr; Gloria Estefan; José Feliciano; Trini López.

ANGELA VALENZUELA

American educator and scholar

Valenzuela's work focuses on eradicating racism against Latinos in U.S. school systems. She is best known for her book Subtractive Schooling: U.S.-Mexican Youth and the Politics of Caring, *which examines how educational policies subtract needed resources from low-income, Latino immigrant students.*

Latino heritage: Mexican
Born: 1949; San Angelo, Texas
Areas of achievement: Education; scholarship

EARLY LIFE

Angela Valenzuela (an-JEL-ah vah-lehn-SWAY-lah) was born and raised in San Angelo, Texas.

School children in that community were often placed in tracking systems that classified students as grade level, below grade level, or above grade level. While Anglo students were usually placed in grade level or above grade level tracks, Latinos, including Valenzuela, were often categorized as being at or below grade level. Valenzuela was aware that Anglo students were taking field trips to Washington, D.C., and attaining better opportunities than she could hope for. She even recognized at a young age that her parents, teachers, and counselors did not encourage her to exceed in academics. In fact, her parents even advised her to drop out during her senior year to get married and have children, which she declined to do. Instead, Valenzuela enrolled in an English program, which required her to do research at the Angelo State University library, and this program influenced her aspirations to attain a college education.

After she graduated from high school in 1977, Valenzuela attended Angelo State University. In her junior year of college, Valenzuela's mother shared her desire to attend college. Valenzuela graduated cum laude with a B.A.

degree in English in 1981; her mother graduated magna cum laude in 1985. In 1989, Valenzuela married Emilio Zamora, a University of Houston associate professor of history, with whom she had two children, Clara and Luz.

LIFE'S WORK

Soon after earning her bachelor's degree, Valenzuela went on to attain two M.A. degrees: one in sociolinguistics from the University of Texas in 1983 and the other in sociology from Stanford University in 1985. In 1990, Valenzuela received her Ph.D. in sociology from Stanford University. From 1989 to 1990, she worked as a lecturer at Rice University in Houston, Texas. She was soon promoted to assistant professor at Rice, remaining in this position from 1990 to 1998. While in Houston, Valenzuela conducted research at local schools on the success rates of Mexican American immigrants. Her own experience with prejudice in the Texas public school system encouraged her to examine how Latino students could attain academic success.

The Mexican American Studies Department at the University of Houston invited Valenzuela to teach there as a visiting scholar during the 1998-1999 academic year. Valenzuela went on to become an associate professor in the Department of Curriculum and Instruction and the Center for Mexican American Studies at the University of Texas at Austin. In 2006, she attained full professorship in this university's departments of Cultural Studies, Curriculum and Instruction, and Educational Administration. Valenzuela also received a Fulbright Scholar award which enabled her to teach at the College of Law at the University of Guanajuato in Guanajuato, Mexico, during the 2007-2008 academic year. While in Guanajuato, she conducted research on immigration, human rights, and binational relations.

Valenzuela later became a Cissy McDaniel Parker Fellow in the Departments of Curriculum and Instruction and Educational Administration at the University of Texas at Austin, and she was the university's associate vice president for university-school partnerships. In 2010, she was named the new director of the National Latino Education Research Agenda Project, which works to create a teacher education pipeline for Latino youth nationwide

Valenzuela is best known for publishing her research, *Subtractive Schooling: U.S.-Mexican Youth and the Politics of Caring* (1999), which examines how school systems' use of assimilation and other similar strategies subtracts resources from low-income, Latino immigrant students. She proposes that school systems become additive through the use of bicultural pedagogy. In 2000, the book received both the American Educational Research Association Outstanding Book Award and an honorable mention from the Gustavus Myers Outstanding Book Awards; the following year, Valenzuela was honored with the American Educational Studies Association Critics' Choice Award.

Valenzuela has served as coeditor of the *International Journal of Qualitative Studies in Education* and *Anthropology and Education Quarterly*. She has also edited *Leaving Children Behind: How "Texas-Style" Accountability Fails Latino Youth* (2005).

SIGNIFICANCE

Valenzuela's research primarily focuses on the areas of sociology of education, minority youth in schools, educational policy, and urban education reform. This research earned her a Scholar Award from the Texas Association of Chicanos in Higher Education in 2000, as well as several other awards, encouraging her to become more involved in refining educational policy as

it pertains to minority students. Specifically, Valenzuela works as an adviser to state legislatures, focusing on areas of assessment, limited-English-proficient youth, bilingual education, school vouchers, and school finance. Ultimately, she hopes to change state education policies to better serve not just Latinos but all students.

Margaret E. Cantú-Sánchez

FURTHER READING

Foley, Douglas, and Angela Valenzuela. "Critical Ethnography: The Politics of Collaboration." *The Landscape of Qualitative Research* (2008): 187-307. Valenzuela reveals how she not only engages in research but also attempts to put her theories into action by working on various legislative policies with state representatives and senators.

Valenzuela, Angela. "Uncovering Internalized Oppression." In *Teach Boldly! Letters to Teachers About Contemporary Issues in Education*, edited by Dennis Earl Fehr and Mary Cain Fehr. New York: Peter Lang, 2009. Valenzuela reveals her own experience with internal discrimination as she recalls how she joined other schoolmates in oppressing a newly arrived Mexican immigrant girl because she continued to follow the traditions of her country.

Vara, Richard. "Professor's Perspective: Her Experiences with Education Provide Insight for a Study Focused on Hispanic Youth." *Houston Chronicle*, September 16, 1997, p. D1. Describes how Valenzuela became interested and began her research into subtractive schooling. Vara also provides brief critiques of Valenzuela's work as revealed by her colleagues and family.

See also: Edna Acosta-Belén; Eduardo Padrón; Patricia Zavella.

FERNANDO VALENZUELA

Mexican-born baseball player

Valenzuela was a pitching phenomenon who became a pop-culture icon through his dominance on the diamond. His pitching career ran from 1980 to 1997. As a highly visible athlete, he was influential in fostering pride in Latino identity.

Latino heritage: Mexican

Born: November 1, 1960; Etchohuaquila, Mexico

Also known as: Fernando Valenzuela Anguamea; El Toro
Areas of achievement: Baseball

EARLY LIFE

Fernando Valenzuela (VAH-lehnz-WAY-lah) was born on November 1, 1960, in Etchohuaquila, Mexico. As an avid baseball player, Valenzuela excelled beyond his local peers and soon advanced to the

Fernando Valenzuela. (AP Photo)

Mexican professional leagues. At the age of seventeen, he began playing professional baseball for the Guanajuato team of the Mexican Central League.

Within a year of his professional debut, Valenzuela attracted the attention of scouts from Major League Baseball (MLB). Mike Brito, a talent scout from the Los Angeles Dodgers, recruited Valenzuela in 1978 from the Leones de Yucatán baseball club. In 1979, the Dodgers purchased Valenzuela's Mexican contract, initially allowing him time to develop in a Class-A farm club in Lodi, California, and then in a Class-AA club in San Antonio, Texas.

LIFE'S WORK

In September, 1980, Valenzuela was called up to the Dodgers' major-league team, where he immediately became one of the most celebrated rookies of the era. In addition to helping the Dodgers reach the National League West Division title in 1980, Valenzuela led the team to a 1981 World Series victory over the New York Yankees. Valenzuela's success combined with his charismatic personality made the young Mexican wildly popular among Dodger fans. The hype that surrounded him was referred to as "Fernandomania."

Valenzuela thrived on the attention he received in Los Angeles. With his signature glance to the sky before each pitch, the left-handed Valenzuela perfected his delivery and became one the most feared pitchers in the National League. Using his trademark screwball, Valenzuela racked up 180 strikeouts and finished with an earned run average of 2.48 in 1981. For this performance, Valenzuela became the first pitcher in MLB history to win both the National League rookie of the year award and the National League Cy Young Award. Fans also recognized Valenzuela's achievements by voting him into several All-Star games. Indeed, Valenzuela's popularity proved influential when he was a National League All-Star selection for six consecutive seasons, from 1981 to 1986.

In addition to Valenzuela's phenomenal pitching, he hit remarkably well for a pitcher. His batting statistics in 1981 and 1983 earned him the coveted Silver Slugger award, an honor given to the best offensive player at each position.

By the close of the 1980's, Valenzuela was considered a veteran pitcher. Although sportswriters claimed that his career was declining, he proved that he was still a valuable pitcher on June 29, 1990, when he recorded a no-hitter against the St. Louis Cardinals. Despite Valenzuela's late-career achievement, his tenure as a Dodger came to an end in 1991 when he was released.

Valenzuela went on to spend the next several years moving between the Mexican Leagues and a variety of MLB teams, including the California Angels, Baltimore Orioles, San Diego Padres, and the St. Louis Cardinals. In 1997, Valenzuela officially retired from Major League Baseball as a Cardinal.

Since his retirement, Valenzuela has held a variety of jobs, including working as a guest commentator for the Dodgers' Spanish-language radio broadcasts and as an assistant coach for the Mexican team in the World Baseball Classic in 2006 and 2009.

SIGNIFICANCE

Valenzuela was not only a dominant pitcher who helped his team win a World Series—he also was a cultural icon who inspired a devoted following. He became a Dodger at a time when Latinos made up a large segment of the team's fan base. Baseball historians have even noted that the late Dodgers owner Walter O'Malley had commented on the need for a "Mexican Sandy Koufax" who would engage the large Latino population of Los Angeles. Having tapped into this

Fernandomania

When twenty-year-old Fernando Valenzuela played his first full season as a Dodger in 1981, Los Angeles was a bustling city of baseball fans absorbed in the race for the National League pennant. Valenzuela's heavy-set build and long, shaggy hair appeared slightly out of place among a team of physically fit athletes. Although he had made his debut late in the previous season, Dodger fans—and indeed the rest of Major League Baseball—had yet to see the caliber of ball-player Valenzuela could be. In his first eight appearances, Valenzuela accumulated seven victories with an earned run average of 0.50, sparking widespread excitement over the rookie sensation. Latino fans in particular came in droves to watch the talented young Mexican baseball player. A cottage industry of souvenir sellers sprang up around Dodger Stadium and Los Angeles, offering baseball cards, posters, baseball jerseys with Valenzuela's number 34 embroidered on the back, Valenzuela bobble-head figurines, and T-shirts reading "*Orale* Fernando!"—"Right on, Fernando!"

As the team reveled in the publicity Valenzuela brought to the Dodgers, they also capitalized on this excitement by promoting his Latino heritage. Nicknamed "El Toro" (the Bull), Valenzuela often was introduced to the strains of Spanish music fit for bullfighters. The crowds responded with homemade banners reading "Viva Valenzuela" and by chanting his name. In this way, Valenzuela became a cultural icon of athletic success for Mexican Americans in Los Angeles, as well as an object of pride for Latinos throughout the Americas.

population, Valenzuela enjoyed immense popularity throughout his career and provided a positive image with which young and often less-fortunate Latinos could identify.

Salvador Jimenez Murguia

FURTHER READING

Bretón, Marcos, and José Luis Villegas. *Away Games: The Life and Times of a Latin Baseball Player.* Albuquerque: University of New Mexico Press, 2000. A telling story of the Latino experience within Major League Baseball, told through the memoirs of Dominican-born shortstop Miguel Tejada. Throughout this book, several references are made to Fernando Valenzuela's successes and his status as a role model for other Latinos.

Burgos, Adrian. *Playing America's Game: Baseball, Latinos, and the Color Line.* Berkeley: University of California Press, 2007. A rich and detailed book about the politics of race and baseball. Burgos provides well-researched account of the Los Angeles Dodgers' 1979 acquisition of Valenzuela.

Regalado, Samuel O. *Viva Baseball!: Latin Major Leaguers and Their Special Hunger.* Champaign: University of Illinois Press, 1998. A history of Latinos in Major League Baseball from the 1800's through the 1990's. This book includes an entire chapter on Fernandomania.

See also: Juan Marichal; Dennis Martínez; Pedro Martinez; Johan Santana; Luis Tiant.

ISMAEL VALENZUELA

American jockey and horse trainer

Valenzuela, a Hall of Fame Jockey, led some of the top thoroughbreds to victories in major competitions. He won both the Kentucky Derby and Preakness Stakes in 1958 and 1968, but he lost the Belmont Stakes, and the Triple Crown, in both years.

Latino heritage: Mexican

Born: December 24, 1934; McNary, Texas

Died: September 2, 2009; Arcadia, California

Also known as: Milo

Area of achievement: Sports

EARLY LIFE

Ismael Valenzuela (ees-mah-EHL vah-lehn-SAY-lah) was born December 24, 1934, in McNary, Texas. He was one of twenty-two children born to Angel Valenzuela and Mari de Jesus Rios Valenzuela, who had immigrated to the United States from Mexico. Shortly after Valenzuela's birth, the family returned to Mexico, where he was raised on a farm and herded sheep and cattle. His took his first ride when he was three and his father put him on a horse. Valenzuela discovered that he liked riding, and he later realized that he also enjoyed racing and competing.

At the age of twelve, Valenzuela traveled to El Paso, Texas, where he found a job exercising horses and cleaning stalls. In 1947, Valenzuela moved to Tucson, Arizona, where he raced quarter horses before switching to thoroughbreds. He won his first race on April 8, 1951, at Rillito Park in Tucson. He went on to compete in thoroughbred races at tracks in Colorado, California, and on the East Coast.

LIFE'S WORK

In 1958, Valenzuela was the top rider in Jamaica, New York, which enabled him to ride in that year's Kentucky Derby. He won this race while riding Tim Tam, a colt. The day after the race, he went to New York City for a television appearance on *The Ed Sullivan Show*. Two weeks later, Valenzuela and Tim Tam won the Preakness Stakes. Tim Tam was favored to win that year's Belmont Stakes. As the horses were heading home, Valenzuela had perfectly positioned Tim Tam a length and a half off the lead of Cavan, the eventual winner. Valenzuela felt Tim Tam take a bad step; the horse fractured his right foreleg and hobbled to the finish line. Valenzuela recalled that, "I tried to ease him up, but he still wanted to run. He finished second, and I couldn't pull him up until the clubhouse turn. Then I felt the tears start to come." Valenzuela saved Tim Tam's life by dismounting and keeping the injured leg off the ground until medical help arrived. Tim Tam never raced again, although he lived for another twenty-four years.

In the early 1960's, Valenzuela regularly rode Kelso, one of the best race horses of the twentieth century, and it was on this horse that Valenzuela experienced his greatest success. He rode Kelso to twenty-two wins in thirty-five important races. He and the horse set other records. Kelso eventually won more money than any horse in thoroughbred history to that date, and he was named Horse of the Year for five consecutive years beginning in 1960. Valenzuela also was honored for his performance. In 1963, he was the recipient of the George Woolf Memorial Jockey Award, which is presented to a top thoroughbred jockey in North America who demonstrates high standards of personal and professional conduct, on and off the racetrack.

In 1966, Valenzuela won the Canadian International Stakes. Two years later, Valenzuela and the horse Forward Pass finished second to Dancer's Image in the Kentucky Derby. Dancer's Image, however, was later disqualified after this horse tested positively for drugs—the only disqualification in the history of the Kentucky Derby. As a result, Forward Pass was declared the victor. Valenzeula and Forward Pass went on to win the Preakness Stakes, but the horse failed to capture the Triple Crown when it finished second in the Belmont Stakes.

After winning 2,545 races, Valenzuela retired in 1980, living with his family in a home near Santa Anita Park racetrack in Arcadia, California. He became a horse trainer and then began teaching yearlings how to race. In December, 1999, Rose Delia, his wife of forty-five years, died suddenly of liver failure. She had been taking the doctor-prescribed drug Rezulin for her diabetes. A few months after her death, the U.S. Food and Drug Administration pulled Rezulin off the market, concluding that its use had caused ninety cases of liver failure, sixty-three deaths, and seven nonfatal organ transplants.

In 2008, Valenzuela was elected to the National Museum of Racing and Hall of Fame. In poor health because of complications from diabetes, he could not travel to Saratoga Springs, New York, for the induction ceremony on August 4, 2008. Instead, he was inducted in a special ceremony at Santa Anita Park on June 22, 2008.

Valenzuela died on September 2, 2009, at the age of seventy-four, and was buried in the Live Oak Memorial Park Cemetery in Monrovia, California.

SIGNIFICANCE

Ismael Valenzuela won more than 130 major horse races, earning purses of more than $20 million. He rode with a powerful yet smooth style that was often compared to that of the legendary jockey Eddie Arcaro, and he was especially good at racing two-year-old horses to victory.

Michael J. Bennett

FURTHER READING

Blood-Horse Publications. "Kelso's Five Horse of the Year Titles." In *Horse Racing's Top One Hundred Moments*. Lexington, Ky.: Author, 2006. Recounts Kelso's illustrious racing history, including information about Valenzuela and a photograph of him atop this champion horse.

Toby, Milton C. *Dancer's Image: The Forgotten Story of the 1968 Kentucky Derby*. Charleston, S.C.: The History Press, 2011. This history of the 1968 Kentucky Derby includes information about Valenzuela's ride on Forward Pass, the horse who was eventually declared the winner.

See also: Angel Cordero, Jr.; Laffit Pincay, Jr.

LILIANA VALENZUELA

Mexican-born translator and writer

Internationally acclaimed as an English-to-Spanish literary translator who has translated many of the great U.S. Latino writers of the late twentieth and early twenty-first centuries, Valenzuela has also built a reputation as a gifted poet, short-story writer, and essayist.

Latino heritage: Mexican
Born: June 1, 1960; Mexico City, Mexico
Also known as: Liliana Valenzuela Aguilera
Areas of achievement: Literature; poetry

EARLY LIFE

Liliana Valenzuela (lee-lee-AN-ah vah-lehn-SWAY-lah) was born in Mexico City, Mexico, to Alfonso Valenzuela Díaz and Marcela Aguilera Alonso. She grew up in Mexico City and attended high school at Colegio Ciudad de Mexico. In 1978, she won an American Field Service scholarship to study in Denmark for one year at Maribo Gymnasium, where she learned Danish. In 1981, while studying cultural anthropology at the Universidad Iberoamericana in Mexico City, Valenzuela met and married George Eckrich, and moved to Austin, Texas. She graduated from the University of Texas at Austin with a bachelor's degree in cultural anthropology in 1984 and a master's degree in this subject in 1988. During her time as a student, she was awarded a Junior Fellows Research Grant in 1984 to fund fieldwork in Mexico. Valenzuela became an American citizen in 1988.

After her oldest child was born, Valenzuela made the decision to become a translator so she could work from her home and be available to her child. In 1993, she was certified by the American Translators Association to translate from English into Spanish. She named her translation agency La Malinche Translations after the often traduced translator and lover of Hernán de Cortés; La Malinche bore the first meztizo child and is considered both the betrayer and the mother of modern Mexico. This was a natural name choice for Valenzuela, who had studied and written about native rituals in Acatlán, where the indigenous peoples held Malinche in a positive light, and she would continue to write about and from the perspective of Malinche. The initial commissions Valenzuela received for translations were business, technical, and academic treatises. She moved to translating art show catalogs and books,

but she had already begun writing and publishing her own creative work and wanted to develop a practice of literary translation.

LIFE'S WORK

By 2011, Valenzuela had become one of the premier translators of American Latino writers into Spanish for the burgeoning market for these authors in Mexico and Latin America. The educated elite in Mexico had disdained U.S. Latino writers for many years, believing them boorish peasants who chose not to speak and write good Spanish. However, as a result of the Chicano movement of the 1970's, these same intellectuals later clamored for the energetic and always unpredictable books by these authors, especially the women, such as Sandra Cisneros and Julia Alvarez. These works were uniquely difficult to translate because of the use of language code-switching, Spanglish, and street slang and because their authors often played with syntax and colloquial vernacular. Valenzuela developed a reputation for working closely with the authors to match their initial intent and produce masterful translations. She translated major works by Cisneros, Alvarez, Denise Chávez, Nina Marie Martínez, Ana Castillo, Dagoberto Gilb, Richard Rodriguez, Rudolfo Anaya, Cristina García, Gloria Anzaldúa, Alex Espinoza, as well as a number of emerging Latino writers. She also recorded the audiobook editions of the Spanish translations of Cisneros's classic *The House on Mango Street* (1984) and of Espinoza's *Still Water Saints* (2007). She has been a director of the American Translators Association, and in 2006 she received the Alicia Gordon Award for Word Artistry in Translation from the American Foundation for Translation and Interpretation.

Valenzuela received awards in the same period for her own poetry, short fiction, and essays, including fellowships for the Vermont Studio Center and Macondo Writing Workshop, the Chicano Literary Award in Fiction, a Texas Commission on the Arts grant, the Christina Sergeyevna Award, the Mary Oliver Award, the Border/Lines Award, and the Carpeta de Poesía Luz, Voces Selectas Poetry Chapbook Prize. Valenzuela was also a guest editor for *Borderlands: A Texas Poetry Review* and reviewed books for *Criticas*, *The Texas Observer*, *Austin Chronicle*, and *Translation*

Journal, among others. She published three chapbooks, *Bocas palabras* (1997), *Mujer frontera, mujer Malinche* (2002), and *The Poetry of Rice Fields: A Long Poem* (2003), and was working on a bilingual memoir in 2011. Her creative output included Spanish, English, and bilingual poems, stories, and essays. As she moved into the second decade of the twenty-first century, Valenzuela increased the use of English in her work for practical reasons, although she stated on several occasions that she could never abandon writing in her birth language.

Significance

A major translator into Spanish of U.S. Latino literary writers, Valenzuela made use of her talents as a creative writer to put great artistry into her Spanish translation work. She was in the forefront of the movement to reject demands to force the linguistic code-switching of U.S. Latino writers into the straitjacket of formal Spanish and instead worked to find new ways to render in Spanish the linguistic invention and playfulness of the writers she translated.

Linda Rodriguez

Further Reading

Salas, Abel. "Writer/Translator Liliana Valenzuela." *Austin Chronicle,* Nov.8, 1996. This interview with Valenzuela gives the reader a good sense of her personality and her professional drive.

Valenzuela, Liliana. *Mujer frontera, mujer Malinche.* Austin, Tex.: Luz Bilingual, 2002. A bilingual edition of Valenzuela's poems dealing with womanhood, sexuality, and the intersection between the two.

_____. "My Two Tongues: On How I Came to Have a Forked Tongue." In *How I Learned English: Fifty-five Accomplished Latinos Recall Lessons in Language and Life*, edited by Tom Miller. Washington, D.C.: National Geographic Books, 2007. A funny yet bittersweet account of life on the gulf between two cultures.

_____. *The Poetry of Rice Fields*. Austin, Tex.: Luz Bilingual, 2003. A long meditation on sisterhood, motherhood, sensuality, and the beauty in small details.

See also: Rudolfo Anaya; Gloria Anzaldúa; Ana Castillo; Denise Chávez; Sandra Cisneros; Cristina García; Richard Rodriguez.

Roberto Valero

Cuban-born poet, writer, and educator

An exile from Cuba, Valero came to the United States, where he wrote poetry and essays in Miami and then in Washington, D.C. He later earned a doctoral degree, taught at the university level, and lectured and read widely in Europe and Latin America.

Latino heritage: Cuban
Born: 1955; Matanzas, Cuba
Died: September 23, 1994; Washington, D.C.
Also known as: Roberto Rodríguez Valero; Julio Real
Areas of achievement: Poetry; literature; education

Early Life

Roberto Rodríguez Valero (roh-BEHR-toh rahd-REE-gehs vah-LEHR-oh) was born in Matanzas, Cuba, a community about sixty miles from Havana, the island's capital. Matanzas, a center of Afro-Cuban culture, is known as "the Athens of Cuba" because of the large number of poets who came from there. During the mid-1970's, Valero attended the University of Havana, where the motto over the gates read: "This university is only for

revolutionaries." Valero, who wished to become a writer, did not earn a degree. Like many students, teachers, and intellectuals, he chafed under the rule of Fidel Castro and became increasingly disenchanted with socialism.

Valero and others were outspoken in their criticism of a repressive university life. The curriculum was disorganized; class content was heavily political and had no relevance to the students' intended careers. University students had little freedom, even when not in the classroom. They were often required to gather en masse to welcome visitors who wished to witness the results of communism at first hand, or to assemble and enthusiastically applaud Castro's harangues. Students suffered in silence until early 1980, when a group of dissenters used a bus to crash through barriers in order to seek asylum at the Peruvian embassy in Havana. Hundreds of people joined the protest, and Valero was one of more than eleven hundred individuals crowded onto the embassy grounds hoping for sanctuary.

The demonstration took the government by surprise. In April, Castro announced that anyone who wanted could leave the island. Valero became part of a mass exodus of Cubans, the third such migration that occurred since the revolution of 1959 (there would be a fourth exodus in the early 1990's). The dissidents left for the United States and elsewhere from the port of Mariel, west of Havana; hence, they were called "Marielitos." Between April and October 31, 1980, when the port was closed, some 125,000 Cubans went into exile, most of them traveling by watercraft in an operation that became known as the Mariel boatlift. Among the voluntary exiles were many Cubans—Juan Abreau, Reinaldo Arenas, Miguel Correa, Carlos Alfonzo, Reinaldo García Ramos, Carlos Victoria, Felipe García Villamil, and Valero—who were destined to become important writers, musicians, artists, actors, dancers, and filmmakers.

Life's Work

Valero landed in Miami, Florida, where he worked as a waiter and at other jobs to earn money and enjoyed newfound freedoms of expression and sexuality. It was difficult overcoming the public perception of the Marielitos, because the media reported that Castro had emptied prisons and mental institutions and sent the inmates into exile with the other immigrants. (Records indicate that some twenty-three hundred refugees had prison records, though most crimes were political, and many of those confined in institutions were homosexuals, considered deviants in Cuba.) Valero in his spare time wrote poetry and essays, sometimes under the pseudonym Julio Real. He won a literary prize from the University of Miami for an article about an openly gay friend, fellow writer, and exile, entitled "The Homeless Humor of Reinaldo Arenas." Valero cofounded *Mariel* literary magazine, published from 1983 to 1986. He released his first poetry collection, *Desde un oscuro ángulo* (*From an Obscure Angle*) in 1982, and followed up with a second collection, *En fin, la noche* (*Finally, the Night*), in 1984 and a collection of poetic prose, *Dharma* (1985). He married Maria Badias, a painter and the translator of his poems into English, and the couple had two daughters.

Valero studied on a fellowship at Georgetown University, where he earned a doctoral degree. He then taught Spanish-American literature at George Washington University, and he released a novel, *This Lenten Wind*, and two additional poetry collections: *Venias* (1990; *You Were Coming*) and *No estare en tu camino* (1991; *I Will Not Stand in Your Way*). A popular speaker, he was in great demand to read his poems at venues throughout the United States, in Europe, and in Latin America. In 1994, he fell ill and, like other Cuban exiles, such as painters Carlos Alfonzo and Ernesto Briel and writers Reinaldo Arenas, Humberto Dionisio, and Luis Boza, Valero became a victim of acquired immunodeficiency syndrome (AIDS), at that time an incurable disease. Valero died from complications of AIDS at the age of thirty-nine.

Significance

Known primarily for writings that mercilessly excoriated the Cuban government, Roberto Valero also wrote nostalgically about his homeland and explored the human condition in his poetry. One of his best-known poems is an epic " . . . But No One Knows His Name," which examines the relationship between humanity and the deities. Other poems, like "Roberto," "Phone Call," "Exile," and "Islands Are Evil and Nobody Knows It," are more personal and ironically humorous. Valero, a Cintras Fellow, won the Letras de Oro Literary Prize in 1989. Well respected in the literary community, Valero during his short life left a body of writing that has been favorably compared to the work of poet Federico García Lorca.

Jack Ewing

Further Reading

Gracia, Jorge J. E., Lynette M. F. Bosch, and Isabel Alvarez Borland, eds. *Identity, Memory, and Diaspora: Voices of Cuban-American Artists, Writers, and Philosophers*. Albany: State University of New York Press, 2009. This collection of interviews with leading Cuban-American intellectuals and creatives touches on many of the issues, subjects, and themes common to the work of these exiles.

Greenhill, Kelly M. *Weapons of Mass Migration: Forced Displacement, Coercion, and Foreign Policy*. Ithaca, N.Y.: Cornell University Press, 2010. A well-researched study of the causes and effects of movements of large groups of people —like the Marielitos—from one place to another for political purposes.

Rieff, David. *The Exile: Cuba in the Heart of Miami*. New York: Touchstone, 2002. An examination of the impact of relocation, both on individual immigrants and on the community to which many Cubans were transplanted.

See also: Reinaldo Arenas; Lorna Dee Cervantes; Cristina García; Oscar Hijuelos; Eduardo Machado; Gary Soto.

RIMA DE VALLBONA

Costa Rican-born writer and scholar

Perhaps the best-known female fiction writer of Central American origin, Vallbona has written novels and short-story collections that speak uncompromisingly of the struggles of women in male-dominated realms. A scholar and professor, she has also produced studies on lesser-known and troubled Latin American female writers.

Latino heritage: Costa Rican
Born: March 15, 1931; San José, Costa Rica
Also known as: Rima Gretchen Rothe
Areas of achievement: Literature; scholarship

EARLY LIFE

Rima de Vallbona (REE-mah deh vahl-BOH-nah) was born Rima Gretchen Rothe in San José, Costa Rica, to Ferdinand Rothe and Emilia Strasburger, who were of German origin. She grew up in the suburb of Guadalupe, then a rural village of coffee farms, pastures, and adobe houses. Though her family belonged to the upper-middle class, Vallona attended the local school with the children of peasants and laborers. During World War II, her father died and her family came to taste poverty at first hand. Vallbona credits these experiences with her becoming aware of society's inequality and injustice, which infused her literary work with a sense of protest.

Vallbona received scholarships to study abroad, first at the Sorbonne, from which she earned her French teacher's diploma in 1953, and then at the University of Salamanca, from which she earned a diploma in Hispanic philology in 1954. Upon her return to Costa Rica, she taught French in high school and continued her studies at the University of Costa Rica. In 1956, she married Carlos Vallbona, with whom she had four children, and moved to the United States. While living in Texas and raising her young children, she managed to complete her master's degree in philosophy from the University of Costa Rica in 1962.

Adapting to life in the United States was difficult and frustrating, particularly because the Texas residency laws prohibited Vallbona from teaching for five years. In order to cope with isolation and the lack of a professional life, she began working on her first novel, *Noche en vela* (1968; *Night Wide Awake*), which introduced a common theme in her work: female characters disillusioned and unable to communicate with the world around them. After many years of teaching and writing, Vallbona went back to school to earn a Ph.D. in modern languages from Middlebury College in 1981, traveling to Vermont every summer for ten years to be able to complete her degree.

LIFE'S WORK

After writing *Noche en vela*, Vallbona launched a successful and steady literary career that has included the publication of two other novels, *Las sombras que perseguimos* (1983; *The Shadows We Chase After*) and *Mundo, demonio y mujer* (1991; *World, Demon, and Woman*), and nine short-story collections, all written in Spanish. Her stories and poems have also been published in numerous literary magazines and anthologies in Europe and throughout the Americas.

To English readers, Vallbona's best-known work is *Flowering Inferno: Tales of Sinking Hearts* (1994), a translation of her 1992 short story collection *Los infiernos de la mujer y algo más*. However, Vallbona's larger body or work has been widely read beyond the Spanish-speaking world, having been translated into English, French, Portuguese, and German. Literary critics have responded well to her narrative, helping to keep her work relevant for more than four decades. U.S. and Latin American scholars have published three volumes about Vallbona's fiction and several university theses have been written about her work.

Vallbona's books have received several honors, including the Costa Rican National Novel Prize (1968), the Jorge Luis Borges Short Story Award (Argentina, 1977), and the Southwest Conference of Latin American Studies Prize (United States, 1982). She was also named a member of the North American Academy of the Spanish Language in 1997.

Another important facet of Vallbona's career is her work as an educator and scholar. She was on the faculty of the University of St. Thomas in Houston from 1964 until her retirement in 1995, and in this position she organized the Spanish Department and served as its first chair. She also became the Cullen Foundation Professor of Spanish in 1989. During her tenure at St. Thomas, she produced six studies and anthologies of "silenced" women, including the seventeenth-century Spanish nun Catalina de Erauso and the talented but tormented Costa Rican writers Yolanda Oreamuno and Eunice Odio.

SIGNIFICANCE

By reflecting a deep feminist commitment and continuously exploring new levels of women's concerns, Rima de Vallbona's literary production and scholarly enterprises have been pioneering works among Latin American and Latina writers. Her narrative questions the roles and norms established for women by patriarchal societies, loudly voicing women's demands for freedom in the modern world. Some of her female characters break new ground as they replace traditional patriarchal myths with vibrant experiences and unique achievements in self-fulfillment. The impact of Vallbona's work as a committed artist and teacher has been recognized in the United States and throughout the Spanish-speaking world in multiple ways, including the bestowing of a civil merit award by King Juan Carlos I of Spain in 1988 for her efforts to spread Hispanic culture. Additionally, in 2011, California State University-Dominguez Hills dedicated its thirty-fourth International Literature Symposium to Vallbona's work.

Mauricio Espinoza-Quesada

FURTHER READING

Erro-Peralta, Nora, ed. *Beyond the Border: A New Age in Latin American Women's Fiction*. Gainsville: University Press of Florida, 2000. Inclusion of Vallbona's short story "The Secret World of Grandma Anacleta" in this volume is testament to her standing among contemporary Latin American women writers.

Jaramillo Levi, Enrique, ed. *When New Flowers Bloomed: Short Stories by Women Writers from Costa Rica and Panama*. Pittsburgh, Pa.: Latin American Literary Review Press, 1991. Includes Vallbona's short stories "The Good Guys" and "The Wall" and aptly places her work in the context of Central American literary production.

Vallbona, Rima de. *Flowering Inferno: Tales of Sinking Hearts*. Pittsburgh, Pa.: Latin American Literary Review Press, 1994. This is the best resource for English readers to delve into Vallbona's narrative and to read her celebrated short stories dealing with the suffering and resistance of women.

See also: Rudolfo Anaya; Lourdes Casal; Rosario Ferré; Arturo Islas; José Montoya; Mary Helen Ponce; Tomás Rivera; Bernice Zamora.

PEDRO DEL VALLE

Puerto Rican-born military leader

The first Latino to reach the rank of major general in the Marine Corps, Valle served in World War I and then in the occupations of Haiti and Nicaragua. During World War II, he was the commanding general of the First Marine Division during the battles of Guadalcanal, Guam, and Okinawa. Following the war, he became a leader of the anticommunist movement.

Latino heritage: Puerto Rican

Born: August 28, 1893; San Juan, Puerto Rico

Died: April 28, 1978; Annapolis, Maryland

Also known as: Pedro Augusto Jose del Valle Barcay Muñoz

Areas of achievement: Military; activism

EARLY LIFE

Born Pedro Augusto Jose del Valle Barcay Muñoz in Puerto Rico when the island was still a Spanish possession, Pedro del Valle (PEH-droh dehl VAH-yeh) was the son of Francisco del Valle, a physician and former mayor of San Juan. In 1900, two years after Puerto Rico was annexed by the United States, the family moved to Maryland, and soon thereafter Pedro del Valle became a U.S. citizen. He attended public schools in Baltimore and completed his high school education at the Mercersburg Academy in Pennsylvania. In 1910, he obtained an appointment by the Puerto Rican governor to attend the U.S. Naval Academy in Annapolis, Maryland. After graduating from the academy in 1915, he was commissioned as second lieutenant of the Marine Corps.

LIFE'S WORK

In 1916, the twenty-three-year-old Valle participated in the U.S. occupation of Santo Domingo, for which he was awarded the Legion of Merit. During World War I, he commanded the Marine detachment on the U.S.S. *Texas* in the North Atlantic, and he was present at the surrender of the German High Seas Fleet. During the 1920's, he was stationed in Haiti, and he then participated in the guerrilla wars against Augusto Sandino in Nicaragua. Returning to the United States in 1929, he attended the Field Officers Court at the Marine Corps School in Virginia. In 1931, he helped the Marines to develop strategies for an amphibious assault, and the next year his essay, "Ship-to-Shore in Amphibious Operations," appeared in the *Marine Corps Gazette*.

In 1933, following the Cuban Sergeants' Revolt, Valle worked as an intelligence officer in Havana, Cuba. From 1935 to 1937, he served as the assistant naval attaché at the U.S. Embassy in Rome. After accompanying Italian forces as U.S. observer of the Italian-Ethiopian War of 1936-1937, he published a comprehensive history of the conflict, *Roman Eagle over Ethiopia* (1940). He was then sent to attend the Army War College in Washington, D.C., and, following graduation, he was appointed executive officer of the Division of Plans and Policies of the Marine Corps. In March, 1941, he was named commanding officer of the Eleventh Marine Artillery Regiment.

Several months after the United States entered World War II, Valle's regiment was dispatched to participate in the defense of Guadalcanal, where it played a major role in the bloody Battle of Tenaru. Valle was awarded the Legion of Merit for his leadership in the battle, and on October 1, 1942, he was promoted to the rank of brigadier general. During 1943, he served as the commander of Marine Forces overseeing Guadalcanal and other islands in the Solomon Archipelago. During the summer of 1944, he commanded the Third Artillery of the Third Amphibious Corps in the battle for Guam. He then served as the commanding general of the First Marine Division during the last major battle of the war, Okinawa, where he directed the capture of the strategically important Shuri Castle. He was awarded a Distinguished Service Medal for his part in the military victory and subsequent occupation of Okinawa. Following the restoration of peace, Valle returned to the Marine headquarters, where he held the position of inspector general director of personnel until his retirement on January 1, 1948.

Entering civilian life, Valle accepted a position as vice president of International Telephone and Telegraph (ITT) in Egypt, and later served for two years as the company's chief executive officer for all of South America. Always a man of conservative values, he increasingly established close relations to a variety of conservative political and religious groups. Agreeing with Senator Joseph McCarthy's fears of communist subversion, Valle tried to convince the Central Intelligence Agency to create a network of vigilante minutemen, but his suggestions were ignored. He also expressed strong anti-Semitic views, even accepting the authenticity of *The Protocols of the Elders of Zion* (which is almost universally discredited as a fake), and he opposed U.S.

participation in the United Nations. In 1951, he left ITT in order to work for conservative causes.

In 1953, Valle joined with other committed anticommunists to form the Defenders of the American Constitution (DAC), an educational organization that produced a regular paper, *Task Force*. In addition, in 1953, he entered Maryland's Republican primary for governor, but he received few votes, in part because of his association with persons considered to be right-wing extremists. In addition to his work with the DAC, he supported other conservative organizations, including the Christian Crusade, the Committee to Restore the Constitution, and the Liberty Lobby. For many years he was a popular speaker among conservative and patriotic groups throughout the country. Following his death at the age of eighty-four in 1978, he was buried at the United States Naval Academy Cemetery and Columbarium. A collection of his speeches, writings, and correspondence is located at the University of Oregon in Eugene.

SIGNIFICANCE

An outstanding commander who was the first Latino to become a major general, Valle was a role model who helped to break down negative stereotypes of Latinos in the military. Although his extremely conservative ideology and particularly his anti-Semitism have been widely rejected for good reasons, it should be noted that many people found his fears of communist infiltration to be reasonable during the height of the Cold War. Even many of his critics, moreover, can appreciate his dedication to the values of patriotism, responsibility, and hard work. The study of Valle demonstrates the great diversity that is found among persons of Latino heritage.

Thomas Tandy Lewis

FURTHER READING

Bemis, Frank M., and Pedro del Valle. *Reminiscences of Pedro Augusto del Valle*. New York: Columbia University Library, 1966. An oral history interview that discusses Valle's military career and efforts to promote Christianity and anticommunism.

Bendersky, Joseph W. *Jewish Threat: Anti-Semitic Politics of the U.S. Army*. New York: Basic Books, 2001. Includes material relating to Valle's ideas about a Jewish oligarchy that controlled the United States for half a century.

Leckie, Robert. *Okinawa: The Last Battle of World War II*. New York: Penguin, 2010. Includes information about Valle's role in the brutal event.

Mintz, Frank. *The Liberty League and the American Far Right: Race, Conspiracy, and Culture.* Westport, Conn.: Greenwood, 1985. A useful account of the right-wing movements in which Valle played an important part.

Valle, Pedro A. del. *Semper Fidelis: An Autobiography.* Hawthorne, Calif.: Christian Book Club of America,

1976. Fascinating discussion of Valle's military career and participation in the anticommunist movement.

See also: Roy Benavidez; Luis R. Esteves; Horacio Rivero, Jr.

LETICIA VAN DE PUTTE

American politician

Van de Putte began serving in the Texas legislature in 1991. She has chaired the Texas senate Democratic Caucus, a position in which she gained national attention when senate Democrats left the state in 2003 in order to delay a vote on congressional redistricting.

Latino heritage: Mexican

Born: December 6, 1954; Tacoma, Washington

Also known as: Leticia Rosa San Miguel Van de Putte; Leticia Rosa Magdalena Aguilar San Miguel

Area of achievement: Government and politics

EARLY LIFE

Leticia Rosa San Miguel Van de Putte, better known as Leticia Van de Putte (leh-TISH-ah van deh put-TEH), was born in Tacoma, Washington, to Isabelle "Belle" and Daniel San Miguel, Jr. At the time she was born, Van de Putte's father was serving in the U.S. Army and stationed at Fort Lewis, Washington. When she was three months old, her parents relocated to San Antonio, Texas. Van de Putte attended the local public schools, graduating from Thomas Jefferson High School in 1973.

While Van de Putte was growing up, her mother, Belle, attended college to earn a degree in education. A music teacher at San Antonio schools, Belle was the primary breadwinner in the family. The San Miguel family lived in close proximity to members of their extended families and Van de Putte spent much time playing with her cousins. She also joined the Girl Scouts because it was one of the few youth organizations in San Antonio that accepted blacks, Hispanics, and Jews. She tried dance, was active in neighborhood sports activities because there were not many school athletic activities for girls, and took piano lessons. In school, Van de Putte served on the student council. Her parents divorced when she was a senior in high school, and her mother married Juan Ortiz in 1982.

Van de Putte enrolled in St. Mary's University in San Antonio in 1973. She majored in science with the goal of becoming a pharmacist like her grandfather. In 1974, at the urging of her friends, she entered the Miss Fiesta Pageant sponsored by the city of San Antonio. She was named alternate first runner-up but ended up carrying out the duties of Miss Fiesta because the winner could not. She represented San Antonio at festivals around the state. A year and half after beginning her studies at St. Mary's, Van de Putte transferred to the University of Houston to attend pharmacy school. She married Pete Van de Putte, a San Antonio high school

Leticia Van de Putte. (AP Photo)

music teacher, in October, 1977. She entered the College of Pharmacy at the University of Texas at Austin in the fall of 1978 and graduated in the spring of 1979.

LIFE'S WORK

Following graduation, Van de Putte went to work as a pharmacist consultant for T. L. Vorden Baumen and Associates in San Antonio. She then served a clinical rotation at San Antonio's State Hospital from 1980 to 1982. For the next two years she worked at her grandfather's pharmacy. While working as a pharmacist she learned about people, the needs of her community, and the community's problems. After complaining about a public urination problem in the area around the pharmacy, San Antonio mayor Henry G. Cisneros appointed her to Centro 21, an advisory board created to revitalize downtown. When Van de Putte saw a problem in her community, she complained and was placed on a board or commission to help find solutions.

By 1987, she owned the Loma Park Pharmacy on Culebra Street, a predominanty Latino area on San Antonio's west side. As her business and family grew, she became more involved in politics and community affairs. In 1990, the Democratic nominee for state representative from her district was appointed to a seat on the state Court of Appeals. Since the seat became vacant after the primary election, it was up to the Democratic Party to find a replacement to run in the general election in November. After talking with several of the candidates and finding that they did not address the issues she found important, Van de Putte's husband suggested that she run for the seat. Out of a large field of candidates, she was nominated by the Democratic Party precinct chairs in the district. She was elected easily and took office in the state's seventy-second legislature in January, 1991.

While in the Texas House of Representatives, Van de Putte served on the Committee on Human Services. Her career as a pharmacist raised questions about a conflict of interest because this committee oversaw legislation regulating drug vendor contracts for the state agency that managed Medicaid. Even though the federal government found that she did not have a conflict of interest, Van de Putte sold the pharmacy in 1994.

At the end of her first term in the House, Van de Putte was presented with the opportunity to run for an open seat in the Texas senate. Health issues convinced her not to run for the senate in 1992. In 1999, the senate seat became vacant and a special election was scheduled for November. Endorsed by the *San An-*

tonio Express News, Van de Putte was elected to fill the remainder of the term. She had to run for reelection in 2000, and she was reelected in that year, as well as in 2002 and 2006.

Van de Putte has served as the chair of the senate Democratic Caucus. In 2003, she led senate Democrats on a trip to New Mexico to break a quorum and delay a vote on a mid-decade redistricting plan. From 2007 to 2009, she served as president of the National Council of State Legislatures, the first Texan and the first Hispanic woman to lead the organization. She considered running for governor in 2010, but in June, 2009, Van de Putte decided to run for reelection to the Texas senate.

SIGNIFICANCE

As a Texas legislator, Van de Putte has worked to represent her constituents, as well as advocate for the needs of children, veterans, and senior citizens. She has authored legislation on quality educational opportunities and quality health care. Her bills have also reformed the welfare system in Texas and provided insurance for children. Her work has been recognized by her many awards for being an effective, hardworking, and influential Texas legislator.

John David Rausch, Jr.

FURTHER READING

Bickerstaff, Steve. *Lines in the Sand: Congressional Redistricting in Texas and the Downfall of Tom DeLay*. Austin: University of Texas Press, 2007. A detailed account of the mid-decade redistricting fight in Texas in 2003. The story includes the actions of senate Democrats led by Van de Putte.

Hart, Patricia Kilday. "Session Player." *Texas Monthly* 29, no. 7 (July, 2001): 89, 134-136. A diary of Van de Putte's reflections on her first term in the Texas senate, documenting the challenges she faced as a wife, mother, and Latina legislator.

_____. "The Unkindest Cut." *Texas Monthly* 31, no. 10 (October, 2003): 44-52. Recounts the mid-decade congressional redistricting process in Texas that led the Democratic members of the Texas senate to leave the state in order to break a quorum and delay consideration of the issue.

Navarro, Sharon A. *Latina Legislator: Leticia Van de Putte and the Road to Leadership*. College Station: Texas A&M University Press, 2008. Detailed biography of Van de Putte, cast as a case study of a female Latino legislator. Includes references to political science research on women in politics and the political activities of minority communities in the United States.

See also: Joe J. Bernal; Joaquín Castro; Julián Castro; Irma Rangel.

ERASMO VANDO

Puerto Rican-born playwright, journalist, and activist

Vando was a founder of Spanish-language theater in New York City, a journalist for newspapers in New York and Puerto Rico, a poet, a founder and president of the Association of Puerto Rican Writers and Journalists, and a founder of the political party Movimiento Pro Independencia (MPI).

Latino heritage: Puerto Rican

Born: June 2, 1896; Ponce, Puerto Rico

Died: October 31, 1988; Santurce, Puerto Rico

Also known as: Erasmo Vando Rodriguez; Vando; Erasmo del Vando

Areas of achievement: Theater; journalism; activism

EARLY LIFE

Erasmo Vando Rodriguez (eh-RAHS-moh VAHN-doh) was born in Ponce, Puerto Rico, on June 2, 1896, to Erasmo Vando Hurtado and Alberta Rodriguez. He was the youngest of nine children.

In 1898, during the Spanish-American War, the United States invaded Ponce. Vando's first memory was of his ailing father wielding a sword to protect his family against American soldiers who had invaded his home. This traumatic incident helped inform his political views, and at an early age he became a fervent proponent of Puerto Rican independence.

When Vando was six years old, his mother was hospitalized and he was sent to live with his maternal aunt and her husband, Alfredo Garnier, who worked as a barber for the army. The family accompanied him from base to base, necessitating Vando's enrollment in various schools. He refused to pledge allegiance to the American flag during school assemblies and in 1912 was expelled from the Central High School of Santurce. Nonetheless, he received his high school diploma.

In his early twenties, Vando opened a grocery store and a restaurant. When both failed to produce an income, he joined a brigade of Puerto Rican workers heading to Fort Jackson, South Carolina. Upon arrival, they were segregated by race. Vando, outraged, organized a protest and wrote a letter to President Woodrow Wilson demanding change. The end of World War I eleven days later, terminated their contract, leaving the matter of segregation to be resolved decades later.

LIFE'S WORK

Arriving in New York City in 1919, Vando encountered unemployment and misery. He wrote an open letter to Luis Muñoz Marín, president of the Puerto Rican Senate, lamenting the plight of the forgotten Puerto Ricans abroad. He eventually found work at the Henry Heide Candy Company, where he remained for twenty-three years, enhancing the company's flavor base with tropical fruits. This gainful employment straddled the Depression, and he was able to help his less-fortunate compatriots. One popular anecdote has him giving his overcoat to a friend in need and never wearing one again.

Vando became a founder of Spanish-language theater in New York City, contributing as a director, playwright, and actor. He directed the Compañia Teatrál Puertorriqueña and in 1929 produced poet and dramatist Gonzalo O'Neill's *Bajo una sola bandera*, a play that advocated the independence of Puerto Rico and helped unite the dissident sociopolitical factions of the Puerto Rican community. In producing plays by writers such as Luis Lloréns Torres and Manuel Méndez Ballester, he was instrumental in the establishment of a Puerto Rican national theater. His own plays included *De Puerto Rico al metropolitan o el Caruso Criollo* (1928), in the *teatro bufo* tradition (a form of Cuban comic theater), and the undated works *Madre Mía*, *El Mago,* and *Chateau Margaux*. Some plays were staged as fund-raisers to benefit the various political clubs.

While in New York, Vando married three times: to Mercedes García; then to Vieques-born Anita Vélez Rieckehoff, with whom he had a daughter; and finally to Emelí Vélez Soto, with whom he had three children.

Vando was a small man with a booming voice that served him well on the stage as well as on the soapbox. A persuasive public speaker, he was able to rally huge crowds. As a founder and president of the Juventud Nacionalista Puertorriqueña (Puerto Rican Nationalist

Youth), he organized marches, protests, and rallies throughout the city. He helped found the Association for the Independence of Puerto Rico; was president of the Puerto Rican Brotherhood of America, which in 1929 claimed more than 6,000 members; and was active in other clubs, including the Committee for Puerto Rican Political Prisoners, the Spanish Workers Center, Chilean Workers Club, and the Cuban Club. In addition, he was a founder of the Association of Puerto Rican Writers and Journalists. His columns appeared in *La Voz*, *Gráfico*, and other Spanish-language newspapers in the city.

In 1945, Vando and Emelí returned to Ponce, where he worked as a journalist for *El Día*, a local paper, and *El Mundo*, the largest national paper. They joined the Partido Independentista Puertorriqueño (Puerto Rican Independence Party, or PIP), on whose behalf Vando wrote and broadcasted radio shows. Despite various leadership roles within the party, he left it in 1959 to help found the Movimiento Pro Independencia (MPI), which became the Puerto Rican Socialist Party (PSP) in 1971. Through his involvement in the PSP, he became a delegate to the United Nations Decolonization Committee. Because of his political activities, Vando was kept under surveillance for forty-five years by the Bureau of Special Investigations of the Department of Justice of Puerto Rico.

Vando continued to write plays: *Amor en el batey: Melodrama de costumbres Puertorriquenas*, was produced in Ponce in 1950. He also appeared in the first Puerto Rican film, *Tres vidas en el recuerdo* (1957). Writing poetry remained a lifelong activity. Many of his poems were published in periodicals and newspapers under the pen name Dovan Amores, an anagram of his name. His book of poems, *Amores*, was published posthumously in 1996. Vando died on October 31, 1988, at the age of ninety-two.

SIGNIFICANCE

Vando was an advocate for Puerto Ricans in New York City during the first half of the twentieth century. Through his work as an activist, playwright, director, producer, actor, journalist, and poet, he made significant contributions to the cultural, social, and political life of the Puerto Rican diaspora. He was a founder of Spanish-language theater in New York City, a founder of several political parties that championed the cause of Puerto Rican independence, and he chronicled the struggles of his people and the plight of his homeland in his plays, newspaper columns, and poetry.

Gloria Vando

FURTHER READING

Bates, Juandrea. "'In Fraternity We Will Once Again Be Men': Remaking Puerto Rican Migrant Masculinity in Early Twentieth Century New York." Austin: University of Texas, 2008. Quoting Vando in the title, the author explores the interactions of masculinity, poverty, racism, and socialism.

Kanellos, Nicolás. *A History of Hispanic Theatre in the United States: Origins to 1940*. Austin: University of Texas,1990. An in-depth history of Spanish-language theater from the mid-nineteenth century to the onset of World War II.

Vando, Erasmo. Erasmo Vando Papers. Archives of the Puerto Rican Diaspora, Centro de Estudios Puertorriqueños, Hunter College, City University of New York. Vando's archives (letters, writings, flyers, programs, photographs, and publications) are a vital resource for an understanding of the Puerto Rican community in New York from 1919-1945.

See also: Pedro Albizu Campos; Rubén Berríos; Lydia Cabrera; Victor Hernández Cruz; José de Diego; Lolita Lebrón; Luis Muñoz Marín; Lola Rodríguez de Tió.

TIBURCIO VÁSQUEZ

American outlaw and folk hero

Vásquez is one of the most famous Latino bandits in the United States. Many myths surround his life, several portraying him as a folk hero. His criminal career lasted for more than twenty years. Vásquez claimed he was trying to drive "invading Americans" out of California, so Mexico could reclaim it.

Latino heritage: Mexican
Born: August 11, 1835; Monterey, California
Died: March 19, 1875; San Jose, California
Area of achievement: Crime

EARLY LIFE

Tiburcio Vásquez (tee-BUR-see-oh VAHS-kehz) is one of the most well-known Latino outlaws and folk heroes. It is impossible to separate the myths from the facts about his life; many sources give conflicting information. He was born in Monterey California, but his birth date is unclear; later in life, while he was in prison, Vasquez told a reporter from the *Los Angeles Star* his birth year was 1835 and he told a reporter from the *Los Angeles Herald* it was 1837. His tombstone lists only a year, 1835. Vásquez's parents, José Hermenegildo Vásquez and Maria Guadalupe Cantua, had five other children—three sons and two daughters. Vásquez's father owned a small area of land and worked as a farmer. Vásquez's great-grandfather is believed to have been part of the 1776 Juan Bautista de Anza expedition, which was the first European attempt to establish an overland route from Mexico to California's Pacific coast. Vásquez attended school, spoke English and Spanish, and could read and write proficiently. His criminal career began as a teenager in 1854 (some sources say 1852 or 1853). Vásquez was at a dance when a fight broke out between several Latino, American, and Irish men. Constable William Hardmount was shot and killed trying to break up the fight. Vásquez fled with Anastacio Garcia, a dangerous bandit. Garcia taught Vásquez how to be an outlaw and bandit. Vásquez often explained his crimes as his effort to reclaim California from the invading Caucasian Americans, who began to arrive after the discovery of gold in 1848.

LIFE'S WORK

Vásquez began his life of crime as a robber and horse thief. He was arrested the first time in 1857 and sentenced to five years in San Quentin prison. Vásquez escaped during a breakout in June, 1859, but he was recaptured the following month, after being caught stealing horses. The escape added an another year to Vásquez's sentence, and he was released in 1863. Vásquez was suspected in the murder of a butcher in 1864, but there was insufficient evidence for an arrest. Following a robbery a few years later, Vásquez was back in prison. After his release in 1870, he was wounded in at least two separate gunfights; one with a friend whose wife Vásquez was having an affair with and the other with a sheriff. Vásquez routinely recruited new members for his gang, and in 1871 he met Abdon Leiva. It was not until 1873 that Vásquez became known throughout California and the rest of the country. In August, 1873, Vásquez and his gang robbed a store in Tres Pinos. They stole more

than two thousand dollars and eleven horses. In the process of the crime, three bystanders were shot and killed. The gang robbed a store near Millerton in November, and the entire town of Kingston in December. By February, 1874, the reward for capturing Vásquez alive was eight thousand dollars. He was captured May 15, 1874, after a tip led sheriffs to the ranch where he was hiding. Vásquez was put on trial the following January, for the murders during the Tres Pinos robbery. Several reporters interviewed Vásquez, during which he claimed never to have killed anyone. While he never married, Vásquez did admit having a year-old child with Rosaria Leiva, the wife of a gang member. Vásquez had a reputation for being a womanizer, reportedly seducing and impregnating his own niece. Hundreds flocked to the jail to catch a glimpse of the bandit each day. The jury convicted him in two hours, sentencing Vásquez to death by hanging. Vásquez was executed in San Jose March 19, 1875, in front of a large paying audience.

SIGNIFICANCE

Vásquez is remembered as both a hero to Mexican Americans and a murdering outlaw. He is described as being average looking, five foot seven inches tall, and uncommon enough to blend into a crowd. Despite this, Vásquez was a notorious womanizer, even having affairs with wives of his friends. A rock formation in Los Angeles County has been renamed Vásquez Rocks because the bandit used them as a hideout in the months before his last capture. The park is located only forty miles north of Los Angeles and has been used in several films and television shows. Vásquez Canyon, created by a tributary of Big Tujunga Creek, is another of the bandit's favorite hideouts that has been renamed in his honor.

Jennifer L. Campbell

FURTHER READING

Boessenecker, John. *Bandido: The Life and Times of Tiburcio Vásquez*. Norman: University of Oklahoma Press, 2010. A biography of Vásquez, exploring why he became a bandit, why the Hispanic community protected him, and whether he was a cold-blooded murderer or a Robin Hood figure. Boessenecker attempts to undercover the real story of Vásquez, hidden beneath decades of myths and legends. Well researched, scholarly, yet suitable for the general reader.

Crongeyer, Sven. *Six Gun Sound*. Fresno, Calif.: Linden, 2006. The early history of the Los Angeles County sheriff's department. Includes a chapter detailing Vásquez's various arrests, prison sentences, escapes, trial, and eventual hanging. Written by a deputy sheriff, well researched, and suitable for the general readers.

MacLean, Angus. *California Banditos.* Sanger, Calif.: Word Dancer Press, 2004. This reprint from 1977 is a collection of legends about Vásquez, told as entertaining narratives. Also includes the author's attempts to distinguish the truth behind the myths.

Secrest, William. *California Desperadoes.* Sanger, Calif.: Word Dancer Press, 2000. Thoroughly researched, based on newspaper accounts, courthouse records, and other historic documents. The chapter on Vásquez includes personal letters and the transcript of an interview between the bandit and a reporter in 1874. Firsthand accounts of the bandit from law enforcement and others who knew him are also included.

See also: Gregorio Cortez; Juan Cortina; Joaquín Murieta.

JACI VELASQUEZ

American singer

Velasquez is a contemporary Christian pop singer and actor. Her music has earned her several awards and number-one hits.

Latino heritage: Mexican
Born: October 15, 1979; Houston, Texas
Also known as: Jaquelyn Davette Velasquez
Areas of achievement: Music

EARLY LIFE

Jaci Velasquez (veh-LAHS-kehz) was born Jaquelyn Davette Velasquez on October 15, 1979, in Houston, Texas, to David and Diana Velasquez; Jaci Velasquez is the youngest of five children. Her father had been a member of the Southern gospel group the Four Galileans and the Latino gospel group the Amigos. In 1988, Velasquez and her parents toured the Southwest as the Velasquez Family, and Velasquez, then nine years old, was featured in the song "The Master of the Wind." Because of their touring schedule, her mother homeschooled Velasquez starting in the fourth grade. By the time she was thirteen, Velasquez was doing her own concerts. She performed at the White House in 1992, but her big break came a year later during a performance at Houston's First Baptist Church. A representative of Myrrh Records heard her perform, and Velasquez was offered her first recording contract.

LIFE'S WORK

Velasquez released her first album, *A Heavenly Place*, in 1996. The certified-gold album was a creative collaboration between Velasquez and some of the top songwriters, studio musicians, and producers in the Christian music industry. The musical style of the songs was more adult contemporary than teen-oriented pop and only lightly tinged with Latin influences. One song on the album cowritten by Velasquez was the ode to virginity, "I Promise." The song drew the attention of the True Love Waits campaign, a national organization dedicated to promoting chastity before marriage, which approached

Jaci Velasquez. (Getty Images)

her about becoming a spokesperson. The album earned her the 1997 Gospel Music Association (GMA) Dove Award for New Artist of the Year, the same award her father had won as a member of the Four Galileans in 1970. "On My Knees" won the Dove for Song of the Year in 1998. She also released a book of inspirational and devotional readings cowritten with Thom Granger also titled *A Heavenly Place* (1998).

Her follow-up album, *Jaci Velasquez*, made clear to audiences that rather than the next Latina teen pop sensation, Velasquez, now eighteen, was being marketed to her non-Hispanic peers' parents. One critic suggested that the album producers were having her try on different costumes to see what the audience likes best. Even though this album was not a critical favorite, it impressed Dove voters enough to earn Velasquez the Female Vocalist of the Year award.

In 1999, Velasquez stepped outside the Christian music industry and released *Llegar a Ti* on a mainstream label. The album contained six Spanish versions of songs from previous albums and five new songs that were less overtly Christian. The album's title track became the first song by a self-described Christian artist to reach number one on *Billboard*'s Hot Latin Tracks chart. It also won a Dove Award for Best Spanish Language Album in 2000. She followed this success with another Spanish language release, *Mi Corazon*, in 2001. This album also produced a number-one single with "Como Se Cura Una Herida."

Although Velasquez admitted she had no deep roots in Hispanic culture, being three generations removed from her father's Mexican ancestors and raised in accordance with mainstream American culture, Velasquez spent a year engaging Hispanic audiences in the American Southwest, Mexico, Puerto Rico, and the Dominican Republic. Her main message was about sexual purity for teenage girls, saying that they could still be pretty and talented without dressing provocatively and being sexually active, an attitude she believed ran counter to the message of most Latin pop artists.

Between the two Latin projects, Velasquez released *Crystal Clear* (2000), another collection of adult contemporary, inspirational songs for Myrrh. The album includes two songs with a strong Latin influence, reminiscent of those of Gloria Estefan.

In 2003, Velasquez released the album *Unspoken*, which showed a slightly different side of the singer.

She was more involved in the songwriting, so the songs come across as more personal. The music is less adult contemporary and more youthful, rhythm and blues-influenced pop. She also made her film debut in *Chasing Papi*, playing a spoiled heiress who is one of three women involved with the same man. She also married Darren Potuck in August, 2003. The couple divorced in 2005.

Beauty Has Grace, Velasquez's fifth English-language album (including a Christmas album released in 2001), was released in 2005, with more than half of the tracks being penned by her. It was the result of a bold stylistic shift, from adult contemporary Latin pop to an alternative-sounding Brit pop in the vein of Coldplay. In 2006, she married Nic Gonzales of the band Salvado,and they had two sons.

In 2008, Velasquez was chosen as one of the Fifteen Prominent Hispanic-Americans in the Arts in America by the U.S. State Department's Bureau of International Information Programs. She also released her sixth English-language album, *Love Out Loud*, that year. *Love Out Loud* represented a return to the sonic style of her first albums.

SIGNIFICANCE

Velasquez is one of the few significant Latinas in the Christian music industry. Although she confesses to having little connection with her Hispanic roots, her mission at the beginning of her career was to be a role model to young Hispanic girls. Her seven English albums have produced sixteen number-one hits, six additional Top Ten hits, and earned her seven Dove Awards.

Eric S. Strother

FURTHER READING

"My Mom Is Such a Strong Woman . . . and She's Beautiful." *Hispanic* 14, no. 5 (2001): 24. Interview with Velasquez.

Velasquez, Jaci, and Thom Granger. *A Heavenly Place*. Whitby, Ont.: Fireside, 1998. Inspirational readings with some personal stories.

Warren, Linda. *CCM Life Lines: Jaci Velasquez*. Eugene, Oreg.: Harvest House, 2000. Biography, mostly culled from magazine interviews.

See also: Mariah Carey; Sheila E.; Gloria Estefan; Linda Ronstadt.

LORETA JANETA VELÁZQUEZ

Cuban-born soldier

After the outbreak of the American Civil War, Velázquez disguised herself as a man and joined the Confederate army. She fought in several battles, only being discovered as a woman after she was injured. She also worked as a spy for the Confederacy, infiltrating the U.S. Secret Service.

Latino heritage: Cuban and Spanish
Born: June 26 1842; Havana, Cuba
Died: 1897; Unknown
Also known as: Lieutenant Harry Buford
Area of achievement: Military

EARLY LIFE

The majority of information known about Loreta Janeta Velázquez (loh-REH-tah jah-NEH-tah veh-LAHS-kehz) comes from her autobiography, *The Woman in Battle,* published in 1876. She was born in Havana, Cuba, on June 26, 1842. Her father was a Spanish government official and her mother was French American. Velázquez had three older brothers and two older sisters. In 1844, the family moved from Cuba to Mexico (to an area that is now part of Texas), where her father owned plantations. Her father fought for Mexico in the Mexican-American War and became very bitter toward Americans.

After the war, the family moved back to Cuba. In her memoirs, Velázquez recalls that she always wanted to be a man when she was a child; she idolized Joan of Arc. Velázquez was educated by an English governess until 1849, when she was sent to Catholic school in New Orleans. While there, she lived with an aunt, who spent two years teaching her to read, write, and speak English. Velázquez had an arranged engagement to a Spanish man named Raphael. However, she felt trapped and did not love him. Instead, she fell in love with William, the boyfriend of her schoolmate, and eloped with him. They were married April 5, 1856, when Velázquez was just fourteen years old. She returned to her aunt's home and kept the marriage a secret until the following October. She had her first child in 1857 before following her husband westward. By 1860, they had three children and were living in St. Louis. The third baby died shortly after birth; the two older children died later that year of fever.

LIFE'S WORK

Political, economic, and social tensions within the United States had been rapidly growing in the years before the 1860 election. The election of Abraham Lincoln as president led to the secession of a number of Southern states, which formed the Confederate States of America. Velázquez's husband, William, was from Texas, so he resigned from the U.S. Army after Texas's secession on February 1, 1861, to join the Confederate army. William was sent to Richmond shortly after the couple's fifth wedding anniversary.

Velázquez had a Memphis tailor make her two Confederate uniforms, adding extra padding inside the coat to conceal her shape. Upon reaching New Orleans, Velázquez needed a disguise that was more comfortable. She got a French tailor to make six wire-net shields to disguise her body. She also used a false mustache and beard to disguise herself as Lieutenant Harry Buford. Velázquez then traveled to Arkansas and recruited 236 men for a regiment. She claims to have delivered the regiment to her husband in Florida for him to command. William was killed a few days later in a training accident.

Failing to purchase a commission into the army, Velázquez fought as an independent officer, which she

Loreta Janeta Velázquez. (© Bettmann/Corbis)

Women Who Fought as Men in the U.S. Civil War

During a time before equal rights for the sexes, military jobs were restricted to men. Women who wanted to aid the war effort joined Sanitary Commissions, aid groups, or became nurses. However, for some women, being confined to a hospital was not enough. These women, like Loreta Janeta Velázquez, became spies or disguised themselves as men in order to enlist in the armed forces. It is unclear from the war records how many women fought in the war; estimates range from hundreds to thousands. Most of them were from the poorer classes, in their late teens or early twenties, and first-generation Americans or immigrants themselves. Sarah Rosetta Wakeman and Jennie Hodgers enlisted for the money, in order to feed their families. Many others, like Malinda Blalock and Frances Clayton, followed their husbands and boyfriends to war. The death of husbands and loved ones also led some women, such as Charlotte Hope, to enlist, hoping to avenge the deaths. Some of the women, like their male counterparts, joined for the sole purpose of adventure. Ones like Velázquez enlisted because of a strong sense of patriotic duty, which sometimes included the belief of being the second Joan of Arc. A number of women were discovered while trying to enlist, others when they were wounded or became ill, and some not until their death. After being detected, the women were arrested, sent home, or forced to work as nurses. If discovered after being captured, they often were the first prisoners exchanged or sent back across the lines wearing dresses.

felt gave her more freedom. She was wounded during the First Battle of Bull Run (Manassas, Virginia) on July 21, 1861, the first major battle of the war. Her injuries were not severe, and she refused medical attention out of fear of being discovered. After the battle, Velázquez went to Washington, D.C., dressed as a woman, to become a spy. She even claimed to have met Lincoln. Velázquez returned to the army as Lieutenant Buford whenever she grew tired of dressing as a woman. In her memoirs, she brags about the attention she received from other women while disguised as Buford. During the Battle of Shiloh, Velázquez claims to have fought valiantly as Buford and spied as a woman at night. She claims to have gotten close enough to Ulysses Grant that she could have killed him but felt it would have been murder. While helping bury the dead, she was wounded by a shell and discovered to be a woman by the army doctor.

Giving up on her army career, Velázquez obtained a British passport and allegedly became a drug smuggler and blockade runner. She then says that the Confederate government hired her to infiltrate the Union's Secret Service as a double agent. According to Velázquez, she was hired by the Secret Service and assigned to discover a Confederate spy—herself. This position allowed her to travel freely throughout the Union. While doing so, Velázquez attempted to organize a rebellion among Confederate prisoners of war. In the last months of the war, she traveled to Ohio, Canada, London, and Paris, arriving in New York City the day after General Robert E. Lee's surrender in April 1865.

After the war, Velázquez traveled through Europe and the former Confederacy. She married her third husband and moved to Venezuela but returned shortly after his death. It was in Texas that she wrote and published her memoirs in 1876. Velázquez wrote the book in order to earn enough money to support herself and her son. The book drew heavy criticism and skepticism; among the most vehement of its critics was Confederate General Jubal Early. Despite having lost her notes, Velázquez's tome is more than six hundred pages long and includes details about the weather and specific conversations. There also is no record of a Harry Buford serving in the Confederate army. Some historians believe that she used the alias Alice Williams, who was reported to have fought as Lieutenant Henry Beford or Bensford. Others claim that Velázquez heard the stories of Williams and passed them off as her own. The book cannot be proven or disproven but appears to be at least a highly fictionalized version of the truth. Velázquez is believed to have died in 1897, but little is known about her outside of her memoirs.

SIGNIFICANCE

Velázquez saw the American Civil War as her chance to live out her dream of being a man and fighting for a cause like her hero, Joan of Arc. Her defiance of the gender norms of her era allowed her to experience a very different life, one filled with excitement and adventure. Her memoirs have made her one of the most well-known women who fought and spied for the Confederacy and one of the most famous Cuban Americans to do so as well.

Jennifer L. Campbell

FURTHER READING

Hall, Richard. *Women on the Civil War Battlefront.* Lawrence: University Press of Kansas, 2006. A well-researched work written by a pioneer in the field that discusses the various roles women played during the Civil War: as soldiers, spies, nurses, scouts, and smugglers.

Velázquez, Loreta Janeta. *The Woman in Battle.* Richmond, Va.: Dustin, Gilman and Company, 1876. Reprint. Charleston, S.C.: Nabu Press, 2010. Velázquez recounts her adventures during the Civil War as Harry Buford, a spy, double agent, and blockade runner. She also includes her family history and life before and after the war. Much of her book is considered factually suspect.

Winkler, H. Donald. *Stealing Secrets.* Naperville, Ill.: Cumberland House, 2010. A work focusing on female spies during the Civil War, including Velázquez. The author discusses how these woman helped change the course of the war. Based on newspapers, journals, diaries, letters, and memoirs from the war.

See also: Santos Benavides; David G. Farragut; Guy Gabaldon.

LUPE VELEZ

Mexican-born actor

Velez is best known for her performances as Carmelita Lindsay in The Girl from Mexico *(1939) and its sequels, also known as the Mexican Spitfire series. She had a multifaceted career as a singer, dancer, and actor from the silent era into the 1940's.*

Latino heritage: Mexican
Born: July, 18, 1908; San Luis Potosí, Mexico
Died: December 13, 1944; Beverly Hills, California
Also known as: María Guadalupe Velez de Villalobos; Mexican Spitfire
Areas of achievement: Acting; dance; music

EARLY LIFE

María Guadalupe Velez de Villalobos was born in San Luis Potosí, Mexico, to Josefina Velez, an opera singer and Jacobo Villalobos Reyes, an officer in the military. Velez's father believed that his daughter's spirited behavior would harm her chances in life, and at the age of thirteen, she was sent to study at a convent in San Antonio, Texas. Despite all his efforts, Velez's fiery attitude and willful behavior could not be controlled, causing embarrassment for one of Mexico's prominent families.

Velez's father refused to allow her to use her family surname when she told him that she wanted to make a career in the theater, so she adopted her mother's maiden name as her stage name. She made her debut as a dancer at the age of sixteen at the Teatro Principal in Mexico City in 1925. She embraced the new flapper style with her bobbed hair, love of jazz, consumerism, and overt displays of sexuality. Velez's actions made her extremely popular but also shocked her family, especially her father. At the age of seventeen, Velez left Mexico for the United States. However, she was denied entry at first because of her age. She returned to Mexico and pleaded with the authorities in Mexico and the United States to let her enter the country; after many rounds of discussions, she was finally allowed into the United States in 1926.

LIFE'S WORK

Velez arrived in Los Angeles with no money but quickly found employment at the Hollywood Music Box Revue,

Lupe Velez. (Hulton Archive/Getty Images)

where she was discovered by Hollywood producer Hal Roach, who was impressed with her performance and her beauty. Roach cast her in small roles in his comedy shorts. Her big break came in 1927 when she was cast opposite Douglas Fairbanks in *The Gaucho*. Her performance in the film and the film itself were well-received by critics and audiences alike.

Velez's beauty and success led to her being cast as a Greek peasant girl in *Stand and Deliver* (1928) and as sultry chanteuse in D. W. Griffith's film *Lady of the Pavements* (1929). However, it was her performance alongside Gary Cooper as Lola, an upper-class señorita, in *The Wolf Song* (1929) that made her a star. Velez's performance embodied the volatile, hot-blooded, sexually promiscuous woman of color, a stock character that was popular with American audiences in the late 1920's. Hollywood cultivated this image for Velez on screen and off to ensure her popularity but also to marginalize her importance in the industry. She made her first English-language sound film, *Tiger Rose*, in 1929. However, fears that her voice sounded too ethnic led to Velez being cast in leading parts in the Spanish-language versions of Hollywood films. When she did appear in mainstream films, she was cast as the fiery "other woman" who acted as a foil to the white heroine.

Velez began the first of her many tumultuous public Hollywood romances with costar Gary Cooper during the making of *The Wolf Song*. Her relationship with Cooper lasted until he married Veronica Cooper, a wealthy heiress who worked as an actor in Hollywood under the name Sandra Shaw. At the height of her popularity and fame, Velez also was linked to Ronald Coleman, John Gilbert, and Ricardo Cortez before marrying Johnny Weismuller, an Olympic athlete and star of the Tarzan films, in 1933. Their marriage was not an easy one. The couple separated three times, and each time, Velez began divorce proceedings on the grounds of physical and mental cruelty. She rescinded the claims each time and remained married to Weismuller.

The conflict in their marriage not only harmed Velez's private life but also her professional life. In 1934, RKO Studios refused to renew her contract on the grounds that her public fighting with Weismuller was harmful to the company and to her overall image. She tried to sue the company but was not successful. Velez adopted the four-year-old child of her eldest sister in 1935 in an attempt to rehabilitate her image. Still, Velez found it difficult to find work at any of the major or minor studios, so she left the United States to make films in England and France. In 1936, she returned to

Velez and the Latin "Spitfire" Stereotype

For many white Americans, the word "spitfire" evokes the image of a curvaceous, hypersexual, irrational, emotionally unstable Latina. This image was employed by Hollywood to normalize the idea of whiteness as ideal and in the process to create a recognizable generic figure such as that of Carmelita Lindsay as played by Lupe Velez in the Mexican Spitfire series at RKO Studios from 1939 to 1943. However, Velez's character was not simply a stereotype. Velez's image as a hypersexual woman in her private life and career was played for laughs in the series, but what sets her films apart from other films of that period was their acceptance of the idea of a mixed-race marriage and the ways the films questioned the belief that such marriages were improper. More importantly, these films featured a Latina performer who represented a positive image of Latino culture and the image of women in the home and in the workplace.

America to appear in RKO's Bert Wheeler and Robert Woolsey comedy *High Flyers* (1937). She then returned to Mexico in 1938 to make her debut in Mexican film, starring in *La zandunga*.

Velez divorced Weismuller in 1939, and RKO offered her a contract to appear in a series of B-films known as the Mexican Spitfire series. From 1939 to 1943, she made eight films featuring the character Carmelita Lindsay. In 1944, she returned to Mexico to star in *Nana*, and after completion of the filming, she announced that she was going to star in a play in New York. During this period she began dating an unknown twenty-seven-year-old French actor, Harold Raymond. Velez announced that she and Raymond were engaged in November, 1944, but two weeks later, gossip columnist Louella Parsons reported that the engagement and the relationship were over.

On December 13, two days after hosting a large party in her home for her family and friends, Velez committed suicide by taking an overdose of a prescription drug. She was several months pregnant with Raymond's child, and according to the notes she left for Raymond and her housekeeper, she could not face the idea of trying to raise a child born out of wedlock.

SIGNIFICANCE

Velez's struggles with her sexuality, ethnicity, and her place within the Hollywood star system illustrate the difficulties faced by Latinas in America as well as women in general at a time when gender norms typically relegated women to subservience and domesticity. Still, her fiery performances and popularity as the embodiment of emergent female sexuality influenced future models of American femininity for Latinas, women in general, and the Hollywood system. Velez's chaotic and tragic life has provided inspiration to experimental artists such as Andy Warhol and Kenneth Anger, who both used Velez's struggles as a means to investigate the idea of performance and its effect on the formation of sexual identity.

Michael Brian Faucette

FURTHER READING

Beltran, Mary C. *Latina/o Stars in U.S. Eyes: The Making and Meanings of Film and TV Stardom*. Urbana: University of Illinois Press, 2009. Offers a historical and cultural approach to the question of how Latinos have been depicted in mainstream media culture.

Freguso, Rosa Linda. "Lupe Velez: Queen of the B's" in *From Bananas to Buttocks: The Latina Body in Popular Culture and Film*, edited by Myra Mendible. Austin: University of Texas Press, 2007. A collection of essays that examines the cultural, political, social, gendered, and economic uses of the Latina body in American culture and media.

Rodgriguez, Clara E. *Heroes, Lovers, and Others: The Story of Latinos in Hollywood*. New York: Oxford University Press, 2004. This book briefly covers the history of representations of Latinos from the silent era to the 1990's in Hollywood. Analyzes key performers as well as lesser-known Latinos.

See also: Dolores del Río; José Ferrer; Mel Ferrer; Rita Hayworth; Fernando Lamas; Carmen Miranda; Anthony Quinn; César Romero.

ELENA VERDUGO

American actor

Best known as nurse Consuelo Lopez in the long-running television medical drama series Marcus Welby, M.D., *in the 1960's and 1970's, Verdugo excelled in a wide variety of entertainment venues, including film, music, dance, radio, and television. Although sometimes listed among performers who were victims of stereotyping, she played throughout her lengthy career characters from many ethnicities and backgrounds.*

Latino heritage: Mexican
Born: April 20, 1926; Paso Robles, California
Also known as: Elena Angela Verdugo
Areas of achievement: Radio and television; acting; dance

EARLY LIFE

Elena Verdugo (ay-LAY-nah vehr-DEW-goh) was born Elena Angela Verdugo in a region of Califonia where her family had lived since the 1770's. She began to learn Mexican folk-dancing at the age of three, started formal dance training at the age of five, and debuted as a child actor the following year in *Cavalier of the West* (1931). Beginning in her early teen years, she danced in a number of diverse films, for example the musical *Down Argentine Way* (1940), the bull-fighting epic *Blood and Sand* (1941), and the war film *To the Shores of Tripoli* (1942). In 1942, she played her first major role, that

of the Tahitian girl Ata, who serves as a model for the painter Paul Gaugin in *The Moon and Sixpence*. Around the same time, she also sang briefly with the orchestra of Spanish bandleader Xavier Cugat and performed on one of his biggest hit recordings, "Tico-Tico."

Her next film role was also that of a Polynesian woman in *Rainbow Island* (1944). That same year, she took on her most famous screen role, that of the Romany (Gypsy) girl Ilonka in Universal's *House of Frankenstein*. Although she would forever after be associated with Universal Studios and its horror-film franchise and would work for Universal steadily, she never signed a contract, purportedly because executives insisted that she lose weight, something Verdugo steadfastly refused to do. An irony of her contentious relationship with Universal is that her Verdugo ancestors once owned the property on which the studios stand.

LIFE'S WORK

Verdugo's role in *House of Frankenstein* made her an icon for fans of early horror films. Although she danced and sang in the film, it was her fine acting abilities that were displayed for perhaps the first time. Ilonka is the love interest of Larry Talbot (Lon Chaney, Jr.), the werewolf introduced in *The Wolf Man* (1941), and her actions and attitudes presage much of the innovation in horror film and literature that would emerge later in the

1960's and 1970's, in which good-hearted, right-minded characters are often depicted as tolerant and sympathetic toward the "monsters" among them. Ilonka falls in love with Talbot, and even after she discovers that he is a werewolf, she does not reject or desert him; her love remains steadfast as she tries to help him battle his curse. As Ilonka, Verdugo enacts for the first time a ritual that quickly became part of popular werewolf lore: In order to free Talbot forever from his lycanthropic fate, she, as one who truly loves him, shoots him with a gun loaded with silver bullets. This now-formulaic trope of how to dispatch a werewolf is for the most part a creation of Universal scriptwriters and is not found in European folklore. Nevertheless, it provides Verdugo with a touching, terrifying scene, one which she plays with great pathos and believability.

After her role in *House of Frankenstein*, Verdugo continued to work regularly in films, sometimes portraying Latina women, as in *Strange Voyage* (1946) and *The Big Sombrero* (1949), and sometimes playing "Anglos" (people of a non-Latino ethnicity), as in *Little Giant* (1946) and the Charlie Chan mystery *The Sky Dragon* (1949). However, in 1952, Verdugo's career took an important turn away from films when she accepted her

Elena Verdugo. (Michael Ochs Archives/Getty Images)

first role in television: three appearances in the syndicated espionage series *Dangerous Assignment*, starring another silver-screen veteran, Brian Donlevy. Although she continued to appear in films occasionally during the 1950's, notably in *Cyrano de Bergerac* (1950), in *The Pathfinder* (1952), and in the title role of *Panama Sal* (1957), most of the rest of her career was spent in television.

Shortly after completing her work on *Dangerous Assignment*, Verdugo became the first Latina to play the starring role in a television series. The series was a situation comedy called *Meet Millie*, which ran from October of 1952 until March of 1956 on CBS. It was an almost prototypal American sitcom. Verdugo portrayed Millie Bronson, a secretary in New York City, and the supporting characters were typical of the genre: a boyfriend, an irascible boss, a meddling mother, and an eccentric neighbor. Nevertheless, it was a milestone for Latino actors as well as for Verdugo, who would never have to worry about falling victim to typecasting as a Latina or other "exotic" character. After *Meet Millie* was cancelled in 1956, Verdugo appeared frequently in other popular television series of the 1950's and 1960's, both comedies and dramas. Perhaps her most memorable role guest-starring in a situation comedy was that of Janice Tuttle, a sexy and flirtatious real-estate agent on an episode of *The Bob Cummings Show* in 1958. In 1959, she played a diametrically opposite role, U.S. Air Force captain Maggie Gallagher, in an episode of the aviation drama, *Steve Canyon*.

In the late 1950's and early 1960's, Verdugo began to take on recurring roles in series: *The Red Skelton Hour* (1956-1960), *The New Phil Silvers Show* (1964), *Many Happy Returns* (1964-1965), and *Mona McCluskey* (1965-1966). In these comedies, she played Anglos or characters of indeterminate ethnicity, but her best television role before her success in *Marcus Welby, M.D.*, was that of the Latina innkeeper Gerry, manager of a hotel called the Gran Quivera, opposite Richard Egan in *Redigo* (1963), a drama series about ranchers in the modern American Southwest. She began her most important television portrayal, that of Consuelo Lopez, in the fall of 1969 and continued to play the compassionate but level-headed nurse until the show's cancellation in 1976. During 1971 and 1972, she was nominated for a Golden Globe award for Best Supporting Actress in a Drama and was twice nominated for an Emmy Award in the same category. She reprised the role in the made-for-TV reunion film, *The Return of Marcus Welby, M.D.*, in 1984.

Consuelo Lopez, R.N.

In many ways, Elena Verdugo's role of Consuelo Lopez, nurse, office manager, and confidant for two Anglo doctors in *Marcus Welby, M.D.*, is reminiscent of another breakthrough nurse's role of the era, that of Diahann Carroll as Julia Baker in *Julia* (1968-1971), the first series headlined by an African American woman not playing a domestic servant. Like Carroll, Verdugo had been the first actor of her ethnicity to star in a television series—*Meet Millie* in the 1950's—and the producers and writers of *Welby* handled Consuelo's ethnic heritage much as those of *Julia* handled that of their title character: Her background was treated as an integral part of her role and identity, but rarely in confrontational or overtly political ways. In both series, the "ethnic" nurse is paired with an older, Anglo-white, patriarchal but likable doctor played by a veteran film star: Lloyd Nolan in *Julia* and Robert Young in *Welby*. Although Verdugo appeared in almost every episode of the long-running series, Consuelo was only rarely the focal character. Nonetheless, when the scriptwriters did give the nurse center stage, the episodes were often very good and respectful of Latino culture. The best of these appeared in the series' first season on January 27, 1970. Entitled "The Legacy," it featured Latina film legend Dolores del Río as Consuelo's aristocratic mother, Carlotta Lopez de Guadalupe. The story provided sharp and telling contrasts between the philosophical, thoughtful approach Carlotta and Consuelo take toward a medical crisis with that of an "uptight" Anglo woman played by another film veteran, Janet Blair.

SIGNIFICANCE

Throughout her long and diverse career, Verdugo established herself as a multitalented, highly versatile performer. In her films, she played numerous ethnicities and became part of the folkloric heritage of the classic Universal horror films of the 1930's and 1940's. In the 1950's, she became the first Latina to star in her own television series, and in the 1970's she became the most visible Latina on prime-time television through her portrayal of nurse Lopez on *Marcus Welby, M.D.*, one of the most highly rated series of the decade.

Thomas Du Bose

FURTHER READING

Arroyo, Juliet. *Early Glendale*. San Francisco: Arcadia, 2005. Contains a chapter on Verdugo's family history in California.

Kalisch, Philip Arthur. *Images of Nurses on Television*. New York: Springer, 1983. Provides context and comparison for Verdugo's role of Consuelo Lopez.

Riley, Philip J., ed. *House of Frankenstein* (Universal Flimscripts Series, Volume 6). Chesterfield, N.J.: Magicimage Filmbooks, 1990. The script of Verdugo's most famous film.

Weaver, Tom, and Michael and John Brunar. *Universal Horrors*. 2d ed. Jefferson, N.C.: McFarland, 1990. History and overview of the studio at which Verdugo filmed most of her films of the 1930's and 1940's.

See also: Lynda Carter; Dolores del Río; Carmen Zapata.

BOB VILA

American television personality and entrepreneur

Vila, a master craftsman and guru of home improvement, has made American homeowners believe they could accomplish many home renovations as do-it-yourself projects with the right step-by-step guide. Vila hosted the Emmy Award-winning television series This Old House *for ten years and then started his own television production company. Vila is the author of eleven books, has his own line of tools, and has a Web site that offers home-improvement videos and tips for all homeowners.*

Latino heritage: Cuban
Born: June 20, 1946; Miami, Florida
Also known as: Robert J. Vila
Areas of achievement: Radio and television; business

EARLY LIFE

Robert J. Vila (VEE-lah) was born in the summer of 1946 in Miami, Florida. Vila attended Miami Dade Junior College and received a bachelor of science degree in journalism and communications from the University of

Bob Vila. (AP Photo)

Florida in 1969. Following graduation, Vila traveled in Europe and volunteered with the Peace Corps in Panama from 1971 through 1973. Upon his return, he lived in Boston and attended the Boston Architectural Center, a school offering degrees and continuing education in architectural and interior design and in landscape architecture design. He opened a residential remodeling business in Boston. In 1975, Vila married Diana Barrett, and they had three children.

LIFE'S WORK

In 1979, at age thirty-three, Vila was asked to join the show *This Old House* at WGBH television station, the Public Broadcasting Service (PBS) affiliate in Boston. Vila had gained some notoriety after restoring a Victorian Italianate home in Newton Center, Massachusetts, and winning the *Better Homes and Gardens* Heritage House of 1978 Award. A Boston reporter wrote a positive article about Vila's work, so WGBH asked Vila to appear in a thirteen-part television series featuring detailed, step-by-step renovations in the Newton Center house. The show was so popular in Boston that PBS tapped it for nationwide coverage on public television. While Vila was with *This Old House*, the show had

some eleven million viewers and received five Emmy Awards. Vila hosted the show for ten years but left to establish his own show and television production company, BVTV, Inc. WGBH added a new host, but Vila's episodes were syndicated on cable as reruns called *The Old House Classics.* Vila started a new show called *Bob Vila's Home Again.* In 2005, he launched another show called *Bob Vila.*

In 1999, America was enamored with restoration. Vila worked with *Home and Garden Television* (HGTV) to complete a year-long tour of the United States with the cable television series *Restore America.* From July 4, 1999, to July 4, 2000, Vila traveled to all fifty states to view historic homes, gardens, and public buildings. He helped the neighborhoods and television viewers celebrate history and heritage while promoting preservation.

Vila showed homeowners how to invest sweat equity in do-it-yourself projects to decrease costs. In 2010, Vila's Web site offered viewers access to more than a thousand home-renovation videos; the site includes videos on the topics of sustainable landscaping, finishing a basement, babyproofing a house, and building an addition for an elderly parent. Shows from *Bob Vila's Home Again* include full-length videos, showcasing various types of home renovations in different geographic regions of the United States.

Two years after he became the host of *This Old House,* Vila put his journalism and communications degree to work by writing a book. His first book, *This Old House: Restoring, Rehabilitating, and Renovating an Older House* was published by Little, Brown, a venerable publishing house established in 1837, which had published work by authors such as Louisa May Alcott and Emily Dickinson. This book explains the week-by-week process of renovating a 110-year-old home, from beginning to finish. Vila wrote a five-volume series called *Bob Vila's Guide to Historic Homes of America*, publishing a total of eleven books between 1980 and 2002.

Over the years Vila diversified his work by joining with sponsors such as Sears or Bellawood, which carried prefinished hardwood floors. He also sold his own line of tools on his Web site and on the Home Shopping Network. Vila has guest-starred on television shows such as the situation comedy *Home Improvement* with Tim Allen and played in several films. Vila has been a regular guest on NBC's *Today Show* and CBS's *Early Show.* He produced his own series called *Bob Vila's Guide to Historic Homes* for cable network A&E.

SIGNIFICANCE

Vila is credited with popularizing home improvement, which attracted so many American homeowners. He encouraged restoration and renovation whenever possible to preserve old homes and strengthen the heritage of American neighborhoods. Vila and his wife are active philanthropists, supporting Habitat for Humanity, the Hemingway Preservation Foundation, and the Vila Foundation. He serves on the board of the Fledging Fund, a charity he and his wife founded to support vulnerable families and communities.

Marylane Wade Koch

FURTHER READING

Lees, Al. "Shop Talk: *This Old House* Revisited." *Popular Science* 222, no. 4 (April, 1993): 164. A candid view of Vila from his early days as a new television host and renovator in Boston, when PBS broadcast *This Old House* on 90 percent of its network.

Norville, Deborah. *Thank You Power: Making the Science of Gratitude Work for You.* Nashville, Tenn.: Thomas Nelson, 2007. Norville encourages a positive approach to life, concentrating on what one has, not on what one does not have, and uses Vila and his work as positive examples.

Vila, Bob. *This Old House: Restoring, Rehabilitating, and Renovating an Older House.* Boston: Little, Brown, 1980. Comprehensive step-by-step homeowner guide to renovating an older home that serves as a companion book to the PBS series *This Old House.*

See also: Linda Alvarado; George Lopez; Nina Tassler.

ALMA VILLANUEVA

American writer and educator

Villanueva is an award-winning poet and novelist whose works reflect her own struggles with prejudice, sexual abuse, the deaths of loved ones, divorce, and male domination.

Latino heritage: Mexican

Born: October 4, 1944; Lompoc, California

Also known as: Alma Luz Villanueva; Luz Villanueva

Areas of achievement: Literature; poetry

EARLY LIFE

Alma Villanueva (AHL-mah vee-yah-NWAY-vah) was born in Lompoc, California, on October 4, 1944, to her Mexican mother, Lydia Villanueva. She never knew her father, who was of German ancestry. Villanueva's Mexican grandfather was a newspaper editor in Hermosillo, Mexico; a poet and a minister, he also held a college degree in philosophy. Villanueva's main family influences were her mother, her mother's sister Ruth Villanueva, and particularly her maternal grandmother Jesus Villanueva. Jesus—a Yaqui Indian from Sonora— was the daughter of a healer and a visionary; she reared Alma in the Mission District of San Francisco, taught Alma the Mexican traditions, encouraged Alma's writing, and ensured that Alma knew of her German ancestry. Jesus also helped Alma learn English, Spanish, and some Yaqui prayers. Jesus died, however, when Alma was eleven. After Jesus died, Alma lived wherever she could and experienced abuse and molestation.

Villanueva dropped out of school, married, and at age fifteen gave birth to her first child. While her husband served with the U.S. Marines, Villanueva took whatever jobs she could find. She worked often as a secretary and a model to help support her family, which soon included three children: Antoinette, Ed, and Marc Goulet. Despite her many responsibilities, in 1965 Villanueva was able to attend some classes at the City College of San Francisco. She also found time to continue writing.

After her divorce, she and her children relocated for four years to an isolated central California farm in the Sierras. There she read, studied, and communed with nature. She listed her religion as "Native Person of the Earth."

LIFE'S WORK

In 1977, the Place of Herons Press published Villanueva's first book of poetry, *Blood Root.* This book included "Poems," which earned Villanueva the First Place Chicano Literary Prize in Poetry from the University of California at Irvine in 1977. "Poems" also was included in the anthology *Third Chicano Literary Prize, 1976-1977* (1977). By 2010, Villanueva's writings had been published in more than twenty anthologies and textbooks.

In 1978, Motheroot Publications published her forty-page, autobiographical poem *Mother, May I?* In this work, Villanueva shares her experiences of being molested, of having a child at a young age, and of growing up female in a male-dominated society. Her writings and studies continue to acknowledge her Native American sense of affinity with nature and the strength and power of the female influence, despite male control and dominance. In the 1980's, when she was in her late thirties, Villanueva and her second husband, Chicano artist Wilfredo Castano, had a child, Jules Villanueva-Castano. At this time, she and her family lived in a secluded area along the California coast.

In 1984, Villanueva earned her M.F.A. from Norwich University. The same year, Place of Herons Press published *Life Span*, her third poetry collection and her second book for this company. Her fourth poetry collection, *La Chingada*, followed in 1985. In these works, Villanueva continued to assert the strength of women through her example and her writings. In 1988, she published her first novel, *The Ultraviolet Sky*. For this work she received the American Book Award from the Before Columbus Foundation; the novel also earned her a listing in *Five Hundred Great Books by Women*. Her second novel *Naked Ladies* (1994) brought her the PEN Oakland fiction award, and she went on to publish five additional novels. Her short stories and poems continued to appear in many journals and publications, and her recordings and videos have been well received by the public.

By 2010, Villanueva had been teaching at Antioch University in Los Angeles for more than ten years. Before this, she had taught for four years at the University of California at Santa Cruz and for two years at Cabrillo College in Aptos, and she has held many assignments at other colleges and universities. She had also been a member of the panel on fiction of the National Endowment for the Arts and a member of such organizations as the Southern Poverty Law Center, Nuclear Freeze, and Greenpeace.

SIGNIFICANCE

Educator, writer, activist, and mother Alma Villanueva demonstrates through her university classes, her writings, and her own example how women can survive the prejudice of others, sexual abuse, the deaths of loved ones, divorce, and the domination that Chicanas and all women face. Her concerns are also evident through her memberships in such organizations as Greenpeace, Amnesty International, Native American Rights, and Save the Children.

Anita Price Davis

FURTHER READING

Koppelman, Susan. *Between Mothers and Daughters: Across a Generation.* New York: Feminist Press at the City University of New York, 2004. Includes Villanueva's short story "The Choice," in which a young woman must decide if she should abort her pregnancy.

Madsen, Deborah. *Understanding Contemporary Chicana Literature.* Columbia: University of South Carolina Press, 2000. The chapter on Villanueva discusses her life, recurrent themes of womanhood and culture, and her search for identity in a male-dominated culture.

Villanueva, Alma. *Mother, May I?* Pittsburgh, Pa.: Motheroot, 1978. Villanueva's long, autobiographical poem emphasizes her communion with nature and her struggle to overcome abuse, loss of family, powerlessness, and other difficulties typical of Chicanas in a male-dominated culture.

_____. *Soft Chaos.* Tempe, Ariz. Bilingual Press, 2006. In this poetry collection, Villanueva explores many unpleasant topics that she personally has had to confront in life. She also describes the turbulent life of a typical wife, mother, and lover.

See also: Gloria Anzaldúa; Norma Elia Cantú; Denise Chávez; Lucha Corpi; Victor Villaseñor; Helena María Viramontes.

DANNY VILLANUEVA

American football player and entrepreneur

Villanueva spent eight years in the National Football League as a punter and place kicker with the Los Angeles Rams and the Dallas Cowboys. He retired from football at age twenty-nine and cofounded the media giant now known as Univision.

Latino heritage: Mexican
Born: November 5, 1937; Tucumcari, New Mexico
Also known as: Daniel Dario Villanueva
Areas of achievement: Football; business; radio and television

EARLY LIFE

Daniel Dario Villanueva (VIH-lah-new-AY-vah) was born on November 5, 1937, in Tucumcari, New Mexico, the ninth of twelve children born to Mexican immigrants. He grew up in Calexico, California, and played college football at New Mexico State University, where he was a kicker.

Villanueva was not drafted by a National Football League (NFL) team out of college and went to work as a schoolteacher. One day, he was conducting class at Las Cruces High School when a young girl walked in and told him that Mr. Elroy Hirsch was on the phone. Hirsch was a former wide receiver and running back for the Los Angeles Rams and had taken a position in the club's front office. The call had to be a prank, he thought, or some kind of new-teacher hazing. He instructed the messenger to tell Hirsch that he was busy.

The vice principal finally arrived to tell Villanueva to take the call because the Rams were, in fact, calling him. Villanueva never thought he would make it to the NFL, but Rams scout Chuck Benedict had attended a New Mexico State game to watch one of Villanueva's teammates, Pervis Atkins, and saw Villanueva kick a 49-yard field goal. Benedict wrote Villanueva's name down in his notes.

Villanueva kicked for Rams coach Bob Waterfield, a pro football Hall of Fame member as a quarterback and kicker. "Bob sat there quietly with a toothpick in his mouth and . . . so I kicked and I kicked and I kicked and I kicked," Villanueva later said. "I don't recall the exact number anymore, but it was thirty-something in a row and I never missed. And he said, '"I've seen enough."'"

LIFE'S WORK

Kicking for Los Angeles from 1960 to 1964, Villanueva averaged 45.5 yards per punt in 1962, a team record that stood for forty-five years. He also set a team record for the longest field goal, 51 yards, which he shares. It was not a smooth cultural transition for the man known as "El Kickador." He never understood that nickname, or why bullfighting music played every time he walked onto the field at the Los Angeles Memorial Coliseum; however, Villanueva believed that any publicity was good publicity, so he mugged for a training camp photo in which he sat on a blocking dummy, sombrero on his head, guitar in his hands.

During that era, Latinos were a rare presence in football, and black and white players traveled on separate buses. Once, a teammate announced, "All black guys get on that bus, white guys get on that bus, and Danny, you take a cab.'"

Traded to Dallas in 1965, Villanueva kicked 56 points after touchdown without a miss in 1966. He retired before the 1968 season. On New Year's Eve in 1967, Villanueva and his Cowboys teammates traveled to Lambeau Field for the NFL championship game in minus-48-degree temperature with windchill. The game, which became known as the Ice Bowl, ended up being Villanueva's last. When it was over, Villanueva tossed his parka and shoes into a bag instead of leaving them in the locker room. At age twenty-nine, he was tired and finished with football.

A favor Villanueva did helped to push him onto a different path. During the Rams' training camp, he taught a boy how to kick. The boy's father introduced Villanueva to Burt Avedon, the first manager of KMEX-TV (channel 34), a Spanish-language station in Los Angeles. He also met Ford Motor Company executives who sponsored him on five-minute sports shows on the station. Villanueva needed the money. He had earned just $5,500 in his first season with the Rams, and his biggest football paycheck was $18,000.

Villanueva had worked for *The Los Angeles Examiner* in high school, reporting on high school games. At New Mexico State, he was editor of the student paper and did part-time work setting up the sports section for the local newspaper, *The Las Cruces Sun*. Later on, he became news director of KMEX and then general manager.

At the time, there were many separate Spanish-language television stations in Los Angeles, San Antonio, and New York. Villanueva's group bought a station in Miami in the early 1970's and merged all of the individual Spanish stations in the area. This combined group became the Spanish International Communications Corporation (SICC). Then, along with the network division, the Spanish International Network (SIN), the two were combined and became Univision. Univision has become a major nationwide network. Villanueva also is a senior partner in Los Angeles-based Bastion Capital.

SIGNIFICANCE

Villanueva found success in multiple fields. He was one of the NFL's first Hispanic kickers. He kicked a game-winning field goal against the Washington Redskins in 1966 that helped the Dallas Cowboys reach the play-offs for the first time. He held the Rams' single-season record for punt average (45.5) for forty-five years. After his playing career ended, he helped launch a successful media empire with his role in the founding of Univision.

Michael J. Bennett

FURTHER READING

Buck, Ray. "Danny Villanueva's Greatest Kicks, Then and Now." *The Fort Worth Star-Telegram*, June 6, 2008. Lengthy profile of Villanueva that chronicles the highlights of his years with the Cowboys.

Libman, Gary. "Danny Villanueva, President of KMEX-TV: He Gets His Kicks Serving Latino Community." *The Los Angeles Times*, September 29, 1985. Describes Villanueva's post-football career and dedication to serving his community.

Pedrero, Wendy. "Daniel Villanueva, Chairman and President, Bastion Capital Corporation: A Philanthropist with the Latino Community in His Heart." *Latino Leaders*, June/July, 2004. Provides an overview of Villanueva's youth and football career and describes his philanthropic activities.

See also: Manny Fernández; Tom Flores; Martín Gramática; Joe Kapp; Eddie Saenz.

ANTONIO VILLARAIGOSA

American politician

Photogenic and charismatic, Villaraigosa enjoyed a meteoric ascent through the political ranks of the Los Angeles Democratic Party, becoming in 2005 the city's first Hispanic mayor in more than a century. Vigorously pursuing infrastructure improvements in an era of economic restraints, Villaraigosa positioned himself for a place in national politics.

Latino heritage: Mexican
Born: January 23, 1953; Los Angeles, California
Also known as: Antonio Ramón Villaraigosa; Antonio Ramón Villar, Jr
Area of achievement: Government and politics

EARLY LIFE

Antonio Ramón Villaraigoso (an-TOH-nee-oh rah-mon VEE-ah-rah-GOH-sah) was born Antonio Ramón Villar, Jr., in the working-class Hispanic neighborhoods of Boyle Heights in East Los Angeles. The oldest of four children, Villaraigoso was raised by a single mother, a first-generation Mexican American who did menial work to support her family. Villaraigosa had little relationship with his Mexican father, a violent alcoholic who abandoned the family before Villaraigosa was five. Villaraigosa struggled in school, although he excelled in a variety of sports. Classes seldom interested him, but he was caught up in the sweeping vision of the era's Civil Rights movement. Before he was even fifteen, he picketed on behalf of farmworkers under union organizer César Chávez, and he led school walkouts supporting the right of African American students to form a student organization.

At sixteen, a benign tumor on his spinal column briefly paralyzed him. Frustrated by the lengthy rehabilitation, he grew restless in school, his grades dropped, and after he was suspended for getting into a fight, he dropped out entirely during his junior year. However, at the encouragement of his mother and a tutor who saw

Antonio Villaraigosa. (AP Photo)

promise in his political activism, Villaraigosa returned to high school and graduated. He attended East Los Angeles College for a semester before matriculating at the University of California at Los Angeles (UCLA). His passion for political activism remained. He joined Movimiento Estudiantil Chicano de Aztlán (MEChA), a radical student political action organization dedicated to Chicano pride, and he led student protests against the American military presence in Southeast Asia.

LIFE'S WORK

Villaraigosa graduated from UCLA with a degree in history. Certain he wanted a career in public service working

Los Angeles's Growing Hispanic Population

During the first decade of the twenty-first century, the Latino population of Los Angeles became the city's majority demographic, coinciding with the political rise of Antonio Villaraigosa. Before Villaraigosa's successful mayoral run, the political strategy for Hispanic candidates running for citywide offices had been to pitch ethnic pride and themselves as representative cultural voices. Such strategy pitted one ethnic group against another.

In the wake of the 1990's, during which Los Angeles was wracked by racial tensions, the city was primed for an alternative vision. Villaraigosa recast the city's growing Hispanic population as part of, rather than separate from, the city's larger urban populace. Villaraigosa offered not some quixotic rainbow metaphor for racial cooperation but rather a pragmatic reality—economics, not ethnicity, should direct the city's future. He argued that lower-income whites, as well as disenfranchised African Americans and Hispanics, shared the same problems: high unemployment, deteriorating public schools, inadequate mass transit, substandard air quality, dwindling water supplies, alarming street crime, substandard housing, limited access to higher education, and systemic bigotry. By placing Hispanic concerns within that broader coalition, Villaraigosa emerged as a political force despite the stubborn xenophobia of anti-immigrant rhetoric that swept California after the September 11, 2001, terrorist attacks. Although accused of toning down his "Hispanic-ness" as a way to appeal to a wider demographic and to advance his own political ambition, Villaraigosa, by repositioning the Hispanic bloc, became a national political figure despite accusations of marital infidelities that would have derailed the political fortunes of most politicians.

for minority rights, he completed his law degree in 1985 from the Peoples College of Law, a nonprofit community-run night school in Los Angeles that focused on training promising minority students as legal advocates specializing in civil rights law. Villaraigosa himself never passed the bar, but he became a prominent activist with the American Civil Liberties Union (ACLU) and in local unions, most notably with the United Teachers of Los Angeles. He married a schoolteacher named Corina Raigosa in 1987, and the couple merged their last names in a show of respect and equality. In 1990, Villaraigosa was elected to Los Angeles's powerful transportation authority, where he learned at first hand of the significant infrastructure problems facing the sprawling city and the need for improved public transportation to ease the area's choking gridlock.

Persuaded by colleagues who recognized his charisma to run for elected office, Villaraigosa in 1994 ran for the California State Assembly from the Forty-fifth District. Although the district was overwhelmingly Hispanic (almost 70 percent), Villaraigosa obtained a winning majority by also appealing to the district's minority white and African American voters based on shared economic conditions. Once in the assembly, Villaraigosa wasted little time, introducing efforts to address underfunded school systems, modernize water quality facilities, preserve thousands of urban acres for parks, and improve health insurance coverage for lower-income families. He sparked immediate interest within his Democratic Party and was selected in his first term as its majority whip. Four years later, he was elected speaker of the assembly, the first person from Los Angeles to hold this position in a generation, gaining Villaraigosa much national media attention. Term limits prevented Villaraigosa from seeking a third term. Returning to Los Angeles in 2001, he lost in a tight and often ugly race to attorney James Hahn for the Democratic mayoral nomination. Undaunted, two years later he ran successfully for the city council, representing the Fourteenth District, which included the Boyle Heights neighborhoods where he had grown up.

The new city councilman quickly distinguished himself, most notably by vigorously working to resolve a potentially crippling transit strike. He was tapped in 2004 to cochair the presidential campaign of U.S. senator John Kerry. Building on the momentum from that national exposure, Villaraigosa remounted his efforts for the Los Angeles mayoralty, challenging Hahn in 2005. Facing criticism for not delivering on campaign promises to expand the city's police force and to address the city's persistent transportation problems, Hahn was additionally vulnerable because he had dismissed the city's African American police chief. Running a visionary campaign that sought to bring together the city's ethnic groups, Villaraigosa was elected mayor. On July 1, 2005, he was sworn in as the city's first Hispanic mayor in more than a century. His election made national news; he was profiled in major news magazines and news shows as one of the Democrats' rising stars at a time when the party was looking for new direction.

Villaraigosa dedicated his first term to three initiatives: expanded funding for public schools; a larger police force of ten thousand officers to help reduce the city's crime rate; and greater compliance with international environmental guidelines for improving air quality, particularly diesel fuel pollution and coal usage, and conserving water usage. Villaraigosa staked much of his first-term agenda on an ambitious $40 billion renovation of the city's much maligned mass transit system and crumbling infrastructure, including, most controversially, an expansion of the city's subway system. In 2008, city voters passed a sales tax hike to partially fund Villaraigosa's plan.

Despite an impressive record, Villaraigosa faced stinging criticism for the perception that he sought the spotlight and was grooming himself for national politics. He offered the Democratic Party's response to President George W. Bush's state of the union address in 2006, served as the national cochair of Hillary Clinton's losing presidential bid in 2008, and was an adviser on economic matters in President-elect Barack Obama's transition team. More problematically, Villaraigosa endured a media firestorm in 2007 over revelations of an affair with a local television reporter, his subsequent divorce proceedings, and later revelations of additional infidelities. Consequently, his 2009 reelection was far closer than many political pundits expected; even though he was an incumbent, he received only 55 percent of the vote. Given the two-term limit on the mayor's office, Villaraigosa in his second term continued the programs from his ambitious first term, most notably shepherding mass transit renovation, the largest such program ever undertaken by an American city.

SIGNIFICANCE

An ambitious and campaign-savvy politician, Villaraigosa used the machinery of local politics to project himself onto the national political stage, despite persistent allegations of moral lapses and criticism of self-promotion and opportunism. He emerged in the mid-2000's as the first national Hispanic politician, the face and the voice of the dominant emerging voting bloc in America. In the post-Obama world of the Democratic Party, he positioned himself to take advantage of new opportunities for minority candidates. His vision to update Los Angeles's public transportation system—a crusade he often acknowledged was close to his heart because his mother had ridden city buses for years— would be a satisfying capstone to most political careers. Villaraigosa's full significance will be determined by how he spends his political capital in the next decades of his public life.

Joseph Dewey

FURTHER READING

Fulton, William. *The Reluctant Metropolis: The Politics of Urban Growth in Los Angeles*. Baltimore: Johns Hopkins Press, 2001. Broad and careful study of the ethnic makeup of Los Angeles politics and ethnic tensions just before the emergence of Villaraigosa.

Douzet, Frederick, Thad Kousser, and Kenneth Miller, eds. *The New Political Geography of California*. Berkeley: University of California Institute Press, 2008. Helpful study that provides essential documentation for the changing reality of California politics in the wake of the emerging Hispanic majority. Includes statewide data and information about Villaraigosa's mayoral races.

Ochoa, Enrique C., and Gilda L. Ochoa. *Latino Los Angeles: Transformations, Communities, and Activism*. Tempe: University of Arizona Press, 2005. As Hispanic populations have risen, cities in the American Southwest have adjusted to that demographic politically, culturally, and economically. This book uses Los Angeles as template for those accommodations, providing a critical context for understanding the political appeal of Villaraigosa.

See also: Cruz Bustamante; Gloria Molina; Loretta Sánchez; Hilda L. Solis.

JOSÉ ANTONIO VILLARREAL

American writer and educator

Villarreal's novel Pocho was the first work featuring Chicano characters to be released by a mainstream publisher, and he parlayed his early success into a long career as a writer and educator in both the United States and Mexico.

Latino heritage: Mexican
Born: July 30, 1924; Los Angeles, California
Died: January 13, 2010; Siskiyou County, California
Areas of achievement: Literature; education

EARLY LIFE

José Antonio Villarreal (hoh-ZAY an-TOE-nee-oh VEE-yah-ray-AL) was the son of a Mexican-born former revolutionary soldier, José Heladio Villarreal, and Felícitas Ramírez Villarreal. After serving in the Mexican Revolution under Pancho Villa, José Heladio and his family immigrated to the United States in 1921 to become migrant farmworkers. José Antonio, born in Los Angeles, was the elder of two sons and grew up with fifteen sisters. During harvest time, the entire family, which spoke only Spanish, lived outdoors in tents and moved throughout California following seasonal crops. In the late 1920's, the family finally settled in Santa Clara, south of San Francisco, where José Antonio attended elementary and high school.

In early 1942, not long after the bombing of Pearl Harbor, seventeen-year-old Villarreal received his father's permission to drop out of school and enlist in the U.S. Navy. He served in the Pacific Theater aboard the U.S.S. *Tawasa*, and he left the service in 1946 with the rank of quartermaster first-class. Returning home, he enrolled at the University of California at Berkeley, graduating with a bachelor's degree in English in 1950. By the time Villarreal left college, he had already begun writing, and he published his first short story in 1947 in *Pegasus*, a literary journal. After graduation, Villarreal continued to write while working at a variety of jobs, including bus driver and cannery worker. In 1953, he married Barbara Gentles, and the couple had three children, Ian, Kelly. and Caleb. Villarreal pursued graduate study in the late 1950's.

LIFE'S WORK

In 1959, Villarreal attracted literary attention with the release of his debut novel, *Pocho*, published by Doubleday, one of the first works of fiction to detail the experiences of Mexican Americans. A critical success that would be reprinted several times in both English and Spanish over the next twenty-five years, the novel enabled Villarreal to gain entry into the corporate world as a writer. He became a consultant and technical writer at Lockheed Aircraft in Palo Alto, and he worked from 1960 to 1968 in several locations for the corporation, writing speeches and proposals and editing company publications. He also wrote nonfiction articles regarding aspects of Mexican American history for *Holiday* and *West* magazines and for the *Los Angeles Times* and the *San Francisco Review*.

In 1968, Villarreal moved to Boulder, Colorado, where for three years he was the supervisor of technical publications and public relations at Ball Brothers Research Corporation. He continued to contribute essays and nonfiction, writing articles for *Empire Magazine*, part of the *Denver Post*. In 1971, Villarreal entered the field of education, teaching courses in English at the University of Colorado at Boulder. He moved to the University of Texas at El Paso to teach English and serve as writer-in-residence during the 1972-1973 academic year.

Feeling the call of his heritage, Villarreal moved to Mexico, where in 1973 he became a naturalized citizen. In Mexico City he became editor in chief of *Now in Mexico*, a travel publication, and he subsequently moved to Guadalajara, where he spent a year working as a translator and radio newscaster. In 1974, Doubleday published his second novel, *The Fifth Horseman*, which was centered upon his father's experiences in the Mexican Revolution.

In the mid-1970's, Villarreal returned to the United States, teaching at the University of Santa Clara from 1975 to 1976 and Texas A&I University in 1976. Following a year writing in Zacatecas, Mexico, his parents' hometown, he accepted jobs both north and south of the border, teaching literature, composition, or English as a second language at numerous colleges for twelve years. These colleges included the University of the Americas (Mexico City, 1977-1978), American School Foundation (Mexico City, 1977-1982), Centro de Estudios Universitarios (San Angel, Mexico, 1977), University of Mexico (Mexico City, 1978-1979), University of California at Riverside (1978), Pan American University (Edinburg, Texas, 1982-1984), California State University, Los Angeles (1985-1986), Texas State

Pocho

The title of José Antonio Villarreal's first and best-known novel, *Pocho*, is often a derogatory term used by those born in Mexico to denigrate Chicanos who have forgotten their roots. It can also be a term of pride among Mexican Americans who are happy to straddle both cultures. Both connotations are present in Villarreal's novel.

Pocho was the first in an intended classical tetralogy: a sweeping saga in four parts that would follow a Mexican family over several generations. Only the first and second parts were completed during Villarreal's lifetime; his second novel, *The Fifth Horseman* (1973), is a prequel to *Pocho*, dealing with a fictional account of Villarreal's father's participation in the Mexican Revolution. His third novel, *Clemente Chacón* (1984), while dealing with Mexican Americans, introduces a new set of unrelated characters, and is not part of the tetralogy. Villarreal's unpublished manuscript, "The Center Ring," is believed to continue the themes and advance the story begun in *Pocho*, and may someday be published.

A multilayered semiautobiographical tragedy, *Pocho* focuses on central character Richard Rubio's life between the mid-1920's and the early 1940's. Richard is the son of the philandering Juan Rubio, a light-skinned *criollo* (of pure Spanish blood) and veteran of the Mexican Revolution who is married to Consuelo, a dark-skinned *indio* (Indian) of Mayan ancestry. Richard resembles his mother more than his father, both in appearance and action. The Rubio family lives and works in a culturally diverse California neighborhood. Richard's growth and education parallels Villarreal's. As he ages, Richard becomes aware of various conflicts that impact his consciousness: American culture versus Mexican culture, the traditions of the older versus the younger generation, the secular versus the religious, rural versus urban worlds, the relative worth of light skin versus dark skin in society, and honor versus dishonor.

Though the story of *Pocho* is on the surface simple, the various forces playing upon the characters' psyches give it depth. A key dramatic event is Juan Rubio's seduction of Macedonia, the wife of a lower-class neighbor, Cirilo, and of Pilar, Cirilo's young niece, to whom teenaged Richard is attracted. Having caused dishonor, Juan is in turn the victim of dishonor when his unmarried daughter Luz sleeps around. In a fit of rage, Juan destroys his house and possessions, and the Rubio family is forcefully dispersed.

Though later criticized for failing to address the prejudices Chicanos routinely experienced, *Pocho* had a different agenda: the presentation of a Mexican American family's internal struggles told in a realistic and artistic fashion. In that goal, the novel succeeded and continues to resonate to this day.

Technical College (1991-1992), and College of the Siskiyous (Weed, California, 1992-1994).

Villarreal's third and final novel, *Clemente Chacón*, was published in 1984. In his later years, he returned to California, living in Siskiyou County along the Oregon border, within sight of volcanic Mount Shasta. He continued to contribute occasional articles and fictional pieces until his death in 2010 at the age of eighty-five, leaving a number of completed novels and short stories unpublished.

SIGNIFICANCE

Born of humble origin into a family of migrant farmworkers, José Antonio Villarreal had a burning desire to become a writer. He continued an education begun late and interrupted by war, and because of family and employment obligations he experienced only modest success in his chosen occupation before the publication of his first novel in 1959. This novel, *Pocho,* achieved acclaim as the well-crafted opening salvo in an eventual barrage of what would become known as Chicano literature—works that focused on the lives of Mexican Americans.

Never an especially prolific published writer, Villarreal nonetheless made regular contributions to both fiction and nonfiction that were highly anticipated and generally well received. More than a half century after its first appearance, *Pocho* is required reading in numerous ethnic study courses, and Villarreal's body of work has formed the basis for many theses and dissertations.

Equally respected as an educator, Villarreal during a teaching career that spanned more than two decades inspired countless students in both the United States and Mexico to turn their unique experiences into literature. In recognition for his commitment to excellence in both writing and education, Houston International University in 1989 awarded Villarreal an honorary doctorate of humane letters.

Jack Ewing

FURTHER READING

Douglas, Christopher. *A Genealogy of Literary Multiculturalism*. Ithaca, N.Y.: Cornell University Press, 2009. A study of the relationship between literature and culture from anthropological and sociological points of view.

Kanellos, Nicolás. *Hispanic Literature of the United States: A Comprehensive Reference*. Santa Barbara, Calif.: Greenwood Press, 2003. This book provides an overview of five hundred years of Hispanic writings in North America, including chapters on themes and trends, brief biographies of important Latino writers, and descriptions of significant works.

Meier, Matt S., Conchita Franco Serri, and Richard A. Garcia. *Notable Latino Americans: A Biographical Dictionary*. Santa Barbara, Calif.: Greenwood Press, 1997. A reference that includes more than 125 biographies of Latino individuals, like Villarreal, who have contributed to American society.

See also: Angela de Hoyos; Rolando Hinojosa; Felipe de Ortego y Gasca; Gregory Rabassa; Pedro Juan Soto; Piri Thomas.

VICTOR VILLASEÑOR

American writer

After the Chicano movement of the 1960's and early 1970's, Villaseñor became one of the first major English-speaking public voices of the Chicano community. He made great contributions to the American public's awareness of Chicano issues and problems through his novels and screenplays, and he especially distinguished himself for his fictionalized biographical novels of his family, which inspired a sense of pride in the Chicano heritage.

Latino heritage: Mexican
Born: May 11, 1940; Carlsbad, California
Also known as: Víctor Edmundo Villaseñor
Area of achievement: Literature

EARLY LIFE

Born to Juan Salvador Villaseñor and Guadalupe ("Lupe") Gómez in Carlsbad, California, Víctor Edmundo Villaseñor (vee-yah-sehn-YOHR) was moved as a young child to a ranch in Oceanside, California, where he was raised with his three sisters and his brother and where he would reside for most of his life. As a student in local public schools Villaseñor experienced great difficulty in learning, both because of his poor English (he spoke Spanish exclusively until going to school) and because of difficulties in reading, which were later diagnosed as dyslexia.

Becoming discouraged with his poor performance, Villaseñor dropped out of high school at the age of eighteen and began to work, first on his family's ranch, then on local farms, and finally in construction projects. Frequently the object of racial slurs and prejudice, he longed to deepen his understanding of his Mexican cultural heritage. Villaseñor went to Mexico for a little over one year, where he worked at humble tasks but experienced the richness of the Mexican culture.

Upon Villaseñor's return to the United States in 1960, a cousin encouraged him to finish high school and

Victor Villaseñor. (AP Photo)

then to enroll in the newly founded University of San Diego. Still filled with feelings of rage because of the mistreatment he received for being Chicano, he took up boxing, but he also found himself drawn to the reading he had seemingly never been able to do. Villaseñor's professors encouraged him and assuaged his self-doubts and feelings of intellectual inadequacy. During the following summer, he returned to Mexico and met a group of people who were culturally engaged and avid readers. They exposed Villaseñor to Mexican art, music, literature, and history. For the first time in his life, the young man experienced a sense of joy and pride in his Mexican and Chicano heritage. He read his first classic work of literature, Homer's *Iliad* (c. 750 BCE; English translation, 1611), as well as works by F. Scott Fitzgerald and Antoine de Saint-Exupéry.

Villaseñor reluctantly returned to the United States, filled with a profound sense of anger and frustration because of the condition of the Chicanos there, who were generally poor and uneducated. He soon read a book that changed his life, James Joyce's *A Portrait of the Artist as a Young Man* (1916); Villaseñor recognized that literature was a medium through which he could combat injustice, express his deepest desires, honor his family heritage, and inspire his fellow Chicanos. Supporting himself through construction work, he continued his education at Santa Clara University and increasingly dedicated himself to writing.

LIFE'S WORK

Villaseñor wrote nine novels and sixty-five short stories over the course of ten years (1963-1973) and received some 250 letters of rejection before his first novel, *Macho!* (1973), was published by one of the largest presses in the United States, Bantam. The book chronicles the plight of a young Mexican who illegally enters the United States but later returns to Mexico a changed man, one who will no longer tolerate the culture of machismo. Continuing to explore the theme of social injustice, Villaseñor next wrote *Jury: The People vs. Juan Corona* (1977), an examination of the murder trial of the protagonist, a Mexican American accused of a murder spree in Yuba City, California.

Villaseñor's most famous novel, *Rain of Gold* (1991), was an instant critical success, and, with *Wild Steps of Heaven* (1996), *Thirteen Senses: A Memoir* (2001), and *Beyond Rain of Gold* (2011), forms an epic series of works that explore the history of Villaseñor's family from their struggles in Mexico to their migration to the United States and their difficulties and sufferings in their new homeland. These are complemented by his novels *Burro Genius: A Memoir* (2004) and *Crazy Loco Love: A Memoir* (2006), which are Villaseñor's accounts of his personal struggles while growing up.

Among Villaseñor's most popular books for young people is *Walking Stars: Stories of Magic and Power* (1994). He also has cowritten other collections of stories for children, such as *Mother Fox and Mr. Coyote* (2004), *Little Crow to the Rescue* (2005), *The Frog and His Friends Save Humanity* (2005), and *Goodnight, Papito Dios* (2007).

SIGNIFICANCE

Villaseñor is one of the most prolific and widely read Chicano authors in the United States. Many of his works have received great critical acclaim and have been incorporated into the literature curricula of high schools and universities. His novels popularized the political turmoil, poverty, prejudice, discrimination, and powerlessness endured by Mexican Americans, yet offered a vision of progress, hope, and happiness. Villaseñor also made significant contributions to children's literature in the form of bilingual editions of short stories that reflect elements of Chicano culture. A popular and frequent speaker, Villaseñor is widely recognized as a clear advocate for the celebration of Chicano life and culture in the United States.

Mark T. DeStephano

FURTHER READING

Jiménez, Francisco. *The Identification and Analysis of Chicano Literature*. New York: Bilingual Press, 1979. A classic work that makes mention of Villaseñor various times, in different contexts.

Kraup, Monika. *Rewriting North American Borders in Chicano and Chicana Narrative*. New York: Peter Lang, 2001. A brief discussion of Villaseñor's early, influential novel, *Macho!*

Shirley, Carl R., and Paula W. *Understanding Chicano Literature*. Columbia: University of South Carolina Press, 1988. The authors offer a brief analysis of Villaseñor's novel *Macho!*, attempting to evaluate it in terms of other Chicano works.

See also: Arturo Islas; Francisco Jiménez; Alejandro Morales; John Rechy; Tomás Rivera; Alma Villanueva; Bernice Zamora.

HELENA MARÍA VIRAMONTES

American writer and feminist

A writer committed to illustrating the plight of disadvantaged Latinas in the United States, Viramontes has written short stories, novels and co-edited anthologies that have met with critical acclaim. Her early story, "The Cariboo Cafe" (1985), about a Nicaraguan woman deranged by the loss of her boy, has been widely studied.

Latino heritage: Mexican
Born: February 26, 1954; East Los Angeles, California
Areas of achievement: Literature; women's rights

EARLY LIFE

A third-generation Mexican American, Helena María Viramontes (VEE-rah-MOHN-tehs) was born on February 26, 1954, to Serafín Bermúdez Viramontes and María Luisa LaBrada Viramontes. Her father held the lowly construction job of hod carrier, transporting bricks for bricklayers. Her mother was a homemaker. To make ends meet for their nine children, Viramontes's parents also worked as harvesters in the fields of California.

Viramontes resented her strict, Catholic father. She and her sisters were closer to their more lenient, Mormon mother. When Viramontes entered elementary school, she was forbidden to speak Spanish there. She graduated from Garfield High School in Los Angeles in 1971 and became involved in the Chicano movement. She was particularly concerned with the plight of Mexican Americans and Mexican immigrants to America.

Viramontes graduated from Immaculate Heart College in Los Angeles, known then for its ultra-liberal politics, with a bachelor of arts degree in English in 1975. Working part time, she entered the creative writing graduate program of the University of California at Irvine (UCI). In 1977, her first published short story, "Requiem for the Poor," won first prize for fiction from *Statement* magazine. Viramontes won the prize again with "The Broken Web" in 1978. In 1979, her short story "Birthday" won UCI's Chicano Literary Contest in the fiction category.

Strongly committed to writing about the personal, social and economic challenges faced by Latinas, Viramontes felt disillusioned by UCI's more traditional creative writing program and left it in 1981. In 1983, she married Eloy Rodríguez, a biologist. By 2010, the couple had two children, daughter Pilar and son Eloy Francisco.

LIFE'S WORK

Viramontes published her first collection of short stories, *The Moths, and Other Stories*, in 1985. It immediately established her as an acclaimed Chicana writer. The title story, "The Moths," about a Chicana teenager tending to her dying grandmother in an atmosphere of Magical Realism, became widely anthologized. "The Cariboo Cafe" became a favorite of literary critics.

Acting on her desire to support young Chicana writers, Viramontes coedited with María Herrera-Sobek the influential anthology *Chicana Creativity and Criticism: Charting New Frontiers in American Literature* (1988). It featured poetry, prose, literary criticism, and art by Chicanas. An expanded second edition came out in 1996.

In 1989, Viramontes received a National Endowment for the Arts fellowship and a Sundance Institute fellowship. She wrote the screenplay *Paris Rats in E.L.A.* (1993), which was made into an experimental film at the American Film Institute. Returning to UCI, Viramontes received her master of fine arts degree in creative writing in 1994. In 1995, she joined the faculty of Cornell University in the creative writing program, later becoming a full professor.

In 1995, Viramontes had a productive year. She published her first novel, *Under the Feet of Jesus*, which tells the story of Chicano migrant farmworkers. Among its many characters is teenager Estrella, who struggles to come of age in a harsh social environment. Together with Herrera-Sobek, Viramontes coedited the anthology *Chicana (W)rites: On Word and Film*, highlighting Chicana accomplishments in literature and cinema. Her novel won Viramontes the 1996 John Dos Passos Prize for Literature.

In 2000, Immaculate Heart College Center (successor to Immaculate Heart College) named Viramontes its alumna of the year. That same year, St. Mary's College of Notre Dame awarded Viramontes an honorary doctorate. In 2006, she was honored with the Luis Leal Award at the Santa Barbara Festival of Books. In 2007, she was made a Ford Fellow by the United States Artists Foundation in recognition of her outstanding work as Latina writer and educator.

Viramontes' second novel, *Their Dogs Came with Them*, came out in 2007. The title refers to the Spanish conquistadors and their canines. Viramontes set her novel in a slightly fictionalized East Los Angeles barrio neighborhood from 1960 to 1970. It tells an almost un-relentingly dark story in which young Latina characters face a harsh social environment of gang violence, male abuse, and no clear future. Inspired by the historical aerial medfly pest sprayings of Los Angeles, Viramontes invents a Quarantine Authority whose helicopters shoot at stray dogs at night when barrio citizens are confined to their homes during curfew.

SIGNIFICANCE

Viramontes's short stories and novels have made her an important contemporary Latina writer. Her characters and plots starkly portray the fates of oppressed Latinas of all ages. "The Moths" and "The Cariboo Cafe" have been included in many college literature anthologies. Readers and critics alike have been impressed by Viramontes's powerfully imagined characters, who suffer as a result of political and economic systems the author depicts as deeply unjust. In Viramontes's texts, hope arises only from moments of female solidarity. They spring up sporadically and unexpectedly and appear all the more beautiful for their rarity.

R. C. Lutz

FURTHER READING

Saldívar-Hull, Sonia. "'I Hear the Women's Wails and I Know Them to Be My Own': From *Mujer* to Collective Identities in Helena María Viramontes's U.S. Third World." *Feminism on the Border: Chicana Gender Politics and Literature.* Berkeley: University of California Press, 2000. Offers close scholarly analysis of Viramontes's early short stories, particularly "The Cariboo Cafe" and praises Viramontes's political opposition to patriarchy.

Sandoval, Anna Marie. "Acts of Daily Resistance in Urban and Rural Settings: The Fiction of Helena María Viramontes." In *Towards a Latina Feminism of the Americas: Repression and Resistance in Chicana and Mexicana Literature.* Austin: University of Texas Press, 2008. Offers scholarly analysis of Viramontes's fiction and celebrates her work for featuring acts of resistance in both urban and rural settings.

Viramontes, Helena María. "You Carry the Border with You: Conversation with Helen María Viramontes." Interview by Elizabeth Mermann-Jozwiak and Nancy Sullivan. In *Conversations with Mexican American Writers: Languages and Literatures in the Borderlands*, edited by Elizabeth Mermann-Jozwiak and Nancy Sullivan. Jackson: University Press of Mississippi, 2009. The editors talk with Viramontes about her work, particularly *Their Dogs Came with Them*, as well as Viramontes's goals and objectives as politically committed Latina writer and the role of memory in her fiction.

See also: Gloria Anzaldúa; Martha P. Cotera; Rosario Ferré; Cristina García; Cherríe Moraga; Judith Ortiz Cofer; Mary Helen Ponce; Estela Portillo Trambley; Alma Villanueva.

RAQUEL WELCH

American actor

Welch was the personification of feminine beauty and sex appeal in the 1960's and 1970's. In later years, she has demonstrated her ability as an actor and business-woman.

Latino heritage: Bolivian

Born: September 5, 1940; Chicago, Illinois

Also known as: Jo Raquel Welch; Jo Raquel Tejada; Raquel Curtis; Raquel Weinfeld; Raquel Palmer

Areas of achievement: Acting; radio and television; theater

EARLY LIFE

Jo Raquel Welch (rah-KEHL) was born Jo Raquel Tejada in Chicago, Illinois. Her father, Armando Carlos Tejada Urquizo, was a Bolivian immigrant and aeronautical engineer. Her mother, Josephine Sara Hall Tejada, was the daughter of architect Emery Stanford Hall, whose family can be traced back to the seventeenth century. Welch was the oldest of three children. She was baptized in the Presbyterian Church and has remained a practicing Christian throughout her life.

The family moved to La Jolla, California, when Armando went to work in San Diego's General Dynamics Corporation. Welch studied dance and participated in drama and cheerleading at La Jolla High School, where she was an outstanding student. Gifted with beauty and a stunning figure, she was a natural for local teenage beauty contests, and the strict discipline she learned from her athletic and theatrical training enabled her to win first prizes in California's rigorous competitions, including the 1957 Fairest of the Fair contest.

Raquel Welch. (AP Photo)

In 1958, Welch graduated from high school and briefly attended San Diego State College. However, she dropped out to pursue an acting career. She married her boy friend, James Welch, and had two children: son Damon, born in 1959, and daughter Latanne Renee, born in 1961. Latanne is an actor who performs under the name Tahnee Welch. Damon is a computer engineer. Welch and her husband divorced in 1964. She has had three subsequent husbands: Peter Curtis, a producer and director; André Weinfeld, a photographer and journalist who also was involved in film; and Richard Palmer.

LIFE'S WORK

In 1959, Welch began her professional career, performing the lead in the annual production of Hemet, California's Ramona Pageant. Then San Diego's KFMB hired her to present the weather. After her divorce, she briefly went to Dallas, where she worked as a department-store model and a cocktail waitress.

Welch returned to Hollywood after several weeks and was able to find bit parts in films and television. In 1965, Twentieth Century-Fox gave her a contract, and she was cast as one of the leads in the science-fiction thriller *Fantastic Voyage* (1966). Afterward, she made a number of films in Europe, most of which received little notice; however, the remake of *One Million Years B.C.* (1966) by Britain's Hammer Film Productions brought her instant fame. The film emphasized Welch's voluptuous figure—its main advertising poster featured a full-length picture of her in a revealing costume. She immediately became an international sex symbol. Dozens of magazines had her portrait on the cover, and her stardom in film was assured. In 1966, *Life* magazine named her the most photographed woman of the year. *Playboy* called her the most desired women of the 1970's. She also was a popular member of Bob Hope's company of stars who toured Vietnam to entertain the American troops fighting there.

Welch's physical attributes and beauty were the only consideration in her early film career. In the 1967 British-made comedy *Bedazzled*, she played Lust, one of the seven deadly sins that frequent the Devil's apartments. In Fox's *100 Rifles* (1969) she made film history by appearing in one of mainstream cinema's first interracial love scenes with actor and football player Jim Brown.

Welch had ambition to play serious dramatic roles outside her image as a sex symbol. However, her fist such venture, *Myra Breckinridge* (1970), was a critical disaster. The studio blamed her for being uncooperative and returned to casting her in minor films that emphasized her sex appeal. Nevertheless, her performance as Constance in the *The Three Musketeers: The Queen's Diamonds* (1973) won her the Golden Globe for Best Actress in a Comedy. In 1981, she was given the opportunity for another major role in the film *Cannery Row* (1982) for Metro-Goldwyn-Mayer (MGM). Then the studio suddenly dropped her a few days before shooting, giving the role to a younger actor. Welch sued, and MGM then claimed that she had been fired for being difficult and unprofessional. After a long trial, Welch won a settlement of almost $11 million, which was later overturned.

Welch had much more success on television. Her variety special *Raquel!* (1970), with many famous guest stars, was well-received. She made films for television including *Right to Die* (1987), about a woman with amyotrophic lateral sclerosis (Lou Gehrig's disease), for which she was again nominated for a Golden Globe.

After Welch's ordeal with MGM, she went to New York and appeared on the Broadway stage, starring in the musical *Woman of the Year* (1981). In 1997, she replaced Julie Andrews in the musical *Victor/Victoria* (1995). The theater critics greeted Welch's performances with acclaim.

Recognizing her all-around talents, the Los Angeles Hispanic Women's Council named Welch its woman of the year for 1990. The star's success made her famous and wealthy but also made her fodder for paparazzi and gossip columnists, who frequently reported on her marriages and love affairs.

"Like Being a Convict": Welch on Her Status as a Sex Symbol

When Raquel Welch appeared in a fur bikini on the posters for the film *One Million Years B.C.* (1966), she achieved international stardom. However, her newfound fame was a mixed blessing. She immediately became a sex symbol for the age, a favorite pinup of the Vietnam War era much like Betty Grable during World War II. She was stereotyped as a glamor girl fit only for B-films and minor roles. The studios cast her as Lust, one of the seven deadly sins, in *Bedazzled* (1967) and as the female lead (a character called "Jugs") in the comedy *Mother, Jugs, and Speed* (1976). Although she enjoyed these comedies, she longed for a chance to be seen as a serious, dramatic actor. In later years, she finally got the chance on the stage and in television.

Welch appeared as a guest star on a number of televisions shows. She was a regular in the series *Central Park West* in the 1990's and played Aunt Dora in the 2002 PBS series *American Family*, about a Los Angeles Latino family. In 2008, she played the temptress Charlene in the CBS sitcom *Welcome to the Captain*. She also performed concerts as a singer, made a number of popular exercise tapes, and has appeared in infomercials for exercise equipment and beauty products. She also marketed a successful line of wigs, jewelry, and skin-care products. In 2007, the Make-up Art Cosmetics (M.A.C.) company featured her as one of their models, and in 2010, she appeared in advertisements for Foster Grant sun glasses.

Significance

Welch was a major actor in the late 1960's and 1970's. She personified feminine beauty, glamor, and sex appeal. Although she was confined mainly to B-films, she was an international celebrity. Welch also became a successful businesswoman, again in large part because of her reputation as a beauty.

Frederick B. Chary

Further Reading

"Myra/Raquel: The Predator of Hollywood," *Time*, November 28, 1969. A lengthy cover story discussing Welch's life and career.

Welch, Raquel. "Q&A with Raquel Welch." Interview by Rebecca Winters. *Time,* February 23, 2004. A brief interview in which Welch discusses her role as a sex symbol.

_____. *Raquel: Beyond the Cleavage*. New York: Raquel Welch Productions, 2010. Welch's autobiography contains fitness and beauty advice and discusses her attitudes toward children, family and life in general.

See also: María Conchita Alonso; Catherine Bach; Lynda Carter; Coco Fusco; Sonia Manzano.

William Carlos Williams

American poet and physician

Williams was a pediatrician and physician whose poetry gradually earned him recognition as one of America's greatest literary figures. His multicultural heritage, extensive travel, associations with other writers, and close ties to his hometown all informed and enriched his writing.

Latino heritage: Spanish and Puerto Rican
Born: September 17, 1883; Rutherford, New Jersey
Died: March 4, 1963; Rutherford, New Jersey
Areas of achievement: Poetry; medicine

Early Life

William Carlos Williams, the elder of two boys, was born into an immigrant, multicultural household in Rutherford, New Jersey, on September 17, 1883. His father, William George Williams, an English businessman, was well-traveled, cosmopolitan, and a lover of William Shakespeare and Dante Alighieri. His mother, the former Raquel Hélène Rose Hoheb, a descendant of Basques on her mother's side and Dutch Sephardic Jews on her father's, had been born into a Spanish-speaking home in Mayagüez, Puerto Rico, and raised in Santo Domingo. As a child, Williams's first language was Spanish, his second French, and English only his third. His middle name honored his mother's brother, Carlos Hoheb, a surgeon in Santo Domingo.

Williams's family traveled frequently to Europe, especially Switzerland and France, including a stay from 1897 to 1899, during which Williams studied at the Lycée Condorcet in Paris. In 1899, his parents enrolled him in the progressive Horace Mann School in Manhattan. After graduating, he entered the School of Dental Medicine at the University of Pennsylvania (Penn) in 1902 but soon transferred to its School of Medicine. While in Philadelphia, he met poets Ezra Pound, then a fellow Penn student, and H. D. (Hilda Doolittle), then a student at Bryn Mawr College, and was a member of the Mask and Wig dramatic society at Penn.

After receiving his M.D. degree from Penn in 1906, Williams interned for two years at the French Hospital in Manhattan, where several physicians were Puerto Rican friends of his family and most of his patients were immigrants who spoke little or no English. He cut short a second internship in 1909 by resigning from Nursery and Children's Hospital in Manhattan rather than obey orders to falsify records. Upon returning from a pediatric residency in Leipzig, Germany, he established a

William Carlos Williams.
(Time & Life Pictures/Getty Images)

private medical practice in Rutherford in 1910 and specialized in pediatrics and obstetrics there for the rest of his career.

In 1909, Williams proposed marriage to Charlotte Herman, who chose his younger brother Edgar instead. Confused and brokenhearted, he proposed to her younger sister Flossie, whom he hardly knew, and married her on December 12, 1912.

LIFE'S WORK

Having begun to write poetry in both English and Spanish, Williams self-published his first book, *Poems*, in Rutherford in 1909. Pound managed the publication of Williams's second book, *The Tempers*, in 1913. Williams subsidized the publication of his third, *Al que quiere!*, in 1917. Thereafter, his road to literary acceptance became easier.

Around 1915, Williams established his routine of practicing medicine on weekdays, writing on weeknights, and spending weekends in Manhattan with poets such as Wallace Stevens and Marianne Moore and artists such as Marcel Duchamp. He found inspiration for the rhythms and forms of his poems in cubism, Dada,

jazz, and other avant-garde movements. He also made occasional trips to Europe, where he visited Pound, James Joyce, Man Ray, and various French painters. One result of these associations was a mutual influence between his poetry and early Surrealist painting.

Williams, like Pound, Doolittle, and T. S. Eliot, rebelled against the strict verse forms that, with notable exceptions such as Walt Whitman's *Leaves of Grass* (1855), had hitherto dominated English-language poetry. Together they created the Imagist movement, in which poetry became primarily the vehicle for sharp, clear, sometimes ambiguous mental images, as if the poet were painting on the canvas of the reader's mind. Williams, however, reacted against Pound's and Eliot's esoteric allusions and sought instead, like Robert Frost, to anchor his poetry in immediate experience, ordinary things, and locally familiar phenomena. He joined Moore and Stevens in rejecting poetry that appealed only to academics and tried to make poetry speak plainly to the intelligent laity, who understood only everyday language.

Williams's poem, "A Sort of a Song," contained his literary motto, "Compose. (No ideas but in things) Invent!" by which he meant that his images and language should be precise, trenchant, and denotative rather than allusive. Taking Moore's advice to experiment with the rhythms and verse forms of the ancient Greek poet Sappho, Williams developed what he called the "variable foot," so that the meter of his poems would resemble common American speech. His poems thus flirted with the boundary between poetry and prose. He even identified some of his most important works, such as *Kora in Hell: Improvisations* (1920), *Spring and All* (1923), and *Paterson* (1946-1958), as consisting of prose poems. Other major works include *Pictures from Brueghel* (1962) and *The Great American Novel* (1923).

Even though Williams was partly incapacitated by a heart attack in 1948 and several subsequent strokes, he suffered persecution during the Joseph McCarthy era and as a result was hospitalized for clinical depression in 1953. Williams died in his sleep at home on March 4, 1963.

SIGNIFICANCE

Williams was a prolific and multifaceted writer. Besides contributing poetry to magazines and journals, he published twenty-one books of poetry, mostly collected works, as well as novels, drama, short stories, nonfiction, and several autobiographical works. Volumes of his correspondence with Pound and many other poets have been published, and major archival collections at

Yale University, the University of Delaware, and the State University of New York at Buffalo provide additional material. General recognition of Williams's literary accomplishments did not arrive until he was in his sixties, yet he quickly ranked among the most admired of American poets. He strived through both his writing and his medical practice to instill humanistic, patient-centered values in medicine. He was a pioneer in the empathy that began in the late twentieth century to replace paternalism as the foundation of the physician-patient relationship. This aspect of his work can be discerned in his most famous poem, "The Red Wheelbarrow."

Politically and culturally Williams was an internationalist and a socialist. He was critical of the influence of the upper classes on civilization, society, and justice. He welcomed what he perceived as his duty to enhance human progress by fostering younger poets such as Allen Ginsberg, Denise Levertov, Gary Snyder, and Harold Harwell Lewis. As such, he was the de facto godfather of several avant-garde movements in American poetry, notably the San Francisco Renaissance, the Beats, and Black Mountain. The heart of his legacy is the legitimation of free verse and the development of a uniquely American idiom accessible to everyone, not just erudite readers of poetry.

Eric v.d. Luft

Influence of Williams's Mother on His Writing

William Carlos Williams's mother, Raquel Hélène Rose Hoheb, known as "Elena," was a sophisticated, purposeful woman who brought to her husband and their two sons a deep, romantic appreciation of painting, music, language, and multiculturalism that pervaded Williams's world view for his entire life. Her mother's ancestors, the Hurrards, had emigrated from the Basque country to Bordeaux, France, and eventually to Martinique in the French Caribbean. Her father, Solomon Hoheb, had emigrated from the Netherlands to Martinique, and from there to Santo Domingo, Puerto Rico, where Elena grew up. William George Williams, an Englishman fluent in Spanish, met her and brought her to the United States to marry him.

Elena spoke Spanish and French fluently but was not so proficient in English. Before her marriage, she had studied painting and music in Paris and Geneva. She became the pianist and choir accompanist at the Unitarian Church in Rutherford. She maintained that she could communicate with the dead. Such spiritualism was not unusual in the late nineteenth and early twentieth centuries, having such adherents as Arthur Conan Doyle and Alfred Russel Wallace. Williams wrote at least one poem, "Eve," about his mother's frequent spiritual trances. Other poems also provide evidence that he regarded the unpredictability of his mixed ethnicity as among his best assets.

FURTHER READING

Ahearn, Barry. *William Carlos Williams and Alterity: The Early Poetry*. New York: Cambridge University Press, 2008. Discusses Williams's association with Ezra Pound and the origins of the Imagist movement.

Baldwin, Neil. *To All Gentleness: William Carlos Williams, the Doctor Poet*. Baltimore: Imprint Editions/Black Classic Press, 2008. Explores New Jersey influences on Williams's work.

Berry, Wendell. *The Poetry of William Carlos Williams of Rutherford*. Berkeley: Counterpoint, 2011. Berry compares his own experiences as a poet of Henry County, Kentucky, with Williams's as a poet of Rutherford, New Jersey.

Copestake, Ian D. *The Ethics of William Carlos Williams's Poetry*. Rochester, N.H.: Camden House, 2010. Traces the influence of Ralph Waldo Emerson and Unitarianism on Williams.

Halter, Peter. *The Revolution in the Visual Arts and the Poetry of William Carlos Williams*. Cambridge: Cambridge University Press, 2009. Considers the symbiotic relationship between Williams's poetry and several movements within early twentieth-century European painting.

Marz, Julio. *The Spanish American Roots of William Carlos Williams*. Austin: University of Texas Press, 1994. Seeks to establish Williams as a proponent of Latino values, an interpreter of Latino culture, and a poet whose oded messages in English bore witness to his Latino heritage.

Williams, William Carlos. *The Autobiography of William Carlos Williams*. New York: Random House, 1951. Williams's autobiography is a useful resource on his life and work.

_____. *Yes, Mrs. Williams: A Personal Record of My Mother*. New York: New Directions, 1982. A supplement to Williams's autobiography that discusses his mother's Hispanic traditions and their relationship.

See also: Fernando Alegría; Sara Estela Ramírez; Clemente Soto Vélez.

Y

VICENTE MARTINEZ YBOR

Spanish-born entrepreneur and founder of Ybor City, Florida

An entrepreneur in the nineteenth-century hand-rolled cigar industry, Ybor established the town of Ybor City on the outskirts of Tampa, Florida, as a modified company town to support his cigar factory. He encouraged other cigar makers to locate there, transforming his small hamlet into the "Cigar Capital of the World." His management style encouraged the preservation of Cuban heritage, helping to create a unique Cuban American culture.

Latino heritage: Spanish
Born: September 7, 1818; Valencia, Spain
Died: December 14, 1896; Ybor City, Florida
Also known as: Vicente Martinez-Ybor
Area of achievement: Business

EARLY LIFE

Vicente Martinez Ybor (EE-bohr) was born on September 7, 1818, in Valencia, Spain. He migrated in 1853 to Havana, Cuba, where he founded his first cigar factory. There, skilled workers hand-rolled cigars from tobacco leaves for Ybor's brand, El Principe de Gales (The Prince of Wales).

The cigar venture was a financial success. By the 1880's, Ybor had become a supporter of Cuban independence from Spain. As revolutionary violence intensified, Ybor feared that his support for independence might lead to his arrest, so he joined thousands of his fellow Cubans in exile in Key West, Florida. Ybor built

a new cigar factory and soon was back in business. A series of violent strikes and a disastrous fire that destroyed much of Key West's business district forced Ybor to move his operations up the coast to Tampa in 1886.

LIFE'S WORK

Ybor and his partner, Eduardo Manrara, reestablished his cigar factory in a section of Tampa that would become known as Ybor City as other cigar makers set up business there, making Tampa famous as the "Cigar Capital of the World." In the spring of 1886, two hundred cigar workers and their families arrived. To connect Ybor City to nearby Tampa, Ybor and Manrara founded the Tampa Street Railway Company, which was 3 1/2 miles long and provided vital access for the cigar factories to the port at Tampa. By December, 1886, Ybor's factory was producing 900,000 hand-rolled cigars per month.

Ybor's plan was to create a modified version of the company town. In contrast to most company towns, in which workers and their families rented housing from the company and shopped in company stores, Ybor believed that workers should own their own homes. Ybor built small shotgun houses (*casitas*), which he sold to his employees at a price slightly above cost, and allowed them to pay for their new homes through payroll deductions. He also encouraged retail shops, laundries, and other small businesses to set up shop to provide for all the needs of his town's residents. Rapid growth began to close the gap of scrub land that separated Ybor City and Tampa, and in 1887 Ybor City was annexed. It was officially named the Fourth Ward, but residents continued to know it as Ybor City.

Ybor believed that these efforts would result in a permanent, stable labor force for his factory and end the practice of workers returning to Cuba periodically. Ybor also encouraged other cigar makers to move their operations to Ybor City, so that he could benefit from an increased labor pool. As an incentive, he offered a discount on land and a free building to prospective factory owners who agreed to create a certain number of jobs. Cigar makers in New York, Key West, and Cuba were quick to see the advantages of relocation, and soon Ybor City boasted a dozen cigar factories and related businesses, laundries, and hundreds of Cuban families.

Cuban culture flourished in Ybor City. Cuban restaurants, two Spanish-language newspapers, and the nature of work in the cigar factories reinforced the Cuban way of life. In the factories, workers joined the unions and mutual aid societies that were common in Havana and continued the tradition of the *lectores* (readers), who read aloud from a wide variety of materials as the cigar makers rolled the leaves. Because the workers rolled the cigars by hand, the workplace was quiet. Newspapers, novels, and political tracts all were popular and provided education along with entertainment.

Ybor ran his operation as a *patron*, or father figure, taking a personal interest in the lives of his workers. He often served as godfather to children, readily offered cash advances to workers who had fallen on hard times, or paid funeral costs when necessary. In return, Ybor expected a compliant and grateful work force. Ybor also supported the cause of Cuban independence

in the 1890's as the workers of Ybor City organized themselves into juntas and reveled in patriotic speeches and fund-raising. After Ybor's death in 1896, the cigar industry underwent a period of consolidation during which the patronage style of management gave way to industrialized production, and ownership of the factories shifted to large corporations.

SIGNIFICANCE

Ybor left behind a lasting legacy in Ybor City. Although the cigar industry eventually faded, the town that he founded allowed Cuban culture to blend with American culture and traditions to create a unique place and people. In recognition of its special character, Ybor City has been designated a National Historic Landmark District.

Robert E. McFarland

FURTHER READING

Lastra, Frank. *Ybor City: The Making of a Landmark Town*. Tampa: University of Tampa Press, 2006. This rambling account of Ybor City from its founding to the 1980's includes information on Ybor.

Mormino, Gary, and George E. Pozzeta. *The Immigrant World of Ybor City: Italians and Their Latin Neighbors, 1885-1985*. Gainesville: University of Florida Press, 1998. Although focused on Italian immigrants, this scholarly study includes a great deal of information about Ybor and Ybor City.

Pacheco, Ferdie. *Ybor City Chronicles*. Gainesville: University of Florida Press, 1994. A memoir of growing up in Ybor City that provides lengthy descriptions of Cuban culture.

See also: Gertrudis Barceló; Esteban Ochoa; Ángel Ramos.

JOSE YGLESIAS

American writer, journalist, and entrepreneur

One of the first Cuban American writers to be published by a major North American press, Yglesias is best known for his novels depicting tampeño (Latino from Tampa) life and exploring themes of socioeconomic mobility and cultural hybridity.

Latino heritage: Cuban and Spanish
Born: November 29, 1919; Tampa, Florida
Died: November 7, 1995; New York, New York
Areas of achievement: Literature; journalism; business

EARLY LIFE

Jose Yglesias (hoh-ZAY ee-GLEH-zee-ahs) was born in West Tampa, Florida, on November 29, 1919, to a Cuban American mother and a Spanish father, both of whom worked in cigar factories. Yglesias moved to the Ybor City section of Tampa with his mother and maternal grandfather in 1921 when his father left the United States upon developing encephalitis. In 1937, Yglesias moved to New York, where he worked at odd jobs and became involved in the movement in support of the

Spanish Republic. He served in the U.S. Navy from 1942 to 1945. From 1946 to 1947, he attended Black Mountain College on the G.I. Bill.

LIFE'S WORK

Yglesias worked as a film critic for the *Daily Worker* from 1948 to 1950. In 1950, he married Helen Basine. In 1953, he began working at Merck, Sharpe, and Dohme International, first as a translator and eventually as assistant vice president. He left the job in 1963 in order to write full time, first in New York and, after 1969, in North Brooklin, Maine, where he moved with Helen, his son, and his stepchildren—all of whom, like his grandchildren, are writers.

In addition to writing articles for *The Atlantic*, *Esquire*, *The Nation*, *The New Yorker*, and *The Sunday Times Magazine*, Yglesias published English translations of works by Juan Goytisolo and Gabriel Celaya, among others. Yglesias also wrote four works of nonfiction concerning his travels abroad. The first of these, *The Goodbye Land* (1967), narrates an encounter with his father's family during a trip to Spain. In 1968, Yglesias published *In the First of the Revolution*, which examines the Cuban Revolution through the changes it has produced in the small town of Mayarí. Yglesias continued his political writing in *Down There* (1970), which discusses left-wing politics in Cuba, Brazil, Chile, and Peru and offers a critique of North American politics from the transnational perspective of a *tampeño* in Latin America. *The Franco Years* (1977) is based on interviews with people who lived through the dictatorship in Spain.

Yglesias's first novel, *A Wake in Ybor City* (1963), deals with ideological and generational conflict in a Cuban American family in the months before the Cuban Revolution. *The Truth About Them* (1971), a fictionalized account of Yglesias's family's history, also takes the Tampa Latin community as its subject.

Many of his novels are concerned with moral discomfort with socioeconomic privilege. In *An Orderly Life* (1968), he tells the story of a *tampeño* in the corporate world, trying to reconcile the material prosperity of his adult life with the left-wing politics of his youth. *Double Double* (1974) deals with the fraught relationship between an upper-class liberal intellectual and the radicalism of the 1960's, while *The Kill Price* (1976) juxtaposes the decadence of the main characters with movements for Chicano and indigenous Chilean rights.

In *Home Again* (1987), a *tampeño* writer renegotiates his identity when he returns to his hometown after spending his adult life among the Northeastern

upper class. Its sequel, *Tristan and the Hispanics* (1989), narrates the writer's upper-class New York grandson's efforts to work through his own hybridity upon meeting his working-class Cuban American relatives in Tampa.

Written while Yglesias was suffering from cancer and published posthumously, *The Old Gents* (1996) tells the story of a dying man in love for the last time. *Break-In* (1996), also published after Yglesias's death, discusses race relations in the contemporary United States through the relationship between an elderly working-class Cuban American and an African-American teenager from a housing project in Tampa.

In 1989, the Gehenna Press and the Ememite Press published 115 copies of Yglesias's short story "One German Dead" with illustrations by Leonard Baskin. Other short stories by Yglesias were collected and published posthumously in *The Guns in the Closet* (1996). Additionally, his stories were included in *The Best American Short Stories: The Yearbook of the American Short Story* in 1972 and 1975.

In the 1980's, Yglesias began to write for the theater. In 1983, his trilogy on Ybor City received a staged reading at the Coconut Grove playhouse in 1989 and has also been read at the Public Theater and the Circle Repertory Company in New York. Another play, *New York 1937*, was performed in 1990 at the Jewish Repertory Theater in New York. Yglesias divorced in 1992, and he died of prostate cancer on November 7, 1995, at Beth Israel Hospital in New York.

SIGNIFICANCE

Yglesias is considered one of the first Latino and the first Cuban American author to be published by a major U.S. commercial press. A prolific writer, he was one of the first to write about *tampeños* in English, exploring the multilayered cultural heritage of the often-overlooked pre-1959 Cuban American community, while at the same time registering the ways in which people negotiate between multiple identities. Deceptively simple, his novels make use of received ideas about different groups in order to explore and subvert ethnic and class hierarchies in the United States.

Tom Genova

FURTHER READING

Terkel, Studs. "Jose Yglesias." In *Hard Times: An Oral History of the Great Depression*. New York: Pantheon, 1970. Yglesias's testimonial on his political education in Ybor City during the 1930's.

Yglesias, Jose. *The Goodbye Land.* New York: Pantheon, 1967. Yglesias's account of his trip to Spain and his discovery of his paternal family.

Yglesias, Rafael. "Foreword." In *A Wake in Ybor City* by Jose Yglesias. Houston, Tex.: Arte Pú-blico, 1998. A portrait of Jose Yglesias written by his son.

See also: Cristina García; Oscar Hijuelos; Richard Rodriguez; Victor Villaseñor.

RAUL YZAGUIRRE

American civil rights activist and diplomat

Yzaguirre is a civil rights activist, champion of Latino culture, and U.S. ambassador to the Dominican Republic. For thirty years, he was the president and executive director of the National Council of La Raza, the most influential American organization advocating on behalf of U.S. Latinos.

Latino heritage: Mexican

Born: July 22, 1939; San Juan, Texas

Also known as: Raul Humberto Yzaguirre; Raul H. Yzaguirre; Raul Izaguirre

Areas of achievement: Government and politics; activism; social issues; diplomacy

EARLY LIFE

Raul Humberto Yzaguirre (rah-OOL um-BEHR-toh ee-zuh-GIHUH-ray) was born to Ruben Antonio Yzaguirre and Eva Linda Morin Yzaguirre, Mexican Americans living in the Rio Grande Valley in south Texas. He was raised in McAllen, Texas, where at an early age he became aware that Mexican Americans were excluded from politics. As a young boy he witnessed social injustice, as Mexican Americans were forced to live under a curfew, and he was forced to carry an identity card. In one instance, Yzaguirre's grandfather was almost lynched when traveling home from work after dark. Yzaguirre began community organizing at age fifteen, when he founded an auxiliary chapter of a local veterans' organization, G.I. Forum Juniors. He graduated from Pharr San Juan-Alamo High School in 1958, and that year he enlisted in the U.S. Air Force Medical Service, in which he served four years. In 1964, he founded the National Organization for Mexican American Services.

He then enrolled at the University of Maryland but transferred to George Washington University, where he met his future wife, Audrey H. Bristow. The couple would eventually have six children. In 1968, he earned a B.S. degree and began a career in public service.

That same year, Yzaguirre approached the Ford Foundation about forming the Southwest Council of La Raza. He was initially turned down, but he sought the aid of various scholars, including Ernesto Galarza, Julian Samora, and Herman Gallegos, and ultimately with their research he was able to help organize the Southwest Council in 1968, with funding from the Ford Foundation. By 1972, the organization had changed its emphasis to become more national in scope and was renamed the National Council of La Raza (NCLR). Yzaguirre also persuaded NCLR to adopt various models of corporate governance and to move its central offices to Washington, D.C.

Raul Yzaguirre. (AP Photo)

LIFE'S WORK

Yzaguirre became president of NCLR after the Ford Foundation in 1973 demanded changes in the organization's management under Executive Director Henry Santiestevan. Since at this time the Ford Foundation was the principle funding source for the nonprofit organization, Santiestevan resigned his office, and in 1974 Yzaguirre was elected executive director by the board of directors, a position he held for thirty years. He immediately expanded the NCLR's focus to include non-Mexican American Latinos, which eventually became an official policy of the organization. Expanding membership brought in other Latinos, including large numbers of Puerto Ricans and Cubans. Under Yzaguirre, the organization also created a Policy Analysis Center in 1980 and boasted more than three hundred chapters in forty-one states, Puerto Rico, and Washington, D.C., with major hubs in important Latino urban areas: Atlanta, Chicago, Los Angeles, New York, Phoenix, Sacramento, San Antonio and San Juan, Puerto Rico.

Yzaguirre and the NCLR suffered a setback during the presidency of Ronald Reagan, when the organization's government funding was cut; as a result, many of NCLR's affiliate offices had to be closed, and the group concentrated its efforts in Washington, D.C. By 1982, NCLR funding had dropped from $5 million to $1.7 million, the number of employees had declined from 100 to 32, and the number of affiliates was reduced from 124 to 74, with some of these affiliates unstaffed. On the NCLR Web site, Yzaguirre refers to this era as "the most difficult period of my life."

The NCLR's centralized, national approach to policy underwent another period of change after adoption of the 1996 Personal Responsibility and Work Opportunity Reconciliation Act, better known as the "Welfare Reform Act." As a result of this law, the states were given the primary responsibility to determine funding for public services. In response, Yzaguirre reformed the NCLR, beginning a new commitment to state-level advocacy.

In addition to his work with the NCLR, Yzaguirre has served on other public policy boards and on presidential advisory panels. For three years, from 1976 to 1979, he chaired the Forum of National Hispanic Organizations, and in 1977 he cofounded the National Neighborhood Coalition and was the first Latino to serve on its executive committee. Never one to avoid controversy, Yzaguirre publicly criticized President Jimmy Carter's immigration policies; his remarks led to his dismissal as chair of the Hispanic Advisory Commission to the Immigration and Naturalization Service. Yzaguirre also denounced President George H. W. Bush's affirmative action stance and U.S. Senator John Kerry's lack of Latino participation during his 2004 presidential run. In 1994, Yzaguirre was appointed to serve on President Bill Clinton's panel, the Initiative on Race. Yzaguirre, however, criticized Clinton for appointing very few Hispanics to key positions and for signing the Welfare Reform Act on August 22, 1996; to protest this act, Yzaguirre resigned as chair of Clinton's Advisory Commission on Educational Excellence for Hispanic Americans.

In 2005, Yzaguirre joined the faculty of Arizona State University as the Presidential Professor of Practice in Community Development and Civil Rights. He also serves on the board of the university's North American Center for Transborder Studies, an organization that promotes North American cooperation and prosperity. In 2009, President Barack Obama nominated Yzaguirre to serve as U.S. ambassador to the Dominican Republic, and Yzaguirre was confirmed to this position the following year.

Yzaguirre is a sought-after commentator in the national media, and he has authored or coauthored articles in various magazines, including *Hispanic*, *Foreign Policy*, *Crisis*, and the *Nonprofit and Voluntary Sector Quarterly*. He has been a lifetime member of the Council on Foreign Relations, and he has served on the boards of various organizations, including Volunteers of America, Sears, Roebuck and Co., the United Way of

---

Yzaguirre and the National Council of La Raza

By 2010, the National Council of La Raza (NCLR), which Raul Yzaguirre had helped found and had managed from 1974 to 2004, had grown into a 35,000-member, 300-affiliate organization, with a staff of 125, a budget of $28 million (more than $90 million in assets), and a variety of funding sources. Yzaguirre, the face of the NCLR and the voice of more than forty million Latinos for thirty years, has always been an advocate for the rights of the forgotten Latinos, migrant workers, and immigrants who are otherwise swept into the cracks of the system. He has been responsible for an increase in federal financing for education programs for the poor and for tax breaks for low-income workers. Since 1996, he and the NCLR have encouraged the federal government to restore tens of billions of dollars in welfare benefits to legal immigrants.

America, the National Hispanic Leadership Agenda, the Salvation Army, and the American Association of Retired Persons (AARP).

SIGNIFICANCE

Throughout his life, Yzaguirre has demonstrated a commitment to public service, and his work has earned him numerous awards and honors. In 1979, he was the first Hispanic to receive a Rockefeller Public Service Award for Outstanding Public Service, and in 1986 he won the Common Cause Public Service Award. From 1989 to 1990, he held a fellowship at Harvard University's John F. Kennedy School of Government. In the 1990's, Yzaguirre received the Order of the Aztec Eagle (1993), the highest honor awarded by Mexico to citizens of another nation; the Hubert H. Humphrey Civil Rights Award (1993); and the Charles Evan Hughes Gold Medal Award (1998). His coauthorship of a report titled *Willful Neglect: The Smithsonian Institution and U. S. Latinos* (1994) led to the establishment of the Smithsonian Center for Latino Initiatives in 1998. In 2003, he was awarded the Congressional Hispanic Caucus Institute Medallion of Excellence and the Aetna Voice of Conscience. In 2005, the NCLR headquarters building in Washington, D.C., was named after him, and that same year, the Raul Yzaguirre Policy Institute was founded at the University Texas-Pan American.

Anthony J. Fonseca

FURTHER READING

Byrne, Dara N., et al. *The Unfinished Agenda of the Selma-Montgomery Voting Rights March*. Hoboken, N.J.: John Wiley and Sons, 2005. On pages 110-112, Yzaguirre offers a brief explanation of the goals of the NCLR.

Carbajal, Frank, and Humberto Medina. *Building the Latino Future: Success Stories for the Next Generation*. Hoboken, N.J.: John Wiley and Sons, 2008. Pages 29-30 offer detailed information about Yzaguirre.

Crutchfield, Leslie R., and Heather McLeod Grant. *Forces for Good: The Six Practices of High-Impact Nonprofits*. Hoboken, N.J.: John Wiley and Sons, 2008. Pages 165-166 detail the history of Yzaguirre's NCLR leadership.

"Raul Yzaguirre." In *Encyclopedia of World Biography*. Vol. 24. Detroit: Gale, 2005. A detailed biography of Yzaguirre, including information about his early years.

Yzaguirre, Raul, and Mari Carmen Aponte. *Willful Neglect: The Smithsonian Institution and U. S. Latinos*. Washington, D.C.: The Smithsonian Institution, 1994. Concludes that the Smithsonian Institution displays a "pattern of willful neglect" to the nation's Latinos.

See also: César Chávez; José Ángel Gutiérrez; Dolores Huerta; Marí-Luci Jaramillo; Vilma Socorro Martínez.

BERNICE ZAMORA

American poet, writer, and educator

Widely recognized as a seminal figure in Chicana poetry, Zamora has also written essays, short stories, children's stories, literary criticism, and monologues for actors. She has taught classes in literature and creative writing at Stanford University, the University of California at Berkeley, and Santa Clara University.

Latino heritage: Mexican
Born: January 20, 1938; Aguilar, Colorado
Also known as: Bernice Ortiz Zamora; Bernice Ortiz
Areas of achievement: Literature; poetry

EARLY LIFE

Bernice Ortiz Zamora (buhr-NEES or-TEEZ sah-MOHR-ah) was born Bernice Ortiz in the small town of Aguilar, Colorado, and spent her early years in small mining communities in southern Colorado. By the time Zamora was seven, her family had moved to Denver, and when she was twelve they relocated to Pueblo. Although her parents spoke both Spanish and English at home, she learned to read English at an early age, and teachers at her Catholic school encouraged Zamora's parents to have her educated in English.

Largely shielded from racism in the Catholic primary school system, Zamora was no longer able to escape it once she began attending public school because of her family's worsening financial situation. The shame of being shunned by one boy for being "Mexican" was an abrupt awakening to the social realities of the time.

In order to help her family, Zamora worked full time in the evenings during her high school years. Education was important to her, and she later continued her studies, entering college at age twenty-eight, despite being married with two daughters.

It was in college that Zamora discovered the joy of writing poetry, inspired by Emily Dickinson. After graduating with her B.A. in English and French from Southern Colorado University, she began working toward her M.A. at Colorado State University, Fort Collins, finishing her degree in 1972. Her short story, "Flexión," was published in the journal *Caracol* that same year. Zamora's incipient sense of biculturalism, which came to be one of the enduring themes of her work, was sparked as she studied literature in multiple languages. In 1974, after a year of doctoral studies at Marquette University, she divorced at the age of thirty-six and moved to California, where she would begin graduate work at Stanford University and teach at several universities. By then she was active in the Chicano movement.

LIFE'S WORK

Zamora is perhaps best known for her seminal 1976 poetry collection *Restless Serpents*, written in collaboration with the late José Antonio Burciaga. That same year, she presented her paper "Archetypes in Chicano Literature" at the annual conference of the prestigious Modern Language Association; this essay was later published in the literary journal *De colores*. By 1977, Zamora had served as guest editor for the Chicano journal *El fuego de Aztlán*, and in 1979 she helped edit *De colores* in Albuquerque, New Mexico. In 1980, she was coeditor, with José Armas, of *Flor y Canto IV and V: An Anthology of Chicano Literature*, and she actively participated in public readings of her work.

After suffering health problems, Zamora returned to California in 1982, vowing to leave academic life behind; however, in 1985 she completed her doctoral dissertation, *Mythopoeia of Chicano Poetry: An Introduction to Cultural Archetypes*, receiving her Ph.D. in English and American literatures from Stanford. Zamora eventually returned to teaching and joined the faculty at Santa Clara University in 1990. In 1992, she published several of her monologues in *New Chicana/ Chicano Writing I*. Significantly, Zamora's much-anticipated second book of poetry, *Releasing Serpents*, was published in 1994 and juxtaposed her work from *Restless Serpents* with her newest poems.

In addition to her poetry, which Zamora has acknowledged is her favorite genre, her other notable publications include literary criticism and essays. One illuminating example is "Against Extinction: The Native American and Indo-Hispanic Literary Discourse," Zamora's contribution to the 1996 critical anthology *Cross-Addressing: Resistance Literature and Cultural Borders*. In 1997, she published her self-reflective essay on her own writing, Chicano discourse, and the need for a new critical approach to Chicano literature, "Silence at Bay," in Lucha Corpi's anthology *Máscaras*.

Zamora's poetry, essays, and fiction are characterized by their intensely personal tenor. She has described childhood poverty, racism, machismo, and marital difficulties, in addition to the Chicano movement of the 1960's and 1970's, as significant influences and motivators. The recurring themes of social justice, race, gender, and class are important yet still secondary to Chicano culture in terms of their prominence in her works. Her poetry includes monolingual English and Spanish pieces, as well as numerous poems that feature code-switching between the two languages, highlighting Zamora's keen awareness of the cultural hybridity inherent in Chicano identity. Little is known about Zamora's activities since the death of her

father in 1999. By 2000, Zamora had largely retreated from public life.

SIGNIFICANCE

Zamora is a canonical Chicana poet, literary critic, and educator, having taught at the University of California at Berkeley, Stanford University, and Santa Clara University, among other colleges. Her poetry, targeted towards a bilingual audience, reflects a hybrid reality representative of Chicano identity. Many of her poems have been anthologized and many have been translated into several languages, including Spanish, German, Italian, and French. The winner of Santa Clara University's Sisterhood Is Powerful award in 1997 in recognition of her contributions to the status of women at this university, Zamora is known for her empowering female-centered discourse.

Yolanda A. Doub

FURTHER READING

Madsen, Deborah L. *Understanding Contemporary Chicana Literature: Bernice Zamora, Ana Castillo, Sandra Cisneros, Denise Chávez, Alma Luz Villanueva, Lorna Dee Cervantes*. Columbia: University of South Carolina Press, 2000. This in-depth reading guide for contemporary Chicana literature includes a detailed introduction defining Chicana feminist theory and a full chapter on Zamora's work.

Sánchez, Marta E. "Inter-Sexual and Intertextual Codes in the Poetry of Bernice Zamora." *MELUS* 7, no. 3 (Fall, 1980): 55-68. Analysis of poetic discourse in three poems that represent English-American and Mexican-Chicano cultural traditions from Zamora's canonical first book, *Restless Serpents*.

Vogeley, Nancy. "Bernice Zamora: Self and Community." In *Releasing Serpents*, by Bernice Zamora. Tempe, Ariz.: Bilingual Press, 1994. A critical introduction to Zamora's much-anticipated second book, this essay offers analysis of the works and of Zamora's significance in the history of Chicano literature.

See also: Rudolfo Anaya; Lorna Dee Cervantes; Lucha Corpi; Mary Helen Ponce; Estela Portillo Trambley.

CARMEN ZAPATA

American actor, activist, and writer

Zapata's multifaceted career has included being an actor, a producer, a translator, a narrator, and a lecturer. She began her career on the Broadway stage, was featured in many film roles, and starred in a children's television show Villa Alegre. Zapata was a founder of a Los Angeles theater company later known as the Bilingual Foundation of the Arts' Teatro de Carmen Zapata.

Latino heritage: Mexican and Argentinean

Born: July 15, 1927; New York, New York

Also known as: Carmen Margarita Zapata; Marge Cameron

Areas of achievement: Theater; acting; radio and television; activism

EARLY LIFE

Carmen Margarita Zapata (KAR-muhn mar-gah-REE-tuh sah-PAH-tah) was one of three daughters born to Julio Zapata, a Mexican immigrant, and Ramona (Roca), an Argentinean. The family lived in New York City's Spanish Harlem and spoke Spanish. Carmen Zapata's lack of prior exposure to the English language made the first few years of school challenging for her. As a child, Zapata took violin, piano, and dancing lessons and also participated in school choirs and plays. She studied at the Actors Studio in New York, a nonprofit organization for directors, playwrights, and actors, under Uta Hagen, a German American actor and acting teacher.

Zapata's professional career began with a role in the chorus of *Oklahoma*, a 1946 Broadway musical. When the show toured, Zapata played a leading role as Annie. During the late 1940's and 1950's, Zapata performed in *Bloomer Girl* (1946), *Bells Are Ringing* (1956), *The Innkeeper's Daughter* (1956), and *Guys and Dolls* (1957). She married writer Roy A. Friedman (sometimes listed as Freedman) in 1957. In the early 1960's, Zapata performed parts in *Bye Bye Birdie* (1960), *Carnival* (1961), and *Stop the World—I Want to Get Off* (1962). She and Friedman divorced in 1963. When she was not on Broadway, Zapata danced, sang, and had comedy acts in East Side nightclubs, where she used the stage name Marge Cameron. Zapata was selected as a performer in Duke Ellington's *Pousse-Café,* which previewed on March 10, 1966, and closed on March 19.

LIFE'S WORK

Sometime after the failure of *Pousse-Café* and the subsequent death of her mother, Zapata relocated to Hollywood, California. In her film debut in 1968, Zapata, as Marge Cameron, played the part of a prostitute in *Sol Madrid.* She appeared in many films throughout the 1970's, 1980's, and 1990's, including her roles as Juana in *Hail Hero!* (1969), Mrs. Harero in *Portnoy's Complaint* (1972), a nurse in *Peter and Tillie* (1972), Lottie in *Bad Charleston Charlie* (1973), Maria in *I Will . . . I Will for . . . Now* (1976), Mrs. Landeros in *Boulevard Nights* (1979), Mama Figueroa in *How to Beat the High Co$t of Living* (1980), and Elena in *Vultures* (1983). She acted onstage as Emilla in *Fanlights* in 1980. Perhaps her best-known film role is that of a choir nun in both *Sister Act* (1992) and *Sister Act Two: Back in the Habit* (1993). She played a small role in *Death in Granada* (1996). While in Los Angeles, Zapata taught drama at East Los Angeles College's Department of Theater Arts and also at the Academy of Stage and Cinema Arts.

Zapata initially hoped that using a pseudonym would help her avoid being typecast in traditional Hispanic roles, allowing her more film prospects; nevertheless, it was difficult for her to obtain acting

Carmen Zapata. (AP Photo)

Bilingual Foundation of the Arts

In 1970, Carmen Zapata, actor, playwright, and stage director Margarita Galban, and set designer Estela Scarlata rented a downtown Los Angeles theater and scrounged around for equipment, staging, and costumes. Three years later, this small itinerant theater, the Teatro Carmen Zapata, became home for the Bilingual Foundation of the Arts (BFA). Beginning in 1979, the BFA, a nonprofit theater company and cultural organization, produced and staged alternating English and Spanish versions of their programs. This production approach was a novel one that promoted Hispanic culture and tradition. For more than three decades, Zapata was the organization's president and producing director. Her career included introducing Hispanic authors and culture to students enrolled in the Los Angeles Unified School District. The BFA's *Teatro Para Los Jovenes,* Teen Theater Project, is a theater-in-education program for at-risk secondary school students. In addition to the Theater for Youth, the BFA has a Theater for Children that serves elementary school students. Zapata's work at the BFA has served to promote Hispanic directors, actors, and writers and has helped garner new talent for the industry. The BFA became a cultural institution in Los Angeles.

opportunities in nonstereotypic film roles. This issue led Zapata to help found an ethnic minority committee of the Screen Actors Guild and to join the Nosotros Foundation, an organization of Hispanic actors. In addition to her film roles, Zapata had hundreds of television appearances, including parts in the *New Dick Van Dyke Show, Married with Children, Love American Style, The Trials of Rosie O'Neil, The Streets of San Francisco, Falcon Crest, Man and the City, Archie Bunker's Place, Adam-12, The Mod Squad, McMillan and Wife, Batman, Charlie's Angels, Bonanza, Flamingo Road, Marcus Welby, M.D., Trapper John, M.D., Viva Valdez, Matt Houston,* and *Santa Barbara.* Perhaps her best-known television role was Doña Luz in Public Broadcasting Service's *Villa Alegre (Happy Village),* a bilingual children's program. She appeared in more than a dozen television films, including as Maria in *The Couple Takes a Wife* (1972), as Lorenza in *Homeward Bound* (1980), as Clara in *How to Murder a Millionaire* (1990), and as a flower seller in *A Street Car Named Desire*(1995). While she obtained many small parts, Zapata continuously endeavored to improve her working opportunities beyond the traditional

roles of maid or mother. She hoped for fewer shadow roles and more leads.

In 1985, Zapata helped narrate the documentary *Las madres de la plaza de mayo (The Mothers of Plaza de Mayo)* about mothers who protested because they believed their offspring had been kidnapped by the government of Argentina. Three years, later she narrated *In the Shadow of the Law,* a Public Broadcasting Service documentary on the plight of illegal Mexican immigrants. She also helped write *Chicana* (1989), *The Panama Deception* (1992), *Power, Politics and Latinos* (1992), *Por la vida: Street Vending and the Criminalization of Latinos* (1994), and other similar works. Supporting these documentaries shows Zapata's sincere interest in her culture.

With encouragement from director Margarita Galban, Zapata returned to New York and obtained a lead role in the 1960 Broadway play *Cada quien su vida (To Each His Own Life).* This job sparked Zapata's interest in Spanish-language theater. Finding limited availability of Spanish stage plays, Zapata helped translate Federico García Lorca's trilogy *Bodas de sangre* (pr. 1933, pb. 1935; *Blood Wedding,* 1939)*; Yerma* (pr. 1934, pb. 1937; English translation, 1941); *La casa de Bernarda Alba* (wr. 1936, pr., pb. 1945; *The House of Bernarda Alba,* 1947) and Fernando de Rojas's *Comedia de Calisto y Melibea* (1499, revised edition 1502; as *Tragicomedia de Calisto y Melibea,* commonly known as *La Celestina;* first English translation, *Celestina,* 1631).

In honor of her professional skills, Zapata won the *Dramalogue* 1984 Best Actress Award for best dramatic performance in *Blood Wedding* and was also nominated for an Emmy Award for her role in the television program *The Lawyers.* She has received a Boy Scouts of America Community Leadership Award, a Governor's Award for the Arts, an Outstanding Woman in Business Award from Women in Film, a Mexican American Foundation Award, a Civil Order of Merit from Juan Carlos, King of Spain, the Cross of Isabel, La Católica; and an honorary doctorate from Sierra University. She received the 1997 Hispanic Heritage Award for Lifetime Achievement. In 2003, Zapata earned a Hollywood Walk of Fame star for her theater performances.

SIGNIFICANCE

With a career in entertainment that has prospered over six decades, Zapata has worked on stage, in films, and on television, as an actor, a producer, a writer, a teacher, a translator, and an advocate of Hispanic culture. Her work in the community has involved guest-lecturing, fund-raising, and serving on foundations, boards, councils, and panels for a wide range of services, including the Boy Scouts, United Way, Special Olympics, the Mexican American Opportunity Foundation, and several endowments for the arts. Often dubbed the First Lady of Latino/Hispanic Theater, Zapata has received numerous awards for her efforts. Her work in the community has included being a guest speaker on college campuses and at charitable fund-raisers.

Cynthia J. W. Svoboda

FURTHER READING
Malaspina, Ann. "Carmen Zapata." In *Latinas! Women of Achievement*, edited by Diane Telgen and Jim

Kamp. Detroit, Mich.: Visible Ink Press, 1996. Biographical resource on Latin American women that includes an overview of Zapata's achievements.
Mendoza, Sylvia. *The Book of Latina Women: 150 Vidas of Passion, Strength, and Success*. Avon, Mass.: Adams Media, 2004. Covers Zapata's accomplishments in the world of entertainment.
Laezman, Rick. *One Hundred Hispanic Americans: Who Changed American History*. Milwaukee, Wis.: World Almanac Library, 2005. This collection of Spanish American biographies includes a concise summary of Zapata's accomplishments.

See also: Jessica Alba; Katy Jurado; Lupe Velez.

PATRICIA ZAVELLA

American educator and scholar

A cultural anthropologist with a Ph.D. from the University of California, Berkeley, Zavella is known for her leadership as a woman of color among both feminists and Chicano scholar activists and for her ethnographic research on Chicana women and transnational migrant labor processes among U.S. workers from Mexico.

Latino heritage: Mexican
Born: November 28, 1949; Tampa, Florida
Also known as: Patricia Juanita Zavella; Pat Zavella
Areas of achievement: Scholarship; education; activism; women's rights

EARLY LIFE
Patricia Juanita Zavella (zah-VAY-yah) is the eldest of twelve children born in Tampa, Florida, to an Hispana mother from southern Colorado and a Tejano father from the border region of Laredo, Texas. She is a fifth-generation Mexican American.

The daughter of a farmer-coal miner, Zavella's mother, Isabel Aurora Martínez Zavella Schnebelen, was born premature in a Delagua, Colorado, mining camp during the Great Depression and was raised in Colorado Springs during a time when local signs in eating establishments read "No Mexicans or dogs." Patricia Zavella's father, Antonio Abram Zavella, originally named Antonio Abram Zavala, was orphaned at a young age when his parents from Nuevo Laredo, Mexico, died. Raised by his elder sister, he led a troubled youth until

he joined the U.S. Air Force at sixteen by providing erroneous evidence of his age. It was an Air Force bureaucrat who changed the name from Zavala to Zavella, suggesting it sounded "more Italian." Zavella rationalized that the new name reflected less social stigma and he never changed it back.

Though Patricia Zavella often changed schools while growing up, relocating to air bases across the United States, she excelled as a student and was praised for her self-discipline and intellect. Though rambunctious as a youngster, in her adolescence Zavella grew increasingly quiet and responsible. As the eldest child, she cared for her younger siblings like a second mother, keeping the household under control.

As Zavella matured, her curiosity and love of knowledge led her to take refuge in the library books she brought home weekly. College seemed an unlikely path, however, because neither of her parents completed college. Her mother did not work outside the home when the children were young; her father completed some college and worked as an electronics technician, eventually running a television repair shop. Nonetheless, it was Zavella's father who insisted she postpone marriage until age twenty-five, pushing her to excel academically and suggesting she become a scientist.

LIFE'S WORK
In 1971, Zavella earned her first degree: an associate of arts in social sciences from Chaffey College in Alta Loma, California. She transferred to Pitzer College in

1973, declaring a major in anthropology and fulfilling a longtime dream of learning about cultural variation and societal differences around the globe. Her educational attainment coalesced with the national Chicano movement, which propelled her to undertake an examination of the social condition of Chicana cannery workers in the Santa Clara Valley as part of the requirements for advanced degrees at the University of California, Berkeley, where she received both her master's and doctoral degrees in 1975 and 1982, respectively.

In 1983, Zavella was appointed assistant professor to the Community Studies Department at the University of California, Santa Cruz. After being granted tenure and promotion to associate professor in 1989, she was promoted quickly to full professor in 1993 and subsequently served as department chair of Community Studies in 1994 and later as director of the Chicano/Latino Research Center in 1999. In 2010, she was made chair of the Latin American and Latino Studies Department at the University of California, Santa Cruz.

Zavella is best known as one of the earliest voices disaggregating the category "women" within feminist analyses and exposing gender differences by economic class, ethnic group (particularly among Latino subgroups), and sexuality. She is an expert on U.S. borderland issues with Mexico, transnational migration, Chicanos/Latinos, and the anthropology of work. In addition to these areas, she has taught on such topics as poverty, labor, family, social networks, sexuality, and ethnographic research methods.

Significance

A prolific scholar, Zavella published nine books. Two of these were as sole author; three books as cowriter, including *Telling to Live: Latina Feminist Testimonios* (2001), which won the Gustavus Myers Outstanding Book Award; and four books as coeditor. Her early work, *Women's Work and Chicano Families: Cannery Workers of the Santa Clara Valley,* published by Cornell University Press in 1987, transformed the field

of anthropology and Chicano studies with a detailed ethnography of Chicana workingwomen and their familial relationships. Her book based on several years of anthropological field research with undocumented immigrants from Mexico is titled *"I'm Neither Here nor There": Mexicans' Quotidian Struggles with Migration and Poverty* (2011). It examines the diversity of Mexican migrants, their subsistence struggles, and their perceptions of the perils involved in border crossing as they negotiate new identities in the United States. In addition, Zavella has published two dozen academic journal articles and book chapters for edited volumes, many of which were reprinted in other books. Her conference presentations at professional meetings number well more than one hundred. Zavella's academic honors include the illustrious National Association for Chicana and Chicano Studies (NACCS) Scholar of the Year award and recognition for leadership among Latino farm worker communities.

Michelle Madsen Camacho

Further Reading

Arredondo, Gabriela F., et al. *Chicana Feminisms: A Critical Reader.* Durham, N.C. : Duke University Press, 2003. Contains Zavella's essay "Talkin' Sex," which discusses sexuality and the Mexican cultural framework.

Zavella, Patricia. "Ana's Choice." *Ms.* (Winter, 2009). Moving account of the trials of immigrants to the United States, along with Zavella's opinions on how the U.S. government should handle the crisis at the borders.

_____. "Silence Begins at Home." In *Telling to Live: Latina Feminist Testimonios* by the Latina Feminist Group. Durham, N.C.: Duke University Press, 2001. Personal narrative about Zavella's early home life and her social and cultural influences.

See also: Edna Acosta-Belén; María Herrera-Sobek; Angela Valenzuela.

Appendixes
&
Indexes

CHRONOLOGICAL LIST OF ENTRIES

All personages appearing in this list are the subjects of articles in Great Lives from History: Latinos. *The arrangement of personages in this list is chronological on the basis of birth years. Subjects of multiperson essays are listed seprarately.*

1701-1850

Joseph Marion Hernández (May 26, 1788)
Antonio José Martínez (January 7, 1793)
José Antonio Navarro (February 27, 1795)
Gertrudis Barceló (c. 1800)
Pío Pico (May 5, 1801)
David G. Farragut (July 5, 1801)
Juan Seguin (October 27, 1806)
Juan Bautista Alvarado (February 14, 1809)
Vicente Martinez Ybor (September 7, 1818)
Román Baldorioty de Castro (February 28, 1822)
Santos Benavides (November 1, 1823)

Juan Cortina (May 16, 1824)
José Policarpo Rodríguez (January 26, 1829)
Joaquín Murieta (c. 1830)
Esteban Ochoa (March 17, 1831)
Francisco Oller (June 17, 1833)
Ignacio Manuel Altamirano (November 13, 1834)
Tomás Estrada Palma (July 9, 1835)
Tiburcio Vásquez (August 11, 1835)
Eugenio María de Hostos (January 11, 1839)
Loreta Janeta Velázquez (June 26, 1842)
Lola Rodríguez de Tió (September 14, 1843)

1851-1900

José Martí (January 28, 1853)
José Celso Barbosa (July 27, 1857)
Luis Muñoz Rivera (July 17, 1859)
Miguel Antonio Otero (October 17, 1859)
Octaviano Larrazolo (December 7, 1859)
Sandy Nava (April 12, 1860)
George Santayana (December 16, 1863)
Elfego Baca (February 10, 1865)
José de Diego (April 16, 1866)
Aristídes Agramonte (June 3, 1868)
Julio Arce (January 9, 1870)
Teresa Urrea (October 15, 1873)
Arturo Alfonso Schomburg (January 24, 1874)
Ricardo Flores Magón (September 16, 1874)
Gregorio Cortez (June 22, 1875)
Aurelio Herrera (June 17, 1876)
Cleofas Martinez Jaramillo (December 6, 1878)
Luisa Capetillo (October 28, 1879)
Leo Carrillo (August 6, 1880)
Sara Estela Ramírez (c. 1881)
William Carlos Williams (September 17, 1883)
José Méndez (March 19, 1887)

Harold Medina (February 16, 1888)
Fernando E. Rodríguez Vargas (February 24, 1888)
Dennis Chavez (April 8, 1888)
José Raúl Capablanca (November 19, 1888)
Evaristo Ribera Chevremont (February 16, 1890)
Pedro Albizu Campos (September 12, 1891 or June 29, 1893)
Mabel Alvarez (November 28, 1891)
Rafael Hernández (October 24, 1892)
Mercedes de Acosta (March 1, 1893)
Luis R. Esteves (April 30, 1893)
Pedro del Valle (August 28, 1893)
Fabiola Cabeza de Baca Gilbert (May 16, 1894)
Erasmo Vando (June 2, 1896)
Juano Hernández (July 19, 1896)
Carlos E. Castañeda (November 11, 1896)
Felisa Rincón de Gautier (January 9, 1897)
Luis Muñoz Marín (February 18, 1898)
Alonso Perales (October 17, 1898)
Ramón Novarro (February 6, 1899)
Lydia Cabrera (May 20, 1899)
Juan Tizol (January 22, 1900)

1901-1910

Jesús Colón (January 20, 1901)
Nicolás Guillén (July 10, 1902)
Ángel Ramos (October 3, 1902)

Jesús María Sanromá (November 7, 1902)
Pura Belpré (February 2, 1903)
Claudio Arrau (February 6, 1903)

Beatriz Noloesca (August 20, 1903)
Luis A. Ferré (February 17, 1904)
Clemente Soto Vélez (January 4, 1905)
Dolores del Río (August 3, 1905)
Ernesto Galarza (August 15, 1905)
Severo Ochoa (September 24, 1905)
Gilbert Roland (December 11, 1905)
George I. Sánchez (October 4, 1906)

César Romero (February 15, 1907)
Luis Leal (September 17, 1907)
José Arcadio Limón (January 12, 1908)
Lupe Velez (July, 18, 1908)
Carmen Miranda (February 9, 1909)
José Aceves (December 22, 1909)
Fray Angélico Chávez (April 10, 1910)
Horacio Rivero, Jr. (May 16, 1910)

1911-1920

Noro Morales (January 4, 1911)
Luis W. Alvarez (June 13, 1911)
Narciso Martínez (October 29, 1911)
José Ferrer (January 8, 1912)
María Montez (June 6, 1912)
Edward Hidalgo (October 12, 1912)
Albert V. Baez (November 15, 1912)
Mel Almada (February 7, 1913)
Sixto Escobar (March 23, 1913)
Lorenzo Homar (September 10, 1913)
Héctor García (January 17, 1914)
Oscar Collazo (January 20, 1914)
Julia de Burgos (February 17, 1914)
Jorge Bolet (November 15, 1914)
Fernando Lamas (January 9, 1915)
Anthony Quinn (April 21, 1915)
Gus C. Garcia (July 27, 1915)
Américo Paredes (September 3, 1915)

Joseph M. Montoya (September 24, 1915)
Edward R. Roybal (February 10, 1916)
Henry Barbosa González (May 3, 1916)
Lydia Mendoza (May 21, 1916)
Bill Melendez (November 15, 1916)
Desi Arnaz (March 2, 1917)
Gus Arriola (July 17, 1917)
Mel Ferrer (August 25, 1917)
Eduardo Catalano (December 19, 1917)
Fernando Alegría (September 26, 1918)
Rita Hayworth (October 17, 1918)
Lolita Lebrón (November 19, 1919)
Jose Yglesias (November 29, 1919)
Julian Samora (March 1, 1920)
Paul Gonsalves (July 12, 1920)
Baruj Benacerraf (October 29, 1920)
Ricardo Montalbán (November 25, 1920)

1921-1930

Ástor Piazzolla (March 11, 1921)
Raymond Barrio (August 27, 1921)
Gregory Rabassa (March 9, 1922)
David Cardús (August 6, 1922)
Eddie Saenz (September 21, 1922)
Minnie Minoso (November 29, 1922)
José Sarria (December 12, 1922)
Tito Puente (April 20, 1923)
Victor Perez-Mendez (August 8, 1923)
Katy Jurado (January 16, 1924)
Bobby Ávila (April 2, 1924)
Olga Albizu (May 31, 1924)
José Antonio Villarreal (July 30, 1924)
Celia Cruz (October 21, 1924)
Joseph A. Unanue (March 14, 1925)
Claudio Spies (March 26, 1925)
Elizabeth Martínez (December 12, 1925)

Carlos Castaneda (December 25, 1925)
Guy Gabaldon (March 22, 1926)
Elena Verdugo (April 20, 1926)
Felipe de Ortego y Gasca (August 23, 1926)
Reies López Tijerina (September 21, 1926)
Cesar Pelli (October 12, 1926)
Lauro Cavazos (January 4, 1927)
Estela Portillo Trambley (January 16, 1927)
Joe J. Bernal (March 1, 1927)
Olga San Juan (March 16, 1927)
César Chávez (March 31, 1927)
Julian Nava (June 19, 1927)
Carmen Zapata (July 15, 1927)
Eligio de la Garza II (September 22, 1927)
Art Aragon (November 13, 1927)
Charlie Palmieri (November 21, 1927)
Helen Fabela Chávez (January 21, 1928)

Rubén Salazar (March 3, 1928)
Pancho Gonzales (May 9, 1928)
Manuel Luján, Jr. (May 12, 1928)
Corky Gonzáles (June 18, 1928)
Marí-Luci Jaramillo (June 19, 1928)
Pedro Juan Soto (July 11, 1928)
Hilda Hidalgo (September 1, 1928)
Piri Thomas (September 30, 1928)
Rolando Hinojosa (January 21, 1929)
Oscar I. Romo (January 29, 1929)
Richard E. Cavazos (January 31, 1929)
Ray Barretto (April 29, 1929)

Royes Fernández (July 15, 1929)
Patrick Flores (July 26, 1929)
Margarita Bradford Melville (August 19, 1929)
Herman Badillo (August 21, 1929)
Dolores Huerta (April 10, 1930)
Maria Irene Fornes (May 14, 1930)
Marisol (May 22, 1930)
Antonio Orendain (May 28, 1930)
Martin Sheen (August 3, 1930)
José A. Cárdenas (October 16, 1930)
Jaime Escalante (December 31, 1930)

1931-1940

John Rechy (March 10, 1931)
Rima de Vallbona (March 15, 1931)
John Gavin (April 8, 1931)
Martha Bernal (April 13, 1931)
David Domingo Sabatini (May 10, 1931)
Irma Rangel (May 15, 1931)
Teresa Bernardez (June 11, 1931)
Rita Moreno (December 11, 1931)
Rodolfo F. Acuña (May 18, 1932)
José Montoya (May 28, 1932)
Lalo Schifrin (June 21, 1932)
Oscar de la Renta (July 22, 1932)
Ralph Amado (November 23, 1932)
Chita Rivera (January 23, 1933)
Willie Champion (June 21, 1933)
Linda Cristal (February 23, 1934)
Francisco Ayala (March 12, 1934)
Raúl R. Salinas (March 17, 1934)
Luis Aparicio (April 29, 1934)
Francisco Rodón (June 6, 1934)
Manuel Cardona (July 9, 1934)
Roberto Clemente (August 18, 1934)
Jerry Apodaca (October 3, 1934)
Arturo Gómez-Pompa (October 21, 1934)
Ismael Valenzuela (December 24, 1934)
Robert Martinez (December 25, 1934)
Alfredo M. Arreguín (January 20, 1935)
Oscar Zeta Acosta (April 8, 1935)
Felipe Alou (May 12, 1935)
Lourdes G. Baird (May 12, 1935)
Roy Benavidez (August 5, 1935)
Virgilio Elizondo (August 26, 1935)
Chi Chi Rodriguez (October 23, 1935)
Nicholasa Mohr (November 1, 1935)

Joseph A. Fernández (December 13, 1935)
Tomás Rivera (December 22, 1935)
José D. García (January 3, 1936)
Miriam Colón (August 20, 1936)
Juan Estanislao Cotera (November 13, 1936)
Luis Rafael Sánchez (November 17, 1936)
Hector Elizondo (December 22, 1936)
Tom Flores (March 21, 1937)
Mario Cantú (April 2, 1937)
Trini López (May 15, 1937)
Diana Montes de Oca Lopez (August 26, 1937)
Orlando Cepeda (September 17, 1937)
Juan Marichal (October 20, 1937)
Rudolfo Anaya (October 30, 1937)
Danny Villanueva (November 5, 1937)
Alma Flor Ada (January 3, 1938)
Martha P. Cotera (January 17, 1938)
Bernice Zamora (January 20, 1938)
Mary Helen Ponce (January 24, 1938)
Joe Kapp (March 19, 1938)
Lourdes Casal (April 5, 1938)
Arturo Islas (May 24, 1938)
Tony Oliva (July 20, 1938)
Rosario Ferré (September 28, 1938)
Nicky Cruz (December 6, 1938)
Carolina Herrera (January 8, 1939)
Arturo Madrid (January 20, 1939)
Flaco Jiménez (March 11, 1939)
George Castro (March 23, 1939)
Lionel Sosa (May 27, 1939)
Rubén Berríos (June 21, 1939)
Raul Yzaguirre (July 22, 1939)
Jorge Mas Canosa (September 21, 1939)
Lee Trevino (December 1, 1939)

Angela de Hoyos (January 23, 1940)
Justino Díaz (January 29, 1940)
George Romero (February 4, 1940)
Victor Villaseñor (May 11, 1940)
Frank Lorenzo (May 19, 1940)
Luis Miguel Valdez (June 26, 1940)

Luis Alfonso Jiménez, Jr. (July 30, 1940)
José Antonio Burciaga (August 23, 1940)
Raquel Welch (September 5, 1940)
Samuel A. Ramirez, Sr. (September 20, 1940)
Walter Alvarez (October 3, 1940)
Luis Tiant (November 23, 1940)

1941-1950

Joan Baez (January 9, 1941)
Anne Maino Alvarez (April 14, 1941)
Toney Anaya (April 29, 1941)
Juan Boza (May 6, 1941)
Ritchie Valens (May 13, 1941)
Vikki Carr (July 19, 1941)
Miguel Algarín (September 11, 1941)
Liliana Porter (October 6, 1941)
Leo Tanguma (November 5, 1941)
Nicholas Dante (November 22, 1941)
Ron Arias (November 30, 1941)
Pat Mora (January 19, 1942)
María Herrera-Sobek (January 21, 1942)
Guillermo B. Cintron (March 28, 1942)
Elma González (June 6, 1942)
Gaspar Enríquez (July 18, 1942)
Jerry Garcia (August 1, 1942)
Isabel Allende (August 2, 1942)
Eduardo Mata (September 5, 1942)
Lupe Ontiveros (September 17, 1942)
Gloria Anzaldúa (September 26, 1942)
Eugenia Kalnay (October 1, 1942)
Yolanda M. López (November 1, 1942)
Angel Cordero, Jr. (November 8, 1942)
Norma Martinez-Rogers (c. 1943)
Gary D. Keller (January 1, 1943)
Jose Alberto Fernandez-Pol (March 17, 1943)
Mario Molina (March 19, 1943)
Marian Lucy Rivas (May 6, 1943)
Francisco Jiménez (June 29, 1943)
Geraldo Rivera (July 4, 1943)
Amalia Mesa-Bains (July 10, 1943)
Reinaldo Arenas (July 16, 1943)
Sylvia Morales (July, 1943)
Julio Iglesias (September 23, 1943)
Vilma Socorro Martínez (October 17, 1943)
Vicente José Llamas (February 14, 1944)
Danny Trejo (May 16, 1944)
Juan Bruce-Novoa (June 20, 1944)
Eduardo Padrón (June 26, 1944)

Richard Rodriguez (July 31, 1944)
Antonia Novello (August 23, 1944)
Alma Villanueva (October 4, 1944)
Alejandro Morales (October 14, 1944)
José Ángel Gutiérrez (October 25, 1944)
Nicolás Kanellos (January 31, 1945)
Michael A. Mares (March 11, 1945)
Daniel Acosta (March 25, 1945)
Lucha Corpi (April 13, 1945)
Mimi Fariña (April 30, 1945)
Leobardo Estrada (May 6, 1945)
José Feliciano (September 10, 1945)
Rod Carew (October 1, 1945)
Gregg Barrios (October 31, 1945)
Isaac Goldemberg (November 15, 1945)
Bob Vila (June 20, 1946)
Manny Fernández (July 3, 1946)
Cheech Marín (July 13, 1946)
Linda Ronstadt (July 15, 1946)
Arte Moreno (August, 1946)
Judith F. Baca (September 20, 1946)
Mel Martínez (October 23, 1946)
Miguel Piñero (December 19, 1946)
Jesse Treviño (December 24, 1946)
Laffit Pincay, Jr. (December 29, 1946)
Norma Elia Cantú (January 3, 1947)
Edward James Olmos (February 24, 1947)
Federico Peña (March 15, 1947)
Donna de Varona (April 26, 1947)
Henry G. Cisneros (June 11, 1947)
Linda Chavez (June 17, 1947)
Carlos Santana (July 20, 1947)
France Anne Córdova (August 5, 1947)
Alurista (August 8, 1947)
Carlos Morton (October 15, 1947)
Bill Richardson (November 15, 1947)
Jim Plunkett (December 5, 1947)
Reyes Cárdenas (January 6, 1948)
Edna Acosta-Belén (January 14, 1948)
Esmeralda Santiago (May 17, 1948)

Antonia Hernández (May 30, 1948)
Gloria Molina (May 31, 1948)
Paquito D'Rivera (June 4, 1948)
Dave Concepción (June 17, 1948)
Joaquín G. Avila (June 23, 1948)
Henry F. Díaz (July 15, 1948)
Rubén Blades (July 16, 1948)
Manuel Ramos Otero (July 20, 1948)
Denise Chávez (August 15, 1948)
Carmen Lomas Garza (September 12, 1948)
Rosie Casals (September 16, 1948)
Yolanda Tarango (September 26, 1948)
Ana Mendieta (November 18, 1948)
Daniel DeSiga (December 12, 1948)

Victor Hernández Cruz (February 6, 1949)
Raúl Juliá (March 9, 1949)
Marie Arana (September 15, 1949)
Richard Henry Carmona (November 22, 1949)
Patricia Zavella (November 28, 1949)
Angela Valenzuela (c. 1949)
Julia Alvarez (March 27, 1950)
Franklin Ramón Chang-Díaz (April 5, 1950)
Willie Colón (April 28, 1950)
Oralia Garza de Cortés (May 1, 1950)
Sonia Manzano (June 12, 1950)
Gwendolyn Díaz (July 25, 1950)
John F. Alderete (October 28, 1950)

1951-1960

César Cedeño (February 25, 1951)
Linda Alvarado (June 15, 1951)
Sidney M. Gutierrez (June 27, 1951)
Lynda Carter (July 24, 1951)
Carmen Tafolla (July 29, 1951)
Oscar Hijuelos (August 24, 1951)
Poncho Sánchez (October 30, 1951)
Tony Labat (November 14, 1951)
Jimmy Santiago Baca (January 2, 1952)
Judith Ortiz Cofer (February 24, 1952)
Gary Soto (April 12, 1952)
Ileana Ros-Lehtinen (July 15, 1952)
Alberto Ríos (September 18, 1952)
Cherríe Moraga (September 25, 1952)
Joaquín Andújar (December 21, 1952)
Cruz Bustamante (January 4, 1953)
Antonio Villaraigosa (January 23, 1953)
Giannina Braschi (February 5, 1953)
Francisco Dallmeier (February 15, 1953)
Eduardo Machado (June 11, 1953)
Ana Castillo (June 15, 1953)
Jane L. Delgado (June 17, 1953)
Luis Gutiérrez (December 10, 1953)
Amalia Mondríguez (December 15, 1953)
Helena María Viramontes (February 26, 1954)
Catherine Bach (March 1, 1954)
Freddie Prinze (June 22, 1954)
Sonia Sotomayor (June 25, 1954)
Luis J. Rodríguez (July 9, 1954)
Lorna Dee Cervantes (August 6, 1954)
Norma V. Cantú (November 2, 1954)
Willie Hernández (November 14, 1954)

Leticia Van de Putte (December 6, 1954)
Sandra Cisneros (December 20, 1954)
Adriana C. Ocampo (January 5, 1955)
Paul Rodríguez (January 19, 1955)
Ken Salazar (March 2, 1955)
Fernando Bujones (March 9, 1955)
Dennis Martínez (May 14, 1955)
Jimmy Smits (July 9, 1955)
Alberto Gonzales (August 4, 1955)
Luis Alberto Urrea (August 20, 1955)
Ralph Alvarez (c. 1955)
Barbara Carrasco (c. 1955)
Maggie Rivas-Rodriguez (c. 1955)
Roberto Valero (c. 1955)
Andy Garcia (April 12, 1956)
Pedro Guerrero (June 29, 1956)
Ruth Behar (c. 1956)
Nancy Lopez (January 6, 1957)
Nina Tassler (June 19, 1957)
María Conchita Alonso (June 29, 1957)
Margarita Colmenares (July 20, 1957)
Martín Espada (August 7, 1957)
Gloria Estefan (September 1, 1957)
Hilda L. Solis (October 20, 1957)
John Phillip Santos (c. 1957)
Ellen Ochoa (May 10, 1958)
Cristina García (July 4, 1958)
Anthony Muñoz (August 19, 1958)
Julio Franco (August 23, 1958)
Wilfred Benitez (September 12, 1958)
Evelyn Cisneros (November 18, 1958)
Rolando Blackman (February 26, 1959)

Ramon E. Lopez (September 7, 1959)
Elizabeth Peña (September 23, 1959)
Carlos Noriega (October 8, 1959)
Sheila E. (December 12, 1959)
Loretta Sánchez (January 7, 1960)
María Martínez-Cañas (May 19, 1960)

Liliana Valenzuela (June 1, 1960)
Coco Fusco (June 18, 1960)
Louis Mendoza (August 25, 1960)
Fernando Valenzuela (November 1, 1960)
Elizabeth Avellán (November 8, 1960)

1961-1970

Narciso Rodriguez (January 27, 1961)
George Lopez (April 23, 1961)
Andrés Galarraga (June 18, 1961)
Maria Hinojosa (July 2, 1961)
Rafael López (August 8, 1961)
Luis Alfaro (c. 1961)
Virgil Suárez (January 29, 1962)
Emilio Estevez (May 12, 1962)
Tony Fernandez (June 30, 1962)
Esai Morales (October 1, 1962)
Jon Secada (October 4, 1962)
Bobby Bonilla (February 23, 1963)
Rich Rodriguez (May 24, 1963)
Benjamin Bratt (December 16, 1963)
Ozzie Guillén (January 20, 1964)
Gigi Fernández (February 22, 1964)
José Canseco (July 2, 1964)
John Leguizamo (July 22, 1964)
Rosie Pérez (September 6, 1964)
Rafael Palmeiro (September 24, 1964)

Lalo Alcaraz (c. 1964)
Oscar Cásares (c. 1964)
Charlie Sheen (September 3, 1965)
Laura Contreras-Rowe (March 8, 1966)
Sandy Alomar, Jr. (June 18, 1966)
Soledad O'Brien (September 19, 1966)
Roberto Alomar (February 5, 1968)
Robert Rodriguez (June 20, 1968)
Yuyi Morales (November 7, 1968)
Sammy Sosa (November 12, 1968)
Junot Díaz (December 31, 1968)
James Perez (c. 1968)
Alisa Valdes-Rodriguez (February 28, 1969)
Jennifer Lopez (July 24, 1969)
Rudy Galindo (September 7, 1969)
Monica Brown (October 24, 1969)
Sacramento Pimentel (c. 1969)
Jeff Garcia (February 24, 1970)
Mariah Carey (March 27, 1970)
Rigoberto González (July 18, 1970)

1971-1990

Selena (April 16, 1971)
Pedro Martinez (October 25, 1971)
Ricky Martin (December 24, 1971)
Manny Ramirez (May 30, 1972)
Cameron Diaz (August 30, 1972)
Félix Trinidad (January 10, 1973)
Oscar De La Hoya (February 4, 1973)
Carolina Monsiváis (May 12, 1973)
Tedy Bruschi (June 9, 1973)
Rebecca Lobo (October 6, 1973)
Miguel Tejada (May 25, 1974)
Joaquín Castro (September 16, 1974)
Julián Castro (September 16, 1974)
Eva Longoria (March 15, 1975)
Alex Rodriguez (July 27, 1975)
David Ortiz (November 18, 1975)
Martín Gramática (November 27, 1975)

Tony Gonzalez (February 27, 1976)
Eduardo Nájera (July 11, 1976)
Manu Ginóbili (July 28, 1977)
Félix Sánchez (August 30, 1977)
Freddy Sanchez (December 21, 1977)
Zoë Saldana (June 19, 1978)
Johan Santana (March 13, 1979)
Carlos Arroyo (July 30, 1979)
Jaci Velasquez (October 15, 1979)
Scott Gomez (December 23, 1979)
Albert Pujols (January 16, 1980)
Tony Romo (April 21, 1980)
Jessica Alba (April 28, 1981)
Diana Taurasi (June 11, 1982)
Miguel Cabrera (April 18, 1983)
America Ferrera (April 18, 1984)

MEDIAGRAPHY

FILMS

Title: *American Me*
Date: 1992
Director: Edward James Olmos
Summary: Fictionalized account of the Mexican Mafia in the California prison system from the 1950s through the 1980s. Starring Olmos.

Title: *. . . And the Earth Did Not Swallow Him*
Date: 1995
Director: Severo Pérez
Summary: Based on Tomás Rivera's 1971 novel . . . Y no se lo tragó la tierra, this film depicts a migrant Mexican American family. Starring Jose Alcala.

Title: *Blood In, Blood Out*
Date: 1993
Director: Taylor Hackford
Summary: This film about poet Jimmy Santiago Baca depicts Chicano prison gangs in Los Angeles. Starring Jesse Borrego and Benjamin Bratt.

Title: *Born in East L.A.*
Date: 1987
Director: Cheech Marín
Summary: A Mexican American (Marín) is mistakenly deported to Mexico.

Title: *The Chalice of Courage*
Date: 1915
Director: Rollin S. Sturgeon
Summary: This feature-length silent film features Myrtle Gonzalez, regarded as the first Latina actor in Hollywood.

Title: *Chasing Papi*
Date: 2003
Director: Linda Mendoza
Summary: Womanizer Thomas Fuentes (Eduardo Verástegui) discovers his three Latina girlfriends are plotting revenge.

Title: *Chop Shop*
Date: 2007
Director: Ramin Bahrani
Summary: This film is about Alejandro, a Latino orphan who lives with his sister in a junkyard on the fringes of New York. Starring Alejandro Polanco.

Title: *The Cisco Kid and the Lady*
Date: 1939
Director: Herbert I. Leeds
Summary: Cisco (César Romero) rescues a child whose father has been killed by bandits.

Title: *La ciudad (The City)*
Date: 1998
Director: David Riker
Summary: Chronicles the lives of four Hispanic immigrants living in New York City. Starring Anthony Rivera, Miguel Maldonado, and Joseph Rigano.

Title: *Colors*
Date: 1988
Director: Dennis Hopper
Summary: A veteran police officer (Robert Duvall) and his rookie partner (Sean Penn) patrol Los Angeles. Costarring Maria Conchita Alonso.

Title: *Copacabana*
Date: 1947
Director: Alfred E. Green
Summary: In this film, a talent agent (Groucho Marx) and his Latin American performer (Carmen Miranda) conspire to perform at New York City's famous Copacabana nightclub.

Title: *Cuban Fireball*
Date: 1951
Director: William Beaudine
Summary: Estelita (Estelita Rodriguez) is a Cuban factory worker who inherits an American oil company and finds romance with Tommy Pomeroy (Warren Douglas).

Title: *Dangerous Minds*
Date: 1995
Director: John N. Smith
Summary: A teacher (Michelle Pfeiffer) and her Latino students in an inner-city high school are affected by gang violence.

Title: *A Day Without a Mexican*
Date: 2004
Director: Sergio Arau

Summary: Mock documentary that examines the ramifications after all Mexicans disappear from California overnight. Starring Yareli Arizmendi.

Title: *Desperado*
Date: 1995
Director: Robert Rodriguez
Summary: In this sequel to the film *El Mariachi*, the mariachi (Antonio Banderas) avenges his lover's murder. Costarring Salma Hayek and Joaquim de Almeida.

Title: *El Mariachi*
Date: 1992
Director: Robert Rodriguez
Summary: A traveling mariachi (Carlos Gallardo) is mistaken for a criminal and pursued by a violent gang. Costarring Consuelo Gómez and Jaime de Hoyos.

Title: *Fools Rush In*
Date: 1997
Director: Andy Tennant
Summary: Culture clashes threaten the happiness of a businessman (Matthew Perry) who marries a Mexican American photographer (Salma Hayek).

Title: *The Gay Caballero*
Date: 1940
Director: Otto Brower
Summary: The Cisco Kid (César Romero) and Gordito return to town, only to discover that Cisco is presumed dead.

Title: *The Gay Desperado*
Date: 1936
Director: Rouben Mamoulian
Summary: Mexican bandito Braganza (Leo Carrillo) kidnaps an American heiress (Ida Lupino) and an opera singer (Nino Martini) performing as a cowboy.

Title: *The Girl from Mexico*
Date: 1939
Director: Leslie Goodwins
Summary: Carmelita Fuentes (Lupe Velez), a Mexico City performer, endeavors to marry an American talent agent (Donald Woods).

Title: *Hot Pepper*
Date: 1933
Director: John G. Blystone
Summary: Two former Marines (Edmund Lowe and Victor McLaglen) become attracted to the same woman, Pepper (Lupe Velez).

Title: *In Caliente*
Date: 1935
Director: Lloyd Bacon
Summary: A magazine editor (Pat O'Brien) gives a Mexican dancer (Dolores del Río) a bad review. Costarring Leo Carrillo.

Title: *King of the Bandits*
Date: 1947
Director: Christy Cabanne
Summary: In this film, the Cisco Kid (Gilbert Roland) and Pancho (Chris Pin Martin) must find the criminal responsible for stage coach robberies in Arizona.

Title: *The Kissing Bandit*
Date: 1948
Director: Laslo Benedek
Summary: This musical film is about Ricardo (Frank Sinatra), the son of a Mexican bandit. Also starring Kathryn Grayson.

Title: *La Bamba*
Date: 1987
Director: Luis Miguel Valdez
Summary: Biography of Ritchie Valens (Lou Diamond Phillips), the young migrant farmworker who became a successful rock-and-roll musician. Also starring Esai Morales and Elizabeth Peña.

Title: *Mad Hot Ballroom*
Date: 2005
Director: Marilyn Agrelo
Summary: In this documentary, Latino and African American students from New York City elementary schools learn ballroom dancing and compete in a city-wide dance competition.

Title: *Maria Full of Grace*
Date: 2004
Director: Joshua Marston
Summary: A pregnant Colombian teenager (Catalina Sandino Moreno) smuggles cocaine into America to earn money for her family.

Title: *Mexican Spitfire*
Date: 1940
Director: Leslie Goodwins

Summary: Dennis (Donald Woods) and Carmelita (Lupe Velez) are newlyweds who must deal with her explosive Latin temper.

Title: *Mi vida loca*
Date: 1993
Director: Allison Anders
Summary: Longtime friends find their relationship shattered by betrayal and violence in East Los Angeles. Starring Angel Aviles and Seidy Lopez.

Title: *The Motorcycle Diaries*
Date: 2004
Director: Walter Salles
Summary: Depicts Che Guevara's 1952 motorcycle road trip across South America. Starring Gael García Bernal, Mercedes Morán, and Rodrigo de la Serna.

Title: *My Family*
Date: 1995
Director: Gregory Nava
Summary: Chronicles three generations of a Mexican American family. Starring Esai Morales, Jennifer Lopez, Edward James Olmos, Lupe Ontiveros, and Jimmy Smits.

Title: *El norte*
Date: 1983
Director: Gregory Nava
Summary: Two young Mayans from Guatemala travel through Mexico on their way to California.

Title: *Once Upon a Time in Mexico*
Date: 2003
Director: Robert Rodriguez
Summary: In this third El Mariachi film, the mariachi (Antonio Banderas) must thwart a corrupt Central Intelligence Agency agent (Johnny Depp) and prevent the overthrow of the government.

Title: *The Perez Family*
Date: 1995
Director: Mira Nair
Summary: Unrelated Cuban refugees pretend to be a family to secure an American immigration sponsor. Starring Marisa Tomei and Alfred Molina.

Title: *Quinceañera*
Date: 2006
Directors: Richard Glatzer and Wash Westmoreland

Summary: Fourteen-year-old Magdalena's pregnancy precludes her quinceañera (fifteenth birthday) celebration. Starring Emily Rios, Jesse Garcia, and Chalo González.

Title: *Real Women Have Curves*
Date: 2002
Director: Patricia Cardoso
Summary: A Mexican American teenager (America Ferrera) struggles to balance her Latina identity with her American dreams. Also starring Lupe Ontiveros.

Title: *Salsa*
Date: 1988
Director: Boaz Davidson
Summary: A Puerto Rican mechanic (Robby Rosa) spends his nights salsa dancing in the local clubs.

Title: *Salt of the Earth*
Date: 1954
Director: Herbert J. Biberman
Summary: In this film, based on the Empire Zinc Mine strike in New Mexico, Mexican American workers seek fair treatment. Starring Juan Chacón and Rosaura Revueltas.

Title: *Selena*
Date: 1997
Director: Gregory Nava
Summary: Biography of Tejano singer Selena, who topped Latin and American music charts before her murder. Starring Jennifer Lopez.

Title: *Sin nombre*
Date: 2009
Director: Cary Fukunaga
Summary: A Honduran teenager begins a fateful train ride on her journey to America. Starring Paulina Gaitan and Edgar Flores.

Title: *Spanglish*
Date: 2004
Director: James L. Brooks
Summary: A Mexican woman and her daughter immigrate to California and work for a wealthy family. Starring Paz Vega and Adam Sandler.

Title: *Stand and Deliver*
Date: 1988
Director: Ramón Menéndez

Summary: This film is a dramatization of Jamie Escalante's (Edward James Olmos) experience teaching calculus to Latino high school students in California.

Title: *Sueño*
Date: 2005
Director: Renée Chabria
Summary: A Mexican immigrant (John Leguizamo) in Los Angeles becomes involved with two women (Elizabeth Peña and Ana Claudia Talancón).

Title: *The Take*
Date: 2007
Director: Brad Furman
Summary: An armored-truck driver (John Leguizamo) shot during a heist in East Los Angeles seeks revenge on his attackers.

Title: *Tony, the Greaser*
Date: 1911
Director: William F. Haddock
Summary: In this silent film, Tony (William Clifford) is a Mexican who encounters a rancher and his daughter.

Title: *Tortilla Soup*
Date: 2001
Director: María Ripoll
Summary: A Mexican American chef (Hector Elizondo) is the widowed father of three daughters. Also starring Jacqueline Obradors, Elizabeth Peña, and Tamara Mello.

Title: *Traffic*
Date: 2000
Director: Steven Soderbergh
Summary: Examines the American war on drugs through a variety of interconnected plots set in Mexico and the United States. Starring Michael Douglas, Benicio Del Toro, and Catherine Zeta-Jones.

Title: *Trial*
Date: 1955
Director: Mark Robson
Summary: A law professor (Glenn Ford) defends a Chicano teenager (Rafael Campos) accused of murdering a wealthy Caucasian woman.

Title: *Viva Zapata!*
Date: 1952
Director: Elia Kazan
Summary: An account of the life of Emiliano Zapata, the Mexican revolutionary who led a rebellion in the early 1900s. Starring Marlon Brando and Anthony Quinn.

Title: *Zoot Suit*
Date: 1981
Director: Luis Miguel Valdez
Summary: Chronicles the Sleepy Lagoon murder case that resulted in the infamous zoot-suit riots. Starring Edward James Olmos and Daniel Valdez.

TELEVISION (SERIES, MINISERIES, MADE-FOR-TELEVISION FILMS)

Title: *American Latino TV*
Dates: 2002-
Summary: Profiles prominent Latinos who have an impact on American culture through entertainment, arts, science, and sports. Hosts include Daisy Fuentes and Valerie Ortiz.

Title: *And Starring Pancho Villa as Himself*
Date: 2003
Summary: This made-for-television film presents a biographical account of the Mexican revolutionary Villa (Antonio Banderas).

Title: *The Ballad of Gregorio Cortez*
Date: 1982
Director: Robert M. Young
Summary: Television film retelling of the saga of real-life outlaw Gregorio Cortez (Edward James Olmos), who killed a Texas sheriff and fled on horseback to Mexico.

Title: *The Brothers Garcia*
Dates: 2000-2003
Summary: Series focusing on the Garcias, a Mexican American family living in San Antonio. Starring Alvin Alvarez, Bobby Gonzalez, and John Leguizamo.

Title: *Chico and the Man*
Dates: 1974-1978
Summary: Chico Rodriguez (Freddie Prinze), a young Chicano, works in a garage with a cantankerous mechanic (Jack Albertson).

Title: *CHiPs*
Dates: 1977-1983
Summary: This series about the California Highway Patrol (CHiP) follows motorcycle patrolmen Frank "Ponch" Poncherello (Erik Estrada) and Jon Baker (Larry Wilcox).

Title: *The Cisco Kid*
Dates: 1950-1956
Summary: This series, the first television series filmed in color, is based on the1940's radio series about desperado Cisco (Duncan Renaldo) and his sidekick, Pancho (Leo Carrillo).

Title: *The Cisco Kid*
Date: 1994
Summary: This made-for-television film based on the 1950's television series features the Cisco Kid (Jimmy Smits) and Pancho (Cheech Marín).

Title: *Dora the Explorer*
Dates: 2000-
Summary: In this bilingual animated series, the Latina character Dora teaches viewers Spanish words. Voices of Caitlin Sanchez and Kathleen Herles.

Title: *George Lopez*
Dates: 2002-2007
Summary: Sitcom starring Latino comedian George Lopez as a Los Angeles manufacturing manager with an eccentric family. Also starring Belita Moreno and Valente Rodriguez.

Title: *Go, Diego! Go*
Dates: 2005-2011
Summary: In this bilingual animated series, Diego, a Latino boy, introduces Spanish words and rescues animals. Voices of Jake T. Austin and Rosie Pérez.

Title: *Handy Manny*
Dates: 2006-2011
Summary: In this bilingual animated series, Manny Garcia (voice of Wilmer Valderrama) is a repairman who introduces Spanish words and explains Latino culture.

Title: *I Love Lucy*
Dates: 1951-1957
Summary: Classic series featuring Lucille Ball as a housewife who aspires to stardom and Desi Arnaz as her Cuban-born bandleader husband, Ricky Ricardo.

Title: *Kingpin*
Date: 2003
Summary: Miniseries depicting the Cadena family, a powerful Mexican American drug-trafficking cartel. Starring Yancey Arias, Angela Alvarado, and Bobby Cannavale.

Title: *Lackawanna Blues*
Date: 2005
Summary: HBO television film chronicling Ruben Santiago, Jr.'s childhood in a boardinghouse during the 1950's and 1960's in Lackawanna, New York.

Title: *Mind of Mencia*
Dates: 2005-2008
Summary: In this sketch-comedy series, comedian Carlos Mencia uses humor to examine issues of race, social class, culture, and politics.

Title: *The Original Latin Kings of Comedy*
Date: 2002
Summary: Prominent Latino comedians perform in this HBO documentary. Starring George Lopez, Cheech Marin, Joey Medina, Alex Reymundo, and Paul Rodriguez.

Title: *The Princess & the Barrio Boy*
Date: 2000
Summary: In this made-for-television film, Sirena (Marisol Nichols) is a wealthy Hispanic woman who becomes involved with Sol (Nicholas Gonzalez), a man from East Los Angeles.

Title: *Ugly Betty*
Dates: 2006-2010
Summary: This series, based on the Colombian telenovela *Yo soy Betty, la fea*, is about Mexican American Betty Suarez (America Ferrera), a bright but badly dressed assistant at a high-fashion magazine.

Pamela Mueller-Anderson

LITERARY WORKS

The works listed below are categorized by genre and offer students and teachers alike some of the best resources for the study of literature by Latinos.

ESSAYS AND NONFICTION

Acosta, Mercedes de. *Here Lies the Heart*, 1960. Acosta's controversial personal memoir which describes her passions and loves as an avowed lesbian.

Ada, Alma Flor. *Under the Royal Palms: A Childhood in Cuba*, 1998. Stories from Ada's experiences of growing up in Camagüey, Cuba.

Alegría, Fernando. *Una especie de memoria*, 1983. Recollections of Alegría's love of his native Chile through the years of his childhood and youth and of the political upheaval that was raging in Chile at this time.

Allende, Isabel. *Paula*, 1994 (English translation, 1995). A memoir and account of the sudden illness and death of Paula, Allende's twenty-eight-year-old daughter.

Anzaldúa, Gloria. *This Bridge Called My Back*, 1981. Anzaldúa wrote some of the forewords to this important critical collection of essays about women—especially immigrants—and their challenges in everyday life.

Arenas, Reinaldo. *Antes que anochezca*, 1992 (*Before Night Falls*, 1993). Arenas's autobiography.

Baca, Jimmy Santiago. *A Place to Stand*, 2001. Baca reflects on his time in prison, his religious conversion, and his rehabilitation through education and writing.

Baldorioty de Castro, Román. *Memoria presentada a la Comisión Provincial de Puerto Rico*, 1868. Baldorioty's report to the Secretariat of Fairs and Expositions regarding his representation of Puerto Rico at the Paris Universal Exposition of 1867.

Behar, Ruth. .*An Island Called Home: Returning to Jewish Cuba*, 2007. Behar examines what it meant to be Jewish in Cuba before Fidel Castro. She discusses her experience of the Jewish community both in her native Cuba and in Miami and New York after Castro's rise to power.

Braschi, Giannina. *Empire of Dreams*, 1994. The writer explores the contours of everyday life and views them through the lens of a complex modernity, exploring culturally sensitive issues, such as sexuality, alterity, and gender roles.

Cabrera, Lydia. *El monte*, 1968. Seminal work on the various forms of African religious belief and practice that persist among members of the Afro-Cuban community.

_____. *Yemayá y Ochún*, 1974. An extremely significant sociological study of two African goddesses, their cults in Cuba, and their influence on later devotion to the Virgin Mary on the island.

Castañeda, Carlos. *Journey to Ixtlán*, 1972. Discussion of the way to truly "see" and appreciate the spiritual reality of the world.

_____. *A Separate Reality*, 1971. Continued spiritual discussions with Don Juan Matus, as well as later reflections.

_____. *The Teachings of Don Juan: A Yaqui Way of Knowledge*, 1968. The author's experiences with Don Juan Matus, a Yaqui Indian magic man, and the spiritual insights he gained through their conversations together.

Colón, Jesús. *A Puerto-Rican in New York, and Other Sketches*, 1961. Personal observations of Colón, a Puerto Rican, upon his arrival in New York in the first decades of the twentieth century.

Cotera, Martha P. *The Chicana Feminist*, 1977. A study of the Chicana women's movement that includes a historical survey and essays that discuss feminist political involvement.

_____. *Diosa y Hembra: The History and Heritage of Chicanas in the U.S.*, 1976. One of the first works written by a Chicana to call attention to the problem of machismo and to celebrate the life and work of Chicanas.

Cruz, Nicky. *Run, Baby, Run*, 1968. A memoir of Cruz's struggles as a young Latino on the streets of New York, who fights against the lure of drugs and crime.

_____. *Soul Obsession*, 2005. Account of Cruz's religious conversion and the role of God in his personal transformation.

Espada, Martín. *Zapata's Disciple*, 1998. Essays with a strong social-justice bent that explore some of the portrayals of Latinos in American culture and urge a change of thinking and political and social reform.

Ferré, Rosario. *Sitio a Eros: Quince ensayos literarios,* 1986. Fifteen essays on various topics in literary criticism.

González, Rigoberto. *Butterfly Boy: Memories of a Chicano Mariposa*, 2006. Account of the author's growing up as poor, Chicano, and gay and his slow process of self-acceptance.

González de Mireles, Jovita. *America Invades the Border Town*, 1930. An article that examines the struggle by Tejanos to gain their equality in the American political and social systems.

Hostos, Eugenio María de. *La educación científica de la mujer*, 1873. Hostos's call for the universal education of women, as an essential step in becoming a progressive and modern society.

_____. *Moral social*, 1888. One of Hostos's finest works, *Moral social* is a discussion of the need for high moral standards if a society is to progress. Especially directed to the people of his native Puerto Rico.

Jaramillo, Cleofas Martínez. *Romance of a Little Village Girl*, 1955. Jaramillo's rich and detailed autobiography, which recounts the events of her life in New Mexico and offers musings on suffering, family, love, and her faith.

_____. *Shadows of the Past*, 1941. Reflections on the traditions and customs of Mexican families, which the author hopes to preserve for the younger generations, who are quickly becoming Anglicized and are losing the richness of their heritage.

Jiménez, Francisco. *Breaking Through*, 2001. Written for younger readers, an autobiographical account of the pain and difficulties endured by "Frankie's" Chicano family as they suffer poverty and the trials of dealing with immigration authorities.

_____. *Reaching Out*, 2008. A recounting of the author's college years, as he suffered homesickness, alienation, and a fear of failure as an outsider to American culture.

Leal, Luis. *Aztlán y México: Perfiles literarios e históricos*, 1985. One of Leal's most important works, which is representative of the breadth and depth of his scholarship, this is also one of the great scholarly works to examine the literary and historical contributions of Chicanos.

_____. *México: Civilizaciones y culturas*, 1955. A seminal work studying the vast number of different civilizations that have existed in Mexico, as well as the great diversity of cultures.

Machado, Eduardo. *Tastes Like Cuba: An Exile's Hunger for Home*, 2007. Machado's memoir of his family's escape from Cuba and his struggle to stay con-

nected to his Cuban heritage through the island's cuisine.

Montoya, José. *In Formation: Twenty Years of Joda*, 1992. Celebration of Chicano tradition, especially the role of the family in grounding Chicano identity and personal integrity.

Moraga, Cherrie. *This Bridge Called My Back*, 1981. Moraga wrote some of the forewords to this important critical collection of essays about immigrants and other women and their challenges in everyday life.

_____. *Waiting in the Wings: Portrait of a Queer Motherhood*, 1997. Recounts Moraga's decision, as a lesbian, to have a child. Chronicles her pregnancy and the difficult early years of her son's life.

Ortego y Gasca, Philip D. *We Are Chicanos: An Anthology of Mexican-American Literature*, 1973. An early anthology that introduced many to the writings of Chicanos and the concerns of the Chicano movement.

Ortiz Cofer, Judith. *The Latin Deli*, 1993. Essays and poems about Cofer's family and neighborhood and reflections about the immigrant experience.

_____. *Silent Dancing: A Partial Remembrance of My Puerto Rican Childhood*, 1990. Memories of the poet's childhood in Paterson, New Jersey, and in Puerto Rico, as well as social commentary about issues of concern to the Latino community.

Paredes, Américo. *A Texas-Mexican Cancionero: Folksongs of the Lower Border*, 1976. A brilliant sociological study of the importance of Texas-Mexican songs in the transmission of values and the preservation of a sense of heritage among the local "Texicans."

Ponce, Mary Helen. *Hoyt Street: An Autobiography*, 1993. Memoir of Ponce's childhood years growing up during the 1940's in the Chicano community of Pacoima, California.

_____. *Taking Control*, 1987. Chicanas confront their demons and try to "take control" of their destinies and change their plight in society.

Rabassa, Gregory. *If This Be Treason: Translation and Its Dyscontents, a Memoir*, 2005. A fascinating memoir of one of the most celebrated Spanish-English translators ever to ply the trade.

Santayana, George. *The Life of Reason*, 1905-1906 (5 vols.). A classic work in the history of philosophy that is primarily dedicated to the development of analytical philosophy.

_____. *Realms of Being*, 1942. A brilliant study of epistemology and its practical effects in daily life.

_____. *The Sense of Beauty*, 1896. Santayana's great philosophical classic in which he presents his theory of aesthetics.

_____. *Skepticism and Animal Faith*, 1923. Santayana's epistemological attack against idealism and his defense of realism.

Santiago, Esmeralda. *Almost a Woman*, 1998. The second part of Santiago's retelling of her life, covering her years as an older adolescent and young adult, with further exploration of her family life and her Puerto Rican identity.

_____. *The Turkish Lover*, 2004. Santiago recalls the Turkish boyfriend of her youth and tackles the problem of abusive relationships.

_____. *When I Was Puerto Rican*, 1994. Memoir of Santiago's childhood and teenage years and her exploration of the meaning of her Puerto Rican identity.

Santos, John Phillip. *The Farthest Home Is an Empire of Fire: A Tejano Elegy*. The story of the López and Vélez families of Santos's mother's heritage, who are difficult to trace because of their early assimilation to Anglo culture and which provokes questions of cultural identity for the author.

_____. *Places Left Unfinished at the Time of Creation*, 1999. A somewhat fictionalized biography of Santos's father's family and an exploration of his Chicano heritage.

Soto, Gary. *Living Up the Street: Narrative Recollections*, 1985. Soto describes his childhood as a Chicano living in Fresno, California, and recounts the personal challenges of those years.

Thomas, Piri. *Down These Mean Streets*, 1967. Autobiographical account of Thomas's growing up in Spanish Harlem and the events that led to his incarceration.

_____. *Savior, Savior, Hold My Hand*, 1972. Thomas's autobiographical account of the events in his life after he was released from prison and returned to face the rank prejudice and hatred of the streets.

_____. *Seven Long Times*, 1974. Thomas's prison memoir, in which he describes the human degradation he encountered while in custody and how he came to a religious conversion that brought him hope and gave him a renewed sense of purpose in life.

Urrea, Luis Alberto. *Across the Wire: Life and Hard Times on the Mexican Border*, 1993. Gut-wrenching accounts of the poverty, corruption, and suffering that Urrea encountered in his life and work along the U.S.-Mexico border.

_____. *By the Lake of Sleeping Children*, 1996. The story of poor Mexicans who live in the dumps of Tijuana and survive by picking from the city's refuse.

_____. *The Devil's Highway: A True Story*, 2004. Recounts the friendship that develops between a group of Mexicans who become lost in the Arizona desert.

_____. *The Hummingbird's Daughter*, 2005. Remarkable account of Teresita Urrea, the "Saint of Cabora," who was raped and killed but, according to local folklore, arose in her coffin and went on to lead her life as a renowned healer.

_____. *Nobody's Son: Notes from an American Life*, 2002. Urrea's autobiographical account of his parents' meeting and the family's ambivalence and struggle with their racial differences.

Vallbona, Rima de. *Noche en vela*, 1968. Journey of discovery by a woman who seeks to know herself better.

Villaseñor, Victor. *Burro Genius: A Memoir*, 2004. Memoir of Villaseñor's painful experiences during his childhood school days, when he was struggling with English and facing the contempt of his classmates and many of his teachers.

_____. *Rain of Gold*, 1991. An occasionally fictionalized history of three generations of Villaseñor's extended family, as they moved from Mexico to California, where they sought to build a new life for themselves.

_____. *Thirteen Senses: A Memoir*, 2001. Villaseñor tells the story of the early years of his parents courtship and marriage, set against the background of history of the first decades of the twentieth century in Mexico and California.

Yglesias, José. *The Franco Years*, 1975. Factual account of the plight of the Spanish people living under the oppression of the Francisco Franco regime from 1939 until Franco's death in 1975.

Zeta Acosta, Oscar. *Autobiography of a Brown Buffalo*, 1972. Zeta's comical yet stunningly trenchant autobiographical account of his early life and his involvement in Chicano activism as a lawyer.

_____. *The Revolt of the Cockroach People*, 1973. A hilarious and irreverent recounting of the actions of militant Chicanos, for whom Zeta acted as legal counsel.

NOVELS

Ada, Alma Flor. *A pesar del amor*, 2003. The story of the fourth generation of the Salvatierra family intertwined with events in their native Cuba from 1868 to 1936.

Alegría, Fernando. *Caballo de copas*, 1951. Set in San Francisco, the story of an immigrant who has come to make a better life for himself, buys a race horse, and gambles his future on the horse's success.

_____. *Camaleón*, 1950. Description of the corruption of the political system in Chile.

_____. *Lautaro*, 1944. Story of Lautaro, the great Araucanian leader who fought against the Spanish conquistadors under Pedro de Valdivia in Chile.

_____. *Lautaro, joven libertador de Arauco*, 1946. Alegría's revisiting of the story of the Araucanian hero Lautaro.

_____. *Recabarren*, 1938. The life of socialist and then communist organizer Luis Emilio Recabarren, who, tragically, committed suicide.

Allende, Isabel. *La casa de los espíritus*, 1982 (The House of Spirits, 1985). The story of the Trueba family of Chile from the nineteenth century through the upheavals of the coup d'etat by Augusto Pinochet Ugarte, peppered with the visions of the family's clairvoyant women.

_____. *Eva Luna*, 1987 (English translation, 1988). The life and adventures of Eva, a woman who charts her way through the difficulties of life by telling stories. She joins up with Rolfe, a German who tries to escape from the horrors of his native Germany through filmmaking.

_____. *Hija de la fortuna*, 1999 (*Daughter of Fortune*, 1999). The story of Eliza Sommers, a Chilean woman who befriends Tao, the Chinese cook on the ship she is taking to the United States to participate in the California gold rush of 1849.

_____. *Retrato en sepia*, 2000 (*Portrait in Sepia*, 2001). The story of Aurora del Valle, a woman of Chilean descent living in California, who looks back over the history of her affluent Chilean family in the late nineteenth and early twentieth centuries.

Altamirano, Ignacio Manuel. *Clemencia*, 1869. Describes the loves, jealousies, and betrayals, both personal and political, of Clemencia, Isabel, Enrique, and Fernando, in the years 1863 to 1864, when Emperor Maximilian's troops were attacking the Mexican resistance.

_____. *La navidad en las montañas*, 1871. The love story of Carmen and Pablo, is told in the light of the author's wish for a Catholic reform of Mexico.

_____. *El zarco*, 1901 (*The Blue-Eyed Fellow*, 2007). A study of the good Pilar and Nicolás, the evil Manuela, and the "Blue-Eyed Bandit" (el zarco), set in Mexico from 1861 to 1863. Pays remarkable attention to the historical details of the Mexican struggle against the French and provides breathtaking descriptions of the Mexican countryside.

Alvarez, Julia. *How the Garcia Girls Lost Their Accent*, 1991. A series of short tales about the four García sisters and their struggles to adapt to life in the Bronx, New York, as they fight against racism and social pressures while recalling their prosperity in the Dominican Republic.

_____. *In the Time of the Butterflies*, 1994. A fictionalized account of the Mirabal sisters, who were murdered by government security agents for their subversive activities against the regime of Dominican dictator Rafael Trujillo.

_____. *Yo!*, 1997. The story of Yolanda (Yo), an author, whose Dominican family and friends describe her in vignettes that are told throughout the narrative.

Anaya, Rudolfo A. *Bless Me, Ultima*, 1972. Ultima, a wise curandera, goes to live with the Marez family in her old age and becomes a spiritual guide for their son Antonio, as he makes the perilous passage from childhood into young adulthood.

_____. *Heart of Aztlán*, 1976. Vivid description of the life of the Chavez family, who move from Mexico to Albuquerque, New Mexico, and struggle to maintain their cultural traditions in a sometimes hostile environment.

_____. *Tortuga*, 1979. Inspired by Anaya's experience in a serious swimming accident, a fictional account of a boy who has been badly injured, suffers great pain, and must wear a cast that reminds him of the shell of a turtle.

Arana, Marie. *Cellophane*, 2006. Don Víctor Sobrevilla, founder of a Peruvian paper empire, also discovers the formula for cellophane, which leads to transparent and painful confessions in the family.

_____. *Lima Nights*, 2009. Saga of Carlos Bluhm and Juana María Fernández, who come from completely different social backgrounds and whose twenty-year relationship goes from illicit love and passion to increasing alienation and clear signs of growing apart.

Arenas, Reinaldo. *Celestino antes del alba*, 1967 (*Celestino Before Dawn*, 1987). A young boy, Celestino, narrates the story of how he cannot stop writing everywhere and on everything. One day he sees a reflection of himself, Celestino, in a well and has found his "inner self." Celestino's world is one of spirits and wondrous occurrences.

_____. *Otra vez el mar*, 1982 (*Farewell to the Sea*, 1986). A story told in two voices, that of an unknown woman who is disenchanted with the Cuban communist regime and with her life, as she suspects that her husband, Héctor, is being unfaithful, and that of Héctor, a poet and revolutionary who is also frustrated with the lack of national progress.

Azuela, Mariano. *Los de abajo*, 1915 (*The Underdogs*, 1929). Exploration of the feelings and attitudes of the poor campesinos who fight in the Mexican Revolution, questioning whether the cause offers them true hope for the future.

_____. *Mala yerba*, 1909. A literary portrayal of the plight of poor farm workers, who are mistreated and underpaid by the wealthy landowners.

Barrio, Raymond. *The Plum Plum Pickers*, 1969. Story of Chicano agricultural workers and their families who suffer from poor wages and a lack of the basic necessities of life.

Braschi, Giannina. *Yo-Yo Boing!*, 1998. A novel structured as a multivoiced collection of monologues and dialogues in English, Spanish, and Spanglish that raises issues of personal and communal identity.

Brown, Monica Alexandria. *My Name Is Celia/Me llamo Celia: The Life of Celia Cruz/La vida de Celia Cruz*, 2004. A beautifully illustrated book in English and Spanish about the life of the Cuban-born salsa singer Celia Cruz.

_____. *My Name Is Gabito/Me llamo Gabito: The Life of Gabriel García Márquez/La vida de Gabriel García Márquez*, 2007. Another in a series of bilingual children's books about the lives of famous Latin American and Latino writers and cultural figures, this volume introduces young people to the life and works of author and critic Gabriel García Márquez.

_____. *My Name Is Gabriela/Me llamo Gabriela: The Life of Gabriela Mistral/La vida de Gabriela Mistral*, 2005. A bilingual children's introduction to the life of Chilean poet Gabriela Mistral.

_____. *Pele, King of Soccer/Pelé, el rey del fútbol*, 2008. This beautiful bilingual book teaches children about the life of famed Brazilian soccer star Pele.

Cantú, Norma Elia. *Canícula: Snapshots of a Girlhood en la Frontera*, 1995. Cantú's fictional re-creation of her early childhood in Laredo, Texas, based on the use of a series of actual photographs.

Casares, Oscar. *Amigoland*, 2009. Set in a small Texas town north of the Mexican border, Amigoland tells the story of the three Rosales brothers, their estrangement from one another, and their struggles with the internal demons that haunt them and keep them isolated.

Castillo, Ana. *The Mixquiahuala Letters*, 1986. Explores the relationship between two strong women: Alicia, who is an artist, and Teresa, who is a writer. The two form strong bonds of respect and friendship.

_____. *Sapogonia: An Anti-Romance in 3/8 Meter*, 1994. The fictional tale of Máximo Madrigal, who has abandoned his native land, Sapogonia, and struggles with his new identity as a mestizo.

_____. *So Far from God*, 1994. A tale of how Sofi's three-year-old daughter dies, is resurrected, and affects the lives of the other three daughters in this Chicano family in New Mexico.

Chávez, Denise. *Face of an Angel*, 1994. Soveida Dosamantes writes a handbook for waitresses and recalls her own struggle as a woman who has served at the beck and call of men throughout her life.

_____. *Loving Pedro Infante*, 2002. Tere Avila, a member of the Pedro Infante Fan Club, watches the Mexican star's films with her best friend, Irma, as the two women share their frustrations with life and love but take consolation in their Mexican heritage.

Cisneros, Sandra. *Caramelo*, 2002. Young Celaya tells the saga of her Mexican family, the Reyes, which spans over three turbulent generations and is filled with rich details of Mexican life.

_____. *The House on Mango Street*, 1984. Young Esperanza Cordero speaks about her family and about the poverty and violence among Latinos in her neighborhood in Chicago.

Corpi, Lucha. *Cactus Blood*, 1995. Chicana detective Gloria Damasco investigates the suspicious suicide of Sonny Mares, an old friend from the United Farmworkers' strike.

_____. *Delia's Song*, 1989. A young Chicana leaves her family to go to college. After a long succession of loves, political involvements, and further studies, she completes her doctorate and pursues a career as a writer.

_____. *Eulogy for a Brown Angel: A Mystery Novel*, 1992. Mystery tale about the search for the murderer of a three-year-old boy in Los Angeles during a national Chicano moratorium.

Díaz, Junot. *The Brief Wonderous Life of Oscar Wao*, 2007. Oscar, an overweight and retiring boy of Dominican heritage who is obsessed with computer games and dreams of becoming a great writer, must deal with the antics of his family and friends and, most important, the family curse.

Ferré, Rosario. *Flight of the Swan/El vuelo del cisne*, 2001. When a Russian ballet company is stranded in Puerto Rico because of the 1917 revolution, its leader, the aging ballet instructor known as Madame, falls in love with a young Puerto Rican revolutionary, Masha, who becomes a convinced Bolshevik. She is brought back to reality by one of her students.

_____. *The House on the Lagoon*, 1995. Isabel decides to write the histories of her and her husband's families, and, in the process, describes Puerto Rico's history of social injustice and racial prejudice.

_____. *The Youngest Doll*, 1991. The struggle of a woman to free herself from the overweening patriarchal structure of her family and of Puerto Rican society.

Galarza, Ernesto. *Barrio Boy*, 1971. The journey of a boy from a tiny town in Mexico to a Chicano barrio in Sacramento, California, which is filled with interesting challenges and adventures.

García, Cristina. *The Agüero Sisters*, 1997. The story of the two Agüero sisters: Reina, who supports the Fidel Castro revolution, and Constancia, who fled for the United States and became thoroughly Americanized. Recounts the sisters' eventual reunion and sharing of family history.

_____. *Dreaming in Cuban*, 1992. The story of three generations of Del Pino women from Cuba, their lives, their loves, and the significance of their Cuban heritage in the life of each.

_____. *Monkey Hunting*, 2003. The saga of the Chens, a Chinese family who have immigrated to Cuba, who suffer through the turbulence of historical events both in China and in Cuba.

Goldemberg, Isaac. *The Fragmented Life of Don Jacobo Lerner*, 1976. Members of a Jewish family in Peru tell the life of Don Jacobo Lerner, an immigrant from Czarist Russia.

_____. *El nombre del padre*, 2001. Shortly before World War II, two Russian Jews arrive in San Sebastián

and find themselves condemned for being Jews, as well as accused of being communists.

González, Rigoberto. *The Mariposa Club*, 2009. The story of four openly gay Latino high school boys who found the Mariposa Club, their school's first lesbian-gay-bisexual-transgender (LGBT) organization. When an act of homophobic violence is perpetrated, all attention focuses on the boys and their leadership.

González de Mireles, Jovita. *Caballero: A Historical Novel*, 1996. A tale of the Mexican War of 1848, as seen from the Mexican perspective. The story focuses on two young people who fall in love--a Mexican girl and an Anglo boy-- and describes their attempts to cross racial barriers.

Hijuelos, Oscar. *Empress of the Splendid Season*, 1999. Lydia España, a spoiled daughter of a wealthy Cuban family, is sent to New York as a punishment for breaking the strict family social code, and she must now earn a living as a cleaning woman to keep her family together.

_____. *The Fourteen Sisters of Emilio Montez O'Brien*, 1993. Exploration of the lives and loves of the members of the Montez O'Brien family of mixed Irish and Cuban heritage, which is composed of fourteen daughters and one son.

_____. *The Mambo Kings Play Songs of Love*, 1990. Two Cuban brothers, César and Néstor Castillo, immigrate to New York City, form their own band, the Mambo Kings, and experience the high life of clubs and even a television appearance with Desi Arnaz.

_____. *Mr. Ives' Christmas*, 1995. A heartwarming tale of Mr. Ives, who slowly brings himself to forgive the young man who gunned down his seventeen-year-old son.

_____. *Our House in the Last World*, 1983. Héctor Santino, the son of Cuban immigrants, learns about his Cuban heritage by listening to the recollections of his parents, and he comes to love their traditions.

_____. *A Simple Habana Melody*, 2002. Israel Levis, the composer of the song "Rosas Puras," returns to his hometown in Cuba, and he is overwhelmed by memories of his childhood that clash with the realities of the suffering in his later life at the hands of the Nazis in Europe.

Hinojosa, Rolando. *Estampas del valle y otras obras*, 1973. The first of Hinojosa's Klail City Death Trip series, this novel is composed of impressions of Chicano life in Belken County, Texas, close to the

Mexican border, during the economic depression of the 1950's.

———. *Klail City y sus alrededores*, 1976 (*Klail City*, 1987). Humorous accounts of everyday life in the fictional small Texas city, with particular attention given to the Chicanos' unique forms of expression.

———. *Korean Love Songs from Klail City Death Trip*, 1978. Composed of several long poems, the novel focuses on Texas Chicano Rafa Buenrostro's experiences as a soldier in the Korean War.

———. *We Happy Few*, 2006. A novel of academic intrigue, racism, and campus politics about the relations between faculty members and the administration of Belken State University in Klail City, Texas.

Hostos, Eugenio María de. *La peregrinación de Bayoán*, 1863. A Puerto Rican romantic novel written in the form of a diary, which mixes love with the political reality of Puerto Rico under Spanish rule.

Islas, Arturo. *Migrant Souls*, 1991. The struggle of Josie Salazar, who fights against her own family's prejudice against the darker members of their family, including herself, and her struggle to survive in her Texas homeland.

———. *La Mollie and the King of Tears*, 1996. Chicano Louis Mendoza, who lives in San Francisco and is an enthusiast for all things English, speaks from his hospital bed to an unknown visitor about his life.

———. *The Rain God: A Desert Tale*, 1984. The story of Mama Chona, who comes to Texas fleeing from the Mexican Revolution of 1910, and the joys, fears, and struggles of the next two generations of her family to make progress in America.

Mohr, Nicholasa. *Nilda*, 1986. A young Puerto Rican girl, Nilda, must learn to cope with the insults of authority figures and comes to find support in her large family.

Morales, Alejandro. *The Brick People*, 1988. An imaginative fictional elaboration of the history of Chicanos and Anglos who work together at the Simons Brick Factory #3 in Southern California, describing the issues of race that arise as a consequence.

———. *Caras viejas y vino nuevo*, 1975. Two teenage boys experience the harsh realities of a Latino barrio that is the locus of violence, frustration, and desperate poverty.

———. *La verdad sin voz*, 1979 (*Death of an Anglo*, 1988). An Anglo doctor is killed while serving the Chicano community, which raises questions among the Chicanos as to what it means to be Chicano and what it means to sacrifice oneself for La Raza.

Paredes, Américo. *George Washington Gómez: A Mexicotexan Novel*, 1990. The struggle of a young Chicano "Texican," who fights against poverty, theft, and regular abuses of power by local Anglo authorities and struggles to preserve his Mexican heritage.

———. *The Shadow*, 1998. A story of the struggle between Antonio Cuitla, a leader of the people in a poor Mexican village, and Don José, the cruel landowner who oppresses the workers.

Ponce, Mary Helen. *The Wedding*, 1989. The preparation and performing of Blanca's wedding, offering many insights into the interests and personalities of the Chicano community which is her home.

Portillo Trambley, Estela. *Trini*, 1986. A young Mexican woman is abandoned by her mother and works her way through the northern badlands of Mexico into the United States, where she hopes to make a better way of life for herself and her children.

Ramos Otero, Manuel. *La novelabingo*, 1976. Constructed like a bingo game with the chapters being the "numbers" that are called, this novel is a search for the meaning of puertorriqueñidad in modern society.

Rechy, John. *City of Night*, 1963. The saga of young male prostitutes who live and work in urban settings of danger, intrigue, violence, and sometimes affection, throughout the United States.

———. *The Miraculous Day of Amalia Gómez*, 1991. The story of Amalia Gómez, who has been repeatedly abused sexually by members of her Mexican family. She struggles to maintain her faith and hope in the face of overwhelming tragedy and suffering.

———. *Numbers*, 1968. Middle-aged Johnny Rio, once a desired man on the gay streets of Los Angeles, returns to the scene of his former glories to try to revive his sexual allure.

———. *Rushes*, 1979. Endore spends an evening in a gay leather bar seeking intimacy and maybe even some sex but winds up joining in a sadomasochistic orgy.

Rivera, Tomás. *. . . y no se lo tragó la tierra*, 1971. The experiences of a young boy who suffers through the pain of racism and mistreatment by Anglo farm owners and who must learn to endure the constant need to move in order to find work and make a living.

Sánchez, Luis Rafael. *La guaracha del macho Camacho*, 1976. The rhythm of a Macho Camacho's guaracha plays on radios, televisions, and record players all over San Juan, Puerto Rico, and guides the movements, thoughts, and words of several individuals whose lives are portrayed.

Santayana, George. *The Last Puritan: A Memoir in the Form of a Novel*, 1935. A fictional account of the life of Oliver Alden, who struggles to free himself from the strictures of responsibility and duty to family, friends, and his studies.

Santiago, Esmeralda. *América's Dream,* 1996. América González flees her abusive lover and alcoholic mother and goes to Westchester, New York, to work as a housekeeper, but she must eventually face the demons of her past.

Soto, Pedro Juan. *Usmaíl*, 1959. The story of Usmaíl, a mixed-race boy who is abandoned by his father, whose mother dies, and who must now make a living on the Puerto Rican island of Vieques, which has been largely taken over by the United States Navy.

Suárez, Virgil. *The Cutter*, 1999. After years of service to the Fidel Castro regime as a sugarcane cutter, Julián is promised that he may join his parents in the United States, but when he protests that news of his grandmother's death has been withheld, he plans a secret escape to America.

_____. *Latin Jazz*, 1989. A Cuban family comes to the United States on the Mariel Boatlift and struggles to find their place in American society.

Suárez y Romero, Anselmo. *Francisco*, 1880. The love story of two slaves, Francisco and Dorotea, whose masters do whatever they can to keep the lovers apart.

Tafolla, Carmen. *What Can You Do with a Rebozo?*, 2008. A children's book in which a family explains many things that can be done with a rebozo, a traditional Mexican shawl.

Valdés-Rodríguez, Alisa. *The Dirty Girls Social Club,* 2003. The lives of six Latinas in their late twenties who narrate how their fortunes in love and profes-

sions are moving towards their fulfillment, yet are fraught with difficulties.

_____. *Hater*, 2006. Aimed at young adults, Hater is a first-person narrative of Paski, a beautiful and somewhat psychic Latina, who competes with her rival, Jessica, for her boyfriend.

_____. *Playing with Boys*, 2004. Three Latinas in a band try to get ahead but find plenty of challenges with the men in their lives.

Villanueva, Alma Luz. *Naked Ladies*, 1994. A novel that addresses many contemporary social problems, including acquired immunodeficiency syndrome (AIDS), discrimination against women and gays, breast cancer, infidelity, and racial prejudice, as told through the lives of multiple characters.

_____. *The Ultraviolet Sky*, 1988. Rosa, a teacher and a painter, changes the direction of her life, especially in her pursuit of love, and fights against the disapproval of her family and friends. She ultimately recognizes that she must go it alone.

Viramontes, Helena María. *Under the Feet of Jesus*, 1995. The life of Mexican migrant workers as seen through the eyes of Estrella, a thirteen-year-old girl who endures the hardships of her family's life and still offers a vision of hope.

Yglesias, José. *An Orderly Life*, 1968. The well-ordered life of Rafe Sabas comes apart when a friend from the past, Jerry, collapses emotionally and the two men finally speak bluntly about their histories.

_____. *Tristan and the Hispanics*, 1989. Tristan, a serious Yale University student, goes to Miami to arrange for his grandfather's cremation. He meets his Cuban relatives, who turn his world upside down, leading him to discover the meaning of his heritage.

PLAYS

Baca, Jimmy Santiago. *Bound by Honor*, 1993. The terrible effects of gang violence on three Chicano friends from East Los Angeles.

Fornés, María Irene. *The Conduct of Life*, 1985. A Latin American lieutenant uses military strategy to juggle his simultaneous relationships with his mistress and his wife.

_____. *Fefu and Her Friends*, 1977. The unusual lives of eight strong-willed women who meet in a country house in New England to plan a fund-raising event.

_____. *Promenade*, 1965. The adventures of two escaped prisoners who wander in the city.

_____. *Sarita*, 1984. The story of Sarita, a woman whose relationship with her husband, Mark, and her son, Melo, is tainted by an abusive parallel relationship with her lover since childhood, Julio.

_____. *There! You Died*, 1963. Theatrical remake of Fornés's Tango Palace (1960), the story of Leopold, who cannot escape his essential need for Isidore's love, no matter how much he must submit himself to Isidore's authority.

Machado, Eduardo. *Broken Eggs,* 1984. Although the Márquez family, who are immigrants from Cuba, have found success in America, they cannot forget their native land and culture and pine to return.

_____. *The Cook*, 2003. Gladys, the cook of the wealthy Batislano family that flees Cuba, cares for the family mansion for forty years, only to be forgotten by her mistress, Adria, and accused of living in a house that is not hers.

_____. *Havana Is Waiting,* 2000. A writer named Federico returns to Cuba after thirty years with his friend Fred, meets Ernesto, who has lived his whole life in Havana, and begins an animated dialogue about the political and social realities of Fidel Castro's Cuba.

Moraga, Cherrie. *Watsonville: Some Place Not Here/ Circle in the Dirt: El pueblo de East Palo Alto,* 2002. Two plays that portray the resistance of poor Chicano communities to the power structures of the Anglo political system in Watsonville and East Palo Alto, both in California.

Portillo Trambly, Estela. *Sor Juana, and Other Plays*, 1983. Interesting exploration of the life and times of Sor Juana Inés de la Cruz, perhaps Mexico's greatest literary mind.

Sánchez, Luis Rafael. *La pasión según Antígona Pérez*, 1970. A tragedy based on Sophocles' character Antigone, this play tells the true story of Olga Viscal Garriga, a mother of three and a member of the Puerto Rican Nationalist Party who was imprisoned for civil disobedience.

Valdez, Luis. *La Bamba*, 1985. Screenplay recounting the life and death of Chicano rock and roll artist Richie Valens.

_____. *La Pastorela*, 1975. A recreation of the Three Kings' pilgrimage to adore the Christ child.

_____. *Zoot Suit*, 1981. Dramatic representation of the murder of a Chicano in Los Angeles in 1942 and the Zoot Suit Riots that soon erupted as a response to the racial prejudice and violence experienced by local Chicanos.

POETRY COLLECTIONS

Acosta, Mercedes de. *Moods: Prose Poems*, 1919. The poet, of Cuban and Spanish heritage, writes of faith, love, feelings, weariness, peace, and dreams in this early collection of beautiful verse.

Ada, Alma Flor. *Gathering the Sun: An Alphabet in Spanish and English*, 1997. Children learn a Spanish word for each letter of the alphabet and hear two poems, one in English and one in Spanish, that describe the importance of what is being defined in terms of the lives of agricultural workers.

Alegría, Fernando. *Changing Centuries: Selected Poems by Fernando Alegría*, 1984. The poet evokes historical moments and figures from across the Americas, interspersing these accounts with personal musings about life and his own travels.

Algarín, Miguel. *Body Bee Calling from the Twenty-first Century,* 1982. Poems about life on the Lower East Side of New York with a view to the future, as well as the past and the present.

_____. *On Call*, 1980. Reflections on the nature of identity and the meeting of cultures as expressed through innovative forms of verse.

_____. *Survival supervivencia*, 2009. Poems written in English, Spanish, and Spanglish that bring Algarín's family, friends, and neighborhood to life, while also addressing social and political struggles.

_____. *Time's Now/Ya es tiempo*, 1985. Poetic explorations about life in New York City, many with marked religious themes and reflections.

Altamirano, Ignacio Manuel. *Rimas*, 1880. Poetry that celebrates nature and love.

Alurista. *As Our Barrio Turns: Who the Yoke B On?,* 2000. Personal poems that describe the poet's everyday surroundings: family, friends, his neighborhood, and the problems and challenges that confront the Chicanos who live in the area.

_____. *Et tú...Raza?*, 1996. Poetic reflections on Alurista's past political activities and hopes to change the American system of government, now tempered with age.

_____. *Floricanto en Aztlán*, 1971. Alurista's first collection of poetry, in which he combines elements from Spanish, English, and pre-Columbian languages to express his identification with his Chicano heritage and sense of alienation from mainstream America.

_____. *Nationchild Plumaroja, 1969-1972*, 1972. A call to arms for Chicanos to take pride in their heritage and resist the oppression of Anglo America.

_____. *Return: Poems Collected and New*, 1982. The poet explores many aspects of his life, speaking frankly and with great feeling.

_____. *Spik in glyph?*, 1981. A collection of poems in which Alurista plays with strange verbal combinations, mixing Spanish and English to produce comic effect, and, at the same time, thought-provoking linguistic juxtapositions.

_____. *Timespace Huracán: Poems, 1972-1975*, 1976. Thoughts on the importance of pre-Columbian myths and the values of the Mexican people in forging a better future for Chicanos in the United States.

_____. *Z Eros*, 1995. A collection of poetry in which Alurista diverges somewhat from his customary concentration on political and social themes to addresses aspects of erotic love.

Alvarez, Julia. *Homecoming*, 1984. Poems celebrating Alvarez's Dominican heritage, the challenges of living the immigrant experience, and the beauty of nature.

_____. *The Other Side/El otro lado*, 1995. Reflections on Alvarez's departure from her native land and on the changes she notices in her identity after her return to the Dominican Republic as an immigrant to the United States.

_____. *The Woman I Kept to Myself*, 2004. Autobiographical poems on Alvarez's childhood, on her work as an author, and on the bittersweet experiences of love, marriage, death, and faith.

Anaya, Rudolfo A. *The Adventures of Juan Chicaspatas*, 1985. A comic epic based on a marijuana-induced dream of the historical figures, mythical and real, great and small, from Mexico and the Southwest United States.

Anzaldúa, Gloria. *Borderlands/La frontera: The New Mestiza*, 1987. Writing in Spanish and English, Anzaldúa intersperses prose and poetry in her personal reflections and critical analysis of questions of racial, linguistic, gender, national, and sexual identity .

Baca, Jimmy Santiago. *Immigrants in Our Own Land*, 1979. Baca captures the raw anger and frustration of Chicanos, who are treated like immigrants in America that they believe to have been their traditional homeland of Aztlán.

_____. *Martin and Meditations on the South Valley*, 1987. Verses that highlight the suffering, anger, and sense of oppression experienced by poor working Chicanos, who are often treated with hatred and disrespect.

Burgos, Julia de. *Canción de la verdad sencilla*, 1982. A collection of lyric poems that speak of love, nature, and the wonder of life.

_____. *El mar y tú: Otros poemas*, 1954. Poems composed in Burgos's final years that celebrate life, nature, and erotic love.

_____. *Poema en veinte surcos*, 1938. Verses published during Burgos's lifetime which treat nature, love, and life. This book's publication paid for her mother's medical expenses.

Cárdenas, Reyes. *Chicano Territory: Poems*, 1975. Poetic memoir of Cárdenas's youth and Chicano family life.

_____. *Elegies for John Lennon*, 2006. Verses written in praise of Lennon, the famous Beatle who was also known for his social activism.

_____. *I Was Never a Militant Chicano*, 1986. Whimsical poetic reflections on Chicano identity and the pride of race that does not feel the need to become outwardly involved in politics.

Casal, Lourdes. *Los fundadores: Alfonso y otros cuentos*, 1973. Poems about life as an exile and the struggles of adapting to a new culture.

_____. *Palabras juntan revolución*, 1981. Poetry evoking Casal's Cuban homeland, filled with bittersweet recollections of escape from the island and exile in the United States.

Castillo Ana. *My Daughter, My Son, The Eagle, The Dove*, 2000. A modern version, in verse, of ancient Nahuatl chants, which is richly illustrated and expresses the hope of success for younger generations of Chicanos.

_____. *My Father Was a Toltec, and Selected Poems, 1973-1988*, 1995. Poetry in English and Spanish that recalls the poet's Toltec heritage, her family, and the challenges that confront modern Chicanos in the United States.

Catalá, Rafael. *Cienciapoesía*,1984. Experimental verses expressing themes of social justice.

Cervantes, Lorna Dee. *Drive: The First Quartet—New Poems, 1980-2005*, 2006. Bilingual poems that range from criticism of global injustices to love, family, and recollections of the writer's childhood and youth.

_____. *Emplumada*, 1981. Poetic explorations of the life of the East Bay and of San Jose, California, especially as seen through the perspective of Chicano immigrants who work in the area's fields and factories.

_____. *From the Cables of Genocide: Poems on Love and Hunger*, 1991. A collection of poetry that depicts scenes of the significant people and places in Cervantes's life and which addresses various social injustices.

Corpi, Lucha. *Palabras de mediodía /Noon Words*. Poems about Corpi's Mexican heritage, love, and the power of literature.

De Hoyos, Angela. *Arise Chicano!, and Other Poems*, 1975. A bilingual call to arms for Chicanos to embrace their culture and confront the Anglo world that appears to be disinterested in them and their way of life.

_____. *Chicano Poems: For the Barrio*, 1975. De Hoyos describes the painful reality of racial and linguistic prejudice. He calls for Chicanos to stand up for their status as being among the first peoples of America, long before the arrival of Europeans.

_____. *Woman, Woman*, 1987. An interesting poetic consideration of the differences between men and women and how these differences affect the Chicano way of life and political movement.

Espada, Martín. *City of Coughing and Dead Radiators*, 1993. A powerful poetic portrayal of the plight of indigent urban Latinos in the United States.

_____. *Imagine the Angels of Bread*, 1996. Verse with a strong political and mystical bent that urges readers to imagine a world without the social injustice brought on by human insecurity and prejudice.

_____. *The Immigrant Iceboy's Bolero*, 1982. Sympathetic poetic portrayals of the difficulties confronted by poor, working-class Latino immigrants, highlighted by photographs taken by the poet's father, Frank Espada.

_____. *Rebellion Is the Circle of a Lover's Hands*, 1990. Sardonic poems that condemn the injustices perpetrated against poor Latinos in the cities of the United States.

_____. *Trumpets from the Islands of Their Eviction*, 1987. Poetry that recalls some of the political situations that have prompted emigration from many parts of the world and the significance of immigration for the United States.

Esteves, Sandra María. *Bluestown Mockingbird Mambo*, 1990. Poems about the Puerto Rican immigrant experience in New York, as well as reflections on love and life.

_____. *Contrapunto in the Open Field*, 1998. A celebration of the poet's Puerto Rican heritage and her love of life.

_____. *Tropical Rains: A Bilingual Downpour*, 1984. Poems in English, Spanish, and Spanglish that explore the question of racial and linguistic identity and heritage.

_____. *Yerba buena: Dibujos y poemas*, 1980. Collection of poems celebrating Esteves's Latino heritage and her struggle to maintain it through years of racism and, especially, the insistence of others that she abandon her native Spanish and speak English.

Goldemberg, Isaac. *Hombre de paso/Just Passing Through*, 1981. Poems that evoke Goldemberg's

Jewish heritage and Jewish religious practices as he experienced them in a Hispanic American context.

González, Rigoberto. *Other Fugitives and Other Strangers*, 2006. Poetic and linguistic explorations of erotic love as expressed through the beauty of exotic similes.

_____. *So Often the Pitcher Goes to Water Until It Breaks*, 1999. González's vision of Latinos in their everyday circumstances, with reflections on youth, faith, and coming-of-age.

Guillén, Nicolás. *Cantos para soldados y sones para turistas, 1937, and España: Poema en cuatro angustias y una esperanza*, 1937. Poetry inspired by the violence and horrors of the Spanish Civil War.

_____. *Motivos de son*, 1930. Inspired by the Afro-Cuban form of music called son, Guillén's verses aim to bring the reader into the Afro-Cuban world.

_____. *Sóngoro Cosongo*, 1931. Poems that capture the daily life and rhythmic speech patterns of Afro-Cubans, especially as these are echoed in music.

_____. *West Indies Ltd.*, 1934. Poetry with a political bent that expresses the poet's concerns for social and governmental justice.

Hernández Cruz, Víctor. *The Mountain in the Sea: Poems*, 2006. Explorations in English, Spanish, and Arabic of Spanish history and culture as these were handed down to Hispanic Americans and how this heritage defines contemporary Latinos.

_____. *Panorama*. Writing in Spanish and English, Hernández Cruz addresses issues of Latino and American culture, as well as the living conditions of Puerto Rican immigrants, especially in New York.

_____. *Papo Got His Gun*, 1966. A Puerto Rican teenager tries to find his personal and national identity amid the violence and hatred of the New York streets.

_____. *Snaps*, 1969. Poetry inspired by "snapshots" of Hernández Cruz's barrio and by the Latin music and dance that invites people to snap their fingers.

Monsiváis, Carolina. *Somewhere Between Houston and El Paso: Testimonies of a Poet*, 2001. Poems that describe Chicano life and its struggles in Texas.

Montoya, José. *El sol y los de abajo, and Other R.C.A.F. Poems*, 1992. Poems celebrating Chicano history and heritage that urge Chicanos to engage in political involvement.

Ortiz Cofer, Judith. *Reaching for the Mainland and Selected New Poems*, 1995. Poems on the immigrant experience and the feeling of living between two worlds that are completely different.

_____. *Terms of Survival: Poems*, 1987. Poetry in Spanish and English about growing up Latina and dealing with family, friends, society, and the challenges of life.

Ramírez, Sara Estela. *"Diamantes negros," "A Juárez," "Huye," and "Surge,"* 1908-1910. Published in literary journals and newspapers, these four poems are among the most influential of Ramírez's compositions, which urge Texicans to take pride in their Mexican heritage and fight for the rights of all people, especially women and other downtrodden individuals.

Ramos Otero, Manuel. *Invitación al polvo*, 1991. Death provides the backdrop for reflections on life, love, and mysteries of sexual attraction.

_____. *El libro de la muerte*, 1985. Poetic explorations about the meaning of life and the realities of death.

Ribera Chevremont, Evaristo. *El caos de los sueños*, 1974. A book of free-verse poems that explore the full range of human emotions, parting from the mystery world of dreams.

_____. *Desfile romántico*, 1914. Lyric poems that speak of love, life, and the hope of the future.

_____. *La hora del orífice*, 1929. A collection of poems through which Ribera Chevremont showcases his fascination with different hues of light and color.

_____. *Tierra y sombra*, 1930. A poetic celebration of the beauty of nature and the subtleties of its contrasts.

Rivera, Tomás. *The Searchers: Collected Poetry,* 1990. Poetic reflections on life written in English and Spanish.

Rodríguez de Tió, Lola. *La Boriqueña*, 1868. The lyrics to Puerto Rico's national anthem.

_____. *Mi libro de Cuba*, 1893. Poems celebrating the poet's love for Cuba and its struggle for freedom from Spanish oppression.

_____. *Mis cantares*, 1876. Verses that reflect Rodríguez de Tió's patriotism and the influence of the poetry of José Martí, Rubén Darío, and the incipient modernist movement.

Salinas, Raúl (also known as Raúlrsalinas). *East of the Freeway: Reflections de mi pueblo, Poems*, 1995. Recalling the Beat Generation and the jazz generation, Salinas's poems portray Chicano life in the city and urge involvement in political and social causes.

_____. *Indo Trials: a Xicano Odyssey through Indian Country*, 2007. Poems composed by Salinas in honor of his life and work with Native Americans, describing various aspects of Indian life.

_____. *Un Trip Through the Mind of Jail y otras excursiones: Poems*, 1980. A collection of Salinas's radical poems, many of which were composed in jail, denouncing American society for victimizing those who have been incarcerated and praising Fidel Castro and the Black Panther movement.

Santos, John Phillip. *Songs Older than Any Known Singer: Selected and New Poems*, 2007. Poems that speak to many dimensions of Santos's Mexican heritage, including poetic tales that mix mythical stories with strange happenings and factual details from events in Mexican history.

Soto, Gary. *The Elements of San Joaquin*, 1977. A poetic discussion of the plight of Chicano farm workers and their families in California's San Joaquin Valley.

_____. *The Tale of Sunlight*, 1978. Poems set in a cantina in the state of Guerrero, Mexico, which express the observations of Manuel Zaragoza, a poor farmer who nonetheless treasures the beauty of the Mexican landscape and the richness of Mexican culture.

Soto Vélez, Clemente. *Arboles*, 1955. A poetic celebration of Puerto Rican nature, its power, and its presence in everyday human life.

_____. *Caballo de palo*, 1976. The poet's reflection on his life and the lives of his fellow Puerto Ricans.

_____. *La tierra prometida*, 1979. Poetic protest against American imperialism in Puerto Rico and its adverse effects.

Suárez, Virgil. *Banyan*, 2001. Suárez evokes his childhood, his time with his father, and the many rich details of his Cuban heritage, from Cuban history to thoughts about the Cuban community in exile.

_____. *In the Republic of Longing*, 1999. Poetry serves as the means to express Suárez's longing to understand his Cuban roots, especially as he struggled to understand his exiled and immigrant status during his childhood in Miami.

Tafolla, Carmen. *Curandera*, 1983. Written in English, Spanish, and Spanglish, these poems recall Tafolla's childhood and her Tejana life and heritage.

_____. *Sonnets and Salsa*, 2001. Poetic exploration of the beauty of the Sonora Desert and the Mexicans and Chicanos who have called it home.

_____. *Sonnets to Human Beings, and Other Selected Works*, 1992. Poetic musings about ethnicity and universal human nature, informed by current world events.

Villanueva, Alma Luz. *Desire*, 1998. Villanueva explores some of her deepest longings, both personal and political, and seeks to integrate them in the poetic search for identity and the meaning of life.

_____. *Planet with Mother, May I?*, 1993. Poems that explore the meaning of family and the process of self-discovery.

_____. *Soft Chaos*, 2009. Poetry treating many aspects of Yaqui and Latino life, in which Villanueva offers insights into the mysteries of love, suffering, passion, and solitude, set against the horrors of human cruelty perpetrated during the twentieth century.

_____. *Vida, Poetry*, 2002. Villanueva's reflections on the meaning of life and the role of her heritage in giving meaning to her existence.

Williams, William Carlos. *Spring and All*, 1923. Poems evoking the images and spirit of Williams's native New Jersey, set again the backdrop of beautiful images of the natural world.

_____. *The Tempers*, 1913. Verse capturing the voices of the ordinary people of Williams's town of Rutherford, New Jersey, including many immigrants, such as that of his own Puerto Rican mother.

Zamora, Bernice. *Releasing Serpents*, 1994. Imaginative poetry with some inventive imagery.

_____. *Restless Serpents*, 1976. Verse that explores the nature of being Chicana, the relations between men and women, the inspiration of faith, and the power of writing and poetry.

SHORT-STORY COLLECTIONS

Ada, Alma Flor. *Derechos del Niño*, 2000. Short stories for young people about children and human rights.

Altamirano, Ignacio Manuel. *Cuentos de invierno*, 1880. A collection of four novellas that deal with various aspects of love.

Anaya, Rudolfo A. *The Silence of the Llano: Short Stories*, 1982. After the death of his wife, a man closes himself off from his daughter and the world. When he gets a hold of himself, he finds it is too late, as his daughter has just been raped.

Cabrera, Lydia. *¿Por qué? . . . Cuentos negros de Cuba,* 1948. An influential selection and study of Afro-Cuban myths as passed on in Cuba.

Casares, Oscar. *Brownsville: Stories*, 2003. A collection of short stories that portray everyday life in Brownsville, Texas, and the culture of the borderlands between Texas and Mexico.

Chávez, Denise. *The Last of the Menu Girls,* 1986. Collection of stories set in New Mexico about the many diverse experiences of Rocío Esquibel as she passes through the stages of life.

Cisneros, Sandra. *Woman Hollering Creek, and Other Stories*, 1991. Stories about Mexican American women, their families, and their struggle to love themselves and their Chicano culture.

Díaz, Junot. *Drown*, 1996. Short stories about Díaz's family, Dominican heritage, and the struggles of growing up in his new home, New Jersey.

Ferré, Rosario. *Papeles de Pandora.* Stories about the struggles of woman to gain a voice and have greater participation in the patriarchal social structure of Puerto Rico.

González, Rigoberto. *Men Without Bliss*, 2008. Stories about the challenges faced by men—especially Latino men—and how it is expected that they endure suffering and hardships in silence.

Jiménez, Francisco. *The Circuit.* Written for young children, these stories recount the difficult life of Jiménez's family. His parents, poor Mexican immigrants, moved from farm to farm seeking work, and this relocation created instability for young Frankie.

Keller, Gary D. *Tales of El Huitlacoche*, 1984. Humorous and, at times, irreverent stories that present some of the ironies of Chicano and Mexican life.

Mohr, Nicholasa. *In Nueva York*, 1988. Stories about Puerto Rican immigrants in Spanish Harlem and how they adapt to their new environment.

_____. *A Matter of Pride, and Other Stories*, 1997. Short stories that provide a humorous yet moving picture of some of the different types of Latinos who inhabit New York, Puerto Rico, and the Dominican Republic.

_____. *Ritual of Survival: A Woman's Portfolio*, 1985. Stories about six Puerto Rican women who are dealing with the frustrations of their lives and how they develop unique strategies to overcome them.

Morales, Alejandro. *The Rag Doll Plagues*, 1992. Three generations of Hispanic doctors serve the Mexican and Chicano communities in the midst of devastating plagues, the last of which, AIDS, has been produced in an American laboratory and exported to Africa as an instrument of political and social diversion.

Paredes, Américo. *The Hammon and the Beans, and Other Stories*, 1994. Spoken in the voices of children, these stories describe the poverty, violence, and discrimination that haunt the lives of many Chicanos on a daily basis.

Portillo Trambley, Estela. *Rain of Scorpions,* 1975. Nine stories that present different aspects of Mexican legend and folklore, as these affect the everyday life of the Chicano community.

Ramos Otero, Manuel. *Concierto de metal para un recuerdo y otras orgías de soledad*, 1971. A collection of short stories that contain many surreal and imaginative images, contrary to the reigning literary canons of the day.

_____. *Página en blanco y staccato*, 1987. Short stories and poems which discuss the search for national and sexual identity.

Sánchez, Luis Rafael. *En cuerpo de camisa,* 1966. A controversial collection of stories that praises city life, with all its contradictions, ironies, humor, and tragedy, and denounces rural life and its strictures.

Soto, Pedro Juan. *Spiks*, 1956. Short stories that explore the experiences of Puerto Ricans who come to New York and are subjected to racism, poverty, and hatred.

Suárez, Virgil. *Welcome to the Oasis*, 1992. Stories of Cuban immigrants of varying ages who find that, because of the ease with which one can become corrupted, life in America can be just as treacherous as it was in the Cuba they left behind.

Tafolla, Carmen. *The Holy Tortilla and a Pot of Beans,* 2008. Chicanos in Texas experience the power of family and friends as they go through marvelous and terrible events in their everyday lives.

Thomas, Piri. *Stories from El Barrio,* 1978. Humorous accounts of childhood and youth as a Puerto Rican immigrant on the streets of New York.

Urrea, Luis Alberto. *Six Kinds of Sky*, 2002. Six short stories that examine life among the garbage pickers of Mexico and the Sioux of the northwestern United States, focusing on the social ills that afflict them.

Vallbona, Rima de. *Mujeres y agonías,* 1982. A series of short stories that examine the challenges facing Hispanic American women in their everyday lives.

Viramontes, Helena María. *The Moths, and Other Stories*, 1985. Stories that probe issues, such as the search for sexual identity, machismo, abortion, terminal illness, and the role of faith in the lives of Chicanas.

_____. *Their Dogs Came with Them*, 2007. The life of Latinos in East Los Angeles during the 1960's and 1970's is captured in these stories, which are replete with details of the struggle for common people to survive and make a living for themselves and their families.

Yglesias, José. *The Guns in the Closet*, 1996. Unusual stories of Latino life along the eastern seaboard of the United States, which are filled with humor and pathos.

Mark DeStephano

Organizations and Societies

U.S.-based organizations of a nonpolitical, nonsectarian nature are included here. Information is provided for national-level organizations because regional and local information often is found through national organizations. The organizations included here were identified through Internet searches conducted in 2011.

Entries are arranged into three categories: educational and cultural organizations, civic and social associations, and metasites. Organizations are international groups with a U.S. presence or are U.S.-based organizations with a national or international scope. The educational and cultural organizations included here unite people of all Hispanic or Latino nationality groups in all regions of the United States for educational and artistic purposes or to enhance opportunities for an education that benefits those persons who might be interested in the arts or intellectual activity. The civic and social associations listed here unite people who have civic pride or an interest in community and social activities aimed at advancing the Latino community. Metasites contain lists of links to all types of Hispanic or Latino nationality groups. Entries within each category are arranged alphabetically. Because URLs frequently change, the accuracy of these sites is not guaranteed; however, long-standing sites, such as those of university departments, national organizations, and government agencies, generally maintain links when sites move or upgrade their offerings.

EDUCATIONAL AND CULTURAL ORGANIZATIONS

American Association of Teachers of Spanish and Portuguese (AATSP), National Office
900 Ladd Road
Walled Lake, MI 48390
Phone: (248) 960-2180
Fax: (248) 960-9570
AATSPoffice@aatsp.org
http://www.aatsp.org

AATSP promotes the study and teaching of the Spanish and Portuguese languages and their corresponding Hispanic, Luso-Brazilian, and other related literatures and cultures at all levels of education. AATSP encourages, supports, and directs programs and research projects involving the exchange of pedagogical and scholarly information. Through extensive collaboration with educators, professionals, and institutions in other countries, AATSP contributes to a better and deeper understanding between the United States and the Spanish-and Portuguese-speaking nations of the world.

The ASPIRA Association, National Office
1444 I Street, NW, Suite 800
Washington, DC 20005
Phone: (202) 835-3600
Fax: (202) 835-3613
info@aspira.org
http://www.aspira.org

The ASPIRA Association promotes the empowerment of the Puerto Rican and Latino communities by developing and nurturing the leadership, intellectual, and cultural potential of its youth so they may contribute their skills and dedication to the fullest development of Puerto Rican and Latino communities everywhere.

Hispanic Association of Colleges and Universities (HACU), National Headquarters
8415 Datapoint Drive, Suite 400
San Antonio, TX 78229
Phone: (210) 692-3805
Fax: (210) 692-0823
hacu@hacu.net
http://www.hacu.net

HACU fulfills its mission by promoting the development of member colleges and universities; improving access to and the quality of postsecondary educational opportunities for Hispanic students; and meeting the needs of business, industry, and government through the development and sharing of resources, information, and expertise.

Hispanic Educational Technology Services (HETS)
Phone: (787) 766-2600, ext. 8911 (Yubelkys Montalvo, executive director)
Fax: (210) 692-0823
yumontalvo@suagm.edu (Yubelkys Montalvo)

http://www.hets.org

HETS is the first bilingual consortium dedicated to serving the higher education needs of the fast-growing Hispanic communities. HETS provides its members with the opportunity to participate in collaborative projects; to network with a culturally diverse community; to benefit from services specifically tailored for students, faculty members, academic leaders, and professionals; to access useful online educational resources; to participate in special interest workshops and training sessions; and to obtain input from experts in technology and online education.

Hispanic Genealogical Society

P.O. Box 231271
San Antonio, TX 77223-1271
joguerra@hispanicgs.com (Jose Guerra, president)
http://hispanicgs.com

The Hispanic Genealogical Society was formed to foster knowledge, training, help, and pride in the search for Hispanic ancestors.

Hispanic Scholarship Fund (HSF)

55 2nd Street, Suite 1500
San Francisco, CA 94105
Phone: (877) HSF-INFO
scholar1@hsf.net
http://www.hsf.net

HSF's mission is to strengthen America by advancing the college education of Hispanic Americans. The fund delivers a range of programs to Hispanic families and students through community outreach and education, affordability via scholarships, and college retention and career opportunities.

Latin American Studies Association (LASA)

416 Bellefield Hall
University of Pittsburgh
Pittsburgh, PA 15260
Phone: (412) 648-7929
Fax: (412) 624-7145
lasa@pitt.edu
http://lasa.international.pitt.edu/

LASA is the largest professional association in the world for individuals and institutions engaged in the study of Latin America.

The Mexican American Legal Defense and Educational Fund (MALDEF), National Headquarters

634 South Spring Street, 11th Floor
Los Angeles, CA 90014
Phone: (213) 629-2512
www.maldef.org/contact
http://www.maldef.org

MALDEF is the nation's leading Latino legal civil rights organization. Often described as the "law firm of the Latino community," MALDEF promotes social change through advocacy, communications, community education, and litigation in the areas of education, employment, immigrant rights, and political access.

National Association for Chicano and Chicana Studies (NACCS)

P.O. Box 720052
San Jose, CA 95172-0052
Phone: (408) 924-5310
Fax: (408) 920-0711
Executive_Director@naccs.org (Julia E. Curry Rodriguez)
http://www.naccs.org

NACCS is the academic organization that serves academic programs, departments, and research centers that focus on issues pertaining to Mexican Americans, Chicanos, and Latinos. The association was formed in 1972, during the height of the Chicano movement, and it called for the development of a space where scholarship and Chicano students could develop their talents in higher education.

National Association of Latino Arts and Culture (NALAC)

1208 Buena Vista
San Antonio, TX 78207
Phone: (210) 432-3982
Fax: (210) 432-3934
info@nalac.org
http://nalac.org

NALAC is the nation's leading nonprofit organization exclusively dedicated to the promotion, advancement, development, and cultivation of the Latino arts field. In this capacity, NALAC stimulates and facilitates intergenerational dialogues among disciplines, languages, and traditional and contemporary expressions.

CIVIC AND SOCIAL ASSOCIATIONS

American GI Forum (AGIF), National Office
Dottie Bruton, 2870 North Speer Boulevard #103
Denver, CO 80211
Phone: (866) 244-3628
Fax: (303) 458-1634
agifnat@gmail.com
http://www.agifusa.org

AGIF is the largest federally chartered Hispanic veterans organization in the United States. The forum is actively involved in such issues as employment, housing, civil rights, women's programs, and youth activities and it is supported by the respected voice and advocacy of a national membership of proven American patriots. AGIF's corporate advisory board (AGIFCAP) provides technical advice and financial support.

César E. Chávez Foundation, Headquarters
316 West Second Street, Suite 600
Los Angeles, CA 90012
Phone: (213) 362-0260
Fax: (213) 362-0265
manguiano@nfwsc.org (Maria Anguiano)
http://chavezfoundation.org

The mission of the Cesar E. Chavez Foundation, a nonprofit charitable organization, is to maximize human potential to improve communities by preserving, promoting, and applying the legacy and universal values of civil rights leader César Chávez.

Cuban American National Council (CNC)
1223 SW 4th Street
Miami, FL 33135
Phone: (305) 642-3484 (Guarione M. Diaz, president)
Fax: (305) 642-3484
gmd@cnc.org (Guarione M. Diaz, president)
http://www.cnc.org

CNC is a nonprofit organization providing human services to people in need from all racial and ethnic groups. CNC assists individuals to become self-reliant and builds bridges among America's diverse communities.

Dominican American National Roundtable
1050 17th Street, NW, Suite 600
Washington, DC 20036
Phone: (202) 238-0097
Fax: (202) 536-5253
info@danr.org
http://danr.org

DANR is a nonpartisan, nonprofit corporation that seeks to bring together the different voices of all people of Dominican origin in the United States. The roundtable is a national forum for analysis, planning, and action to advance the educational, economic, legal, social, cultural, and political interests of Dominican Americans. It aims to ensure for U.S. Dominicans the full exercise of the rights and freedoms guaranteed in the Constitution of the United States. With those objectives in mind, DANR is committed to enriching the quality of life in the United States by highlighting the contributions of Dominicans to the larger American society.

League of United Latin American Citizens (LU-LAC), National Office
2000 L Street, NW, Suite 610
Washington, DC 20036
Phone: (202) 833-6130
Fax: (202) 833-6135
http://lulac.org/contact
http://lulac.org

LULAC's mission is to advance the economic condition, educational attainment, political influence, housing, health, and civil rights of the Hispanic population of the United States.

MANA: A National Latina Organization
1146 19th Street, NW, Suite 700
Washington, DC 20036
Phone: (202) 833-0060
Fax: (202) 496-0588
hermana2@aol.com
http://www.hermana.org

MANA: A National Latina Organization, is a nonprofit advocacy organization established in 1974. MANA's mission is to empower Latinas through leadership development, community service, and advocacy. MANA fulfills its mission through programs designed to develop the leadership skills of Latinas, promote community service by Latinas, and provide Latinas with advocacy opportunities. Support for these programs is derived from members, corporations, foundations, and government grants.

National Alliance for Hispanic Health
1501 16th Street, NW
Washington, DC 20036

Phone: 202-387-5000
Fax: (202) 797-4353
alliance@hispanichealth.org
http://www.hispanichealth.org

The mission of the National Alliance for Hispanic Health is to improve the health of Hispanic communities and work with others to secure health for all. The alliance is the nation's foremost source of information on Hispanic health and a science-based and community-driven advocate for health.

National Council of La Raza (NCLR), Headquarters

Raul Yzaguirre Building
1126 16th Street, NW
Suite 600
Washington, DC 20036-4845
Phone: 202) 785-1670
Fax: 202) 776-1792
comments@nclr.org
http://www.nclr.org

The National Council of La Raza, the largest national Hispanic civil rights and advocacy organization in the United States, works to improve opportunities for Hispanic Americans.

National Hispanic Council on Aging (NHCOA)

The Walker Building
734 15th Street, NW, Suite 1050
Washington, DC 20005
Phone: 202-347-9733
Fax: 202-347-9735
nbcoa@nhcoa.org
http://www.nhcoa.org

NHCOA is the nation's premier constituency-based organization that advocates, celebrates, and enhances the quality of life for Hispanic older adults, their families, and their communities. NHCOA's top priorities are health, economic security, empowerment, and housing.

National Puerto Rican Coalition, Inc. (NPRC)

1444 I Street, NW, Suite 800
Washington, DC 20005
Phone: 202-223-3915
Fax: 202-429-2223
nprc@nprcinc.org
http://www.bateylink.org

NPRC's mission is to systematically strengthen and enhance the social, political, and economic well-being of Puerto Ricans throughout the United States and in Puerto Rico, with a special focus on the most vulnerable.

METASITES & FURTHER READING

National Hispanic Corporate Council (NHCC)

http://www.nhcchq.org/index

The mission of NHCC is to provide best-in-class solutions and foster professional networks by maximizing the Hispanic market opportunity among Fortune 1000 corporations.

United States-Mexico Chamber of Commerce

http://www.usmcoc.org

The United States-Mexico Chamber of Commerce is the leading binational business organization working to build mutually beneficial trade and investment relationships in the Americas. The organization's mission is to promote business between the United States and Mexico.

Further Reading

Encyclopedia of Associations. Detroit, Mich.: Gale. Available in print or by electronic subscription, this work contains extensive contact and membership information for all types of national and international nonprofit membership groups. Print volumes are arranged in the following parts: international, regional, state, and local organizations.

Willette F. Stinson

RESEARCH CENTERS AND LIBRARIES

Due to space constraints, the select U.S.-based libraries and research centers, including individual programs and consortia that have been designated a National Resource Center for Latin American Studies by the U.S. Department of Education's International Education Programs Service, scratch the surface of the many libraries and research centers that support Latin American studies. Internet sites providing access to extensive lists or detailed reference materials are provided under the headings "Metasites" and "Further Reading." Each site was visited by Salem Press in 2011. Because URLs frequently change or are moved, the accuracy of these sites cannot be guaranteed; however, long-standing sites, such as those belonging to academic institutions, national organizations, and government agencies, generally maintain links when sites move or upgrade their offerings.

LIBRARIES AND RESEARCH CENTERS

Center for Latin American Studies (CLAS), Ohio State University

309 Oxley Hall
1712 Neil Avenue
Columbus, OH 43210
Phone: (614) 688-4285; 688-3963
Fax: (614) 292-4273
clas@osu.edu
http://clas.osu.edu

CLAS at Ohio State University has a primary mission of serving, facilitating, and stimulating the intellectual needs of the faculty and students involved in Latin American studies in order to foster cutting-edge instruction and research on Latin American languages, cultures, societies, histories, politics, economics, and the arts.

Center for Latin American Studies (CLAS), Stanford University

Bolivar House
582 Alvarado Row
Stanford, CA 94305
Phone: (650) 723-4444
Fax: (650) 723-9822
boho-calendar-join@lists.stanford.edu
http://www.stanford.edu/group/las/home

The mission of the CLAS is to support research and teaching by the faculty and students of Stanford University in all fields of study.

Center for Latin American Studies (CLAS), University of Arizona

Marshall Building
Suite 280
University of Arizona
Tucson, Arizona 85721-0158
Phone: (520) 626-7242
Fax: (520) 626-7248
clas@mail.sbs.arizona.edu
http://clas.arizona.edu

CLAS at the University of Arizona hosts an outstanding faculty with particular strengths in Mexico, Brazil, environmental studies, border studies, indigenous studies, and women's studies.

Center for Latin American Studies (CLAS), University of California, Berkeley

2334 Bowditch Street #2312
Berkeley, CA 94720
Phone: (510) 642-2088
Fax: (510) 642-3260
clas@berkeley.edu
http://clas.berkeley.edu

CLAS at UC Berkeley is a National Resource Center dedicated to promoting research and community awareness about issues affecting Latin America.

Center for Latin American Studies, University of Florida

319 Grinter Hall
PO Box 115530
Gainesville, FL 32611
Phone: (352) 392-0375
Fax: (352) 392-7682
info@latam.ufl.edu
http://www.latam.ufl.edu

The center's mission is to advance knowledge about Latin America and the Caribbean and its peoples throughout the hemisphere, as well as to enhance the scope and quality of research, teaching, and outreach in Latin American, Caribbean, and Latino studies at the University of Florida.

Center of Latin American Studies, University of Kansas

1440 Jayhawk Boulevard
Suite 320
Lawrence, KS 66045-7574
Phone: (785) 864-4213
Fax: (785) 864-3800
latamst@ku.edu
http://latamst.ku.edu

The Center of Latin American Studies supports the publication of the Latin American Theatre Review, a journal dedicated to the scholarly study of dramatic performance in Latin America. An annual newsletter, the Kansas Latin Americanist, highlights recent campus activities and faculty and student research on Latin America and also publicizes new outreach materials and current funding, travel, and research opportunities.

Center for Latin American Studies, University of Miami

1111 Memorial Drive
Coral Gables, FL 33124
Phone: (305) 284-1854
Fax: (305) 284-2796
umclas@miami.edu
http://www.as.miami.edu/clas

The Center for Latin American Studies at the University of Miami works to integrate the energies, ideas, and experiences of scholars, students, and other individuals who share a common while diverse interest in Latin America and the Caribbean—their peoples, societies, environments, and global connections—fostering new knowledge, dialogue and cooperation, innovative education, and constructive, forward-looking engagement.

Center for Latin American Studies (CLAS), University of Pittsburgh

4200 Wesley W. Posvar Hall
University of Pittsburgh
Pittsburgh, PA 15260
Phone: 412-648-7392
Fax: 412-648-2199
clas@ucis.pitt.edu
http://www.ucis.pitt.edu/clas/index.html

The mission of CLAS is to expand and enrich academic resources at the University of Pittsburgh relating to Latin America and the Caribbean. These resources provide the means for students to become experts about Latin America and the Caribbean and for faculty to pursue research, enhance their expertise, and disseminate new knowledge on the region.

Center for Latin American Studies, Vanderbilt University

VU Station B #351806
2301 Vanderbilt Place
Nashville, TN 37235-1806
Phone: (615) 322-2527
Fax: (615) 322-2305
clas@vanderbilt.edu
http://www.vanderbilt.edu/clas

While CLAS at Vanderbilt University maintains one of the strongest concentrations of Brazilianists of any university in the United States, the center's faculty also has particular strengths in Mesoamerican anthropology and archaeology, the study of democracy building and economic development, Latin American literature and languages, and African populations in Latin America and the Caribbean.

Center for Latin American and Caribbean Studies (CLACS), Indiana University

College of Arts and Sciences
1125 East Atwater Avenue
Bloomington, IN 47401
Phone: (812) 855-9097
Fax: (812) 855-5345
clacs@indiana.edu
http://www.indiana.edu/~clacs/index.shtml

CLACS at Indiana University is a pivotal site for interdisciplinary research, instruction, and outreach focused on Latin America and the Caribbean. CLACS offers minor and area certificate degrees; a master's degree; three-year dual degree programs in business administration, library science, and public affairs; and a doctoral minor and certificate.

Center for Latin American and Caribbean Studies (CLACS), New York University

53 Washington Square South
Floor 4W
New York, NY, 10012
Phone: 212-998-8686
Fax: 212-995-4163
clacs.info@nyu.edu
http://clacs.as.nyu.edu/page/home

Located in the heart of New York City's Greenwich Village, CLACS at New York University serves as a bridge to local and global communities. The center creates a network of people interested in the region and collaborates to further expand Latin American and Caribbean studies.

Center for Latin American and Caribbean Studies (CLACS), University of Illinois
201 International Studies Building, MC-481
910 South 5th Street
Champaign, IL 61820
Phone: (217) 333-3182
Fax: (217) 244-7333
clacs@illinois.edu
http://www.clacs.illinois.edu

CLACS at the University of Illinois is a Title VI National Resource Center in consortium with the University of Chicago Center for Latin American Studies funded by the U.S. Department of Education. Established in 2009, the center promotes research on Brazil by organizing conferences and offering fellowships. In addition, the facility encourages collaborative research between University of Illinois faculty and Brazilian colleagues and supports instruction on Brazil.

Columbia University Libraries, Latin American and Iberian Studies
307 International Affairs
420 W. 118th Street
New York, NY 10027
Phone: (212) 854-3630
Fax: (212) 854-9099
latam@libraries.cul.columbia.edu
http://www.columbia.edu/cu/lweb/indiv/latam

The university collects materials published in or about Latin America and Iberia across many disciplines. The collection is strong in coverage of Mexico, Brazil, the Spanish Caribbean, and the countries of the Southern Cone. Subject strengths include architecture, economic development, history, languages and literature, political science, sociology, and anthropology.

The Consortium in Latin American and Caribbean Studies at the University of North Carolina at Chapel Hill and Duke University
Institute for the Study of America at UNC-Chapel Hill
Chapel Hill, NC 27599-3205
Phone: (919) 966-1484
Fax: (919) 962-0398
http://isa.unc.edu/contact/contact_form.asp
http://uncdukeconsortium.org

The consortium seeks to encourage and facilitate collaboration and cooperation in all aspects of Latin American and Caribbean studies across the two campuses and across disciplines. A focus on interdisciplinary work is one of the consortium's hallmarks.

Council on Latin American and Iberian Studies (CLAIS), Yale University
The Whitney and Betty MacMillan Center for International and Area Studies
34 Hillhouse Avenue
Suite 232
P.O. Box 208206
New Haven, CT 06520
Phone: (203) 432-3422
Fax: (203) 432-9381
latin.america@yale.edu
http://www.yale.edu/macmillan/lais

CLAIS organizes a weekly lecture series, sponsors research abroad, coordinates outreach programs, convenes international conferences, and edits conference results for scholarly publication. In addition, the council works to strengthen ties with institutions throughout Latin America, Spain, and Portugal and is a member of the New England Council on Latin American Studies and the Latin American Studies Association.

Hispanic Reading Room
Library of Congress
Thomas Jefferson Building, Room LJ240
101 Independence Avenue, SE
Washington, DC 20540-4850
Phone: (202) 707-5397
Fax: (202) 707-2005
http://www.loc.gov/rr/askalib/ask-hispanic-eng2.html
(Hispanic Division Inquiry Form)
http://loc.gov/rr/hispanic

The Hispanic Reading Room, as it is usually called, serves as the primary access point for research relating to those parts of the world encompassing the geographical areas of the Caribbean, Latin America, and Iberia; the indigenous cultures of these areas; and people throughout the world historically influenced by Luso-Hispanic heritage, including Latinos in the U.S. and people of Portuguese or Spanish heritage in Africa, Asia, and Oceania.

Institute of Latin American Studies (ILAS), Columbia University
Columbia University
420 West 118th Street, 8th Floor IAB
MC 3339
New York, NY 10027
Phone: (212) 854-4643
Fax: (212) 854-4607
http://ilas.columbia.edu

ILAS is the center for research, teaching, and discussion on Latin America at Columbia University. The institute's main goal is to bring together and provide resources for Columbia faculty, students, and visiting scholars, recognizing the diversity of their interests and approaches while strengthening their links with Latin America and with communities of Latin American origin in the United States.

Inter-University Program for Latino Research (IU-PLR)
230 McKenna Hall
Notre Dame, IN 46556
Phone: (574) 631-3481
iuplr@nd.edu
http://iuplr.nd.edu/index.php

IUPLR is a national consortium of university-based centers dedicated to the advancement of the Latino intellectual presence in the United States. IUPLR works to expand the pool of Latino scholars and leaders and increase the availability of policy-relevant Latino-focused research.

Latin American and Caribbean Center (LACC), Florida International University
Modest A. Maidique Campus
Deuxieme Maison, 353
11200 SW 8th Street
Miami, FL 33199
Phone: (305) 348-2894
Fax: (305) 348-3593
lacc@fiu.edu
http://casgroup.fiu.edu/lacc

LACC was founded in 1979 in order to promote the study of Latin America and the Caribbean in Florida and throughout the United States. The center forges linkages across the Americas through high-quality education; research aimed at better understanding of the most urgent problems confronting the region; national and international outreach; and meaningful dialogue between different ethnic communities, nationalities, and cultures that claim the Americas as their homeland.

Latin American and Caribbean Studies (LACS), University of Michigan
2607 International Institute Building
1080 South University Street
Suite 2620
Ann Arbor, Michigan 48109-1106
Phone: 734-463-0553

Fax: 734-615-8880
lacs@umich.edu
http://www.ii.umich.edu/lacs

LACS established a Quechua language program in 1997 that offers one of the world's only full-year, three-level courses in the most extensively spoken indigenous language in the Americas. LACS has achieved national recognition for its growth as an academic program and a center of excellence in area research through support from the U.S. Department of Education.

Latin American and Iberian Institute (LAII), University of New Mexico
801 Yale Boulevard NE
MSC02 1690
Albuquerque, NM 87131
Phone: (505) 277-2961
Fax: (505) 277-5989
laii@unm.edu
http://laii.unm.edu

The LAII's mission is to create a stimulating environment in order to produce and exchange knowledge of Latin America within and beyond the University of New Mexico.

The Pew Hispanic Center
1615 L Street, NW
Suite 700
Washington, DC 20036-5610
Phone: 202.419.3600
Fax: 202.419.3608
info@pewhispanic.org
http://pewhispanic.org

The Pew Hispanic Center is a project of the Pew Research Center, a nonpartisan "fact tank" that provides information on the issues, attitudes, and trends shaping America and the world. It is supported by the Pew Charitable Trusts.

The Population Research Center (PRC), University of Texas at Austin
1 University Station, G1800
Austin, TX 78712-0544
Phone: (512) 471-5514
Fax: (512) 471-4886
mhayward@prc.utexas.edu (Mark Hayward, director);
    trejo@eco.utexas.edu (Stephen Trejo, assoc. director)
http://www.utexas.edu/cola/centers/prc

The PRC is an interdisciplinary research unit of the University of Texas at Austin. The center's purpose is to provide the resources and culture that are necessary to facilitate the highest level of population-related research and training activities among its faculty members and students. A number of researchers' projects focus on the demography of Latin America and the U.S. border.

Roger Thayer Stone Center for Latin American Studies, Tulane University
100 Jones Hall
New Orleans, LA 70118
Phone: (504) 865-5164
rtsclas@ti;ame.edu
https://stonecenter.tulane.edu

According to its Web site, Tulane University's Latin American studies "program is today comprehensive with faculty in almost every region and discipline essential to understanding Latin America. The Mississippi-Gulf-Caribbean region is the epicenter of cultural and historical converging and radiating flows of a vast cultural and geographic network embracing Europe, Africa, the Pacific Rim, and North and South America." The university has programs in African and African diaspora studies; the Atlantic world; comparative Southern studies; and Cuban, Brazilian, and Francophone Caribbean studies.

UCLA Latin American Institute
10343 Bunche Hall
Box 951447
Los Angeles, CA 90095-1447
Phone: 310-825-4571
Fax: 310-206-6859
latinamctr@international.ucla.edu
http://www.international.ucla.edu/lai

The UCLA (University of California, Los Angeles) Latin American Institute, situated in a major U.S. gateway to the region, is committed to excellence in its exchange of knowledge with students, specialists, and the surrounding community. The institute equips leaders

and scholars with the information and skills required for understanding complex Latin American societies.

University of Wisconsin Consortium
University of Wisconsin-Madison
Latin American, Caribbean and Iberian Studies (LACIS)
209 Ingraham Hall
1155 Observatory Drive
Madison, WI 53706
Phone: (608) 262-2811
Fax: (608) 265-5851
llacis@intl-institute.wisc.edu
http://www.lacis.wisc.edu
University of Wisconsin-Milwaukee
Center for Latin American and Caribbean Studies (CLACS)
2513 E. Hartford Avenue
Pearse Hall 168
Milwaukee, WI 53201-04131155
Phone: (414) 229-4401
Fax: (414) 229-2879
clacs@uwm.edu
http://www4.uwm.edu/clacs

The University of Wisconsin (UW) Consortium, a partnership between the Latin American, Caribbean and Iberian Studies (LACIS) Program at UW-Madison and the Center for Latin American and Caribbean Studies (CLACS) at UW-Milwaukee, serves as a major resource for the state of Wisconsin, the Upper Midwest, and the nation. The mission of the UW Consortium, both as a resource center and as an academic program, is three-fold: To train Latin Americanist specialists for academic, government, and private sectors; to support Latin Americanist students and faculty in their intellectual development so they can become and remain superior language and area specialists; and to serve as a local, regional, and national resource center that provides outreach, support services, and information to other university units, primary and secondary school teachers and students, undergraduate teachers and students, government, and civic, community, and business constituencies.

METASITES & FURTHER READING

Handbook of Latin American Studies Online
Hispanic Division, Library of Congress
Washington, DC 20540-4851
hlas@loc.gov
http://lcweb2.loc.gov/hlas

The Handbook of Latin American Studies (HLAS) is a bibliography on Latin America consisting of works se-

lected and annotated by scholars. Edited by the Hispanic Division of the Library of Congress, the multidisciplinary Handbook alternates annually between the social sciences and the humanities. With the introduction of HLAS Online, the Handbook became available in three formats: the original print volumes, now published by the University of Texas Press; a CD-ROM produced and updated by the

Fundación Histórica TAVERA in Madrid, Spain; and an Internet version. Updated weekly, HLAS Online provides rapid, comprehensive access to future, current, and retrospective volumes of the Handbook. HLAS depends upon the voluntary work of its more than 130 contributing editors, all of whom are recognized scholars in their fields.

Latin American Network Information Center (LANIC)

University of Texas at Austin
Teresa Lozano Long Institute of Latin American Studies
1 University Station D0800
Austin, Texas 78712
http://lanic.utexas.edu/info/comment/
lin@mail.utexas.edu (Ning Lin, Director)
http://lanic.utexas.edu

LANIC's editorially reviewed directories contain more than ten thousand unique URLs, one of the largest guides for Latin American content on the Internet. LANIC's mission is to facilitate access to Internet-based information to, from, or on Latin America. Its target audience includes people living in Latin America, as well as those around the world who have an interest in this region. While many of LANIC's resources are designed to facilitate research and academic endeavors, the site has also become an important gateway to Latin America for primary and secondary school teachers and students, private and public sector professionals, and other people looking for information about this region.

Latin American Studies Network (LASNET), University of Texas

lasnet-request@uts.cc.utexas.edu

http://lanic.utexas.edu/info/faq/#LASNET

LASNET is an electronic mailing list of more than six hundred Latin Americanists from a wide variety of academic disciplines. The purpose of LASNET is to facilitate the transmission of information among Latin Americanists worldwide. Discussions on the list can be carried out in English, Spanish, or Portuguese. Once subscribed, members of the list can send and receive messages posted to all LASNET participants.

REFORMA: The National Association to Promote Library and Information Services to Latinos and the Spanish-Speaking

P.O. Box 4386
Fresno, CA 93744
Phone: (480) 734-4460
officemgr@reforma.org
http://www.reforma.org

Established in 1971 as an affiliate of the American Library Association, REFORMA has actively sought to promote the development of library collections to include Spanish-language and Latino-oriented materials, the recruitment of more bilingual and bicultural library professionals and support staff, the development of library services and programs that meet the needs of the Latino community, the establishment of a national information and support network among individuals who share the organization's goals, the education of the U.S. Latino population in regard to the availability and types of library services, and lobbying efforts to preserve existing library resource centers serving the interests of Latinos.

FURTHER READING

Byrd, Susannah Mississippi. *¡Bienvenidos! ¡Welcome!: A Handy Resource Guide for Marketing Your Library to Latinos*. Chicago: ALA Editions, 2005. Byrd helps librarians create a comprehensive marketing and outreach strategy that will attract diverse Latino audiences, providing insight into what collections and programs have been successful in libraries with a large base of Spanish-language users, as well as tried and true methods to gain knowledge about their local Hispanic communities.

Stonich, Susan C., ed. *Endangered Peoples of Latin America: Struggles to Survive and Thrive*. Westport, Conn.: Greenwood Press, 2001. Readers are offered rare insight into indigenous and marginalized groups in Mexico, Central America, and South America as

this volume focuses on more than thirteen endangered peoples, from the Mayans of Central Quintana Roo in Mexico to the Quechua of the Peruvian Andes.

Tenenbaum, Barbara A., et al., eds. *Encyclopedia of Latin American History and Culture*. New York: C. Scribner's Sons, 1996. A five-volume encyclopedia of history and culture with topical entries, plus entries for each Latin American country. Some entries are followed by bibliographies.

Tompkins, Cynthia Margarita, and David William Foster, eds. *Notable Twentieth-Century Latin American Women: A Biographical Dictionary*. Westport, Conn.: Greenwood Press, 2001. This dictionary focuses on Latin American, Spanish- and Portuguese-speaking women, most of whom were born after

1900. It also includes lengthy biographies and suggestions for further reading.

Williamson, Edwin, ed. *The Penguin History of Latin America.* New York: Penguin Books, 1992. Offers a broad but comprehensive overview of the history of Latin America, from the conquistadores to the 1990's.

Willette F. Stinson

BIBLIOGRAPHY

This bibliography offers resources about Latinos, beginning with general reference and then arranged alphabetically by areas of achievement.

GENERAL REFERENCE

Benson, Sonia G., ed. *Reference Library of Hispanic America.* 4 vols. Farmington Hills, Mich.: Gale Group, 2003.

Bergad, Laird W., and Herbert S. Klein. *Hispanics in the United States: A Demographic, Social, and Economic History, 1980-2005.* New York: Cambridge University Press, 2010.

Graham, Joe S., comp. *Hispanic-American Material Culture: An Annotated Directory of Collections, Sites, Archives, and Festivals in the United States.* New York: Greenwood Press, 1989.

Kanellos, Nicolas. *Handbook of Hispanic Cultures in the United States.* 4 vols. Houston.: Arte Público Press, 1993-1994.

Oboler, Suzanne, and Deena J. González, eds. 4 vols. *The Oxford Encyclopedia of Latinos and Latinas in the United States.* New York: Oxford University Press, 2005.

Stavans, Ilan, and Harold Augenbraum, eds. 4 vols. *Encyclopedia Latina: History, Culture, and Society in the United States.* Danbury, Conn.: Grolier Academic Reference, 2005.

Tienda, Marta, and Faith Mitchell, eds. *Hispanics and the Future of America: Panel on Hispanics in the United States [and] Committee on Population,* Division of Behavioral and Social Sciences and Education. Washington, D.C.: National Academies Press, 2006.

ART AND CREATIVE EXPRESSION

Otfinoski, Steven. *Latinos in the Arts.* New York: Facts On File, 2007.

Vigil, Angel. *Una Linda Raza: Cultural and Artistic Traditions of the Hispanic Southwest.* Golden, Colo.: Fulcrum, 1998.

ART

Briggs, Charles. *The Wood Carvers of Córdova, New Mexico: Social Dimensions of an Artistic "Revival."* Knoxville: University of Tennessee Press, 1980.

Cockcroft, James D., and Jane Canning. *Latino Visions: Contemporary Chicano, Puerto Rican, and Cuban American Artists.* New York: Franklin Watts, 2000.

Gómez-Quintero, Raysa E. Amador, and Mireya Pérez Bustillo. *The Female Body: Perspectives of Latin American Artists.* Foreword by Elena Poniatowska. Westport, Conn.: Greenwood Press, 2002.

Herrera, Olga U. *Toward the Preservation of a Heritage: Latin American and Latino Art in the Midwestern United States.* Notre Dame, Ind.: Institute for Latino Studies, 2008.

Keller, Gary D., et al. 2 vols. *Contemporary Chicana and Chicano Art: Artists, Works, Culture, and Education.* Tempe, Ariz.: Bilingual Press/Editorial Bilingue, 2002.

Riggs, Thomas, ed. *St. James Guide to Hispanic Artists: Profiles of Latino and Latin American Artists.* Detroit: St. James Press, 2002.

Sullivan, Edward J. *The Language of Objects in the Art of the Americas.* New Haven, Conn.: Yale University Press, 2007.

LITERATURE AND JOURNALISM

Bardeleben, Renate von, ed. *Gender, Self, and Society: Proceedings of the IV International Conference on the Hispanic Cultures of the United States.* New York: Peter Lang, 1993.

Bloom, Harold, ed. *Hispanic-American Writers.* 2d ed. New York: Bloom's Literary Criticism, 2009.

Day, Frances Ann. *Latina and Latino Voices in Literature: Lives and Works.* Westport, Conn.: Greenwood Press, 2003.

Editors of Salem Press. *Notable Latino Writers.* 3 vols. Pasadena, Calif.: Author, 2006.

Fabre, Genviève, ed. *European Perspectives on Hispanic Literature of the United States.* Houston: Arte Público Press, 1988.

Febles, Jorge, ed. *Into the Mainstream: Essays on Spanish American and Latino Literature and Culture.* Newcastle, United Kingdom: Cambridge Scholars, 2006.

Gruesz, Kirsten Silva. *Ambassadors of Culture: The Transamerican Origins of Latino Writing.* Princeton, N.J.: Princeton University Press, 2002.

Gutiérrez, Ramón, and Genaro Padilla, eds. 4 vols. *Recovering the U.S. Hispanic Literary Heritage.* Houston: Arte Público Press, 1993-2002.

Kanellos, Nicolás, ed. *The Greenwood Encyclopedia of Latino Literature*. Westport, Conn.: Greenwood Press, 2008.

Kanellos, Nicolás, and Hevetia Martell. *Hispanic Periodicals in the United States, Origins to 1960: A Brief History and Comprehensive Bibliography*. Houston: Arte Público Press, 2000.

Krstovic, Jelena, ed. *Hispanic Literature Criticism*. 2 vols. Detroit: Gale Research, 1994.

Luis, William. *Dance Between Two Cultures: Latino Caribbean Literature Written in the United States*. Nashville, Tenn.: Vanderbilt University Press, 1997.

Martinez, Julio, ed. and comp. *Chicano Scholars and Writers: A Bio-Bibliographical Directory*. Metuchen, N.J.: Scarecrow Press, 1979.

Martinez, Sara E., ed. *Latino Literature*. Santa Barbara, Calif.: Libraries Unlimited, 2009.

Pérez Firmat, Gustavo. *Tongue Ties: Logo-Eroticism in Anglo-Hispanic Literature*. New York: Palgrave Macmillan, 2003.

Valdivia, Angharad, N., ed. *Latina/o Communication Studies Today*. New York: Peter Lang, 2008.

West-Durán, Alan, ed. 2 vols. *Latino and Latina Writers*. New York: Charles Scribner's Sons, 2004.

Wood, Jamie Martinez. *Latino Writers and Journalists*. New York: Facts On File, 2007.

MUSIC

Avant-Mier, Roberto. *Rock the Nation: Latin/o Identities and the Latin Rock Diaspora*. New York: Continuum, 2010.

Boggs, Vernon W. *Salsiology: Afro-Cuban Music and the Evolution of Salsa in New York City*. New York: Greenwood Press, 1992.

Clark, Walter Aaron, ed. *From Tejano to Tango: Latin American Popular Music*. New York: Routledge, 2002.

Cohen, Norm, ed. *Ethnic and Border Music: A Regional Exploration*. Westport, Conn.: Greenwood Press, 2007.

Dower, Catherine. *Puerto Rican Music Following the Spanish American War: 1898, the Aftermath of the Spanish American War and Its Influence on the Musical Culture of Puerto Rico*. Lanham, Md.: University Press of America, 1983.

Gerard, Charley. *Music from Cuba: Mongo Santamaria, Chocolate Armenteros, and Cuban Musicians in the United States*. Westport, Conn.: Praeger, 2001.

Manuel, Peter, ed. *Essays on Cuban Music: North American and Cuban Perspectives*. Lanham, Md.: University Press of America, 1991.

Pacini Hernandez, Deborah. *Oye Como va! Hybridity and Identity in Latino Popular Music*. Philadelphia: Temple University Press, 2009.

Pacini Hernandez, Deborah, Héctor Fernández-L'Hoeste, and Eric Zolov, eds. *Rockin' las Americas: The Global Politics of Rock in Latin/o America*. Pittsburgh, Pa.: University of Pittsburgh Press, 2004.

Peña, Manuel. *The Mexican American Orquesta: Music, Culture, and the Dialectic of Conflict*. Austin: University of Texas Press, 1999.

Rivera, Raquel Z., Wayne Marshall, and Deborah Pacini Hernandez, eds. *Reggaeton*. Durham, N.C.: Duke University Press, 2009.

Robb, John Donald. *Hispanic Folk Music of New Mexico and the Southwest: A Self-Portrait of a People*. Norman: University of Oklahoma Press, 1980.

Salazar, Max. *Mambo Kingdom: Latin Music in New York*. New York: Schirmer Trade Books, 2002.

THEATER, FILM, AND TELEVISION

Berg, Charles Ramirez. *Latino Images in Film: Stereotypes, Subversion, Resistance*. Austin.: University of Texas Press, 2002.

Nericcio, William Anthony. *Tex(t)-Mex: Seductive Hallucinations of the "Mexican" in America*. Austin: University of Texas Press, 2007.

Noriega, Chon A., ed. *Chicanos and Film: Essays on Chicano Representation and Resistance*. New York: Garland., 1992.

Ranucci, Karen, and Julie Feldman, eds. *A Guide to Latin American, Caribbean, and U.S. Latino Made Films and Video*. Lanham, Md.: Scarecrow Press, 1998.

Reyes, Luis, and Peter Rubie. *Hispanics in Hollywood: A Celebration of One Hundred Years in Film and Television*. Hollywood, Calif.: Lone Eagle, 2000.

Richard, Alfred Charles, Jr. *Censorship and Hollywood's Hispanic Image: An Interpretive Filmography, 1936-1955*. Westport, Conn.: Greenwood Press, 1993.

_____. *The Hispanic Image on the Silver Screen: An Interpretive Filmography from Silents into Sound, 1898-1935*. New York: Greenwood Press, 1992.

BIOGRAPHIES AND CASE STUDIES

Acuña, Rodolfo F., and Guadalupe Compean, eds. 3 vols. *Voices of the U.S. Latino Experience*. Westport, Conn.: Greenwood Press, 2008.

Davis, Marilyn P. *Mexican Voices/American Dreams: An Oral History of Mexican Immigration to the United States*. New York: H. Holt, 1990.

Melendez, Miguel "Mickey." *We Took the Streets: Fighting for Latino Rights with the Young Lords.* New York: St. Martin's Press, 2003.

Rivera, John-Michael. *The Emergence of Mexican America: Recovering Stories of Mexican Peoplehood in U.S. Culture.* New York: New York University Press, 2006.

Rodriguez, Jaime Javier. *The Literatures of the U.S.-Mexican War: Narrative, Time, and Identity.* Austin: University of Texas Press, 2010.

Rosales, F. Arturo, ed. *Testimonio: A Documentary History of the Mexican American Struggle for Civil Rights.* Houston: Arte Público Press, 2000.

Siems, Larry, ed. and trans. *Between the Lines: Letters Between Undocumented Mexican and Central American Immigrants and Their Families and Friends.* Preface by Jimmy Santiago Baca. Hopewell, N.J.: Ecco Press, 1992.

Torres, Andrés, and José E. Velázquez, eds. *The Puerto Rican Movement: Voices from the Diaspora.* Philadelphia: Temple University Press, 1998.

Wagenheim, Kal, and Olga Jiménez de Wagenheim, eds. *The Puerto Ricans: A Documentary History.* Princeton, N.J.: Markus Wiener, 1994.

COMMUNITIES

Arreola, Daniel D., ed. *Hispanic Spaces, Latino Places: Community and Cultural Diversity in Contemporary America.* Austin: University of Texas Press, 2004.

DeAnda, Roberto M., ed. *Chicanas and Chicanos in Contemporary Society.* Boston: Allyn & Bacon, 1995.

Gonzalez-Pando, Miguel. *The Cuban Americans.* Westport, Conn.: Greenwood Press, 1998.

Oboler, Suzanne. *Ethnic Labels, Latino Lives: Identity and the Politics of (Re)presentation in the United States.* Minneapolis: University of Minnesota Press, 1995.

Padilla, Felix M. *Latino Ethnic Consciousness: The Case of Mexican-Americans and Puerto Ricans in Chicago.* Notre Dame, Ind.: University of Notre Dame Press, 1985.

Pap, Leo. *The Portuguese-Americans.* Boston: Twayne, 1981.

Pérez E. González, Maria E. *Puerto Ricans in the United States.* Westport, Conn.: Greenwood Press, 2000.

Rivera, Raquel Z. *New York Ricans from the Hip Hop Zone.* New York: Palgrave Macmillan, 2003.

Sanchez, José Ramón. *Boricua Power: A Political History of Puerto Ricans in the United States.* New York: New York University Press, 2007.

EDUCATION

Donato, Rubén. *The Other Struggle for Equal Schools: Mexican Americans During the Civil Rights Era.* Albany: State University of New York Press, 1997.

Gándara, Patricia, and Frances Contreras. *The Latino Education Crisis: The Consequences of Failed Social Policies.* Cambridge, Mass.: Harvard University Press, 2009.

Garcia, Eugene E. *Hispanic Education in the United States: Raíces y Alas.* Lanham, Md.: Rowman & Littlefield, 2001.

Martinez, Corinne, Zeus Leonardo, and Carlos Tejeda, eds. *Charting New Terrains of Chicana(o)/Latina(o) Education.* Cresskill, N.J.: Hampton Press, 2000.

Padilla, Felix M. *The Struggle of Latino/a University Students: In Search of a Liberating Education.* New York: Routledge, 1997.

Padilla, Raymond V., and Rudolfo Chávez Chávez, eds. *The Leaning Ivory Tower: Latino Professors in American Universities.* Albany: State University of New York Press, 1995.

FOOD AND CULTURE

Canfield, Jack, Mark Victor Hansen, and Susan C. Sánchez. *Chicken Soup for the Latino Soul: Celebrating la Comunidad Latina.* Deerfield Beach, Fla.: Health Communications, 2005.

Cordova, Regina, and Emma Carrasco. *Celebración: Recipes and Traditions Celebrating Latino Family Life.* New York: Doubleday, 1996.

Counihan, Carole M. *A Tortilla Is Like Life: Food and Culture in the San Luis Valley of Colorado.* Austin: University of Texas Press, 2009.

Janer, Zilkia. *Latino Food Culture.* New York: ABC-CLIO/Greenwood Press, 2008.

Sanjur, Diva. *Hispanic Foodways, Nutrition, and Health.* Boston: Allyn & Bacon, 1995.

HISTORY AND POLITICS

Abalos, David T. *Latinos in the United States: The Sacred and the Political.* 2d ed. Notre Dame, Ind.: University of Notre Dame Press, 2007.

Acuña, Rodolfo. *Occupied America: A History of Chicanos.* 4th ed. New York: Longman, 2000.

Antón, Alex, and Roger E. Hernández. *Cubans in America: An Exciting, Vibrant History of a People in Exile.* New York: Mallard, 2002.

Barreto, Matt A. *Ethnic Cues: The Role of Shared Ethnicity in Latino Political Participation.* Ann Arbor: University of Michigan Press, 2010.

Beers, Henry Putney. *Spanish and Mexican Records of the American Southwest: A Bibliographical Guide to Archive and Manuscript Sources.* Tucson: University of Arizona Press, 1979.

Beltrán, Cristina. *The Trouble with Unity: Latino Politics and the Creation of Identity.* New York: Oxford University Press, 2010.

Cabán, Pedro A., et al. *The Latino Experience in U.S. History.* Paramus, N.J.: Globe Fearon, 1994.

Cardona, Luis Antonio. *A History of the Puerto Ricans in the United States of America.* Rev. and enlarged ed. Bethesda, Md.: Carreta Press, 1995.

Chavez, Linda. *Out of the Barrio: Toward a New Politics of Hispanic Assimilation.* New York: Basic Books, 1991.

Cisneros, Henry G., and John Rosales, eds. *Latinos and the Nation's Future.* Houston: Arte Público Press, 2009.

DeSipio, Louis. *Counting on the Latino Vote: Latinos as a New Electorate.* Charlottesville: University Press of Virginia, 1996.

DeVarona, Frank, ed. *Hispanic Presence in the United States: Historical Beginnings.* Miami: National Hispanic Quincentennial Commission/Mnemosyne, 1993.

Didion, Joan. *Miami.* New York: Simon & Schuster, 1987.

Enck-Wanzer, Darrel, ed. *The Young Lords: A Reader.* New York: New York University Press, 2010.

Fernández-Shaw, Carlos M. *The Hispanic Presence in North America from 1492 to Today.* Translated by Alfonso Bertodano Stourton, et al. New York: Facts On File, 1999.

González, Juan. *Harvest of Empire: A History of Latinos in America.* New York: Viking, 2000.

Gutiérrez, David G., ed. *The Columbia History of Latinos in the United States Since 1960.* New York: Columbia University Press, 2004.

Hutchinson, Earl Ofari. *The Latino Challenge to Black America.* Los Angeles: Middle Passage Press, 2007.

Kanellos, Nicolás, and Cristelia Pérez. *Chronology of Hispanic-American History: From Pre-Columbian Times to the Present.* New York: Gale Research, 1995.

Kanellos, Nicolás, and Bryan Ryan, eds. *Hispanic American Chronology.* New York: U.X.L., 1996.

Mariscal, George, ed. *Aztlán and Viet Nam: Chicano and Chicana Experiences of the War.* Berkeley:

University of California Press, 1999.

Menendez, Bob. *Growing American Roots: Why Our Nation Will Thrive as Our Largest Minority Flourishes.* New York: New American Library, 2009.

Mira, Manuel. *The Forgotten Portuguese.* Franklin, N.C.: Portuguese-American Historical Research Foundation, 1998.

Navarro, Sharon Ann, and Armando Xavier Mejia, eds. *Latino Americans and Political Participation: A Reference Handbook.* Santa Barbara, Calif.: ABC-CLIO, 2004.

Novas, Himilce. *Everything You Need to Know About Latino History.* 3d ed. New York: Plume, 2007.

Ochoa, George, and Carter Smith. *Atlas of Hispanic-American History.* Rev. ed. New York: Facts On File, 2008.

Platt, Lyman D. *Hispanic Surnames and Family History.* Baltimore: Genealogical, 1996.

Shorris, Earl. *Latinos: A Biography of the People.* New York: W. W. Norton & Co., 2001.

Stavans, Ilan. *Latino History and Culture.* New York: Collins, 2007.

Vigil, Maurilio E. *Hispanics in Congress: A Historical and Political Survey.* Lanham, Md.: University Press of America, 1996.

Villarreal, Roberto E., and Norma G. Hernandez, eds. *Latinos and Political Coalitions: Political Empowerment for the 1990s.* New York: Greenwood Press, 1991.

Villarreal, Roberto E., Norma G. Hernandez, and Howard D. Neighbor, eds. *Latino Empowerment: Progress, Problems, and Prospects.* New York: Greenwood Press, 1988.

Whalen, Carmen Teresa, and Victor Vázquez-Hernández, eds. *The Puerto Rican Diaspora: Historical Perspectives.* Philadelphia: Temple University Press, 2005.

HUMOR

Aldama, Frederick Luis. *Your Brain on Latino Comics: From Gus Arriola to Los Bros Hernandez.* Austin: University of Texas Press, 2009.

De la Fuente, Cristián, and Federico Lariño. *Hot, Passionate, and Illegal? Why (Almost) Everything You Thought About Latinos Just May Be True.* New York: New American Library, 2010.

Garcia, Nasario, ed. and transl. *Chistes! Hispanic Humor of Northern New Mexico and Southern Colorado.* Santa Fe: Museum of New Mexico Press, 2004.

IMMIGRATION

Aranda, Elizabeth M. *Emotional Bridges to Puerto Rico: Migration, Return Migration, and the Struggles of Incorporation.* Lanham, Md.: Rowman & Littlefield, 2007.

Baganha, Maria Ioannis Benis. *Portuguese Emigration to the United States, 1820-1930.* New York: Garland, 1990.

Balderrama, Francisco E., and Raymond Rodriguez. *Decade of Betrayal: Mexican Repatriation in the 1930s.* Rev. ed. Albuquerque: University of New Mexico Press, 2006.

Bonilla, Frank, et al., eds. *Borderless Borders: U.S. Latinos, Latin Americans, and the Paradox of Interdependence.* Philadelphia: Temple University Press, 1998.

Canul, Rafael D. *Mexican Illegal Aliens: A Mexican American Perspective.* Edited by John Cise. Mountain View, Calif.: Floricanto Press, 2005.

Duany, Jorge. *The Puerto Rican Nation on the Move: Identities on the Island and in the United States.* Chapel Hill: University of North Carolina Press, 2002.

Eckstein, Susan. *The Immigrant Divide: How Cuban Americans Changed the U.S. and Their Homeland.* New York: Routledge, 2009.

Espada, Frank. *The Puerto Rican Diaspora: Themes in the Survival of a People.* New York: El Museo del Barrio, 1983.

Faber, Eli. *A Time For Planting: The First Migration, 1654-1820.* Baltimore: Johns Hopkins University Press, 1992.

Fitzpatrick, Joseph P. *Puerto Rican Americans: The Meaning of Migration to the Mainland.* 2d ed. Englewood Cliffs, N.J.: Prentice-Hall, 1987.

Hattam, Victoria. *In the Shadow of Race: Jews, Latinos, and Immigrant Politics in the United States.* Chicago: University of Chicago Press, 2007.

Hefner, Tony. *Between the Fences: Before Guantánamo, There was the Port Isabel Service Processing Center.* New York: Seven Stories Press, 2010.

James, Ian Michael. *Ninety Miles: Cuban Journeys in the Age of Castro.* Lanham, Md.: Rowman & Littlefield, 2006.

Johnson, Benjamin Heber. *Revolution in Texas: How a Forgotten Rebellion and Its Bloody Suppression Turned Mexicans into Americans.* New Haven, Conn.: Yale University Press, 2003.

Jouët-Pastré, Clémence, and Leticia Braga, eds. *Becoming Brazuca: Brazilian Immigration to the United States.* Cambridge, Mass.: Harvard University Press, 2008.

Levine, Robert M. *Secret Missions to Cuba: Fidel Castro, Bernardo Benes, and Cuban Miami.* New York: Palgrave, 2001.

Maciel, David R., and Maria Herrera-Sobek, eds. *Culture Across Borders: Mexican Immigration and Popular Culture.* Tucson: University of Arizona Press, 1998.

Maril, Robert Lee. *Living on the Edge of America: At Home on the Texas-Mexico Border.* College Station: Texas A&M University Press, 1999.

O'Reilly Herrera, Andrea, ed. *Remembering Cuba: Legacy of a Diaspora.* Austin: University of Texas Press, 2001.

Pachon, Harry, and Louis DeSipio. *New Americans by Choice: Political Perspectives of Latino Immigrants.* Boulder, Colo.: Westview Press, 1994.

Pedraza, Silvia. *Political Disaffection in Cuba's Revolution and Exodus.* New York: Cambridge University Press, 2007.

Ramos, Jorge. *A Country for All: An Immigrant Manifesto.* Translated from the Spanish by Ezra Fitz. New York: Vintage Books, 2010.

Rivera-Batiz, Francisco, and Carlos E. Santiago. *Island Paradox: Puerto Rico in the 1990s.* New York: Russell Sage Foundation, 1996.

Rodriguez, Gregory. *Mongrels, Bastards, Orphans, and Vagabonds: Mexican Immigration and the Future of Race in America.* New York: Vintage Books, 2008.

Schwab, Stephen Irving Max. *Guantánamo, USA: The Untold History of America's Cuban Outpost.* Lawrence: University Press of Kansas, 2009.

Suro, Roberto. *Strangers Among Us: How Latino Immigration Is Transforming America.* New York: Alfred A. Knopf, 1998.

Thompson, Gabriel. *There's No José Here: Following the Hidden Lives of Mexican Immigrants.* New York: Nation Books, 2007.

Torre, Carlos Antonio, Hugo Rodriguez Vecchini, and William Burgos, eds. *The Commuter Nation: Perspectives on Puerto Rican Migration.* Rio Piedras, P.R.: Editorial de la Universidad de Puerto Rico, 1994.

Torres, Maria de los Angeles. *In the Land of Mirrors: Cuban Exile Politics in the United States.* Ann Arbor: University of Michigan Press, 1999.

Weyr, Thomas. *Hispanic U.S.A.: Breaking the Melting Pot.* New York: Harper & Row, 1988.

LAW AND CRIME

Bender, Steven W. *Greasers and Gringos: Latinos, Law, and the American Imagination.* New York: New York University Press, 2003.

Bourgois, Philippe. *In Search of Respect: Selling Crack in El Barrio.* 2d ed. New York: Cambridge University Press, 2003.

Diaz, Tom. *No Boundaries: Transnational Latino Gangs and American Law Enforcement.* Ann Arbor: University of Michigan Press, 2009.

Diaz-Cotto, Juanita. *Gender, Ethnicity, and the State: Latina and Latino Prison Politics.* Albany: State University of New York Press, 1996.

Haney López, Ian F. *Racism on Trial: The Chicano Fight for Justice.* Cambridge, Mass.: Belknap Press of Harvard University Press, 2003.

López, Gerald P. *Rebellious Lawyering: One Chicano's Vision of Progressive Law Practice.* Boulder, Colo.: Westview Press, 1992.

Martinez, Ramiro, Jr. *Latino Homicide: Immigration, Violence, and Community.* New York: Routledge, 2002.

Mendoza-Denton, Norma. *Homegirls: Language and Cultural Practice Among Latina Youth Gangs.* Malden, Mass.: Blackwell, 2008.

LINGUISTICS

Cruz, Bill, et al. *The Official Spanglish Dictionary: Un User's Guia to More than Three Hundred Words and Phrases That Aren't Exactly Español or Inglés.* Illustrations by David Le Batard. New York: Fireside, 1998.

Fought, Carmen. *Chicano English in Context.* New York: Palgrave, 2003.

Fusco, Coco. *English Is Broken Here: Notes on Cultural Fusion in the Americas.* New York: New Press, 1995.

Harris, Tracy K. *Death of a Language: The History of Judeo-Spanish.* Newark: University of Delaware Press, 1994.

Kalmar, Tomás Mario. *Illegal Alphabets and Adult Biliteracy: Latino Migrants Crossing the Linguistic Border.* Mahwah, N.J.: L. Erlbaum Associates, 2000.

Morales, Ed. *Living in Spanglish: The Search for a New Latino Identity in America.* New York: St. Martin's Press, 2002.

Stavans, Ilan. *Spanglish: The Making of a New American Language.* New York: Rayo, 2003.

Tobar, Héctor. *Translation Nation: Defining a New American Identity in the Spanish-Speaking United States.* New York: Riverhead Books, 2005.

POLITICAL AND RACIAL DISCRIMINATION

Acuña, Rodolfo. *Sometimes There Is No Other Side: Chicanos and the Myth of Equality.* Notre Dame, Ind.: University of Notre Dame Press, 1998.

Dávila, Arlene. *Latino Spin: Public Image and the Whitewashing of Race.* New York: New York University Press, 2008.

DeGenova, Nicholas, and Ana Yolanda Ramos-Zayas. *Latino Crossings: Mexicans, Puerto Ricans, and the Politics of Race and Citizenship.* New York: Routledge, 2003.

Garcia, Jorge J. E., ed. *Race or Ethnicity? On Black and Latino Identity.* Ithaca, N.Y.: Cornell University Press, 2007.

Garcia, Jorge J. E., and Pablo De Greff, eds. *Hispanics/Latinos in the United States: Ethnicity, Race, and Rights.* New York: Routledge, 2000.

Gomez, Laura E. *Manifest Destinies: The Making of the Mexican American Race.* New York: New York University Press, 2008.

Gordon, Linda. *The Great Arizona Orphan Abduction.* Cambridge, Mass.: Harvard University Press, 2001.

Menchaca, Martha. *Recovering History, Constructing Race: The Indian, Black, and White Roots of Mexican Americans.* Austin: University of Texas Press, 2001.

Portales, Marco. *Crowding out Latinos: Mexican Americans in the Public Consciousness.* Philadelphia: Temple University Press, 2000.

Skerry, Peter. *Mexican Americans: The Ambivalent Minority.* New York: Free Press, 1993.

Stafford, Jim. *Puerto Ricans' History and Promise: Americans Who Cannot Vote.* Philadelphia: Mason Crest, 2006.

Telles, Edward E., and Vilma Ortiz. *Generations of Exclusion: Mexican Americans, Assimilation, and Race.* New York: Russell Sage Foundation, 2008.

PROFESSIONS, LABOR, EMPLOYMENT, AND BUSINESS

Bacon, David. *The Children of NAFTA: Labor Wars on the U.S./Mexico Border.* Berkeley, Calif.: University of California Press, 2005.

Benitez, Cristina, and Marlene González. *Latinization and the Latino Leader: How to Value, Develop, and Advance Talented Professionals.* Ithaca, N.Y.: Paramount Market, 2011.

Chong, Nilda, and Francia Baez. *Latino Culture: A Dynamic Force in the Changing American Workplace.* Yarmouth, Maine.: Intercultural Press, 2005.

DeFreitas, Gregory. *Inequality at Work: Hispanics in the U.S. Labor Force.* New York: Oxford University Press, 1991.

Griffith, David, and Manuel Valdés Pizzini. *Fishers at Work, Workers at Sea: A Puerto Rican Journey*

Through Labor and Refuge. Philadelphia: Temple University Press, 2002.

Knouse, Stephen B., Paul Rosenfeld, and Amy Culbertson, eds. *Hispanics in the Workplace*. Newbury Park, Calif.: Sage, 1992.

Korzenny, Felipe, and Betty Ann Korzenny. *Hispanic Marketing: A Cultural Perspective*. Burlington, Mass.: Elsevier/Butterworth-Heinemann, 2005.

Newton, David E. *Latinos in Science, Math, and Professions*. New York: Facts On File, 2007.

Renteria, Tamis Hoover. *Chicano Professionals: Culture, Conflict, and Identity*. New York: Garland, 1998.

Rivera, Geraldo. *The Great Progression: How Hispanics Will Lead America to a New Era of Prosperity*. New York: Celebra, 2009.

Sedillo López, Antoinette, ed. *Latino Employment, Labor Organizations, and Immigration*. New York: Garland, 1995.

Valle, Isabel. *Fields of Toil: A Migrant Family's Journey*. Pullman: Washington State University Press, 1995.

Vargas, Zaragosa. *Labor Rights Are Civil Rights: Mexican American Workers in Twentieth-Century America*. Princeton, N.J.: Princeton University Press, 2005.

RELIGION

Agosín, Marjorie, ed. *Passion, Memory, and Identity*. Albuquerque: University of New Mexico Press, 1999.

Ben-Ur, Aviva. *Sephardic Jews in America: A Diasporic History*. New York: New York University Press, 2009.

Birmingham, Stephen. *The Grandees: America's Sephardic Elite*. New York: Syracuse University Press, 1997.

Cohen, Martin A., and Abraham J. Peck, eds. *Sephardim in the Americas: Studies in Culture and History*. Tuscaloosa: University of Alabama Press, 1993.

Dahm, Charles W. *Parish Ministry in a Hispanic Community*. New York: Paulist Press, 2004.

Diaz-Mas, Paloma. *Sephardim: The Jews from Spain*. Translated by George K. Zucker. Chicago: University of Chicago Press, 1992.

Diaz-Stevens, Ana Maria, and Anthony M. Stevens-Arroyo. *Recognizing the Latino Resurgence in U.S. Religion: The Emmaus Paradigm*. Boulder, Colo.: Westview Press, 1998.

Dobrinsky, Herbert C. *A Treasury of Sephardic Laws and Customs: The Ritual Practices of Syrian, Moroccan, Judeo-Spanish, and Spanish and Portuguese Jews of North America*. New York: Yeshiva University Press, 1986.

Dolan, Jay P., and Jaime R. Vidal, eds. *Puerto Rican and Cuban Catholics in the U.S., 1900-1965*. Notre Dame, Ind.: University of Notre Dame Press, 1994.

Eisenberg, Ellen, Ava F. Kahn, and William Toll. *Jews of the Pacific Coast: Reinventing Community on America's Edge*. Seattle: University of Washington Press, 2009.

Espinosa, Gastón, and Mario T. Garcia, eds. *Mexican American Religions: Spirituality, Activism, and Culture*. Durham, N.C.: Duke University Press, 2008.

Hordes, Stanley M. *To the End of the Earth: A History of the Crypto-Jews of New Mexico*. New York: Columbia University Press, 2005.

Jacobs, Janet Liebman. *Hidden Heritage: The Legacy of the Crypto-Jews*. Berkeley: University of California Press, 2002.

Malamed, Sandra Cumings. *The Jews in Early America: A Chronicle of Good Taste and Good Deeds*. McKinleyville, Calif.: Fithian Press, 2003.

_____. *The Return to Judaism: Descendants from the Inquisition Discovering Their Jewish Roots*. McKinleyville, Calif.: Fithian Press, 2010.

Maldonado, David, Jr., ed. *Protestantes/Protestants: Hispanic Christianity Within Mainline Traditions*. Nashville, Tenn.: Abingdon Press, 1999.

Matovina, Timothy, and Gerald E. Poyo, eds. *Presente! U.S. Latino Catholics from Colonial Origins to the Present*. In collaboration with Cecilia González Andrieu, Steven P. Rodriguez, and Jaime R. Vidal. New York: Orbis Books, 2000.

Mizrahi, Judith. *Seven Hundred Three American Sephardim: Diversity Within Cohesiveness*. New York: Gemini Books, 1993.

Ortiz, Manuel. *The Hispanic Challenge: Opportunities Confronting the Church*. Downers Grove, Ill.: InterVarsity Press, 1993.

Poyo, Gerald E. *Cuban Catholics in the United States, 1960-1980: Exile and Integration*. Notre Dame, Ind.: University of Notre Dame Press, 2007.

Valentin, Karen, and Edwin Aymat. *The Flavor of Our Hispanic Faith*. Valley Forge, Pa.: Judson Press, 2008.

Wilson, Catherine E. *The Politics of Latino Faith: Religion, Identity, and Urban Community*. New York: New York University Press, 2008.

SCIENCE, HEALTH, AND MEDICINE

Aguirre-Molina, Marilyn, and Carlos W. Molina, eds. *Latina Health in the United States: A Public Health Reader*. San Francisco: Jossey-Bass, 2003.

Delgado, Melvin, ed. *Alcohol Use/Abuse Among Latinos: Issues and Examples of Culturally Competent Services*. New York: Haworth Press, 1998.

DeStefano, Anthony M. *Latino Folk Medicine: Healing Herbal Remedies from Ancient Traditions*. New York: Ballantine Books, 2001.

Peña, Devon G. *Mexican Americans and the Environment: Tierra y Vida*. Tucson: University of Arizona Press, 2005.

Rosenwaike, Ira, ed. *Mortality of Hispanic Populations: Mexicans, Puerto Ricans, and Cubans in the United States and in the Home Countries*. New York: Greenwood Press, 1991.

Valdez, R. Burciaga, et al. *Cancer in U.S. Latino Communities: An Exploratory Review*. Santa Monica, Calif.: Rand, 1993.

SEX AND GENDER ROLES

Asencio, Marysol, ed. *Latina/o Sexualities: Probing Powers, Passions, Practices, and Policies*. New Brunswick, N.J.: Rutgers University Press, 2010.

Sifuentes-Jáuregui, Ben. *Transvestism, Masculinity, and Latin American Literature: Genders Share Flesh*. New York: Palgrave, 2002.

Taylor, Diana, and Juan Villegas, eds. *Negotiating Performance: Gender, Sexuality, and Theatricality in Latin/o America*. Durham, N.C.: Duke University Press, 1994.

GAY LATINOS

Chávez-Silverman, Susana, and Librada Hernández, eds. *Reading and Writing the Ambiente: Queer Sexualities in Latino, Latin American, and Spanish Culture*. Madison: University of Wisconsin Press, 2000.

Diaz, Rafael M. *Latino Gay Men and HIV: Culture, Sexuality, and Risk Behavior*. New York: Routledge, 1998.

Guzmán, Manolo. *Gay Hegemony/Latino Homosexualities*. New York: Routledge, 2006.

Hames-Garcia, Michael, and Ernesto Javier Martinez, eds. *Gay Latino Studies: A Critical Reader*. Durham, N.C.: Duke University Press, 2011.

LaFountain-Stokes, Lawrence. *Queer Ricans: Cultures and Sexualities in the Diaspora*. Minneapolis: University of Minnesota Press, 2009.

Rodriguez, Juana Maria. *Queer Latinidad: Identity Practices, Discursive Spaces*. New York: New York University Press, 2003.

Torres, Lourdes, and Immaculada Pertusa, eds. *Tortilleras: Hispanic and U.S. Latina Lesbian Expression*. Philadelphia: Temple University Press, 2003.

LATINAS

Del Alba Acevedo, Luz, et al. *Telling to Live: Latina Feminist Testimonios–the Latina Feminist Group*. Durham, N.C.: Duke University Press, 2001.

Fountas, Angela Jane, ed. *Waking up American: Coming of Age Biculturally, First-Generation Women Reflect on Identity*. Emeryville, Calif.: Seal Press, 2005.

Marting, Diane E., ed. *Spanish American Women Writers: A Bio-Bibliography*. New York: Greenwood Press, 1990.

Moreno, Robyn, and Michelle Herrera Mulligan, eds. *Border-Line Personalities: A New Generation of Latinas Dish on Sex, Sass, and Cultural Shifting*. New York: Rayo, 2004.

Peña, Milagros. *Latina Activists Across Borders: Women's Grassroots Organizing in Mexico and Texas*. Durham, N.C.: Duke University Press, 2007.

Rivera, Carmen S. *Kissing the Mango Tree: Puerto Rican Women Rewriting American Literature*. Houston: Arte Público Press, 2009.

Stoner, K. Lynn, and Luis Hipólito Serrano Pérez, eds. and comps. *Cuban and Cuban-American Women: An Annotated Bibliography*. Wilmington, Del.: Scholarly Resources, 2000.

Trujillo, Carla, ed. *Living Chicana Theory*. Berkeley, Calif.: Third Woman Press, 1998.

Vargas, Lucila. *Latina Teens, Migration, and Popular Culture*. New York: Peter Lang, 2009.

LATINO MEN

Abalos, David T. *The Latino Male: A Radical Redefinition*. Boulder, Colo.: Lynne Rienner, 2002.

Gonzalez, Ray, ed. *Muy Macho: Latino Men Confront Their Manhood*. New York: Anchor Books, 1996.

Mirandé, Alfredo. *Hombres y Machos: Masculinity and Latino Culture*. Boulder, Colo.: Westview Press, 1997.

SOCIAL IDENTITY

Benitez, Cristina. *Latinization: How Latino Culture Is Transforming the U.S.* Ithaca, N.Y.: Paramount Marketing, 2007.

Donovan, Sandy. *The Hispanic American Experience*. Minneapolis: Twenty-First Century Books, 2011.

Flores, Juan. *From Bomba to Hip-Hop: Puerto Rican Culture and Latino Identity*. New York: Columbia University Press, 2000.

Flores, William V., and Rina Bénmayor, eds. *Latino Cultural Citizenship: Claiming Identity, Space, and Rights.* Boston: Beacon Press, 1997.

Fox, Geoffrey E. *Hispanic Nation: Culture, Politics, and the Constructing of Identity.* Secaucus, N.J.: Carol, 1996.

Limón, Jose E. *American Encounters: Greater Mexico, the United States, and the Erotics of Culture.* Boston: Beacon Press, 1998.

Menard, Valerie. *The Latino Holiday Book: From Cinco de Mayo to Dia de los Muertos–the Celebrations and Traditions of Hispanic Americans.* Foreword by Cheech Marin. New York: Marlowe & Co, 2000.

O'Brien, Soledad, and Rose Marie Arce. *Latino in America.* New York: New American Library, 2009.

Rodriguez, Gloria G. *Raising Nuestros Niños: Bringing up Latino Children in a Bicultural World.* New York: Fireside Books, 1999.

Sanchez, George J. *Becoming Mexican American: Ethnicity, Culture, and Identity in Chicano Los Angeles.* New York: Oxford University Press, 1995.

SPORTS

Friedman, Ian C. *Latino Athletes.* New York: Facts On File, 2007.

Porter, David L., ed. *Latino and African American Athletes Today: A Biographical Dictionary.* Westport, Conn.: Greenwood Press, 2004.

WEB SITE DIRECTORY

Online resources for further study of Latinos are listed below.

America.gov Archive: Hispanic Americans Contributing to the American Mosaic

http://www.america.gov/st/washfile-english/2006/September/20060915190750AEneerG0.6483576.html

Provides information on notable Hispanic Americans in art, literature, fashion design, architecture, sports, entertainment, and politics.

American Women's History: A Research Guide: Hispanic American Women

http://frank.mtsu.edu/~kmiddlet/history/women/wh-hispanic.html

American Women's History is created by Ken Middleton of the Middle Tennessee State University Library. The page devoted to Hispanic American Women links users to information about the lives and accomplishments of these women, including oral histories and old photographs.

Association for Library Service to Children: Welcome to the Pura Belpré Award Home Page

http://www.ala.org/ala/mgrps/divs/alsc/awardsgrants/bookmedia/belpremedal/index.cfm

The Pura BelpréAward is the focus of this Web site, and Latino authors and illustrators who received this prestigious award, such as Pam Muñoz Ryan and Eric Velasquez, are featured.

Biography.com: Celebrating Hispanic Heritage

http://www.biography.com/hispanic-heritage/index.jsp

An easy-to-navigate resource, abundant with information on influential Hispanic figures. Provides access to visually appealing slide shows and photograph galleries.

California Cultures: Everyday Life: Hispanic Americans

http://www.calisphere.universityofcalifornia.edu/calcultures/ethnic_groups/subtopic3g.html

This section of Calisphere, a digital library maintained by the University of California, features historic photographs depicting the lives of Hispanic Americans from the 1940's through the 1970's. Users can click the smaller images to view enlarged photographs.

California State University Northridge Oviatt Library: Latino Cultural Heritage Digital Archives

http://digital-library.csun.edu/LatArch

Using this Web site, viewers can access information about Latino history, such as digitized documents and photographs.

The Christian Science Monitor: Latino Politicians Gain Clout in U.S.

http://www.csmonitor.com/2005/0519/p01s01-uspo.html

This article takes an in-depth look at Latinos' involvement in politics and the unique experiences of Hispanic politicians.

Digital History: Chronology of Mexican American History

http://www.digitalhistory.uh.edu/modules/mex_am/chronology.html

Provides a time line marking important events from 1527 to 1994.

The Economist: Latinos and American Politics: Power in Numbers

http://www.economist.com/node/15213228

Contains an enlightening article about Latinos' engagement in politics.

Educating Change: Latina Activism and the Struggle for Educational Equity

http://www.brown.edu/Research/Coachella/introduction.html

Maintained by Brown University, this site provides information on the Chicano movement and the educational injustices faced by Mexican children in California. Particularly insightful are the historic photographs and video interviews of women who strove to improve the educational situation of Mexican students.

ESPN: Take Notice of Latinas as Leaders in the Sports World

http://sports.espn.go.com/espn/hispanicheritage2007/columns/story?id=3039570

An article describing the feats of various Latina athletes.

Fact Monster: Famous Firsts by Hispanic Americans
http://www.factmonster.com/ipka/A0933896.html

A visually appealing Web page with information on Hispanic Americans who were pioneers in government, literature, film, military, sports, and other areas.

Fact Monster: Notable Hispanic-American Scientists
http://www.factmonster.com/spot/hhmbio4.html

Aimed at younger viewers, this site informs users about prominent Hispanic American scientists, such as Severo Ochoa, Mario Molina, and Luis Walter Alvarez. The page's links lead to more details about each scientist.

Famous Firsts by Hispanic Americans
http://personnel.ky.gov/NR/rdonlyres/84B3E416-D76C-46F8-BC84-2562CF10D863/0/FamousFirstbyHispanicAmericans.pdf

Lists the remarkable achievements and contributions made by trailblazing Hispanic Americans, such as Alberto Gonzales, Edward Hidalgo, and Tom Fears.

The Forty-two Most Influential Latino Politicians: Hispanic Power
http://www.latinamericanstudies.org/latinos/politicians.htm

An article from *Latino Leaders*, a national magazine about successful Latinos. The article provides background information about prominent Latino political figures.

Girls Incorporated: Latinas in the United States.: Social Issues
http://www.girlsinc.org/downloads/Latinas_US_SocialIssues_factsheet.pdf

A fact sheet containing statistical information about the social and economic conditions of Latinas.

Harvard University Faculty of Arts and Sciences: Introduction: Immigration from Latin America and Caribbean
http://www.fas.harvard.edu/~gstudies/latin/curriculum/intro.htm

The article on this Web page contains information pertaining to Latin American and Caribbean immigrants, including some discussion of the achievements of well-known Latino individuals.

HistoryLink.org: Muralist Art and Activism in Washington's Latino Community
http://www.historylink.org/index.cfm?DisplayPage=output.cfm&file_id=7879

An informative essay about the muralist art movement in the state of Washington, including images of artwork and information about the Mexican American artists involved in this movement.

Houston Area Digital Archives: Preserving Library Collections
http://digital.houstonlibrary.org/cdm4/results.php?CISOOP1=exact&CISOBOX1=leonel+castillo&CISOFIELD1=CISOSEARCHALL&CISOROOT=all&t=s

Maintained by the Houston Public Library, these digital archives contain images, audiovisual content, and informative descriptions about distinguished Hispanic individuals. Users can turn to the archive search feature when seeking specific information.

KUOW Puget Sound Public Radio: Increasing Numbers of Latino Politicians Running in Northwest
http://www.kuow.org/program.php?id=16019

Offers a transcript of an interview with a Latino politician and political science professors who discuss Latinos' involvement in politics in the northwestern United States.

Latino Guide: A Guide to Literature by Students for Students
http://www.ccc.commnet.edu/latinoguide/index.htm

Created by students at Capital Community College in Hartford, Connecticut, this site provides information on U.S. Latino authors and poets and their works. Links to further information on a few authors are included.

Law Library of Congress: National Hispanic Heritage Month
http://www.loc.gov/law/help/commemorative-observations/hispanic-heritage.php

Provides interesting background information about National Hispanic Heritage Month.

Library of Congress: Hispanic Americans in Congress, 1822-1995
http://www.loc.gov/rr/hispanic/congress/introduction.html

Delves into the history of Hispanic Americans in Congress, highlighting important milestones that they achieved.

Library of Congress: Hispanic Reading Room
http://www.loc.gov/rr/hispanic

This online resource provides information on Hispanic culture and history. Especially valuable are the digital collections,Webcasts, and guides for students and teachers.

Life: Hispanic-American Firsts

http://www.life.com/gallery/31882/image/89039468#index/0

Life magazine's Web site contains a collection of photographs of Hispanic American trailblazers, such as Antonia Novello, Severo Ochoa , and Rita Moreno.

The Museum of Modern Art: Survey of Archives of Latino and Latin American Art

http://www.moma.org/learn/resources/latino_survey/index

Particularly useful on this online resource is the sidebar of links to different archives featuring Latino and Latin American artwork. Clicking on a link leads users to more details about the archive and enables them to browse a collection of art images.

National Archives Hispanic American Records

http://www.archives.gov/research/hispanic

These archives offer links to digitized artifacts, such as letters and other historic documents pertaining to Hispanic Americans.

National Education Association: Famous Hispanics Hall of Fame

http://www.nea.org/home/Famous-Hispanics-Hall-of-Fame.html

Features a lesson plan aimed at teaching students about noted Hispanic figures. There are also links to additional lessons covering Hispanic culture.

National Hispanic Christian Leadership Conference: Latino Religion in the United States: Demographic Shifts and Trends

http://www.nhclc.org/news/latino-religion-us-demographic-shifts-and-trend

This article takes an insightful look at religious statistics pertaining to Latinos in the United States.

National Hispanic Heritage Month: Heritage, Diversity, Integrity and Honor: The Renewed Hope of America

http://hispanicheritagemonth.gov

Hosted by the Library of Congress, this online resource gives viewers a perspective on Hispanic culture and history. The site includes links to teacher resources and pertinent audio and visual content.

National Public Radio: New and Established Writers Redefine Chicano Lit

http://www.npr.org/2011/01/27/133277380/New-And-Established-Writers-Redefine-Chicano-Lit

Through this Web page, users can read the transcript of an interview featuring two Mexican American authors. An audio version of the interview is also offered.

The New York Times: Mexican-Americans: Forging a New Vision of America's Melting Pot

http://www.nytimes.com/2001/02/11/weekinreview/the-nation-mexican-americans-forging-a-new-vision-of-america-s-melting-pot.html

This article discusses the impact of the Mexican American population on the United States.

The New York Times: Women's Sports; Hispanic Female Athletes Are Few and Far Between

http://www.nytimes.com/2002/11/06/sports/womens-sports-hispanic-female-athletes-are-few-and-far-between.html

Discusses the trends in sports participation among Hispanic women.

Pew Hispanic Center: Chronicling Latinos Diverse Experiences in a Changing America

http://pewhispanic.org

A go-to resource for retrieving up-to-date statistical information regarding Hispanics in the United States. Information can be easily accessed by selecting a specific topic, such as education, economics, labor, and politics.

Poetry.org : Poetry, Poems, Bios and More

http://www.poets.org/poet.php/prmPID/246

This Web site contains information on poets of Latino heritage, such as Martín Espada, Sandra Cisneros, Jack Agros, and Victor Hernández Cruz. Users can easily search for a specific poet and view his or her photograph, poems, and personal profile.

Pro Football Hall of Fame: Photo Gallery: NFL's Hispanic Heritage

http://www.profootballhof.com/photos/nfls-hispanic-heritage/2010/9/29

Features a slide show with photographs of Hispanics who have played in the National Football League (NFL).

Public Broadcasting Service: American Experience: Zoot Suit Riots

http://www.pbs.org/wgbh/amex/zoot/index.html

This section of the Public Broadcasting Service Web site accompanies an episode of *American Experience* which focused on the Zoot Suit Riots in Los Angeles. The site provides links to a time line and photo gallery about this event.

Public Broadcasting Service: The Border: Interactive Time Line

http://www.pbs.org/kpbs/theborder/history/interactive-timeline.html

Through this online resource, users can access a visually appealing, clickable time line to obtain information about historic events involving Latinos.

Public Broadcasting Service: Latin Music USA

http://www.pbs.org/wgbh/latinmusicusa

An engaging Web site that enables users to hear the sounds of Latin music, read about Latin music genres, and watch pertinent videos.

Rhythm Wheels: History of Latino-Caribbean Music

http://csdt.rpi.edu/latino/rhythm/rythm_Timeline.html

Rhythm Wheels, a Web site maintained by Rensselaer Polytechnic Institute, contains this section providing a time line with information on Latino-Caribbean music from Cuba, the Dominican Republic, and Puerto Rico.

San Jose State University: Mexican-American Tradition and Protest

http://gallery.sjsu.edu/mexican_amerixan_tradition/index.html

Clicking the links at the top of this Web page enables users to explore the artwork of Mexican American artists.

Scholastic, Inc.: Bring Hispanic Heritage Month to Life

http://www2.scholastic.com/browse/collection.jsp?id=386

Scholastic, Inc., a publisher of educational materials, created this Web resource for teachers. It features links to activities, lesson plans, and other resources designed to help students learn about Latino culture.

Scholastic, Inc.: Celebrate Hispanic Heritage

http://teacher.scholastic.com/activities/hispanic/athlete.htm

Geared toward students and teachers, this online resource offers information and photographs of, and personal quotes by, notable Hispanic individuals.

Sealift: U.S. Navy Military Sealift Command: Honoring Hispanic Heroes

http://www.msc.navy.mil/sealift/2004/September/perspective.htm

This page in the Web site for the U.S. Navy Military Sealift Command recognizes several Hispanic individuals for their service in the military and shares their personal stories and experiences.

Smithsonian Education: Hispanic Heritage Teaching Resources

http://www.smithsonianeducation.org/educators/resource_library/hispanic_resources.html

Aimed at teachers, this easy-to-navigate online resource offers lessons and activities pertaining to Hispanic culture.

Smithsonian Institution: Hispanic American Artists

http://collections.si.edu/search/results.jsp?q=Hispanic+American+artists

This section of the institution's Collections Search Center is a rich source for information on Hispanic American artists. It allows users to access digitized photographs and transcripts of artists' oral history interviews.

Smithsonian Latino Center: Latino Patriots in American Military History

http://latino.si.edu/education/latinopatriots.htm

Contains links to historic documents about Latinos in the military, as well as bilingual content and lesson plans.

State Library of North Carolina: Celebrating Hispanic Heritage: Prominent Hispanic North Carolinians and Hispanic Firsts

http://statelibrarync.org/news/2010/09/celebrating-hispanic-heritage-prominent-hispanics

Highlights the achievements of several notable Hispanic figures.

Teaching Tolerance: Latino Civil Rights Time Line, 1903 to 2006

http://www.tolerance.org/latino-civil-rights-timeline

A project of the Southern Poverty Law Center, the Teaching Tolerance Web site includes this time line delineating events pertaining to Latino civil rights.

United Food and Commercial Workers International Union: Latino Activists

http://www.ufcw.org/hispanic_heritage_month/chicano_civil_rights_movement/index.cfm

This Web page offers photographs of Latino activists, such as Rodolfo "Corky" Gonzáles, Reies López Tijerina, and Henry Cisneros, as well as specific details on their major activities and achievements.

University of Michigan: Exploring the Chicana Feminist Movement

http://www.umich.edu/~ac213/student_projects07/latfem/latfem/whatisit.html

Several pages of this Web site contain information on the Chicana feminist movement.

University of Texas Libraries: VOCES Oral History Project

http://www.lib.utexas.edu/voces

Enables users to access information on Latinos who served in the military during World War I, the Korean War, and the Vietnam War, including their oral histories, full-size photographs, and videos of military veterans.

USA Today: Trail Blazers for Hispanic Women

http://www.usatoday.com/sports/2005-03-29-hispanic-footsteps_x.htm

Features an article that discusses how Hispanic female athletes inspire Hispanic women and girls.

USA Track and Field Committee on Diversity and Leadership Development: In Honor of Hispanic Heritage Month

http://www.usatfdiversity.org/links-in-honor-of-hispanic-heritage-month

Focuses on Hispanic atheletes, admininstrators, and coaches in the sport of track and field.

U.S. Department of Agriculture: I Want to Learn More About Hispanic Americans in Agriculture

http://riley.nal.usda.gov/nal_display/index.php?info_center=8&tax_level=2&tax_subject=3&want_id=354&topic_id=1030&placement_default=0

Aimed at students and teachers, this page, created by the department's National Agricultural Library, includes links to documents on Hispanic Americans in agriculture. It features resources about prominent individuals, such as César Chávez, Dolores Huerta, Ernesto Galarza, and Eligio "Kika" de la Garza.

U.S. Department of Agriculture Natural Resources Conservation Service: The First Hispanic-American Politicians, Baseball Players, and More

http://www.tx.nrcs.usda.gov/about/civilrights/famous_first.html

Highlights the success of Hispanic American individuals who paved the way for others in film, music, government, sports, and other areas.

U.S. Department of Defense: Defense Department Honors Hispanic Heroes

http://www.defense.gov/news/newsarticle.aspx?id=28305

This article focuses on Hispanics who served in the military.

U.S. Department of State: Notable Hispanic Athletes in the United States.

http://photos.state.gov/galleries/amgov/30145/hispanic_sports

Through this Web site, users can access a photo gallery of famous Hispanic sports figures. In addition to photographs, the site provides description of the athletes' accomplishments and links to relevant articles.

Brooke Posley

CATEGORY INDEX

Category Index

LATINOS

1032

GEOGRAPHICAL INDEX

Subject Index

Academy Awards; Ferrer, José, 360; Moreno, Rita, 638; Quinn, Anthony, 732

Aceves, José, 1–2

Acosta, Daniel, 2–4

Acosta, Mercedes de, 4–6

Acosta, Oscar Zeta, 6–9

Acosta-Belén, Edna, 9–10

acting; Alba, Jessica, 15; Alonso, María Conchita, 37; Aragon, Art, 72; Arnaz, Desi, 80; Bach, Catherine, 103; Blades, Rubén, 143; Bratt, Benjamin, 152; Carey, Mariah, 191; Carrillo, Leo, 198; Colón, Miriam, 261; Cristal, Linda, 279; del Río, Dolores, 300; Diaz, Cameron, 305; Elizondo, Hector, 319; Estevez, Emilio, 332; Ferrer, José, 359; Ferrer, Mel, 361; Ferrera, America, 363; Fusco, Coco, 373; Garcia, Andy, 383; Gavin, John, 400; Hayworth, Rita, 442; Hernández, Juano, 448; Juliá, Raúl, 489; Jurado, Katy, 491; Kapp, Joe, 498; Lamas, Fernando, 506; Leguizamo, John, 514; Longoria, Eva, 521; Lopez, George, 523; Lopez, Jennifer, 525; López, Trini, 533; Marín, Cheech, 552; Miranda, Carmen, 602; Montalbán, Ricardo, 613; Montez, María, 617; Morales, Esai, 629; Moreno, Rita, 637; Novarro, Ramón, 661; Olmos, Edward James, 677; Ontiveros, Lupe, 679; Peña, Elizabeth, 697; Pérez, Rosie, 704; Quinn, Anthony, 731; Rodríguez, Paul, 779; Roland, Gilbert, 792; Romero, César, 793; Saenz, Eddie, 810; Saldana, Zoë, 817; San Juan, Olga, 822; Sheen, Charlie, 858; Sheen, Martin, 860; Smits, Jimmy, 862; Trejo, Danny,

900; Velez, Lupe, 940; Verdugo, Elena, 942; Welch, Raquel, 958; Zapata, Carmen, 971

activism; Acosta, Oscar Zeta, 6; Acuña, Rodolfo F., 10–12; Ada, Alma Flor, 12–14; Alfaro, Luis, 26; Alurista, 42; Avila, Joaquín G., 93; Baca, Jimmy Santiago, 99; Baez, Joan, 108; Baldorioty de Castro, Román, 113; Belpré, Pura, 124; Bratt, Benjamin, 152; Burciaga, José Antonio, 161; Cantú, Mario, 173; Cantú, Norma V., 176; Capetillo, Luisa, 181; Cárdenas, José A., 182; Casal, Lourdes, 202; Chávez, César, 231; Chávez, Helen Fabela, 241; Collazo, Oscar, 255; Colmenares, Margarita, 257; Colón, Jesús, 259; Corpi, Lucha, 271; Cortina, Juan, 274; Cotera, Martha P., 277; de Hoyos, Angela, 290; Delgado, Jane L., 298; Espada, Martín, 327; Fariña, Mimi, 339; Flores Magón, Ricardo, 364; Galarza, Ernesto, 379; Garcia, Gus C., 386; García, Héctor, 389; Garza, Carmen Lomas, 397; Garza de Cortés, Oralia, 398; Gómez-Pompa, Arturo, 409; Gonzáles, Corky, 414; Gutiérrez, José Ángel, 436; Gutiérrez, Luis, 438; Hernández, Antonia, 444; Hidalgo, Hilda, 461; Hostos, Eugenio María de, 471; Huerta, Dolores, 472; Juliá, Raúl, 489; Lebrón, Lolita, 512; Lobo, Rebecca, 519; Martí, José, 556; Martínez, Elizabeth, 564; Martínez, Vilma Socorro, 575; Mas Canosa, Jorge, 581; Melville, Margarita Bradford, 590; Monsiváis, Carolina, 612; Montalbán, Ricardo, 613;

Montoya, José, 619; Morales, Esai, 629; Muñoz Rivera, Luis, 646; Olmos, Edward James, 677; Orendain, Antonio, 681; Perales, Alonso, 701; Pérez, Rosie, 704; Rivas-Rodriguez, Maggie, 757; Rivera, Tomás, 764; Rodríguez de Tió, Lola, 788; Rodríguez, Luis J., 775; Rodríguez, Paul, 779; Rodriguez, Richard, 783; Salinas, Raúl R., 818; Samora, Julian, 821; Sánchez, George I., 827; Santana, Carlos, 836; Sarria, José, 847; Sheen, Martin, 860; Smits, Jimmy, 862; Soto Vélez, Clemente, 875; Tanguma, Leo, 883; Tarango, Yolanda, 885; Thomas, Piri, 891; Tijerina, Reies López, 895; Urrea, Teresa, 910; Valle, Pedro del, 929; Vando, Erasmo, 933; Yzaguirre, Raul, 966; Zapata, Carmen, 971; Zavella, Patricia, 973

affirmative action, 12, 244, 576, 745, 784, 967

Agramonte, Arístides, 14–15

Aguilar San Miguel, Leticia Rosa Magdalena. *See* Van de Putte, Leticia

Aim High: Extraordinary Stories of Hispanic and Latina Women (Contreras-Rowe), 266

a.k.a. Pablo (television program), 780

Alamo, The (film), 228, 279

Alamo, the, 215, 657, 854

Alarcón, Norma, 68

Alba, Jessica, 15–16, 901

Albizu Campos, Pedro, 17–19, 255, 513, 876

Albizu, Olga, 19–21

Alcaraz, Lalo, 21–23

Alderete, John F., 23–24

Alegría, Fernando, 25–26

Alfaro, Luis, 26–28

Algarín, Miguel, 28–29, 717